AF769842

Microcomputer Architecture and Programming

Microcomputer Architecture and Programming

Editor:

Gerard Ian Prudhomme

ArclerPress

www.arclerpress.com

Microcomputer Architecture and Programming

Editor: Gerard Ian Prudhomme

© 2017 Arcler Press LLC

708 3rd Avenue, 6th Floor
New York
NY 10017
United States of America
www.arclerpress.com

ISBN: 978-1-68094-466-2

Library of Congress Control Number: 2016951350

This book contains information obtained from highly regarded resources. Reprinted material sources are indicated. Copyright for individual articles remains with the authors as indicated. A Wide variety of references are listed. Reasonable efforts have been made to publish reliable data and views articulated in the chapters are those of the individual contributors, and not necessarily those of the editors or publishers. Editors or publishers are not responsible for the accuracy of the information in the published chapters or consequences of their use. The publisher believes no responsibility for any damage or grievance to the persons or property arising out of the use of any materials, instructions, methods or thoughts in the book. The editors and the publisher have attempted to trace the copyright holders of all material reproduced in this publication and apologize to copyright holders if permission has not been obtained. If any copyright holder has not been acknowledged, please write to us so we may rectify.

Notice: Registered trademark of products or corporate names are used only for explanation and identification without intent of infringement.

Arcler Press LLC publishes wide variety of books and eBooks. For more information about Arcler Press and its products, visit our website at www.arclerpress.com

About the Editor

Gerard Ian Prudhomme

Gerard I. Prudhomme has a graduate degree (M.S.) for Computer Science from University College London (UCL). He has also worked as a software programmer and tech writer for different Fortune 500 companies, and studied at UCL, Harvard, and Oxford.

Contents

List of Contributors

David Díaz
Dep. Lenguajes y Ciencias de la Computacio´n, Universidad de Ma´laga, Ma´laga, Spain

Francisco J. Esteban
Servicio de Informa´tica, Universidad de Co´rdoba, Co´rdoba, Spain

Pilar Hernández
Instituto de Agricultura Sostenible (IAS-CSIC), Co´rdoba, Spain

Juan Antonio Caballero
Dep. Estadı´stica, Universidad de Co´rdoba, Co´rdoba, Spain,

Antonio Guevara
Dep. Lenguajes y Ciencias de la Computacio´n, Universidad de Ma´laga, Ma´laga, Spain

Gabriel Dorado
Dep. Bioquı´mica y Biologı´a Molecular, Universidad de Co´rdoba (Campus de Excelencia Internacional Agroalimentario), Co´rdoba, Spain

Sergio Gálvez
Dep. Lenguajes y Ciencias de la Computacio´n, Universidad de Ma´laga, Ma´laga, Spain

Mohsen Dorraki
Department of Electrical Engineering, Amirkabir University of Technology, Tehran, Iran

Gregory K. Cambrel
Department of Electrical and Computer Systems Engineering, Faculty of Engineering, Monash University, Victoria, Australia

Derek Abbott
School of Electrical and Electronic Engineering, University of Adelaide, South Australia, Australia

M. Fernando Gonzalez-Zalba
Hitachi Cambridge Laboratory, Cambridge CB3 0HE, United Kingdom

Chiara Ciccarelli
Cavendsih Laboratory, University of Cambridge, Cambridge, United Kingdom

Liviu P. Zarbo
Institute of Physics, The Academy of Science of the Czech Republic, v.v.i, Cukrovarnick'a 10, 162 53 Praha 6, Czech Republic

Andrew C. Irvine
Cavendsih Laboratory, University of Cambridge, Cambridge, United Kingdom

Richard C. Campion
School of Physics and Astronomy, University of Nottingham, Nottingham NG7 2RD, United Kingdom

Bryan L. Gallagher
School of Physics and Astronomy, University of Nottingham, Nottingham NG7 2RD, United Kingdom

Tomas Jungwirth
Institute of Physics, The Academy of Science of the Czech Republic, v.v.i, Cukrovarnick'a 10, 162 53 Praha 6, Czech Republic
School of Physics and Astronomy, University of Nottingham, Nottingham NG7 2RD, United Kingdom

Andrew J. Ferguson
Cavendsih Laboratory, University of Cambridge, Cambridge, United Kingdom

Joerg Wunderlich
Hitachi Cambridge Laboratory, Cambridge CB3 0HE, United Kingdom
Institute of Physics, The Academy of Science of the Czech Republic, v.v.i, Cukrovarnick'a 10, 162 53 Praha 6, Czech Republic

Antoni Morro
Electronic Engineering Group, Physics Department, Universitat de les Illes Balears, Palma de Mallorca, Balears, Spain

Vincent Canals
Electronic Engineering Group, Physics Department, Universitat de les Illes Balears, Palma de Mallorca, Balears, Spain

Antoni Oliver
Electronic Engineering Group, Physics Department, Universitat de les Illes Balears, Palma de Mallorca, Balears, Spain

Miquel L. Alomar
Electronic Engineering Group, Physics Department, Universitat de les Illes Balears, Palma de Mallorca, Balears, Spain

Josep L. Rossello
Electronic Engineering Group, Physics Department, Universitat de les Illes Balears, Palma de Mallorca, Balears, Spain

Erico N. de Souza
Big Data Analytics Institute, Faculty of Computer Science, Dalhousie University, Halifax, NS, Canada

Kristina Boerder
Biology Department, Dalhousie University, Halifax, NS, Canada

Stan Matwin
Big Data Analytics Institute, Faculty of Computer Science, Dalhousie University, Halifax, NS, Canada
Institute of Computer Science, Polish Academy of Sciences, Warsaw, Poland

Boris Worm
Biology Department, Dalhousie University, Halifax, NS, Canada

Hwa Jen Yap
Department of Mechanical Engineering, Faculty of Engineering, University of Malaya, Kuala Lumpur, Malaysia

Zahari Taha
Faculty of Mechanical Engineering, Universiti Malaysia Pahang, Pekan, Pahang, Malaysia

Siti Zawiah Md Dawal
Department of Mechanical Engineering, Faculty of Engineering, University of Malaya, Kuala Lumpur, Malaysia

Siow-Wee Chang
Bioinformatics Program, Institute of Biological Sciences, Faculty of Science, University of Malaya, Kuala Lumpur, Malaysia

Nazila Norouzi
Department of Bioengineering, University of California, Riverside, Riverside, CA, United States of America

Heran C. Bhakta
Department of Bioengineering, University of California, Riverside, Riverside, CA, United States of America

William H. Grover
Department of Bioengineering, University of California, Riverside, Riverside, CA, United States of America

Arram Bae
Graduate School of Culture Technology, Korea Advanced Institute of Science and Technology, Daejeon, Republic of Korea

Doheum Park
Graduate School of Culture Technology, Korea Advanced Institute of Science and Technology, Daejeon, Republic of Korea

Yong-Yeol Ahn
School of Informatics and Computing, Indiana University, Bloomington, Indiana, United States of America

Juyong Park
Graduate School of Culture Technology, Korea Advanced Institute of Science and Technology, Daejeon, Republic of Korea

Liang Wu
School of Information Engineering, China University of Geosciences, Wuhan, China
National Engineering Research Center for GIS, Wuhan, China

Lei Xue
School of Information Engineering, China University of Geosciences, Wuhan, China

Chaoling Li
Development and Research Center, China Geological Survey, Beijing, China

Xia Lv
Development and Research Center, China Geological Survey, Beijing, China

Zhanlong Chen
School of Information Engineering, China University of Geosciences, Wuhan, China

Mingqiang Guo
School of Information Engineering, China University of Geosciences, Wuhan, China

Zhong Xie
School of Information Engineering, China University of Geosciences, Wuhan, China
National Engineering Research Center for GIS, Wuhan, China

Ali Seyed Shirkhorshidi
Department of Information Systems, Faculty of Computer Science and Information Technology, University of Malaya, 50603, Kuala Lumpur, Malaysia

Saeed Aghabozorgi
IBM Analytics, Platform, Emerging Technologies, IBM Canada Ltd., Markham, Ontario L6F 1C7, Canada

Teh Ying Wah
Department of Information Systems, Faculty of Computer Science and Information Technology, University of Malaya, 50603, Kuala Lumpur, Malaysia

Ling Yin
Shenzhen Institutes of Advanced Technology, Chinese Academy of Sciences, Shenzhen, Guangdong, China

Qian Wang
Shenzhen Institutes of Advanced Technology, Chinese Academy of Sciences, Shenzhen, Guangdong, China

Shih-Lung Shaw
Department of Geography, The University of Tennessee, Knoxville, TN, United States of America
State Key Laboratory of Information Engineering in Surveying, Mapping, and Remote Sensing, Wuhan University, Wuhan, Hubei, China

Zhixiang Fang
State Key Laboratory of Information Engineering in Surveying, Mapping, and Remote Sensing, Wuhan University, Wuhan, Hubei, China

Jinxing Hu
Shenzhen Institutes of Advanced Technology, Chinese Academy of Sciences, Shenzhen, Guangdong, China

Ye Tao
Department of Urban Planning and Design, The University of Hong Kong, Hong Kong, China

Wei Wang
Shenzhen Institutes of Advanced Technology, Chinese Academy of Sciences, Shenzhen, Guangdong, China

Yang J
Institute of Computer Science and Technology, Harbin Engineering University, Harbin, China

Chen L
Institute of Computer Science and Technology, Mudanjiang Teachers College, Mudanjiang, China

Zhang J
Institute of Computer Science and Technology, Harbin Engineering University, Harbin, China

Xiaolei Ma
School of Transportation Science and Engineering, Beijing Key Laboratory for Cooperative Vehicle Infrastructure, Systems, and Safety Control, Beihang University, Beijing, China,
Jiangsu Province Collaborative Innovation Center of Modern Urban Traffic Technologies, SiPaiLou #2, Nanjing, China,

Haiyang Yu
School of Transportation Science and Engineering, Beijing Key Laboratory for Cooperative Vehicle Infrastructure, Systems, and Safety Control, Beihang University, Beijing, China,
Jiangsu Province Collaborative Innovation Center of Modern Urban Traffic Technologies, SiPaiLou #2, Nanjing, China,

Yunpeng Wang
School of Transportation Science and Engineering, Beijing Key Laboratory for Cooperative Vehicle Infrastructure, Systems, and Safety Control, Beihang University, Beijing, China,
Jiangsu Province Collaborative Innovation Center of Modern Urban Traffic Technologies, SiPaiLou #2, Nanjing, China,

Yinhai Wang
Department of Civil and Environmental Engineering, University of Washington, Seattle, Washington, United States of America

Bo Liu
Faculty of Geomatics, East China Institute of Technology, 330013, Nanchang, PR, China
State Key Laboratory of Information Engineering in Surveying, Mapping and Remote Sensing, Wuhan University, 430079, Wuhan, PR, China

Dajun Li
Faculty of Geomatics, East China Institute of Technology, 330013, Nanchang, PR, China

Yuanping Xia
Faculty of Geomatics, East China Institute of Technology, 330013, Nanchang, PR, China

Jian Ruan
Faculty of Geomatics, East China Institute of Technology, 330013, Nanchang, PR, China

Lili Xu
Faculty of Geomatics, East China Institute of Technology, 330013, Nanchang, PR, China

Huanyi Wu
Faculty of Geomatics, East China Institute of Technology, 330013, Nanchang, PR, China

Derek E. Smith
National Ecological Observatory Network, Boulder, Colorado, United States of America

Stefan Metzger
National Ecological Observatory Network, Boulder, Colorado, United States of America
Institute of Arctic and Alpine Research, University of Colorado, Boulder, Colorado, United States of America

Jeffrey R. Taylor
National Ecological Observatory Network, Boulder, Colorado, United States of America
Institute of Arctic and Alpine Research, University of Colorado, Boulder, Colorado, United States of America

Xueyan Zhou
College of Computer Science and Technology, Harbin Engineering University, Harbin, China
College of Engineering, Harbin University, Harbin, China

Jing Yang
College of Computer Science and Technology, Harbin Engineering University, Harbin, China

Zehong Lin
College of Engineering, Harbin University, Harbin, China

Jianpei Zhang
College of Computer Science and Technology, Harbin Engineering University, Harbin, China

Xiaomeng Wang
Institute of Remote Sensing and Digital Earth, Chinese Academy of Sciences, Beijing, China
University of Chinese Academy of Sciences, Chinese Academy of Sciences, Beijing, China

Ling Peng
Institute of Remote Sensing and Digital Earth, Chinese Academy of Sciences, Beijing, China

Tianhe Chi
Institute of Remote Sensing and Digital Earth, Chinese Academy of Sciences, Beijing, China

Mengzhu Li
College of Economics and Management, Southwest University, Chongqing, China

Xiaojing Yao
Institute of Remote Sensing and Digital Earth, Chinese Academy of Sciences, Beijing, China
University of Chinese Academy of Sciences, Chinese Academy of Sciences, Beijing, China

Jing Shao
Institute of Remote Sensing and Digital Earth, Chinese Academy of Sciences, Beijing, China
University of Chinese Academy of Sciences, Chinese Academy of Sciences, Beijing, China

Zhen Zhou
Institute of Remote Sensing and Information Application, Zhejiang University, Hangzhou, China
Key Laboratory of Agricultural Remote Sensing and Information System, Zhejiang Province, Hangzhou, China

Jingfeng Huang
Institute of Remote Sensing and Information Application, Zhejiang University, Hangzhou, China
Key Laboratory of Environmental Remediation and Ecological Health, Ministry of Education, Zhejiang University, Hangzhou, China

Jing Wang
Institute of Remote Sensing and Information Application, Zhejiang University, Hangzhou, China
Key Laboratory of Agricultural Remote Sensing and Information System, Zhejiang Province, Hangzhou, China

Kangyu Zhang
Institute of Remote Sensing and Information Application, Zhejiang University, Hangzhou, China
Key Laboratory of Agricultural Remote Sensing and Information System, Zhejiang Province, Hangzhou, China

Zhaomin Kuang
Guangxi Zhuang Autonomous Region Institute of Meteorological and Disaster-Mitigation Research, Nanning, China

Shiquan Zhong
Guangxi Zhuang Autonomous Region Institute of Meteorological and Disaster-Mitigation Research, Nanning, China

Xiaodong Song
Institute of Remote Sensing and Information Application, Zhejiang University, Hangzhou, China
Key Laboratory of Agricultural Remote Sensing and Information System, Zhejiang Province, Hangzhou, China

Slavko Žitnik
Laboratory for Data Technologies, University of Ljubljana and Optilab d.o.o., Ljubljana, Slovenia

Lovro Sˇubelj
Laboratory for Data Technologies, University of Ljubljana, Ljubljana, Slovenia

Marko Bajec
Laboratory for Data Technologies, University of Ljubljana, Ljubljana, Slovenia

Osvaldo Navarro
Departamento de Ciencias Computacionales, Instituto Nacional de Astrofı´sica, O´ ptica y Electro´nica, Sta. Ma. Tonantzintla, Puebla, Me´xico

Rene´ Cumplido
Departamento de Ciencias Computacionales, Instituto Nacional de Astrofı´sica, O´ ptica y Electro´nica, Sta. Ma. Tonantzintla, Puebla, Me´xico

Luis Villasen˜ or-Pineda
Departamento de Ciencias Computacionales, Instituto Nacional de Astrofı´sica, O´ ptica y Electro´nica, Sta. Ma. Tonantzintla, Puebla, Me´xico

Claudia Feregrino-Uribe
Departamento de Ciencias Computacionales, Instituto Nacional de Astrofı´sica, O´ ptica y Electro´nica, Sta. Ma. Tonantzintla, Puebla, Me´xico

Jesu´ s Ariel Carrasco-Ochoa
Departamento de Ciencias Computacionales, Instituto Nacional de Astrofı´sica, O´ ptica y Electro´nica, Sta. Ma. Tonantzintla, Puebla, Me´xico

Ivan Komarov
Department of Mechanical Engineering, Complex Systems Simulation Lab, University of Wisconsin-Milwaukee, Milwaukee, Wisconsin, United States of America

Ali Dashti
Department of Mechanical Engineering, Complex Systems Simulation Lab, University of Wisconsin-Milwaukee, Milwaukee, Wisconsin, United States of America

Roshan M. D'Souza
Department of Mechanical Engineering, Complex Systems Simulation Lab, University of Wisconsin-Milwaukee, Milwaukee, Wisconsin, United States of America

Preface

Initial computer software was hard wired. Programs were difficult to implement. To re-create computer software required altering the equipment by hand, that began to take quite a long time with a myriad of possible mistakes. Memory space was merely useful for holding information. The phrase micro usually describes the CPU of a microcomputer, including the arithmetic logic unit (ALU).

Von Neumann recommended that information and also software ought to be kept with each other in memory space. This is now known as a Von Neumann structure. Software, and also information, are symbolized in memory space in the same manner. The primary complaint directed towards this approach is that safety issues may occur while directions may be exploited as though these were information, and also vice versa. A CPU is linked to memory space and also I/O by buses which carry data between the units. It is typically used on one LSI microchip. Microcomputers utilize a time clock, a microprocessor unit (MPU), interfaces to memory space, and also exterior input/output units. The first chapter views a novel parallelization strategy, aligning sequences in architectures with many cores. Chapter 2 analyzes a uniform transmission line. Chapter 3 scrutinizes a hybrid single-electron device. Chapter 4 suggests a parallel architecture of stochastic-logic pulse-based blocks. Chapter 5 puts emphasis on Satellite-based Automatic Information Systems. Chapter 6 evaluates robotic work cell design. Chapter 7 peruses microfluidic chips. Chapter 8 probes advanced data modeling and analysis. Chapter 9 evaluates digital information in geological fields. Chapter 10 gives an outline of clustering algorithms. Chapter 11 figures out mobile phone location data. Chapter 12 analyzes heterogeneous information networks. Chapter 13 views deep learning theory for data-driven research. Chapter 14 features formalization and reasoning of topological relations. Chapter 15 scrutinizes assessments of data quality. Chapter 16 is designed to develop social network information tracing. Chapter 17 scrutinizes floating car data and urban-scale traffic monitoring. Chapter 18 deals with remote sensing data. Chapter 19 explains coreference resolution. Chapter 20 analyzes Sequential Pattern Mining. Chapter 21 studies a graphics processing unit (GPU)-based k-NNG algorithm.

Editor
Gerard Ian Prudhomme
Hawaii, US

CHAPTER 1

MC64-CLUSTALWP2: A HIGHLY-PARALLEL HYBRID STRATEGY TO ALIGN MULTIPLE SEQUENCES IN MANY-CORE ARCHITECTURES

David Díaz,[1] Francisco J. Esteban,[2] Pilar Hernández,[3] Juan Antonio Caballero,[4] Antonio Guevara,[1] Gabriel Dorado,[5] and Sergio Gálvez[1]

[1] Dep. Lenguajes y Ciencias de la Computacio´n, Universidad de Ma´laga, Ma´laga, Spain

[2] Servicio de Informa´tica, Universidad de Co´rdoba, Co´rdoba, Spain

[3] Instituto de Agricultura Sostenible (IAS-CSIC), Co´rdoba, Spain

[4] Dep. Estadı´stica, Universidad de Co´rdoba, Co´rdoba, Spain,

[5] Dep. Bioquı´mica y Biologı´a Molecular, Universidad de Co´rdoba (Campus de Excelencia Internacional Agroalimentario), Co´rdoba, Spain

ABSTRACT

We have developed the MC64-ClustalWP2 as a new implementation of the Clustal W algorithm, integrating a novel parallelization strategy and significantly increasing the performance when aligning long sequences in architectures with many cores. It must be stressed that in such a process, the detailed analysis of both the software and hardware features and peculiarities is of paramount importance to reveal key points to exploit and optimize the full potential of parallelism in many-core CPU systems. The new parallelization approach has focused into the most time-consuming stages of this algorithm. In particular, the so-called progressive alignment has drastically improved the performance, due to a fine-grained approach where the forward and backward loops were unrolled and parallelized. Another key approach has been the implementation of the new algorithm in a hybrid-computing system, integrating both an Intel Xeon multi-core CPU and a Tilera Tile64 many-core card. A comparison with other Clustal W implementations reveals the high-performance of the new algorithm and strategy in many-core CPU architectures, in a scenario where the sequences to align are relatively long (more than 10 kb) and, hence, a many-core GPU hardware cannot be used. Thus, the MC64-ClustalWP2 runs multiple alignments more than 18x than the original Clustal W algorithm, and more than 7x than the best x86 parallel implementation to date, being publicly available through a web service. Besides, these developments have been deployed in cost-effective personal computers and should be useful for life-science researchers, including the identification of identities and differences for mutation/polymorphism analyses, biodiversity and evolutionary studies and for the development of molecular markers for paternity testing, germplasm management and protection, to assist breeding, illegal traffic control, fraud prevention and for the protection of the intellectual property (identification/traceability), including the protected designation of origin, among other applications.

INTRODUCTION

The amount of genomic data is growing exponentially, due to the advances in technology and the evolution in the so-called "Next-Generation" Sequencing (NGS), including the latest second- and third-generation equipment. Thus, the former bioinformatics tools from the genic era are evolving to handle the current genomic data. These include alignment algorithms for sequence comparison like the Needleman-Wunsch [1] pairwise global-alignment algorithm, which has evolved both from a biological point of view, as the Smith-Waterman local aligners [2] or Gotoh affine gaps [3], and also

Citation: Díaz D, Esteban FJ, Hernández P, Caballero JA, Guevara A, Dorado G, et al. (2014) MC64-ClustalWP2: A Highly-Parallel Hybrid Strategy to Align Multiple Sequences in Many-Core Architectures. PLoS ONE 9(4): e94044. doi:10.1371/journal.pone.0094044.

from a computational point of view, as the Hirschberg linear space approach [4] or Driga FastLSA [5].

Yet, these computational improvements in pairwise-alignment algorithms cannot properly handle long or very long sequences, like some partial or complete chromosomes and genomes. Thus, some heuristic strategies have been developed to overcome the large amount of memory and execution time required to align such sequences. The Fast Alignment Sequence Tools (FAST)-All (FASTA) [6] and Basic Local Alignment Search Tool (BLAST) [7] are examples of this trend. The heuristics are able to obtain approximate alignments with acceptable accurate results in much less time, so they can be useful to compare long sequences. Nonetheless, the quality of the alignment may be compromised in some instances [8], and therefore non-heuristic aligners may be needed to guarantee the optimal alignment from a computational point of view.

Additionally, the "optimal" pairwise aligners can be ported to new computing architectures to overcome the previous limitations. Though an alternative to speedup algorithms is to use supercomputers, grid computing and clustering using several nodes [9], more affordable options are available nowadays. That is the case of the multi-core architectures, where several threads or processes run independent code in parallel, albeit requiring the programmers to develop new approaches when porting, adapting and optimizing the existing alignment algorithms to the new parallel architectures. In fact, the number of cores is increasing exponentially, giving birth to the concept of "many-core" architectures, where tens, thousands and even millions of them are available.

At this point it is important to distinguish between multi-core and many-core microprocessors. Thus, in many-core architectures, the execution cores are small Central Processing Units (CPU) with fewer resources than a standard multi-core CPU; so in order to extract the full potential of the former, specific parallelism strategies for them should be developed. Besides, the many-core microprocessors can be classified into two different groups: many-core Graphical Processing Units (GPU), and many-core CPU. The former ones have thousands of Stream Processors Units (SPU), sometimes named cores, distributed in a hierarchical way: a GPU has several Thread Processing Clusters (TPC), where each one consists of an array of Stream Multiprocessor Units (SMU), having each one eight SPU. The resources are shared between the SMU in these models. On the contrary, the many-core CPU microprocessors have a matrix of uniform CPU with their own resources, usually interconnected via a high-throughput network. A graphical comparison of both architectures can be seen in Figure 1. Unfortunately, such architectural differences require also different programming methodologies, being the Compute-Unified Device Architecture (CUDA) a specific model to exploit the parallelism in General-Purpose GPU (GPGPU) [10] and the standard C being usually deployed in many-core CPU architectures. In the field of cluster computing, the C language is sometimes complemented by some kind of standard or proprietary Application Program Interface (API), to extend some parallelism abilities like message passing, shared memory or abstract channel communications.

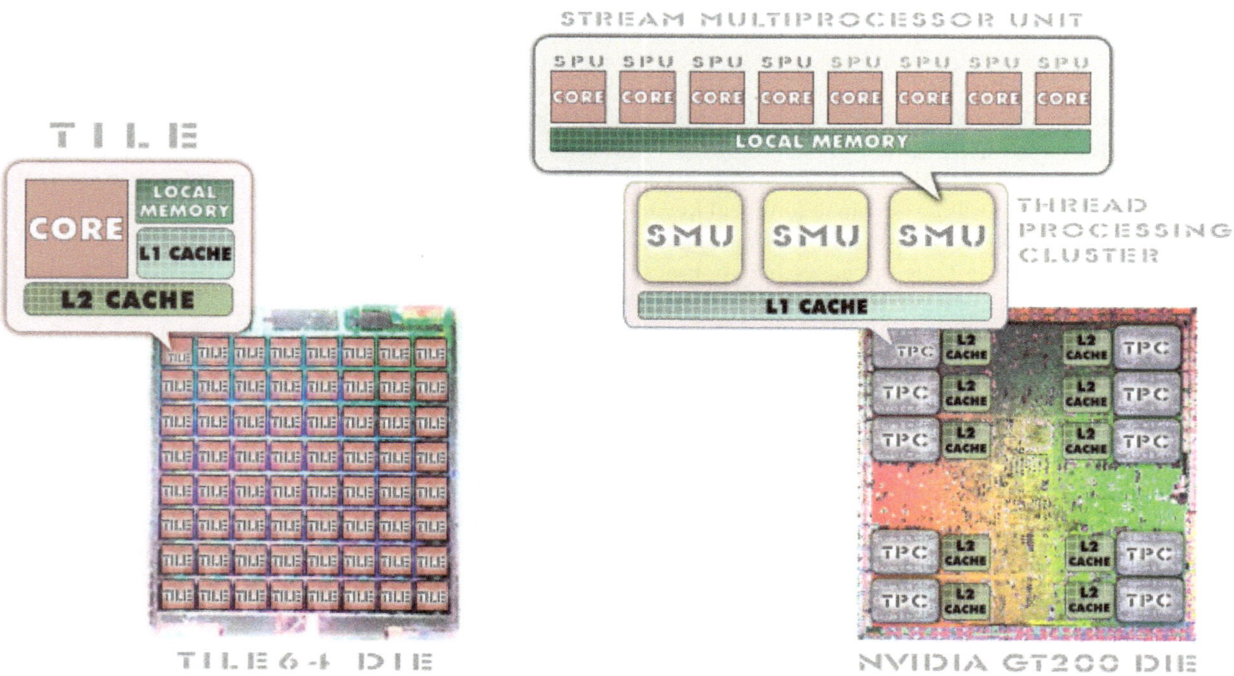

Figure 1. Block diagram of many-core CPU and GPU architectures. The shown dies are boarded on nVidia GT 200 GPU series and Tilera Tile64 Peripheral Component Interconnect express (PCIe) cards. The cores in the many-core CPU architectures are interconnected through a high-bandwidth mesh, whereas the ones in the many-core GPU are isolated.

There are experimental and commercial many-core CPU models. They include the Adapteva Epiphany IV with 64 cores [11], the Sun Microsystems UltraSPARC T2 Pro with eight cores and eight threads per core [12], and the models from Intel, the leader company in this research field with the Many-Integrated Cores (MIC) architecture. At first, they created the Intel Terascale microprocessor with 80 cores [13], and then experimental models like the Single-chip Cloud Computing

(SCC) [14] with 48 cores and the Knights Ferry [15] with 32 cores. From the experience obtained from this models and the Larrabee hybrid CPU-GPU project, a new model codenamed Knights Corner and eventually named Xeon Phi was developed with 61 cores and 22 nm 3-D tri-gate process fabrication process. The second generation of Xeon Phi products (Knights Landing) is expected in the near future as a coprocessor or a host processor (CPU), manufactured with 14 nm node technology and second-generation 3-D tri-gate transistors.

Following this trend, Tilera has developed a many-core CPU architecture known as the Tile64 microprocessor, being a 90 nm Reduced Instruction Set Computing (RISC) System-on-Chip (SoC) microprocessor with 64 general-purpose CPU called tiles, each one being able of running an independent operative system (Linux). Each core runs at 500–866 MHz and can reach a global 0.166 Tera-Instructions Per Second (TIPS). The tiles are interconnected through a high-throughput network called intelligent Mesh (iMesh) with 31 Terabits per second (Tbps) bandwidth. As seen in Figure 1, each tile contains its own Level 1 (8 KB for data and 8 KB for instructions) and Level 2 (64 KB) caches. Furthermore, all the Level 2 caches become a larger Level 3 common cache [16]. Lately, Tilera has announced a future branch of microprocessors called Tile-Gx [17] with 16 to 100 cores using a 40 nm fabrication process.

Thus, thanks to the emerging many-core technologies, new approaches are available to address the increasing demand of computational power. This allows to tackle the bioinformatics analyses required for the exponentially increasing data generated by the new sequencing methodologies. That is the case of the previously mentioned Needleman-Wunsch (NW) [1] and Smith-Waterman (SW) [2] pairwise aligners, where GPU parallel approaches have been presented by Manavski [18] and Liu [19]. However, most of these implementations are designed to align a single query sequence against a huge number of small sequences like those from peptides (eg., proteins), yet cannot align sequences longer than 59,000 residues. This is due to the intrinsic “Single Instruction, Multiple Data” (SIMD) characteristics of the GPGPU, where pipelining allows a great speedup factor, yet intense memory usage may lead to bottlenecks.

Indeed, although some many-core CPU microprocessors with tens of cores have recently arisen, there are only a few bioinformatics developments deployed in such architectures, as the ones that we have previously published for the Tile64 microprocessor [20]–[22]. Such developments were carried out with TILExpress-20G cards including the Tile64 microprocessor and 8 GB of RAM, for which we have empirically demonstrated some limits: 7.8 GB for Solid State Disk (SSD), 2.8 GB for local memory and 1.9 GB for shared memory. Such cards have high-bandwidth communication ports and a very good performance per watt [20]. Among others, we have developed a parallel version of the NW/SW algorithm, named Multicore64-NeedlemanWunsch/SmithWaterman (MC64-NW/SW), using a FastLSA strategy [5], which we have thoroughly optimized taking into account the hardware and algorithm features and peculiarities. This implementation achieved a gain of ~1,000% against the same algorithm on a x86 multi-core architecture, allowing to align sequences of one Megabase (Mb) length in 23 minutes approximately [20], [22].

In this report, we have extended our work to the popular Multiple-Sequence Alignment (MSA) algorithm known as Clustal W. The new parallel version of Clustal W exploits the high-throughput parallelism in many-core CPU architectures, optimizing the most time-consuming stage of the original algorithm. This has been accomplished taking into account both the existing parallel versions of the Clustal W for multi-core and many-core GPGPU architectures, as well as our previous experience when developing the parallel MC64-NW/SW [20]. Thus, the new algorithm, called MC64-ClustalWP2 for Many-Core64-Clustal W Phase 2 (of parallelization), was implemented for the Tilera Tile64 microprocessor, as described below.

Different benchmarks were run to test the new algorithm against the previous developments and to quantify its performance. Since the MC64-ClustalWP2 algorithm was developed to align relatively large sequences, for instance, from 10 kilobases (kb) to 300 kb, it was tested with a family of organisms whose genome lengths fall into such a range. It should be noted that this approach would require an excessive execution time in a multi-core system or would not even be allowed in a GPGPU architecture, due to the length of the sequences. The MC64-ClustalWP2 source code is available under the General Public License (GPL) license at the <http://galactus.uma.es/manycore> web site [23], where the algorithm can be also remotely invoked through web services.

Multiple-Sequence Alignments

The multiple-sequence alignments allows the comparison of two or more sequences, in contrast to the pairwise aligners like Smith-Waterman, which are limited to just a couple of them. Therefore, the former are particularly useful to identify identities (similarities) and divergences (differences) between many sources, allowing to build evolutionary phylogenetic trees (dendrograms). Thus, the identification of small and large variations, mutations or polymorphisms like base changes and insertions/deletions (indels), duplications or amplifications, recombinations and rearrangements like translocations can be exploited to develop molecular markers for identification, including germplasm management and protection, paternity testing, marker-assisted selection and breeding, illegal traffic control, fraud prevention and traceability. This can be applied to the Protected Designation of Origin (PDO), which is a label of food products from some geographical areas, showing particular organoleptic or otherwise desirable characteristics, conferring them a higher quality than similar products from other sites.

However, generating a Dynamic-Program Matrix (DPM) in the sense of “optimal” pairwise aligners, but for more than two sequences, means a Nondeterministic Polynomial (NP) complete complexity problem in computation, and therefore no fast solution to it is known by definition. For this reason, several heuristic strategies were developed to simulate the behavior of the n-dimensional matrix, using a batch of pairwise alignments and simpler DPM. That is the case of MULTAN [24], being a Waterman [25] or Clustal [26] method. The latter has become very popular, due to its original performance and further developments and improvements. The Clustal algorithm is based on a progressive-alignment strategy of all the sequences, aligned by the order determined by a previously-calculated phylogenetic tree, generated from the similarities and differences among the sequences in an all-vs-all comparison matrix.

The first version of MULTAN was programmed in the FORTRAN language, but later on it was re-programmed in the C language, and a few new functionalities were added, like the generation of a dendrogram in the final stage [27]. More notable changes were introduced in the new Clustal W [28], which received the "W" for "weighting", since in this version the sequences were weighted in order to increase the sensibility of the algorithm. Later on, the version 2 was ported into C++, including two new minor-relevant features [29]. Besides the Clustal, there are other multiple-sequence alignment algorithms, like the T-Coffee [30] and MUSCLE [31], which may obtain accurate-enough results for large sequences using heuristics, modifying the progressive alignment method and adding new refinements.

Furthermore, as with pairwise aligners, quicker MSA heuristic methods which do not rely on a DPM have been also developed, as the Multi-LAGAN general anchoring-based method[32]. In addition, new multiple-sequence alignment approaches have been published, including the so-called genome MSA methods, capable of dealing with very long similar sequences, like MGA [33] or MAVID [34]. These methods are very fast, but they are usually not accurate when the aligned sequences have highly polymorphic regions (e.g., with high mutation-rates). Therefore, they can be useful to align restricted or local similar regions, but not to globally align any set of sequences [35]. More recent methods like the progressive Mauve [36] are able to deal with some sequence variations (like rearrangements), but not with all of them, as is the case for duplications [37]. A further review of the most important MSA algorithms can be found at [38].

On the other hand, the Clustal W design is divided into three main stages: the distance matrix generation, the guide tree generation and the progressive alignment. It can be easily determined that the most time-consuming stages are the first and the last ones [39]. Indeed, they require most of the computation time as the number of sequences or their length increase. Therefore, their optimization represents the first theoretical choice to improve the algorithm performance. Thus, the Clustal W has been parallelized for SGI computers [40], multi-core platforms using threads [41], the hybrid multi-core Cell chip [42] and scalable clusters using the Message Passing Interface (MPI) [43]. However, none of them has really exploited the parallelism in the third stage, as it is pointed out in the next section.

Clustal W Behavior Analyses

In order to properly optimize the Clustal W parallelization, each stage of the algorithm should be carefully analyzed. Traditionally, the Clustal W has been used to align short sequences of nucleic acids (DNA or RNA) and peptides, with high-performance implementations of Clustal W exploiting parallelism to obtain the best results for larger number of such sequences. However, as the MC64-ClustalWP2 focuses on longer DNA sequences (for instance, from 10 kb to 300 Mb), the parallelization and optimization strategies should be different.

As previously noted, the Clustal W is divided into three main stages, shown at the top ofFigure 2. The first stage fulfills the cells of a distance matrix with a score that represents the distance between every pair of sequences. Each score is calculated running a pairwise-alignment operation. The second stage generates a guide tree using a clustering method, like the Neighbor-Joining (NJ) [44] and, finally, the third stage progressively generates the multiple alignment, following the topology of the guide tree.

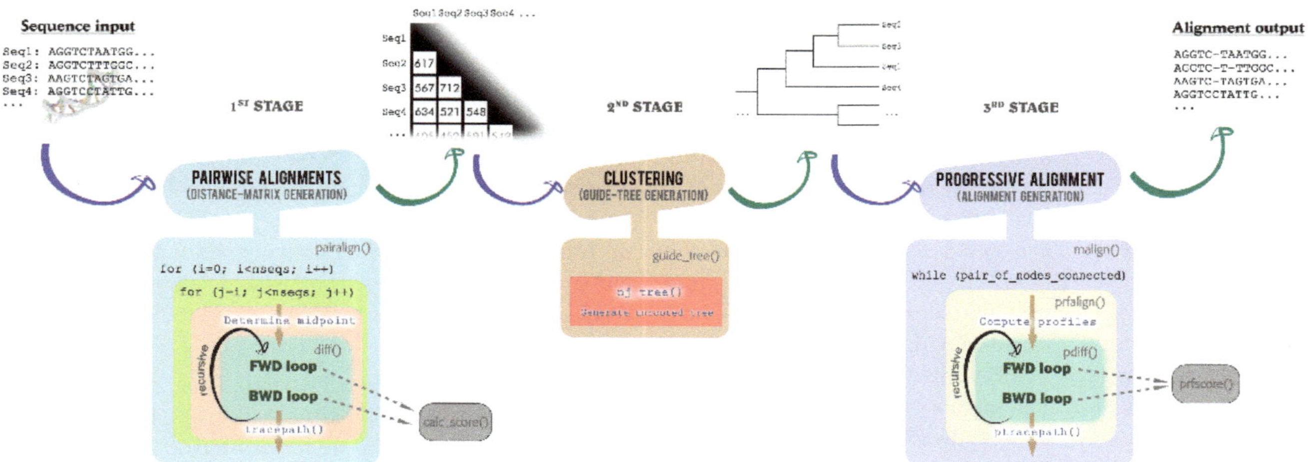

Figure 2. Global behavior of the Clustal W algorithm and its three main stages. The top part shows the three main stages of the Clustal W showing both the data used and generated in each one. In the bottom part, the functions and high-level pseudo-code reveal the similarities between the most time-consuming and representative parts of the algorithm.

The pairwise alignments of the first main stage are calculated using the local Myers-Miller algorithm [45], a Smith-Waterman pairwise aligner that implements affine-gap penalties [3]. Its space complexity is linear, at the expense of doubling the execution time when compared to other standard pairwise aligners. The multiple alignment of n sequences requires to complete the distance matrix, performing n/2*(n−1) alignment operations between each pair of sequences. There are no dependencies between them, so they can be executed in parallel. The MPI-alike implementations for Personal Computer (PC) clusters usually assume this coarse-grained approach [46]. A more fine-grained approach is used by the MSA-CUDA [47], as each pairwise alignment is partially distributed among several executing threads, thus obtaining two levels of parallelism. Each alignment returns a score value, which is then stored into the corresponding cell of the distance matrix. In addition, the actual pairwise alignments are also required by Clustal W to fine-tune the distance matrix values.

The clustering stage builds a phylogenetic tree from the previously calculated distance matrix, returning an unrooted tree with the evolutionary distances between branches. This is the less time-consuming stage [39] and, when working with only a few sequences (n<100), it can be considered negligible, as its complexity only relies on the number of sequences to align. In any case, the algorithm used for this node-clustering phase is the Neighbor-Joining (NJ) method [44], which has been previously parallelized for GPU many-core systems [48]. Other methods like the Unweighted Pair Group Method with Arithmetic Mean (UPGMA) [49]can also be used.

Finally, the progressive-alignment stage globally aligns sequences in an iterative way, following the path described by the unrooted-guide-tree topology. This stage starts aligning the closest pairs of leaf sequences. Then, the resulting pairwise alignments must be aligned again, following the closest path given by the guide tree. This high-level alignment strategy is called profile-profile alignment, where a profile is obtained from a previous intermediate of the multiple alignment, following a path from the leaves to the top of the tree. Thus, a profile alignment presents a more advanced scoring system and is more computationally expensive than a common-pairwise alignment. Furthermore, dependencies in the tree do not allow parallelizing all alignments, as occurs in the first stage. Therefore, only independent parallel-branches of the tree can be simultaneously executed, and thus may be restricted by the tree shape. This low-parallelization factor is determined by the log n in a well-balanced tree of n nodes for the best-case scenario. In a deeper level, the core of the aligner can be divided as well into two independent loops to be run separately, corresponding to the forward and backward loops [50]. Some implementations take advantage of this fact to run both loops in parallel, as the ClustalW-MPI [43]. The result produced by this stage is the full alignment.

A New Strategy to Parallelize Clustal W: MC64-ClustalWP2

In order to exploit the parallelism in the many-core architectures, the tasks to be executed must be spread among all the available cores, which should communicate between themselves at a high speed. Thus, the first step carried out in this work was considering Clustal as three main tasks to be independently parallelized. In addition, as we focus on aligning a few long sequences, the second stage can be ignored, because its execution time can be considered negligible. An exhaustive analysis of the Clustal W allowed us to identify the progressive alignment source-code that should be rewritten, in order to have a structure very close to that of the pairwise-alignments stage. A bird's eye Clustal W structure of such approach is shown at the bottom of Figure 2.

This chart reveals the inherent similarity between the first and the last stage, where the alignment of a pair of sequences is replaced by the alignment of a pair of profiles. These profile alignments make use of a more-advanced scoring system, and they are far-more computational expensive. In particular, the score calculus function, prfscore(), the hot spot of the aligner, is a time-consuming vector multiplication (whereas in the first stage, the corresponding operation is a straightforward access to an array cell).

A New Parallel Approach of the Pairwise-Alignments Stage

In order to parallelize the first ClustalW stage in a previous work, we replaced it with an iterative call to the MC64-NW/SW pairwise aligner [21], obtaining more than a 60% performance speedup against the ClustalW-MPI executed in a quad-core Xeon system [43]. The resulting algorithm, named MC64-ClustalW, was a coarse-grained strategy, as only individual alignments were parallelized. Besides, a considerable percentage of the tiles were idle at the beginning and at the end of each alignment, due to the wave-front growth behavior of the algorithm. Furthermore, only a tile was used in the backward stage of a pairwise alignment, being therefore a waste of resources.

Following the Tile64 terminology, a geometry is a set of adjacent cores that forms a rectangular shape, behaving as an independent subset of the Tile64 chip from a functional point of view. The Tile64 can be partitioned into several geometries, but any tile can only belong to a particular geometry at a given time. In the present work, we propose a much more advanced and fine-grained approach, being a new phase in our efforts to improve the performance of Clustal W, in which the parallelism is exploited at two levels: i) several alignments are calculated simultaneously in different geometries of cores; and ii) inside each of them, the alignment is computed in parallel by all the cores contained in it.

To achieve this new run-distribution requires a higher-level controller to schedule alignments among all groups of geometries. This new design unrolls the two main loops in the pairalign() function, and replaces the original linear-space approach with a call to the MC64-NW/SW which, in turn, uses an advanced FastLSA strategy. With this unrolling method, each pairwise alignment is assigned to an available geometry, in the same way as our previous MC64-NW/SW works [20]. Therefore, the number of pairwise alignments that can be simultaneously calculated corresponds to the number of geometries into which the Tile64 core-array is divided. Nonetheless, forward and backward stages of the pairwise alignment are separated: geometries of n workers calculate the full DPM for the forward stage (*F-xx geometries* from this point on), but geometries of only one worker perform the backtracking and alignment generation (*B-xx geometries* from this point on). Thus, several working geometries of these two classes collaborate to calculate all the alignments, taking the most out of every available tile. Meanwhile, the high-level controller schedules and manages all the pending jobs. Furthermore, the temporary grid-cache data must be shared between their geometries, in order to communicate a forward stage job with its backward stage counterpart.

A New Parallel Approach of the Progressive-Alignment Stage

With MC64-ClustalWP2 we propose as well a new parallelization strategy for the progressive-alignment stage. As stated above, Figure 2 shows that the progressive alignment is actually a Myers-Miller-like alignment algorithm, whose two main loops can be unrolled in a similar way as the pairwise alignment was done. Therefore, we propose to transform the linear-space recursive Myers-Miller into a quadratic-space sequential Needleman-Wunsch. In both cases, the corresponding progressive affine-gap algorithm must be applied. In a similar way as with the first stage, this sequential dynamic-programming strategy has been parallelized using the FastLSA approach, in order to reduce the constant multiplicative factor.

However, two levels of parallelism cannot be achieved in this progressive-alignment stage, because each alignment profile depends on the previous ones; these dependencies are given by the guide tree. Our parallel approach transforms the prfalign() function into a new parallel program, using the same FastLSA strategy to distribute a single alignment to all the available tiles in the many-core system. Thus, applying the wave-front parallel strategy and selecting an optimal *k value*, the speedup will depend on the number of available processing resources, as long as the scalability factor is very close to that of our previous MC64-NW/SW [20].

In this design, a controller tile is in charge of the management of the grid cache and the distribution of jobs among the rest of available worker tiles. The profiles of the original Clustal W are still used, so the profile initialization is performed by the controller tile, whereas the workers call the original prfscore() calculus-function profile. The new implementations of both the pairwise and progressive aligners, as well as their relative speedups, are discussed in the next sections.

Deployment of the MC64-ClustalWP2 on the Tile64 Many-Core Microprocessor

The main asset of the many-core CPU Tile64 System-on-Chip is the execution of parallel programs, due to its 64 cores/tiles running at 866 MHz in a TILExpress-20G card. The drawback is that inherently sequential code is poorly performed by a single tile. Considering that the Clustal W contains purely sequential blocks of code, yet being potentially parallelizable, we have based our implementation on a heterogeneous programming model. In such an approach, the code is commonly executed in the host CPU, using many-core GPU cards as code accelerators, effectively exploiting the best complementary potential of each kind of microprocessor. Different standards and programming methodologies have been proposed to unify and schedule the tasks in these systems, like the OpenCL [51]. Albeit, no one supports the Tile64 architecture yet, due to the novelty of the many-core CPU technologies.

The Clustal W 1.83 source code, written in the C programming language, has been carefully adapted to support the heterogeneous programming approach, generating a x86-Tile64 implementation of the MC64-ClustalWP2 parallel algorithm. Thus, the MC64-ClustalWP2 is composed by three executables: one runs in the host and two run in the Tile64. The main one is executed in the host; it processes the input parameters, sets the internal variables and orchestrates the three stages of the algorithm, eventually producing the multiple alignment. The three stages of the Clustal W are scheduled between the host CPU and the many-core CPU, as follows:

- The pairwise alignments are launched in the Tile64 environment, following the schema previously described. The pairwise-alignments overseer is the previously named "high-level controller", a Perl script launched in the host to supervise the work distribution among the geometries.
- Once every pairwise alignment and its score are obtained, the host performs the clustering algorithm, whose execution time is negligible compared to the other stages, since the number of sequences is reduced. Therefore, the parallelization is not worth the effort in this stage. The result is the phylogenetic tree.
- Again, each profile alignment of the progressive-alignment stage is executed in the Tile64 microprocessor, following the job distribution previously stated. Every intermediary result is processed by the host, in order to calculate the next one, until the final multiple alignment is obtained.

Therefore, this hybrid work distribution exploits both architecture strengths, thus running the sequential code in the PC host and the parallel code in the Tile64 microprocessor. The complete workflow can be seen in the Figure 3. Following this approach, the implementation requires communicating both platforms for pairwise and progressive alignments.

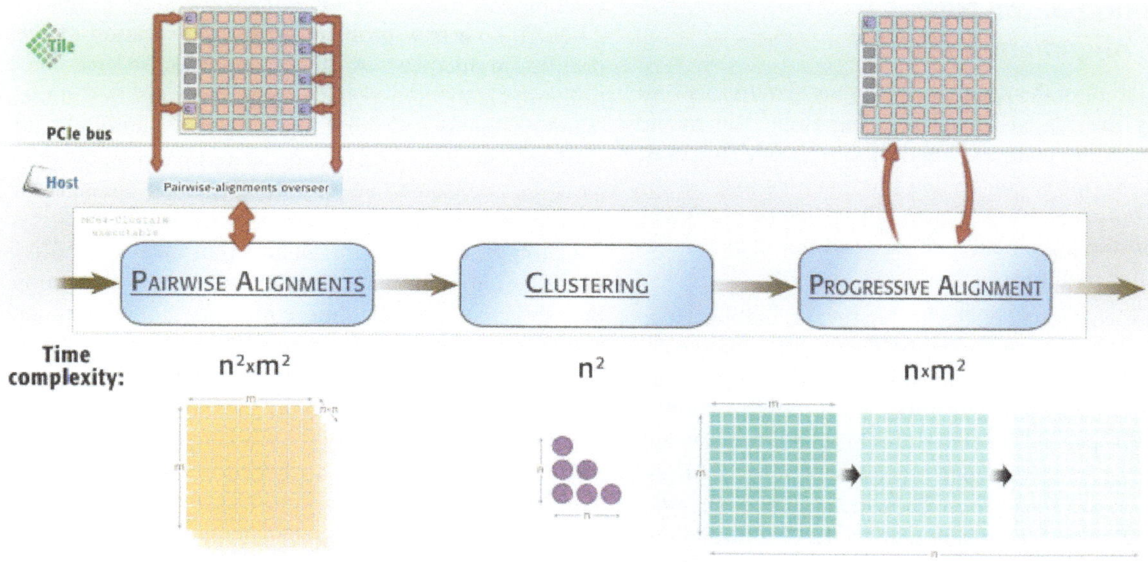

Figure 3. Heterogeneous programming model of the MC64-ClustalWP2 and each stage complexity. The executable algorithm is run in the host machine: the pairwise-alignments stage communicates with an external host program, which schedules the alignments among tiles. The clustering stage is executed in the host, and the progressive-alignment stage is controlled by the host, by calculating each profile alignment in the Tile64 microprocessor. The time complexity of each stage is shown in the lower part.

Implementation of the New Pairwise-Alignments Stage

The MC64-ClustalWP2 pairwise aligner design requires two different job classes to be run in the many-core platform; they deal with the forward and backward stages, respectively. In order to balance the developing effort versus the performance gain, the starting point was our local MC64-NW/SW pairwise aligner [20], where the necessary modifications were carried out to adapt it to the new requirements.

Both stages were decoupled, but keeping the same controller-worker strategy. So, in order to run any job, at least two tiles are needed in each stage: one acting as the stage controller and the other executing the code of the worker stage. With this approach, the same executable runs a forward or a backward stage, depending on a flag parameter: the forward stage is launched on a *F-xx geometry*, whereas the backward stage is launched on a *B-xx*one. This requires to share data between the two controllers of the same alignment (now decoupled), by temporarily storing the grid cache and the internal variables in the TILExpress-20G card 8 GB SSD file system. On the other hand, the original MC64-NW/SW used 6 bytes per cell, since gap penalties are never greater than 128 [5]. However, the pairwise alignment in Clustal W uses bigger values, so the grid-cache cell structure was modified as well to support it. Now, 12 bytes are used and the absolute values are stored instead of the relative differences in the case of the two auxiliary matrices. This is translated into more memory/file-system usage and less performance, due to the Tile64 instruction characteristics. As a collateral effect, the optimal *k values* calculated in the MC64-NW/SW parallelization are invalid and must be recalculated.

Taking into consideration that four cores are reserved for the internal management of the chip and communications with the host, the 60 remaining available cores are distributed into a number of static geometries. Different empirical tests have demonstrated that the optimal geometries to use are four forward stage geometries of 7×2 tiles and two backward stage geometries of 2×1 tiles. The rationale of such result is that the forward stage is far more computationally expensive than the backward one. Nonetheless, when the number of pairwise alignments is between five and eight, it is better to use eight 7×1 F-xx geometries, because this optimizes the workload by avoiding a second batch of alignments with idle geometries.

To achieve two levels of parallelism, a "high-level" controller is needed to manage several alignments simultaneously; this controller appears in Figure 3 with the name Pairwise-alignments overseer. This controller runs in the host because it must communicate with the tile-monitor command-line tool which Tilera provides in its Multicore Development Environment (MDE), in order to manage the tile geometries. To take apart this functionality from the Clustal W source code, this task is carried out by a Perl script, which is called from the host main executable with the proper parameters: sequences to align, scoring matrix, etc.

Although other kinds of communications would be possible, like a telnet access, a client-server approach using the available Ethernet ports or a serial console, the communication between the Perl script and the Tile64 is performed via the more straightforward tile-monitor command line tool: when the Perl script starts a new tile-monitor session, it takes input/output communication channels through which the commands and results are sent. The Perl script manages pending jobs and available geometries, in order to schedule workload. Finally, when every pairwise alignment has been calculated, the MC64-ClustalWP2 pairalign() function gets all of them from the Perl script. Starting from them, the scoring matrix is computed as the original Clustal W does.

Implementation of the New Progressive-Alignment Stage

The implementation of the progressive aligner requires as well communicating the MC64-ClustalWP2 program, run in the host, with the parallel code executed in the Tile64. However, an intermediate script is not needed this time, as long as the algorithm has only one level of parallelism (every tile works for the same profile alignment and, thus, no fine-grained tile-monitor control is required).

This stage is controlled by the host main executable, which launches each profile alignment on the Tile64 environment. To do this, many internal variables must be shared between these both hardware environments. In total, 37 different variables and structures are needed, in order to rebuild the profiles and run the algorithm in the Tile64; other five are updated and returned to the host. To perform these communications and, at the same time, to avoid spreading dependencies throughout the code, we have built an intermediate layer library, called MC64-NWProfile_ParameterManagement, that encapsulates data structures and communication functions. This layer carries out communications using properly-formatted plain-text files. This facilitates uploading the required data into the Tile64, as well as download from it when required. In addition, the MC64_ParameterManagement provides the implementation of the profile-alignment algorithm, which is executed in the Tile64 microprocessor, as seen in Figure 3. Thus, the Clustal W malign() remains nearly the same, but the prfalign() function has been replaced by the needed calls to the parameter management library functions, which wait for the Tile64 program to finish before continuing.

The profile alignment algorithm for the Tile64 microprocessor has been developed starting from the MC64-NW/SW code, and applying several major changes to align profiles instead of sequences. For internal purposes, we have called MC64-NWProfile this new sub-algorithm, due to its global behavior. Each profile is a bi-dimensional structure of 35×m, where the height (35) is determined by all the possible residues plus gaps, whereas the width (m) is determined by the profile length; i.e., the length of the globally aligned sequences in the block. The progressive alignment is based on the alignment of these structures, with the prfscore() function determining the score for position i,j of the DPM from the vector multiplication of the profile1[i] row and the profile2[j] row.

Firstly, the MC64-NWProfile computes the profiles using the internal variables passed to it. Once calculated, the algorithm follows the same controller-workers approach than the MC64-NW/SW, using a similar wave-front parallelism. However, the prfscore() is now a vector-multiplication operation instead of an indirect-access operation. Additionally, the cells are 12 bytes instead of 6 bytes, so the job-partition optimal *k values* for each pair of profiles are completely different from those calculated in the pairwise-alignments stage. Thus, new optimal *k values* for significant profiles lengths must be pre-calculated, and, when a pair of profiles is to be aligned, the actual *k value* is interpolated from these ones.

To calculate a cell's content in this parallel approach, each worker requires accessing to the profile structures to compute the scores and alignment. However, for relatively long sequences, each profile can take several megabytes (for example, to align 200 kb sequences, each profile requires 24 MB), so a new problem arises: the location of these two profiles in memory. A direct approach to overcome such limitation is to store a single copy of the profiles in the shared memory, being accessible by both the controller and every worker. Yet, unfortunately, the shared memory access is very slow (can consume tens of CPU cycles) in comparison to the local memory access. Therefore, a better approach is to copy the profiles into the local memory of each tile. This simple modification represents an 8x speedup in execution time, though it requires much more memory (following the 200 kb example, 24 MB×2×59 workers =2.8 GB), and thus restricts the range of valid *k values*. Indeed, both the grid cache and the profile copies coexist in the available 8 GB (used as SSD shared and local memory). As a consequence, the available memory to store the grid cache decreases using this approach, and then, a low *k value* may produce a memory overflow.

In contrast, the MC64-NWProfile obtains a better performance with lower *k values*. Therefore, an intermediate approach is to only copy the necessary fragments for the current job to the worker local memory. Hence, when a worker receives a new job, it brings these fragments of the profiles to the local memory and when finished, it frees the memory. This approach opens the door to use small *k value* sizes, though the handicap is that the same fragments are eventually copied in the same worker several times for each alignment. In spite of this, using low *k values* instead of bigger ones, allows obtaining an additional 1.5x overall speedup, as it has been empirically demonstrated (data not shown). Finally, when the alignment is obtained, the local Clustal W variables are modified and returned to the host, which generates the intermediary multiple alignment and continues the process, following the guide-tree topology to progressively generate the next alignments.

RESULTS AND DISCUSSION

Once the algorithm was developed and implemented using the approach stated above, the MC64-ClustalWP2 was tested to benchmark its performance against the original algorithm and other parallel implementations, using different architectures and approaches. At first, we launched stress tests with ten sequences of different sizes and measured the speedup of the MC64-ClustalWP2 against other Clustal W implementations. A further test was carried out to analyze families of long sequences, which are aligned in much less time than with other general global MSA strategies, as discussed below.

Heterogeneous Tile64/PC MC64-ClustalWP2 Speedup Tests

In order to test the relative performance of the new MC64-ClustalWP2 parallel strategy implementation with the many-core Tile64 microprocessor, the original Clustal W algorithm and other parallel implementations were compared using a set of sequences with different sizes. In particular, the tested algorithms were the Clustal W 1.83 (originally written in C language) [28] and two parallel implementations: the ClustalW-MTV (the latest version of MT-ClustalW for multi-threaded systems) [41] and the ClustalW-MPI (focused on multi-core systems and PC clusters using the MPI library) [43]. The Clustal W many-core GPU implementations, as the MSA-CUDA [47], were excluded from this test, since they are unable to align such large sequences. The dataset used for the experiment is composed of 10 sets of artificial sequences whose lengths range between 25 and 300 kb. The alignment of hundreds or thousands of sequences with lower lengths is not the focus of our parallel approach (and neither its strength), so it is not worthy to carry out any test on such sets of sequences. In these cases, the scientist may choose from a different set of tools specifically developed for the purpose, including the above-mentioned GPU implementations and programs like MAFFT (the PartTree algorithm [52]) and Clustal-Omega [53].

All of the algorithms tested were run in the same environment (Intel Xeon Quad Core 2.0 GHz PC with 8 GB of quad-channel DDR2 memory), providing the same results but with rather different execution times. The MC64-ClustalWP2 used the Tile64 microprocessor on-boarded in a TilExpress-20G card with 8 GB RAM. The execution time and minimum-gain ratio of the MC64-ClustalWP2 algorithm against the other ones is shown for each set of sequences in Figure 4.

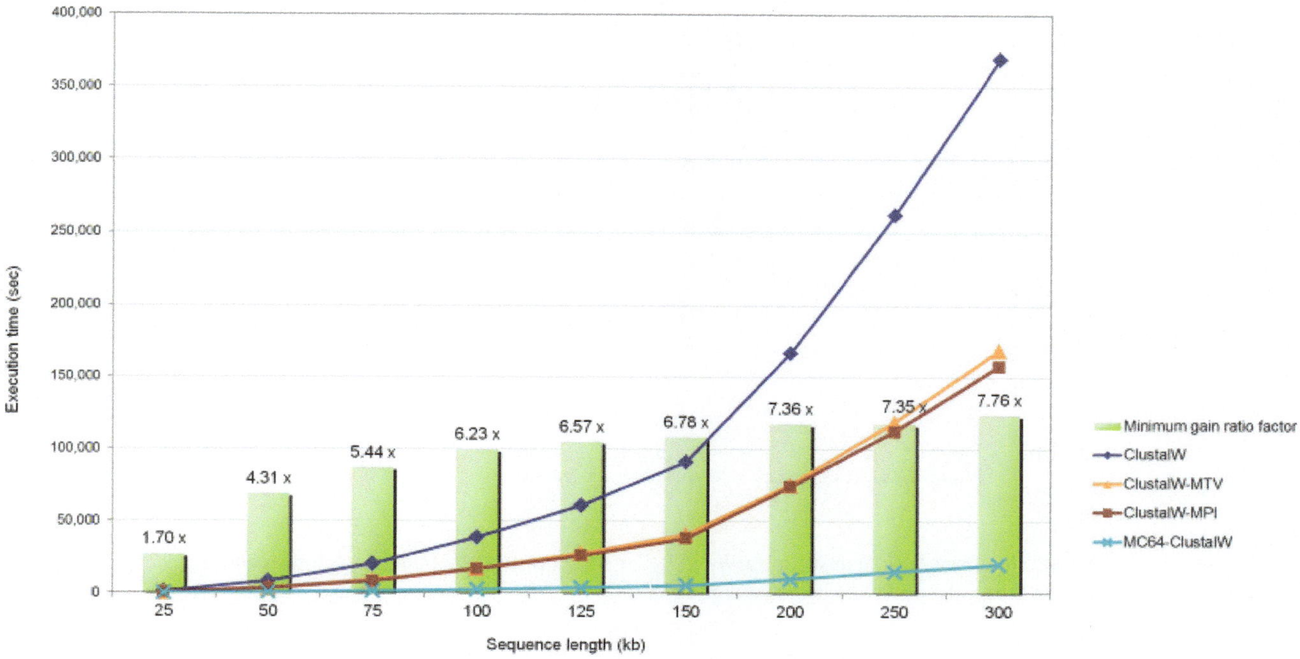

Figure 4. Execution time of the alignment of sets of ten randomly-generated sequences of different sizes, using Clustal W implementations. The tested algorithms are the original Clustal W 1.83, the MC64-ClustalWP2 for Tile64 and PC, and two parallel implementations for x86 systems (MT-ClustalW and ClustalW-MPI). In addition, the minimum gain ratio of the MC64-ClustalWP2 against all the other implementations is exposed for each set of sequences.

The results reveal the best performance of the MC64-ClustalWP2 against every other implementation. This tendency increases with the length of the sequences, because a higher parallelization factor is obtained.

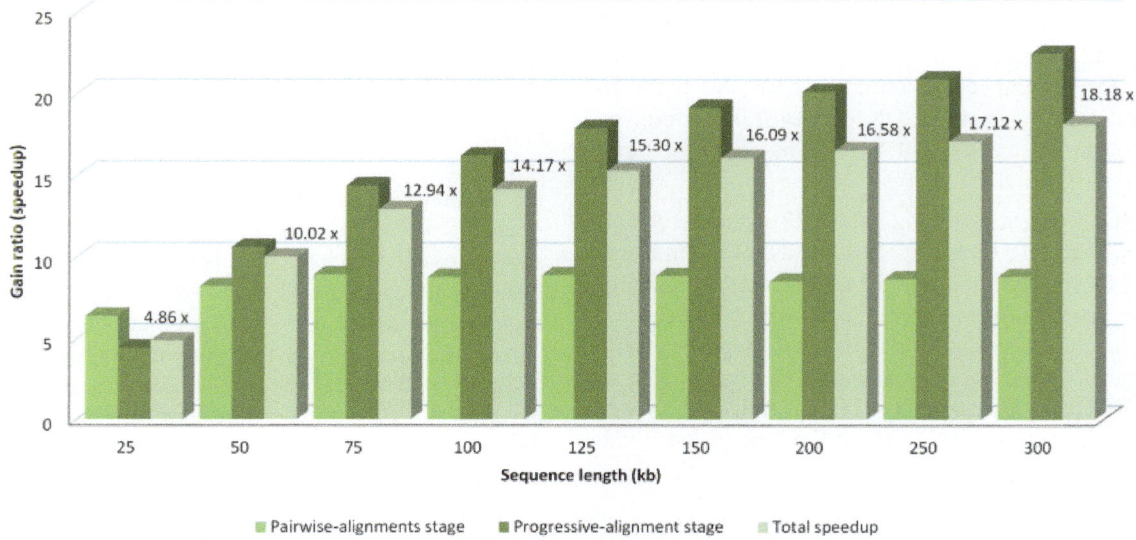

Figure 5. Speedup of the MC64-ClustalWP2 against Clustal W 1.83. The speedup is shown both for each relevant stage and for the full execution when aligning sets of ten randomly-generated sequences of different sizes.

Thus, the MC64-ClustalWP2 reaches a speedup of more than 7x when compared to the best multi-core implementation (ClustalW-MPI). In particular, both multi-core approaches present very similar behaviors with differences only appreciable when aligning 300 kb length sequences. On the other hand, the MC64-ClustalWP2 obtains a speedup factor of more than 18x when compared to the original algorithm. The Figures 5 and 6 show the relative acceleration factor in both the first and third stages against ClustalW and ClustalW-MPI, which reveals that our work-distribution strategy for the third stage yields much more parallelism than other methods.

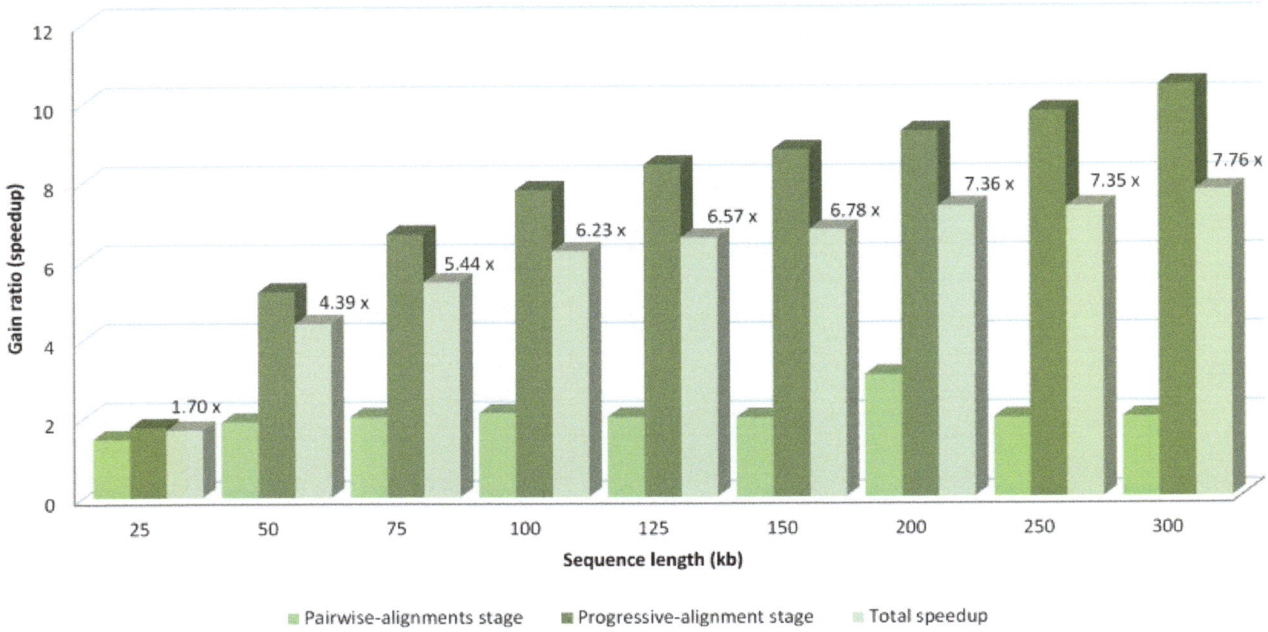

Figure 6. Speedup of the MC64-ClustalWP2 against ClustalW-MPI. The speedup is shown both for each relevant stage and for the full execution when aligning sets of ten randomly-generated sequences of different sizes.

Variation analyses of the Human Herpesvirus 1 Genomes

As a final test, the MC64-ClustalWP2 was used to run an experiment whose execution time is near prohibitive when non-parallel or less-efficient parallel MSA methods are applied. In this stress test, 37 different human herpesvirus 1 (*Herpes simplex* virus type 1; HHV-1) genomes, publicly available at GenBank <http://www.ncbi.nlm.nih.gov/genbank>, were selected to be aligned. The complete genome of the HHV-1 is about 152 kilobase pairs (kbp), and the different strains should *a priori* present several mutation areas, due to the high mutation-rates of this kind of DNA viruses. Therefore, such alignments can be carried out with dynamic-programming algorithms like Clustal W.

The MC64-ClustalWP2 aligned the 37 sequence genomes in 36,103 seconds (10.03 h; 21,742 seconds for the first stage, nearly zero for the second one and 14,360 seconds for the third stage). The final phylogenetic tree is shown in Figure 7. The upper part of the dendrogram includes the reference genome, which appears twice in the database (GenBank accession numbers NC_001806.1 and X14112.1) and was modeled from the strain 17 sequencing (GenBank accession number JN555585.1).

The quality of the alignments provided by any MSA algorithm, including Clustal W, depends on many factors, being an issue open for discussion [38], [54]. As expected in this case, the resulting alignment highlighted the polymorphisms between the virus strains. The most divergent strain was the TFT401 ocular one (GenBank accession number JN420337.1), also showing a low sequencing-coverage [55]. The alignment hereby presented confirms the previously reported sequencing results. As an example, a review of these genomes in relation to their glycoproteins coding genes has been published elsewhere [56].

This alignment was also performed with other global MSA algorithms, and even with other Clustal W implementations (which provides exactly the same alignment), but the quickest among them (ClustalW-MPI) required 274,149 seconds (3.17 days) to complete the alignment, being 7.59 times slower than our approach which, hence, becomes the only one capable to deal with this type of alignments in a reasonable time. On the other hand, some of the MSA algorithms do not generate an evolutionary tree of the genomic sequences, as they are oriented to find only the similar regions. Besides, they lack accuracy when the aligned sequences have highly polymorphic regions (e.g., with high mutation-rates), which is typical for most viruses [35].

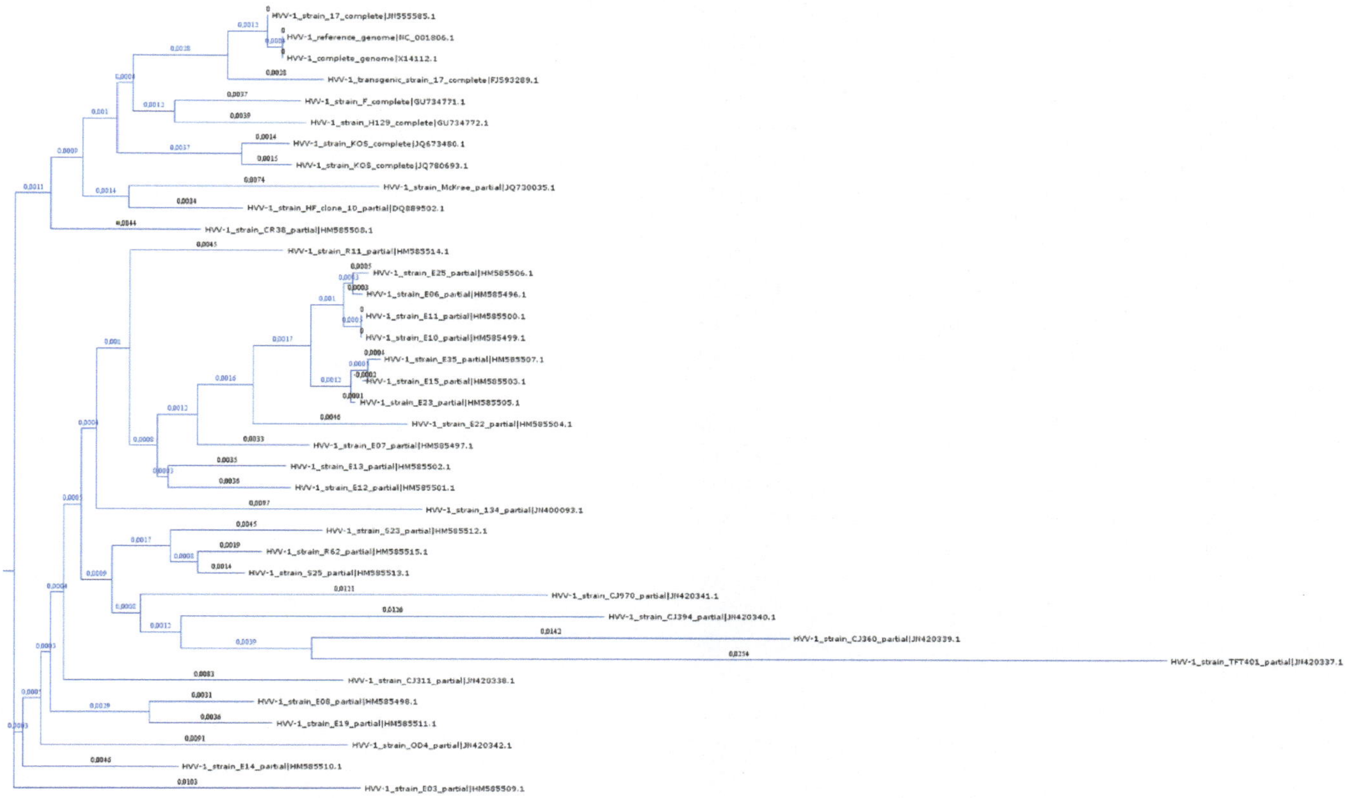

Figure 7. Phylogenetic tree of 37 different genomes of HHV-1. To calculate the multiple alignment of the genomes in this tree, MC64-ClustalWP2 run 7.59 times faster than its closest competitor (ClustalW-MPI).

Conclusions and Future Work

We have developed a new parallel strategy for Clustal W, which is one of the most relevant algorithms in bioinformatics for multiple-sequence alignments and dendrogram generation. This algorithm uses the pairwise-alignment operation as its core. Our work has focused on large sequences, a field where the resources of a GPGPU architecture have proven insufficient but, in contrast, our previous developments in many-core technologies for bioinformatics, like the MC64-NW/SW, have shown a high performance [20], [22]. In this scenario, we have separately redesigned and parallelized the two most time-consuming stages of Clustal W, using a new approach that exploits parallelism in systems with many cores. This new model, named MC64-ClustalWP2, allows aligning large sequences in a relatively short period of time on a personal computer, obtaining a global speedup of more than 18x against the original Clustal W, and more than 7x against the best x86 parallel implementation to date. This allows aligning more and larger sequences and, thus, enhances the range of problems that can be addressed in an affordable time.

The MC64-ClustalWP2 has been implemented for the heterogeneous standalone system x86-Tile64, using the Tile64 many-core microprocessor. Thus, within a single computer, the MC64-ClustalWP2 offers an impressive performance, being scalable to larger many-core systems using the same parallel strategy. This represents also a proof of concept that new parallel strategies can be exploited to harness the new developments in the many-core microprocessors to analyze the increasing amount of data generated by the second- and third-generation sequencing platforms. Thus, the Clustal W dynamic-programming approach that we have developed (MC64-ClustalWP2) can align genomes with highly polymorphic regions [35], which cannot be accomplished by the MSA heuristic aligners of genomes.

These developments allow to identify identities and differences to generate dendrograms for biodiversity and evolutionary studies, and to develop molecular markers like the ones based, for instance, on Single Nucleotide Polymorphisms (SNP), as well as on microsatellites, also known as Short Tandem Repeats (STR) in animals and as Simple Sequence Repeats (SSR) in plants, for germplasm management, breeding, identification and protection of the intellectual property, PDO, illegal traffic control and fraud prevention, as we have described for the olive oil [57].

Additionally, the MC64-ClustalWP2 strategy can be deployed for any many-core system with very little effort, like the current and future Intel Xeon Phi and the Tilera microprocessors. In particular, we have already developed a threaded version of MC64-NW/SW for the Intel i7 processor, and we are planning to use it as starting point to take full advantage of every Intel Xeon Phi core, where several threads must be executed to achieve an instruction-per-cycle performance. Furthermore, the approach can be escalated, both in processor and in memory resources, interconnecting several TilExpress-20G cards through their 10GBase-CX4 connectors to build a powerful cluster of Tile64 microprocessors, with thousands of cores, increasing both the number and the length of the sequences to align. We have already designed such a cluster, which is currently being evaluated [58].

On the other hand, a possible optimization in order to improve even further the parallelism of the first stage is to get rid of the intermediate Perl script and to transfer its high-level controller functionalities to a core of the many-core system. This allows using a single geometry where each worker is independent (i.e., may indistinctively work for any alignment), receiving in each case the data from the input sequences to be aligned. This new approach would maximize the core usage in the first stage, but would require more data transfers and memory resources in the overall system, which is strongly limited to 8 GB of RAM in the case of the Tile64 hardware. As an additional optimization for the alignment of thousands of sequences, the clustering stage could be parallelized as stated in [59]. However, we are not dealing with such an scenario now, since the MC64-ClustalWP2 is oriented to align long sequences.

On the other hand, the MC64-ClustalWP2 should be considered as a complementary tool to heuristic algorithms like the MGA [33] for the alignment of large sequences with highly polymorphic regions. In this regard, a more complex and "intelligent" alignment system could be built in a heterogeneous environment, in order to distribute and optimize the alignment tasks and stages, attending to the sequence characteristics. These developments should enhance the current tools in the bioinformatics arsenal.

Lastly, the MC64-ClustalWP2 algorithm is freely accessible to the scientific community and can be remotely executed on our server (a system that integrates the TilExpress-20G card) by means of a web service at <http://galactus.uma.es/manycore>. In the same way, the MC64-ClustalWP2 project is available under the GNU General Public License (GPL), and its source code can be downloaded from the same website.

Acknowledgments

We are grateful to Tilera for providing hardware and software tools <http://www.tilera.com>.

Author Contributions

Conceived and designed the experiments: DD FJE PH GD SG. Performed the experiments: DD FJE. Analyzed the data: DD FJE PH JC AG GD SG. Contributed reagents/materials/analysis tools: JC AG GD. Wrote the paper: DD FJE PH JC AG GD SG. Software design: DD FJE SG. Web deployment: DD AG SG.

REFERENCES

1. Needleman SB, Wunsch CD (1970) A general method applicable to the search for similarities in the amino acid sequence of two proteins. Journal of Molecular Biology 48: 443–453
2. Smith TF, Waterman MS (1981) Identification of common molecular subsequences. J Mol Biol 147: 195–197
3. Gotoh O (1982) An improved algorithm for matching biological sequences. Journal of Molecular Biology 162: 705–708
4. Hirschberg DS (1975) A linear space algorithm for computing maximal common subsequences. Commun ACM 18: 341–343
5. Driga A, Lu P, Schaeffer J, Szafron D, Charter K, et al. (2006) FastLSA: A Fast, Linear-Space, Parallel and Sequential Algorithm for Sequence Alignment. Algorithmica45: 337–375
6. Pearson WR, Lipman DJ (1988) Improved tools for biological sequence comparison.Proceedings of the National Academy of Sciences of the United States of America 85: 2444–2448
7. Altschul S, Gish W, Miller W, Myers E-M, Lipman D (1990) Basic local alignment search tool. J Mol Biol 215: 403–410
8. Pearson WR (1991) Searching protein sequence libraries: comparison of the sensitivity and selectivity of the Smith-Waterman and FASTA algorithms. Genomics 11: 635–650
9. Mirto M, Fiore S, Epicoco I, Cafaro M, Mocavero S, et al. (2008) A Bioinformatics Grid Alignment Toolkit. Future Generation Computer Systems 24: 752–762
10. Goetzmann JF (2007) Massively Parallel Contact Simulation on Graphics Hardware using NVIDIA CUDA Bacherlor's Thesis. Institute for Computer Science, Universität Mainz.
11. Adapteva (2011) Epiphany Multicore IP. Available:http://www.adapteva.com/index.php?option=com_content&view=article&id=72&Itemid=79 Accessed 2013 Jul 16.
12. Shah M, Barreh J, Brooks J, Golla R, Grohoski G, et al. (2007) UltraSPARC T2: A highly-treaded, power-efficient, SPARC SOC Asian Solid-State Circuits Conference.(ASSCC07): 22–25
13. Mattson TG, Wijngaart RVD, Frumkin M (2008) Programming the Intel 80-core network-on-a-chip Terascale processor. Proceedings of the 2008 ACM/IEEE conference on Supercomputing. Austin, Texas: IEEE Press. pp. 1–11.
14. Intel (2010) The SCC Platform Overview. Available:http://techresearch.intel.com/spaw2/uploads/files/SCC-Overview.pdf Accessed 2013 Jul 16.
15. Intel (2010) Intel's Teraflops Research Chip. Available:http://download.intel.com/pressroom/kits/Teraflops/Teraflops_Research_Chip_Overview.pdf Accessed 2013 Jul 16.
16. Wentzlaff D, Griffin P, Hoffmann H, Bao L, Edwards B, et al. (2007) On-Chip Interconnection Architecture of the Tile Processor. IEEE Micro 27: 15–31
17. Tilera (2011) Product Brief: TILE-Gx 8000 Series. Available:http://www.tilera.com/sites/default/files/productbriefs/TILE-Gx8000Series Brief_0.pdf. Accessed 2013 Jul 16.
18. Manavski SA, Valle G (2008) CUDA compatible GPU cards as efficient hardware accelerators for Smith-Waterman sequence alignment. BMC Bioinformatics 9Suppl 2: S10.
19. Liu Y, Schmidt B, Maskell DL (2010) CUDASW++2.0: enhanced Smith-Waterman protein database search on CUDA-enabled GPUs based on SIMT and virtualized SIMD abstractions. BMC Research Notes 3: 93.
20. Díaz D, Esteban FJ, Hernández P, Caballero JA, Dorado G, et al. (2011) Parallelizing and optimizing a bioinformatics pairwise sequence alignment algorithm

for many-core architecture. Parallel Computing 37: 244–259

21. Esteban FJ, Díaz D, Hernández P, Caballero JA, Dorado G, et al. (2013) Direct approaches to exploit many-core architecture in bioinformatics. Future Generation Computer Systems 29: 15–26
22. Gálvez S, Díaz D, Hernández P, Esteban FJ, Caballero JA, et al. (2010) Next-Generation Bioinformatics: Using Many-Core Processor Architecture to Develop a Web Service for Sequence Alignment. Bioinformatics 26: 683–686
23. Agrifood Biotechnology ("Biotecnología Agroalimentaria") Research Group (2009) Many-core bioinformatics algorithms development. Available:http://galactus.uma.es/manycore/ Accessed 2013 Sep 11.
24. Bains W (1986) MULTAN: a program to align multiple DNA sequences. Nucleic Acids Research 14: 159–177
25. Waterman MS (1986) Multiple sequence alignment by consensus. Nucleic Acids Research 14: 9095–9102
26. Higgins DG, Sharp PM (1988) CLUSTAL: a package for performing multiple sequence alignment on a microcomputer. Gene 73: 237–244
27. Higgins DG, Bleasby AJ, Fuchs R (1992) CLUSTAL V: improved software for multiple sequence alignment. Computer applications in the biosciences: CABIOS 8: 189–191
28. Thompson JD, Higgins DG, Gibson TJ (1994) CLUSTAL W: improving the sensitivity of progressive multiple sequence alignment through sequence weighting, position-specific gap penalties and weight matrix choice. Nucleic Acids Res 22: 4673–4680
29. Larkin MA, Blackshields G, Brown NP, Chenna R, McGettigan PA, et al. (2007)Clustal W and Clustal X version 2.0. Bioinformatics 23: 2947–2948
30. Notredame C, Higgins DG, Heringa J (2000) T-coffee: a novel method for fast and accurate multiple sequence alignment. Journal of Molecular Biology 302: 205–217
31. Edgar RC (2004) MUSCLE: multiple sequence alignment with high accuracy and high throughput. Nucleic Acids Research 32: 1792–1797
32. Brudno M, Do CB, Cooper GM, Kim MF, Davydov E, et al. (2003) LAGAN and Multi-LAGAN: efficient tools for large-scale multiple alignment of genomic DNA. Genome Res 13: 721–731
33. Hohl M, Kurtz S, Ohlebusch E (2002) Efficient multiple genome alignment.Bioinformatics 18: S312–320
34. Dewey CN (2007) Aligning multiple whole genomes with Mercator and MAVID.Methods Mol Biol 395: 221–236
35. Chain P, Kurtz S, Ohlebusch E, Slezak T (2003) An applications-focused review of comparative genomics tools: Capabilities, limitations and future challenges. Briefings in Bioinformatics 4: 105–123
36. Darling AE, Mau B, Perna NT (2010) progressiveMauve: Multiple Genome Alignment with Gene Gain, Loss and Rearrangement. PLoS ONE 5: e11147.
37. Paten B, Earl D, Nguyen N, Diekhans M, Zerbino D, et al. (2011) Cactus: Algorithms for genome multiple sequence alignment. Genome Res 21: 1512–1528
38. Notredame C (2007) Recent Evolutions of Multiple Sequence Alignment Algorithms.PLoS Comput Biol 3: e123.
39. Vandierendonck H, Rul S, Questier M, De Bosschere K (2008) Experiences with Parallelizing a Bio-informatics Program on the Cell BE High Performance Embedded Architectures and Compilers. In:Stenström P, Dubois M, Katevenis M, Gupta R, Ungerer T, editors: Springer Berlin/Heidelberg. pp. 161–175.
40. Mikhailov D, Cofer H, Gomperts R (2001) Performance optimization of Clustal W: parallel Clustal W, HT Clustal, and MULTICLUSTAL. Silicon Graphics, Inc.
41. Chaichoompu K, Kittitornkun S, Tongsima S (2006) MT-ClustalW: multithreading multiple sequence alignment. Proceedings of the 20th Parallel and Distributed Processing Symposium (IPDPS 2006). pp. 8.
42. Vandierendonck H, Rul S, De Bosschere K (2010) Accelerating Multiple Sequence Alignment with the Cell BE Processor. The Computer Journal 53: 814–826
43. Li K-B (2003) ClustalW-MPI: ClustalW analysis using distributed and parallel computing. Bioinformatics 19: 1585–1586
44. Saitou N, Nei M (1987) The neighbor-joining method: a new method for reconstructing phylogenetic trees. Molecular Biology and Evolution 4: 406–425
45. Myers EW, Miller W (1988) Optimal alignments in linear space. Comput Appl Biosci4: 11–17
46. Cheetham J, Dehne F, Pitre S, Rau-Chaplin A, Taillon PJ (2003) Parallel CLUSTAL W for PC clusters. Proceedings of the 2003 international conference on Computational science and its applications: Part II. Montreal, Canada: Springer-Verlag. pp. 300–309.
47. Yongchao L, Schmidt B, Maskell DL (2009) MSA-CUDA: Multiple Sequence Alignment on Graphics Processing Units with CUDA. Proceedings of the 20th IEEE International Conference on Application-specific Systems, Architectures and Processors (ASAP 2009). pp. 121–128.
48. Yongchao L, Schmidt B, Maskell DL (2009) Parallel reconstruction of neighbor-joining trees for large multiple sequence alignments using CUDA. Proceedings of the IEEE International Symposium on Parallel and Distributed Processing (IPDPS 2009). pp. 1–8.
49. Michener CD, Sokal RR (1957) A quantitative approach to a problem of classification. Evolution 11
50. Isaza S, Sanchez F, Gaydadjiev G, Ramirez A, Valero M (2010) Scalability Analysis of Progressive Alignment on a Multicore. Proceedings of the International Conference on Complex, Intelligent and Software Intensive Systems (CISIS 2010). pp. 889–894.
51. Stone JE, Gohara D, Shi G (2010) OpenCL: A Parallel Programming Standard for Heterogeneous Computing Systems. Computing in Science and Engineering. pp. 66–73.
52. Katoh K, Toh H (2007) PartTree: an algorithm to build an approximate tree from a large number of unaligned sequences. Bioinformatics 23: 372–374

53. Sievers F, Wilm A, Dineen D, Gibson TJ, Karplus K, et al. (2011) Fast, scalable generation of high-quality protein multiple sequence alignments using Clustal Omega.Mol Syst Biol 7: 539.

54. Higgins DG, Blackshields G, Wallace IM (2005) Mind the gaps: progress in progressive alignment. Proc Natl Acad Sci U S A 102: 10411–10412

55. Kolb AW, Adams M, Cabot EL, Craven M, Brandt CR (2011) Multiplex sequencing of seven ocular herpes simplex virus type-1 genomes: phylogeny, sequence variability, and SNP distribution. Invest Ophthalmol Vis Sci 52: 9061–9073

56. Norberg P, Bergstrom T, Rekabdar E, Lindh M, Liljeqvist JA (2004) Phylogenetic analysis of clinical herpes simplex virus type 1 isolates identified three genetic groups and recombinant viruses. J Virol 78: 10755–10764

57. Perez-Jimenez M, Besnard G, Dorado G, Hernandez P (2013) Varietal tracing of virgin olive oils based on plastid DNA variation profiling. PLoS One 8: e70507.

58. Esteban F, Díaz D, Hernández P, Caballero J, Dorado G, et al. (2013) MC64-Cluster: A Many-Core CPU Cluster for Bioinformatics Applications. In: Rocha Á, Correia AM, Wilson T, Stroetmann KA, editors. Advances in Information Systems and Technologies: Springer Berlin Heidelberg. pp. 819–825.

59. Du Z, Lin F (2006) pNJTree: A parallel program for reconstruction of neighbor-joining tree and its application in ClustalW. Parallel Computing 32: 441–446

CHAPTER 2

ANALYSIS OF THE TRANSIENT RESPONSE OF A DUAL-FED RC TRANSMISSION LINE

Mohsen Dorraki,[1] Gregory K. Cambrell,[2] and Derek Abbott[3]

[1] Department of Electrical Engineering, Amirkabir University of Technology, Tehran, Iran

[2] Department of Electrical and Computer Systems Engineering, Faculty of Engineering, Monash University, Victoria, Australia

[3] School of Electrical and Electronic Engineering, University of Adelaide, South Australia, Australia

ABSTRACT

The transient analysis of a uniform transmission line of finite length is considered in this paper. For the first time this paper provides an analytical expression for the time-domain response of an RC transmission line, which is stimulated by a step function that is fed into both ends of the transmission line. In particular, we find an analytical expression for the step response at the center of the transmission line, in order to determine the worst-case rise time. This is of interest, for example, in large charge-coupled device (CCD) arrays, where long polysilicon lines are dual-fed in order to mitigate degradation in rise time. The analytical expressions for the RC transmission line are supported by computer-simulated lumped RC models.

INTRODUCTION

Integrated circuits have seen significant progress—from the early developments that contained only a few transistors to modern microprocessors that can contain billions of elements. This development has been made possible by the downscaling of circuit dimensions, which results in increased speed and reduced costs.

The disadvantage of this development is that the resistance of the wires between transistors increases disproportionately when their cross-sectional dimensions are reduced. Consequently, when they are scaled down, signal propagation speed becomes reduced.

Citation: Dorraki M, Cambrell GK, Abbott D (2015) Analysis of the Transient Response of a Dual-Fed RC Transmission Line. PLoS ONE 10(2): e0116993. doi:10.1371/journal.pone.0116993.

Estimating interconnection delay is an important issue for present circuits. Many authors have modeled the wires inside integrated circuits as distributed RC lines. The analysis of finite RC interconnections under a step input is widely discussed in the literature, e.g. [1, 2]. The usual method is to calculate the transfer function, then the time-domain response is extracted for an RC transmission line with a step input. Many authors have adopted different approaches to obtain a time-domain response using the Laplace transform technique [3]. Kahng and Muddu presented the time-domain response for an RC transmission line with source and load impedances [3]. Moreover, they analyzed a finite transmission line for a ramp input [4], using a method based on solving the diffusion equation and applying the method of images [3]. Rao reviewed the step response of the semi-infinite distributed RC line and focused mainly on the step response of a finite-length RC line with a capacitive load termination, which is the most common model for a wire within present-day integrated CMOS chips [5]. Additionally,

Gupta and Patnaik presented an exact analysis of the output response of a distributed RC interconnect under input signals that are polynomial in time [6].

None of these previous studies used the same step input fed simultaneously into both ends of the transmission line, while considering the behavior at the center of the line. This scheme is of interest for long interconnects on chips and also for long electrodes on charged-coupled devices (CCDs). For example, in order to mitigate a slow rise time, a circular clock bus can be fed from both ends, and it becomes of interest to have an analytical expression for the transient response at the center of the bus. Similarly, in order to reduce RC degradation of clock signals along long CCD electrodes, it is possible to feed the clock to both ends of the electrodes [7]. An analytical expression that predicts the worst-case rise time at the center of the electrode is therefore a useful design equation. Another example, where such an analytical expression is potentially useful, is in the design of A and J gates for future silicon quantum computers [8].

The rest of this paper is organized as follows. After reviewing the transient response of a semi-infinite RC transmission line and an RC line of finite length with open-circuit termination, we will derive the transient response of an RC line of finite length that is fed at both ends with the same step function. In particular, we will determine the improvement of the 63% rise time thereby achieved at the center of the line. The analytical expressions will be presented in two forms: a convergent series of trigonometric and exponential functions, and a convergent series of complementary error functions. Furthermore, it will be evident that the same expressions arise by applying the method of superposition. As a final confirmation of the derived analytical expressions, the distributed RC line of finite length is modeled by several lumped RC sections, and the step response at the center of the model is computed and compared with the analytical expressions.

TRANSIENT RESPONSE OF RC TRANSMISSION LINES

Semi-Infinite RC Transmission Line

An RC transmission line is shown in Fig. 1. This may, for example, be the model of a CCD electrode. Ignoring any propagation time due to inductance, the voltage across the line $v(x,t)$ at position x **along the line and at time** t **satisfies the well-known diffusion equation**

$$\frac{\partial^2 v}{\partial x^2} = rc\,\frac{\partial v}{\partial t} \tag{1}$$

together with appropriate boundary conditions and initial condition. Here r **and** c **are the uniform resistance and capacitance per unit length. It is a linear partial differential equation (PDE)**. The corresponding current in the line $i(x, t)$ satisfies the same PDE and is related to the voltage $v(x, t)$ by

$$i = -\frac{1}{r}\frac{\partial v}{\partial x}. \tag{2}$$

A particular integral for the diffusion equation is

$$v(x,t) = a\ \mathrm{erfc}\left((b \pm \frac{x}{L})\Big/\sqrt{\frac{4t}{rcL^2}}\right) + cx + d \tag{3}$$

where a, b, c **and** d **are constants and** $\mathrm{erfc}(\cdot)$ is the complementary error function defined by

$$\mathrm{erfc}(z) = 1 - \frac{2}{\sqrt{\pi}}\int_0^z e^{-y^2}\,dy. \tag{4}$$

A characteristic length L **has been introduced so that the dimensionless (normalized) variables**

$$\chi = \frac{x}{L} \tag{5}$$

And

$$\tau = \frac{t}{rcL^2} \tag{6}$$

can be used throughout the analysis. The corresponding dimensionless diffusion equation is

$$\frac{\partial^2 v}{\partial \chi^2} = \frac{\partial v}{\partial \tau}. \tag{7}$$

The unit step response of a semi-infinite line extending from $x = 0$ **to infinity is found by imposing the boundary conditions**

$$\mathrm{BC1}: v(0,t) = v_{\mathrm{in}}(t) = u(t) \quad \text{for all} \quad t \geqslant 0 \tag{8}$$

$$\mathrm{BC2}: i(\infty,t) = 0 \ \text{ or } \ \frac{\partial v}{\partial x}(\infty,t) = 0 \quad \text{for all} \quad t \geqslant 0 \tag{9}$$

where $u(t)$ is the unit step function, and the initial condition

$$\mathrm{IC}: v(x,0) = 0 \quad \text{for all} \quad 0 < x < \infty. \tag{10}$$

Therefore $a = 1$, **and** b, c **and** d **must be zero, and so the unit step response of the semi-infinite line is**

$$v(x,t) = \mathrm{erfc}\left(\left(\frac{x}{L}\right)\Big/\sqrt{\frac{4t}{rcL^2}}\right) \tag{11}$$

Or

$$v(\chi,\tau) = \mathrm{erfc}(\chi/\sqrt{4\tau}). \tag{12}$$

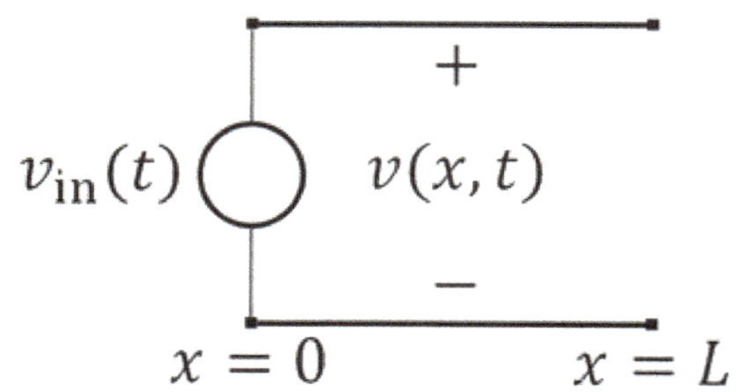

Figure 1. An RC transmission line.

Finite RC Transmission Line with Open-Circuit Termination

Consider an RC transmission line of finite length L **with open-circuit termination, as shown in** Fig. 1, fed with a unit step function of voltage. Rao has solved this case by using the Laplace transform technique [5]. For the Laplace transform of the voltage step response $v(x, t)$ he obtains

$$\mathcal{L}\{v(x,t)\}_s^t = \int_0^\infty v(x,t)e^{-st}\,dt = V(x,s) = \frac{1}{s}\frac{\cosh\left((1-\frac{x}{L})\sqrt{rcL^2s}\right)}{\cosh(\sqrt{rcL^2s})} \quad \textbf{(13)}$$

for $0 \le x \le L$. By directly inverting this Laplace transform Rao obtains the following infinite series for the unit step response:

$$v(x,t) = 1 - \frac{2}{\pi}\sum_{n=1}^{\infty}\frac{1}{(n-\frac{1}{2})}\left[\sin\left((n-\frac{1}{2})\pi(\frac{x}{L})\right)\right]e^{-\left((n-\frac{1}{2})\pi\right)^2 t/(rcL^2)}. \quad \textbf{(14)}$$

Then, by using the expansion

$$\frac{1}{\cosh(y)} = \frac{2e^{-y}}{1+e^{-2y}} = 2\sum_{n=0}^{\infty}(-1)^n e^{-(2n+1)y} \quad \textbf{(15)}$$

so that

$$V(x,s) = \frac{1}{s}\sum_{n=0}^{\infty}(-1)^n\left\{e^{-(2n+\frac{x}{L})\sqrt{rcL^2s}} + e^{-(2n+2-\frac{x}{L})\sqrt{rcL^2s}}\right\} \quad \textbf{(16)}$$

he performs an alternative inversion of the Laplace transform (13) and obtains another, but equivalent, infinite series for the unit step response:

$$v(x,t) = \sum_{n=0}^{\infty}(-1)^n\left\{\operatorname{erfc}\left((2n+\frac{x}{L})/\sqrt{\frac{4t}{rcL^2}}\right) + \operatorname{erfc}\left((2n+2-\frac{x}{L})/\sqrt{\frac{4t}{rcL^2}}\right)\right\}. \quad \textbf{(17)}$$

For the purpose of comparison, the following practical example will be considered here and later in the paper. Let r = **1 Ω/m**, c = **1×10^{-6} F/m and** L = **1×10^{-3} m. The unit step response at the center of this line will be of particular interest. Here,** x = **0.5×10^{-3} m and** $\chi = x/L$ = **0.5. When evaluated at this position, the unit step response reaches (1–1/e)** or 0.63212 of its final value of 1.0 in the time t = **0.36283×10^{-12} s, that is, when** $\tau = t/(rcL^2)$ = 0.36283. This is called the 63% rise time.

For interest, if this practical line were extended to infinity (becoming a semi-infinite line), the 63% rise time at the same position would increase to time t = **0.54538×10^{-12} s, that is, to** $\tau = t/(rcL^2)$ = 0.54538. The increased rise time is due to the need to charge the extra capacitance beyond $x = L$.

On the other hand, if this practical line is fed with the same step function of voltage into both ends of the line, charging of the capacitance within the finite line is potentially faster than when leaving the far end open.

Analysis of Dual-Fed RC Transmission Line

Consider an RC transmission line of finite length L **fed with the same step function of voltage at both ends, as shown in** Fig. 2. The boundary and initial conditions now become

$$\text{BC1}: v(0,t) = u_1 \cdot u(t) \quad \text{for all} \quad t \geqslant 0, \quad \textbf{(18)}$$

$$\text{BC2}: v(L,t) = u_2 \cdot u(t) \quad \text{for all} \quad t \geqslant 0, \quad \textbf{(19)}$$

$$\text{IC}: v(x,0) = 0 \quad \text{for all} \quad 0 < x < L. \quad \textbf{(20)}$$

For generality, individual step amplitudes u_1 **and** u_2 **have been introduced at each end of the RC line. They can both be set to unity at the end of the analysis.**

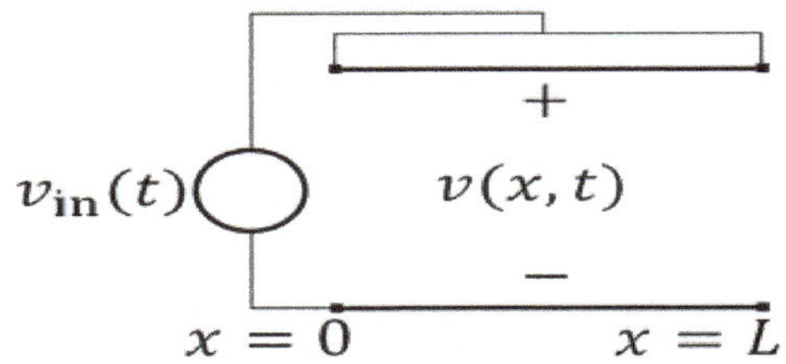

Figure 2. The RC transmission line is identical to that in Fig. 1, except that both ends are fed with the same step function $v_{in}(t)$. The response of interest, $v(x; t)$, is the voltage at the center of the line. The voltage at that position will possess the worst-case rise time.

Taking the Laplace transform of the diffusion Equation (1) **and applying the initial condition** (20) gives the wave equation

$$\frac{\partial^2}{\partial x^2}V(x,s) = rc[v(x,t)e^{-st}]_{t=0}^{t=\infty} + rcs\int_0^\infty v(x,t)e^{-st}dt = rcsV(x,s). \quad \textbf{(21)}$$

Its general solution in the Laplace transform domain is

$$V(x,s) = A(s)\, e^{x\sqrt{rcs}} + B(s)\, e^{-x\sqrt{rcs}} \quad \textbf{(22)}$$

where $A(s)$ and $B(s)$ do not depend on x **and must be determined from the boundary conditions** (18) and (19). Since the Laplace transform of the unit step function is $1/s$, BC1 and BC2 become

$$V(0,s) = A(s) + B(s) = \frac{u_1}{s}, \quad \textbf{(23)}$$

$$V(L,s) = A(s)\, e^{L\sqrt{rcs}} + B(s)\, e^{-L\sqrt{rcs}} = \frac{u_2}{s}. \quad \textbf{(24)}$$

Thus

$$A(s) = \frac{-u_1 e^{-L\sqrt{rcs}} + u_2}{2s\sinh(L\sqrt{rcs})}, \quad \textbf{(25)}$$

$$B(s) = \frac{u_1 e^{L\sqrt{rcs}} - u_2}{2s\sinh(L\sqrt{rcs})} \quad \textbf{(26)}$$

so that

$$V(x,s) = \frac{1}{s}\cdot\frac{u_1\sinh\left((1-\frac{x}{L})\sqrt{rcL^2s}\right) + u_2\sinh\left((\frac{x}{L})\sqrt{rcL^2s}\right)}{\sinh(\sqrt{rcL^2s})} = u_1F(L-x,s) + u_2F(x,s) \quad \textbf{(27)}$$

Where

$$F(x,s) = \frac{1}{s}\cdot\frac{\sinh\left((\frac{x}{L})\sqrt{rcL^2s}\right)}{\sinh\left(\sqrt{rcL^2s}\right)}. \quad \textbf{(28)}$$

The inverse Laplace transform of $F(x, s)$ is

$$f(x,t) = \mathcal{L}^{-1}\{F(x,s)\}_t^s = \frac{1}{2\pi j}\int_{\alpha-j\infty}^{\alpha+j\infty}F(x,s)e^{ts}ds = \frac{1}{2\pi j}\int_{\alpha-j\infty}^{\alpha+j\infty}\frac{1}{s}\cdot\frac{\sinh\left((\frac{x}{L})\sqrt{rcL^2s}\right)}{\sinh\left(\sqrt{rcL^2s}\right)}e^{ts}ds. \quad (29)$$

Though sinhz—√z is not analytic, the ratio of two such functions is lacking any double-valuedness and so there is no need for a cut along the negative-real axis. Note that this ratio has a line of first-order poles along this axis. For $t < 0$, **the** contour of the integration may be closed to the right, the integral at infinity goes to zero, and the value of the contour integral is zero. For $t > 0$, this is not permissible, the integral becoming exponentially large due to the e^{ts} factor. However, the contour may be closed to the left, thus enclosing the line of poles. The value of the new integral at infinity is still zero, and the contour integral that we are interested in takes on the value of the sum of the residues. The simple poles are located at

$$s_n = -\frac{(n\pi)^2}{rcL^2} \tag{30}$$

for each integer $n \geq 1$. **Therefore,**

$$f(x,t) = \frac{x}{L} + \sum_{n=1}^{\infty} \frac{2}{jn\pi} \frac{\sinh(jn\pi x/L) e^{-(n\pi)^2 t/(rcL^2)}}{\cosh(jn\pi)} \tag{31}$$

so that

$$f(x,t) = \frac{x}{L} + \frac{2}{\pi} \sum_{n=1}^{\infty} \frac{(-1)^n}{n} \sin(n\pi x/L) e^{-(n\pi)^2 t/(rcL^2)}. \tag{32}$$

Hence the general step response is

$$v(x,t) = u_1\left(1 - \frac{x}{L}\right) + u_2\left(\frac{x}{L}\right) + \frac{2}{\pi}\sum_{n=1}^{\infty} \frac{(-1)^n}{n} \left[u_1 \sin\left(n\pi\left(1 - \frac{x}{L}\right)\right) + u_2 \sin\left(n\pi\left(\frac{x}{L}\right)\right)\right] e^{-(n\pi)^2 t/(rcL^2)}. \tag{33}$$

Finally, by setting $u_1 = 1$ and $u_2 = 1$, the unit step response of the dual-fed RC line is

$$v(x,t) = 1 + \frac{2}{\pi}\sum_{n=1}^{\infty} \frac{(-1)^n}{n} \left[\sin\left(n\pi\left(1 - \frac{x}{L}\right)\right) + \sin\left(n\pi\left(\frac{x}{L}\right)\right)\right] e^{-(n\pi)^2 t/(rcL^2)}. \tag{34}$$

At the center of the line where $\chi = x/L = 0.5$, the unit step response of the dual fed RC line is

$$v\left(\frac{L}{2}, t\right) = 1 - \frac{4}{\pi} \sum_{n=0}^{\infty} \frac{(-1)^n}{(2n+1)} e^{-\left((2n+1)\pi\right)^2 t/(rcL^2)} \tag{35}$$

Or

$$v(0.5, \tau) = 1 - \frac{4}{\pi} \sum_{n=0}^{\infty} \frac{(-1)^n}{(2n+1)} e^{-\left((2n+1)\pi\right)^2 \tau}. \tag{36}$$

Again let $r = 1\ \Omega/\text{m}$, $c = 1\times10^{-6}$ F/m and $L = 1\times10^{-3}$ m. The unit step response at the center of this dual-fed RC line reaches $(1-1/e)$ or 0.63212 of its final value of 1.0 in the time $t = 0.125795\times10^{-12}$ s, that is, when $\tau = t/(rcL^2) = 0.125795$.

Compared to the case when this line is left open at the far end, the 63% rise time at the center has been reduced by a factor of 2.8843, which is a significant improvement.

Alternative Analysis of Dual-Fed RC Transmission Line

Following a method similar to that presented by Rao in [5], and using the expansion

$$\frac{1}{\sinh(y)} = \frac{2e^{-y}}{1 - e^{-2y}} = 2\sum_{n=0}^{\infty} e^{-(2n+1)y} \tag{37}$$

the Laplace transform (28) can be expanded as

$$F(x,s) = \frac{1}{s}\sum_{n=0}^{\infty} \left\{ e^{-(2n+1-\frac{x}{L})\sqrt{rcL^2 s}} - e^{-(2n+1+\frac{x}{L})\sqrt{rcL^2 s}} \right\}. \tag{38}$$

Then another, but equivalent, infinite series for the general step response of the dual-fed RC line is

$$v(x,t) = \sum_{n=0}^{\infty} \left\{ u_1 \left[\operatorname{erfc}\left((2n + \frac{x}{L}) \Big/ \sqrt{\frac{4t}{rcL^2}}\right) - \operatorname{erfc}\left((2n + 2 - \frac{x}{L}) \Big/ \sqrt{\frac{4t}{rcL^2}}\right)\right] + u_2 \left[\operatorname{erfc}\left((2n + 1 - \frac{x}{L}) \Big/ \sqrt{\frac{4t}{rcL^2}}\right) - \operatorname{erfc}\left((2n + 1 + \frac{x}{L}) \Big/ \sqrt{\frac{4t}{rcL^2}}\right)\right] \right\}. \tag{39}$$

The unit step response is obtained by setting $u_1 = 1$ and $u_2 = 1$. At the center of the line where $\chi = x/L = 0.5$, the unit step response of the dual-fed RC line is

$$v\left(\frac{L}{2}, t\right) = 2\sum_{n=0}^{\infty}\left\{\operatorname{erfc}\left(\left(2n + \frac{1}{2}\right)/\sqrt{\frac{4t}{rcL^2}}\right) - \operatorname{erfc}\left(\left(2n + \frac{3}{2}\right)/\sqrt{\frac{4t}{rcL^2}}\right)\right\} \tag{40}$$

Or

$$v(0.5, \tau) = 2\sum_{n=0}^{\infty}\left\{\operatorname{erfc}\left(\left(2n + \frac{1}{2}\right)/\sqrt{4\tau}\right) - \operatorname{erfc}\left(\left(2n + \frac{3}{2}\right)/\sqrt{4\tau}\right)\right\}. \tag{41}$$

This series has been found to converge faster than the series in Equation (36) **for small values of τ but otherwise gives identical numerical values.**

Some analytical results are shown in Table 1.

Table 1. Analytical results for the unit step response at the center of a dual-fed RC line.

τ	0.01	0.02	0.03	0.05	0.07	0.10	0.12	0.13	0.15	0.20	0.50
$v(0.5, \tau)$ (volt)	0.001	0.025	0.082	0.228	0.363	0.526	0.610	0.647	0.710	0.823	0.991

doi:10.1371/journal.pone.0116993.t001

Analysis of Dual-Fed RC Transmission Line using Superposition

For any bilateral linear electrical network, lumped or distributed, the method of superposition is valid. In particular, the voltage at any point in an RC transmission line that is fed by two independent sources is the algebraic sum of the voltages caused by each independent source acting alone, where the other source is reduced to zero and replaced by its internal impedance. Thus, an ideal voltage source becomes a short-circuit when reduced to zero.

The problem of the dual-fed RC transmission line can now be solved by first finding the step response within the line when it is fed by a unit step voltage source at one end having terminated the other end of the line with a short-circuit. Because of the symmetry of the uniform RC transmission line, the step response when the unit step voltage source and the short-circuit load are swapped can be found by simply changing the position variable x to L—x, where L is the length of the line. By applying superposition, the step response of the dual-fed line is the algebraic sum of the step responses of the line when fed from just one end and terminated at the other end with a short-circuit.

Because of the symmetry of the uniform line the step response at the center will be the same whether it is fed from the left end and short-circuited at the right end or fed from the right end and short-circuited at the left end. Hence, the step response at the center of a dual-fed line is the same as that from a singly-fed line, terminated in a short-circuit, but fed with double the amplitude.

The step response of a forward-fed finite RC transmission line with short-circuit termination at $x = L$ **can obtained by setting $u_2 = 0$ in either** Equation (33) **or** Equation (39). Similarly the step response of a backward-fed finite RC transmission line with short-circuit termination at $x = 0$ can obtained by setting $u_1 = 0$ **in either** Equation (33) **or** Equation (39). By superposition, the general step response of a dual-fed RC line is the algebraic sum of these two individual step responses. But that is exactly what appears in both Equations (33) and (39).

Furthermore, it is easily shown that the step response at the center of a dual-fed RC line is simply halved in amplitude when the source at either end is reduced to zero and replaced by a short-circuit. By linearity, that halved-response can be restored by doubling the amplitude of the remaining source. Shorting the far end of an RC line maximizes the current through the bulk of the transmission line, but at the same time causes the greatest voltage drop towards the far end. It follows that terminating the far end of the line with any finite value of resistance will improve the rise time within the RC line compared to when that far end is left open. The source amplitude can be increased to compensate for the extra voltage drop towards the far end.

TRANSIENT RESPONSE OF LUMPED RC MODELS

A lumped approximation is used to model the distributed RC line as lumped resistors and lumped capacitors, as shown in Fig. 3. As the transmission line is uniform, the lumped model consists of several identical π sections in cascade.

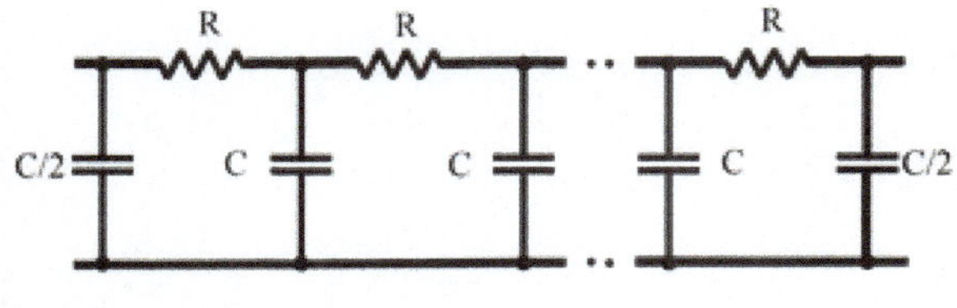

Figure 3. The lumped RC model.

A model with two π sections in cascade is the simplest approximation to the transmission line. A better approximation has four sections, wherein the transmission line is split into two halves, and each half is approximated by two π sections in cascade. The approximation continues to improve as the line is broken into smaller lengths, each piece being represented by a π section. Table 2 lists the computed results for the unit step response at the center of the dual-fed lumped model with N sections where N = 2,4,10 and 20. The example values of $r = 1\ \Omega/m$, $c = 1\times10^{-6}$ F/m and $L = 1\times10^{-3}$ m were used in the computations, but the results are shown for selected values of dimensionless (normalized) time $\tau = t/(rcL^2)$. The results for N = 2,4 and 20 are plotted in Fig. 4.

Table 2. Analytical and lumped model results for the unit step response at the center of a dual-fed RC line.

τ	analytical	$N = 2$	$N = 4$	$N = 10$	$N = 20$
0.01	0.001	0.077	0.021	0.004	0.002
0.02	0.025	0.148	0.069	0.034	0.027
0.03	0.082	0.213	0.129	0.091	0.085
0.05	0.228	0.330	0.258	0.232	0.229
0.07	0.363	0.429	0.378	0.365	0.363
0.10	0.526	0.551	0.528	0.526	0.526
0.12	0.610	0.617	0.608	0.610	0.610
0.13	0.647	0.647	0.643	0.646	0.647
0.15	0.710	0.699	0.704	0.709	0.710
0.20	0.823	0.798	0.815	0.822	0.823
0.50	0.991	0.982	0.989	0.991	0.991

doi:10.1371/journal.pone.0116993.t002

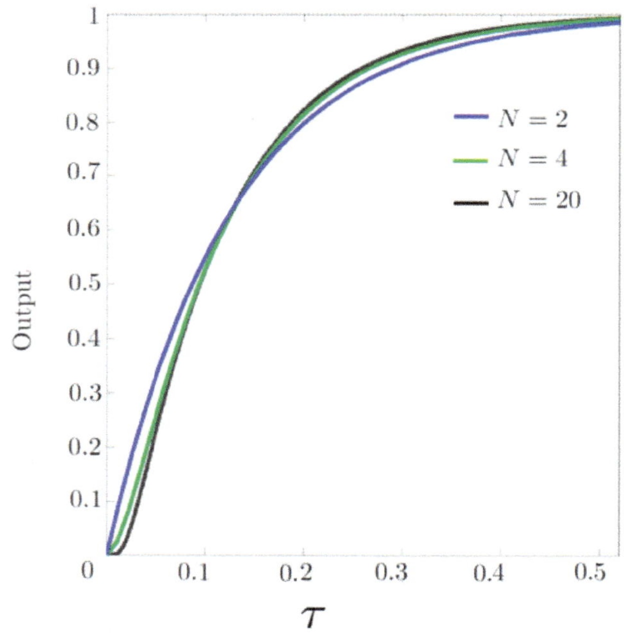

Figure 4. The voltage at the center of the dual-fed line, simulated with N = **2, 4 and 20 sections.**

It is clear from these plots that the lumped approximation improves as the number of sections increases. In practice, for N = **20, the step response closely follows the analytical result.**

For reference, the step responses of the first two models, N = **2 and** N = **4, have explicit expressions:**

$$v_2(0.5, \tau) = 1 - e^{-8\tau} \quad (42)$$

And

$$v_4(0.5, \tau) = 1 - \frac{\sqrt{2}+1}{2} e^{-(32-16\sqrt{2})\tau} + \frac{\sqrt{2}-1}{2} e^{-(32+16\sqrt{2})\tau} \quad (43)$$

The latter is the step response of an overdamped second-order circuit with a natural frequency of 162—√/(rcL2)162/(rcL2) rad/s and a Q-factor of 1/(22—√)=0.3541/(22)=0.354.

CONCLUSION

This paper derives analytical expressions for the transient time response of an RC transmission line under a step excitation fed into both ends of the line. Of particular interest is the response at the center of the line, where the rise time is the longest. Two forms of the analytical expressions are obtained by inverting the Laplace transform in two ways. Both forms are infinite series but one of them converges faster for small values of time. Furthermore, the expressions were presented in a form consistent with the method of superposition.

It is found that the 63% rise time at the center is reduced by a factor of 2.8843 when the RC line is dual-fed compared to the case when it is left open at the far end.

While closed-form analytical expressions now exist for the step response at the center of a dual-fed distributed RC line, lumped models with different numbers of sections were used to approximate the line. We demonstrated that the response errors from the lumped approximations reduce significantly as the number of sections in the π model is increased, 20 sections being enough in practice to closely predict the step response of the distributed line.

AUTHOR CONTRIBUTIONS

Conceived and designed the experiments: MD DA. Performed the experiments: MD. Analyzed the data: MD GKC DA. Contributed reagents/materials/analysis tools: MD GKC DA. Wrote the paper: MD GKC DA.

REFERENCES

1. Peirson RC, Bertnolli EC (1969) Time-domain analysis and measurement techniques for distributed RC structures. Impulse measurement techniques, J. App. Physics, 40:118–122.
2. Sakurai T (1983) Approximation of wiring delay in MOSFET LSI impulse measurement techniques. IEEE Journal of Solid-State Circuits, 18:418–426. doi:10.1109/JSSC.1983.1051966
3. Kahng AB, Muddu S (1994) Delay analysis of VLSI interconnections using the diffusion equation model. Proc. ACM/IEEE Design Automation Conf., 2:563–569.
4. Kahng AB, Muddu S (1997) Analysis of RC interconnections under ramp input. ACM Transactions on Design Automation of Electronic Systems, 2:168–192. doi:10.1145/253052.253137
5. Rao VB (1995) Delay analysis of the distributed RC line. Proc. ACM/IEEE Design Automation Conf., 370–375.
6. Gupta S, Patnaik LM (1999) Exact output response computation of RC interconnects under polynomial input waveforms. Twelfth International Conference on VLSI Design, 160–163.
7. Kamasz SR, Washkurak WD, Weale GP, Ma F, Smith CR et al. (1993) Design and electro-optical characterization of a 1024 × 1024 imager. Proc. SPIE Charge-Coupled Devices and Solid State Optical Sensors III, 1900:147–156. doi: 10.1117/12.148593
8. Ng J, Abbott D (2002) Introduction to solid state quantum computation for engineers.Microelectronics Journal, 33:171–177. doi: 10.1016/S0026-2692(01)00116-1

CHAPTER 3

RECONFIGURABLE BOOLEAN LOGIC USING MAGNETIC SINGLE-ELECTRON TRANSISTORS

M. Fernando Gonzalez-Zalba[1], Chiara Ciccarelli[2], Liviu P. Zarbo[3], Andrew C. Irvine[2] , Richard C. Campion[4] , Bryan L. Gallagher[4] , Tomas Jungwirth[3,4], Andrew J. Ferguson[2] , Joerg Wunderlich[1,3]

[1] Hitachi Cambridge Laboratory, Cambridge CB3 0HE, United Kingdom

[2] Cavendsih Laboratory, University of Cambridge, Cambridge, United Kingdom

[3] Institute of Physics, The Academy of Science of the Czech Republic, v.v.i, Cukrovarnick'a 10, 162 53 Praha 6, Czech Republic,

[4] School of Physics and Astronomy, University of Nottingham, Nottingham NG7 2RD, United Kingdom

ABSTRACT

We propose a novel hybrid single-electron device for reprogrammable low-power logic operations, the magnetic single-electron transistor (MSET). The device consists of an aluminium single-electron transistor with a GaMnAs magnetic back-gate. Changing between different logic gate functions is realized by reorienting the magnetic moments of the magnetic layer, which induces a voltage shift on the Coulomb blockade oscillations of the MSET. We show that we can arbitrarily reprogram the function of the device from an n-type SET for in-plane magnetization of the GaMnAs layer to p-type SET for out-of-plane magnetization orientation. Moreover, we demonstrate a set of reprogrammable Boolean gates and its logical complement at the single device level. Finally, we propose two sets of reconfigurable binary gates using combinations of two MSETs in a pull-down network.

INTRODUCTION

As the downscaling of conventional CMOS technology is bound to reach its fundamental limit new algorithms will be the answer to achieve increasingly higher performance and reduced power consumption. Reconfigurable digital circuits provide a way to extend the functionalities of conventional CMOS by implementing in the same physical space multiple logic operations and therefore increasing the computational complexity. Reconfiguration of the logic functions at each individual device promises even more compact and flexible circuit design [1–5]. However, the implementation of such reconfigurable logic using single-electron transistors (SETs) [6, 7] is appealing because SETs have good scalability, one of the lowest energy-per-switching-event [8] and the possibility to combine their electrical properties with magnetic elements [9–14]. There have been several proposals to implement programmable SET logic by using the charge degree of freedom such as fixed gate voltages [15], non-volatile charge nodes [16, 17] and the spin degree of freedom [18–20].

In this manuscript, we show a proof of principle for reconfigurable Boolean logic based on magnetically-gated circuit elements and we suggest multi-device reconfigurable logic architectures. More particularly, we report the complementary logic operation of a aluminium MSET. The reconfigurable capability of our MSET stems from the magnetization-dependent work function of GaMnAs back gate. When the back-gate is kept at a constant potential the magnetic-field-induced chemical change causes a charge accumulation in the gate electrode which can be readily sensed by the SET as a change in the Coulomb oscillation phase

Citation: Gonzalez-Zalba MF, Ciccarelli C, Zarbo LP, Irvine AC, Campion RC, Gallagher BL, et al. (2015) Reconfigurable Boolean Logic Using Magnetic Single-Electron Transistors. PLoS ONE 10(4): e0125142. doi:10.1371/journal.pone.0125142.

[21, 22]. Although the concept is demonstrated here for MSET devices, the operating principle is general and transferable to any field-effect transistor.

RESULTS

The MSET has two modes of operation: it responds to gate voltage inputs (electric mode) as well as to the orientation of the magnetic moments (magnetic mode). By reorienting the magnetization of the GaMnAs substrate we are able to switch from n-type to p-type MSET. Making use of the magnetic mode we demonstrate two sets of reprogrammable Boolean logic gates implemented at the single device level. Finally, we suggest a strategy to scale the reconfigurable logic operation to the multiple device level.

A schematic cross-section of the proposed aluminium MSET is depicted in Fig 1(a). The key element of this structure is the magnetic gate electrode, an epitaxially grown $Ga_{0.94}$ $Mn_{0.06}$As layer on GaAs that acts as a back-gate with easy-axis directions [110] and [1–10]. A magnetic field $B = 0.7$ T, larger that the saturation field $B_s \approx 0.3$ T, is applied to rotate the magnetization M with respect to the [001] direction (ϕ = 0°). The angle θ with respect to the [1–10] direction is kept equal to 90° in all measurements. The results presented here are independent of the magnitude of B for $B > B_s$. A 100 nm alumina layer is used as gate dielectric on top of which the Al-SET is fabricated. The source and drain leads are separated from the micron-sized island by aluminium oxide tunnel junctions, as it can be observed in the SEM image in Fig 1(b). In this letter the side gates were not used but could provide extra-functionality to the structure.

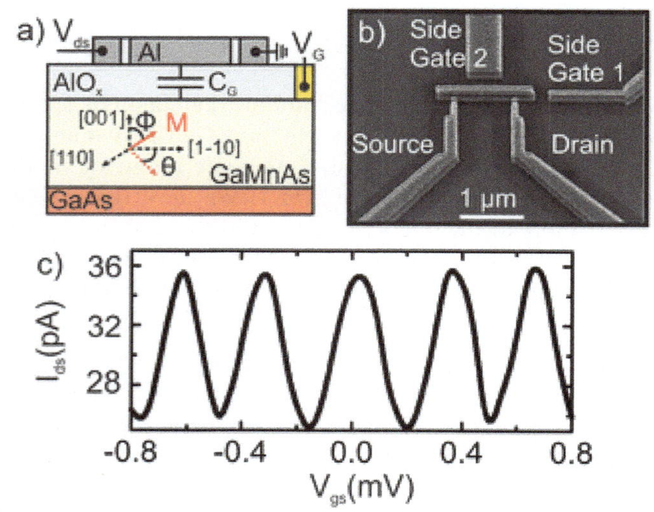

Figure 1. Device structure. (a) Schematic cross-section of the device sketching the magnetization orientation of the (Ga,Mn)As back-gate layer. (b) SEM image of the device. The aluminium island is separated from the source and drain leads by AlO_x tunnel junctions. Side gates were not used in this experiment. (c) Drain current (I_{ds}) oscillations as a function of the back gate voltage (V_{gs}).

In the electric mode of operation we use the back-gate voltage to control the induced-charge in the island of the MSET. Fig 1(c) shows the drain current (I_{ds}) versus back-gate voltage (V_{gs}) at 300 mK. The plot shows a periodic oscillatory behaviour of the current, namely the Coulomb blockade oscillations. Several devices were studied with typical charging energies E_C = 100–300 μeV and gate capacitances C_G = 0.4–1.0 fF. We obtain a I_{ON}/I_{OFF} contrast ratio of up to 1.33 and typical tunnel junction resistances of R_T = 500 kΩ.

The magnetic mode of operation is based on the dependence of the GaMnAs band structure on the orientation of the magnetization due to spin orbit coupling. The magnetization reorientation yields a shift in the GaMnAs work function $\Delta\mu$ which in itself does not produce a response on the MSET. However, when the back gate is held at constant potential a change in μ causes an inward or outward flow of charge in the gate which in turn offsets the Coulomb oscillations. If the work function shift in the magnetic layer is adequate, the phase shift becomes half a period of the Coulomb blockade oscillations and complementary MSETs are obtained. The equation that defines the necessary work function shift for maximum on-off current ratio can be expressed as,

$$\Delta\mu(B)_{max} = \frac{e^2}{2C_G} \quad (1)$$

As well, the minimum potential shift for complementary operation at temperature T can be defined as a gate voltage shift equal to the FWHM of the Coulomb peak [23],

$$\Delta\mu(B)_{min} = \frac{4.35 k_B T C_\Sigma}{C_G} \quad (2)$$

These two equations set the operational parameters in terms of temperature, magnetic field and physical dimensions of the structure.

The complementary operation of the MSET is experimentally demonstrated in Fig 2 for a device with E_C = 300μeV and C_G = 1.0 fF. To switch between complimentary modes we rotate continuously a saturating magnetic field from ϕ = 90°, where the magnetization resides M parallel to the plane along the easy-axis [110] (Fig 2(a)) to ϕ = 0° where the magnetization is out-of-plane (Fig 2(b)). This can be seen in Fig 2(c) where we plot the source-drain current I_{ds} as a function of the magnetization angle ϕ and gate voltage V_{gs} for V_{ds} = 15μV and B = 0.7 T. When the magnetization is in-plane, we select V_{gs} = -61 μV as the logic 0 and V_{gs} = +86 μV as the logic 1 for the n-type SET (see Fig 2(d)). As the magnetic field is rotated to ϕ = 0°, the magnetization is re-oriented in the [001] direction and the GaMnAs work function increases producing a gate voltage shift of ΔV_{gs} = 150 μV [24]. The combination of work function potential shift in the $Ga_{0.94}$ $Mn_{0.06}$ As layer with the 300 μV gate voltage period of the device result in that the magnetically-induced gate voltage shift coincides with half a Coulomb oscillation (fulfilling Eq (1)). The MSET behaves effectively as a p-type SET, Fig 2(e). Therefore we can arbitrarily select the function of the SET from an n-SET for in-plane magnetization ϕ = 90° to a p-type for out-of-plane magnetization ϕ = 0°.

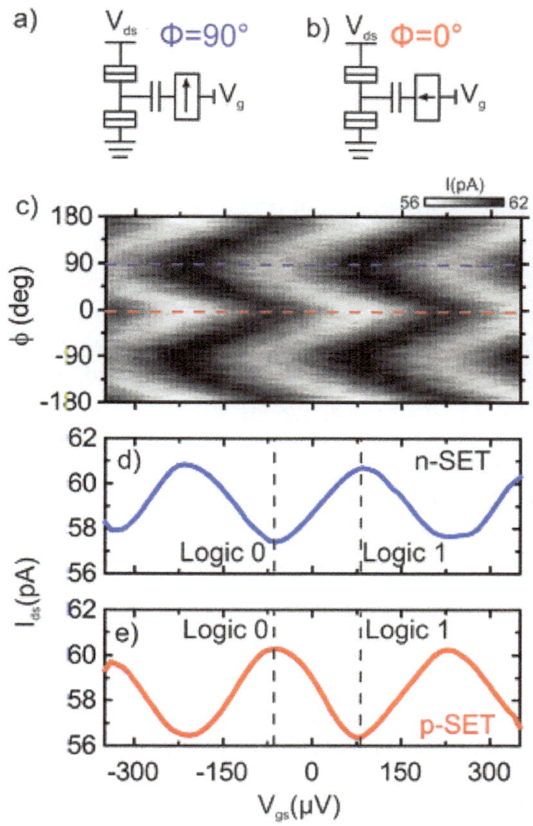

Figure 2. Complementary operation. Schematic diagram of the MSET for different magnetization orientations. (a) ϕ = 0° the magnetization is in-plane and (b) ϕ = 90° the magnetization is out-of-plane. (c) Coulomb blockade oscillations as a function of the direction of the back-gate voltage V_{gs} and the applied magnetic field orientation ϕ for B = 0.7 T. The-dashed blue and red lines indicate the operating points. (d) MSET Ids-Vgs transfer function at ϕ = 0°. The logic 0 (1) has been selected at a low (high) current level, n-type SET. (e) MSET Ids-Vgs transfer function at ϕ = 90°. The logic outputs have been inverted, p-type SET.

We now focus on the logic design that could be implemented at the single device level. It has been shown that any Boolean function of two variables can be implemented on a SET [25]. In this letter, by making use of the magnetic mode of operation, we demonstrate two sets of reprogrammable logic gates. The inputs in this case are the drain voltage (input A) and the gate voltage (input B) and the output is the drain current. In Fig 3(a) we plot the V_{ds}– V_{gs} diagram of the MSET showing the characteristic Coulomb diamonds at ϕ = 0°. Overimposed, we schematically show two logic gates framed in red AND and NAND. The output is drawn as en empty dot if the results is 0 (low current level) and a full dot if the results is 1 (high current level). Upon changing the magnetization angle to ϕ = 90°, the whole diagram is shifted horizontally by ΔV_{gs} = -150 μV and, therefore, at the same input voltages the gate output changes to the two blue-framed logic gates, from (N) AND to (N)OR as depicted by the arrow. The reconfigurable logic gates are demonstrated in the histograms in Fig 3(b)–3(e). In order to discriminate between logic outputs 0 and 1 we select the low(high) current threshold at I_{ds} = 80(90) pA. In Fig 3(b) we represent a histogram of the current output for an AND gate implemented on the edge of the Coulomb diamond. By rotating the magnetization to the in-plane direction (ϕ = 90°) the Coulomb diamonds shift and the logic gate switches function to OR (Fig 3(c)). Moreover, in Fig 3(d) and 3(e) we demonstrate the logical complement set of reprogrammable Boolean gates. The set switches between NAND (ϕ = 0°) and NOR (ϕ = 90°) logic gates.

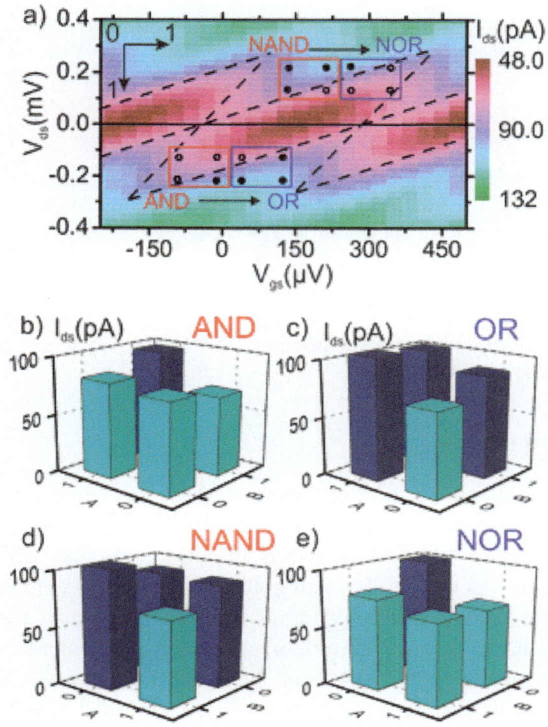

Figure 3. Single-device logic. (a) $V_{ds} - V_{gs}$ map of the drain current for ϕ = 0° showing the characteristic Coulomb diamonds. Red and blue frames sketch the implemented logic gates for ϕ = 0° and 90° respectively. (b-c) AND-OR set of reprogrammable logic gates. AND gate implemented at ϕ = 0° (b) and OR gate at ϕ = 90° (c) with V_{ds} (input A) 0(1) defined as −132(−220) μV and V_{gs} (input B) 0(1) defined as −96(0) μV. (d-e) NAND-NOR set of reprogrammable logic gates. NAND gate implemented at ϕ = 0° (d) and NOR gate atϕ = 90° (e) with V_{sd} (input A) 0(1) defined as 220(132) μV and V_{gs} (input B) 0(1) defined as 128(224) μV.

Finally, we briefly comment on the possibilities for multi-device reconfigurable logic design. As an example, we focus on pull-down networks formed by two elements with a common magnetic back-gate and independently addressable electrical gates. We concentrate on the case of MSET with identical I_{ds}-V_{gs} transfer functions and logic inputs defined by Fig 2(c) and 2(d). The circuit in Fig 4(a) consists of a resistor load and two MSETs in series. In the state ϕ = 0° both MSET are in the p-type state and the network realizes the operation OR. However this gate can be reconfigured by rotating the magnetization, ϕ = 90°. In this situation both MSET are in the n-type state and the logic operation becomes NAND. Similarly, for a pull-down network consisting of two MSETs in parallel, Fig 4(b) the logic gate can be programmed to switch between AND (ϕ = 0°) and NOR (ϕ = 90°) operations.

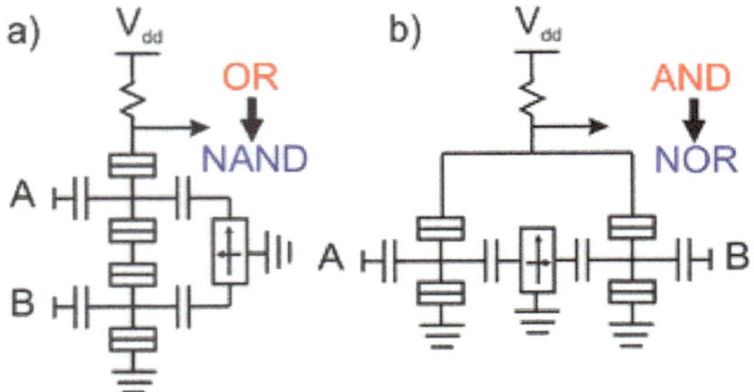

(a)

Inputs A	Inputs B	Output 0°	Output 90°
0	0	0	1
0	1	1	1
1	0	1	1
1	1	1	0

(b)

Inputs A	Inputs B	Output 0°	Output 90°
0	0	0	1
0	1	0	0
1	0	0	0
1	1	1	0

Figure 4. Logic at the multiple device level considering identical SETs and the logic inputs defined in Fig 2. The inputs A and B are defined as taken as the SET gate values. (a) A series pull-down network performs the OR operation at $\phi = 0°$ and NAND at $\phi = 90°$. (b) Parallel pull-down network performs the AND operation at $\phi = 0°$ and NOR at $\phi = 90°$.

DISCUSSION

In conclusion, we have demonstrated the complementary logic operation of an aluminium MSET by making use of magnetization-dependent work function of the GaMnAs magnetic back-gate. By using the source-drain voltage and the gate voltage as binary inputs we showed a set of Boolean gates and its logical complement implemented at the single device level, AND-OR and NAND-NOR gates. Finally, we have described a route to integrate multiple MSET in to integrated reconfigurable logic circuits. Although here we present results on MSETs, magnetic gating could be exploited to switch function in more conventional circuit elements such as CMOS field-effect transistors or novel electronic devices such as graphene ambipolar transistors [26] or spin-hot carrier transistors [27]. For reliable room temperature switching, magnetic materials with work function shifts of the order of 60 mV will be required [28]. Materials with large work function anisotropy such as CoPt alloys could provide that functionality [21]. Moreover, non-volatile logic reconfiguration could be also achieved by making use of the stability of the magnetic moments along non collinear "magnetic easy axes" orientations without applying external magnetic fields or electrical currents.

ACKNOWLEDGMENTS

The authors thank M. Klein, D.A. Williams for fruitful discussion.

AUTHOR CONTRIBUTIONS

Conceived and designed the experiments: MFGZ CC TJ AF JW. Performed the experiments: CC. Analyzed the data: MFGZ. Contributed reagents/materials/analysis tools: LZ AI RC BG. Wrote the paper: MFGZ CC JW.

REFERENCES

1. Strukov DB, Snider GS, Stewart DR, Williams RS. The missing memristor found. Nature. 2008;453: 80–83. doi: 10.1038/nature06932. pmid:18451858
2. Joo S, Kim T, Shin SH, Lim JY, Hong J, Song JD, et al. Magnetic-field-controlled reconfigurable semiconductor logic. Nature. 2013;494: 72–76. doi: 10.1038/nature11817. pmid:23364687
3. Heinzig A, Slesazeck S, Kreupl F, Mikolajick T, Weber WM. Reconfigurable silicon nanowire transistors. Nano Letters. 2012;12: 119–124. doi: 10.1021/nl203094h. pmid:22111808
4. Yu WJ, Kim UJ, Kang BR, Lee IH, Lee EH, Hee Y, et al. Adaptive logic circuits with doping-free ambipolar carbon nanotube transistors. Nano Letters. 2009;9: 1401–1405. doi: 10.1021/nl803066v. pmid:19281215
5. Mol JA, Verduijn J, Levine RD, Remacle F, Rogge S. Integrated logic circuits using single-atom transistors PNAS 2011;108: 13969–13972. doi: 10.1073/pnas.1109935108
6. Kastner MA. The single-electron transistor. Rev Mod Phys. 1992;64: 849–858. doi: 10.1103/RevModPhys.64.849.
7. Gonzalez-Zalba MF, Heiss D, Podd G, Ferguon AJ. App Phys Lett. 2012;101: 103504. doi: 10.1063/1.4750251.
8. .Zhu C, Gu Z, Shang L, Dick RP, Knobel RG. Towards an ultra-low-power architecture using single-electron tunneling transistors. Proceedings of the 44th annual Design Automation Conference. 2007; 312.
9. Ono K, Shimada H, Ootuka Y. Enhanced magnetic valve effect and magneto-Coulomb oscillations in ferromagnetic single electron transistors. J Phys Soc Japan. 1997;66: 1261. doi: 10.1143/JPSJ.66.1261.
10. Barnas J, Martinek J, Michalek G, Bulka B R, Fert A. Spin effects in ferromagnetic single-electron transistors. Phys Rev B. 2000;62: 12363. doi: 10.1103/PhysRevB.62.12363.
11. Shirakashi J, Takemura Y. Ferromagnetic single-electron transistor with multiple tunnel junctions. J Mag Soc Japan. 2001;25: 783. doi: 10.3379/jmsjmag.25.783.
12. Jalil MBA, Tan SG, Ma MJ. Enhanced magneto-Coulomb effect in asymmetric ferromagnetic single electron transistors. J App Phys. 2009;105: 07C905 doi: 10.1063/1.3055271.
13. Takiguchi M, Shimada H, Mizugaki Y. Correlation between polarity of magnetoresistance ratio and tunnel resistance in ferromagnetic single-electron transistor with superconductive island. J J App Phys. 2014;53: 043101 doi: 10.7567/JJAP.53.043101.
14. Kirchner S, Si Q. Quantum criticality out of equilibrium: Steady state in a magnetic single-electron transistor. Phys Rev Lett. 2009;103: 206401 doi: 10.1103/PhysRevLett.103.206401. pmid:20365995
15. Tucker JR. Complementary digital logic based on Coulomb blockade. J App Phys. 1992;72: 4399–4413. doi: 10.1063/1.352206.
16. Ishikuro H, Hiramoto T. Influence of quantum confinement effects on single electron and single hole transistors. In: Electron Devices Meeting, 1998. IEDM '98. Technical Digest., International. 1998; 119–122.
17. Uchida K, Koga J, Ohba R, Toriumi A. Programmable single-electron transistor logic for low-power intelligent

Si LSI. In: Solid-State Circuits Conference, 2002. Digest of Technical Papers. ISSCC. 2002 IEEE International. 2002;1: 206–460.

18. Wunderlich J, Jungwirth T, Irvine AC, Kaestner B, Shick AB, Campion RP, et al. Coulomb blockade anisotropic magnetoresistance and voltage controlled magnetic switching in a ferromagnetic GaMnAs single electron transistor. J Magn Magn Mater. 2007;310: 1883–1888. doi: 10.1016/j.jmmm.2006.10.676.
19. Dery H, Dalal P, Cywinski L, Sham LJ. Spin-based logic in semiconductors for reconfigurable large-scale circuits. Nature. 2007;447: 573–576. doi: 10.1038/nature05833. pmid:17538616
20. Hai PN, Sugahara S, Tanaka M. Reconfigurable logic gates using single-electron spin transistors. Japn J Appl Phys. 2007;46: 6579–6585. doi: 10.1143/JJAP.46.6579.
21. Wunderlich J, Jungwirth T, Kaestner B, Irvine AC, Shick AB, Stone N, et al. Coulomb blockade anisotropic magnetoresistance effect in a (Ga,Mn)As single-electron transistor. Phys Rev Lett. 2006;97: 077201. doi: 10.1103/PhysRevLett.97.077201. pmid:17026268
22. Ciccarelli C, Zarbo LP, Irvine AC, Campion RP, Gallagher BL, Wunderlich J, et al. Spin gating electrical current. App Phys Lett. 2012;101: 122411–122414. doi: 10.1063/1.4752013.
23. Beenakker CWJ. Theory of coulomb-blockade oscillations in the conductance of a quantum dot. Phys Rev B. 1991;44: 1646–1656. doi: 10.1103/PhysRevB.44.1646.
24. In-plane rotations between [110] and [1–10] directions were explored leading to $\Delta\mu = 46$ μeV insufficient for complementary operation.
25. Klein M, Lansbergen GP, Mol JA, Rogge S, Levine RD, Remacle F. Reconfigurable logic devices on a single dopant atom-operation up to a full adder by using electrical spectroscopy. ChemPhysChem 2009;10: 162–173. doi: 10.1002/cphc.200800568. pmid:19115322
26. Wang H, Hsu A, Wu J, Kong J, Palacios T. (2010.) Graphene-based ambipolar RF mixers. IEEE Elec Dev Lett. 2010;31: 906 doi: 10.1109/LED.2010.2052017.
27. Mizuno Y, Ohya S, Hai PN, Tanaka M. Spin-dependent transport properties in GaMnAs-based spin hot-carrier transistors. Appl Phys Lett. 2007;90: 62505/1–3 doi: 10.1063/1.2724771.
28. Betz AC, Barraud S, Wilmart Q, Placais B, Jehl X, Sanquer M, et al. High frequency characterisation of thermionic charge transport in silicon-on-insulator nanowire transistors. App Phys Lett 2014;104: 043106. doi: 10.1063/1.4863538.

CHAPTER 4

ULTRA-FAST DATA-MINING HARDWARE ARCHITECTURE BASED ON STOCHASTIC COMPUTING

Antoni Morro, Vincent Canals, Antoni Oliver, Miquel L. Alomar, and Josep L. Rossello

Electronic Engineering Group, Physics Department, Universitat de les Illes Balears, Palma de Mallorca, Balears, Spain

ABSTRACT

Minimal hardware implementations able to cope with the processing of large amounts of data in reasonable times are highly desired in our information-driven society. In this work we review the application of stochastic computing to probabilistic-based pattern-recognition analysis of huge database sets. The proposed technique consists in the hardware implementation of a parallel architecture implementing a similarity search of data with respect to different pre-stored categories. We design pulse-based stochastic-logic blocks to obtain an efficient pattern recognition system. The proposed architecture speeds up the screening process of huge databases by a factor of 7 when compared to a conventional digital implementation using the same hardware area.

INTRODUCTION

Data explosion is the capability of current technologies to generate large amounts of data at different scientific disciplines. Data volumes are doubling every year in most areas of modern science [1], and its proper analysis is becoming more and more complex. As a matter of fact, data explosion has not led to an information explosion since current data analysis techniques are unable to handle billions of data records in a reasonable period of time. Large scientific databases containing several terabytes of information need to be continuously screened by scientists, and current processor-based techniques are unable to provide an efficient response to this problem. To solve this, different solutions have been developed based on artificial neural networks [2–5], the use of simple metrics [6] or the extraction of simplified datasets from the original data [7].

An alternative to traditional deterministic computational methodologies is the use of stochastic logic, introduced more than 40 years ago [8,9]. Stochastic computing is the result of applying probabilistic laws to logic cells where variables are represented by random pulse streams, thus providing a natural way of representing analog quantities with digital systems [10]. Pulses can be converted to binary numbers by using digital counters (P2B converters) while binary numbers can be translated to stochastic signals by combining a random (or a pseudo-random) number generator and a comparator (B2P converters). Stochastic computing makes use of digital technology to perform complex arithmetic operations with a reduced number of gates. When performing those types of operations, stochastic signals must be completely uncorrelated for a proper behavior.

Citation: Morro A, Canals V, Oliver A, Alomar ML, Rossello JL (2015) Ultra-Fast Data-Mining Hardware Architecture Based on Stochastic Computing. PLoS ONE 10(5): e0124176. doi:10.1371/journal.pone.0124176.

Stochastic computing is useful for those applications requiring parallel-processing techniques [11–14]. Traditional parallel processing architectures have the shortcoming of requiring a large amount of hardware resources. Therefore, the number of tasks that can be executed in parallel within a single chip is relatively small. Stochastic computing could represent a solution to this problem since the hardware used to solve each task is reduced in size if compared to traditional digital implementations. As a result, more complex tasks can be executed in parallel when using stochastic computing elements. The greatest advantage of stochastic computing is the potential of implementing hundreds of smart computing elements in one single integrated circuit, thus obtaining a highly parallelized processing chip with a computing capacity that can be several orders of magnitude higher than traditional binary-logic-based microprocessors.

In this work we generalize the basic stochastic computing principles, thus creating a more general *probabilistic processing*. The primary basic principle of traditional stochastic computing is that the stochastic bit streams must be completely uncorrelated in time and space to obtain the desired arithmetic operations when using simple logic gates. Our extended *probabilistic processing* approach will also use correlated signals in order to implement a set of non-linear operations. This set of non-linear operations can be used for an efficient and fast comparison between signals as we will show later.

Accordingly, *probabilistic computing* is characterized by the combination of two different types of operations:

- Arithmetic operations implemented by uncorrelated signals (such as the multiplication, the division or the addition). These ones are taken from the traditional stochastic computing concepts [8].
- Non-linear operations performed by correlated signals evaluated through logic gates.

The introduction of the possibility of coherence between the signal phases enhances the capacity of stochastic computing by including those non-linear operations that can be applied to perform fast similarity searches. Consequently, complex pattern recognition tasks can be executed in parallel when using probabilistic processing operations.

In this work we present a highly efficient methodology for data mining based on probabilistic processing. High dimensional data is inherently complex in clustering, classification and similarity search [15]. The proposed approach is evaluated showing its application to a similarity search over a huge database. Most data mining algorithms use similarity search as a subroutine core [16–18], and thus the time taken for this task is the bottleneck of virtually all data mining algorithms [19]. Similarity search plays a fundamental role in many data mining and machine learning problems, e.g. text categorization [20], collaborative filtering [21], time-series analysis [22,23], protein sequencing [24] or any application-specific task as petroglyphs comparison [25]. At the same time, the mining of huge datasets implies the use of large computer clusters [26,27]. The proposed approach based on the use of probabilistic processing shows large improvements in terms of hardware resources when compared with conventional solutions.

BASIC PRINCIPLES OF PROBABILISTIC PROCESSING

Stochastic Computing Principles

In stochastic-based computations a global clock provides the time interval during which all stochastic signals are stable (settled to 0 or 1). For each clock cycle, a particular node has a probability p of being in the HIGH state (see Fig 1). Stochastic pulsed signals follow probabilistic laws when evaluated with logic gates. As an example, an AND gate provides at the output the product of its inputs (that is to say, the collision probability between signals) whereas a NOT gate converts a probability p at the input to the complementary $1-p$ at the output. One of the requirements for these stochastic computing blocks is that signals must be un-correlated at different clock cycles and between them. In Fig 2 we show the importance of the temporal de-correlation when implementing arithmetic functions (we use the example of implementing $f(p) = p(1-p)$). The figure illustrates that if the inputs of the AND gate p and $1-p$ are correlated the output is always equal to zero. Such correlations can be eliminated using shift registers to delay signals from one arithmetic level to the next one. In the correct case, the AND gate evaluates properly the product between p and a delayed (and therefore uncorrelated) value of $1-p$.

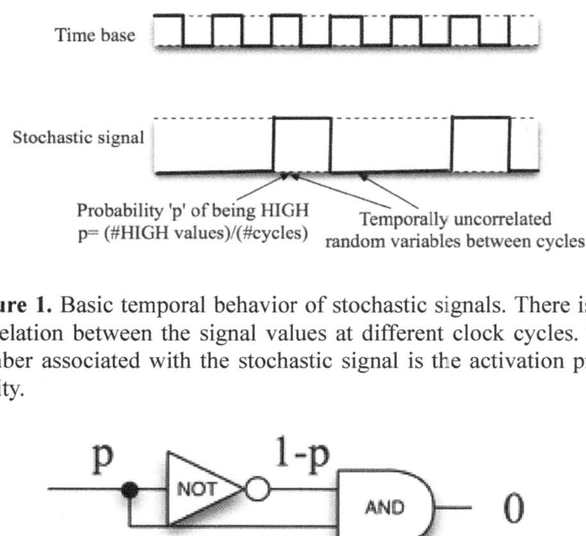

Figure 1. Basic temporal behavior of stochastic signals. There is no correlation between the signal values at different clock cycles. The number associated with the stochastic signal is the activation probability.

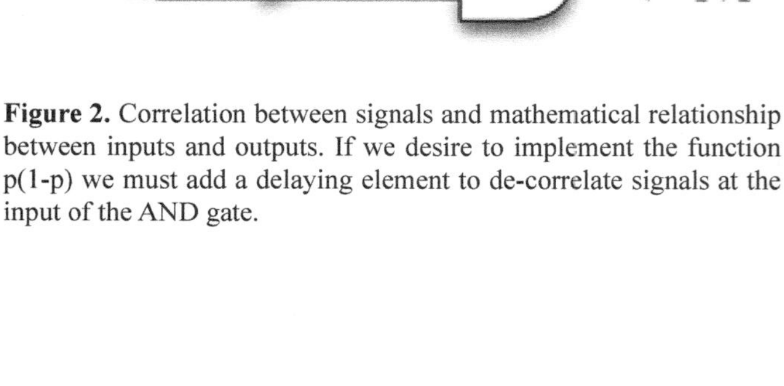

Figure 2. Correlation between signals and mathematical relationship between inputs and outputs. If we desire to implement the function p(1-p) we must add a delaying element to de-correlate signals at the input of the AND gate.

Random Number Generation

The generation of pseudorandom sequences is a key issue for the implementation of probabilistic computing systems since stochastic bit streams are required to convert binary magnitudes to their equivalent stochastic signals. In particular, in order to obtain a random variable from Bernoulli sequences with a known generating probability *p*, we have to compare the binary number to convert (*P*) and the generated random number (*R*). If *P*>*R*, the stochastic pulse will be at high level, otherwise it will be low (Fig 3a).

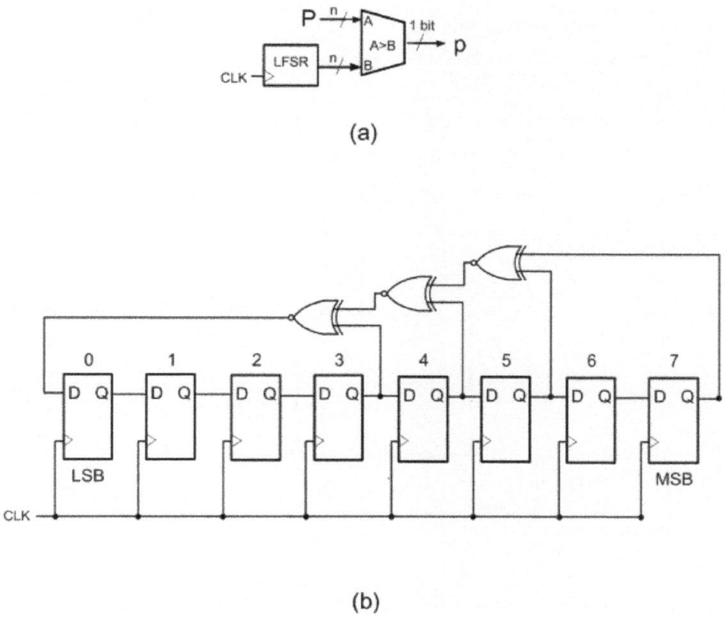

Figure 3. (a) Binary to pulse converter (B2P), an LFSR and a comparator are combined to obtain the pulsed signal. (b) Linear Feedback Shift Register (LFSR) used in the experiments.

A commonly used [28] source of pseudorandom digital noise is the linear feedback shift register (LFSR), which is an array of interconnected flip-flops with feedback to its input from a combination of the outputs of its various stages gated together in EXCLUSIVE-OR gates (see Fig 3b). This linear feedback structure provides uniformly distributed sequences (which have an autocorrelation delta function), but with a finite period of repetition, which has an exponential dependence with the number of bits. Since the sequences are produced deterministically, uncorrelated sources must be generated using different initial values (seeds) for the registers. The feedback configurations enabling maximal-length generators have been given [29,30]. The configuration applied in the present work, which employs a 8-bit shift register, is shown in Fig 3b. The autocorrelation function of a pseudorandom sequence generated by the LFSR used is shown at Fig 4. This function is a set of repeating delta functions separated by the number of bits in the LFSR's sequence length (2^n-1).

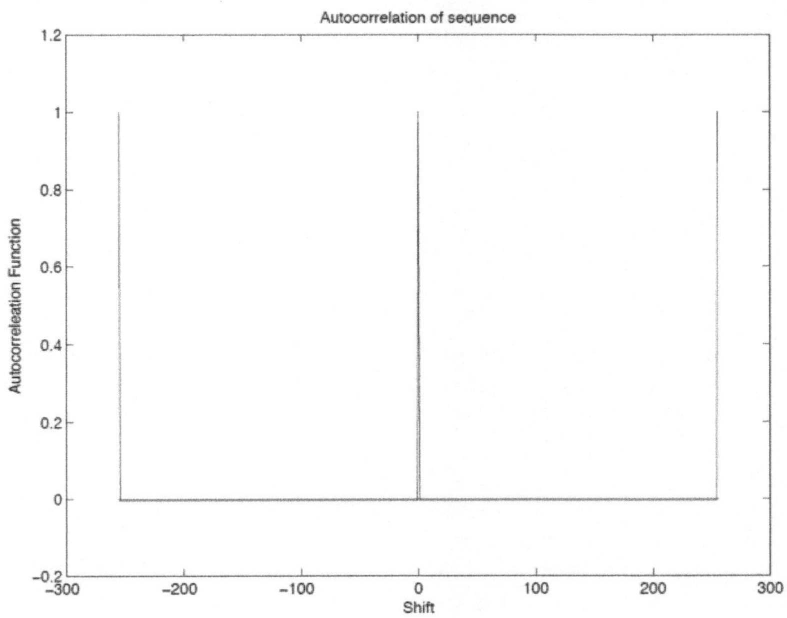

Figure 4. Autocorrelation function. Autocorrelation function of the pseudo-random number generator used in the experiments.

For operations that need un-correlated signals, we define different seeds for each LFSR block. On the other hand, for operations requiring correlated signals we employ the same LFSR output for all stochastic variables.

Generalization of Stochastic Computing

Different kinds of stochastic non-linear functions can be reproduced using stochastic correlated signals. In Fig 5a, we show an example of the implementation of the absolute value of a subtraction ($|p_x-p_y|$). Stochastic signals x and y are derived from binary numbers X and Y when comparing with a random number R, generated using one LFSR. The probability of getting x = '1' or y = '1' (values of p_x and p_y) is proportional to X and Y respectively. Since X and Y are correlated (they share the same LFSR) the probability of getting both signals x and y with a high level (x = y = '1') is min(p_x, p_y), while the probability of getting both signals with a low level (x = y = '0') is min(1- p_x, 1- p_y). These two situations provide a low signal at the XOR output. On the other hand, the probability of getting different values on x and y is equal to $| p_x-p_y|$. In this situation, the XOR output (z) provides a high value with probability $p_z = | p_x-p_y|$.

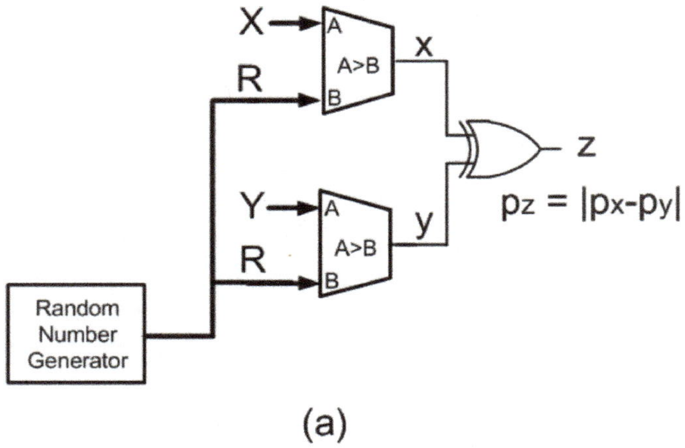

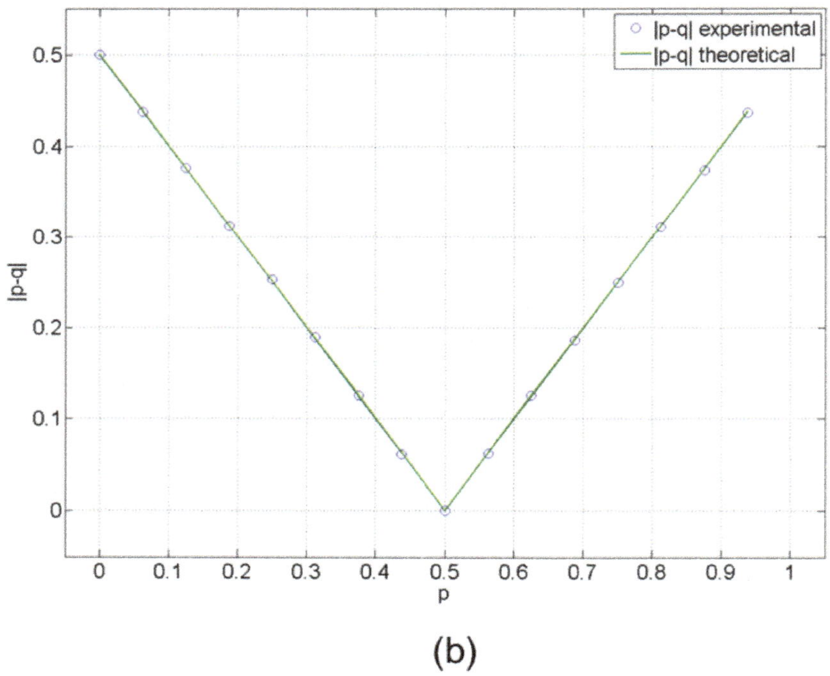

Figure 5. Similarity estimation of X and Y (with correlated signals). In contrast to the un-correlated scheme (case in which X and Y are compared with different random values), a non-linear function is obtained. The probability of the R signal of being between X and Y is proportional to $|P_x-P_y|$ that is the switching activity of the output signal. (a) Probabilistic circuitry for the computation of $|P_x-P_y|$. (b) Experimental results when evaluating $|P_x-P_y|$.

The experimental measurements of this circuit confirm this behavior (see Fig 5b). In general, correlated signals evaluated through logic gates would implement max-min algebra functions. These types of functionalities are ideal for pattern recognition.

Data Mining of Huge Databases

The probabilistic nature of stochastic logic is an advantage for the implementation of probabilistic-based pattern recognition methodologies [2] and pattern matching is in the core of many data mining processes. The purpose is to compare parameters (the features) from different objects with reference vectors that represent different categories. All the features define each object, thus configuring an m-dimensional vector (for m different features).

Fig 6 shows the stochastic circuit used to compare two m-dimensional vectors, providing at the output an estimation of the similarity (s_{jr}) of both objects (vector *'r'* in the database to mine, and the vector defining the category *'j' ($\mathbf{x}_j$)*). A total of *'2m'* binary comparators and also *'m'* randomly selected binary numbers (R_k for the k-th descriptor) are configured in parallel to create a total of *2m* switching bits. Each pair of stochastic bits (x_{jk} and r_k) are compared through XNOR gates connected with a block performing the AND function between the *m* signals, thus providing at its output an estimation of the similarity (s_{jr}) between the vector (**r**) and the category j ($\mathbf{x}_j$).

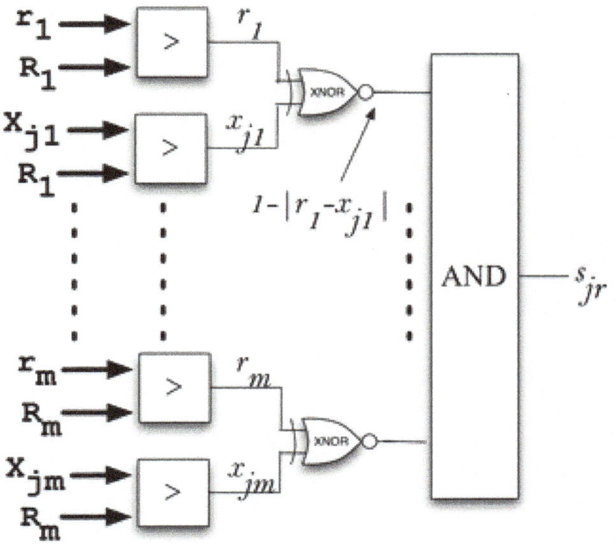

Figure 6. Stochastic architecture for comparing m-dimensional vectors. A total of 'm' random signals are needed for each comparison.

Note the combination of both correlated and uncorrelated stochastic signals to obtain s_{jr} (all the AND inputs must be uncorrelated between them so that we need *'m'* random numbersR_k). This block would represent the typical implementation of a probabilistic processing unit combining both types of signaling. Therefore, the probabilistic signal obtained (s_{jr}) can be expressed as

$$s_{jr} = \prod_{k=1}^{m} \left(1 - |x_{jk} - r_k|\right) \quad (1)$$

The switching activity at the output of the AND block is therefore proportional to the similarity between the object **r** and the category represented by vector $\mathbf{x}_j$. In Fig 7 we show the level curves associated to the Manhattan-based metric used in (1). As it is shown, the selected metric can be considered a good proximity estimator for fast mining of huge databases.

Hundreds of similarity estimators as the one shown in Fig 6 can be configured in parallel in a medium-sized FPGA, thus increasing considerably the mining speed in comparison with traditional processor-based techniques.

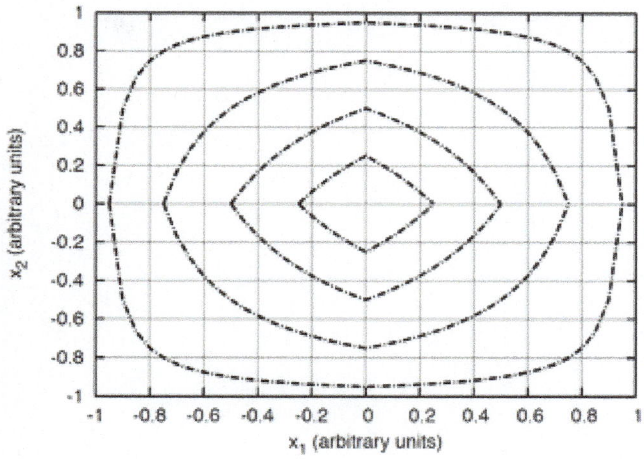

Figure 7. Level curves for the similarity metric used for the case of a two-dimensional space.

Different vectors can be compared in parallel by using a Winner-Take All (WTA) architecture (see Fig 8). From *'n'* different vectors of the database, the circuitry provides at its output the closer to reference vector **r**. Then, relative fraction of the area used by the LFSRs with respect to the total circuit area decreases with the number of vectors $\mathbf{x}_j$ that can be compared.

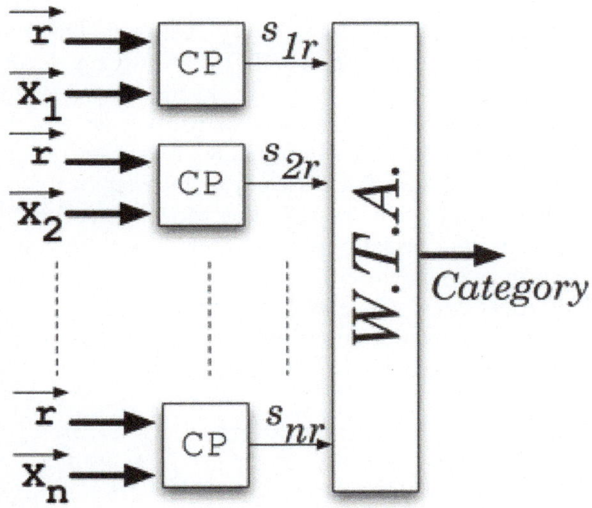

Figure 8. Architecture used to estimate the closest category to the reference vector 'r'. Each comparator (CP) provides at its output a switching signal proportional to the similarity of the two vectors connected to it. The Winner-Take All selects the highest frequency signal.

Thus, at the WTA output the category label *'j'* that is activated is the one with the highest similarity:

$$Category = 'j' | s_{jr} \geq s_{ir} \forall i \in \{1..n\} \quad (2)$$

The WTA can be constructed by using binary counters (module-k) (see Fig 9). Only a maximum number of clock cycles per comparison ($N>k$) are allowed, and therefore the number of cycles needed to overflow fixes a minimum similarity value to be distinguisheds_{min} so that $N \cdot s_{min} = k$. If all the similarities at the input of the WTA (s_{jr}) are lower than s_{min}, the most probable scenario is not to obtain any positive result at the output of the WTA.

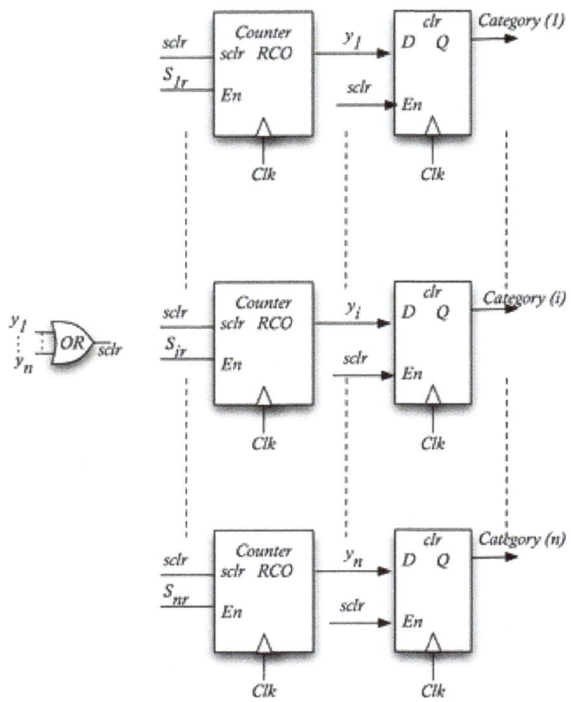

Figure 9. Winner-Take All. Architecture used to select the category associated to the s_{ir} with the higher activity.

For any similarity value $s_{jr}>s_{min}$ between two vectors ($\mathbf{x}_j$ and **r**) we have that the probability of identifying vector ***r*** as belonging to class *'j'* is close to 1. In Fig 10 we show the relationship between the distances of two vectors (|*x-y*|) and the number of cycles (N) needed to obtain an overflow of one of the counters of the WTA. We compare the analytical formula of the theoretical behavior (solid line showing the formula $N = k/s$, where the similarity is s = 1-d since we only vary the distance in one dimension) and the measurements obtained with an ALTERA Cyclone III FPGA (dashed lines). As it can be seen, a close relationship is obtained between the expected behavior and the probabilistic implementation.

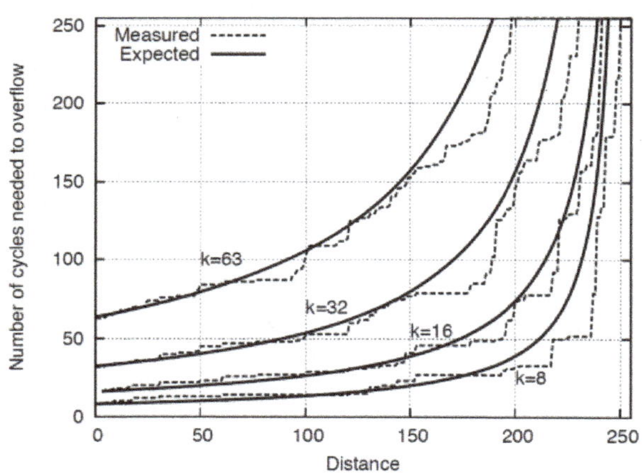

Figure 10. Relationship of distance between vectors (|*x-y*|) and the number of cycles needed to overflow a module-k counter of the WTA. The switching activity of the similarity stochastic signal (s_{jr}) is dependent on the distance ($s = 1-d$). As the higher is the distance, lower will be the switching activity of*s*, and higher the number of cycles needed to overflow the counter.

The probability of identifying vector ***r*** as belonging to class *'j'* can be estimated considering the probability of obtaining more than *'k'* HIGH values from a signal with switching activity *'s_{jr}'*when waiting a total of N cycles (N>k).

$$P_{jr}\left(s_{jr}\right) = P(r \in j) = \sum_{l=k}^{N} \binom{N}{l} s_{jr}^{l}\left(1 - s_{jr}\right)^{N-l}$$

(3)

where N is the total number of cycles used to compare any set of vectors. Function (3) is represented in Fig 11 for the special case in which $k = 16$ and $N = 80$ as a function of the similarity s_{jr}. For this case, $s_{min} = k/N = 0.2$, note that $P_{jr}>0.5$ for $s_{jr}>s_{min}$ in Fig 11.

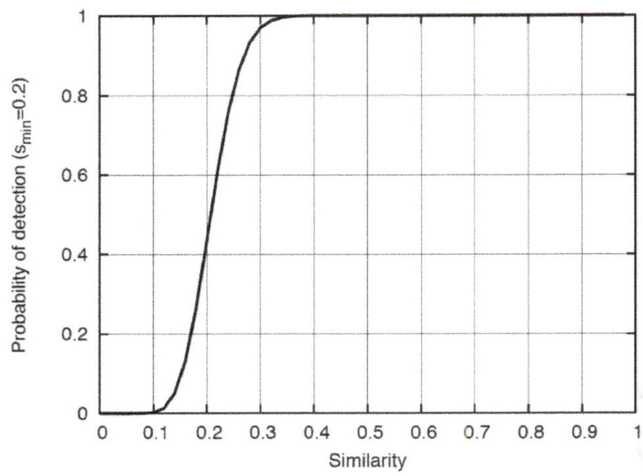

Figure 11. Variation of query identification probability with respect to similarity. An arbitrary threshold of $s_{min} = 0.2$ is selected.

The similarity search function (1) has the inherent advantage of its analytical simplicity. In this sense, given two randomly selected *m*-dimensional vectors $\mathbf{x}_j$ and **r**, it is possible to compute the cumulative distribution function of obtaining a similarity lower than a given selected value *'z'*. From basic probability theory we have that this cumulative distribution function can be estimated as:

$$F_z(z) = \int_{\Omega} dy$$

(4)

where $F_z(z)$ is the probability of obtaining a similarity lower than z, Ω is the volume for which$g(y)<z$, being $g(y)$ the function under consideration (1). Vector ***y*** is composed by all the parameters for which *'g'* is dependent (the components of both $\mathbf{x}_j$ and **r** vectors that are stochastic signals with values between 0 and 1).

After some algebra, and considering (1) for the estimation of Ω and that each parameter is bounded between 0 and 1 we have:

$$F_z(z) = z^2 \sum_{j=1}^{m} \frac{[-2log(z)]^{j-1}}{(j-1)!} = \frac{\Gamma(m, -2log(z))}{\Gamma(m)}$$

(5)

where *'m'* is the dimension of the vectors. If we want to estimate the probability density function $f_z(z)$, we have to derive the cumulative distribution function with respect the selected similarity (z), $f_z(z) = \partial_z F_z(z)$

From expression (5) we can estimate the number of positive identifications from a database with W unknown objects if we select a minimum similarity of s_{min} ($Positives \approx W \bullet (1-F(s_{min}))$). Expression (5) is also very useful to estimate the minimum database width W_{min} needed to identify an object with a specific property (assuming a random database):

$$W_{min} = \frac{1}{1 - s_{min}^2 \sum_{j=1}^{m} \frac{[-2\log(s_{min})]^{j-1}}{(j-1)!}} \quad \textbf{(6)}$$

RESULTS

We implemented the proposed methodology in a FPGA-based PCIe board (ProcStarIV110E-4B) fabricated by GIDEL Ltd (see Fig 12). This board incorporates four ALTERA STRATIX III 110E FPGAs along with 32GB of DDR2 SODIMM memory banks to allocate the database. The communication with the board is done through a PCI-express connector of a PC. The clock frequency of operation of the board is 87.5 MHz and the maximum power dissipation is about 100W.

Figure 12. FPGA-based PCIe board used for the data mining process from GIDEL.

Inside the four FPGA cores we configured a total of 400 similarity comparators per core (design shown in Fig 6), thus implementing a total of 1600 stochastic comparators in the board that operate in parallel. The dimension of the vectors are selected to be $m = 12$. To test the circuit effectiveness, we created a similarity search in a random database with a total of $2.56 \bullet 10^6$ 12-D vectors setting an arbitrary minimum similarity of $s_{min} = 0.2$. The final positive results are shown in Fig 13, where we show, as a function of the similarity 's': the number of vectors of the database with this similarity (dark diamonds), the number of vectors that are finally selected by the circuitry as belonging to class 'c' (circles), the ideal number of vectors to be selected (solid line) and the expected number of vectors to be selected (dashed line $f_z(s_{jr})P_{jr}$). It is visible that the experimental and theoretical results (circles and dashed line) are similar. We also can see that nearly all the vectors with a similarity higher than the selected threshold are identified (circles and solid line). Unfortunately there is a non-negligible fraction of vectors with a similarity lower than s_{min} that are selected (circles with $s<s_{min} = 0.2$). This fact is due to the non-negligible tie of $P_{jr}(s_{jr})$ for $s_{jr}<s_{min}$ and the exponential dependence of $f_z(s_{jr})$ with s_{jr}.

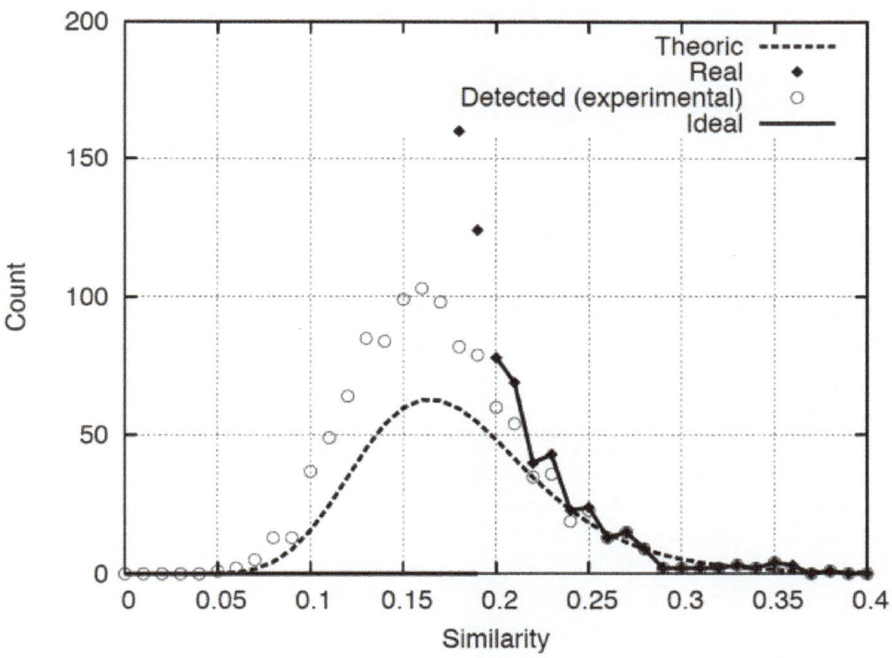

Figure 13. Number of positive identifications from a database with $2.56 \bullet 10^6$ **particles when** s_{min} **= 0.2.**

The solution to erase such *false positives* is to filter-out the final results using software. The impact of this filtering on the database screening timing is small since only a low volume of vectors must be recomputed (rather than the billions of vectors that the database can contain).

The total number of positives to be selected by the stochastic circuitry can be estimated numerically as:

$$Positives = \int_{0}^{1} P_{jr}(s) f_z(s) ds \quad \textbf{(7)}$$

Expression (7) can be used to select an optimal number for k and N to control the number of positive results within reasonable values. In Fig 14 we show the different types of negatives and positives provided by the system. False positives are those positives with a similarity lower than the threshold s_{min}. False negatives are those vectors that, even presenting a higher similarity than s_{min}, are not found by the system. Finally, the true positives and negatives are those vectors that are correctly classified by the system.

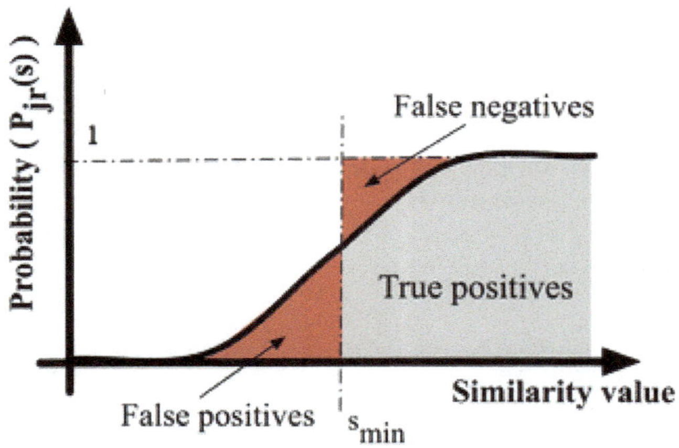

Figure 14. For each computation, a given number of false positives and negatives are provided by the probabilistic system. False positives can be filtered out by software while false negatives are lost.

Although the false positives can be filtered-out by software, the vectors with $s>s_{min}$ that are finally not found by the hardware (false negatives) cannot be recovered (in Fig 13, the false negatives are the difference between the solid line and the circles). In this sense, the precision of the system is defined as the ratio between true positives and the total number of possible positives (true positives + false negatives).

$$\eta = \frac{\int_{s_{min}}^{1} P_{jr}(s) f_z(s) ds}{\int_{s_{min}}^{1} f_z(s) ds} \quad \textbf{(8)}$$

In Table 1 we show the dependence of η with respect to parameter k assuming $f_z = 1$ with $s_{min} = 0.5$. Increasing k increases the efficiency but decreases the screening speed of the circuit. In Table 1 we find the relationship between η and the number of cycles needed to overflow a WTA counter (k value). For most applications, a value of k = 8 provides good results in terms of accuracy and computation time.

Table 1. Relationship between the k value and the precision of the system when fz = 1 and using smin = 0.5 (i.e. N = 2k).

k	Precision (η)
8	0.93
16	0.94
32	0.96
64	0.97
128	0.97

doi:10.1371/journal.pone.0124176.t001

The circuit speed can be estimated from the time needed to screen a database (t_p) with a total of W vectors:

$$t_p = \frac{W \cdot size}{f_{RAM}} + \frac{NT_{clk} W}{1600} + t_{setup} \quad \textbf{(9)}$$

where W is the number of vectors in the database, f_{RAM} is the data transfer frequency of the DDR-DRAM (of the order of 16GB/s for the PCIe used in the experiment), T_{clk} is the global clock period of the circuit (operating at 87.5MHz), *'size'* is the number of bytes per vector (12 bytes in our case), 1600 is the number of stochastic comparators implemented inside the FPGAs, parameter N is the number of clocks used by the WTA to process the inputs (signals s_{jr}), and finally t_{setup} is the setup time needed for board initialization (of the order of 1ms). Finally, the speed of the screening process is estimated as a function of the number of vectors in the database ($f_{proc} = W/t_p$). In Fig 15 we show the screening speed (in millions of comparisons per second) as a function of the database width (in millions of vectors), where the vectors are composed by 12 bytes ($m = 12$). The low speed obtained by the proposed methodology when the database is small is basically due to the fixed setup time of the system.

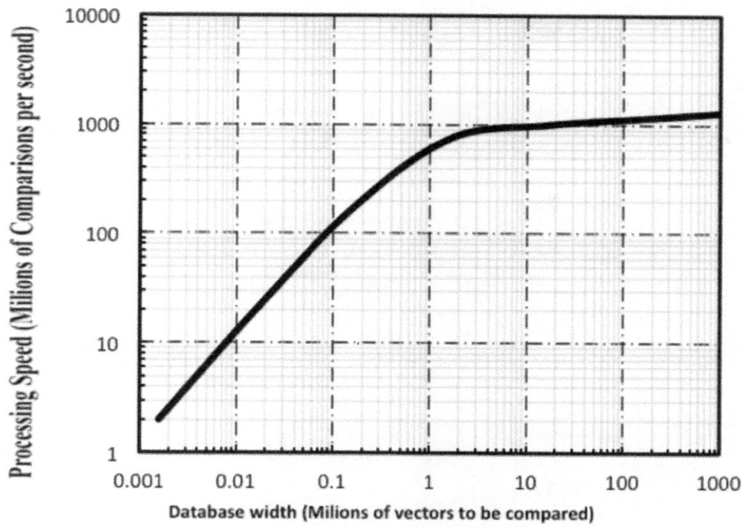

Figure 15. Data mining speed variation with database width when using probabilistic computing. Each comparison implies the processing of two vectors of 12 Bytes each one.

We compared a conventional implementation using binary-based digital hardware of a multi-vector comparator implementing the metric proposed in (1) with the proposed probabilistic system. In Fig 16 we show the conventional implementation of expression (1). Finally, in Fig 17 we compare the result of such similarity comparators with the minimum similarity s_{min}. In Table 2 we compare both implementations in terms of FPGA resources when using an ALTERA Cyclone III EP3C25F324C8 device. The vectors to be compared are fixed to 12 dimensions. As it can be seen, the ratio of Logic Elements needed by the conventional and the probabilistic implementation increases as the number of vectors to be compared grows. The area ratio between both systems is of the order of 56 while the ratio in terms of circuit speed is constant and about 1/k (1/8). Therefore, the probabilistic implementation speeds up the screening process of the database by a factor of 7 when compared to a conventional digital implementation using the same hardware area. In other words, the total performance when using the proposed architecture is higher by a factor of 7. It means that, the lack in speed can be compensated by using less hardware area.

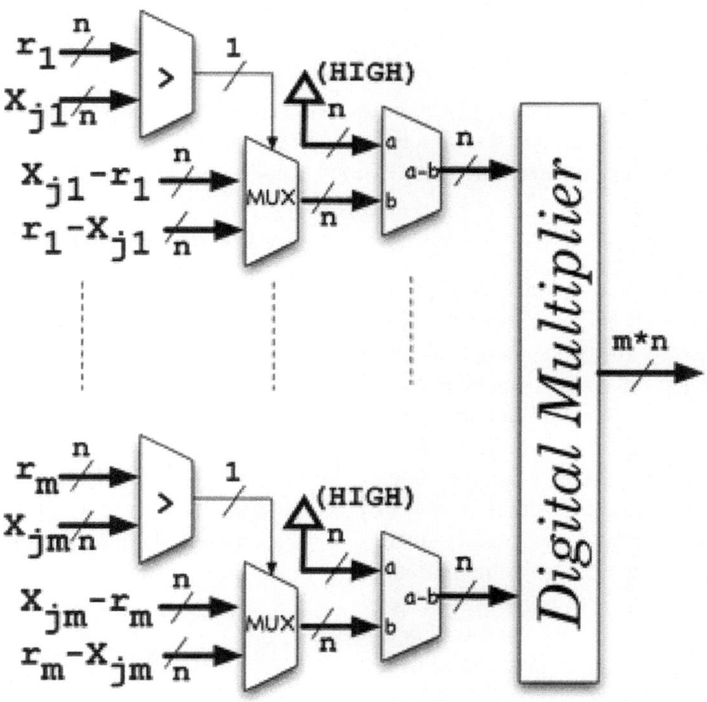

Figure 16. Conventional implementation of a m-dimensional digital comparator where expression (1) is implemented. The first comparator and the multiplexer implement the absolute value function while the multiplier provide the product for all the dimensions.

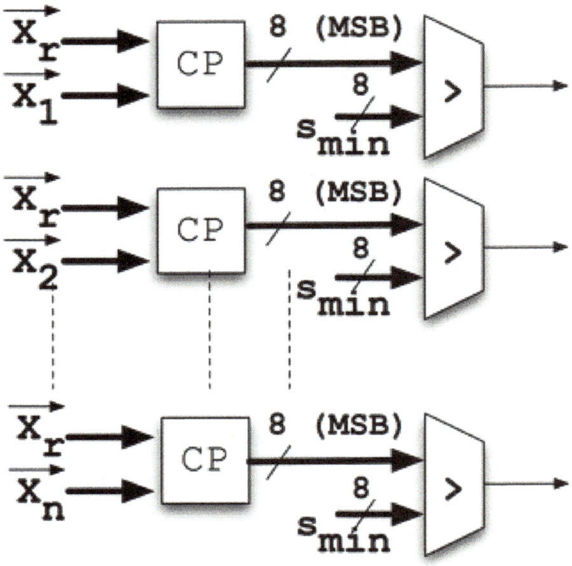

Figure 17. Global comparator between the reference vector and each vector in the database. Block CP is implementing the circuitry shown in Fig 16. The result is compared with s_{min}.

Table 2. Relationship between conventional and probabilistic implementation in terms of FPGA resources for an Altera Cyclone III device.

Number of vectors	Classical			Probabilistic		
	Logic Elements (LE)	Multipliers	Delay time (t_D)	Logic Elements	Multipliers	Delay time (t_D)
2	1.955	126	1	321	0	8
4	13.898	132	1	551	0	8
8	39.142	132	1	1.023	0	8
16	91.464	132	1	1.908	0	8
32	196.076	132	1	3.713	0	8
128	823.814	132	1	14.719	0	8

doi:10.1371/journal.pone.0124176.t002

To sum up, the presented application is an example where stochastic computing is advantageous over conventional computing systems. Since the presented implementation takes advantage of the high parallelism of stochastic computing, less circuit area implies a lower power demand to achieve a determined processing speed.

CONCLUSIONS

We have presented a new and unconventional computing technique for ultra-fast mining of huge databases. The methodology is based on the use of probabilistic pulsed signals. We describe how correlated bit streams can be used to implement non-linear functions like the absolute value function, which have been also developed by other research group [31]. In the final architecture we allow the use of both correlated and uncorrelated stochastic bit streams. The combination of both types of switching signals increases the mathematical capacity of original stochastic computing implementations. The data to be mined is translated to spikes and processed by a simple digital circuitry. The simplicity of the circuitry is used to implement hundreds of stochastic comparators inside Field-Programmable Gate Arrays and oriented to screen huge databases. The final implementation uses an FPGA-based PCIe board for the screening. This implementation uses less hardware resources than conventional digital methodologies (based on binary and not probabilistic logic) and is able to process the order of 13GBytes of information per second (in contrast to the estimated 2GBytes/s of speed that could be achieved by the conventional implementation using the same hardware area). With the 12-dimensional space used to allocate each vector in the example shown in this paper we obtain the order of 1 billion of comparisons per second. A patent application has been done for this new mining methodology [32].

REFERENCES

1. Szalay A, Gray J. (2006) 2020 computing: Science in an exponential world. Nature440: 413–414.
2. Bishop C.M., editor. (2006) Pattern recognition and machine learning. New York: Springer.
3. Fayos J, Fayos C. (2007) Wind data mining by Kohonen neural networks. PLoS ONE2.
4. Stegmayer G, Gerard M, Milone D. (2012) Data mining over biological datasets: An integrated approach based on computational intelligence. IEEE Computational Intelligence Magazine 7: 22–34.
5. Zou J, Han Y, So S-. (2008) Overview of artificial neural networks. Methods in Molecular Biology 458: 15–23.

6. Ballester PJ, Richards WG. (2007) Ultrafast shape recognition for similarity search in molecular databases. Proceedings of the Royal Society A: Mathematical, Physical and Engineering Sciences 463: 1307–1321.

7. Pan F, Wang W, Tung AKH, Yang J. (2005) Finding representative set from massive data. Proceedings—IEEE International Conference on Data Mining, ICDM: 338–345.

8. Gaines BR. (1975) Stochastic and fuzzy logics. Electron Lett 11: 188–189.

9. Gaines R. (1969) Stochastic Computing Systems. Advances in Information Systems Science. Tou,ed., 2:37–172.

10. Kim Y, Shanblatt MA. (1995) Random noise effects in pulse-mode digital multilayer neural networks. IEEE Trans Neural Networks 6: 220–229.

11. Canals V, Morro A, Rosselló JL. (2010) Stochastic-based pattern-recognition analysis.Pattern Recog Lett 31: 2353–2356.

12. Hori M, Ueda M, Iwata A. (2006) Stochastic computing chip for measurement of manhattan distance. Japanese Journal of Applied Physics, Part 1: Regular Papers and Short Notes and Review Papers 45: 3301–3306.

13. Rosselló JL, Canals V, Morro A. (2012) Probabilistic-based neural network implementation. Proceedings of the International Joint Conference on Neural Networks.

14. Li P., Lilja D.J., Qian W., Bazargan K., Riedel M.D. (2014) Computation on stochastic bit streams digital image processing case studies. IEEE Transactions on Very Large Scale Integration (VLSI) Systems, 22: 449–462.

15. Aggarwal CC, Han J, Wang J, Yu PS. (2005) On high dimensional projected clustering of data streams. Data Mining and Knowledge Discovery 10: 251–273.

16. Bayardo RJ, Ma Y, Srikant R. (2007) Scaling up all pairs similarity search. 16th International World Wide Web Conference, WWW 2007: 131–140.

17. Gullo F, Ponti G, Tagarelli A, Greco S. (2009) A time series representation model for accurate and fast similarity detection. Pattern Recognit 42: 2998–3014.

18. Kontos D, Megalooikonomou V. (2005) Fast and effective characterization for classification and similarity searches of 2D and 3D spatial region data. Pattern Recognit38: 1831–1846.

19. Rakthanmanon, T., Campana, B., Mueen, A., Batista, G., Westover, B., Zhu et al. (2012) Searching and mining trillions of time series subsequences under dynamic time warping. Proceedings of the ACM SIGKDD International Conference on Knowledge Discovery and Data Mining: 262–270.

20. Zhen Y, Yeung D-. (2013) Active hashing and its application to image and text retrieval. Data Mining and Knowledge Discovery 26: 255–274.

21. Koren Y. (2008) Factorization meets the neighborhood: A multifaceted collaborative filtering model. Proceedings of the ACM SIGKDD International Conference on Knowledge Discovery and Data Mining: 426–434.

22. Wang X, Smith K, Hyndman R. (2006) Characteristic-based clustering for time series data. Data Mining and Knowledge Discovery 13: 335–364.

23. Li H, Guo C. (2012) Similarity search for time series based on efficient warping measure. Proceedings of the ACM SIGKDD International Conference on Knowledge Discovery and Data Mining.

24. Kaznadzey A, Alexandrova N, Novichkov V, Kaznadzey D. (2013) PSimScan: Algorithm and utility for fast protein similarity search. PLoS ONE 8.

25. Zhu Q, Wang X, Keogh E, Lee S-. (2011) An efficient and effective similarity measure to enable data mining of petroglyphs. Data Mining and Knowledge Discovery23: 91–127.

26. Grossman R, Gu Y. (2008) Data mining using high performance data clouds: Experimental studies using sector and sphere. Proceedings of the ACM SIGKDD International Conference on Knowledge Discovery and Data Mining: 920–927.

27. Zhou P, Lei J, Ye W. (2011) Large-scale data sets clustering based on MapReduce and hadoop. Journal of Computational Information Systems 7: 5956–5963.

28. Kitsos P, Sklavos N, Zewas N, Koufopavlou O. (2001) A reconfigurable linear feedback shift register (LFSR) for the bluetooth system. Proceedings of the IEEE International Conference on Electronics, Circuits, and Systems 2: 991–994.

29. Peterson W. (1961) Error Correcting Codes. Jonh Wiley and Sons.

30. Korn G. (1966) Random-Process Simulation and Measurements. McGraw-Hill Book Co.

31. Alaghi A, Hayes JP. (2013) Exploiting correlation in stochastic circuit design. 2013 IEEE 31st International Conference on Computer Design, ICCD 2013: 39–46.

32. Rosselló JL, Morro A, Canals V. (2012) Sistema digital probabilístico para la exploración y reconocimiento de formas eficiente en grandes bases de datos.

CHAPTER 5

IMPROVING FISHING PATTERN DETECTION FROM SATELLITE AIS USING DATA MINING AND MACHINE LEARNING

Erico N. de Souza[1], Kristina Boerder[2], Stan Matwin[1,3], Boris Worm[2]

[1] Big Data Analytics Institute, Faculty of Computer Science, Dalhousie University, Halifax, NS, Canada

[2] Biology Department, Dalhousie University, Halifax, NS, Canada

[3] Institute of Computer Science, Polish Academy of Sciences, Warsaw, Poland

ABSTRACT

A key challenge in contemporary ecology and conservation is the accurate tracking of the spatial distribution of various human impacts, such as fishing. While coastal fisheries in national waters are closely monitored in some countries, existing maps of fishing effort elsewhere are fraught with uncertainty, especially in remote areas and the High Seas. Better understanding of the behavior of the global fishing fleets is required in order to prioritize and enforce fisheries management and conservation measures worldwide. Satellite-based Automatic Information Systems (S-AIS) are now commonly installed on most ocean-going vessels and have been proposed as a novel tool to explore the movements of fishing fleets in near real time. Here we present approaches to identify fishing activity from S-AIS data for three dominant fishing gear types: trawl, longline and purse seine. Using a large dataset containing worldwide fishing vessel tracks from 2011–2015, we developed three methods to detect and map fishing activities: for trawlers we produced a Hidden Markov Model (HMM) using vessel speed as observation variable. For longliners we have designed a Data Mining (DM) approach using an algorithm inspired from studies on animal movement. For purse seiners a multi-layered filtering strategy based on vessel speed and operation time was implemented. Validation against expert-labeled datasets showed average detection accuracies of 83% for trawler and longliner, and 97% for purse seiner. Our study represents the first comprehensive approach to detect and identify potential fishing behavior for three major gear types operating on a global scale. We hope that this work will enable new efforts to assess the spatial and temporal distribution of global fishing effort and make global fisheries activities transparent to ocean scientists, managers and the public.

INTRODUCTION

A common challenge in ecology is the mapping of dynamic patterns of human activity across vast areas in order to understand and track their ecosystem impacts on regional and global scales [1–3]. While important from a scientific perspective, there are also many other obvious applications, including the monitoring of marine fisheries and the enforcement of spatial management measures, such as marine protected areas (MPAs), ecologically and biologically sensitive areas (EBSAs) as well as fisheries closure zones. While the reception range of coastal monitoring tools such as tower-based applications (tAIS, radar) is limited to inshore areas, long-range tools such as satellite-based AIS (Automatic Identification System) and VMS (Vessel Monitoring System) provide insight into vessel movements elsewhere. VMS was specifically designed to monitor commercial fisheries while

Citation: de Souza EN, Boerder K, Matwin S, Worm B (2016) Improving Fishing Pattern Detection from Satellite AIS Using Data Mining and Machine Learning. PLoS ONE 11(7): e0158248. doi:10.1371/journal.pone.0158248.

AIS was intended as a safety feature to avoid vessel collisions under low visibility. While the use of VMS devices is mandated only for some fleets in individual nations, the International Maritime Organization (IMO) has made the carrying of an AIS transponder mandatory for all vessels larger than 300 gross tons or carrying passengers (SOLAS Chapter V). In addition, national regulations may include other vessel types, such as per recent requirements by the European Union that all fishing vessels bigger than 15m must carry an AIS device [4]. Both VMS and AIS feature on-board transmitters linked to the vessel's GPS to receive and transmit exact position in time and space on long-range radio frequencies to either coastal ground stations or satellites. In the case of AIS, data are also transmitted to other ships in the area that carry the device. VMS usually transmits in time intervals varying from one to several hours, satellite-based AIS (S-AIS) transmissions can be as frequent as every few seconds, enabling the monitoring of fine-scale vessel behavior and movement patterns.

Several attempts have been made to use VMS and AIS data to understand fishing vessel behavior, for example by using simple presence/absence or vessel speed [5] [6]. While speed can be a useful indicator of vessel activity, operational speeds while fishing vary greatly for different fishing gear types such as trawls, longlines or nets. More sophisticated algorithms differentiating fishing from non-fishing activity for different fleets and gears are needed to properly capture and represent the characteristics of the various fishing methods, as stated previously by Natale *et al.* [4] We develop and present such algorithms here, then assess their accuracy in correctly identifying individual fishing events or 'sets' by comparing against expert-labeled data. Finally, we briefly chart potential applications in marine ecology, conservation, and fisheries management.

METHODS

Data Sets

This work is based on a database containing global S-AIS data obtained from AIS-enabled communication satellites since January 2011 until October 2015. Data were obtained under research licence from exactEarth (http://www. exactearth. com/products/exactais). A representation of three several-year tracks and examples of fishing activity patterns for trawling, longlining and purse seining is given in Fig 1. Individual tracks for known trawl, longliner and purse seine fishing vessels were extracted from different regions representing vessels from different nations operating in various parts of the oceans at scales from coastal fishing grounds to circumnavigating the globe.

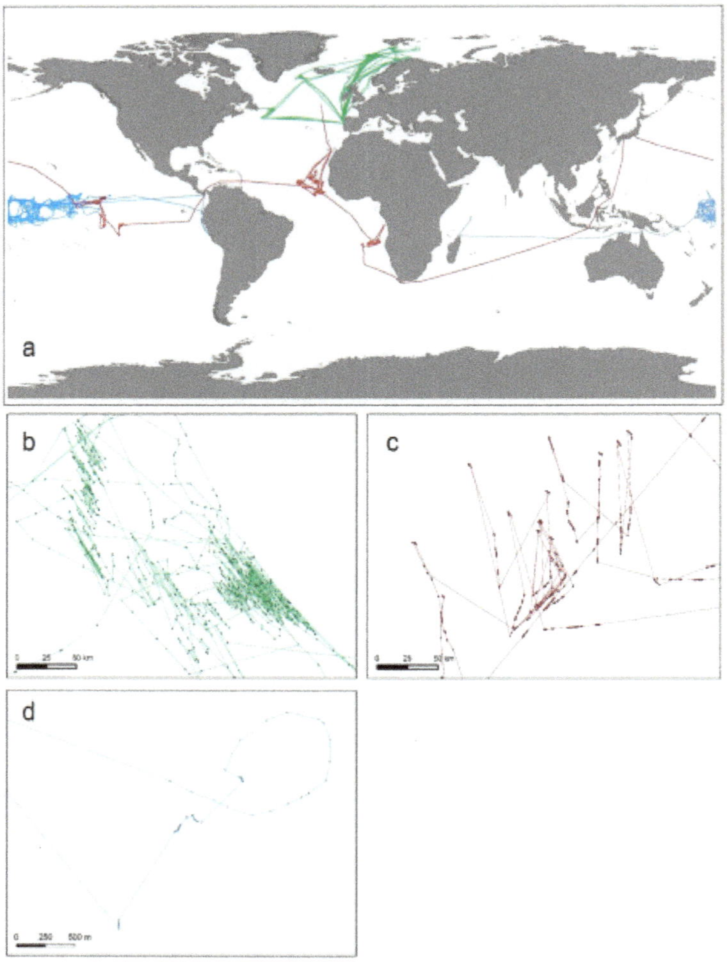

Figure 1. Presentation of raw S-AIS tracks for three individual vessels using different fishing gear types in global overview (A) and more fine-scale representations of potential fishing behavior for a trawler (green, B), longliner (red, C) and purse seiner (blue, D). Dots represent individual S-AIS signal detections, lines interpolated tracks. Note the global-range behavior of longliners, and the more regional basin-wide operations of purse seine and trawl vessels. Map data by Natural Earth.

The trawler data contained an initial sample of 83 vessels operating in the North Pacific and corresponds to 217,860 data points collected in July 2013 used for algorithm development and training. For comparison and testing on a global scale, a second trawler data set, composed of seven vessels operating from January 2011 until October 2015 across various ocean basins was selected. These tracks were much longer than those in the North Pacific, totaling 884,478 data points.

Analyses for longliners comprised data from 16 vessels operating across all major ocean basins from June 2012 until December 2013, corresponding to 573,204 data points.

Data on 7 purse seine vessels comprised 399,545 points from January 2011 until October 2015 representing long-range operations in various areas of the world.

Definition of Fishing Activity by Gear Type

Trawler

Trawling involves dragging one or more nets behind a fishing vessel either on the sea floor (bottom trawling) or in the water column (pelagic or midwater trawling). While trawling, fishing vessels usually slow down and aim to maintain a constant speed to keep the strain on the dragged net as even as possible. Duration of trawling operations depends mostly on the density of the prey and can last from a few minutes up to several hours. The typical length of a trawl will vary between 3 and 5 hours [7]. Here, trawling activity is defined from the moment the net is deployed to when it is retrieved. Trawls are often characterized by slow, steady speeds between 2. 5 and 5. 5 knots. These speed thresholds were determined directly from the distribution of the AIS speed data and correspond to similar values obtained from literature [8–11].

Longliner

Longlining involves the setting of fishing lines (up to 100 km length) equipped with several hundred to several thousands of hooks [12]. Lines can be deployed at various depths with the use of floats and horizontal lines extending to deeper waters. To set the line, the vessel travels only slightly slower than its steaming speed while the line is set. After the last hook is in the water, the line is left in the water for some hours ('soak time'). During this time, the vessel either drifts slowly with the line or sets other lines in the vicinity. To haul the line the vessel reverses and steams back along the line. The whole operation can take up to a day. Speed while hauling is kept mostly constant but can vary according to catch and number of crew working. The time to set a longline depends on the length of the line and the number of crew working it, but the median set time estimated from the 16 vessels used in our analyses was 6. 5 hours. Here a longline set is considered to start with setting of the longline and to end with retrieval of the last hooks. Characteristics used for identification of longline sets comprise spatial-temporal movement patterns in a very restricted area.

Purse Seiner

Purse seines are long nets deployed hanging vertically from floats around schooling fish on or near the surface by the vessel or by a separate skiff. To avoid fish escaping the setting of the seine needs to happen quickly and is done at high speeds averaging around 10 knots. Once the net encircles the school completely, the bottom of the net is pulled shut and the net hauled. Drifting with the net attached, the fish are then retrieved and transferred to the vessel. The duration of this process depends on the amount of catch and can vary from one to several hours [13].

For the purpose of this work, a purse seine set is defined as the time the net is closed around the fish to the end of the fish bailing operation when the net is lifted out of the water. During this time the purse seine vessel stays more or less stationary and speed over ground is generally slow, ranging around 2. 5 knots and less. This threshold was determined based on speed distributions of the AIS data as well as observations from literature [14, 15].

Data Labeling and Pre-processing

All vessel tracks were classified and pre-labeled as potential fishing and non-fishing events by an expert based on information on fisheries characteristics as obtained from literature, analyses of the tracks (speed and movement profiles by gear type, flag, vessel size and area of operation), personal interviews with fishermen and fisheries on-board observers and comparisons to speed and movement profiles from observer data for the Northeast Atlantic. Characteristics include speed over ground, change of direction within a defined area, spatial-temporal movement patterns, operational time and duration of the fishing event. The testing of the algorithms against expert-labeled data was chosen because suitable observer or logbook data for the fleets and time period examined were unavailable to us Expert judgement on vessel behavior based on the aforementioned characteristics might be a conservative approach, as some fishing events will be missed.

In order to improve fishing activity prediction, for each data point we calculated whether it occurred during night or day. In order to estimate the amount of sun light available in a region of the world during a certain UTC-based time, the R package solaR [16] was used, with positive values for sunlight marking the day, zeroes marking the night. To avoid irregular vessel movement patterns very close to shore and in port a 10 km boundary around shorelines was established. The calculation requires the computation of the Haversine distance between each vessel track point and all the points in the shoreline data provided by Natural Earth [17] to establish the minimum distance to shore. This process is computationally expensive and to improve the quality of the calculation, it was decided to use the parallel capabilities provided by the code available in [18].

Algorithm Testing

The algorithms presented here were tested against expert-labeled fishing vessel tracks, separating fishing and non-fishing activity based on observations from operational data, expert knowledge and comparison to other tracking data. Accuracies presented are based on these comparisons.

Each algorithm proposed has different assumptions: the HMM assumes that the user will have part of the data available for training, while the Data Mining (DM) and filtering approaches do not require training. These differences determine how these approaches are tested: the HMM algorithm (applied for trawlers) uses Monte Carlo experiments to measure how it behaves with time variation, and the DM approach uses all data available for testing against expert-labeled data (used for longliner and purse seiner). For the trawling activity the HMM algorithm was tested with a Monte Carlo simulation using the implementation provided by the R package DMwR [19]. North Pacific trawler data set was used for this purpose. This data was the first data set that was available for development and testing of the HMM approach and offered a high variation of vessel behaviors within shorter tracks covering one month of data (July 2013). To ensure the applicability of the HMM trained on this data set, the HMM was subsequently applied and tested on a second data set containing multi-year trawler tracks operating in various parts of the ocean on regional and global scale. The Monte Carlo Simulation partitioned the data in 20 segments; each of these segments was trained with anywhere from 25,000 data to 130,000 points. All tests predicted 100,000 points in the future. The Monte Carlo simulations did not consider the 10 km threshold, as the HMM uses only speed as input. We decided to execute tests with fixed-size windows for training and test to avoid possible overfitting. DMwR [19] package randomly selects 20 data windows according to the user specification for training and test data, where the entire window is dislocated once the training and testing is done, and its respective statistical results are stored. The results of the testing are represented as Prediction (F for fishing) and Prediction (NF for non-fishing) in Tables 1 and 2 and were calculated based on [20]. These two metrics give an estimate of how well the algorithm predicts the desired class using unseen data.

Table 1. Performance measures for the worldwide trawl dataset. NF stands for probable non-fishing and F for probable fishing events. Sensitivity is related with non-fishing detection, and specificity with fishing detection. The column Stat. Diff. Fish Effort shows the t-test statistical comparison (p-value) between the predicted fishing effort time calculated from the algorithm's labels and the expert's labels. The asterisk indicates a significant difference.

Track ID	Track Size	Accuracy	Prediction (F)	Prediction (NF)	Sensitivity	Specificity	% of Fish Activity	Stat. Diff. Fish Effort
1	38258	0.75	0.47	0.96	0.90	0.71	0.42	0.84
2	254323	0.84	0.83	0.85	0.93	0.69	0.70	0.21
3	93670	0.83	0.82	0.95	0.99	0.40	0.89	0.11
4	56287	0.87	0.89	0.80	0.94	0.69	0.77	0.04*
5	55034	0.92	0.51	0.98	0.82	0.93	0.14	0.21
6	285407	0.57	0.28	0.93	0.84	0.51	0.55	0.09
7	101499	0.76	0.01	1.00	1.00	0.76	0.24	0.32
Median±SD		0.83±0.11	0.51±0.32	0.95±0.07	0.93±0.07	0.68±0.17		

doi:10.1371/journal.pone.0158248.t001

Table 2. Performance measures for the 16 longliner vessels in different oceans. NF stands for probable non-fishing and F for probable fishing events. Sensitivity is related with non-fishing detection, and specificity with fishing detection. The column Stat. Diff. Fish Effort shows the t-test statistical comparison (p-value) between the predicted fishing effort time calculated from the algorithm's labels and the expert's labels. Two of the vessels could not be measured because they did not have any labeled fishing activity. The asterisk indicates a significant difference.

Track ID	Track Size	Accuracy	Prediction (NF)	Prediction (F)	Sensitivity	Specificity	% of Fish Activity	Stat. Diff. Fish Effort
1	7935	0.46	0.95	0.25	0.35	0.93	0.70	0.29
2	25558	0.80	0.56	0.87	0.52	0.88	0.80	0.08
3	9642	0.65	0.85	0.57	0.45	0.91	0.71	0.62
4	35258	0.89	0.70	0.93	0.71	0.93	0.81	0.67
5	34993	0.87	0.82	0.89	0.66	0.95	0.79	0.28
6	42566	0.89	0.83	0.90	0.54	0.98	0.88	0.35
7	25287	0.76	0.81	0.73	0.59	0.89	0.68	0.67
8	96314	0.54	0.97	0.48	0.22	0.99	0.87	0.05 *
9	123686	0.89	0.89	0.90	0.81	0.94	0.67	0.54
10	128668	0.74	0.96	0.66	0.49	0.98	0.75	0.82
11	2070	0.54	0.81	0.50	0.20	0.94	0.86	0.80
12	1452	0.95	0.95		1.00	0.00	0.00	NA
13	12405	0.71	0.93	0.43	0.68	0.82	0.44	0.34
14	18169	0.86	0.80	0.87	0.55	0.96	0.83	0.67
15	6421	0.99	0.99		1.00	0.00	0.00	NA
16	2780	0.88	0.93	0.80	0.89	0.86	0.36	0.30
Median±SD		0.83±0.15	0.87±0.11	0.77±0.21	0.57±0.24	0.93±0.04		

doi:10.1371/journal.pone.0158248.t002

DATA ANALYSIS

HMM and Observation Variable Choice for Trawlers

Hidden Markov Models (HMM) represent a probability distribution over a sequence of points [21]. It is assumed that an observation at time t was generated by a hidden state S_t. The second assumption is that given the value in S_{t-1}, the value of S_t is independent of all previous states to $t-1$. Assuming that the observed variable is defined by Y_t in time t, and states S_t are defined as classes {'F','N'}, then the Markov Model is factored in the following way:

$$\Pr(S_{1:T}|Y_{1:T}) = \Pr(S_1)\Pr(Y_1|S_1)\prod_{t=2}^{T}\Pr(Y_t|S_t)\Pr(S_t|S_{t-1}) \quad (1)$$

where $Pr(S_t|S_{t-1})$ represents the the transition matrix giving the probability of a state being changed to another state. In the case of fishing activity, it will represent the probability of changing the vessels' state from fishing to non-fishing, and vice-versa. This transition matrix can be estimated directly from the distribution of fishing and non-fishing labels defined in the data set. $\Pr(Y_t|S_t)$ represents the probability of an observed variable occurring associated with a state S_t in time t. T represents the last speed read in the data set.

In order to build a successful HMM model it is necessary to define which parameters offer the best chance to identify the correct hidden states (fishing or non-fishing). Since speed is a key feature in all ecological work associated with HMM's of animal movement [22], our work also implements an HMM based on speed.

Fig 2 shows the speed distribution for vessels engaged in potential fishing or non-fishing activities (such as steaming, searching and anchoring). These results are comparable to those presented by others for mobile towed gear [23].

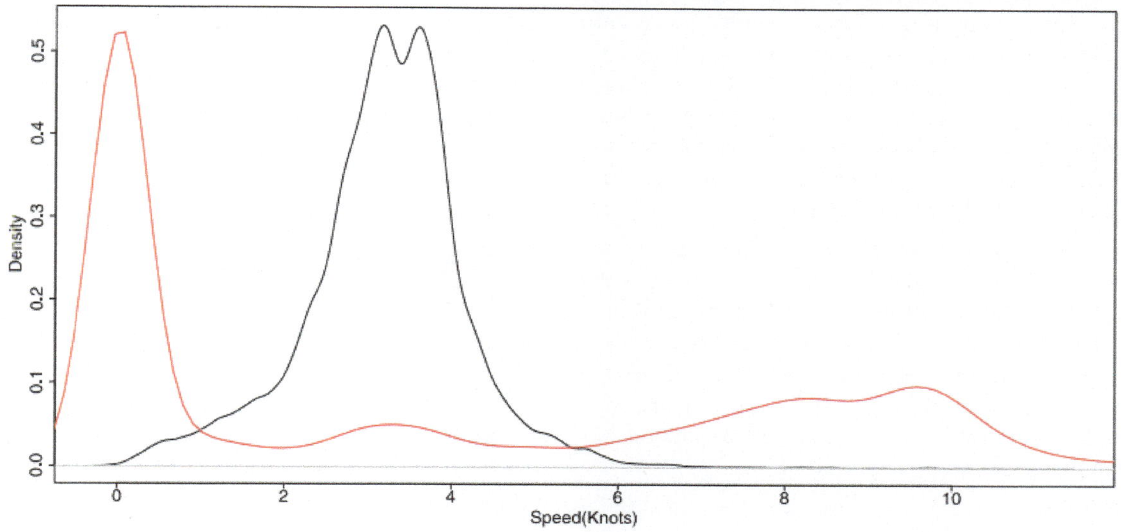

Figure 2. Speed distributions for trawlers during fishing and non-fishing activities. The red line represents probable non-fishing activity, and the black line probable fishing activity.

Data Mining Approach for Fishing Detection with Longliner

The same HMM approach cannot be directly applied to the longliner data set as the speed distribution does not follow a clear pattern as seen in the trawler data (Fig 3). Several parameters contained in the data were tested as potential classifiers, but none proved sufficient to describe fishing and non-fishing activity patterns for longlining.

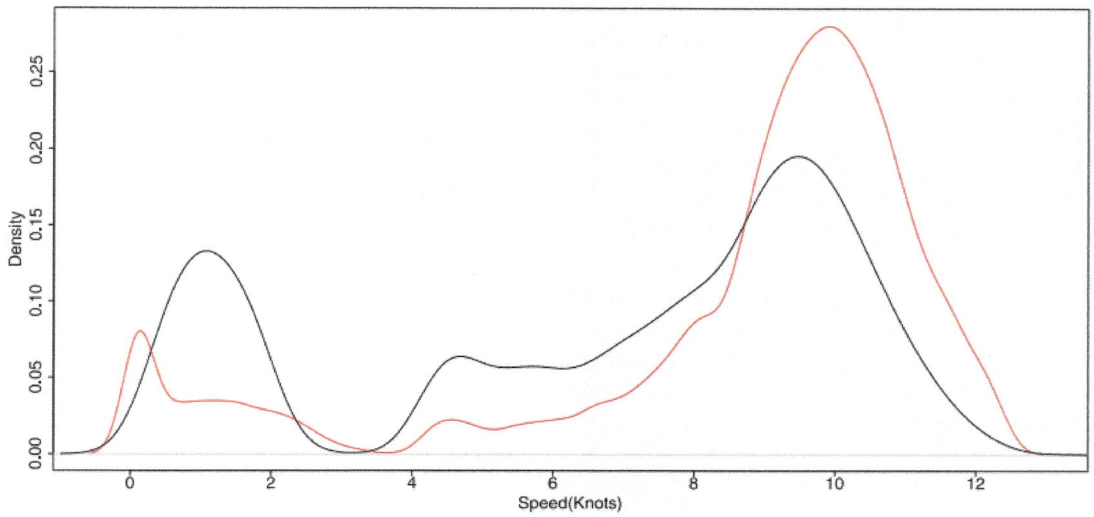

Figure 3. Speed distributions for longliners during fishing and non-fishing activities. The red line represents probable non-fishing activity, and the black line probable fishing activity.

Therefore we opted to develop an alternative approach similar to what biologists have used in studying animal movement tracks. It has been shown that human fishermen tend to show similar movement patterns as animal predators simply because this is the most efficient method to search for and locate prey [15]. Building on this, we decided to use a segmentation technique traditionally applied to animal predators. The Lavielle's segmentation algorithm [24, 25] is widely used by biologists to segment animal tracks in order to identify possible variations in their habitat use.

The Lavielle's algorithm finds the best segmentation of a time series assuming that it is built by K segments defined by the user. The algorithm is not originally designed to work with GPS coordinates, but instead it will segment *any* regular time series data. Before segmentation the whole track was regularized in time to remove gaps in the GPS readings. The regularization assumes equal separation of seven hours between each GPS reading. The separation based on seven hours was defined based on the average time that longliners spent fishing as estimated from the labeled data set.

Lavielle's algorithm searches for a minimum contrast estimator in a problem of change-points estimation, which suggests that Lavielle's algorithm is a drift detector in a time series. The implementation used required the definition of K, which is the number of segments desired by the user as algorithm input, and it was estimated as 70 segments based on various tests. More information about the implementation used may be found inadehabitat package [26] in R.

For each of the segments a second algorithm was used to detect if the segment is composed of straight or curved lines. For each segment, the algorithm calculates the cosine of the relative angle between two consecutive points and calculates an average for all points in the segment. If the average cosine returns a value above 0. 8 or below -0. 8, it indicates that the whole segment is formed by a straight-line movement. All segments that contain the majority of their points classified as straight lines receive a label of non-fishing activity. The segments presenting curved movements are separated to execute a third algorithm to further filter non-fishing activity.

Once the curved segments are separated it is possible to analyze each point to remove possible non-fishing activity classified as fishing. Since the entire curved segment is considered fishing from the straight line algorithm detection, many non-fishing activities will be automatically assumed as fishing. In order to reduce this type of error, two other algorithms are combined to extract these false alarms: First-Passage Time algorithm (FPT) [27] and Utilization Distribution algorithm (UD) [28].

The FPT algorithm [27, 29] uses Brownian Motion theory to find areas where the patterns appear in a trajectory. According to [26], "for a given scale r it is defined as the time required by animals to pass through a circle of radius r". This means that the FPT algorithm searches for the minimum radius r that contains multiple passes of the animal/vessel in the same region. One problem with the approach is that, depending on how long the track is, it does not restrict the size of r, which could result in a longer search for the correct radius. Fortunately, the movement of the vessels inside the curved segments is very restricted, which makes the search for r feasible. After some tests, we found that r using 30 different radii uniformly distributed varying from 0. 1 to 1, offer a acceptable accuracy for FPT. Fauchald and Tveraa [27] extended the FPT algorithm to compute the variance of the$log(FPT)$, which should be high for scales where vessels have multiple passes. As a threshold for our algorithm, if the $Var(log(FPT)) \leq 0.1$ it is a straight line and these points are labeled as non-fishing.

To reduce possible false alarms, the Utilization Distribution algorithm (UD) [28] was used in addition. The UD is defined as a probability distribution [30] using only the longitude and latitude features. In order to estimate this distribution, a kernel method clustering algorithm is used in the coordinate parameters. The idea is to use a bivariate *kernel function* as a distance metric in each GPS location to find the cluster centers. The adehabitatimplementation uses by default the normal kernel function, and we did not change this parameter. This work uses the UD estimations to correct wrong predictions of points wrongly classified as fishing activity to non-fishing activity.

The combination of FPT and UD within the curved data segments offers an extra 1% to 2% accuracy improvement and a reduction of non-fishing activity false alarm comparing to the expert labels.

Filtering Approach for Purse Seiner Fishing Detection

Fishing activity detection for Purse Seiners builds on two assumptions based on literature data (see [14]), personal communication with fisheries observers working on board of various purse seiners and observations from the AIS data. Firstly, the majority of purse seiners do not fish at night, with rare exceptions that are not considered here. Second, that the fishing pattern consists of two main activity patterns, namely the setting of the net at high speeds and the drifting while hauling in the net and retrieving the fish at very low speeds. While the setting of the net is a very short activity that may not be represented in the data due to insufficient satellite coverage, the hauling and bailing can take up to several hours and is thus used to detect and classify potential fishing activity. Using the abovementioned day/night classifier, possible fishing activity was detected using a speed filter for speeds smaller than or equal to 2. 5 knots. Fig 4 presents the speed distribution for purse seiners, for all positions reported at least 10 km from shore and during day. It is noticeable that the majority of probable fishing activity happens with speeds in the range of 0 up to 5 knots, as indicated by the black distribution, and a second distribution peak appears for probable non-fishing activity (around 15 knots) in red.

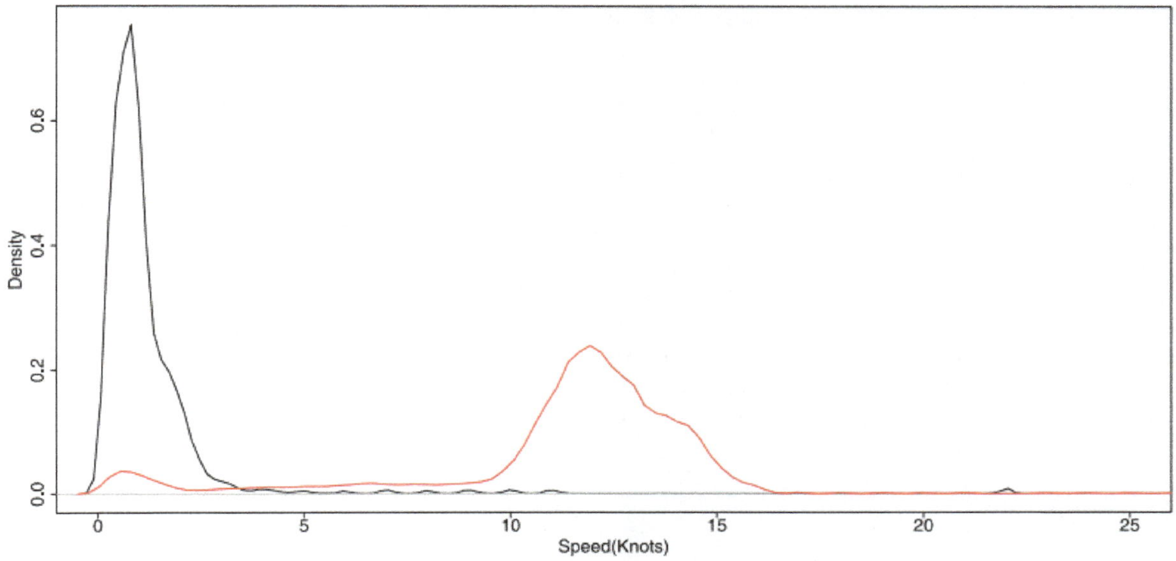

Figure 4. Speed distribution for Purse Seiners. The red line indicates the probable non-fishing activity labeled by the expert, while the black line is the probable fishing activity. This distribution considers only the speeds reported by the vessels 10 km from shore, and during day time.

The 2. 5 knots speed threshold was chosen based on observations from the AIS data and the work of Bez *et al* [14]. The filtering based approach does not require machine learning, but the computation of extra features as described in the data pre-processing section.

RESULTS

Trawler

As presented in Section 2. 4, the solution proposed for trawling vessels is based on the HMM algorithm. As HMMs assume that the data is time dependent the analysis must consider the order of the points. Monte Carlo simulations are the only repeatable testing method that does not change this order. The objective of the repeated test is twofold: 1) to assess the HMM performance, and 2) to identify how many data points are required to correctly predict potential fishing activity.

Fig 5 presents the Monte Carlo average results of the accuracy, recall and Area Under the Curve (AUC) for each class (fishing and not fishing). The HMM keeps the same average accuracy independently on the number of points available for training (close to 88%). The algorithm also improved the recall (defined as the percentage of relevant, correct fishing detections retrieved by the algorithm) of the fishing activity from 58% to above 85% when the algorithm was presented with more data for training, but also reduced the prediction of non-fishing activity from above an average 95% to 87% at the same time. This increase in the number of correct predictions of probable fishing activity indicates that the HMM may be overfitting, with higher number of points available for training. The overfitting aspect of the model can only be evaluated with tests on a different data set.

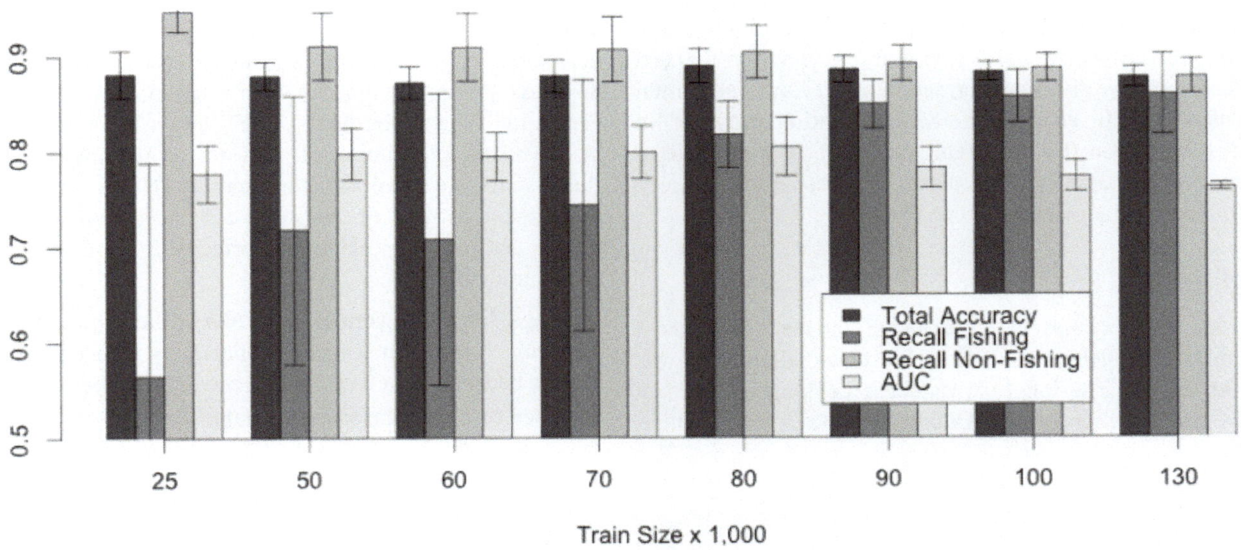

Figure 5. Accuracy/Recall measured for trawlers with HMM using Monte Carlo Simulation. Results do not consider the 10 km coastal distance threshold.

Despite the fact that the Monte Carlo simulations are a good indicator of the algorithm's performance, they do not give the full information about how the algorithm will work with future data sets. To confirm the number of points necessary for training we tested the HMM against data from other parts of the world. The training was done on the 2013 North Pacific data, which contains 25,000 points. The test data was derived from the seven vessels operating across all oceans and years. The algorithm showed low accuracy results when trained with more than 25,000 data points, due to overfitting. This lies in the nature of the Monte Carlo test methodology: the more data available for training also means less data for testing, which reduces the variance (Fig 4). To avoid overfitting, it is advisable to train the HMM with fewer data points to increase its generalization. The results indicate that the HMM can be used to locate probable fishing activity for trawlers using tracks from different areas of the world with a median accuracy of 84%. There was little difference in accuracy for the two subtypes of trawling, pelagic/midwater (average accuracy 75%) and bottom (average accuracy 80. 6%). The sensitivity to detect probable fishing activity (column Sensitivity inTable 1) shows a median of 93% and the respective specificity (the capability to identify probable non-fishing activity) a median of 68%.

Fig 6 presents the results for track number two from Table 1, containing 254,323 points with a total accuracy of 84% and 69% specificity to detect probable fishing activity, as well 93% sensitivity of probable non-fishing activity detection.

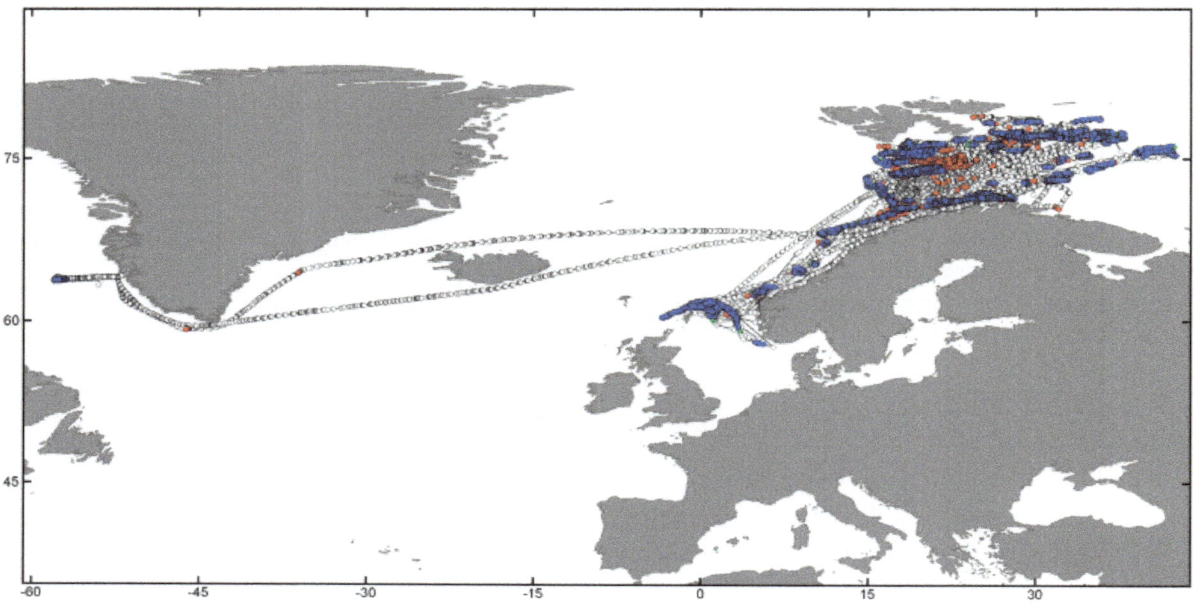

Figure 6. Comparison of the Hidden Markov Model algorithm results to the expert labels. Matching results for fishing activity presented in blue, expert labels in green and the algorithm's fishing activity predictions in red. Empty circles represent non-fishing activity as identified by algorithm and expert. The track corresponds to vessel number 2 in Table 1. Map data by Natural Earth.

As shown by [20], the sensitivity and specificity only concern the current model's capability to classify the test instances, but they give no information about future algorithm performance. With support of the information provided in columns Prediction (F) and Prediction (NF), it is possible to confirm that the algorithm will have high probability to keep the same performance with unseen data.

Longliner

The 16 longliner vessels were tested independently as a mathematical model was fit to the data set and all the data was used for testing. The longliner database contains an average of 76% of movement patterns dedicated to assumed fishing activity. Table 2 summarizes the results of the longliner detection. In general, the median algorithm performance is 83%. As previously presented in Section 2. 4, the columns Prediction (F) and Prediction (NF) shown in Table 2 indicate how well the algorithm will perform on unknown data sets. Results indicate that non-fishing activity (NF) will be correctly predicted in 87% of all cases with 57% accuracy and probable fishing activity (F) is identified correctly 77% of the time with an accuracy of 93%.

Figs 7 and 8 illustrate the results of the fishing prediction for tracks 8 and 1 in Table 2, respectively. These tracks were chosen because these vessels presented the highest and lowest accuracy results in the longliner data.

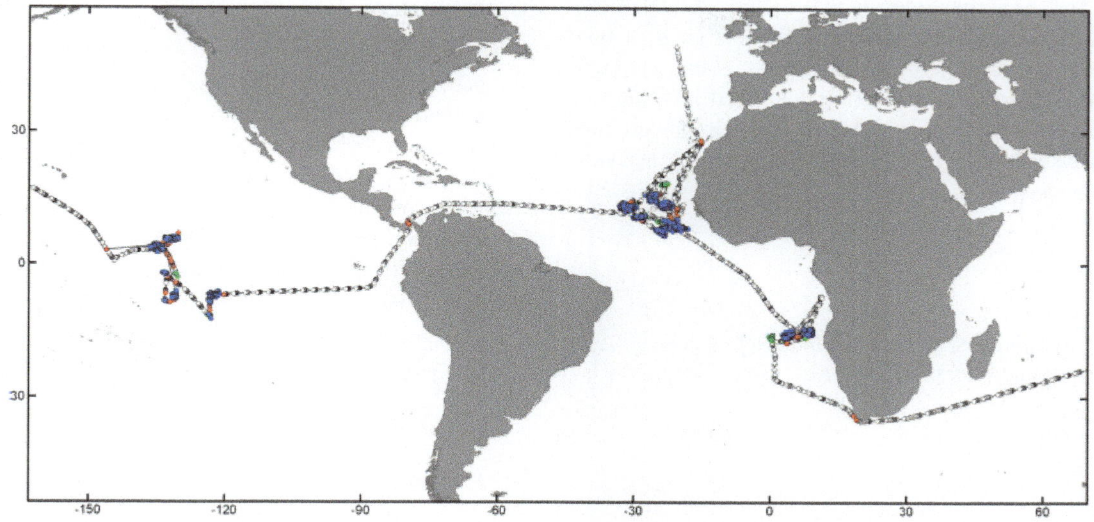

Figure 7. Results for longliner number 8 from Table 2(Accuracy: 89%). Matching results for fishing activity presented in blue, expert labels in green and the algorithm's fishing activity predictions in red. Empty circles represent non-fishing activity as identified by algorithm and expert. Map data by Natural Earth.

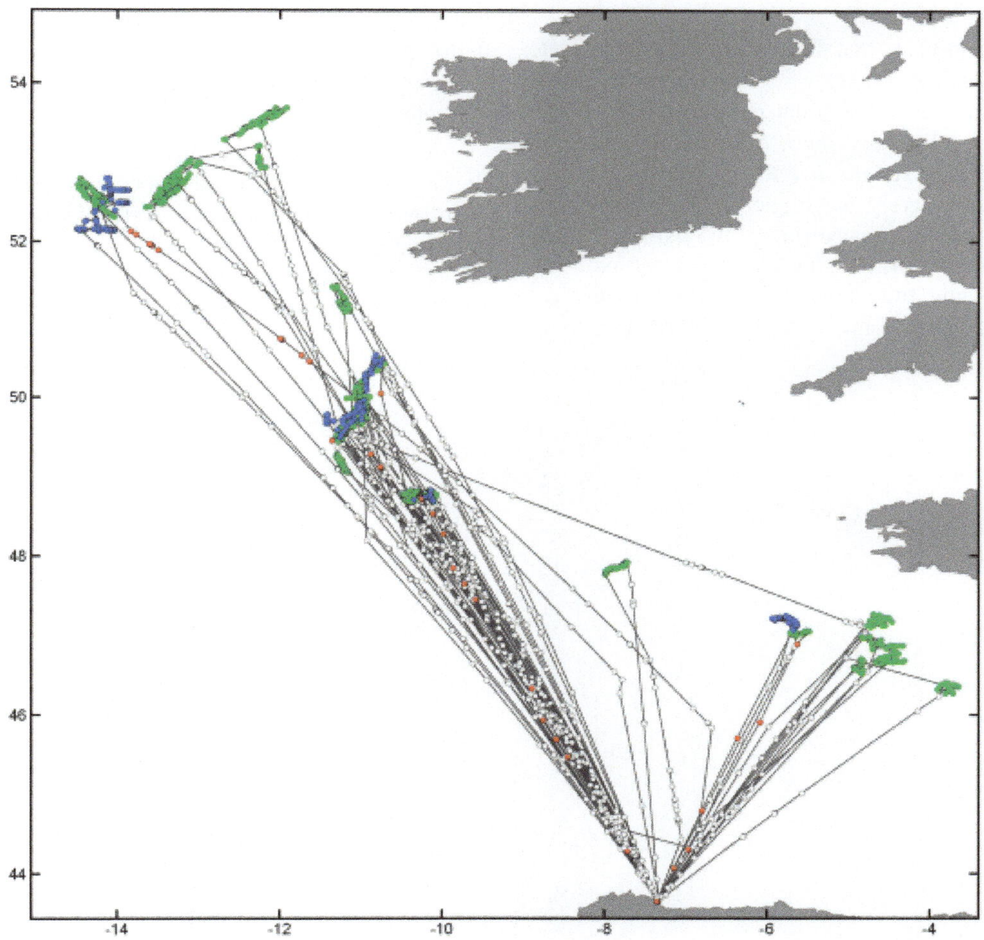

Figure 8. Results for longliner number 1 from Table 2 **(Accuracy: 46%)**. Matching results for fishing activity presented in blue, expert labels in green and the algorithm's fishing activity predictions in red. Empty circles represent non-fishing activity as identified by algorithm and expert. Map data by Natural Earth.

The last column presented in Tables 1 and 2 shows the results of a t-test between the algorithm's predicted Fishing Effort (FE) and the expert's labels. The FE is a measure to estimate how much time the vessel invests in fishing activity and is calculated in two steps: 1) periods of fishing activity for each vessel are tagged at the moments when a change from non-fishing activity to fishing and vice-versa occurred, and 2) for each individual period of fishing the time difference between the first and last AIS messages is calculated. A statistical difference between expert and prediction labels ($p < 0.05$) occurred only in one case ($p = 0.05$, Tables 1 and 2). This indicates that the algorithm is capturing the expert labeling for nearly all of the vessels evaluated. Two of the vessels were not part of the analyses as they did not have any fishing activity labeled by the expert.

Purse Seiner

Table 3 illustrates the results for the Purse Seiner filtering approach. The total median accuracy of the model is 97%, with a standard deviation of 1%. The filter median prediction capability of probable fishing and non-fishing activities is 97% and 94%, respectively. The main difference is in the sensitivity measure associated with probable non-fishing activity, with a median of 99% and a standard deviation of 1%. The specificity associated with probable fishing activity detection is around 71% with a standard deviation of 17%.

Table 3. Result for the purse seiner filtering approach. The seven vessels were randomly chosen from multiple parts of the world. NF stands for probable non-fishing and F for probable fishing events. Sensitivity is related with non-fishing detection, and specificity with fishing detection.

Track ID	Track Size	Accuracy	Prediction (NF)	Prediction (F)	Sensitivity	Specificity	AUC	% of Fish Activity
1	43457	0.95	1.00	0.02	0.95	0.82	0.89	0.05
2	170972	0.98	0.98	0.94	1.00	0.71	0.85	0.05
3	43369	0.96	0.96	0.95	1.00	0.36	0.68	0.02
4	18122	0.94	0.97	0.76	0.96	0.79	0.88	0.13
5	38596	0.99	1.00	0.91	1.00	0.89	0.94	0.03
6	51545	0.97	0.97	0.97	1.00	0.65	0.83	0.05
7	33484	0.97	0.97	0.96	1.00	0.64	0.82	0.05
Median±SD		0.97±0.01	0.97±0.01	0.94±0.34	0.99±0.01	0.71±0.17		

doi:10.1371/journal.pone.0158248.t003

All these results indicate that the model is highly accurate to detect probable fishing activity when comparing to expert labels. The FE metric was not estimated for purse seiners as due to incomplete satellite coverage the total purse seining activity from starting to set the net to the finishing of the haul is rarely seen completely. Subsequently the filtering was designed to capture the hauling portion of the fishing activity only. This makes the FE metric unreliable to estimate the correct probable fishing time intervals. Instead, we present the AUC which is a common metric used in ML to inform on algorithm performance. The median AUC for the purse seiner is 0.85, with a standard deviation of 0.08, which also indicates the model is reliable to identify the minority class.

Fig 9 presents an example of the results found with the filtering technique proposed and corresponds to track number six in Table 3. The track contains 51,545 points and the filtering algorithm reached 97% total accuracy with nearly all probable fishing activity detected. The detection of false alarms is based on the expert's labeling strategy, which classified speeds higher than 2.5 knots as fishing.

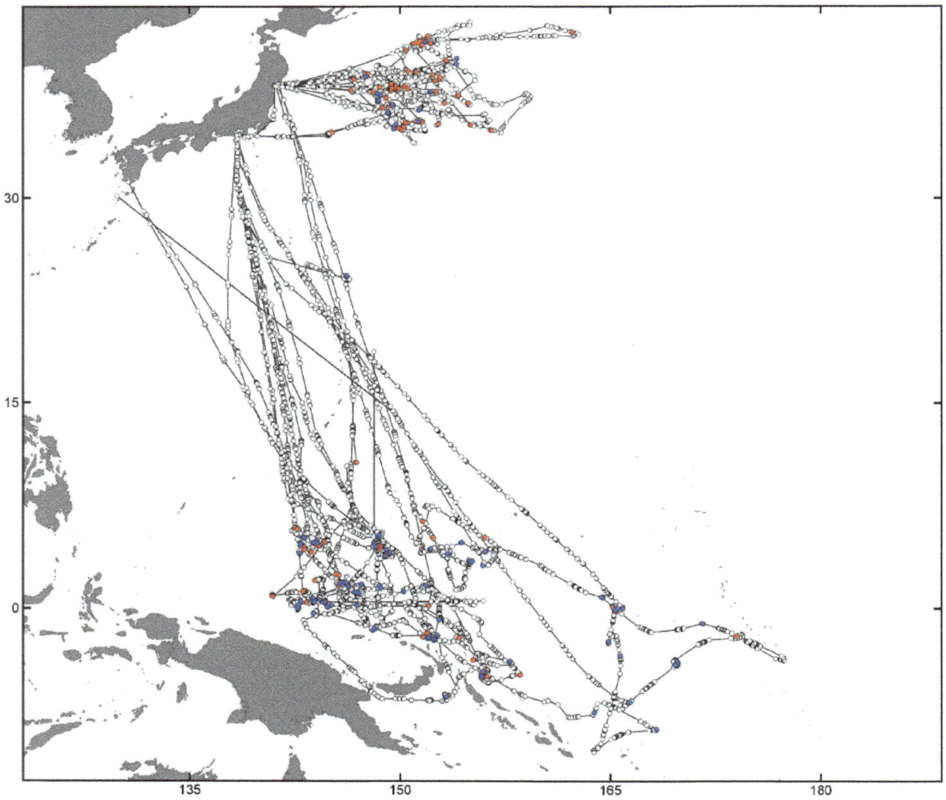

Figure 9. Comparison of the purse seiner algorithm results to the expert labels. Matching results for fishing activity presented in blue, expert labels in green and the algorithm's fishing activity predictions in red. Empty circles represent non-fishing activity as identified by algorithm

and expert. The track corresponds to vessel number 6 in Table 3. Map data by Natural Earth.

DISCUSSION

The aim of this work was to develop automated methods to detect potential fishing behavior from different gear types based on S-AIS track data. As fishing activity for each gear type has its unique pattern and characteristics (compare Fig 1), we developed separate approaches tailored to the specific challenges associated with systematic differences in vessel behavior, speed distribution, and fishing time.

Results indicate that our machine learning and data mining approaches were able to correctly identify a very large fraction (83–97%) of probable fishing events compared to the expert labeled data. Importantly, our algorithms performed similarly well for different fleets in different regions operating from regional to global scales, making this a versatile tool to study the behavior of fishing fleets worldwide. While a number of previous studies have analyzed VMS data for vessel identification and tracking [6, 31, 32], S-AIS data have only been available for a few years and we are aware of only two published attempts to use it for detection and classification of vessel activities [4, 33]. Most previous work was done in engineering and computer science, largely either focusing on the technical aspects of system performance analyses mostly in the context of Maritime Situational Awareness [34–40] or on the computational challenge of complex analyses on big data and the combinations with other tools [33, 41]. While these studies form a valuable basis for the work presented here, no previous study has focused on a comprehensive solution to detect and classify fishing activities on a global scale using a distinction between gear types.

We presented three distinct machine learning, data mining and filtering approaches to detect potential fishing activity for trawlers, longliners and purse seiners, respectively. The method developed for trawlers is based on previous works [31] that showed a HMM is an effective way to predict fishing activity using vessel speed as the critical parameter. Our model works equally well for the two subtypes of trawling we accounted for, pelagic/midwater and bottom trawling. To establish the performance of the trawl algorithm, a Monte Carlo experiment was executed in which the algorithm performs increasingly better when the number of data points available for training increases. The objective to run Monte Carlo simulations is to assess the minimum number of points required to train a stable model, and confirm the model's performance. Unfortunately, Monte Carlo simulations can suffer from overfitting, which is the case when tested models perform very well during the simulation but fail when new data is presented. Monte Carlo simulation results presented inFig 5 indicate that models trained with 80,000 points would offer a more reliable and stable model, but when we tested these models against the data from various parts of the world, the accuracy reduced considerably. In order to confirm if the 80,000 points HMM was overfitting we tested HMM models with higher number of points for training. Results remained much below the accuracies reported by the Monte Carlo simulations, therefore confirming the overfitting assumption. As more generic models can be created with a reduced amount of data to avoid overfitting, we tested the HMM model with 25,000 points and results were very close to those reported by the Monte Carlo simulations for various parts of the world.

For longliner fishing activity detection no clear separation between fishing and non-fishing speeds exists. To detect probable longliner fishing activity, the development of an alternative algorithm was required. Since the proposed method is a Data Mining-based approach, all the data was used for testing, and the results indicate that the proposed method based on previous analyses of animal movement and habitat selection (see [15]) offers a good prediction level to detect a more complex type of fishing pattern. The main results are presented in Table 2 and indicate that the algorithm has good prediction capabilities with a median accuracy of 83%. One disadvantage of the method is the track segmentation algorithm, which requires defining the number of segments beforehand. Further work might consider methods to dynamically partition tracks.

Finally, the purse seiner approach uses another DM algorithm based on a filtering strategy. The filter designed is similar to the one used by McCauley *et al.* [42]. The algorithm filters the data assuming that purse seiners only fish during day, and that fishing activities are characterized by low speeds (lower than 2. 5 knots). Due to this type of behavior, the filter results are well aligned with expert labels, indicating that the filtering approach is well suited to this type of vessel. A limitation of the filter is that it will not capture probable fishing activity with speeds above the 2. 5 knots threshold. This assumption opens the possibility of future research to create techniques that are based on movement shape to detect possible fishing activity at higher speeds.

The labeling for all three methods is point-based, attaching a fishing or non-fishing label to the individual AIS vessel position records. On the basis of these labeled points, fishing time per area can be calculated on any given scale. Future work includes the partitioning of sequences of labeled points into sets for each gear type to adjust the output of the methods presented here to other units commonly used as measures of fishing effort. This can also include further information on the characteristics of fishing vessels as either transmitted with the AIS message or available through vessel registry data bases such as size, tonnage or engine power.

Overall, the algorithms are slightly more likely to detect potential fishing activity than expert labels, reflecting the conservative approach taken in labeling. As most groundtruthed data such as observer and logbook data is proprietary and often impossible to access, manual vessel activity labeling by an expert provides a workable solution. A possible next step to further improve the algorithms is to test and train them on data containing groundtruthed fishing activity recordings such as observer or logbook data if available at a resolution matching that for vessels carrying AIS transponders. This would eliminate any variability potentially introduced through the manual labeling and provide a more precise picture of vessel activities. Despite their flexibility and versatility, the approaches presented here come with limitations and caveats. The biggest weakness is the structure of the S-AIS system itself: not all vessels carry S-AIS transponders and those who do can still tamper with or disable the transponders, or falsify positional or identification data. Manipulated data and switching-off events can be detected using specially designed algorithms, but more comprehensive legislation regarding the use of S-AIS may be needed to address these non-compliance issues on a broader scale, e. g. as suggested by McCauley *et al.* [42]. Another issue regarding S-AIS data is the limited satellite coverage, which at this point provides limited time and space windows for observation, and samples some regions better than others. This inherent problem, however, will be alleviated with the projected launching of several new AIS-enabled satellites in 2016.

The methods presented here were designed to stand on their own but they perform best on pre-processed AIS data, where wrong detections, noise and faulty out-of-bounds data (e. g. observations on land) are removed. There are efforts currently underway to develop better 'de-spoofing' algorithms that can reliably detect faulty or falsified AIS messages with inaccurate information. In combination with such pre-processing and de-spoofing algorithms, our methods will be applied within the framework of 'Global Fishing Watch' (http:// www. globalfishingwatch. org), an open-access online-tool to detect and visualize fishing activity worldwide, with a launch planned for fall 2016. Furthermore, we caveat that algorithm performance varies with the quality of the track, giving better results for long tracks with high detection continuity. The three approaches presented here are designed to be applied for vessels with known gear type so the appropriate method can be chosen. While work on the identification of gear types used by fishing vessels is ongoing, our methods are only partly applicable for vessels using mixed gears and not for other gears than the three addressed here.

In conclusion, the approaches we have developed allow us to detect and identify potential fishing behavior for three main gear types with high accuracy and spatial resolution on a global scale. This opens up a new window of transparency, providing information on ocean uses not only to marine spatial planners and managers as well as the public, but also lays a foundation for future scientific research on vessel behavior for different gear types and sizes. One major challenge lies in expanding behavior identification to small-scale and artisanal fishing vessels which currently remain largely invisible in most tracking systems. Spatial-temporal analyses of long-term tracking data will offer valuable insights into fishing effort intensity and distribution in various areas such as nation's exclusive economic zones, the high seas and areas of special interest like marine protected areas and other areas of biological or managerial interest.

ACKNOWLEDGMENTS

This work was partly funded by the NSERC CREATE Transatlantic Ocean System Science and Technology (TOSST) and the National Science and Engineering Council of Canada. We are grateful for AIS data access and technical support from Exact Earth and MEOPAR and the help of Ron Pelot and Casey Hilliard, as well as a a number of fishermen, fisheries experts and fisheries observers who provided labeling information. We further thank Paul Woods, David Kroodsma, Derek Tittensor and Douglas McCauley for helpful discussion.

AUTHOR CONTRIBUTIONS

Conceived and designed the experiments: ENS KB SM BW. Performed the experiments: ENS KB. Analyzed the data: ENS KB. Wrote the paper: ENS KB SM BW.

REFERENCES

1. Halpern BS, Walbridge S, Selkoe KA, Kappel CV, Micheli F, D'Agrosa C, et al. A global map of human impact on marine ecosystems. Science. 2008;319(5865):948–952. doi: 10. 1126/science. 1149345. pmid:18276889
2. Trebilco R, Halpern BS, Flemming JM, Field C, Blanchard W, Worm B. Mapping species richness and human impact drivers to inform global pelagic conservation prioritisation. Biological Conservation. 2011;144(5):1758–1766. doi: 10. 1016/j. biocon. 2011. 02. 024.
3. Selig ER, Turner WR, Troëng S, Wallace BP, Halpern BS, Kaschner K, et al. Global priorities for marine biodiversity conservation. PloS one. 2014;9(1):e82898. doi: 10. 1371/journal. pone. 0082898. pmid:24416151
4. Natale F, Gibin M, Alessandrini A, Vespe M, Paulrud A. Mapping Fishing Effort through AIS Data. PLoS ONE. 2015 06;10(6):e0130746. doi: 10. 1371/journal. pone. 0130746. pmid:26098430
5. Shui-Kai C, Tzu-Lun Y. Deriving high-resolution spatiotemporal fishing effort of large-scale longline fishery from vessel monitoring system (VMS) data and validated by observer data. Canadian Journal of Fisheries and Aquatic Sciences. 2014;71(9):1363–1370. doi: 10. 1139/cjfas-2013-0552.
6. Gerritsen H, Lordan C. Integrating vessel monitoring systems (VMS) data with daily catch data from logbooks to explore the spatial distribution of catch and effort at high resolution. ICES Journal of Marine Science: Journal du Conseil. 2011;68(1):245–252. Available from: http:// icesjms. oxfordjournals. org/content/68/1/245. abstract. doi: 10. 1093/icesjms/fsq137.
7. Fishing Gear types. Bottom trawls. Technology Fact Sheets;. Accessed: 2015-Nov-13. http://www. fao. org/ fishery/geartype/205/en.
8. Skaar K, Jørgensen T, Ulvestad B, Engås A. Accuracy of VMS data from Norwegian demersal stern trawlers for estimating trawled areas in the Barents Sea. ICES Journal of Marine Science: Journal du Conseil. 2011;p. fsr091. doi: 10. 1093/icesjms/fsr091.
9. Lee J, South AB, Jennings S. Developing reliable, repeatable, and accessible methods to provide high-resolution estimates of fishing-effort distributions from vessel monitoring system (VMS) data. ICES Journal of Marine Science: Journal du Conseil. 2010;67(6):1260–1271. doi: 10. 1093/icesjms/fsq010.
10. Alemany D, Iribarne OO, Acha EM. Effects of a large-scale and offshore marine protected area on the demersal fish assemblage in the Southwest Atlantic. ICES Journal of Marine Science: Journal du Conseil. 2013;70(1):123–134. doi: 10. 1093/icesjms/fss166.
11. Mazzarella F, Vespe M, Damalas D, Osio G. Discovering vessel activities at sea using AIS data: mapping of fishing footprints. In: Information Fusion (FUSION), 2014 17th International Conference on. IEEE; 2014. p. 1–7.
12. Fishing Techniques. Industrial tuna longlining. Technology Fact Sheets;. Accessed: 2015-Nov-13. http://www. fao. org/fishery/fishtech/1010/en.

13. Walker E, Bez N. A pioneer validation of a state-space model of vessel trajectories (VMS) with observers' data. Ecological Modelling. 2010;221(17):2008–2017. doi: 10. 1016/j. ecolmodel. 2010. 05. 007.

14. Bez N, Walker E, Gaertner D, Rivoirard J, Gaspar P, Walters C. Fishing activity of tuna purse seiners estimated from vessel monitoring system (VMS) data. Canadian Journal of Fisheries and Aquatic Sciences. 2011;68(11):1998–2010. doi: 10. 1139/f2011-114.

15. Bertrand S, Burgos JM, Gerlotto F, Atiquipa J. Levy trajectories of Peruvian purse-seiners as an indicator of the spatial distribution of anchovy (Engraulis ringens). ICES Journal of Marine Science: Journal du Conseil. 2005;62(3):477–482. Available from: http://icesjms. oxfordjournals. org/content/62/3/477. abstract. doi: 10. 1016/j. icesjms. 2004. 12. 002.

16. Perpiñán O. solaR: Solar Radiation and Photovoltaic Systems with R. Journal of Statistical Software. 2012;50(9):1–32. Available from:http://www. jstatsoft. org/v50/i09/.

17. Natural Earth;. Accessed: 2015-Nov-12. http://www. naturalearthdata. com/http//www. naturalearthdata. com/ download/10m/physical/ne_10m_coastline. zip.

18. Stack Overflow;. Accessed: 2015-Nov-12. http:// stackoverflow. com/questions/27697504/ocean-latitude-longitude-point-distance-from-shore.

19. Torgo L. Data Mining with R, learning with case studies. Chapman and Hall/CRC; 2010. Available from: http:// www. dcc. fc. up. pt/~ltorgo/DataMiningWithR.

20. Altman DG, Bland JM. Diagnostic tests 2: Predictive values. BMJ. 1994 Jul;309(6947):102. doi: 10. 1136/ bmj. 309. 6947. 102. pmid:8038641

21. Ghahramani Z. Hidden Markov Models. River Edge, NJ, USA: World Scientific Publishing Co. , Inc. ; 2002. p. 9–42. Available from: http://dl. acm. org/citation. cfm?id=505741. 505743.

22. Peel D, Good NM. A hidden Markov model approach for determining vessel activity from vessel monitoring system data. Canadian Journal of Fisheries and Aquatic Sciences. 2011;68(7):1252–1264. doi: 10. 1139/f2011-055.

23. Charles C, Gillis D, Wade E. Using hidden Markov models to infer vessel activities in the snow crab (Chionoecetes opilio) fixed gear fishery and their application to catch standardization. Canadian Journal of Fisheries and Aquatic Sciences. 2014;71(12):1817–1829. doi: 10. 1139/cjfas-2013-0572.

24. Lavielle M. Detection of multiple changes in a sequence of dependent variables. Stochastic Processes and their Applications. 1999;83(1):79–102. Available from:http://www. sciencedirect. com/science/article/ pii/S030441499900023X. doi: 10. 1016/S0304-4149(99)00023-X.

25. Lavielle M. Using penalized contrasts for the change-point problem. Signal Processing. 2005;85(8):1501–1510. Available from:http://www. sciencedirect. com/ science/article/pii/S0165168405000381. doi: 10. 1016/j. sigpro. 2005. 01. 012.

26. Calenge C. The package adehabitat for the R software: tool for the analysis of space and habitat use by animals. Ecological Modelling. 2006;197:1035. doi: 10. 1016/j. ecolmodel. 2006. 03. 017.

27. Fauchald P, Tveraa T. Using First-Passage Time in the Analysis of Area-Restricted Search and Habitat Selection. Ecology. 2003;84:282–288. doi: 10. 1890/0012-9658(2003)084%5B0282:UFPTIT%5D2. 0. CO;2.

28. Worton BJ. Using Monte Carlo Simulation to Evaluate Kernel-Based Home Range Estimators. The Journal of Wildlife Management. 1995;59(4):pp. 794–800. Available from: http://www. jstor. org/stable/3801959. doi: 10. 2307/3801959.

29. Johnson AR, Milne BT, Wiens JA. Diffusion in Fractcal Landscapes: Simulations and Experimental Studies of Tenebrionid Beetle Movements. Ecology. 1992;73(6):pp. 1968–1983. Available from: http://www. jstor. org/ stable/1941448. doi: 10. 2307/1941448.

30. Winkle WV. Comparison of Several Probabilistic Home-Range Models. The Journal of Wildlife Management. 1975;39(1):pp. 118–123. Available from:http://www. jstor. org/stable/3800474. doi: 10. 2307/3800474.

31. Vermard Y, Rivot E, Mahévas S, Marchal P, Gascuel D. Identifying fishing trip behaviour and estimating fishing effort from VMS data using Bayesian Hidden Markov Models. Ecological Modelling. 2010;221(15):1757–1769. doi: 10. 1016/j. ecolmodel. 2010. 04. 005.

32. Witt MJ, Godley BJ. A step towards seascape scale conservation: using vessel monitoring systems (VMS) to map fishing activity. PloS one. 2007;2(10):e1111. doi: 10. 1371/journal. pone. 0001111. pmid:17971874

33. Lehner S, Brusch S, Fritz T. Ship surveillance by joint use of SAR and AIS. In: OCEANS 2009-EUROPE. IEEE; 2009. p. 1–5.

34. Carson-Jackson J. Satellite AIS–Developing Technology or Existing Capability? Journal of Navigation. 2012;65(02):303–321. doi: 10. 1017/ S037346331100066X.

35. Cervera MA, Ginesi A, Eckstein K. Satellite-based vessel Automatic Identification System: A feasibility and performance analysis. International Journal of Satellite Communications and Networking. 2011;29(2):117–142. doi: 10. 1002/sat. 957.

36. Cervera M, Ginesi A, et al. On the performance analysis of a satellite-based AIS system. In: Signal Processing for Space Communications, 2008. SPSC 2008. 10th International Workshop on. IEEE; 2008. p. 1–8.

37. Pallotta G, Vespe M, Bryan K. Vessel pattern knowledge discovery from AIS data: A framework for anomaly detection and route prediction. Entropy. 2013;15(6):2218–2245. doi: 10. 3390/e15062218.

38. Soleimani BH, De Souza EN, Hilliard C, Matwin S. Anomaly detection in maritime data based on geometrical analysis of trajectories. In: Information Fusion (Fusion), 2015 18th International Conference on; 2015. p. 1100–1105.

39. Liu B, De Souza EN, Hilliard C, Matwin S. Ship

movement anomaly detection using specialized distance measures. In: Information Fusion (Fusion), 2015 18th International Conference on; 2015. p. 1113–1120.

40. Liu B, De Souza EN, Matwin S, Sydow M. Knowledge-based clustering of ship trajectories using density-based approach. In: Big Data (Big Data), 2014 IEEE International Conference on; 2014. p. 603–608.

41. Cairns WR. AIS and long range identification & tracking. Journal of Navigation. 2005;58(02):181–189. doi: 10. 1017/S0373463305003267.

42. McCauley DJ, Woods P, Sullivan B, Bergman B, Jablonicky C, Roan A, et al. Ending hide and go seek in the oceans. Science. 2016;351(6278):1148–1150. doi: 10. 1126/science. aad5686.

CHAPTER 6

VIRTUAL REALITY BASED SUPPORT SYSTEM FOR LAYOUT PLANNING AND PROGRAMMING OF AN INDUSTRIAL ROBOTIC WORK CELL

Hwa Jen Yap[1], Zahari Taha[2], Siti Zawiah Md Dawal[1], Siow-Wee Chang[3]

[1] Department of Mechanical Engineering, Faculty of Engineering, University of Malaya, Kuala Lumpur, Malaysia

[2] Faculty of Mechanical Engineering, Universiti Malaysia Pahang, Pekan, Pahang, Malaysia

[3] Bioinformatics Program, Institute of Biological Sciences, Faculty of Science, University of Malaya, Kuala Lumpur, Malaysia

ABSTRACT

Traditional robotic work cell design and programming are considered inefficient and outdated in current industrial and market demands. In this research, virtual reality (VR) technology is used to improve human-robot interface, whereby complicated commands or programming knowledge is not required. The proposed solution, known as VR-based Programming of a Robotic Work Cell (VR-Rocell), consists of two sub-programmes, which are VR-Robotic Work Cell Layout (VR-RoWL) and VR-based Robot Teaching System (VR-RoT). VR-RoWL is developed to assign the layout design for an industrial robotic work cell, whereby VR-RoT is developed to overcome safety issues and lack of trained personnel in robot programming. Simple and user-friendly interfaces are designed for inexperienced users to generate robot commands without damaging the robot or interrupting the production line. The user is able to attempt numerous times to attain an optimum solution. A case study is conducted in the Robotics Laboratory to assemble an electronics casing and it is found that the output models are compatible with commercial software without loss of information. Furthermore, the generated KUKA commands are workable when loaded into a commercial simulator. The operation of the actual robotic work cell shows that the errors may be due to the dynamics of the KUKA robot rather than the accuracy of the generated programme. Therefore, it is concluded that the virtual reality based solution approach can be implemented in an industrial robotic work cell.

INTRODUCTION

According to a survey from the UN Economic Commission for Europe published in "World Robotics 2001" [1], there were approximately 750,000 robots running in industries worldwide. After a decade, the statistics, market analysis, forecasts, case studies and profitability of robot investment published by the International Federation of Robotics (IFR) in "World Robotics 2011" [2] revealed that the annual robot sales in 2010 was 118,337 units. The sales almost doubled compared to that in 2009, during the worldwide economic and financial crisis. The forecasted figures for year 2011 and 2014 were 139,300 and 166,700 respectively. On the other hand, the sale for robots in 2010 was US$ 5.7 billion. It was estimated that the sales value for robot systems in 2010 was US$ 17.5 billion, which includes software, peripherals and systems engineering. On the other hand, over 1,300 labours were struck by moving objects

Citation: Yap HJ, Taha Z, Md Dawal SZ, Chang S-W (2014) Virtual Reality Based Support System for Layout Planning and Programming of an Industrial Robotic Work Cell. PLoS ONE 9(10): e109692. doi:10.1371/journal.pone.0109692.

in their workplace. This appears to be the most common accident which causes injuries, which is due to the complexity of hardware and software. In Sweden and Japan [3], these incidents have been associated with robot operations, such as malfunction to stop, rapid motion of the robot arm, injuries in the workspace during repair and maintenance, illegal entrance to the workspace as well as unpredictable robot work functions to the operator.

In this research, a virtual reality based programming of a robotic work cell (VR-Rocell) is proposed and developed. In general, robot programming methods can be classified as online and offline programming, which is dependent on the presence of the actual robot while the programme is being created. In online programming, the actual robot must be present and used in the teaching process. Offline programming is the most popular method for robot programming as it does not involve real robots. This reduces robot downtime and the production line will be unaffected [4]. The system is designed to improve human-machine interface and is divided into two major sub-systems, namely, VR-Robotic Work Cell Layout (VR-RoWL) and VR-Robot Teaching System (VR-RoT). Open platform architecture is used along with a universal file format. The system uses the teach-points concept for offline programming to generate robot commands, which prevents users from potential uncertain manufacturing environments. The objective of this research is to develop a VR-based system for cell layout planning and design, path teaching, programming and simulation for an industrial robot which will achieve zero robot downtime during path teaching using a generic approach.

SOLUTION APPROACHES FOR AN INDUSTRIAL ROBOTIC WORK CELL

The synergy between virtual reality and robotics in various areas was reviewed in 1999 [5]. It is known that traditional approaches in robot programming are tedious and require knowledge of a specific robot language. Hence, a new virtual reality based system is needed to provide users with a more user-friendly interface by means of high-level programming language. Various solution approaches for industrial robots have been proposed in past studies and are presented in the following sections.

Simulation Solution Approaches

There are various commercial software available which provide solutions for facility layout planning involving robotic work cells. In addition, commercial software have also been specifically developed for industrial robot simulation and visualization. Simulation and visualization of robotic work cells are necessary prior to procurement of hardware. The simulation software allow users to check the reachability, workspace, safety issues as well as other aspects of industrial robots.

In general, facility layout planning software is based on the discrete-event simulation concept, in which the operation of the system corresponds accordingly to the chronological order of events. Discrete-event simulation software provides an overall picture of the simulated robotic work cell, whereby the industrial robot is considered as an event within the cell. Hence, detailed simulation and information of the industrial robot (such as path planning and robot programming) may be unavailable in this type of simulation since robot commands cannot be generated automatically from the simulation results. In addition, the simulation environment does not consider spatial constraints and ergonomic issues. Although this technique is most popular compared to other techniques (e.g. gaming), it has a relatively low stakeholder commitment due to modelling lead time and purpose [6].

Geometric or continuous simulation provides a geometric graphical representation with constant time interval. Unlike discrete-event simulation with irregular time intervals, geometric simulation is more suitable for 3D visualization, offline programming of robots and collision detection during manufacturing processes [7]. Geometric simulation is also called virtual manufacturing [8].

On the other hand, various robotic simulation software have been developed by robot manufacturers such as ABB, KUKA, Fanuc and Mitsubishi. In this research, industrial robots manufactured by KUKA are used. KUKA SimPro is the official software developed specifically for offline programming of KUKA robots. The product is connected to KUKA OfficeLite, which is a virtual KUKA controller and enables real-time cycle time analyses and generation of robot programmes. However, the software requires adequate knowledge of robotic systems and special training. The cost of the software may not be within the financial means of many industries.

There are several generic robotic software available in the market such as Delmia from Dassault Systems, RobCAD from Technomatrix, Robsim from Camelot and Cosimir from Festo. These packages are flexible for various industrial robots produced by different manufacturers and are fully coupled with product life management (PLM). However, the disadvantages of these simulation software are the absence of direct outputs to the actual robots and require strong knowledge of robotic systems. The fundamental criteria which enable the adoption of such software in SMEs and academic sectors are affordability, ease of use and short learning curves [9], in which generic robot software are unable to do so. Furthermore, system integration is particularly a challenging task, whereby compatibility issues between some robot manufacturers and data structure of different software vendors may occur. Thus, simulation software with open architecture are actively developed by many researchers, in which the codes written for the simulation are portable to real robotic platforms [10].

Virtual Manufacturing Solution Approaches

Virtual Manufacturing (VM) is the use of virtual reality technology in real-time manufacturing based simulations in order to optimize product design and processes for a specific manufacturing goal such as design for assembly, quality, lean operations, and/or flexibility. VM is used to generate 3D models and real-time simulations of manufacturing processes to aid the design and production of products. VM is known as the next revolution of global manufacturing [11].

Lawrence Associates [12] introduced three virtual manufacturing paradigms which have been applied by Kim & Choi [13] to solve problems in flexible manufacturing systems. These three paradigms are:

- Design-centred VM: Provides designers/engineers with tools to design products which fulfil the design criteria.

Design-centred VM can be performed early during the conceptual design stage, which is easily modified and tested. This type of VM also uses simulation technology to optimize design specifications such as stress, strain and failure analyses.

- Production-centred VM: Provides the means to develop and analyse alternative production and process plans. Factory models and layout designs can be created to simulate the production process, assembly process, material flow and human factors. Production simulation is capable of simulating manufacturing process models which provides a means for inexpensive, fast evaluation of various processing alternatives.
- Control-centred VM: Evaluates product designs, production plans and control strategies. This VM interactively improves these three aspects through simulations of the control process. It is an additional tool to control models and actual processes, enabling seamless simulation for optimization during the actual production cycle.

Mujber et al. [14] classified the applications of VR in manufacturing into three areas, which are design, operations management and manufacturing process. In the design area, the VM technique has been used to design the die geometry for sheet metal forming in a virtual space. It is also widely used to generate virtual prototypes in order to replace physical prototypes [15]. The time required for design and development can be shortened and costs can be reduced when producing physical prototypes. Furthermore, virtual prototypes can be used to support design and development through simulation and analysis results [16], [17]. The integration of virtual reality with rapid prototyping technology is capable of creating digital prototypes to assist product development.

Moreover, VM technology is widely employed in the planning phase of manufacturing processes. This technology is used to estimate, optimize and minimize the processing time prior to the actual production [18]. In addition, this technology can be used to investigate material and information flow through the virtual operation control concept. The factors affecting the operation of a manufacturing system can be tracked to evaluate design and operational performance. In-house virtual training can be developed for machine tools [19], milling machines [20], turn-milling centres [21], maintenance [22] and so on.

VR application in manufacturing processes covers machining, assembly and inspection. Virtual machining is commonly used to solve cutting processes such as milling, turning and drilling. Collision detection can be checked to prevent accidental collisions which will damage machine tools during actual processes [23]. In addition, VM can be used in assembly planning to investigate the feasibility of assembly processes. The mechanical and physical characteristics of equipment and tooling can be modelled and simulated virtually. Furthermore, the quality, quantity, product cycle and cost can be determined in order to obtain optimum results. Virtual inspection is used to check the physical and mechanical properties of inspection equipment such as collision checks [24].

The effectiveness of VR-based training systems has also been tested. A VR-based training system for Metal Active Gas Welding (MAG) has been developed to integrate virtual robot path teaching system with a practical training system, in which VR-based offline robot programming techniques are implemented. The process paths are triggered, recorded and converted into robot commands for robotic welding. A survey has been carried out on controlled and uncontrolled groups of students in Faculty of Engineering, University of Malaya, in order to evaluate their motivation towards virtual welding learning and conventional welding learning. The results revealed that more than 85% of the students supported the use of VR integrated training system compared to traditional welding training. The respondents agreed that VR technology is a valuable tool and the prototype with VR-based system is feasible to be implemented as a supplement in the welding training programme as well as in path planning for robotic welding [4].

MATERIALS AND METHODS

Due to limited accessibility, high cost and strong demand for technical knowledge for commercial simulation software, a number of research projects have been conducted to develop alternative solution approaches for industrial robots. Several virtual robots have been created in the works of [25]–[27]. However, these systems still require strong technical knowledge. Furthermore, the interactions between humans and virtual robots are very poor, and are limited to conventional input/output devices.

VR-based industrial robotic systems are able to overcome the above mentioned problems[28]. VR technology was used to develop a virtual gripper for robotic inspections such that information of the inspected workpiece (position and orientation) can be defined interactively. The synergy between virtual reality and robots was reviewed and it was concluded that VR in robotics can be attained from haptic interfaces and human factor know-how [5]. Xu et al. [29] developed VR-based robot graphics simulation with built-in collision detection and coordinate translation functions.

Santis and Siciliano [30] developed a physical human-robot interaction model to measure the safety and dependability of robots. This model was implemented to evaluate the perceived safety during robot motion, which is dependent on shape, speed and posture. VR technology was also used to model a complex robotics system to study the perception of safe robot idle time [31]. They found that robot speed and size has an effect on idle time, whereby high robot speed and large-sized robot increases the waiting time of the participants.

Figure 1 shows the proposed model of this research, which is VR-Rocell. The model is designed to integrate the advantages of various simulation systems into a robotic work cell. The model proposes a VR-based layout planning and design for robotic work cell, which is similar to the functions provided by discrete-event simulation software. Furthermore, robot programming is conducted based on the teach-by-demonstrate concept for the VR-based robot teaching system. Robot paths are taught through an intuitive user interface compared to geometric simulation systems. The proposed model is based on open platform architecture, which includes programming language (C++), graphic libraries (OpenGL) and 3D formats (e.g. VRML).

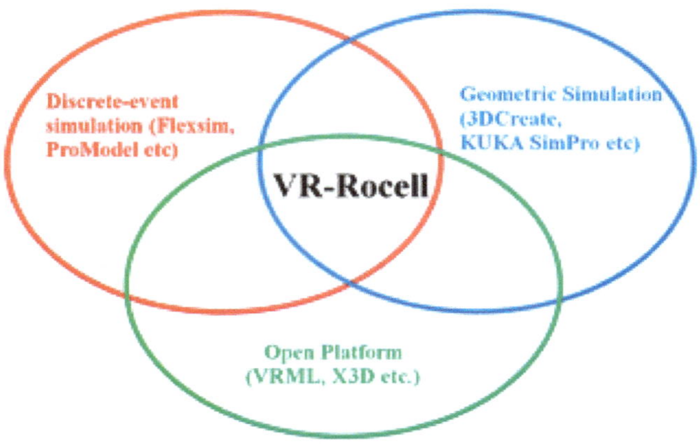

Figure 1. Proposed model of VR-Rocell.

CAD format can be converted into virtual reality (VR) by using either a commercial modelling software, library or database approach [32]. 3D models can be integrated in virtual manufacturing (VM) through Lex lexical analyser generator and Open Graphic Library [33]. However, there are no standard methods or algorithms which convert 3D models from CAD modelling software into VR and/or VM, which is monitored and controlled by the related society. In addition, there are no standard methods or algorithms which convert 3D models from CAD modelling software to virtual manufacturing systems. Therefore, a generic algorithm is proposed to import 3D models into the VR-based system based on an open platform concept. The system can be used in all operating systems such as Windows, Mac and Linux. In addition, the system supports all types of browsers such as Internet Explorer, Mozilla and Google Chrome.

Most of the commercial VR packages use native file formats to create their virtual environment. These formats consist of algorithms and data structures for a particular software, which may not be readable or visualized by others. The universal formats which are loaded into the CAD software are not editable in the native system. The assembly of universal formats cannot be saved back into the universal format. For these reasons, the proposed model consists of four universal file formats, which are supported by all related software. An algorithm is developed to extract and save 3D meshing information into four file formats. File format conversion is possible among the above formats. Thus, the output models from one VM can be transferred or imported to another VM using a universal file format. A database can be built to re-configure a modular-based VM, which further reduces the development time of the new system [33], [34]. The developed VR-based system is designed with simple and user-friendly interfaces to reduce the software training period and is therefore suitable for inexperienced users. Furthermore, the system is created based on an open architecture concept which allows the generated data to be transferred to/from different platforms without loss of information. In this manner, the output data can be viewed and configured by other systems.

The issues on human-computer interface design parameters in virtual environment have also been studied. A systematic axiomatic design method was used to design the virtual environment in order to minimize visual symptoms. The axiomatic design parameters were identified such as colour of background, brightness of virtual lighting, field of view (FOV), speed of virtual objects and display resolution. This method was developed and tested on a virtual robot manufacturing system [35].

Hardware Architecture

In this research, the hardware of the system is divided into two major parts, which are computer workstation and virtual reality hardware. The computer workstation consists of the computer CPU with a dedicated graphics card and is connected to two monitors, video splitters, two projectors, display extension devices and other peripherals (e.g. mouse, keyboard and speaker).

A Virtual Wall system has been built for the virtual reality hardware. The frame is made of an aluminium profile (40 mm×40 mm), which can be easily assembled and disassembled. At the same time, a mirror is used to reduce the projection distance and thus reduces the footprint of the Virtual Wall into half. Five major virtual reality hardware are integrated into the Virtual Wall, namely, 6-degree-of-freedom (6-DOF) tracker system, non-depolarized projection screen, polarized filter, polarized glasses and active-stereo glasses with emitter. The magnetic-type sensor tracker (Polhemus Patriot) is used in this research, which consists of a system electronics unit, a transmitter, a receiver (for head tracking) and a digitizer (user's manipulator). The maximum distance of the sensor tracker at which the resolution and noise performance of the system can be realized is 900 mm at default settings. Even though the useful range can be extended up to 1520 mm, this causes reduction in the accuracy of the data. These hardware are used to visualize and manipulate the virtual objects created in the virtual environment. The ergonomic dimensions (visual and arm reach) of the Virtual Wall needs to be decided. In this research, the visual limit can be neglected for the following reasons:

- Visual position limits: The user can simply walk to the position of his/her choice within the range of the sensor. This means that the user can walk to the left, right, near to or far from the screen if he/she intends to see the virtual objects clearly.
- Visual orientation limits: The 6-DOF sensor is attached to the glasses and virtual environment which will be updated according to his/her viewing angle for all attitudes.

The arm reach is the primary concern for screen position. The horizontal position has no effects on the arm reach since the user can walk either to the left or right if he/she is unable to reach the virtual objects. The vertical position of the projection screen is calculated based on the standing position of the user. The anthropometrics data for the Malaysian population are considered since the system is designed for a manufacturing environment [34]. The vertical position is designed to accommodate 95% of the population from short users (maximum height) to tall users (minimum height) in standing position. The height dimension is within the range of 2.5–97.5 percentiles. The reachable height depends on the shoulder height (H), arm reach forward length (L) and arm reach angle (θ) of the workers. Table 1shows the parameters for standing position based on the anthropometrics data of Malaysian workers. From Table 1, the minimum reachable height can be calculated using the following equation:

$$reach.H = H - L\cos\theta \quad (1)$$

where:

$reach.H$ = reachable height

H = shoulder height

L = arm reach forward length

θ = arm reach angle

Table 1. Parameters for standing position.

Specifications	Male (mm)		Female (mm)	
	Min	Max	Min	Max
Shoulder height, H	1,223.00	1,462.56	1,157.00	1,356.96
Arm reach forward length, L	724.00	920.00	690.56	843.44
Minimum reachable height – assumed the user's hand is vertically pointed down, with the arm reach angle, $\theta = 30°$)	596.00	665.82	558.96	626.52
Maximum reachable height – assumed the user's hand is vertically pointed up, with the arm reach angle, $\theta = 150°$)	1,850.00	2,259.30	1,755.04	2,087.40

doi:10.1371/journal.pone.0109692.t001

Therefore, the minimum vertical reachable height is 665.82 mm and the maximum vertical reachable height is 1,755.04 mm. The design accommodates 95% of Malaysian workers.

Sensor Configuration

The Virtual Wall used by VR-RoWL involves four coordinate systems, namely, user, sensor transmitter, projection screen and virtual environment (VM). A standard reference coordinate system needs to be selected or defined, whereby other systems can be transformed into this coordinate frame. Thus, the projection screen coordinate system is used as the reference frame, as shown in Figure 2. The transformation between frames can be simplified into the following configurations:

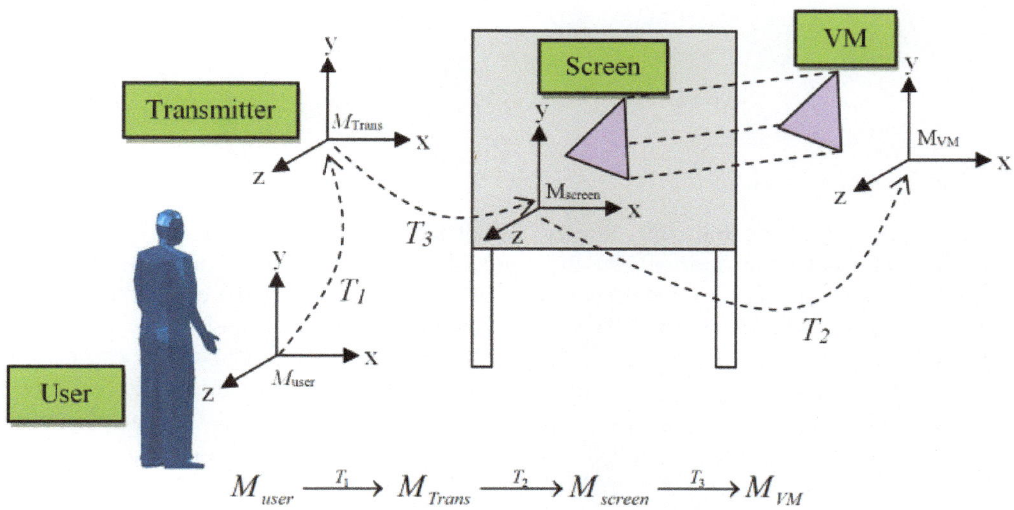

Figure 2. Reference coordinate system for Virtual Wall.

- First, the user's coordinate system needs to be transformed into the transmitter coordinate frame. In this research, the position and orientation of the head and hand are tracked using sensors and the sensors are referred to the transmitter coordinate frame. Furthermore, the default location of the transmitter is programmed at the origin without the rotation angle. Therefore, the transformation matrix T_1 can be obtained through the position and orientation of the user's head/hand which is referenced to the transmitter, and these data can be directly tracked by the 6-DOF sensor and digitizer.
- The virtual scene is projected (clipped) onto the screen. The actual dimensions of the screen are used to set up the OpenGL projection, and the virtual objects will appear on a 1-to-1 scale (full-scale), which is the same as the actual size. The centroid of the projection screen is fixed as the origin of the virtual environment. Hence, the transformation matrix T_2 represents the position and orientation of the virtual objects referenced to the screen, and these data are referred to the global coordinate system of the virtual environment.

Only two coordinate frames need to be considered, which are transmitter and screen. Both coordinate frames are configured as the origin in their respective frame. Consequently, the transformation matrix T_3 can be obtained by measuring the distance and rotation angle of the transmitter which is referenced to the centroid of the screen. The user will feel as though he/she is located within the virtual manufacturing system and uses the same coordinate system through these transformation functions.

ErgoVR station is another configuration used in the robot teaching system (VR-RoT). The ErgoVR station is designed to make the user feel, see and interact with objects in the most natural and ergonomic position. The user will be able to see and interact with virtual objects in the same place, as shown in Figure 3. Thus, the screen coordinate system can be replaced by a new coordinate system, which is termed as the virtual-monitor coordinate system. The transformation of the frame for the VR-RoT can be simplified into the following configurations:

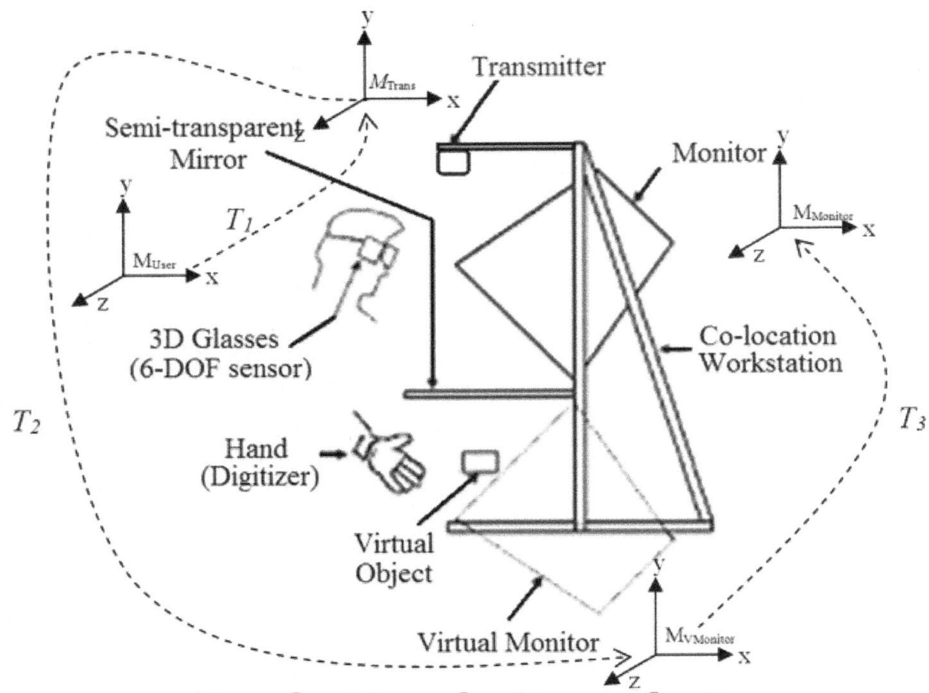

$$M_{user} \xrightarrow{T_1} M_{Trans} \xrightarrow{T_2} M_{VMonitor} \xrightarrow{T_3} M_{Monitor}$$

Figure 3. Coordinate system for ErgoVR workstation.

- Similar to the VR-RoWL condition, the user's coordinate system needs to be transformed into the transmitter coordinate frame. The transformation matrix T_1 is obtained directly from the recorded data.
- Based on the unique design of the co-location workstation, the virtual monitor will appear as the reflection of the actual monitor. Therefore, a mirror transformation matrix (T_3) at x-axis is applied to achieve the desired effect.

Robot Command Generator

The process path generated by the VR-based robot teaching system is recorded in a text file. Following this, the data acquisition and generator are designed to generate the robot commands, in which the generator is programmed specifically for KUKA industrial robots. The command generator is capable of converting the generated path into KUKA readable and executable formats. Hence, the robot commands can be tested by the KUKA OfficeLite simulator before being loaded into the real physical robot.

The software architecture of the KUKA robot system must be identified before conversion between VR-RoT and KUKA robot system can be established. Additionally, KUKA programming language and syntax must be analysed and studied in depth before conversion can be carried out. Each KUKA robot command is formed by two files, i.e. source file (*.*src*) and data file (*.*dat*). The data file contains data of the coordinate points whereas the source file consists of robot motion data such as velocity etc.

In this research, the content of each source file is similar to one another, whereby the motion of the robot will be determined during the actual robot testing. However, the source file is somewhat dependent on the data file. For example, the motion loop controls the dynamics and type of movement from one point to another, whereby the number of loops (counter) must tally with the number of points in the data file. The data file consists of all points in the path. Figure 4 shows the flow chart of the robot command generator.

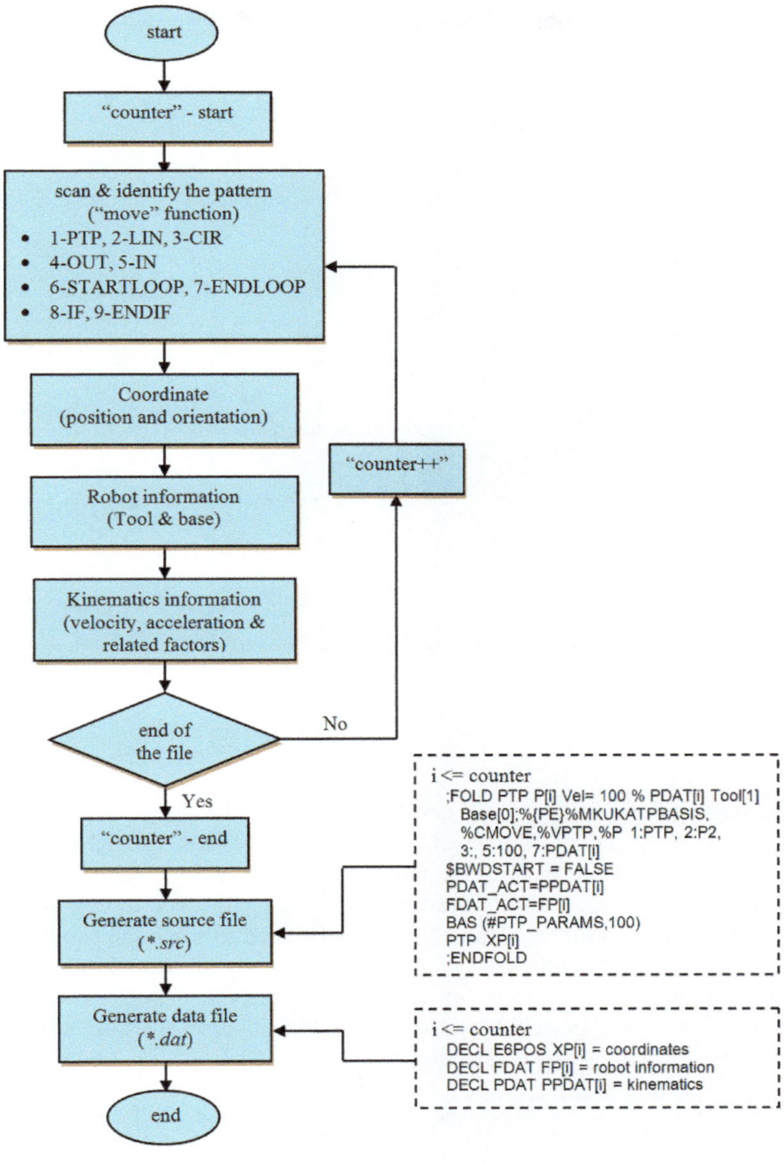

Figure 4. Flow chart of robot command generator.

In general, there are six parameters used to define a point in the KUKA robot command, namely, *x*, *y*, *z*, *pitch*, *yaw* and *roll*. Thus, the coordinates tracked by VR-RoT can be inserted into the data files accordingly. Figure 5 and Figure 6 shows an example of the source file and data file, respectively.

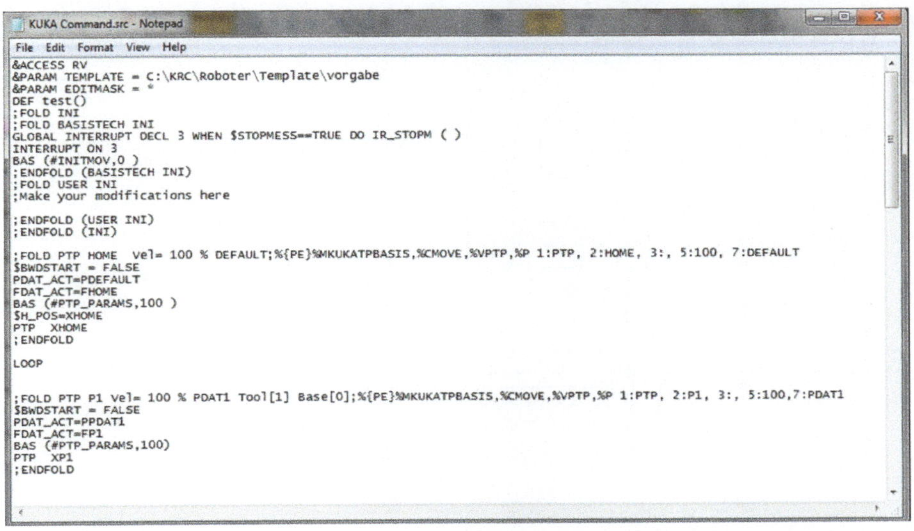

Figure 5. Example of source file (*.src) generated by the VR-based system.

```
&ACCESS RV
&PARAM TEMPLATE = C:\KRC\Roboter\Template\vorgabe
&PARAM EDITMASK = *
DEFDAT test
;FOLD EXTERNAL DECLARATIONS;%{PE}%MKUKATPBASIS,%CEXT,%VCOMMON,%P
;FOLD BASISTECH EXT;%{PE}%MKUKATPBASIS,%CEXT,%VEXT,%P
EXT  BAS (BAS_COMMAND  :IN,REAL  :IN )
DECL INT SUCCESS
;ENDFOLD (BASISTECH EXT)
;FOLD USER EXT;%{E}%MKUKATPUSER,%CEXT,%VEXT,%P
;Make here your modifications

;ENDFOLD (USER EXT)
;ENDFOLD (EXTERNAL DECLERATIONS)
DECL BASIS_SUGG_T LAST_BASIS={POINT1[] "P7      ",POINT2[] "P7          ",CP_PARAMS[] "CPDATO
",PTP_PARAMS[] "PDAT7              ",CONT[] "      ",CP_VEL[] "2.0         ",PTP_VEL[] "50  "}

DECL E6POS XP1={x 1025.000000,y 0.000000,z 1480.000000,a 118.000000,b 37.000000,c 129.000000,
s 2.000000,t 34.000000,e1 0.000000,e2 0.000000,e3 0.000000,e4 0.000000,e5 0.000000,e6 0.000000}
DECL FDAT FP1={TOOL_NO 1,BASE_NO 0,IPO_FRAME #BASE,POINT2[] " " }
DECL PDAT PPDAT1={VEL 100.000000,ACC 50.000000,APO_DIST 100.000000}


DECL E6POS XP2={x 1025.000000,y 0.000000,z 1480.000000,a 118.000000,b 37.000000,c 129.000000,
s 2.000000,t 34.000000,e1 0.000000,e2 0.000000,e3 0.000000,e4 0.000000,e5 0.000000,e6 0.000000}
DECL FDAT FP2={TOOL_NO 1,BASE_NO 0,IPO_FRAME #BASE,POINT2[] " " }
DECL PDAT PPDAT2={VEL 100.000000,ACC 50.000000,APO_DIST 100.000000}


DECL E6POS XP3={x 1025.000000,y 0.000000,z 1480.000000,a 118.000000,b 37.000000,c 129.000000,
s 2.000000,t 34.000000,e1 0.000000,e2 0.000000,e3 0.000000,e4 0.000000,e5 0.000000,e6 0.000000}
DECL FDAT FP3={TOOL_NO 1,BASE_NO 0,IPO_FRAME #BASE,POINT2[] " " }
DECL PDAT PPDAT3={VEL 100.000000,ACC 50.000000,APO_DIST 100.000000}


DECL E6POS XP4={x 1025.000000,y 0.000000,z 1480.000000,a 118.000000,b 37.000000,c 129.000000,
s 2.000000,t 34.000000,e1 0.000000,e2 0.000000,e3 0.000000,e4 0.000000,e5 0.000000,e6 0.000000}
```

Figure 6. Example of data file (*.dat) generated by the VR-based system.

Software Architecture

The virtual reality-based programming of a robotic work cell (VR-Rocell) is developed by solid modelling using commercial CAD software. The 3D models can be saved in a universal file format, either in STL, VRML, XML or OBJ. Following this, these models are integrated into the VR-Robotic Work Cell Layout (VR-RoWL) using a generic approach, in which the assembly models are saved in the VRML format. Virtual models can be transformed and saved in new files. The assembly models can be designed, modified and re-arranged accordingly. The models will be used to teach the robot path via the VR-based Robot Teaching system (VR-RoT). The robot commands and layout information can be loaded into the actual robotic work cell to execute the desired tasks. In addition, the VM models can be saved in different universal file formats. Therefore, the output models from one VM can be transferred or imported to another VM in the universal file format. Figure 7shows the overview of the research.

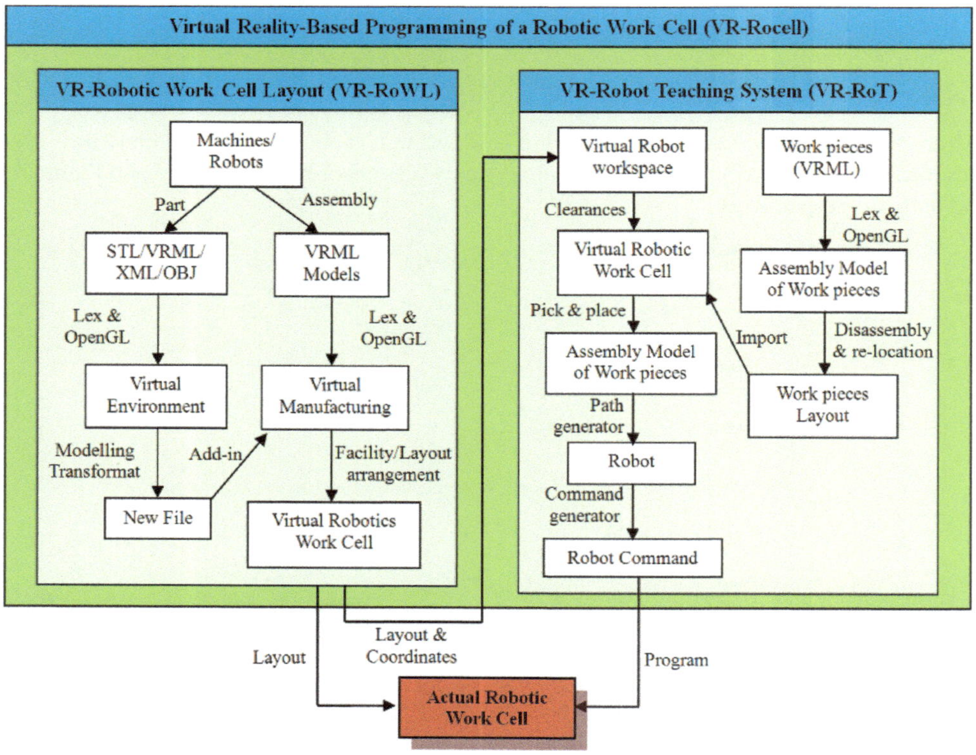

Figure 7. Overview of the project.

3D Models and Coordinate System in VR-RoWL

In the robot layout planning system (VR-RoWL), the layout is re-arranged according to the user's input (via digitizer) in the VRML format. In this case, the models inside the assembly file solely consist of 3-DOF, which allows translation in the horizontal plane (xz-plane) and rotation around the y-axis. This is due to the constraints of the physical (real) environment, such that the models must be placed on the floor with the y-axis always equal to zero. Thus, the machines/robots are unable to rotate around the x- and z-axes.

The global coordinate system in the virtual environment is the fixed reference coordinate system for all virtual objects. The global coordinate system maintains the position and orientation of the models such that they are unaffected by modelling transformation. The coordinate system is located on the virtual floor rather than on any virtual object since the virtual objects are allowed to move and hence, only the coordinates of the transformed models will be updated. The relative distance between the virtual objects can be calculated using vector analysis. As an example, the material handling of a milling machine is handled by an industrial robot while an operator is assigned to the lathe machine. The new layout involves switching the role (location) of the robot and operator. The global coordinate is fixed at the front-centre of the grid and the transformed coordinates (set-A) of the virtual objects are tabulated in Table 2. An additional set of coordinates (set-B) is shown if the industrial robot is selected as the reference frame (local coordinate) for comparison purposes.

Table 2. Global coordinate versus local coordinate in layout design.

	Virtual Object	Original Layout	New Layout
Set A	Forklift	(−900, 0, 400), 135°CCW	(−900, 0, 400), 135°CCW
	Milling	(−200, 0, 1500)	(−200, 0, 1500)
	Lathe	(1000, 0, 1000), 315°CCW	(1000, 0, 1000), 315°CCW
	Robot	(−200, 0, 1000), 270°CCW	***(550, 0, 650), 45°CCW***
	Operator	(550, 0, 650), 135°CCW	***(−200, 0, 1000), 180°CCW***
Set B	Forklift	(600, 0, −700), 225°CCW	***(−120.2, 0, 848.5), 90°CCW***
	Milling	(−500, 0, 0), 90°CCW	***(70.7, 0, 1131.4), 315°CCW***
	Lathe	(0, 0, 1200), 45°CCW	***(565.7, 0, −70.7), 270°CCW***
	Robot	(0, 0, 0)	***(0, 0, 0)***
	Operator	(350, 0, 750), 225°CCW	***(−282.8, 0, 777.8), 135°CCW***

doi:10.1371/journal.pone.0109692.t002

In general, the coordinates of the virtual objects in set-A can be measured directly from the reference point and are independent of each other. Therefore, only the position and orientation of the moving objects (operator and robot) are updated whereas the others are maintained at the same position. In set-B, the robot (local coordinate) is selected as the reference frame, and it is moved and rotated. Consequently, the reference frame changes even though the coordinate of the robot always remains at (0, 0, 0). Hence, the coordinates for other objects need to be re-calculated based on the new position and orientation of the industrial robot. For this reason, set-A is more suitable and practical for use in a flexible manufacturing environment. The global coordinate system is then applied in the VR-RoWL.

3D Models and Coordinate System in VR-RoT

The assembly format is also used in the robot path teaching system. Before proceeding to the path teaching process, the user is required to plan the robot assembly process in advance, which is based on the reverse engineering concept. Firstly, the original assembly model of the workpieces is imported into the virtual environment at the output buffer. Following this, the user has to disassemble the imported assembly models and place the related parts in the assembly area. Finally, the user is required to move the components into the input buffer accordingly. Hence, validation of the assembly models can be carried out in the assembly area and input buffer. Only then the user can demonstrate the assembly process in the virtual environment and this assembly process will be recorded as the robot path.

The imported model is validated, and the vertices and triangle meshing data are checked and compared. The coordinates of the vertices and triangle meshing sequence are also confirmed. Validation of the disassembled model in the assembly area is carried out (Table 3). The imported assembly models are then dismantled and placed in the assembly area accordingly. The layout of the components is used to design the assembly jig and the VR-based robot path teaching system. Finally, the components are moved into the pallet at the input buffer and the output model is validated accordingly.

Table 3. Example of validation in VR-RoT.

Parameter		Original (Solidworks)	Imported (VR-RoT)	Dismantled (VR-RoT)	Exported (Internet browser)
Geometric Information	Number of components	3	3	3	3
	Total vertices	3708	3708	3708	3708
	Total triangles	1236	1236	1236	1236
Vertices' coordinates checking		Yes (same)	Yes (same)	Yes (same)	Yes (same)
Triangle meshing sequence checking		Yes (All CCW)	Yes (All CCW)	Yes (All CCW)	Yes (All CCW)

doi:10.1371/journal.pone.0109692.t003

The origin of the industrial robot coordinate frame is located at its base. However, the local coordinate system is a convenient and common method of robot programming in a virtual environment, and is located at the end effector of the robot arm at the "home" position. If the user likes to change the end effector, the relative distance between the new end effector and work-pieces need to be updated although the origin (robot base) is unaltered. Therefore, the local coordinate system is preferable for use in VR-RoT.

Frame Delay

Real-time updating simulation is an important visual feedback in order to provide a sense of presence in the virtual environment. Moreover, simulation delays will create flickering images, which will cause cyber sickness. In general, delays are caused by insufficient computational load for handling large quantities of polygons in the virtual environment. The situation may become more critical if the user likes to interact with virtual objects in real-time. Furthermore, the active stereo is set at 120 Hz (120 frames-per-second) to create flicker-free stereoscopic images. Therefore, frame delays should be validated by checking the refreshing rate (frames-per-second) in real-time simulations. The validation process is checked with examples of virtual environment and the results are tabulated in Table 4.

Table 4. Validation of frame delay.

Virtual environment	Passive stereo (60 Hz)		Active stereo (120 Hz)	
	without sensor	with sensor	without sensor	with sensor
Five (5) Equipment with Vertices (21,040) and Triangles (38,145)	√	√	√*	√*+
Five (5) Equipment with Vertices (54,107) and Triangles (97,275)	√	√	√*	√*+
Nine (9) Equipment with Vertices (140,116) and Triangles (142,608)	√	√	√*	√*+

doi:10.1371/journal.pone.0109692.t004

The validation results show that the virtual environment created matches the computational load for the selected computer workstation. There are no frame delays when the refreshing rate is tested at 60 frames-per-second (FPS or Hz). The first two frames fall below the rated FPS (marked by "*" in Table 4) when the refreshing rate is doubled. This is attributed to the initial processing of the rendering process, whereby the OpenGL technique "Display List" is used for compiling for later use. This technique evaluates all rendering information (vertices and triangles) and stores the information into the server machine at the beginning of the process. The information created can be re-used without re-evaluating and re-transmitting the data during simulations.

Furthermore, the frame delay remains constant (120 Hz) when the sensors are activated in the active stereo mode. However, the frequencies of the sensors are limited to 60 Hz. Thus, the following methods are used to overcome frame delay:

- The following frame will be updated accordingly when the data is triggered and sent from the sensors. A total of 60 frames will be updated based on the input information from the sensors in an event-mode input model.
- The previous information will be used to update the frames if no data is received. The information is applied to the remaining frames, where the OpenGL is able to simulate the virtual environment until the next input is received (marked by "+" in Table 4).

RESULTS AND DISCUSSION

A case study is conducted at the Robotics Laboratory, Department of Mechanical Engineering, Faculty of Engineering, University of Malaya. The industrial robotic work cell is required to assemble an electronics casing which consists of three components: a main casing and two identical heat sink assemblies. The main casing is made of aluminium and the heat sink assemblies are attached onto the main casing. Each heat sink assembly is a combination of a heat sink and a side plate, which has been assembled prior to the robotic work cell. The work cell initially consists of two industrial robots (KUKA KR6/2). However, due to the high maintenance and performance of the robots (payload: 6 kg only), the existing robots are replaced with KUKA KR16 KS (payload: 16 kg). Therefore, a new layout design is required since both robots have different workspace and reach requirements. The machines and robots are listed in Table 5.

Table 5. Industrial robotic work cell.

No.	Machine/Robot	Task
1	KUKA KR 16 (A)	Pick-and-place
2	KUKA KR 16 (B)	Fastening
3	Assembly jig with pneumatic system	Assembly area for the casing
4	PLCs	Synchronize and control assembly process
5	Pallet with fibre optic sensor	Input buffer and use sensor to trigger process

doi:10.1371/journal.pone.0109692.t005

The assembly process of the electronics casing is identified during the design stage, as shown in Figure 8. Firstly, the main body (*O*-1) is placed at its position in the jig. Following this, the left heat sink assembly (*O*-2) is fixed onto the main body using two screws. Finally, the right heat sink assembly (*O*-2) is fixed onto the main body using two other screws.

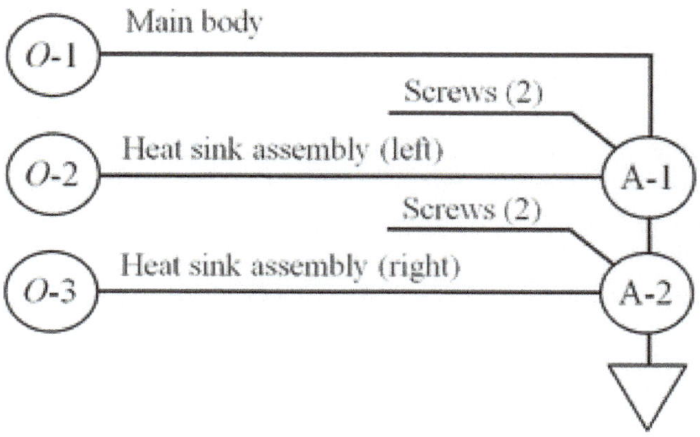

Figure 8. Assembly process chart for case study.

VR-Robotic Work Cell Layout (VR-RoWL)

The 3D models of the robots and related components are developed using commercial CAD modelling software. Following this, these models are imported into the virtual work cell for layout planning, in which the assembly model is saved in the VRML format. The layout of the laboratory needs to be studied in advance. The location of the power supply, entrance (door), windows (if any), materials supply and others should be confirmed before re-arranging the layout of the robotic work cell. In this case study, the upper-right corner of the laboratory is assigned as the global coordinate system. The dimensions of the robotic zone will be used to set up the layout for the VR-RoWL. All components and machines must be located within this zone, with the exception of materials supply mechanisms/machines.

The original assembly model is then imported into the VR-RoWL. The models are free to move within the fixed zone (grid). In general, the robots should be placed in parallel and facing towards the positive *y*-axis direction. The assembly zone is located between the robots and within the workspace of both robots. This layout design can be implemented for various assembly processes involving two robots, whereby the materials supply is located in front of the robots. Therefore, the new layout can be obtained by moving the related machines/robots in the virtual layout. The new layout can be saved in the VRML format, which can be shared between various Internet browsers. The proposed robotic work cell created by the VR-RoWL and the actual laboratory setup are shown in Figure 9.

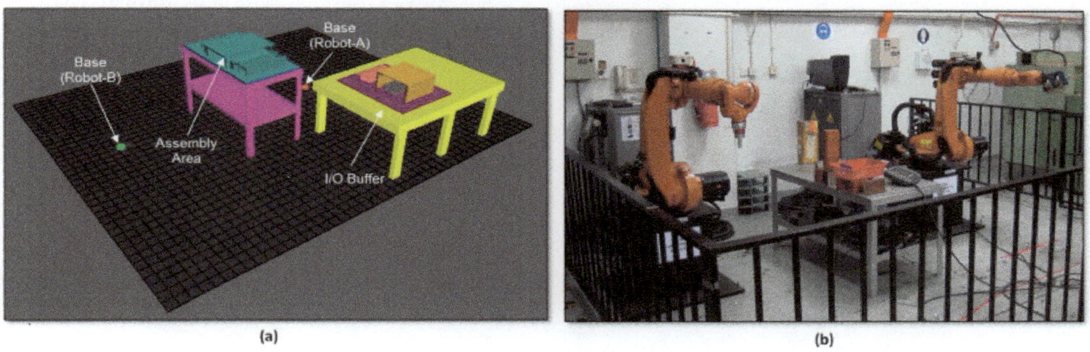

Figure 9. (a) Proposed robotic work cell (b) Actual robotic work cell setup.

The laboratory is set up according to the above mentioned criteria and the proposed new layout design. The actual dimensions of the equipment are measured based on the proposed global coordinate system. Comparisons between the actual coordinates and virtual layout coordinates for the robotic work cell are tabulated in Table 6. There are some constraints while installing the robots and equipment in the actual laboratory setup; one of them being the accuracy of the measurement tools. Thus, the unit used in the actual setup is centimetres (cm) and the tolerance is ±0.5 cm. The orientation of the equipment in the actual installation is difficult to control and therefore the tolerance is set as ± 3° (for all axes). The digital coordinates (virtual layout) do not impose limitations on the environmental conditions (e.g. floor) and instrumentations (e.g. measuring tape).

Table 6. Comparisons between virtual layout and laboratory setup.

No	Equipments	Virtual Layout (x, y) (mm)	Laboratory (x, y) (mm)	Absolute Variation (x, y) (mm)
1	KUKA KR 16 (A)	(1459, 1716)	(1450, 1700)	(9, 12)
2	KUKA KR 16 (B)	(3965, 1713)	(3950, 1700)	(15, 13)
3	Input buffer (Conveyor)	(1556, 3203)	(1570, 3230)	(14, 27)
4	Output buffer (Conveyor)	(1555, 3209)	(1570, 3230)	(15, 21)
5	Assembly jig (Table)	(2515, 2041)	(2530, 2025)	(15, 16)

doi:10.1371/journal.pone.0109692.t006

There are differences between the virtual layout and actual laboratory setup, and the virtual layout provides an overview of the arrangement. There are no measurement tools used in the virtual environment. The user locates the equipment using his/her visual feedback only. For example, the user is unable to "see" a difference of 5 mm in a virtual environment. The user is also unable to "see" whether two robots are exactly located at the same axis (y=1700 mm). This can be improved by applying the "snap-fit" feature, in which each grid is 10 mm.

VR-Robot Teaching System (VR-RoT)

The imported assembly model is located on the input buffer by default. The user is requested to dismantle the assembly model and move the components to the pallet and arrange them accordingly. In this mode, only the final position and orientation of the components will be stored, neglecting the path of the movement. The path planning mode is then activated after assembly planning and the user is requested to either plan the robot path by moving the components (material handling, e.g. suction cup) or demonstrate the process path (material processing, e.g. fastening). The path will be recorded and translated into robot commands. The loaded information will not be substituted by the final location of the components. In addition, there are two basic ways of describing the movement of industrial robots in a robot control system, i.e. angle of the manipulator's joints or location of the end effector. If all joint variables are known, then forward kinematics can be used to determine the position and orientation of the robot's end (tool centre point). However, inverse kinematics is used to calculate the value of each joint variable by knowing the position and orientation of the end effector. Thus, the inverse kinematic model is developed and used in this research [28].

Robot-A is programmed to pick-and-place (PnP) the components between the input buffer and assembly area. There is no force or tactile feedback provided to the developed robot teaching system. The collision detection algorithms are applied to detect whether the end effector touches the components, in which a bounding box will be drawn at the end effector when collision is detected. Furthermore, the colour of the bounding box will change at different stages of the PnP process, as follows:

- No bounding box: No collision is detected (Figure 10 (a)).
- Red (blinking): Collision is detected between the end effector and workpiece, but the PnP process cannot be continued (Figure 10 (b)).
- Yellow (blinking): Collision is detected between the end effector and workpiece, and ready for the PnP process (Figure 10 (c)).
- Green (blinking): The colour of the workpiece will stop blinking when the end effector is activated. The workpiece is now grasped by the end effector and moves together with it (Figure 10 (d)).

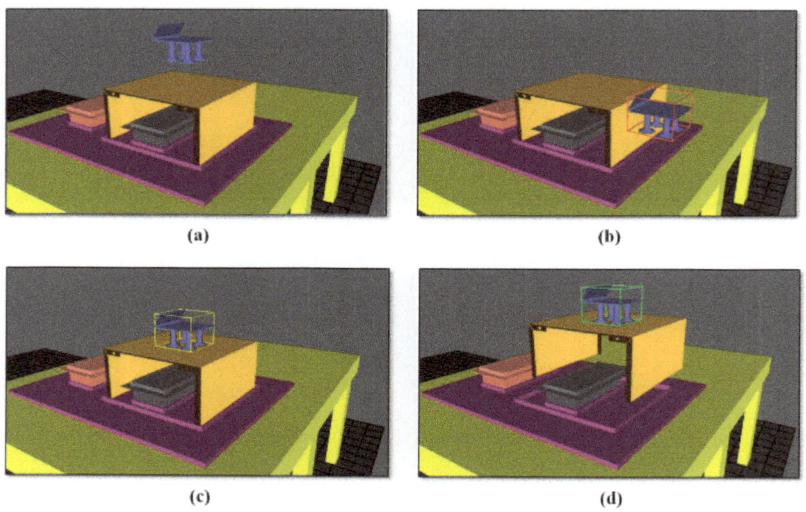

Figure 10. Bounding box for end effector.

In the virtual teaching system, collision detection is enabled when the end effector touches the components or the components collide with the assembly jig. Thus, the end effector always pick-and-place at the right height (z-axis). Only the horizontal positions (x-axis and y-axis) may differ slightly from the exact location, as shown in Table 7.

Table 7. Data of PnP process for Robot-A.

Step	Task	VR generated Coordinate (x, y, z) (mm)	Predefined Coordinate (x, y, z) (mm)	Absolute Variation (x, y, z) (mm)
a1	Pick: Main Body	(1677, −126, 867)	(1670, −120, 867)	(7, 6, 0)
a2	Place: Main Body	(327, −1076, 1200)	(325, −1080, 1200)	(2, 4, 0)
b1	Pick: Heat Sink Assembly (left)	(1283, −115, 750.5)	(1290, −120, 750.5)	(7, 5, 0)
b2	Place: Heat Sink Assembly (left)	(−91, −1078, 994)	(−94, −1080, 994)	(3, 2, 0)
c1	Pick: Heat Sink Assembly (right)	(1635, −116, 750.5)	(1640, −120, 750.5)	(5, 4, 0)
c2	Place: Heat Sink Assembly (right)	(740, −1076, 994)	(744, −1080, 994)	(4, 4, 0)

doi:10.1371/journal.pone.0109692.t007

On the other hand, the fastening paths and coordinates need to be controlled, as the fastening coordinates are fixed. These coordinates can be tracked by the screw holes available in the heat sink assembly, which enables the user to change the sequence of the fastening process. Figure 11 shows the fastening sequence defined in the virtual environment and Table 8 shows the coordinates of the fastening process.

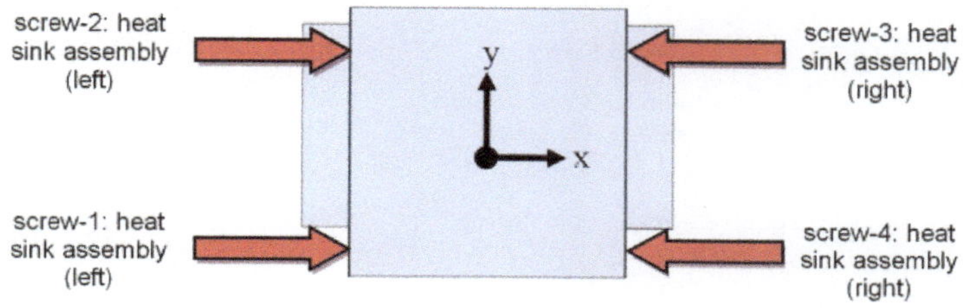

Figure 11. Fastening sequence.

Table 8. Data of fastening process for Robot-B.

Screw	Predefined Coordinate (x, y, z) (mm)	Fastening direction (Robot's Coordinate system)	Fastening Depth (mm)
1	(113.4, 1270, 1190)	positive *x*-axis	10
2	(113.4, 1570, 1190)	positive *x*-axis	10
3	(536.6, 1570, 1190)	negative *x*-axis	10
4	(536.6, 1270,1190)	negative *x*-axis	10

doi:10.1371/journal.pone.0109692.t008

Laboratory Testing

The actual testing is carried out in the Robotics Laboratory. The original work cell consists of two industrial robots of KUKA KR6/2 (payload: 6 kg). The existing robots require higher maintenance and the low payload is unable to fulfil the current requirements. Therefore, the existing robots are replaced with KUKA KR16 KS (payload: 16 kg). Thus, a new layout design is needed since both robots have different workspace, reach, speed and other requirements. Following this, the VR-RoWL model is used to determine and evaluate the layout prior to the actual hardware installation. The robot teaching system (VR-RoT) is used to plan and determine the robot path in advance. The robot process path is taught and the robot commands are generated offline. The layout and process path planned in the VR-RoWL are validated using KUKA SimPro Simulation environment to determine clearance, reach, safety etc. KUKA OfficeLite is used to validate the robot commands generated by the VR-RoT. Figure 12 shows the simulation and validation using KUKA software before being loaded into the actual system.

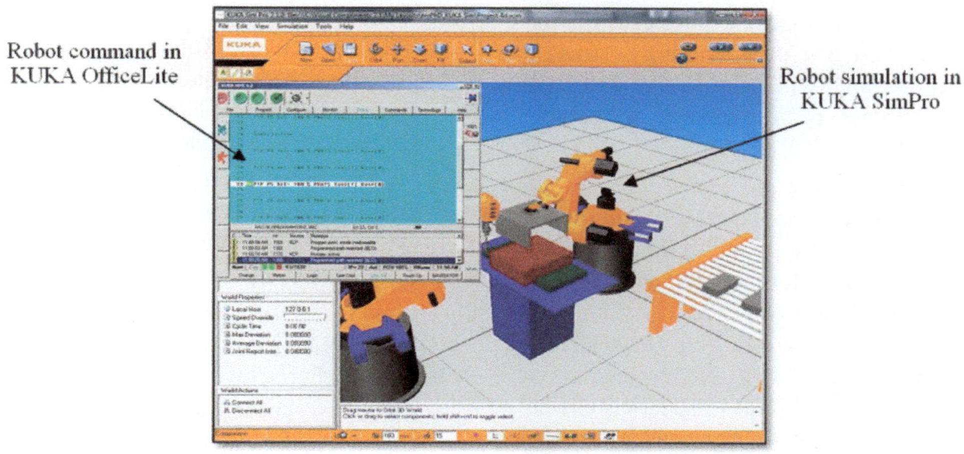

Figure 12. Simulation and validation using KUKA software.

Finally, the actual robots and all equipment are installed at their respective locations based on the layout generated by the VR-system. The KUKA robot commands generated by the VR-based system are saved into a floppy disk and transferred into Robot-A (pick-and-place) and Robot-B (fastening), respectively. The end effector is then attached to each robot. The assembly jig is assembled with a pneumatic system and the input buffer is equipped with a fibre optic sensor. The PLCs are programmed to synchronize and control the assembly process for all equipment.

The robots are operated at 10% of their maximum speed under two conditions (i.e. with and without load) during laboratory testing. The speed is then increased to 30 and 50%

of the maximum speed for both conditions. These changes are made using the control panel of the KUKA robot. The average cycle time of the test (five tests for each condition and speed) is recorded and tabulated in Table 9.

Table 9. Average cycle time for various speeds.

Process	10% of Speed		30% of Speed		50% of Speed	
	with load (sec)	without load (sec)	With load (sec)	without load (sec)	with load (sec)	without load (sec)
1. Trigger the sensor	1.0	1.0	1.0	1.0	-	1.0
2. Robot-A: Pick the components from input buffer and place at assembly area	103.12	102.88	36.56	36.28	-	23.08
3. Position the jig	2.0	2.0	2.0	2.0	-	2.0
4. Robot-B: Fastening the four (4) screws.	49.38	49.12	17.41	17.14	-	11.08
5. Position the jig	2.0	2.0	2.0	2.0	-	2.0
6. Robot-A: Pick the completed assembly at assembly jig and place at output buffer. Return to home position.	38.56	38.36	14.16	13.92	-	8.68
Cycle Time	**196.06**	**195.36**	**73.13**	**72.34**	-	**47.84**

doi:10.1371/journal.pone.0109692.t009

Overall, it can be seen that the cycle time is reduced when the speed of the robots is increased, whereby the relationship between the cycle time and percentage speed of the robot is fairly linear. It is also found that the cycle time without load is slightly faster than that with load, which is about 0.70 and 0.79 sec for 10% and 30% speed, respectively. The suction cup is unable to hold the components firmly when the robot arm travels at high speed (50% speed) and thus the data for 50% speed is unsuitable for load-carrying use in this case study.

CONCLUSIONS

A virtual reality based programming for an industrial robotic work cell has been developed in this research, and is given the name "VR-Rocell". The system is divided into two major sub-systems, namely, VR-Robotic Work Cell Layout (VR-RoWL) and VR-Robot Teaching System (VR-RoT). The system is designed to improve the human-machine interface (human-robot interface), whereby off-line programming is used to generate robot commands which will reduce robot downtime and prevents the programmer from exposure to potential hazardous environment.

The system has been validated and tested using a case study. Several settings and assumptions have been made during the validation process. The generic approach of integrating and converting file formats is validated for both part and assembly files and the frame delay has also been tested. It is found that the algorithms and approaches used are able to generate a flicker-free virtual environment for both passive and active stereoscopic visualization systems. Moreover, a case study has been conducted for an electronics casing assembly. The results reveal that there is an absolute variation of 9–15 mm (x-axis) and 12–27 mm (y-axis) between the virtual layout and actual setup. The virtual path teaching shows an absolute variation of 2–7 mm (x-axis) and 2–6 mm (y-axis). It is found that the variations in dimensions have no effects on the performance of the robotic work cell. Thus, it is concluded that the VR-Rocell can be used in an industrial robotic work cell based on the accuracy and effectiveness achieved in the case study. Future work can be focused on layout and sequence optimization, analysis of human factors in workstation design and multi-criteria decision making for sustainable manufacturing in order to further improve the proposed system.

AUTHOR CONTRIBUTIONS

Conceived and designed the experiments: HJY ZT SZD SWC. Performed the experiments: HJY. Analyzed the data: HJY ZT SZD SWC. Contributed reagents/materials/analysis tools: HJY. Wrote the paper: HJY ZT SZD SWC. Ergonomic model design & development: HJY ZT SZD. Human-computer interface validation: HJY SWC.

REFERENCES

1. IFR (2001) World Robotics: Statistics, market analysis, forecasts, case studies and profitability of robot investment: United Nations Economic Commission for Europe (UNECE), International Federation of Robotics.
2. IFR (2011) World Robotics: Statistics, market analysis, forecasts, case studies and profitability of robot investment: United Nations Economic Commission for Europe (UNECE), International Federation of Robotics.
3. OSHA Japan (1995) Study on accidents Involving industrial robot report no. 5, Labor Standard Bureau: Occupational Safety and Health Department, Japan Ministry of Labour.
4. Choo HK (2014) Virtual Reality-based Training System for Metal Active Gas Welding. Department of Mechanical Engineering: University of Malaya, Malaysia.
5. Burdea GC (1999) Invited review: The synergy between virtual reality and robotics. IEEE Transactions on Robotics and Automation 15: 400–410. doi: 10. 1109/70. 768174
6. Jahangirian M, Eldabi T, Naseer A, Stergioulas LK, Young T (2010) Simulation in manufacturing and business: A review. European Journal of Operational Research 203: 1–13. doi: 10. 1016/j. ejor. 2009. 06. 004
7. Li E, Du TC (2005) Advances in electronic business, volume I Idea Group Publishing.
8. Klingstam P, Gullander P (1999) Overview of simulation

tools for computer-aided production engineering Computers in Industry. 38: 173–186. doi: 10. 1016/ s0166-3615(98)00117-1
9. Neto P, Pires JN, Moreira AP (2010) Robot path simulation: a low cost solution based on CAD; Singapore. pp. 333–338.
10. Staranowicz A, Mariottini GL (2011) A survey and comparison of commercial and open-source robotic simulator software; Greece.
11. Radhakrishnan R, Balasubramanian S (2008) Business process re-engineering: text and cases. New Delhi: Prentice-Hall of India.
12. Lawrence Associates (1994) Technical Report. Virtual Manufacturing User Workshop.
13. Kim SC, Choi KH (2000) Development of Flexible Manufacturing System using Virtual Manufacturing Paradigm. International Journal of the Korean Society of Precision Engineering 1: 84–90.
14. Mujber TS, Szecsi T, Hashmi MSJ (2004) Virtual reality applications in manufacturing process simulation. Journal of Materials Processing Technology 155–156: 1834–1838. doi: 10. 1016/j. jmatprotec. 2004. 04. 401
15. Raneda A, Pessi P, Siuko M, Handroos H, Palmer J, et al. (2003) Utilization of virtual prototyping in development of CMM. Fusion Engineering and Design 69: 183–186. doi: 10. 1016/s0920-3796(03)00333-8
16. Gökdere LU, Benlyazid K, Dougal RA, Santi E, Brice CW (2002) A virtual prototype for a hybrid electric vehicle. Mechatronics 12: 575–593. doi: 10. 1016/ s0957-4158(01)00009-5
17. Guerra D, Ramírez R, Donato L, Molina A (2006) Digital Manufacturing for Aerospace industry: Experimental Aircraft; Mexico.
18. Lee WB, Cheung CF, Li JG (2001) Applications of virtual manufacturing in materials processing. Journal of Materials Processing Technology 113: 416–423. doi: 10. 1016/s0924-0136(01)00668-9
19. Iqbal M, Hashmi MSJ (1999) Application of virtual reality for the training of engineering personnel; Dublin, Ireland. pp. 1959–1966.
20. Crison F, Lécuyer A, d'Huart DM, Burkhardt J-M, Michel G, et al. Virtual technical trainer: learning how to use milling machines with multi-sensory feedback in virtual reality; 2005; Bonn, Germany. pp. 139–145.
21. Zhu L, Wang J, Chen E, Yang J, Wang W (2008) Applications of virtual reality in turn-milling centre; Qingdao, China. pp. 2302–2305.
22. Wang QH, Li JR (2004) A desktop VR prototype for industrial training applications. Virtual Reality 7: 187–197. doi: 10. 1007/s10055-004-0127-z
23. Kadir AA, Xu X, Hämmerle E (2011) Virtual machine tools and virtual machining-A technological review. Robotics and Computer-Integrated Manufacturing 27: 494–508. doi: 10. 1016/j. rcim. 2010. 10. 003
24. Lee WB, Li JG, Cheung CF (2002) Development of a virtual training workshop in ultra-precision machining. International Journal of Engineering Education 18: 584–596.
25. Mitsi S, Bouzakis K-D, Mansour G, Sagris D, Maliaris G (2005) Off-line programming of an industrial robot for manufacturing. International Journal of Advanced Manufacturing Technology 26: 262–267. doi: 10. 1007/ s00170-003-1728-5
26. Fauadi HF, Jumali MS (2008) Modeling and simulation of programmable universal machine for assembly (PUMA) industrial robot for automotive-related assembly process; Kuala Lumpur.
27. Kumar R, Kalra P, Prakash NR (2011) Virtual RV-M1 robot system. Robotics and Computer-Integrated Manufacturing 27: 994–1000. doi: 10. 1016/j. rcim. 2011. 05. 003
28. Yap HJ, Taha Z, Lee JV (2008) VR-based Robot Programming and Simulation System for an Industrial Robot. International Journal of Industrial Engineering – Theory, Application and Practice 15: 314–322.
29. Xu ZJ, Zhao ZX, Wu MH, Liao JB, Tian GY (1997) Virtual reality based robot graphic simulation and virtual manufacturing system; Manchester.
30. Santis AD, Siciliano B (2008) Safety issues for human-robot cooperation in manufacturing systems; Napoli, Italy. pp. 1–12.
31. Or CKL, Duffy VG, Cheung CC (2009) Perception of safe robot idle time in virtual reality and real industrial environments. International Journal of Industrial Ergonomics 39: 807–812. doi: 10. 1016/j. ergon. 2009. 01. 003
32. Whyte J, Bouchlaghem N, Thorpe A, McCaffer R (2000) From CAD to virtual reality: modelling approaches, data exchange and interactive 3D building design tools. Automation in Construction 10: 43–55. doi: 10. 1016/ s0926-5805(99)00012-6
33. Yap HJ, Taha Z, Dawal SZ (2012) A Generic Approach of Integrating 3D Models into Virtual Manufacturing. Journal of Zhejiang University-SCIENCE C (Computers & Electronics) 13: 20–28. doi: 10. 1631/jzus. c11a0077
34. Malaysian Anthropometry (2008) Anthropometric data for the Malaysian adult population. Unpublished data, Centre for Product Design & Manufacture, University of Malaya, Kuala Lumpur.
35. Taha Z, Soewardi H, Dawal SZM (2014) Axiomatic design principles in analysing the ergonomics design parameter of a virtual environment. International Journal of Industrial Ergonomics 44: 368–373. doi: 10. 1016/j. ergon. 2013. 11. 007

CHAPTER 7

ORIENTATION-BASED CONTROL OF MICROFLUIDICS

Nazila Norouzi, Heran C. Bhakta, William H. Grover

Department of Bioengineering, University of California, Riverside, Riverside, CA, United States of America

ABSTRACT

Most microfluidic chips utilize off-chip hardware (syringe pumps, computer-controlled solenoid valves, pressure regulators, etc.) to control fluid flow on-chip. This expensive, bulky, and power-consuming hardware severely limits the utility of microfluidic instruments in resource-limited or point-of-care contexts, where the cost, size, and power consumption of the instrument must be limited. In this work, we present a technique for on-chip fluid control that requires no off-chip hardware. We accomplish this by using inert compounds to change the density of one fluid in the chip. If one fluid is made 2% more dense than a second fluid, when the fluids flow together under laminar flow the interface between the fluids quickly reorients to be orthogonal to Earth's gravitational force. If the channel containing the fluids then splits into two channels, the amount of each fluid flowing into each channel is precisely determined by the angle of the channels relative to gravity. Thus, any fluid can be routed in any direction and mixed in any desired ratio on-chip simply by holding the chip at a certain angle. This approach allows for sophisticated control of on-chip fluids with no off-chip control hardware, significantly reducing the cost of microfluidic instruments in point-of-care or resource-limited settings.

INTRODUCTION

The advantages of microfluidics over conventional lab-scale techniques—reduced reagent consumption, faster reactions, smaller instrument size, enhanced automation, higher throughput, and so on—have enabled applications for microfluidic instruments in fields as diverse as health care, environmental monitoring, and space exploration. The ability to control fluid flow on a microfluidic chip is a fundamental need in these instruments. However, most existing techniques for controlling on-chip fluid flow rely on off-chip hardware. For example, to control the mixing ratio of two fluids in a microfluidic chip, two off-chip pumps (pressure regulators or syringe pumps) are typically required. Valves and pumps can be moved on-chip [1, 2], but microfluidic valves and pumps also require off-chip hardware (usually computer-controlled solenoid valves and pressure or vacuum pumps). Electrical methods for controlling fluids, such as dielectrophoresis [3, 4] and electrowetting, [5] require off-chip electrical power supplies and complicate the fabrication of the microfluidic chip. In each of these approaches, the off-chip hardware required to control on-chip fluid flow can *cost thousands of dollars, consume hundreds of watts of electrical power, and contribute significant bulk to the instrument*. Consequently, many microfluidic instruments remain unsuitable for use in

Citation: Norouzi N, Bhakta HC, Grover WH (2016) Orientation-Based Control of Microfluidics. PLoS ONE 11(3): e0149259. doi:10.1371/journal.pone.0149259.

point-of-care or resource-limited settings, where instrument cost, power consumption, and size must be minimized.

Here we describe a method for precisely controlling fluid flow inside a microfluidic chip that requires *no off chip hardware*. In this method, by simply orientating a microfluidic chip at a certain angle, on-chip fluids can be routed and mixed in any desired ratios. We accomplish this by adding inert compounds that slightly increase the density of certain fluids in the chip. When two fluids of different densities flow together under laminar flow on-chip, the interface between the two fluids quickly reorients itself to be orthogonal to Earth's gravitational force. If the channel containing the fluids then splits into two channels, the amount of each fluid flowing into each channel is a function of the angle of the channels relative to gravity. In this manner, different amounts of different fluids can be routed on-chip simply by changing the orientation of the microfluidic chip as shown in Fig 1.

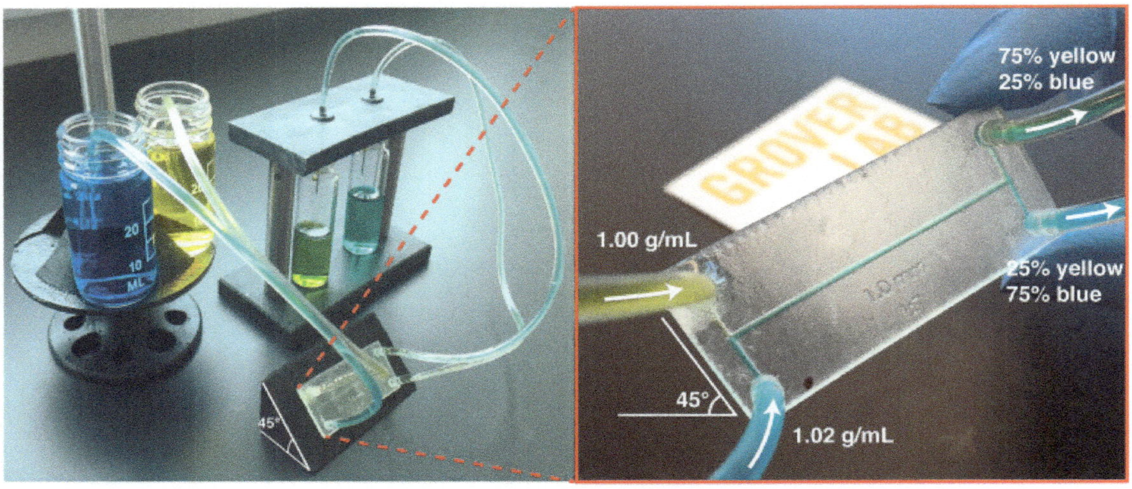

Figure 1. Using the orientation of a microfluidic chip to control the mixing ratio of fluids on-chip.

Two fluids (yellow and blue) flow into the chip; the blue fluid includes an additive (sucrose) that makes the blue fluid 2% more dense than the yellow fluid. When the two fluids flow together in the chip, the fluids rotate to orient the more-dense blue fluid toward Earth's gravity. When the channel then splits, the amount of each fluid flowing in each direction is precisely controlled by the angle of the chip. By using this approach, any desired mixing ratio of the yellow and blue fluids can be obtained simply by holding the chip at a certain angle; no off-chip control hardware is needed.

As a proof-of-concept demonstration, we used the principle of orientation-based microfluidic control in a simple mixer chip that is capable of generating any desired mixing ratio of two fluids. We chose to create a mixer because of the importance of mixing in microfluidic devices. Microfluidic mixers automate the time-consuming process of preparing arbitrary concentrations and mixtures of solutions by hand. Most existing microfluidic mixers utilize either microfluidic valves and pumps [1, 2] or arrays of split-and-combine operations [6, 7]. These mixers have found a variety of uses in microfluidic chips for evolving novel ribozymes [8], cytotoxicity studies [9], estimation of drug efficiency and optimization of biochemical reactions [10, 11]. However, a chip that uses these existing mixers is capable of generating only certain fixed ratios of mixtures; it cannot be used to generate *any* desired concentration or mixing ratio without redesigning the chip. Additionally, mixers containing microfluidic valves and pumps still rely on off-chip hardware for controlling these valves and pumps. Finally, existing valve- and pump-based or split-and-combine mixers consume a relatively large amount of fluid to generate a relatively small amount of the desired mixture. In summary, there is an unmet need for simple, equipment-free methods for generating arbitrary mixtures of fluids in microfluidic chips.

THEORY OF ORIENTATION-BASED MICROFLUIDICS

To explore the effects of chip orientation on fluid flow inside a microfluidic chip, we used finite element analysis software to simulate the behavior of a simple microfluidic chip held at different angles relative to gravity. Our model combines the Navier-Stokes equations, Fick's law of diffusion, and a function that describes the density of a solution as a function of the concentration of a solute [12]. COMSOL Multiphysics (Burlington, MA) was used to simulate a orientation-controlled mixer chip shown in Fig 2. The model simulated the experimental conditions in Fig 3: a microfluidic channel with a circular cross section and 1.0 mm diameter, a less-dense yellow fluid with density 1.00 g/mL, and a more-dense blue fluid with density 1.07 g/mL. The fluid phase in the model is governed by the continuity equation for the incompressible Navier-Stokes equations:

$$\nabla \cdot u = 0 \quad (1)$$

$$\rho u \cdot \nabla u = -\nabla P + \rho g + \nabla \cdot (\mu(\nabla u + \nabla u^T)) \quad (2)$$

where u is the velocity vector, μ is the fluid viscosity, P is the pressure applied to the upstream end of the fluid, ρ is the density of the fluid, and g is the gravitational acceleration of objects on Earth (9.8 m s^{-2}). The solute concentration follows the equation of conservation of mass and Fick's Law of Diffusion:

$$u \cdot \nabla c = \nabla \cdot (D \nabla c) \quad (3)$$

where D is the diffusivity of the solute and c is the concentration of the solute. Eqs 1–3 are coupled through the dependence of a solution's density on its solute concentration, which can be expressed as

$$\rho = \rho_{\text{water}}(1 + Bc) \quad (4)$$

where ρ is the density of the solution, ρ_{water} is the density of pure water (1.00 g/mL), c is the solute concentration, and B is an experimentally-obtained, solute-specific constant that correlates a solution's density with its solute concentration (in this study, B = 127 L/mol for sucrose). Eqs 1–4 are solved for a steady state flow with inlet solute concentrations of 0 mol/L in Inlet 1 and 1 mol/L in Inlet 2.

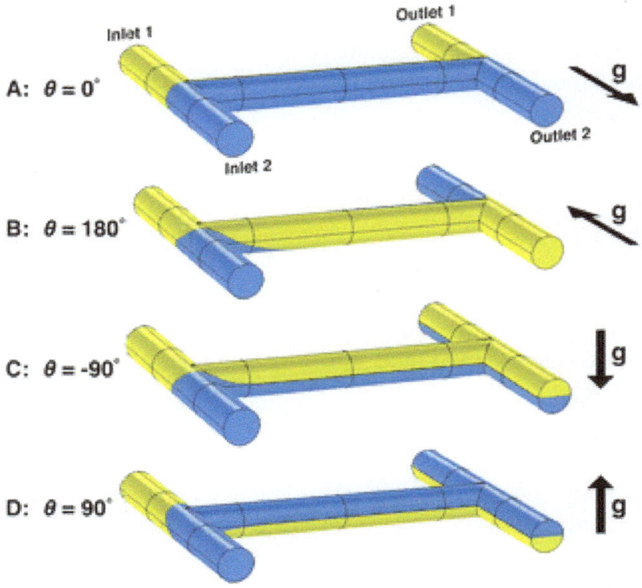

Figure 2. Principle of orientation-based control of microfluidics. These simulations show fluid flowing inside a simple microfluidic channel network containing two inlets and two outlets. Inlet 1 contains a less-dense yellow fluid and Inlet 2 contains a more-dense blue fluid. When the chip is oriented such that Inlet 2 is aligned with the Earth's gravitational force **(A)**, the yellow and blue fluids remain unperturbed and exit the chip in the same directions from which they entered (yellow at Outlet 1 and blue at Outlet 2). However, when the chip is rotated 180° **(B)**, the force of gravity causes the fluids to swap places in the horizontal channel, placing the more-dense blue fluid on the bottom of the channel and the less-dense yellow fluid on the top. Consequently, the two fluids exit in the *opposite* directions from which they entered: Outlet 1 contains blue fluid and Outlet 2 contains yellow fluid. When the chip is oriented at −90° relative to gravity **(C)**, the fluids rotate 90° clockwise to orient the more-dense blue fluid on the bottom of the channel and the less-dense yellow fluid on the top. When the channel splits into two outlets, each outlet receives an identical mixture containing 50% yellow fluid and 50% blue fluid. Finally, when the chip is oriented at 90° **(D)**, the fluids rotate 90° *counter-clockwise* to once more orient the more-dense blue fluid on the bottom of the channel, and again both outlets contain identical mixtures containing 50% yellow and 50% blue. In this manner, the orientation of a microfluidic chip may be used to route fluids in different directions on-chip without using any off-chip control hardware.

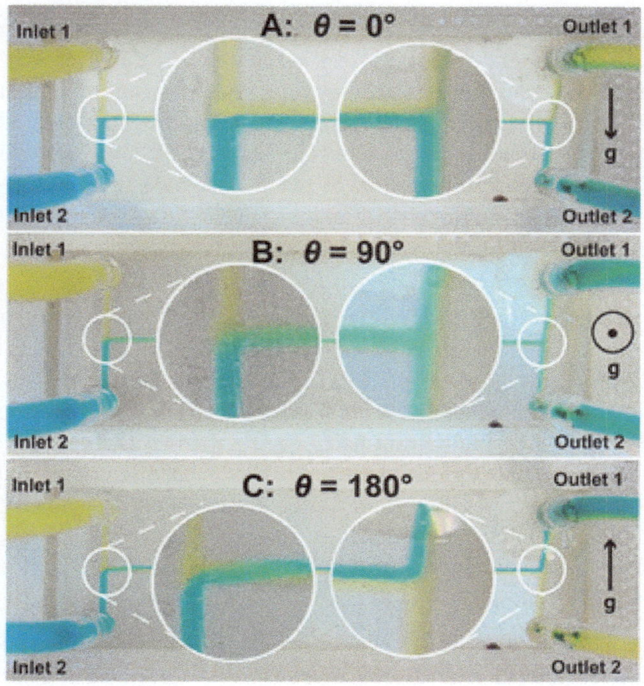

Figure 3. Photographs of a microfluidic mixer chip oriented at different angles θrelative to gravity. In each case Inlet 1 contains a less-dense yellow fluid (water; density ρ = 1.00 g/mL) and Inlet 2 contains a more-dense blue fluid (sucrose solution; ρ = 1.07 g/mL). Whenθ = 0° **(A)** the arrangement of yellow and blue fluids in the horizontal channel remains unchanged, and Outlet 1 contains yellow fluid and Outlet 2 contains blue fluid. However, at θ = 90° **(B)** gravity causes the more-dense blue fluid to move to the bottom of the horizontal channel and the less-dense yellow fluid to move to the top. This twists the contents of the horizontal channel by 90° and causes both outlets to contain identical mixtures containing ~50% blue and ~50% yellow. Finally, at θ = 180° **(C)** the gravity-induced repositioning of the fluids in the horizontal channel causes the fluids to twist by 180°, effectively swapping places in the channel. As a result, the two fluids exit the chip in directions *opposite* from where they entered, with Outlet 1 containing blue fluid and Outlet 2 containing yellow fluid.

The H-shaped microfluidic channel network simulated in Fig 2 has two inlets and two outlets. Inlet 1 contains a yellow fluid with density ρ = 1.00 g/mL, and Inlet 2 contains a slightly-more-dense blue fluid (ρ = 1.07 g/mL). In Fig 2A, the chip is oriented such that Inlet 2 is in the same direction as gravity (so the angle θ between Inlet 2 and gravity is 0°). In this orientation, the force of gravity keeps the more-dense blue fluid flowing along the bottom of the channel and the less-dense yellow fluid flowing along the top of the channel. Consequently, when the channel splits into two outlets, the fluids leave in the same directions they came from: the more-dense blue fluid exits through Outlet 2 in the direction of gravity, and the less-dense yellow fluid exits through Outlet 1.

In Fig 2B, the chip has been rotated about the middle channel axis by 180°. In this configuration, the force of gravity causes the two fluids to quickly swap places in the middle channel so that the more-dense fluid flows along the bottom of the channel and the less-dense fluid flows along the top. When the channel splits, the fluids exit in the *opposite* direction they came from: the more-dense blue fluid entered from Inlet 2 but exits through Outlet 1, and the less-dense yellow fluid entered from Inlet 1 but exits through Outlet 2. In this manner two different fluids can be routed to two different destinations on-chip by orienting the chip at either 0° relative to gravity (Fig 2A) or 180° (Fig 2B).

In Fig 2C, the chip has been rotated by 90° relative to gravity. The force of gravity again causes the fluids to reorient to place the more-dense blue fluid on the bottom and the less-dense yellow fluid on the top (a clockwise rotation of 90°). When the channel splits, both Outlet 1 and Outlet 2 have the same contents: the bottom-half of each channel is filled with more-dense blue fluid, and the top half of each channel is filled with less-dense yellow fluid. After the contents of each exit channel becomes homogeneous by *e.g.* diffusional mixing, both outlets contain identical mixtures consisting of 50% blue and 50% yellow.

Finally, in Fig 2D, the chip has been rotated by −90° relative to gravity. This case is similar toFig 2C; gravity once more causes the two fluids to reorient to place the more-dense blue fluid on the bottom and the less-dense yellow fluid on top (a *counterclockwise* rotation in this case) and the exit channels each contain the same mixture (50% yellow and 50% blue).

The results in Fig 2 can be generalized for any angle of orientation θ. If the less-dense fluid at Inlet 1 contains a solute A with a concentration $[A_0]$, and the more-dense fluid at Inlet 2 contains a solute B with concentration $[B_0]$, the concentrations $[A]$ and $[B]$ in each of the outlet channels are:

$$[A] = [A_0]\frac{\theta}{180} \qquad [B] = [B_0]\left(1-\frac{\theta}{180}\right) \quad \text{at Outlet 1}$$

$$[A] = [A_0]\left(1-\frac{\theta}{180}\right) \qquad [B] = [B_0]\frac{\theta}{180} \quad \text{at Outlet 2} \tag{5}$$

Using the above equations, we can predict the concentrations [A] and [B] flowing in a chip held at any desired angle θ. These equations only apply to a microfluidic chip with circular cross-section channels, although similar equations may be derived for other channel shapes.

MATERIALS AND METHODS

To demonstrate the principle of orientation-based control of fluid flow in a microfluidic chip, we fabricated microfluidic chips similar to the one simulated in Fig 2. Microfluidic chips were designed using SolidWorks (Dassault Systèmes, Vélizy-Villacoublay, France), exported as an.STL file, and printed using a 3D printer (Form 1+, Formlabs, Cambridge, MA). These chips contain a H-shaped microchannel 42 mm long and 1 mm in diameter. The Stereolithography-based printer uses a 405 nm Class 1 laser to polymerize a liquid resin into a solid part. The resin used in this study is a combination of methacrylated monomers and oligomers.

Fig 3 shows our test chip in operation. Inlet 1 contains water, density ρ = 1.00 g/mL, and Inlet 2 contains more-dense sucrose solution, ρ = 1.07 g/mL. Sucrose solutions of precisely known densities were prepared using our software NaCl.py (available for download athttp://groverlab.org). FD&C Blue #1 and Yellow #6 were used specifically for visual characterizations. The inlets were connected by tubing to fluid reservoirs that were held 3 cm above the chip. Since the inlet reservoirs were higher than the outlet reservoirs, a head pressure $P = \rho gh$ developed that pumped fluid flow from the input reservoirs through the chip and to the output reservoirs (g = 9.8 m s^{-2} and h = height difference between input and output reservoirs). The inlet and outlet reservoirs were maintained at the same height regardless of the tilt of the chip. Consequently, the orientation of the chip does not affect the flow rate. No off-chip fluid control hardware like pumps or valves were used.

The phenomenon of orientation-based control depends upon convection, not diffusion, being dominant in the microfluidic system. A dimensionless parameter called the Peclet number, Pe, is used to determine whether convection or diffusion is dominant in a system:

$$Pe = \frac{Lu}{D} \tag{6}$$

where L is the characteristic length, u is the flow velocity, and D is the solute's diffusion coefficient. The calculated Peclet number for our flow rate (~11,000) is much greater than one, indicating that convection is dominant and diffusional mixing between the different fluid streams is negligible.

Chips of different channel geometries were held at different angles. The average residence time of fluid in the chip was calculated to be 0.7 seconds. To make sure that the system reaches steady state, samples were collected from the chip after 1 minute of flow. Samples of 5 mL were collected from each outlet for each orientation and chip geometry. To quantify the resulting mixing ratios, fluids from both outlets were collected and analyzed using an UV-Vis-NIR spectrophotometer (V-670, Jasco, Easton, MD).

EXPERIMENTAL RESULTS

When the chip is oriented on its edge relative to gravity in Fig 3A (θ = 0°), the more-dense blue fluid remains on the bottom of the horizontal channel and the less-dense yellow fluid remains on the top of the channel. Consequently, the fluids exit the mixer chip in the same directions from which they entered (yellow fluid at Outlet 1 and blue fluid at Outlet 2). This case is identical to the simulation shown in Fig 1A. When the chip is held flat relative to gravity in Fig 3B (θ = 90°), the two fluids reorient relative to gravity (rotating 90° clockwise) to place the more-dense blue fluid at the bottom of the horizontal channel and the less-dense yellow fluid on the top of the channel. When the horizontal channel splits, both output channels have the same contents (~50% yellow and ~50% blue, which appears as green in the outlets). This situation is identical to the simulation shown in Fig 2C. Finally, when the chip is oriented on its *other* edge in Fig 3C (θ = 180°), the yellow and blue fluids swap places in the horizontal channel to place the more-dense blue fluid on the bottom and the less-dense yellow fluid on the top. Consequently, the fluids leave the Outlet channels*opposite* from where they entered, with yellow fluid at Outlet 2 and blue fluid at Outlet 1.

To demonstrate orientation-based control of fluid flow over a wide range of angles (not just the three angles shown in Fig 3), the mixer chip was operated at angles from 0° to 180° in 15°

increments. As before, the more-dense blue fluid was a sucrose solution (density = 1.07 g/mL) and the less-dense yellow fluid was water (density = 1.00 g/mL). Fig 4 shows the concentration of each dye in the two output channels. As the mixer chip's angle of rotation $\theta$is varied from 0° to 180°, the concentration of blue fluid rises and yellow fluid drops in Outlet 1, and an opposite trend is observed in Outlet 2. The relationship of concentration on angle of rotation is roughly linear as predicted by Eq 5. This experimental data deviates from the predicted model at angles near 0° and 180°, where the outlet fluids concentrations are not 100% and 0% as predicted but ~90% and ~10% instead. This is likely due to diffusion within the horizontal channel in the mixer chip, which contributes a small amount of mixing between the two fluid streams. The effect of this diffusional mixing is most pronounced at angles near 0° and 180° where the outlets should contain pure (unmixed) fluids according to Eq 5; instead their contents are ~90% pure. Additionally, the relationship of fluid concentration on angle of rotation in Fig 4 is not purely linear but appears to have some higher-order shape. This can be attributed to the cross-sectional geometry of the 3D-printed microfluidic channel because of the limited resolution of the 3D printer. The 1 mm channel was printed using a stereolithography 3D printer with a tolerance of ± 200 μm. This could result in a microfluidic channel that is not perfectly circular and requires a more complex model than the one shown in Eq 5. However, the error bars in Fig 4 confirm that the outlet concentrations are a reproducible and predictable function of the angle of rotation of the chip, and a higher-order function could easily be derived that predicts the fluid concentrations in a chip at any rotation angle θ to within a few percentage points.

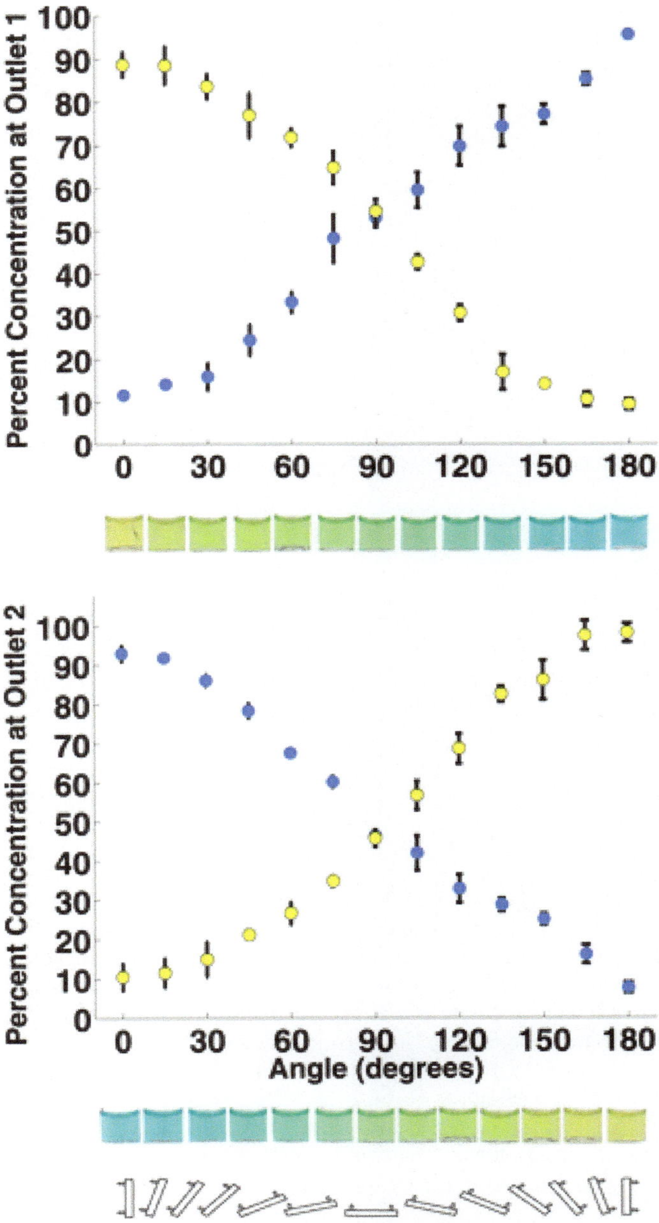

Figure 4. Concentrations of yellow and blue dyes in the mixer chip's two outlets as the angle of rotation of the mixer chip is varied from 0° to 180°. Also shown are photographs of the fluid collected at each outlet and an illustration of the chip's orientation at each angle of rotation. N = 3 measurements for each point; error bars indicate ±1 standard deviation. These results show that mixture composition is a function of the angle of rotation of the chip, and any desired mixture can be generated simply by orienting the chip and the required angle.

To explore the role of channel cross-section shape in orientation-controlled microfluidics, we designed and 3D printed mixer chips with square (1 × 1 mm) and rectangular (1 × 1.25 mm) cross-section channels. We then repeated the experiments from Fig 5A using the square and rectangular chips for rotation angles θ = 0°, 90°, and 180°. The results in Fig 5Aconfirm that the orientation of a chip can still be used to control fluid mixing in chips with square and rectangular cross sections, though increased deviation from the predicted fluid concentrations is observed in the rectangular cross-section chip. This suggests that orientation-based control of microfluidics works best in channels with aspect ratios near one; at higher aspect ratios the channel geometry hinders the desired rotation of fluid in the channel. We were limited to a 1 mm channel diameter since we wanted to explore different geometries and aspect ratios using a 3D printer; however, the same phenomena were observed in a conventional glass microfluidic channel of 180 μm (data not shown). We also examined the behavior of two fluids of different densities flowing in rectangular channels with much higher aspect ratios (cross-sectional dimensions 1 mm × 5 mm; data not shown). The experimental results further support the assertion that orientation-based control of microfluidics is most practical in channels with cross-sectional aspect ratios near one (circular and square channels)

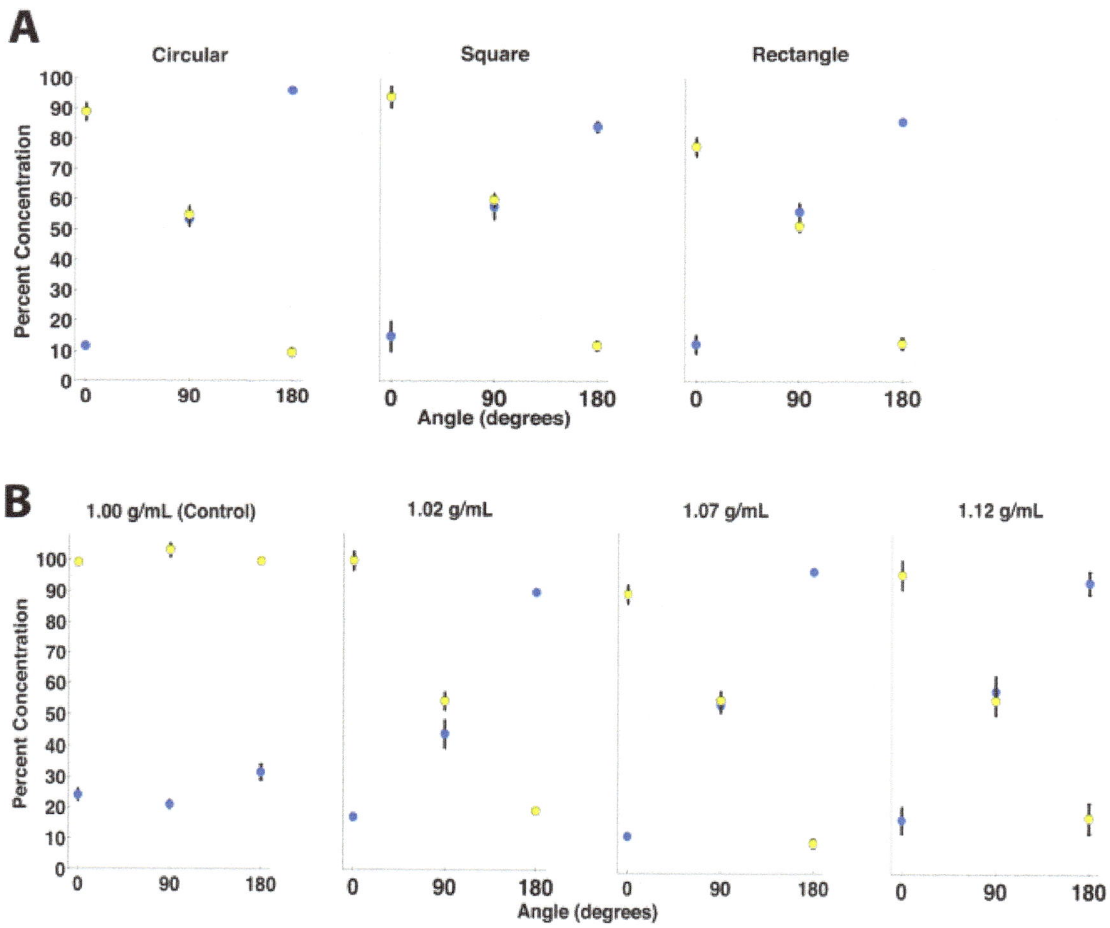

Figure 5. (A) Concentrations of yellow and blue dyes at Outlet 1 in mixer chips held at 0°, 90° and 180°, for chips with circular, square, and rectangular channel cross-sections. Chip orientation can be used to control on-chip fluids in devices with a variety of channel cross-sectional shapes, although performance deteriorates somewhat in the rectangular channel. These results suggest that microfluidic channels with aspect ratios close to one are best suited for orientation-based control. **(B)** Outlet fluid concentrations measured at Outlet 1 while orienting the mixer chip at 0°, 90° and 180° for four different fluid densities at Inlet 1. The density of fluid at Inlet 2 was kept constant at 1.00 g/mL. When there is no difference in fluid densities between the two inlet fluids, fluid reorientation is not observed and orientation-based control cannot be used (Control case). However, if the fluid density in Inlet 1 is just 2% greater than the fluid density in Inlet 2, then the flowing fluids reorient with respect to gravity and orientation-based control is possible.

In addition to channel geometry, fluid density has an effect on our phenomenon. The speed at which rotation occurs is influenced by the density difference. However, in practice we found that all rotations we observed were nearly instantaneous. The channel length was kept excessively long for characterization purposes. However, for a channel diameter of 1 mm, a minimum length of 10 mm is required for the rotation to occur. The larger the difference between fluid densities, the quicker the rotation occurs. Rotation speed could be increased by further increasing the difference between fluid densities; however, the resulting increase in concentration gradients will result in an increase in diffusive flux, potentially allowing for more mixing between the two layers.

To determine how much of a difference in density between the two fluids is necessary to employ orientation-based control, sucrose solutions with different concentrations (and thus different densities) were prepared as shown in Fig 5B. Experiments were performed using solutions with densities of 1.00 g/mL (control), 1.02 g/mL, 1.07 g/mL, and 1.12 g/mL. As before, the density of the second fluid was kept constant at 1.00 g/mL (water). In the control case in Fig 5B, there is no difference in densities between the two fluids in the mixer chip, so no reorientation of the fluids occur within the chip and the fluid concentrations at the outlets are constant regardless of the angle of orientation of the chip; however, when the density of one input fluid is increased by only 2% to 1.02 g/mL, the fluids again reorient with respect to gravity and orientation-based control is demonstrated.

CONCLUSIONS

We demonstrated that the orientation of a microfluidic chip can be used to precisely control the flow of fluids inside the chip. By using the orientation of a chip to control fluid flow instead of on-chip valves or off-chip pumps and regulators, our technique can eliminate a substantial portion of the cost, size, and power-consumption of a microfluidic assay or instrument. Thus, this technique should facilitate the spread of microfluidic technologies to new applications in resource-limited and point-of-care settings.

Orientation-based control of microfluidics does depend upon different fluids in the chip having different densities. However, the amount of density difference necessary to use orientation-based control is very small (only ~2%), and there are many different substances that can be added to a fluid to adjust its density. For applications that do not require precise control of the osmotic strength of fluids, small amounts of solutes like sucrose (as used here) and sodium chloride can be easily and inexpensively added to a fluid to enable orientation-based control. For applications in which the osmotic strength of the fluid *does* need to be controlled, a number of compounds have been developed that increase a fluid's density without affecting its osmotic strength. These include Ficoll, a high molecular weight polysaccharide used in density gradient centrifugation [13]; Percoll, a colloidal silica solution which is biologically inert and also used in density gradient centrifugation [14]; Visipaque (iodixanol), an isotonic, nonionic, nontoxic compound used as an intravenous contrast agent in radiography [15] and metatungstate solutions, a dense, inert and inorganic solutions with low reactivity. By adding small amounts of substances like these to fluids and using the principle of orientation-based control, microfluidic assays can run with little or no off-chip hardware.

A density difference of ~2% is required for fluid reorientation to occur. Increasing the density of a solution by ~2% may change the viscosity of the solution. For example, increasing the density of a sucrose solution by 2% increases the effective viscosity of the solution by 17%. However, this viscosity difference is actually too low to affect the concentration of the output fluid. Karst *et al.* [12] studied fluids of different viscosities flowing alongside each other in laminar flow (as is the case in the horizontal channel of our chip). They found that the ratio of the volumes occupied by each fluid inside the tube is not equal to the ratio of the fluids' flow rates. Moreover, they found that the viscosity of the second fluid has to be at least 100% greater than the viscosity of the first fluid for the ratio of the volumes of the two fluids in the channel to be altered. Therefore, the effect of fluid viscosity is minimal.

Finally, is orientation-based control powerful enough to control real-world microfluidic chips? Certainly chips with hundreds of computer-controlled valves offer a level of fluid control that may be unattainable by orientation-based control (though this level of control comes with a significant cost). However, many real-world microfluidic devices require simpler fluid control and could be controlled using chip orientation. For example, the proof-of-concept mixer chip shown here could be used in a drug toxicity screening assay by exposing cells downstream of the mixer to various concentrations of a drug [16]. This could be accomplished by flowing a drug solution in one inlet and a diluent with 2% greater density in the second inlet, and trapping cells in one of the outlet channels. By orienting the chip at a certain angle and then assessing the viability of the cells, the response of the cells to a particular concentration of the drug could be assessed. Assuming that a chip can be held at an angle with an accuracy of ±5 degrees, the resulting drug concentration should be accurate to about ±10% which is adequate precision for many drug screening assays. This is one of many real-world microfluidic assays and diagnostics that could be performed with little or no off-chip control hardware using orientation-based control.

ACKNOWLEDGMENTS

The authors would like to thank Dr. Brian Storey of the Franklin W. Olin College of Engineering for helpful discussions on finite element analysis of fluids with different physical properties. This work was supported in part by the National Science Foundation's Instrument Development for Biological Research Program under award DBI-1353974. There was no additional external funding received for this study.

AUTHOR CONTRIBUTIONS

Conceived and designed the experiments: NN HCB WHG. Performed the experiments: NN HCB. Analyzed the data: NN HCB WHG. Wrote the paper: NN HCB WHG.

REFERENCES

1. Unger MA, Chou HP, Thorsen T, Scherer A, Quake SR (2000) Monolithic microfabricated valves and pumps by multilayer soft lithography. Science, 288(5463):113–116. doi: 10.1126/science.288.5463.113. pmid:10753110
2. Grover WH, Skelley AM, Liu CN, Lagally ET, Mathies RA (2003) Monolithic membrane valves and diaphragm pumps for practical large-scale integration into glass microfluidic devices. Sensors and Actuators B: Chemical 89(3):315–323. doi: 10.1016/S0925-4005(02)00468-9.
3. Voldman J (2006) Electrical forces for microscale cell manipulation. Annu. Rev. Biomed. Eng 8:425–454. doi: 10.1146/annurev.bioeng.8.061505.095739. pmid:16834563
4. Mugele M, Baret JC (2005) Electrowetting: from basics to applications. Journal of Physics: Condensed Matter 17(28):R705. doi: 10.1088/0953-8984/17/28/r01
5. Cooney CG, Chen CY, Emerling MR, Nadim A, Sterling JD (2006) Electrowetting droplet microfluidics on a single planar surface. Microfluidics and Nanofluidics 2(5):435–446. doi: 10.1007/s10404-006-0085-8.
6. Hardt S, Pennemann H, Schönfeld F (2006) Theoretical

and experimental characterization of a low-reynolds number split-and-recombine mixer. Microfluidics and Nanofluidics 2(3):237–248. doi: 10.1007/s10404-005-0071-6.

7. Neerincx PE, Denteneer RPJ, Peelen S, Meijer HEH (2011) Compact mixing using multiple splitting, stretching, and recombining flows. Macromolecular Materials and Engineering 296(3-4):349–361. doi: 10.1002/mame.201000338.

8. Paegel BM, Grover WH, Skelley AM, Mathies RA, Joyce GF (2006) Microfluidic serial dilution circuit. Analytical chemistry 78(21):7522–7527. doi: 10.1021/ac0608265. pmid:17073422

9. Kim C, Lee K, Kim JH, Shin KS, Lee KJ, Kim TS, et al. (2008) A serial dilution microfluidic device using a ladder network generating logarithmic or linear concentrations. Lab on a Chip 8(3):473–479. doi: 10.1039/b714536e. pmid:18305867

10. Pihl J, Sinclair J, Sahlin E, Karlsson M, Petterson F, Olofsson J, et al. (2005) Microfluidic gradient-generating device for pharmacological profiling. Analytical Chemistry 77(13):3897–3903. doi: 10.1021/ac050218+. pmid:15987089

11. Sugiura Sh, Hattori K, Kanamori T (2010) Microfluidic serial dilution cell-based assay for analyzing drug dose response over a wide concentration range. Analytical Chemistry 82(19):8278–8282. doi: 10.1021/ac1017666. pmid:20822164

12. Karst CM, Storey BD, Geddes JB (2013) Laminar flow of two miscible fluids in a simple network. Physics of Fluids (1994-present) 25(3):033601. doi: 10.1063/1.4794726.

13. Boyum A (1968) Isolation of mononuclear cells and granulocytes from human blood. Scandinavian Journal of Clinical and Laboratory Investigation S21(97):77–89.

14. Pertoft H, Rubin K, Kjellen L, Laurent TC, Klingeborn B (1977) The viability of cells grown or centrifuged in a new density gradient medium, Percoll (TM). Experimental Cell Research 110(2):449–457. doi: 10.1016/0014-4827(77)90311-1. pmid:201479

15. Grynne BH, Nossen JO, Bolstad B, Borch KW (1994) Main results of the first comparative clinical studies on Visipaque. Acta Radiologica. Supplementum 399:265–270.

16. oh YC, Lim TC, Tai D, Xiao G, Noort D, Yu H (2009) A microfluidic 3D hepatocyte chip for drug toxicity testing. Lab on a Chip 9(14): 2026–2035. doi: 10.1039/b900912d. pmid:19568671

CHAPTER 8

THE MULTI-SCALE NETWORK LANDSCAPE OF COLLABORATION

Arram Bae[1], Doheum Park[1], Yong-Yeol Ahn[2], Juyong Park[1]

[1] Graduate School of Culture Technology, Korea Advanced Institute of Science and Technology, Daejeon, Republic of Korea

[2] School of Informatics and Computing, Indiana University, Bloomington, Indiana, United States of America

ABSTRACT

Propelled by the increasing availability of large-scale high-quality data, advanced data modeling and analysis techniques are enabling many novel and significant scientific understanding of a wide range of complex social, natural, and technological systems. These developments also provide opportunities for studying cultural systems and phenomena—which can be said to refer to all products of human creativity and way of life. An important characteristic of a cultural product is that it does not exist in isolation from others, but forms an intricate web of connections on many levels. In the creation and dissemination of cultural products and artworks in particular, collaboration and communication of ideas play an essential role, which can be captured in the heterogeneous network of the creators and practitioners of art. In this paper we propose novel methods to analyze and uncover meaningful patterns from such a network using the network of western classical musicians constructed from a large-scale comprehensive Compact Disc recordings data. We characterize the complex patterns in the network landscape of collaboration between musicians across multiple scales ranging from the macroscopic to the mesoscopic and microscopic that represent the diversity of cultural styles and the individuality of the artists.

INTRODUCTION

Advances in information science and technology have enabled us to amass large-scale data from a wide range of social and cultural phenomena, stimulating the development of advanced data modeling and analysis methods for extracting useful information. This type of large-scale data collection and analysis is not limited to traditional scientific and engineering fields but is reaching into a wider range of fields such as social science and humanities, calling for deep and serious transdisciplinary effort to make full use of its universal impact [1, 2]. Recently, various mathematical and computational techniques have been applied to cultural data sets including recipes, music, paintings, etc. to gain new insights and understanding, further expanding the application in their fields [3–7].

Of many new data modeling frameworks, networks in particular have gained popularity for analyzing systems whose structure and function depend critically on the connections or correlations between their components [8–13]. There are several essential connections between networks and culture that render such network framework necessary for a scientific understanding of culture. First, a cultural product invariably

Citation: Bae A, Park D, Ahn Y-Y, Park J (2016) The Multi-Scale Network Landscape of Collaboration. PLoS ONE 11(3): e0151784. doi:10.1371/journal.pone.0151784.

cites existing products or ideas either explicitly or implicitly. Second, most cultural products are borne out of collaborations between artists and practitioners that act as a conduit for ideas and inspirations. Accordingly there have been notable scientific studies of culture and cultural phenomena from the network perspective focusing on the relationships among cultural products, creators, consumers, etc. [14–16]. In this paper we study the network of the creators and practitioners of culture to understand the patterns of collaborations and associations, and what they tell us about the nature of cultural prominence and diversity. Specifically we analyze the network of western classical musicians by leveraging one of the most comprehensive Compact Disc (CD) recordings databases in a rigorous fashion using established and new methods. While this paper focuses solely on music as the area of application, the analytical framework we propose should be generally applicable to any similar type of network.

Music, one of the most significant and oldest cultural traditions, boasts a rich history of cross-pollination of ideas and practices through time [17, 18]. There have been a number of studies on musician networks: Silva *et al.* studied the Brazilian popular musician network, finding basic properties such as the small-world effect and the power-law degree distribution [19]; Park *et al.* considered two distinct relationship types between contemporary pop musicians (musical similarity and collaboration) and showed that they exhibit vastly different network patterns [20]; Gleiser and Danon studied the social network of jazz musicians and found communities of musicians that correspond to regional differences and racial segregation [21]; and Park *et al.* studied the network of classical composers who formed communities that corresponded to a modern musicological understanding of the history of music [22].

Those works, while having pioneered in the application of network framework to musical data, show two apparent shortcomings. First, many deal with a relatively narrow period in the history of music, mainly the latter half of the 20th century and beyond. Prominently missing is the entire body of western classical music, one of the richest musical traditions [18, 23]. Second, they all ignore that a musical composition is distinct from many other art forms such as paintings or sculptures in that it requires a collaboration or combination between people with differing roles, i.e. individuals or group performers, composers, conductors, etc. Therefore this is a heterogeneous network where the meaning of an edge depends on which node types it connects. By leveraging one of the largest databases on western classical music performance recordings that incorporates the network heterogeneity, this paper aims to shed light on the complex and heterogeneous nature of the network of collaborations in music and, more broadly, culture.

We study the network of western classical musicians to find significant global patterns, to uncover principles that drive the connections between musicians, and to identify local network structures that allow us to represent the rich diversity within culture. Our network is constructed from ArkivMusic (http:/www.arkivmusic.com) database, an online vendor of classical music CDs. For each CD it provides its title, release date, label, and four classes of musicians (composer, performer, conductor, and ensemble) whose compositions or performances were featured on it. After removing the so-called compilation albums that are repackaged collections of previously released recordings, we are left with 67 277 CDs and 75 604 musicians, which can be represented as a bipartite network with 428 728 edges as shown schematically in Fig 1(A). Fig 1(B) shows a small backbone [24] of the network of composers as an example (subsequent analyses are performed on the original bipartite network to minimize loss of information). Specifically, we focus on the network patterns on three scales which we label the *macroscopic*, the *mesoscopic*, and the *microscopic* (see Fig 2).

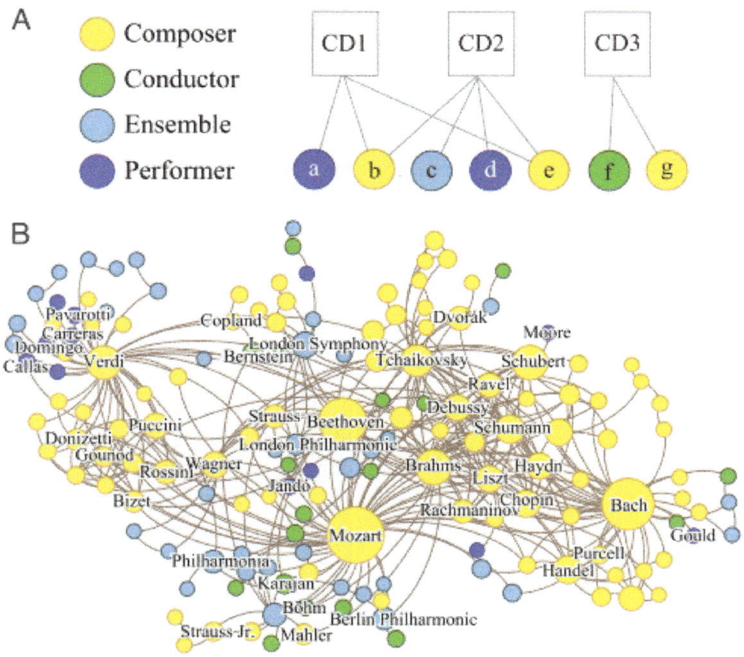

Figure 1. Constructing the network of artists and cultural products. (A) The comprehensive classical music recordings data from ArkivMusic is a bipartite network with edges running between CDs and the musicians. The musician layer (bottom) is a heterogeneous mix of musician classes—composers, conductors, ensembles, and individual performers. (B) A backbone of the network of musicians (CDs omitted via one-mode projection). An edge between musicians means that their compositions or performances were featured on a common CD.

On the macroscopic scale we study the global, bird's-eye view of the network, which allows us to identify those musicians with universal prominence. On the mesoscopic scale we study the modular structure (node subgroups) of the network to find the strength of correlation between node characteristics and connection. Some results from the macroscopic and mesoscopic scales have been previously reported by us in [5], with some updates that reflect the most up-to-date data, although it stands on its own for a completeness and consistency leading to our new and rigorous analysis on the microscopic scale, and on the unified view of the various scales. On the microscopic scale we present how to quantify the relevance of all other musicians to a specific musician, which allows us to identify the smallest, local network landscape. Finally, we conclude by how these multiscale patterns relate to one another, letting us establish a coherent relationship between universality and diversity, two essential yet seemingly contradictory characteristics of culture.

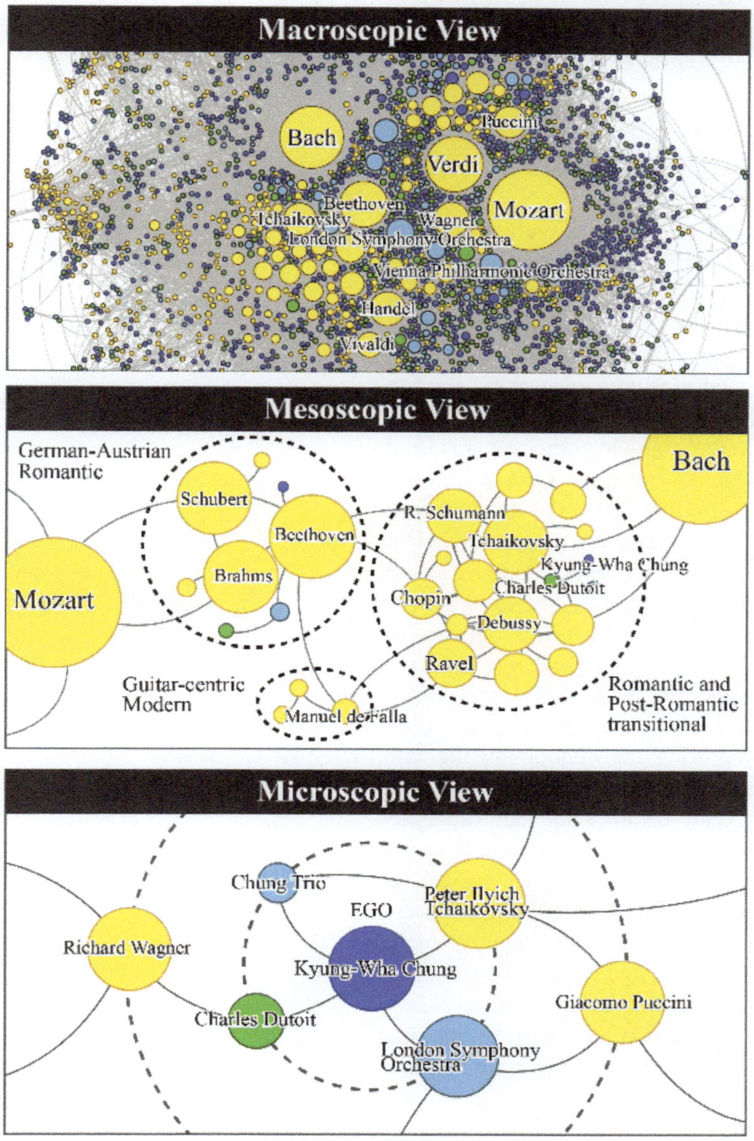

Figure 2. The multiscale views of the network landscape of the classical music network. On the macroscopic level (top), we take a bird's-eye view of the global characteristics of the network. On the mesoscopic scale (middle), we investigate the community structure of the network that reveals the homophily based on musician characteristics such as period and nationality. On the microscopic scale (bottom), we find the local network landscape around a specific musician by quantifying the relevance of others to the musician. This type of multiscale view allows us to correctly characterize the relationships between musicians and their roles in the cultural collaboration network, where a simple global prominence (top) can easily eclipse the rich local structures that represent diverse styles (middle) and individuality of artists (bottom).

MACROSCOPIC NETWORK PATTERNS: GLOBAL CHARACTERISTICS

On the macroscopic scale, our network shows many common characteristics of large-scale complex networks. For instance, the network possesses a giant component comprising 98.8% of all nodes, meaning that most musicians are connected by a path, regardless of their active era or specialties. The average geodesic (the shortest path between two nodes) length is 5.6 while the diameter (longest geodesic length) is 18 in the giant component, showing the small-world property [25, 26]. They are summarized in Table 1.

Table 1. Basic Network Properties.

Total Number of Nodes (CDs and musicians)	142881
— Number of CDs	67 277
— Number of Musicians	75604
- Composers	13148
- Conductors	5167
- Performers	45907
- Ensembles	11382
Number of Edges	428728
Mean Degree of Musicians	5.67
Mean Geodesic Length / Diameter	5.6 / 18
Largest Component Size	141 212 (98.8%)
Power Exponent of Degree Distribution	2.31 ± 0.03

doi:10.1371/journal.pone.0151784.t001

The mean degree of musicians, i.e. the average number of CDs on which a musician's composition or performance is featured, is 5.7. Compared with the total number of CDs 67277, this tells us that the network is very sparse. The distribution of the degree is very skewed, approximately a power law (Fig 3(A)). In Table 2 we show, for each musician class, the ten highest-degree musicians. For instance, Wolfgang Amadeus Mozart (1756–1791) is the most popular composer, featured on 5 288 CDs. The tenor Plácido Domingo (1941—) is the most popular performer, featured on 354 CDs. Herbert von Karajan (1908–1989) and London Symphony Orchestra (founded in 1904) are most prolific recording conductor and ensemble, respectively. If we accept the degree as a simple measure for the importance of a musician, this appears to suggest that these few musicians dominate the rest in terms of musical importance. But this may be the very reason why a macroscopic characteristic such as the degree distribution is insufficient in properly capturing the nuances in the role or importance of a musician; it would be absurd to assert, for instance, that vocalists are more important than organists simply because their degrees are larger. This problem is found again when we look at groups of musicians, shown in Fig 3(B) and 3(C). Fig 3(B) shows us that the degrees of composers from the Romantic period are disproportionately high, whileFig 3(C) shows that highly skewed degree distributions are found amongst composers from the same period across all periods. These findings suggest that it is necessary to examine the nature of groups of musicians that form the smaller-scale structures in the networks.

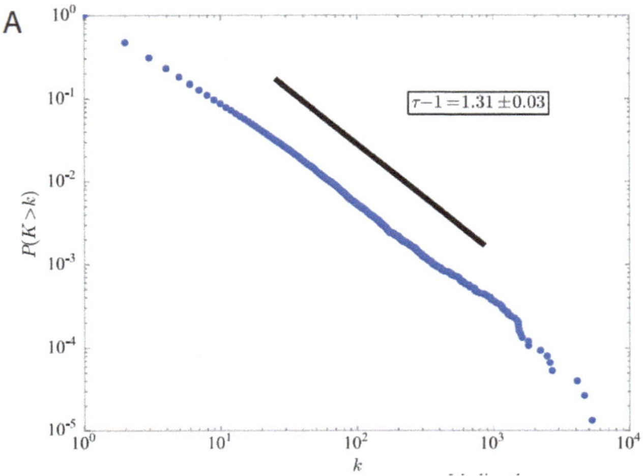

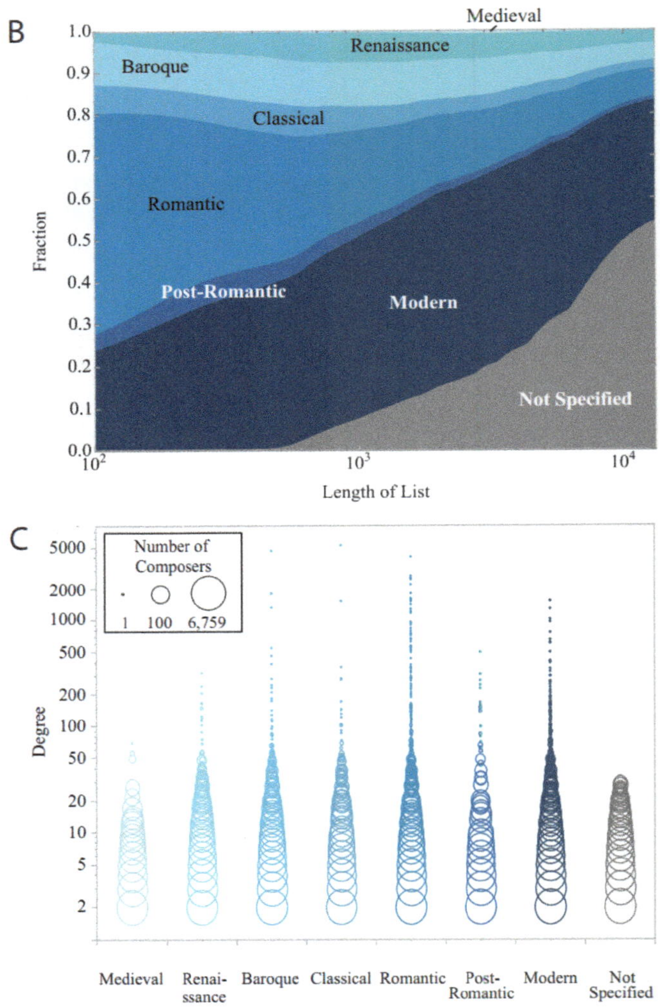

Figure 3. Measuring the macroscopic network structure. On the macroscopic scale the network is characterized by wide variations in the visibility of the musicians, potentially masking diversity and the existence of smaller structures. (A) The cumulative degree distribution $P(K > k)$ of nodes in the bipartite network. It appears to follow a power law $P(K > k) \propto k^{-\tau+1}$ (with $\tau = 2.31 \pm 0.03$), suggesting an extreme level of difference in the visibility or prominence between musicians. (B) Composers from the Romantic period are overrepresented in the lists of highest-degree composers. For instance, nearly 50% of 100 highest-degree composers are from the Romantic period (far left), while it accounts for only 10% of all composers (far right). (C) Significant variations in the degree of musicians are observed within the musical period as well.

Table 2. Ten Highest-Degree Musicians (Composer, Performer, Conductor, Ensemble).

Composer	Performer	Conductor	Ensemble
W. A. Mozart (Classical)	P. Domingo (Tenor)	Herbert Von Karajan	London Symphony Orchestra
J. S. Bach (Baroque)	D. Fischer-Dieskau (Bass)	Leonard Bernstein	Vienna Philharmonic Orchestra
L. Van Beethoven (Romantic)	M. Callas (Soprano)	Sir Neville Marriner	Philhamonia Orchestra
J. Brahms (Romantic)	L. Pavarotti (Tenor)	Claudio Abbado	Berlin Philharmonic Orchestra
F. Schubert (Romantic)	P. Schreier (Tenor)	Eugene Ormandy	London Philharmonic Orchestra
G. Verdi (Romantic)	S. Richter (Piano)	Daniel Barenboim	Royal Philharmonic Orchestra
P. I. Tchaikovsky (Romantic)	J. Jando (Piano)	Neeme Järvi	English Chamber Orchestra
G. F. Handel (Baroque)	N. Gedda (Tenor)	James Levine	Academy of St.Martin in the Fields
R. Schumann (Romantic)	E. Schwarzkopf (Soprano)	Sir Colin Davis	New York Philharmonic
F. Chopin (Romantic)	J. Sutherland (Soprano)	Sir Georg Solti	Milan Teatro Alla Scala Orchestra

doi:10.1371/journal.pone.0151784.t002

MESOSCOPIC NETWORK STRUCTURES: COMMUNITIES

The previous analysis lets us see the global, system-wide characteristics of the network such as the existence of a giant component and the small-world property. The most notable shortcoming was that a few individuals and groups appeared to be dominating the network, masking other important players in music (Fig 3). According to a modern understanding of networks, in fact, the small-world property by no means rules out interesting local structures in a network that represent groups of nodes called "modules" or "communities." A common definition of a network community is a group of nodes that are more densely connected between themselves than to the rest of the network. Communities are therefore a way of partitioning a network into meaningful mesoscopic substructures. Of many useful algorithms for identifying communities [27–30], we apply the Louvain algorithm to our network [28] which yields 614 communities.

In Fig 4 we show the four largest communities, along with their notable musicians' names. An examination of these suggests a positive correlation between musician characteristics and community structures, a sign of homophily or assortative mixing [31–34]. For instance, community A contains many Austrian-German Romantic composers such as Ludwig van Beethoven (1770–1827), Franz Schubert (1797–1828), and Johannes Brahms (1833–1897). Community B, on the other hand, contains Aaron Copland (1900–1990), Samuel Barber (1910–1981), and John Cage (1912–1992) all prominent US-born Modern composers. To properly characterize a community in terms of such musician attributes as nationality and period, we use the following Z-score to quantify the degree of *overrepresentation* of a musician attribute a in community s:

$$Z_a^s \equiv \frac{n_a^s - np_a}{\sqrt{np_a(1-p_a)}}, \tag{1}$$

where n_a^s is the number of musicians with attribute a inside community s, n is the number of all musicians in the network, and p_a is the fraction of musicians who have attribute a in the network. The results for three musician attributes (composer's period, performer's position, and musicians's nationality applicable to all musicians except ensembles) are shown in the boxes in Fig 4, the areas being proportional to the Z-scores. They confirm our previous observations: Romantic composers from Austria and Germany are the most overrepresented in community A, while Modern composers from the USA are so in community B. Community C is another interesting case, with the piano being the most prominent instrument and representing the transitional period spanning Romantic, Post-Romantic, and early European Modern, with Frédéric Chopin (1810–1849), Peter Ilyich Tchaikovsky (1840–1893), Claude Debussy (1862–1918), and Maurice Ravel (1875–1937). Community D, on the other hand, represents the guitar with notable names including Issac Albéniz (1860–1909, Spain), Heitor Villa-Lobos (1887–1959, Brazil) and Andrés Segovia (1893–1987, Spain). It also shows the dominance of Spain and Latin America, known for boasting a strong guitar tradition in modern times. Community D also clearly demonstrates the importance of local structures in understanding how diversity is represented in a cultural network: While undoubtedly a significant component of music, musicians specializing in the guitar are absent or severely underrepresented in Table 2 and Fig 3.

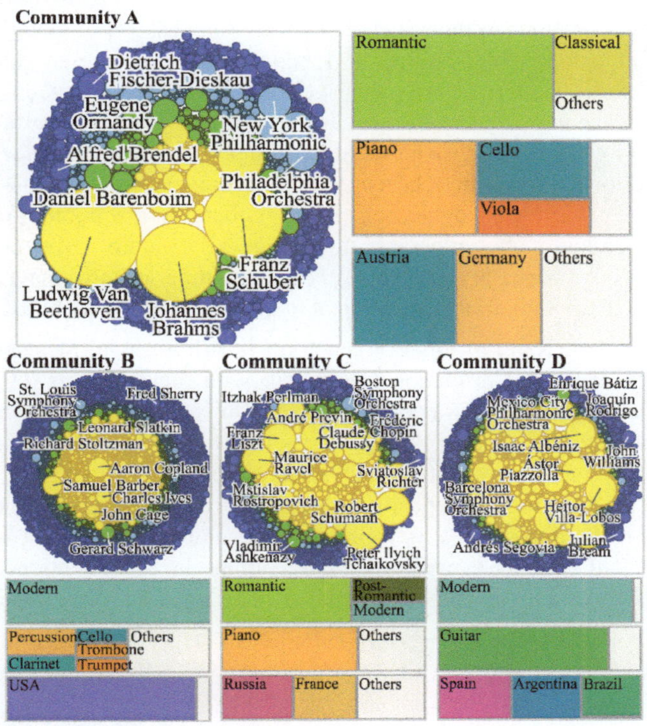

Figure 4. Communities showing the mesoscopic network structure. On the mesoscopic scale the network is characterized by tightly-knit communities. We show four major communities. We show which musician attributes (composer periods, performer positions, and musician nationalities) are overrepresented in each community. Community A, for instance, represents the Austrian-German Romantic

music; B represents the USA-based Modern music; C represents the transitional period between Romantic and Post-Romantic; finally, D represents the classical guitar.

MICROSCOPIC NETWORK STRUCTURES: EGOCENTRIC RELEVANCE

That we had to look into smaller-scale network structures to uncover important aspects of a cultural network prompts us to delve further into an even smaller scale. As mesoscopic means the network structure of groups of nodes, we take microscopic to mean the network structure centered on the individual node of the network. Traditionally, the network arranged around a specific node at the center is called the "egocentric network" and the central node the "ego." Here we focus on determining the significance or relevance of network nodes to the specific ego, and what it can tell us about the nature of musical combinations.

Perhaps the simplest sensible measure of the relevance of a node to another is the geodesic distance between the two. But geodesic distance is well-known to be of limited use for the following reasons: First, since the geodesic distance is an integer and tend to be small due to the small-world property, very made nodes tend to be at the same distance from the ego. This results in a poor resolution, and not many interesting findings can be made. Second, geodesic distance does not consider the existence of multiple paths between two nodes that could also indicate a varying level of relevance between the nodes.

Here we overcome both limitations via two straightforward modifications to the widely-used PageRank [8, 35] of Google that adopts the concept of random walk. We present the detailed steps for clarity. In PageRank, one assumes a random walker who visits the nodes in the network according to the following rule: At each time step, with probability α the walker follows a randomly chosen edge from the currently occupied node (the "walk" dynamic), or with probability $1-\alpha$ it jumps to a randomly chosen node in the network (the "jump" dynamic, no edge necessary). After a very large number of movements, the PageRank of a node is equal to its occupation probability.

PageRank in this original form is still a global measure (its Pearson Correlation Coefficient with the degree is 0.99 in our network), necessitating modifications to measure node's relevance to the ego. This is achieved by modifying the jump dynamic so that the walker jumps to the ego only. This functions to reposition the walker onto the ego so that a node close to ego as well as having more paths leading to it will be visited more often, overcoming the aforementioned shortcomings of geodesic distance. The resulting occupation probability we call **Egocentric PageRank** (EP) P_i^e defined for node i and ego e, which can be mathematically represented as $\mathrm{P}_i^e = \alpha \times \sum_j \frac{A_{ij}}{k_j} \mathrm{P}_j^e + (1-\alpha) \times \delta_i^e$ where A_{ij} is the adjacency matrix, k_j is the degree, and δ_i^e is the Kronecker delta. This is a specific application of personalized PageRank [35], also known as Random Walk with Restart (RWR) [36]. Other examples of random walk-based relevance between two nodes include one based on counting of short-length random walks, which was used for community detection [37]. Now we represent EP in vector and matrix form

$$\vec{\mathrm{P}}^e = (1-\alpha)\left(\mathbf{I} - \alpha \mathbf{A}\mathbf{K}^{-1}\right)^{-1} \cdot \vec{\delta}^e. \quad (2)$$

The Pearson Correlation Coefficient between EP (averaged over all egos) and the degree is 0.19, a much smaller value but it shows that the degree is still influential; it is the nature of the walk dynamics, where a high degree generally increases the chance of the node being occupied by the surfer. With this in mind, we try the following modification to the walk dynamic: The walker now chooses a target node with a probability inversely proportional to its degree. We call the resulting occupation probability the Degree-Neutralized Egocentric PageRank (DNEP) $\mathrm{D}_i^e = \alpha \times k_i^{-1} \sum_j A_{ij} H_j \mathrm{D}_j^e + (1-\alpha) \times \delta_i^e$, given in vector and matrix form as

$$\vec{\mathrm{D}}^e = (1-\alpha)\left(\mathbf{I} - \alpha \mathbf{K}^{-1}\mathbf{A}\mathbf{H}\right)^{-1} \cdot \vec{\delta}^e \quad (3)$$

where $\mathbf{H}$ is a diagonal matrix of $H_j = \left[\sum_l A_{lj} k_l^{-1}\right]^{-1}$, the reciprocal of the sum of the inverse of the degree of node j's neighbors. This degree-neutralized pairwise quantity is reminiscent of similarity measures such as SimRank proposed by Jeh and Widom [38] or the regular equivalence discussed in [8]. Note that, however, our quantity is designed to find the relevance (one could also say generalized closeness) between two nodes by refining PageRank, thereby not their similarity. Now the correlation between degree and DNEP of the nodes is 0.003, showing that the degree effect has been almost eradicated. To see the difference between EP and DNEP, we define the **Egocentric Relevance** (ER) R_i^e to be the linear combination of the two:

$$\mathrm{R}_i^e(\beta) = (1-\beta)\mathrm{P}_i^e + \beta \mathrm{D}_i^e, \quad (4)$$

with $\beta \in [0, 1]$. ER thus changes continuously from EP to DNEP as β is tuned from 0 to 1.

We now apply this method to a prominent violinist Kyung-Wha Chung (1948—) as an example, which is presented in Fig 5 . Fig 5(A)shows how Chung's relevant musicians change as β is tuned from 0 to 1. When $\beta = 0$ (EP), although the top ten list shares seven musicians with Table 1 (Tchaikosky, London Symphony Orchestra, J. S. Bach, Beethoven, Royal Philharmonic Orchestra, W. A. Mozart, and Brahms), it also features those associated with her signature debut album (André Previn and London Symphony Orchestra). EP therefore already succeeds, to some degree, in bringing forth those more intimately revelant to the ego. The top list of relevant musicians according to DNEP is even more drastically different—first of all, it shares no name withTable 1, and one name with (Charles Dutoit) EP (left). On the top of the list is Chung Trio, composed of Chung and her siblings cellist Myung-Wha Chung (1944—) and pianist-conductor Myung-Whun Chung (1953—), ranked only 35th according to EP. This shows that DNEP performs even better than EP at identifying those intimately relevant to the ego: Pianist Krystian Zimerman (1956—) at #4 is very well known for his Gramophone award-winning with Chung; conductor Sir Simon Rattle (1955—) at #10 is famous for his work with Chung and the Vienna Philharmonic. Fig 5(B) shows a more extensive egocentric network landscape around Chung according to DNEP of different musician classes (with degree 30 or larger). The distance from Chung is proportional to the log of the reciprocal of DNEP. Among ensembles the Montreal Symphony Orchestra (founded in 1935) whose violin concerto recording with conductor Charles Dutoit (1936—) and Chung is very famous in the classical music community. Among composers it is Max Bruch (1838–1920) who is the most relevant to Chung. It is due to her recording of Max Bruch's concertos considered to be her signature achievement, pushing out better-known names including Beethoven and Bach. Chung's recordings of Jean Sibelius (1865–1957) and Béla Bartók (1881–1945) are also famous, bringing them close to the center.

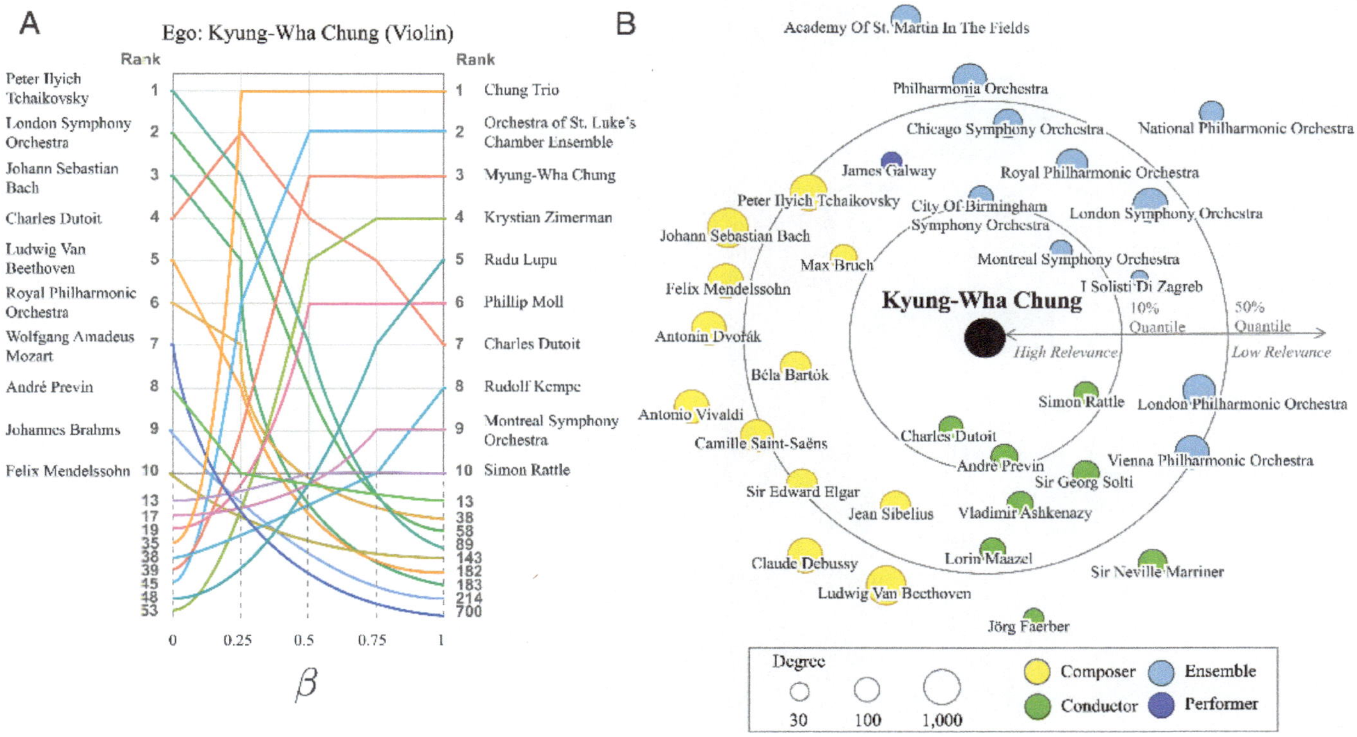

Figure 5. Microscopic network structure centered on an individual musician. (A) The musicians most relevant to violinist Kyung-Wha Chung as an ego determined by Egocentric PageRank (EP, left) and Degree-Neutralized Egocentric PageRank (DNEP, right). Of the ten highest-EP musicians, seven (Tchaikovsky, London Symphony, J. S. Bach, Beethoven, Royal Philharmonic, W. A. Mozart, and Brahms) are also among the ten highest-degree nodes in the overall network. The ten highest-DNEP musicians feature those more specific to the ego, with the Chung Trio (composed of Chung's two siblings) occupying the top spot, with Krystian Zimerman and Simon Rattle known for their collaborations with Chung in high spots. W. A. Mozart, in contrast, falls rapidly in the ranks. (B) A figure showing the egocentric network landscape determined by DNEP ($\beta = 1$) around Kyung-Wha Chung. Highly relevant musicians tend to be lower in degree but more specifically related to her (e.g., composer Max Bruch, conductor Charles Dutoit, Montreal Symphony Orchestra, etc.). High-degree nodes such as Tchaikovsky are pushed outwards, demonstrating the ability of DNEP to differentiate between ego-specific and universally associated musicians.

With the success of EP and DNEP in identifying the egocentric network landscape, we now ask if we can use these measures for a group of nodes as an ego. For instance, one may be interested in those relevant to a specific instrument, not merely one individual. One possibility is to add up a musician i's relevance to all nodes e in the given group of interest G, i.e. $\sum_{e\in G} R_i^e$. Yet, we would also like to identify those broadly relevant to the member of G. We therefore propose the **group-level egocentric relevance** as follow:

$$R_i(G) \equiv -\left[\sum_{v\in G} R_i^v\right] \times \left[\sum_{v\in G} \frac{R_i^v}{\sum_{v\in G} R_i^v} \log_{10} \frac{R_i^v}{\sum_{v\in G} R_i^v}\right], \quad \textbf{(5)}$$

a product of two terms—the sum of relevance and an entropy-like term that gives awards those that are more uniformly relevant to the members of the group. As an example application, we have calculated the relevance of the composers with respect to the five largest performer groups (violinists, cellists, pianists, tenors, and sopranos). Then, we took the top-100 composers in DNEP for each group, and counted how many times (one to five) they are included in the lists as a measure of the composer's versatility. The number of composers and some notable names are given in Fig 6. We see that, perhaps surprisingly, it is only Schubert that is intimately relevant to all five groups, showing his versatility and virtuosity in both instrumental and vocal music. Mozart, Beethoven, J. S. Bach, and Haydn are intimately relevant to four (except the cello for Mozart, and the tenor for the rest). George Frideric Handel (1685–1759), Richard Wagner (1813–1883) and Richard Strauss (1864–1949) are intimately relevant to the tenor and the soprano, likely based on their masterpiece choral compositions and opera. Names relevant to one group can be thought of as highly specialized composers, such as Giuseppe Tartini (1692–1770) and Niccolò Paganini (1782–1840) for the violin, and Frédéric Chopin (1810–1849), Franz Liszt (1811–1886), and George Gershwin (1898–1937) for the piano. We have to keep in mind, however, that Fig 6 is for the five individual performer groups and that those whose major compositions were for ensembles or orchestras are likely underrepresented, which may be the case for Camille Saint-Saëns (1835–1921) who does not appear in the lists.

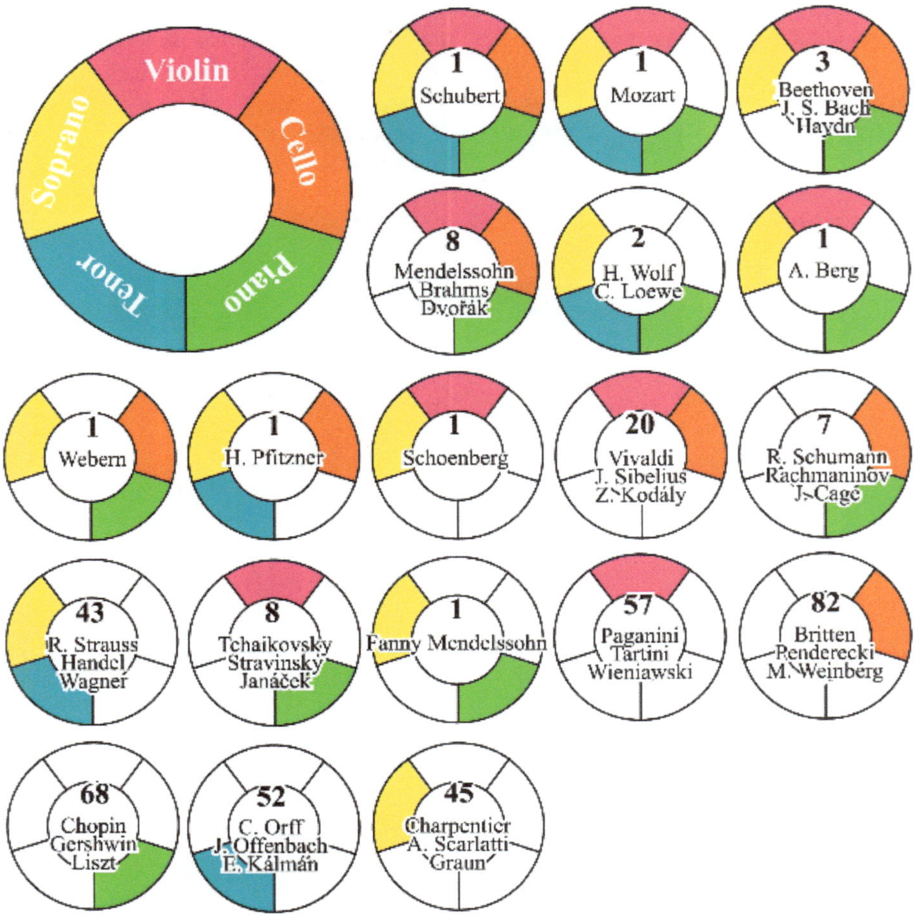

Figure 6. Versatility of composers based on relevance to instrument groups. The number of composers highly relevant (ranked 100th or higher) to any of the five largest instrument groups (violin, cello, piano, tenor, and soprano) is in the circles. Composers relevant to multiple instrument groups in the absence of degree effect tend to be the universally recognized composers, revealing the connection between macroscopic and microscopic network patterns.

The significance of Fig 6 lies in the fact that it shows an explicit connection between the macroscopic and the microscopic network landscape patterns. Since the figure was based on DNEP, a measure that had nearly eradicated the degree effect, it is a representation of the local structures in the classical music network. Interestingly, however, it reproduces many names that were prominent on the macroscopic scale as those who are versatile and relevant to many classes of musicians. Fig 6 suggests that, therefore, universality in culture stems from versatility on the microscopic level which appears as prominence on the macroscopic scale, while diversity represents the existence of many virtuosi in different subfields.

DISCUSSION AND CONCLUSION

Our work shows how we can utilize the network framework to understand the landscape of cultural collaboration and combination based on large-scale databases. In order to properly understand the diversity and universality—two of the most significant aspects of cultural creativity—we needed to take a multi-scale view of the network, incrementally revealing the finer and more complex patterns from the network. On the macroscopic scale we retrieve some common features of social-type network such as the power-law degree distribution and the small-world property. The inadequacy of a single-scale analysis becomes immediately clear in the beginning with the macroscopic analysis; the power-law degree distribution, for instance, suggests a strict ordering of the importance of musicians across the entire network. This is, of course, a problematic view of culture where diversity and heterogeneity are treasured. On the mesoscopic scale we presented quantitatively the correlation between the modular structure of the network and various attribute data (periods, instruments, and nationalities), demonstrating a way to establish connection between information mined from massive digital data and a common musicological understanding of the history of music. We conducted an investigation on a further smaller scale to see how one can characterize the network properties centered on individuals. We developed two versions of egocentric relevance measures to achieve this, enabling us to discover the very musicians uniquely relevant to the ego. This allowed us to finally understand how universality and diversity, two seemingly paradoxical nature of culture, could coexist and be represented in a coherent fasion.

We believe that our work here represents a starting point for exploring the multiscale patterns of cultural networks. With certainly a vast array of crucial questions to be explored therein, the possibility of advances in the scientific studies on cultural and humanities subjects utilizing large-scale data must be significant.

ACKNOWLEDGMENTS

The authors thank Joo Young Oh for helpful discussions.

AUTHOR CONTRIBUTIONS

Conceived and designed the experiments: AB JP YA. Performed the experiments: AB JP DP. Analyzed the data: AB JP DP. Contributed reagents/materials/analysis tools: AB JP DP. Wrote the paper: AB JP DP YA. Data crawl: YA DP.

REFERENCES

1. Miller E. Community cleverness required. Nature. 2008;455:1. doi: 10. 1038/455001a.
2. Lazer D, Pentland AS, Adamic L, Aral S, Barabasi AL, Brewer D, et al. Computational Social Science. Science. 2009;323(5915):721–23. doi: 10. 1126/science. 1167742. pmid:19197046
3. Ahn YY, Ahnert SE, Bagrow JP, Barabási AL. Flavor network and the principles of food pairing. Scientific Reports. 2011;1. doi: 10. 1038/srep00196. pmid:22355711
4. Schich M, Song C, Ahn YY, Mirsky A, Martino M, Barabási AL, et al. A network framework of cultural history. Science. 2014;345(6196):558–562. doi: 10. 1126/science. 1240064. pmid:25082701
5. Bae A, Park D, Park J. The Network of Western Classical Musicians. In: Complex Networks V. Springer; 2014. p. 13–24.
6. Park D, Bae A, Park J. The Network of Western Classical Music Composers. In: Complex Networks V. Springer; 2014. p. 1–12.
7. Klingenstein S, Hitchcock T, DeDeo S. The civilizing process in London's Old Bailey. Proceedings of the National Academy of Sciences. 2014;111(26):9419–9424. doi: 10. 1073/pnas. 1405984111.
8. Newman M. Networks: an introduction. Oxford University Press; 2010.
9. Newman ME. The structure and function of complex networks. SIAM Review. 2003;45(2):167–256. doi: 10. 1137/S003614450342480.
10. Faloutsos M, Faloutsos P, Faloutsos C. On power-law relationships of the internet topology. In: ACM SIGCOMM computer communication review. vol. 29. ACM; 1999. p. 251–262.
11. Holme P, Edling CR, Liljeros F. Structure and time evolution of an Internet dating community. Social Networks. 2004;26(2):155–174. doi: 10. 1016/j. socnet. 2004. 01. 007.
12. Jeong H, Tombor B, Albert R, Oltvai ZN, Barabási AL. The large-scale organization of metabolic networks. Nature. 2000;407(6804):651–654. doi: 10. 1038/35036627. pmid:11034217
13. Grimm V, Revilla E, Berger U, Jeltsch F, Mooij WM, Railsback SF, et al. Pattern-oriented modeling of agent-based complex systems: lessons from ecology. Science. 2005;310(5750):987–991. doi: 10. 1126/science. 1116681. pmid:16284171
14. Uzzi B, Spiro J. Collaboration and Creativity: The Small World Problem. American Journal of Sociology. 2005;111(2):447–504. doi: 10. 1086/432782.
15. Salganik MJ, Dodds PS, Watts DJ. Experimental study of inequality and unpredictability in an artificial cultural market. Science. 2006;311(5762):854–856. doi: 10. 1126/science. 1121066. pmid:16469928
16. Schich M, Meirelles I. Arts, Humanities and Complex Networks. Leonardo. 2012;45(1):77–77. doi: 10. 1162/leon_e_01054
17. Struble JW. The history of American classical music: MacDowell through minimalism. Facts on File; 1995.
18. Taruskin R. Music in the Nineteenth Century: The Oxford History of Western Music. Oxford University Press; 2009.
19. e Silva DdL, Soares MM, Henriques M, Alves MS, de Aguiar S, de Carvalho T, et al. The complex network of the Brazilian Popular Music. Physica A: Statistical Mechanics and its Applications. 2004;332:559–565. doi: 10. 1016/j. physa. 2003. 09. 059.
20. Park J, Celma O, Koppenberger M, Cano P, Buldú JM. The social network of contemporary popular musicians. International Journal of Bifurcation and Chaos. 2007;17(07):2281–2288. doi: 10. 1142/S0218127407018385.
21. Gleiser PM, Danon L. Community structure in jazz. Advances in Complex Systems. 2003;6(04):565–573. doi: 10. 1142/S0219525903001067.
22. Park D, Bae A, Schich M, Park J. Topology and evolution of the network of western classical music composers. EPJ Data Science. 2015;4(1):1–15. doi: 10. 1140/epjds/s13688-015-0039-z.
23. Ross A. The rest is noise: Listening to the twentieth century. Macmillan; 2007.
24. Serrano MÁ, Boguná M, Vespignani A. Extracting the multiscale backbone of complex weighted networks. Proceedings of the National Academy of Sciences. 2009;106(16):6483–6488. doi: 10. 1073/pnas. 0808904106.
25. Milgram S. The small world problem. Psychology Today. 1967;2(1):60–67.
26. Watts DJ, Strogatz SH. Collective dynamics of 'small-world' networks. Nature. 1998;393(6684):440–442. doi: 10. 1038/30918. pmid:9623998
27. Newman ME, Girvan M. Finding and evaluating community structure in networks. Physical Review E. 2004;69(2):026113. doi: 10. 1103/PhysRevE. 69. 026113.
28. Blondel VD, Guillaume JL, Lambiotte R, Lefebvre E. Fast unfolding of communities in large networks. Journal of Statistical Mechanics: Theory and Experiment. 2008; 2008(10):P10008. doi: 10. 1088/1742-5468/2008/10/P10008.
29. Fortunato S. Community detection in graphs. Physics Reports. 2010;486(3):75–174. doi: 10. 1016/j. physrep. 2009. 11. 002.
30. Ahn YY, Bagrow JP, Lehmann S. Link communities reveal multiscale complexity in networks. Nature. 2010;466(7307):761–764. doi: 10. 1038/nature09182.

pmid:20562860

31. Newman ME, Park J. Why social networks are different from other types of networks. Physical Review E. 2003;68(3):036122. doi: 10. 1103/PhysRevE. 68. 036122.
32. Park J, Barabási AL. Distribution of node characteristics in complex networks. Proceedings of the National Academy of Sciences. 2007;104(46):17916–17920. doi: 10. 1073/pnas. 0705081104.
33. Newman ME. Assortative mixing in networks. Physical Review Letters. 2002;89(20):208701. doi: 10. 1103/PhysRevLett. 89. 208701. pmid:12443515
34. Park J, Newman ME. Origin of degree correlations in the Internet and other networks. Physical Review E. 2003;68(2):026112. doi: 10. 1103/PhysRevE. 68. 026112.
35. Page L, Brin S, Motwani R, Winograd T. The PageRank Citation Ranking: Bringing Order to the Web. Stanford InfoLab; 1999. 1999–66.
36. Pan JY, Yang HJ, Faloutsos C, Duygulu P. Automatic multimedia cross-modal correlation discovery. In: Proceedings of the tenth ACM SIGKDD international conference on Knowledge discovery and data mining. ACM; 2004. p. 653–658.
37. Pons P, Latapy M. Computing communities in large networks using random walks. In: Computer and Information Sciences-ISCIS 2005. Springer; 2005. p. 284–293.
38. Jeh G, Widom J. SimRank: a measure of structural-context similarity. In: Proceedings of the eighth ACM SIGKDD international conference on Knowledge discovery and data mining. ACM; 2002. p. 538–543.

CHAPTER 9

A GEOSPATIAL INFORMATION GRID FRAMEWORK FOR GEOLOGICAL SURVEY

Liang Wu[1,2], Lei Xue[1] , Chaoling Li[3] , Xia Lv[3] , Zhanlong Chen[1] , Mingqiang Guo[1] , Zhong Xie[1,2]

[1] School of Information Engineering, China University of Geosciences, Wuhan, China

[2] National Engineering Research Center for GIS, Wuhan, China

[3] Development and Research Center, China Geological Survey, Beijing, China

ABSTRACT

The use of digital information in geological fields is becoming very important. Thus, informatization in geological surveys should not stagnate as a result of the level of data accumulation. The integration and sharing of distributed, multi-source, heterogeneous geological information is an open problem in geological domains. Applications and services use geological spatial data with many features, including being cross-region and cross-domain and requiring real-time updating. As a result of these features, desktop and web-based geographic information systems (GISs) experience difficulties in meeting the demand for geological spatial information. To facilitate the real-time sharing of data and services in distributed environments, a GIS platform that is open, integrative, reconfigurable, reusable and elastic would represent an indispensable tool. The purpose of this paper is to develop a geological cloud-computing platform for integrating and sharing geological information based on a cloud architecture. Thus, the geological cloud-computing platform defines geological ontology semantics; designs a standard geological information framework and a standard resource integration model; builds a peer-to-peer node management mechanism; achieves the description, organization, discovery, computing and integration of the distributed resources; and provides the distributed spatial meta service, the spatial information catalog service, the multi-mode geological data service and the spatial data interoperation service. The geological survey information cloud-computing platform has been implemented, and based on the platform, some geological data services and geological processing services were developed. Furthermore, an iron mine resource forecast and an evaluation service is introduced in this paper.

INTRODUCTION

Following the development of information technology, the revolution in Earth information technology has continued. In the geospatial sciences, various challenges related to data intensity, computing intensity, concurrent access intensity and spatiotemporal intensity have emerged. These challenges require a computing infrastructure that better supports the discovery, accessibility, processing and utilization of data and provides a more reliable and scalable service for massive numbers of concurrent users[1,2]. The same is true in the geological domain, where research and development typically produces and analyzes large volumes of distributed heterogeneous geospatial data sets[3]. The applications and services that use geological spatial data have certain features, such as being cross-region and cross-domain and requiring real-time updating, focus on a certain application

Citation: Wu L, Xue L, Li C, Lv X, Chen Z, Guo M, et al. (2015) A Geospatial Information Grid Framework for Geological Survey. PLoS ONE 10(12): e0145312. doi:10.1371/journal.pone.0145312.

or service (e.g., the evaluation of mineral resource potential, the evaluation of geological disasters and the environment, and the evaluation of underground water)[4]. Furthermore, the geological spatial data that must be mobilized are usually distributed in different regions, different domains and different departments. Distributed geographic information processing (DGIP) has become increasingly important in the past decade with the popularization of computer networks, the growth of distributed data repositories, and the collaboration of researchers, developers, and users among multiple disciplines using geographic information[5]. To implement a collaborative, real-time functioning system, the isolated geological spatial data, services and computing resources should be logically integrated and made shareable. Information must be extracted from accumulated geological spatial data by comprehensively analyzing the data; then, the information should be transformed into knowledge that is significant for geological research[6]. DGIP plays a critical role in integrating the widely distributed geospatial resources to support the envisioned digital earth for utilizing a wide variety of information[7]. Requirements from the global initiatives and the nature of distributed geographic information call for the research and development of effective DGIP[5]. In addition, the sharing of large volumes of data sets encourages researchers and organizations to focus on consensus development of standard protocols and tools to publish and interoperate these large volumes of data sets[8]. Data semantics play an extremely important role in spatial data infrastructure by providing semantic specifications for geospatial data and in this way enabling data sharing and interoperability[9]. However, the management of resources in a distributed computing environment is inherently more difficult[10]. The use of an efficient mechanism to store, manage, retrieve and discover spatial information and services to provide the fusion and strategic decision-making ability of massive dynamic global geospatial information is significant[9,11,12]. Therefore, a GIS platform that is open, integrative, reconfigurable, reusable and elastic would represent an indispensable tool for enhancing geological information processing and services.

Cloud computing overlaps with some concepts of distributed computing and grid computing[13]. The goal of cloud computing lies in sharing of resources; however, resource sharing is not restricted to software and data; it is extensive and includes computing resources, storage resources, and knowledge resources[14,15]. With a cloud computing platform, users requisition computing power, storage, and other services gaining access to a suite of elastic IT infrastructure services as demands[16–18]. In a cloud environment, users have a large pool of easily usable and accessible virtualized resources[15,19]. Cloud infrastructure services, also known as Infrastructure as a Service (IaaS), including physical machines, networks, storage and system software, as virtualized computing resources[1,14,20]. The method of resource organization is an important aspect of a cloud computing environment. In terms of resource management or organization in a distributed environment, there are primarily three models: the resource pool model (a centralized model), the global-local resource model and the peer-to-peer (P2P) model.

Resource pooling is a mechanism for virtualizing and managing resources as a resource pool[21]. It is a centralized strategy for resource allocation and management[22]. The global-local resource model is used in Globus. It consists of four components: a resource agency, a collaboration assigner, a resource information service component and a resource arrangement manager. In the global/local-to-layer model, resource request processing is divided into local and global components[23]. Considering the availability and practicability of a universal description discovery and integration, peer-to-peer architectures have been proposed. A P2P system consists of a number of decentralized distributed network nodes that are capable of sharing resources without centralized supervision[24]. Based on the resource location, there are two main types of P2P structures: the message flooding and the distributed hash table (DHT). In message flooding, the query is propagated to all nodes in the network. However, the quantity of messages in the network rapidly increases as the number of nodes in the network increases, thereby easily resulting in saturation[24,25]. The distributed hash table method has been widely used for resource locating[26–28]. However, it is difficult to maintain the DHT when the node is modified.

Many organizations have begun to adopt cloud computing to better utilize computing resources by taking advantage of its scalability, lower costs, and easy accessibility[29]. Furthermore, various geospatial systems based on cloud computing have been developed. Some organizations have built their applications or systems on a commercial cloud that is provided by Google, Amazon or Microsoft. For example, "ModflowOnAzure" is a scientific modeling service that enables large-scale ensemble runs of groundwater flow models to be easily executed in parallel in the Windows Azure cloud[30]. Combined with the web-processing service, a geoprocessing cloud platform, AWT, that integrates Amazon cloud computing and geoprocessing functions was built to provide geoprocessing competence in a distributed web environment[16]. Various researchers have adopted a distributed computing architecture that is designed to solve a certain geospatial problem. A cloud-based framework for a spatial web portal (SWP) has been proposed to integrate several cloud features to support the SWP operation[31]. A prototype for sharing geographical analysis models that constructs a volunteer-style sharing mode for modeling and computing resources in an open environment on a cloud computing platform has been proposed[32]. The state-of-the-art application, which runs in a cloud computing environment, is composed of a wildfire risk and wildfire spread simulation service. The above two applications are delivered within a web-based interactive platform to fire management agencies as Software as a Service (SaaS)[33]. GeoSearch is a distributed search engine that leverages a series of existing standards, technologies and geospatial cyber infrastructure components to narrow the gap between users and geospatial resource providers/publishers; in addition, it hides the complexity of GCIs[6]. Grid Services for Earth Observation Image Data Processing has been proposed to cater to future Earth observation application requirements for the digital Earth. It provides the capability of addressing application requirements, such as real-time monitoring, time series data processing and processing with user-required characteristics, to meet the requirements of end user applications[34]. Geopot is a cloud-based geolocation data service for mobile applications[35].

Various cloud computing systems for geospatial information have been established; however, numerous problems must be solved, especially in the geological domain.

For instance, in term of spatial data discovery and management, most current systems discover and manage spatial data using its metadata. A centralized repository of metadata with distributed data sources provides extremely fast search results to the user[36]; however, this remains a centralized way of managing the metadata in a distributed environment. In term of spatial data processing, some intermediate result data cannot be discovered by users because this type of data represents a temporary result, which cannot be registered in the system. However, this type of data is sometimes valuable. To address these problems, we designed a p2p node manager and include it in the cloud system to provide resource discovery and management, thereby making each node in the cloud system absolutely independent and distributed. In addition, the p2p node manager creates the concepts of perpetual resources and temporary data resources to manage, register and reuse the valuable intermediate results. In this paper, we propose a readily available, integrated data and service working environment that is based on a cloud computing architecture, the geological survey information cloud-computing platform (GSICCP), to share geological spatial information and geological spatial analysis models. In this environment, the geological ontology theory is imported and used to describe, organize and manage the heterogeneous geological data. Each node in the system remains independent, but the heterogeneous data, services and computing resources on different nodes were integrated and logically shared. The users assembled specified nodes using virtual organization to obtain the on-demand services. Additionally, a node management component based on a P2P pattern was adopted to organize and manage the data, services and computing resources on each node. The remaining sections of the paper are structured as follows. Section 2 proposes a cloud platform architecture for sharing geological information and services. Section 3 introduces a description, organization and management strategy for the heterogeneous geological data. In Section 4, a cloud service workflow and a P2P strategy are proposed to provide users with a transparent service environment. Section 5 introduces some the related performance test results and use cases of geological cloud platform. The prospects for the geological cloud platform are discussed in Section 6.

HIERARCHICAL ARCHITECTURE OF THE GSICCP

Using the Chinese geological ontology description, adopting the P2P architecture, taking the Geographic Information System as the principal source, focusing on resource agglomeration, and employing a cloud concept strategy, we designed a distributed geological survey information cloud-computing platform and organized the hardware, software and data resources by building a resource aggregation standard and protocol on this platform (Fig 1).

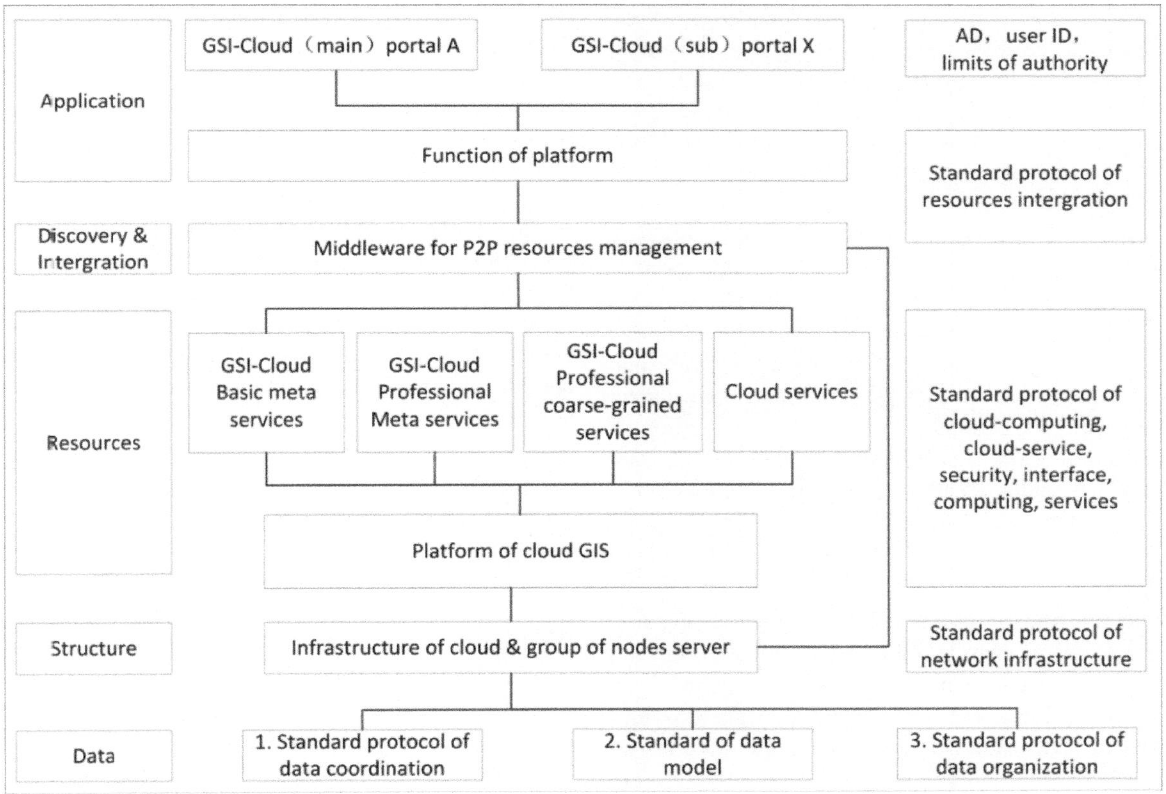

Figure 1. Hierarchical architecture of the geological survey information cloud-computing platform.

According to Fig 1, the GSICCP is divided into the following layers: data, fabric, resources, discovery and integration, application and representation in the vertical direction. The cloud platform architecture is built on multiple compulsive standards that attempt to eliminate an existing resource islet and prevent a new resource islet from appearing. The following are the contents of each layer:

- Data layer: This layer consists of multi-level standard-based databases and is responsible for the integration of multi-source, multi-scale and multi-temporal geological data, including graphical data or data that is organized according to non-standard database models, databases built using multi-period data models, databases organized according to a large databases, or thematic databases organized according to a data warehouse technology. In this layer, we adopt a geological domain ontology theory as the foundation for unified organization, semantics sharing, discovery and integration to build a universal description and organization model for the geological spatial feature data in a distributed environment and to provide a framework for geological data service inter-operation.

- Fabric layer: Grid nodes form the foundation of the GSICCP. This layer connects the infrastructure and node server groups of each professional unit and integrates the hardware and software resources according to the network. The hardware resources primarily include multi-level servers, personal computers, mobile phones and location terminals. The software resources primarily include the operating systems, such as Windows, Linux, Unix, and Aix; the development frameworks, such as.Net; and the GIS platforms such as MapGIS, ArcGIS, and SuperMap. The GSICCP combines a dedicated network and the Internet and employs various security strategies, such as a software firewall, a hardware firewall and other internet security technologies, to build the net system.
- Resources layer: This layer is the foundation of the GSICCP. It consists of pivotal modules, including the GSI-CLOUD resource integration middleware, the GSI-CLOUD meta service libraries for different granularities and functions, the GSI-CLOUD workflow service middleware, and the GSI-CLOUD service engine middleware.
- Discovery and integration layer: This layer is the core module of the GSICCP. The purpose of this layer is to provide a node management method that combines the distributed resources in the cloud environment and universally describe the hardware, software and data resources. In this layer, P2P node management middleware is adopted to implement resource organization and management. This middleware primarily includes a virtual node resource integrator, a cloud node meta service library, a virtual node portal configurator and a temp data resource integration container.
- Application and representation layer: this layer consists of a geological survey information cloud portal and relevant coarse-granularity service modules. The GSICCP achieves the basic functions and provides the basic architecture and public cloud in terms of resource sharing and cooperation (as a public cloud). In this layer, different requirements and professional applications can be deployed on the platform in the form of a service. The users only need to pay attention to their own business process and functions (as a private cloud) without paying attention to how the resources share and cooperate.

ORGANIZATION AND MANAGEMENT OF THE GEOLOGICAL DATA

Geological Ontology

Building a geological data model is the foundation for multi-source, multi-scale, heterogeneous geological spatial data integrated organization and management. The model describes the data content, structure, behavior and semantics to assist in forming a common comprehension. The existing data models or modeling methods emphasize the project requirements and are accompanied by personal database technology limitations. Therefore, this suggests that geological modeling lacks a consistent description of the data and data relationship, the semantic restraint rules related to the formal description, and the data content, structure, behavior and semantics that are governed by the data model. Thus, the abovementioned problems influence the shared understanding of geological scientific data and limit the ability to design a basic data model using various data structures.

The ontology is concerned with a conceptual structure of the methods that we use to describe the world[37,38]. It is an explicit specification of a sharing conceptualization, which is used in an integration task to describe the semantics of information sources and to make the contents explicit. Additionally, it is used to identify and associate the semantically corresponding information concepts[39]. In recent years, the ontology concept has been used in the information domain to solve problems related to knowledge concept expression, knowledge organization structure, knowledge sharing and semantic consistency. These problems play a pivotal role in supporting information reuse, sharing and exchange. Therefore, geological ontology research is important. Geological ontology provides a foundation for geological professional and application standards. Therefore, it is the guiding model for the entire geological data model. Additionally, it is the basis for integrated geological data description, organization and discovery and for achieving inter-operation between different systems, geological ontology supplies, geological knowledge ontology and knowledge mining services for professionals and non-professionals.

Geological ontology research builds the description of objects and relationship between objects in geological domain. The framework of the geological ontology consists of a domain outline table, a basis category table, a main table (a detail table) and a redistribution table (a typical class). The domain outline table consists of the primary categories of the geological ontology classification, and it defines the basis subject category and the arranging sequence. The basis category table consists of the basis broad heading and the second and the third categories. Therefore, it is the classification category framework that helps users understand the general classification situation. The main table is a list that contains various categories. It is the principal part of the ontology, and it is the basis of the classification index. The redistribution table uses the existing common geology categories as a typical class to describe and adopt the assembled technology. The redistribution table uses a simple category number that expresses a simple theme concept, constructs a composite category number according to certain rules, and expresses a complicated concept, which is in the classified table.

Geological Spatial Data Organization and Management

Using the geological ontology theory and the spatial data concept model, geological map data and tile pyramid data models were adopted to organize the geological spatial data in the GSICCP; furthermore, the MapGIS platform was employed to manage the geological data. The MapGIS platform adopts a service-oriented architecture (SOA) and a multi-level structure, and determines the spatial content and its relationship-oriented data organization. Furthermore, it facilitates the effective storage and indexing of the massive spatial data. Therefore, the MapGIS platform supports a distributed spatial data calculation in local and wide area networking environments. To integrate the heterogeneous data from other GIS platforms, such as ArcGIS, SuperMap and GeoStar, the middleware technology was employed to help share the multi-source data on the GSICCP.

The geologic logical data model was built according to the geological survey requirements and an existing data modeling method using the geographic information application model rules (ISO 19109), the geographic spatial application model (ISO 19107), the feature description framework, UML, and the relational database normalization theory. Fig 2 shows the geological spatial data model framework. This framework is a specialized standard for the geological map data model that uses the specialized standard application model rules; additionally, it can be transformed into a multi-scale geological map data model.

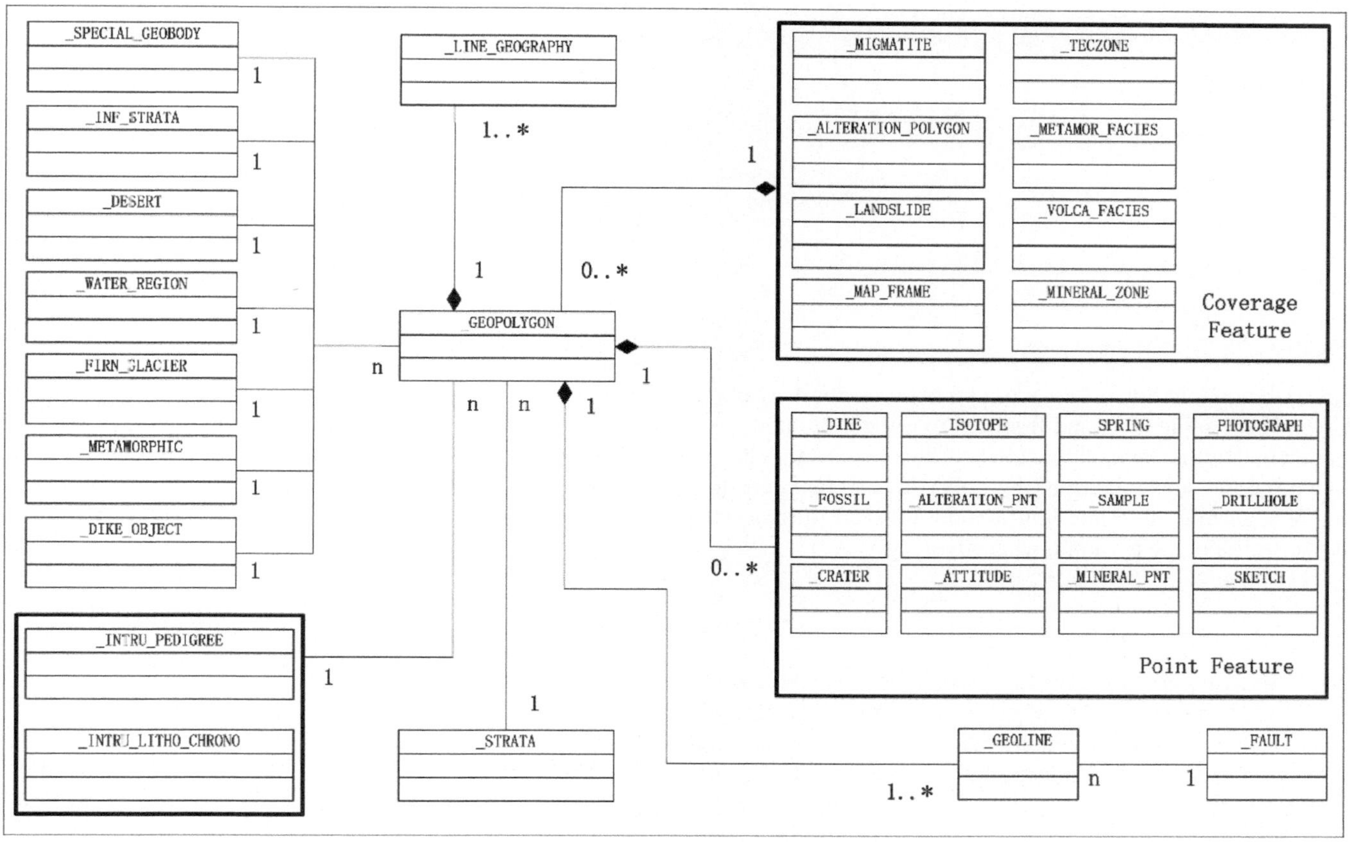

Figure 2. Data model framework of the geologic map.

In the grid stream geological map data service, the tile pyramid model was adopted to organize the multi-scale geological map. As shown in Fig 3, the top pyramid layer in rank 0 shows the original geological map panorama. The tiles in rank 1 are divided according to the rank 0 tile in the 2×2 form and used to generate four tiles in a sequence. The tiles in rank n are divided according to the rank n-1 tile in the 2×2 form. Thus, it is easy to calculate the number of tiles in the L rank according to the following expression:

$$n = \sum_{i=0}^{L-1} 2^i \times 2^i \qquad (L > 0) \tag{1}$$

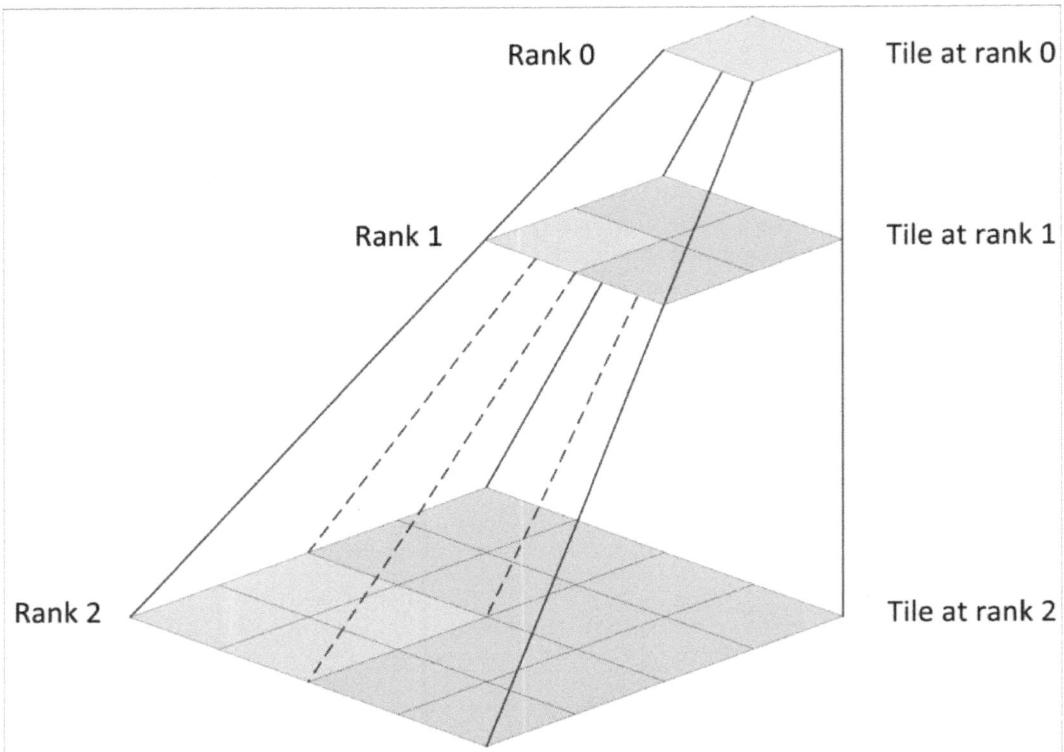

Figure3. Tile pyramid data model.

As shown in Fig 4, the serial number of each tile (from the highest layer at rank 0 to the lowest layer at rank n, from bottom to top in the same layer and from left to right in the same row) increases by a degree, and each serial number corresponds to the table number displayed to the client. The indexing for each tile is completed using a quadtree. The quadtree traverses each node in a top-down approach (rank-by-rank). In each rank, the quadtree traverses the node from left to right. Thus, as shown in Fig 5, the first, second, third and fourth node from left to right in each rank corresponds to the bottom left, bottom right, top left, and top right tile in the pyramid, respectively.

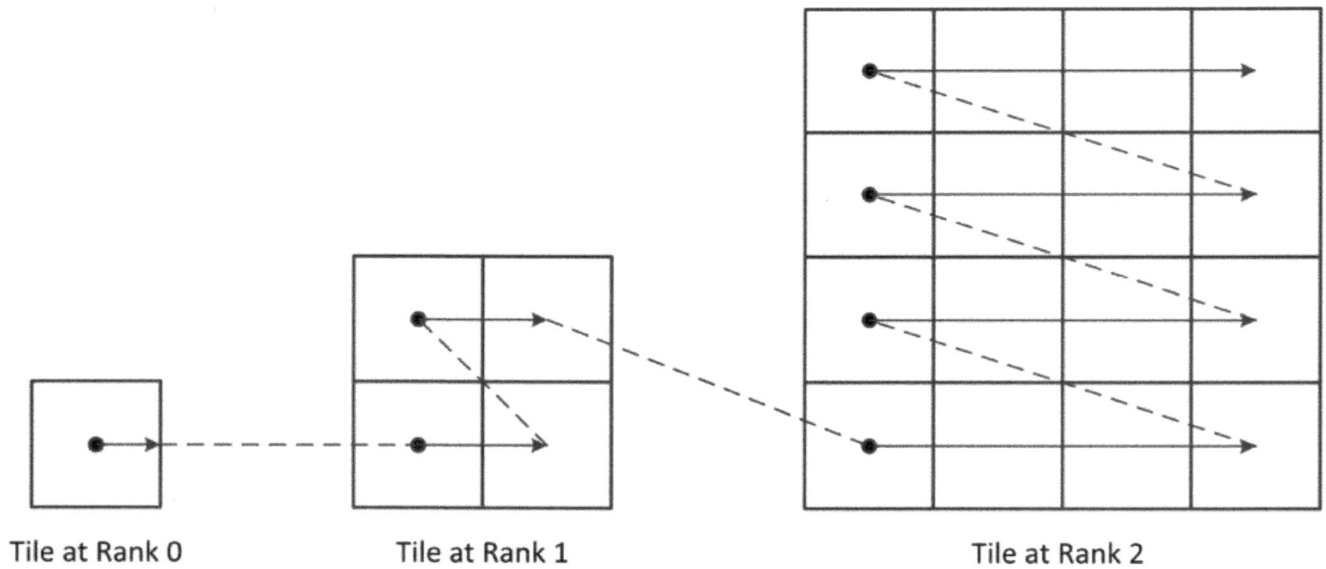

Figure 4. Numbering method for each tile.

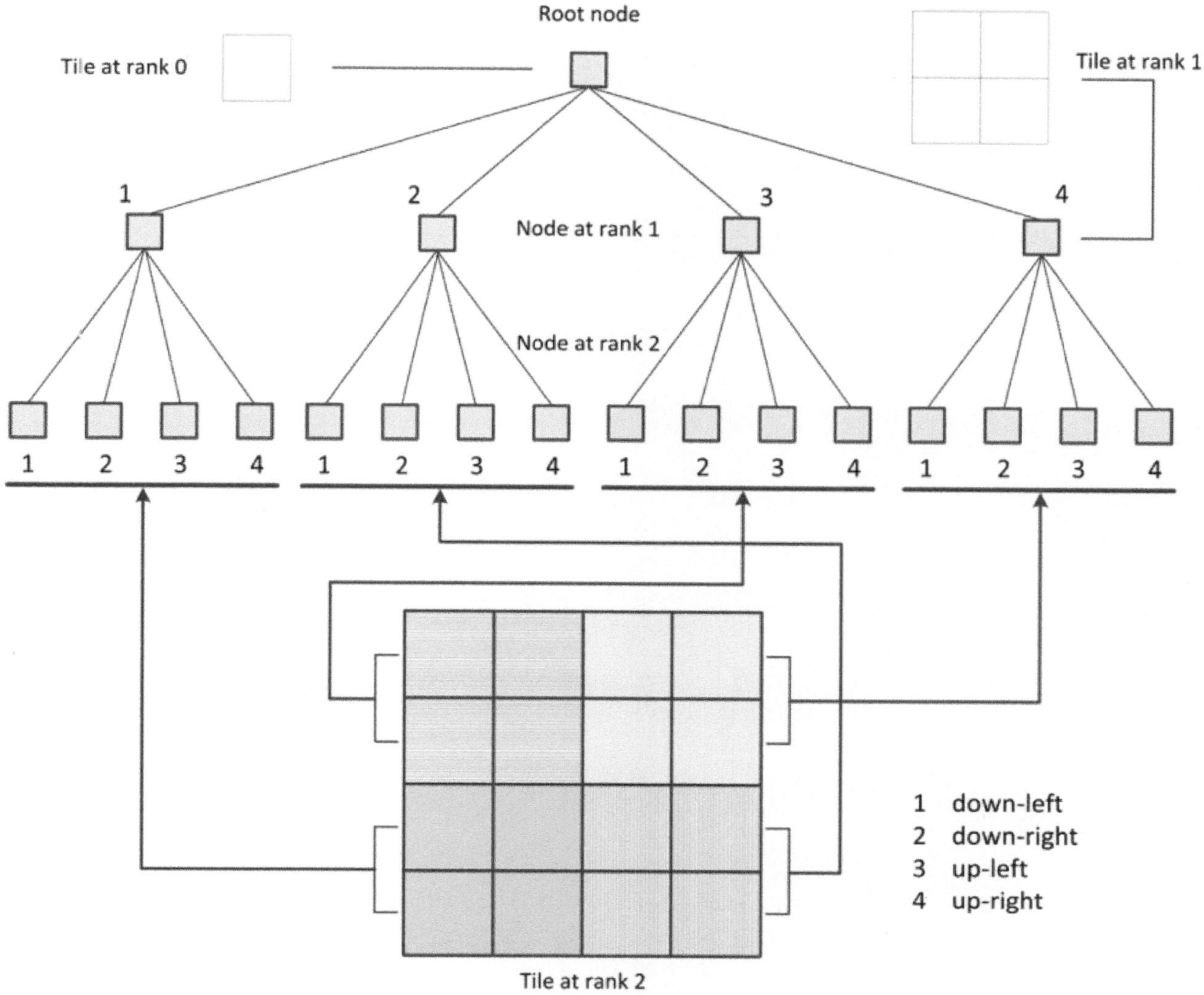

Figure 5. Corresponding relationship between the tile number and the quadtree node.

Workflow and P2P Node Management Mechanism

Hybrid Framework of the GSICCP

The GSICCP is based on the cloud GIS platform, which completes the platform architecture by combining a P2P node management mechanism with the cloud GIS middleware. The cloud application development framework publishes functions to users in the Cloud Service forms and thus provides a customized rapid development process for users. The GSICCP develops a hybrid framework (Fig 6) that integrates the IMS and Cloud GIS WRSF Services based on the WSRF. Furthermore, it provides the GSICCP with an ability to be deployed and run on heterogeneous operating systems such as Windows, Linux and Unix. Additionally, it supports different data formats such as local spatial data formats (e.g., MapGIS HDF) and spatial database formats based on large commercial databases (e.g., Oracle 10g/11g, IBM DB2). In the foundation of the cross-platform GIS C/C++ kernel, the GSICCP packages the low-level GIS functions by adopting JNI technology. Then, the GSICCP publishes the low-level GIS functions as a meta function service in the forms of SOAP and REST and provides a traditional service API and a non-status service API to a higher level of the framework. The open stack is used to package the API, which was provided by the meta function service layer, and generates a series of cloud GIS function components such as the cloud root directory and domain object management, distributed spatial calculating, cloud workflow and user security management components. Based on these cloud function components, the Cloud Application Development Framework is formed. All of the underlying functions are published to the upper layer by the cloud service, thereby allowing users to rapidly customize and develop their own applications in the portal layer using rich client development technologies such as JavaScript and Flex.

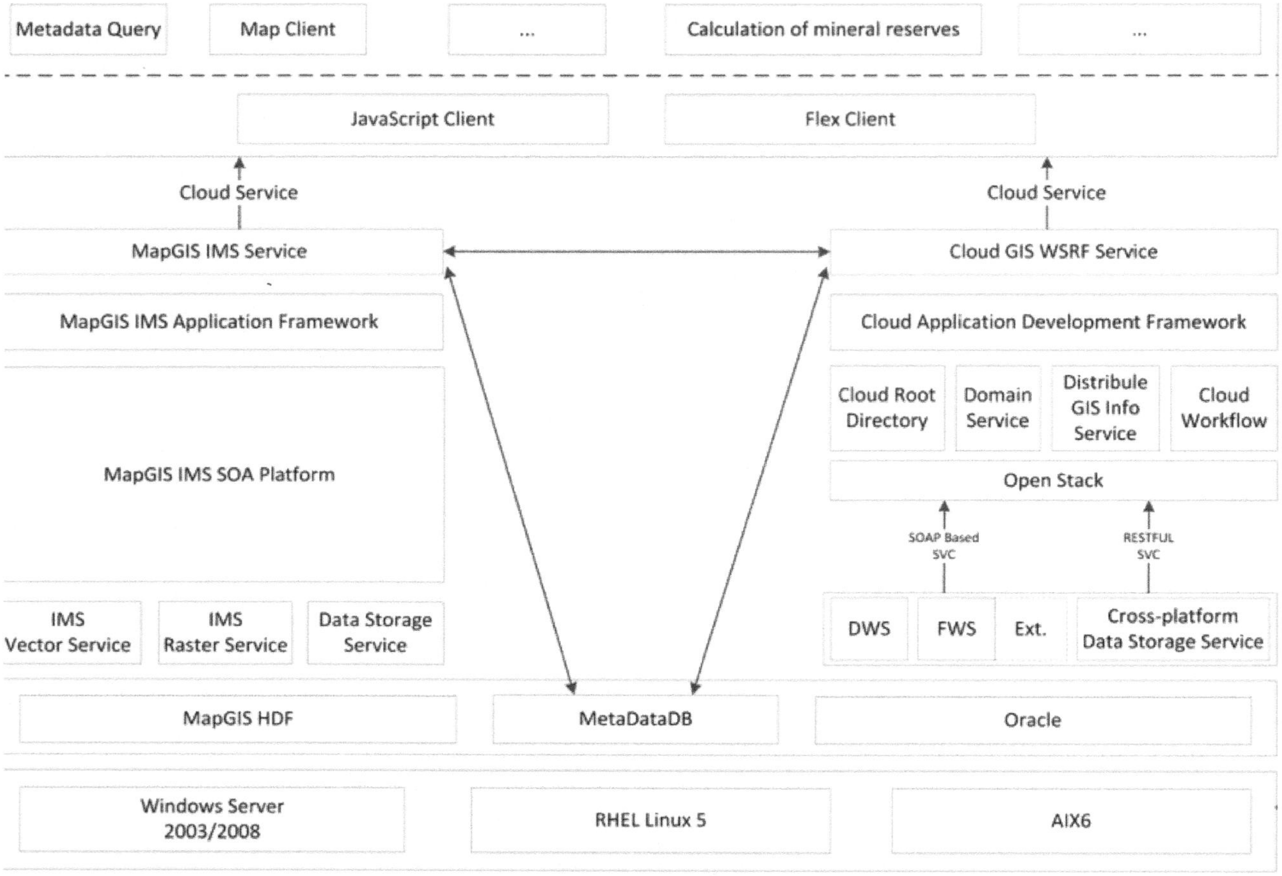

Figure 6. Hybrid framework of the geological survey information cloud-computing platform.

The GSICCP adopts the domain-based business integrated approach, retrieves the eligible resource nodes according to the root directory manager component, builds the dynamic virtual organization in the cloud environment, saves the domain-related information (e.g., domain manager node ID, domain ID, domain node information description, and domain service description), creates the domain resource directory and registers the domain objects on the global domain directory management node. When domain objects are modified, the manager and the global directory service nodes are joined to determine the modified information. If a node in this virtual organization fails to function, the global domain management service generates a new domain management node for this virtual organization.

This type of hybrid integrated architecture maintains the original system stability and intentionally imports the cloud GIS function component, which improves the efficiency and maintainability of each node.

Cloud Service Workflow

In the GSICCP, the Geospatial Cloud Service Workflow System is adopted to promote geospatial information processing from a desktop to a cloud environment. According to the Geospatial Cloud Service Workflow System, various spatial and non-spatial information services are assembled on demand. Thus, the blending of traditional and cloud GIS services is achieved. Using the geospatial cloud service workflow management component, the users conveniently choose multiple geospatial information resources. This provides an important technological guarantee for integrating and sharing geospatial information.

The geospatial information cloud service workflow engine (GICSWE) is the core of the cloud GIS business process management. The GICSWE, according to the business description file parser and workflow execution monitor, controls and manages the GIS service flow data, execution status, flow execution result and the GICSWE architecture, as shown in Fig 7. Considering features of business flow, the global parser and a task processing manager of the GIS workflow were deployed on the same node. The task executer was deployed on another work node to form a distributed architecture. In the client, the users build a model by choosing the proper business flow units from the workflow model library. Then, these units form and generate a service flow description file. The description file will be submitted to a workflow execution manager that has a light load on one cloud node to parse the file globally and to distribute tasks to several nodes. The workflow execution manager will interact with a distributed cloud GIS service executer in real time. The P2P messaging mechanism is utilized to synchronize the execution statuses and results of the workflow between the workflow execution manager and the distributed cloud service executer.

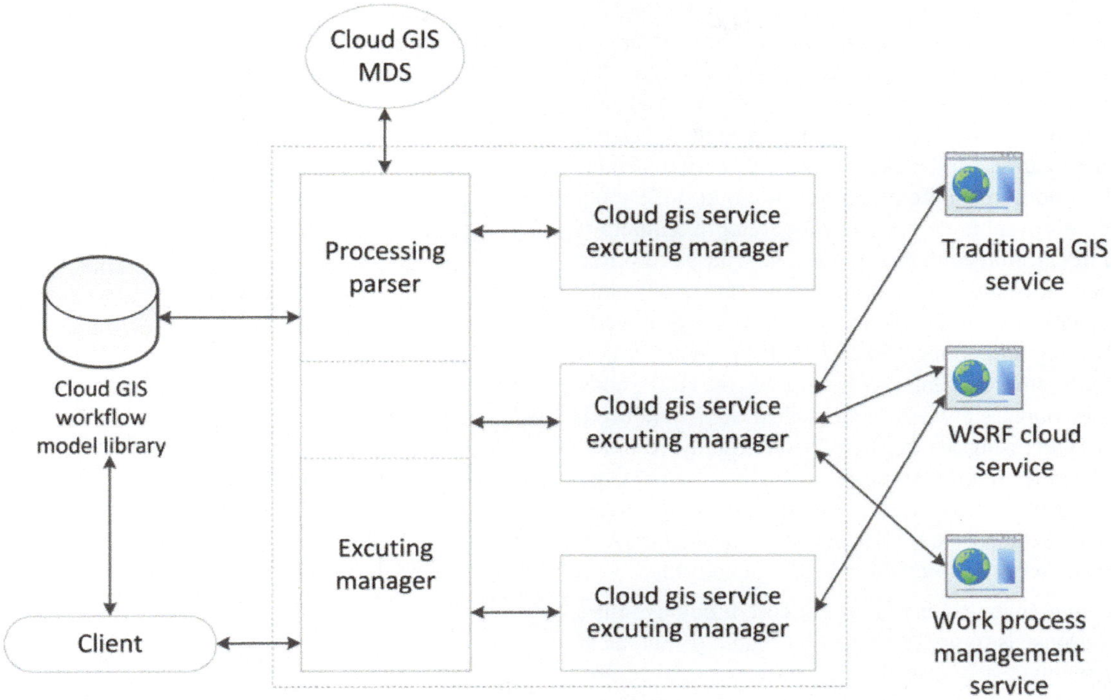

Figure 7. Distributed workflow engine deployment architecture.

P2P Node Manager Mechanism

The P2P node manager (Fig 8) is the middleware of the GSICCP. This middleware is required to provide a service environment that maintains the autonomy of each node without changing the original environment (e.g., operating system, network protocol, or network service). Additionally, the P2P node manager ensures the users' and nodes' security. The lower level data information, hardware information and software information will be shielded by the P2P node manager. Thus, the users will be in fully transparent computing or servicing environments.

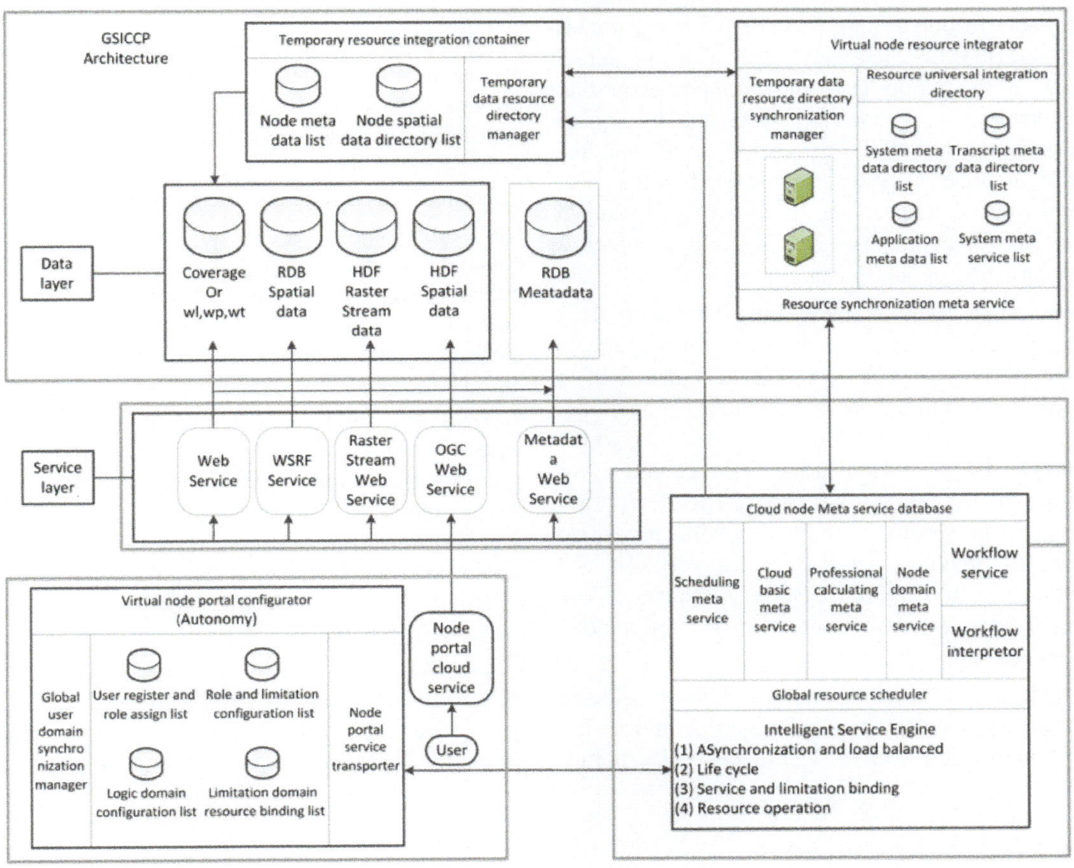

Figure 8. Architecture of the P2P node manager.

In the GSICCP architecture, a node does not represent different servers. The node is a group that consists of servers and personal computers. The nodes are distributed over the entire environment, and they can be physically or logically divided. To provide the features of geological spatial information applications and services, the P2P node manager adopts a virtual node resource integrator, a cloud node meta service library, a virtual node portal configurator, a temporary data resource integration container and an SOA-based resource integration model standard. Additionally, the P2P node manager provides the description, organization, discovery, integration, sharing and cooperation for distributed resources. In the GSICCP environment, according to the P2P node manager, the resource statuses are described and monitored, and all services and resources are shared; additionally, resource efficiency and service quality are improved. On a virtual node, a coarse-granularity meta service is not divided into several fine-granularity meta services. Rather, it is arranged on a suitable machine to run in-line with a loading condition.

The P2P node manager is one of the core modules in the GSICCP. Its purpose is to organize the distributed resources in the cloud and to universally describe the hardware, software and data resources. The node structure is not of a centralized form. By considering the autonomy, sharing and coordination of each node, the environment resources are divided into regional and global resources. The regional resource is managed by each node. The global resource is shared and managed by all cloud platform resources that require synchronization mechanism support. Additionally, the P2P node manager supports the long-lived transaction during the cloud computing process and cloud serving. The function of each component of the P2P node manager is described in the following:

- Virtual node resource integrator: This integrator is used to describe, organize and manage the perpetual resources in the cloud environment and, according to the synchronism, synchronously update the global resources on each node. The virtual node resource integrator includes a system metadata directory list, an application metadata list, a transcript metadata directory, a system meta service list and a universal resource directory synchronism manager.
- Temporary data resource integration container: This container is used to manage the new data resources generated by the service layer. The new data are an intermediate result that is generated during processing. The data will be transformed into perpetual data, which are managed by the virtual node resource integrator according to the synchronization. The temporary data resource integration container consists of a node metadata list, a node spatial data directory list and a temporary data resource directory manager. The contents of each list are the same as in the virtual node resource integrator.
- Cloud node meta service library: This library is used to build a service layer, manage a service and assign an online hardware resource. The meta service library on each node includes 1) a meta service and a meta-computing library, 2) a workflow interpreter, 3) a global resource scheduler, and 4) an intelligent service engine.
- Virtual node portal configurator: This configurator is used to provide a service entrance for users by connecting the users and service layer. The virtual node portal configurator consists of a user register and role assigning list, a role and limitation configuration list, a logical domain configuration list, a limitation and resource binding list, a global user domain synchronization manager and a node portal service transporter.

Distributed Node Portal

The distributed node portal is an exemplification of the P2P pattern and facilitates resource collaboration and sharing between local and other remote nodes. Resource publishing on a local node demonstrates the autonomy of each node. The sharing and collaboration of resources are implemented by sharing the global resources and synchronization of the platform function resources. Each node in the GSICCP belongs to an independent application domain, which includes a main portal for a local node; in addition, the node visits the sub-portal on another node according to this main portal. The distributed node portals follow a decentralized model.

In the node synchronization structure, the node portal only needs to manage the resources on a local node. After finishing the registering of resources, logging out or updating locally, the related message will be pushed into a local message queue. The node portal synchronization manager will receive the registering, logging out or updating message from the message records and will then send the resource information to other nodes according to a related web service. The portal synchronization manager adopts the message mechanism to provide resource registering, logging out, updating, publishing and discovery between different nodes. Each node maintains a message queue. This message queue is different from a traditional message queue such as MSMQ (Microsoft Message Queue). In the MSMQ, the sender packages the content into a container to form a message and then places the message into a public message queue. Then, the node on a local or on a remote node receives the message that is sent to it from the public message queue and processes the message. In the GSICCP, the message queue operation is restricted on a local node; a message does not need to be sent to other nodes. The resource registering, logging out, updating, publishing and discovery operations are completed by invoking related web services on the other nodes. Fig 9 shows the node portal resource synchronism. The resource synchronization is performed between the nodes. For example, there are several nodes in the GSICCP. If new resources are registered on one of the nodes in the GSICCP, the node portal synchronization manager will invoke the metadata service or publish a service on a local node to obtain the content of the resource. Then, this node will invoke the related updating web services that are deployed on the remote node to accomplish the metadata upload.

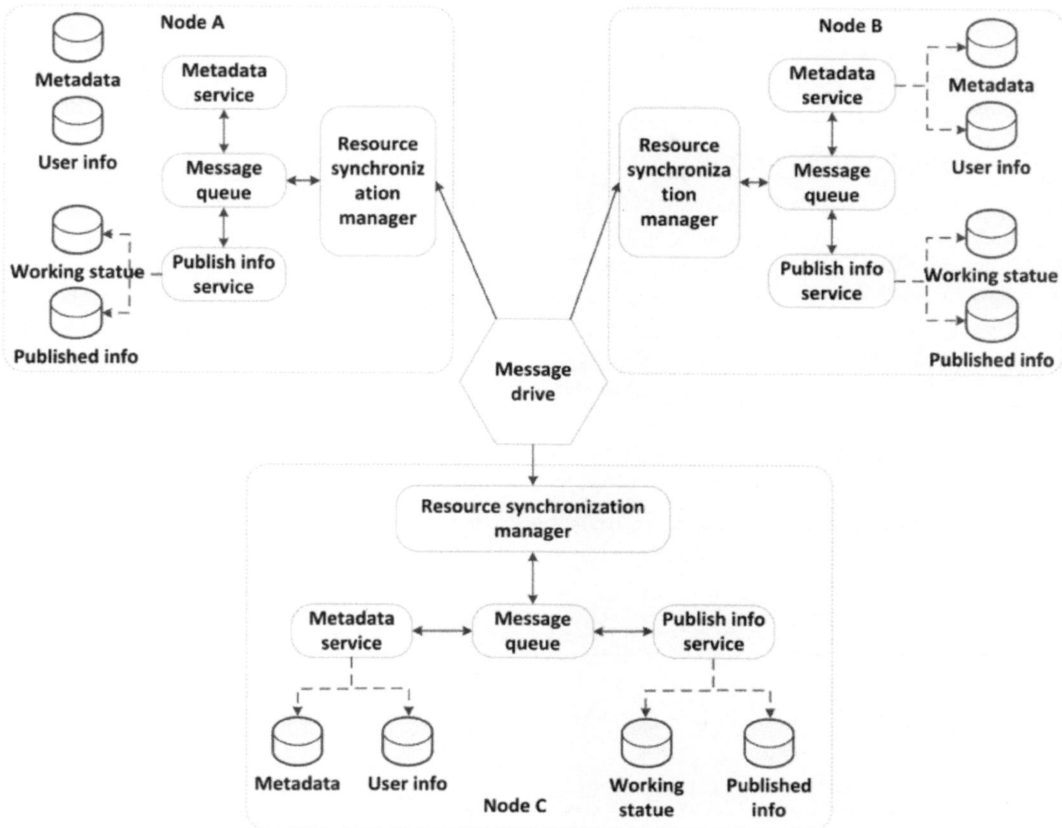

Figure 9. Resource synchronism of the node portal.

Each node operates and manages the data by utilizing data management tools. According to the design, each node in the GSICCP deploys the same metadata service, synchronization tools, meta database and node portal flow resource synchronism, as shown in Fig 10. The portal is one of the most important components of the GSICCP. The portal usually integrates security managing, authorization managing, node resources monitoring, and charging functions. A portal in the GSICCP is different from a routine portal because in the GSICCP, each node portal is P2P instead of being centralized.

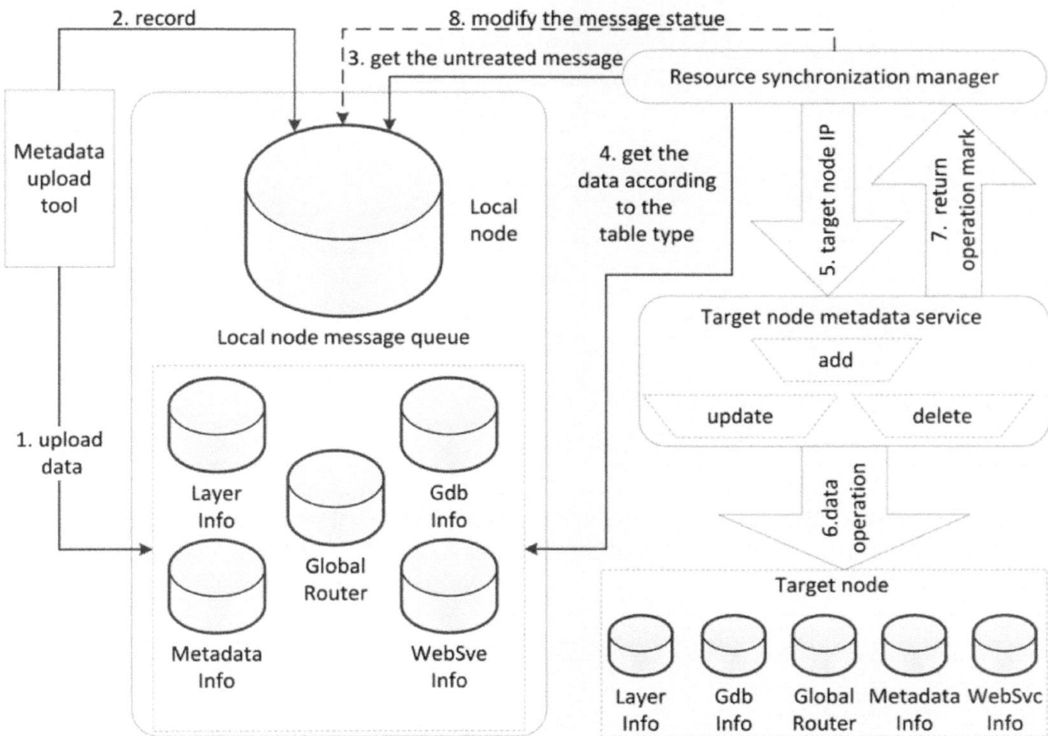

Figure 10. Resource synchronization process.

EXPERIMENTS

Use Case

Multi-mode Geological Data Service

Based on the GSICCP architecture, the nationwide geological data are deployed on different nodes. The computing, data and software resources are virtualized into a logical integrated domain that caters to different user groups. The platform provides multi-level services (http://www.gsigrid.cgs.gov.cn/) such as the geological metadata service; the geological grid stream service; the multi-node, multi-source geological data integrated service; and the geological data visualization in 3D service. Users request these services according to the web service without knowing the data source and data distribution. Then, the users obtain a seamlessly integrated view on a web browser. Some of the most important use cases are discussed below:

(1) Geological metadata service: This service provides the data resource discovery service based on metadata. The metadata system discovery mechanism primarily seeks out the servers that store the data by retrieving the information, querying the metadata and metadata catalog tables, and finally processing the queried data (Fig 11).

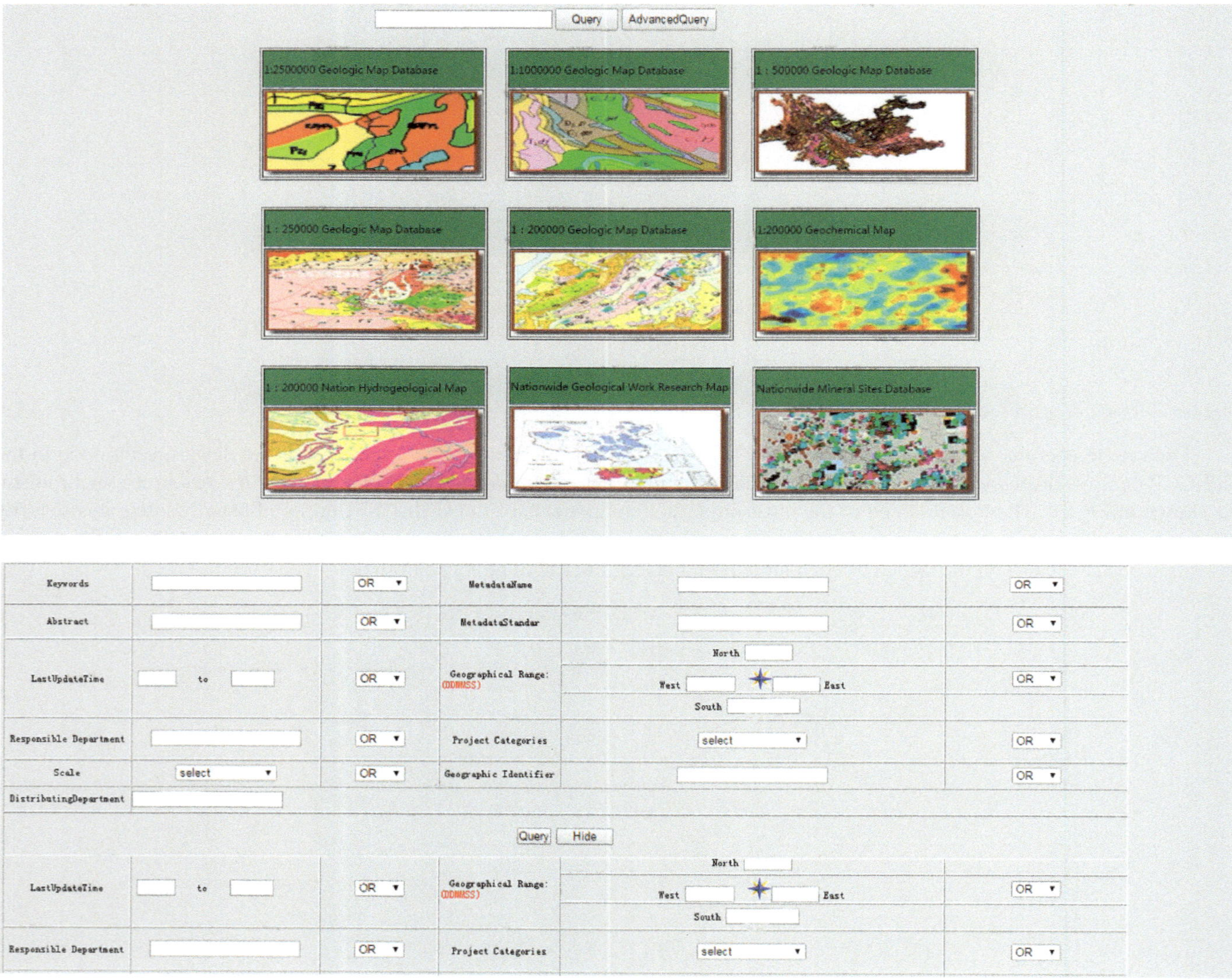

Figure 11. Multiple methods for metadata retrieval.

(2) Geological grid stream service: This service facilitates the transformation, organization and publication of a multi-scale distributed geological map in an image format. A user obtains a service that provides information ranging from a coarse to fine granularity (Fig 12).

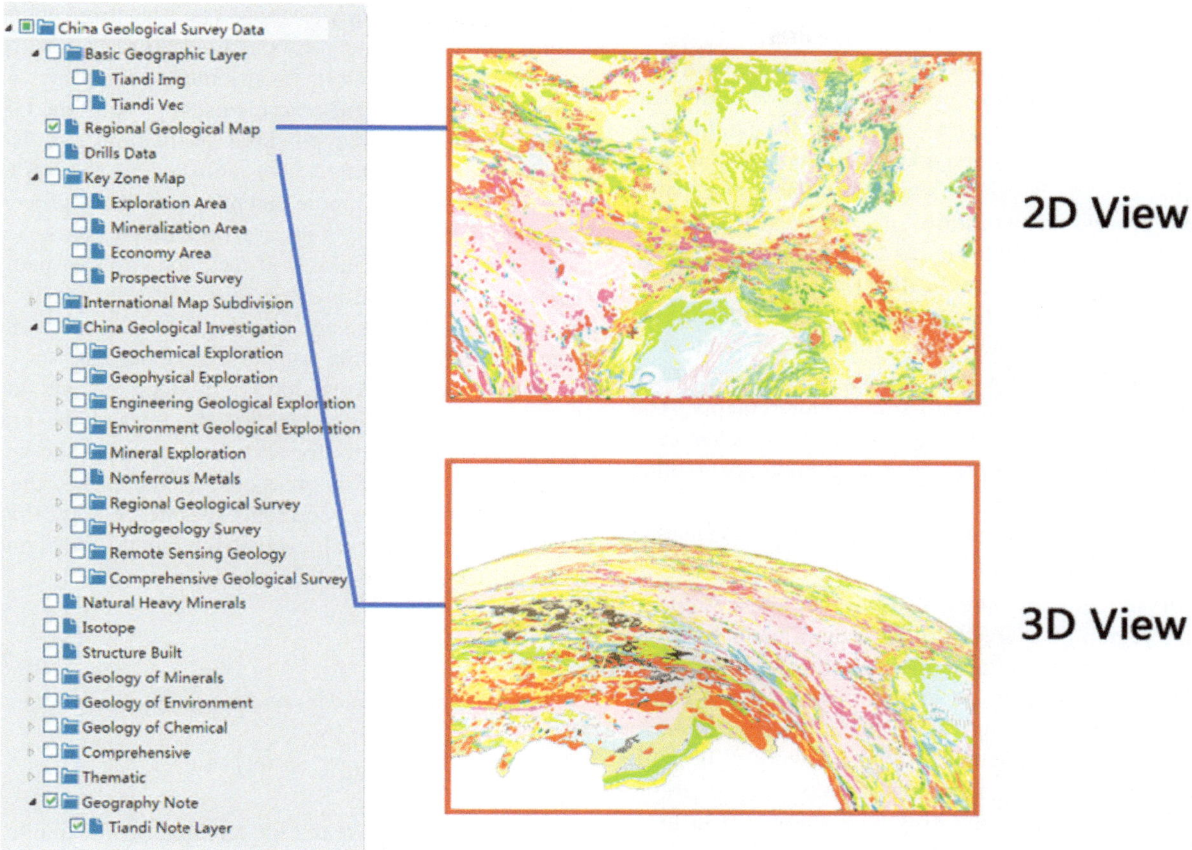

Figure 12. Distributed multi-source, multi-scale geological grid stream service.

(3) Multi-node, multi-source geological data integrated service: This service facilitates the discovery, retrieval and integration of thematic geological data from different nodes and sources. This service includes three types of retrieval methods: a spatial extent-based retrieval, metadata keyword-based retrieval, and web service-based retrieval method. The advantage of this service is that it integrates various types of information in one view. After selecting a target area, the data catalog related to the target area is retrieved from the meta database, and the data is presented in a vector map form (Fig 13).

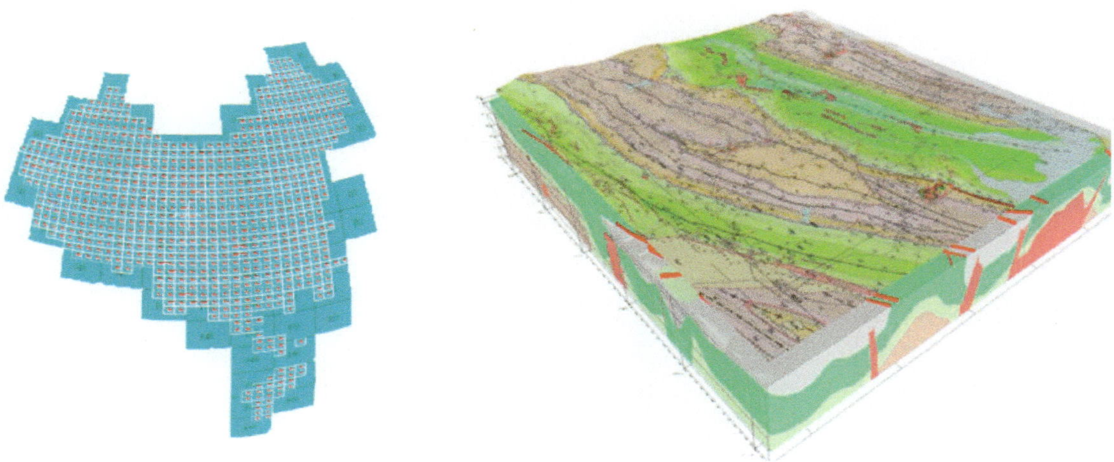

Figure 13. Geological integrated map service.

(4) Geological data visualization in 3D service: Using a 3D graphical interface, the service displays the geological data in a 3D form to users. The geological data are spread on a virtual 3D Earth model. When the display rank changes, the rank of the 3D image changes as well, and the users can rotate the 3D model to browse the geological data anywhere (Fig 12).

Geological Processing Service

The geological information processing service is complicated because it needs to establish the service flow based on a meta service. This service includes the definition, generation, storage, organization, execution management, and achievement of a spatial event and the management of a spatial information processing workflow. The meta services are assembled and invoked arbitrarily to form an execution flow and thus complete the spatial application task. According to the workflow and various middleware technologies, the service flow or a workflow that focuses on a different application or the thematic processing tasks can be packaged into the GSICCP to a certain problems or meet various requirements. The processing work is distributed on different nodes. When each node completes its work, the result of each node is compiled onto the starting node, which returns the final result to the user. Here, we introduce an iron mine resource potential evaluation service flow that is based on the GSICCP.

Mineral exploration aims to discover new mineral deposits in a region of interest[40], wherein mineral potential evaluation plays an important role, the results of mineral potential evaluations represent a significant reference for mineral exploration[4]. When using a traditional approach, the iron mine resource potential evaluation work is difficult because the geological data are distributed across various areas and departments, and multi-type geological data need to be collected, storing and analyzing the data also present a challenge[4,41]. Geo-spatial information technology is widely used in the mining industry, and it is beginning to move from traditional experience-based methods to quantitative analysis and automatic direction science-based methods[42]. However, there are limitations to evaluating the mineral potential only with the use of desktop or web-based geospatial information technology. For instance, one could not solve problems such as those resulting from incomplete information, data integration, information extraction and thematic mapping[43,44]. Distributed computing can be applied to help solve these problems[41]. Using the GSICCP, the iron mine resource potential evaluation task is easily accomplished. A workflow is established on the GSICCP to build the iron mine resource potential evaluation process. The data storage and computing are distributed across multiple nodes. Therefore, it is easy to process the vast geospatial data. The cloud GIS computing service process for the iron mine potential evaluation is shown in Fig 14. To address different seam forms, the volume calculating model can vary. There are three types of seam forms: monocline, syncline, and anticline. The volume calculating model and the graphical representation parameter for each form type are shown in Fig 15. In the following expressions, h represents the lower limit for prediction, M represents the ore geology thickness, and L represents the geological strike length. For monocline, the model for calculating the volume is

$$V = \frac{h}{\sin\alpha} \times M \times L \tag{2}$$

For syncline, the model for calculating the volume is

$$V = \left(\frac{h}{\sin\beta} \times L_1 + \frac{h}{\sin\alpha} \times L_2\right) \times M \tag{3}$$

For anticline, the model for calculating the volume is

$$V = V_2 - V_1 \tag{4}$$

$$V_1 = \frac{4}{3}\pi \times a \times b^2 \times \tan\alpha \tag{5}$$

$$V_2 = \frac{4}{3}\pi \times (a+M) \times (b+M) \times (b\tan\alpha + M) \tag{6}$$

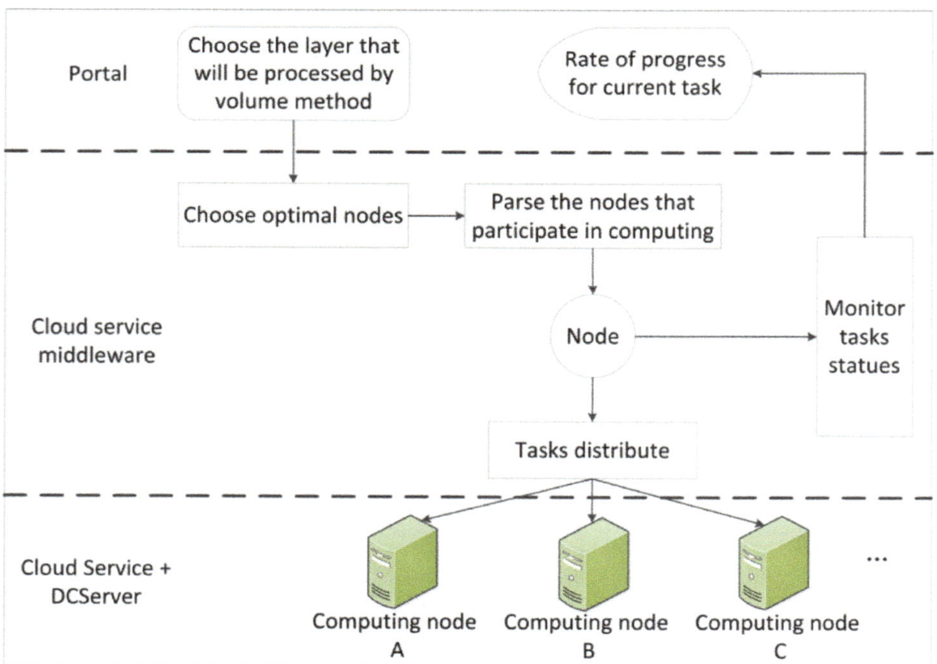

Figure 14. Process of GIS cloud-computing service for iron mine potential evaluation.

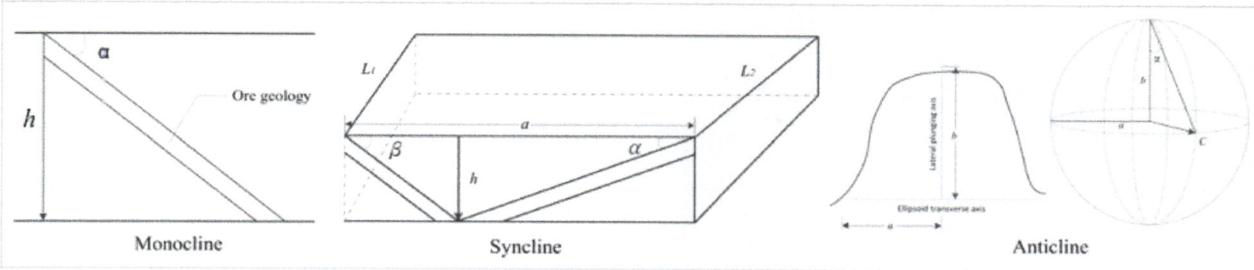

Figure 15. Graphical representation of the volume calculating parameter.

In this example, the data are multi-type, and the data volume is greater than 800 G, as illustrated by Table 1. The actual iron mine resource potential evaluation study, which uses the GSICCP, is shown in Fig 16. The workflow (Fig 17) of the iron mine resource potential evaluation is as follows: 1) choosing and integrating the multi-node data, 2) inputting the basis parameters, 3) calculating the predicted ore volume, 4) finding the target area using the evidence weight method, 5) calculating the volume, 6) summarizing the province data, 7) summarizing the area, 8) summarizing the nationwide data, and 9) outputting the results. After the evaluation process, the workflow is saved for reuse by the users or published as a service for the users.

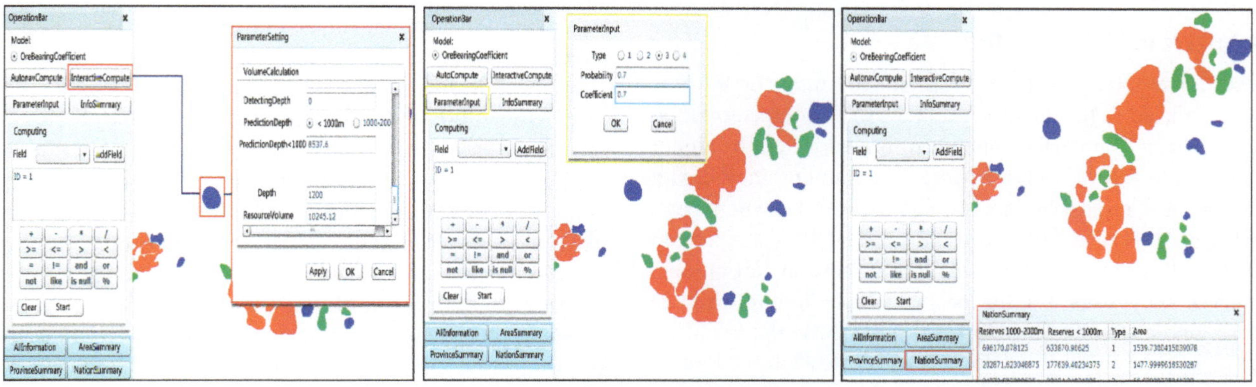

Figure 16. Iron mine potential evaluation on the GSICCP.

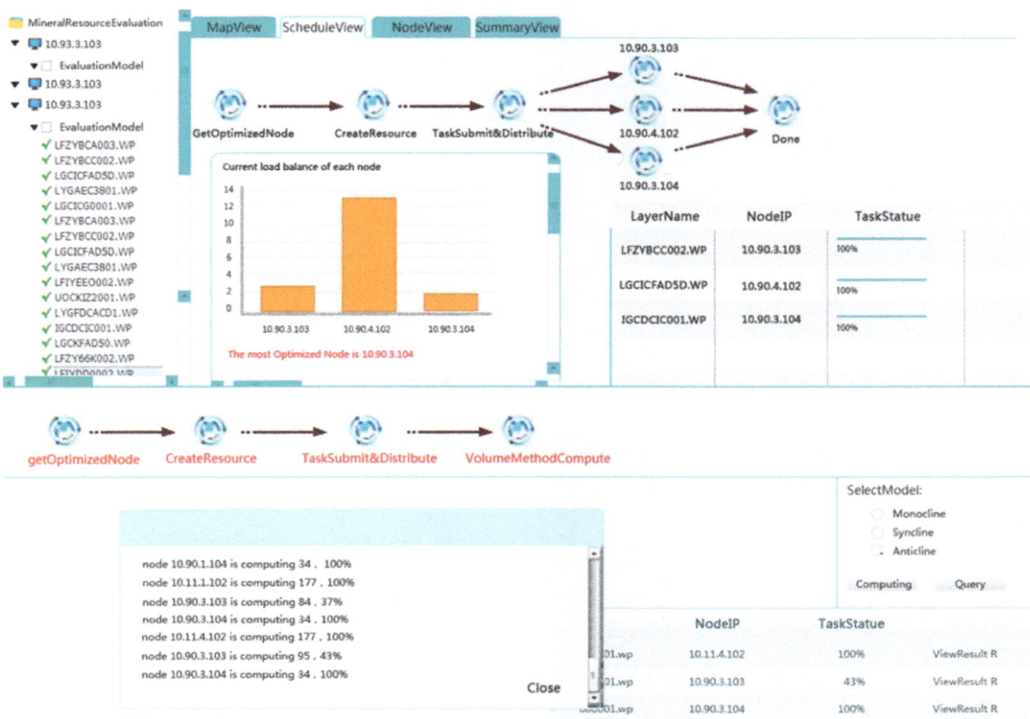

Figure 17. Iron mine potential evaluation workflow.

Table 1. Geological data used in the iron mine resource potential evaluation.

Num	Thematic Map	Classification of Thematic Map	Quantity	Amount
1	Thematic atlas for Metallogenic prediction	prediction result map	135	170
		upgrade of iron ore	35	170
2	Thematic atlas for metallogenic regularity	typical deposits of metallogenic elements	109	387
		typical deposit prediction elements	85	387
		workbench metallogenic elements	103	387
		workbench prediction elements	70	387
		provincial map	20	387
3	Thematic atlas for geological background	deeds material figure	76	160
		building structure diagram	39	160
		the predicted workspace metamorphic structure for construction	16	160
		the predicted workspace intrusion magma working map	14	160
		the predicted workspace deposit structure for construction	9	160
		the predicted workspace structure lithofacies paleogeographic map	4	160
Total	899 metadata			717

doi:10.1371/journal.pone.0145312.t001

Performance Test

Map Service Performance

Requests for a geologic vector map and tile map for Wuhan, China, were used to test the performance of the map service in GSICCP. During the performance test, the entire environment was deployed as follows: 1) Hardware environment: Includes an application server, database server and GIS server, where each server has 32 GB of RAM and 8 3.86 GHz CPUs, connected by a 1000 Mb network. However, due to certain limitations, each server only uses 1 CPU to participate in this test. 2) Software environment: The GSICCP portal was deployed on each application server, the database server utilized the Oracle database to store the spatial data, and MapGIS IGServer (a MapGIS software package for map service publication) was deployed on the GIS server to provide the related spatial information service.

During the map service performance test, different cluster environments and different concurrent numbers were designed to compare the response times. For the tile map test, four types of clusters were built The number of nodes in each cluster was 1, 2, 4, and 8, the concurrent request number in each cluster varies from 200 to 1600. When accessing the geologic tile map for Wuhan, the response time varied with the number of concurrent requests and the number of cluster nodes, the test results are provided in Fig 18 and Fig 19. For the geologic vector map test, five types of cluster were built. The number of nodes in each cluster was 1, 2, 4, 6, 8, and the concurrent request number in each cluster varied from 50 to 200. When accessing the geologic vector map for Wuhan in a geospatial box from 114.125602E to 114.500707E and from 30.453932N to 30.708764N, the response time also varied with the number of concurrent requests and the number of the cluster nodes. The test results are provided in Fig 20 and Fig 21.

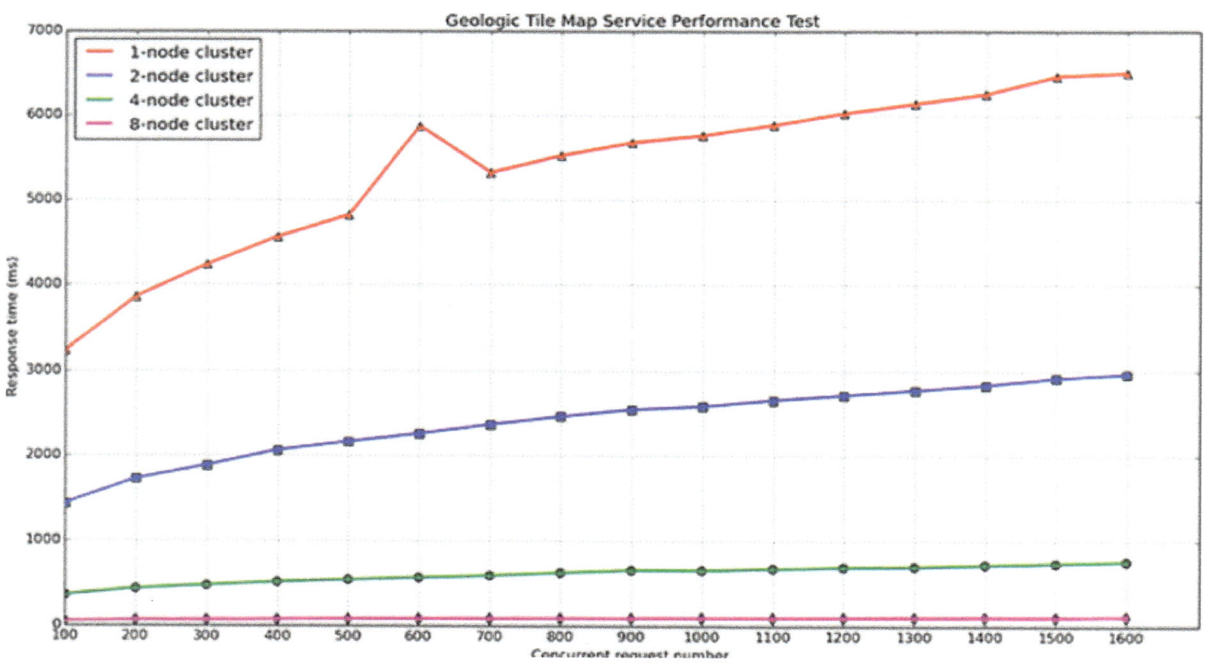

Figure 18. The geologic tile map service performance test results.

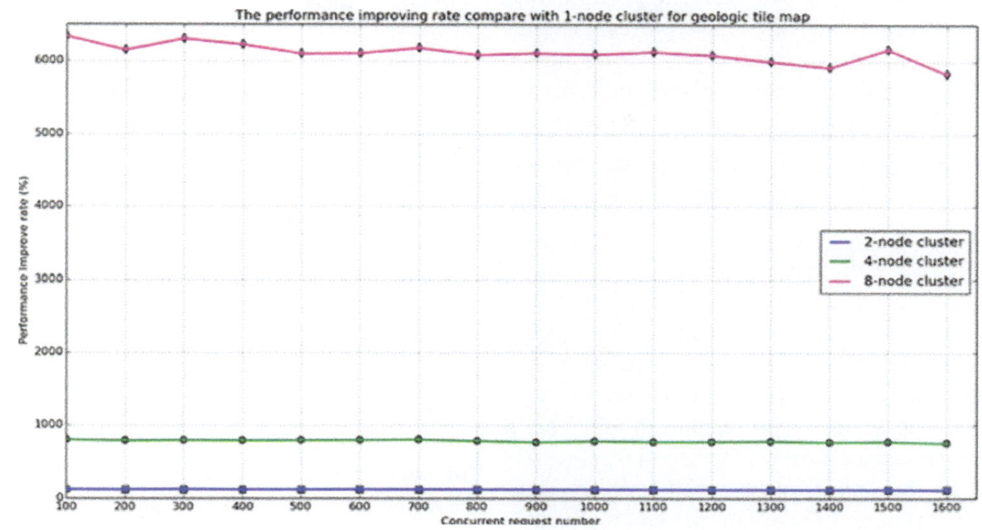

Figure 19. Performance improving rate of tile map service compared with 1-node cluster.

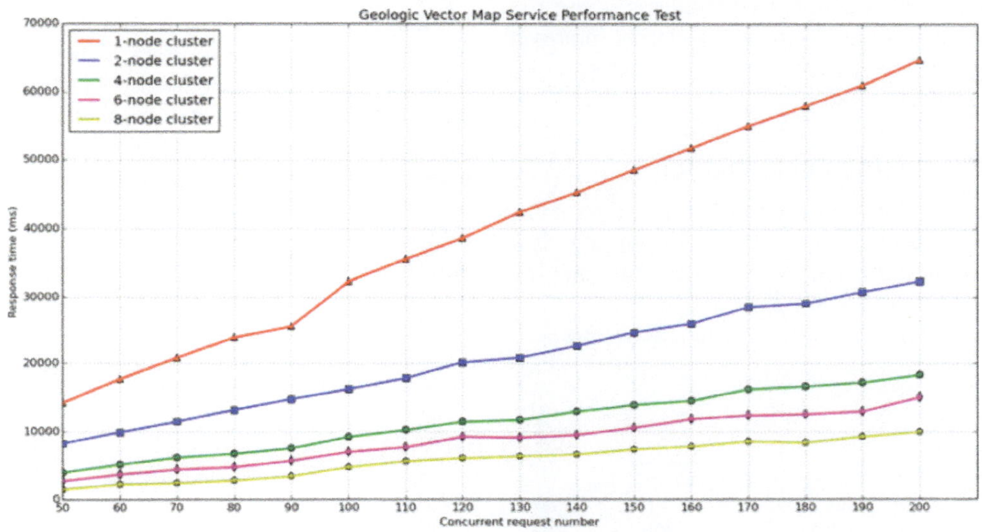

Figure 20. The geologic vector map service performance test results.

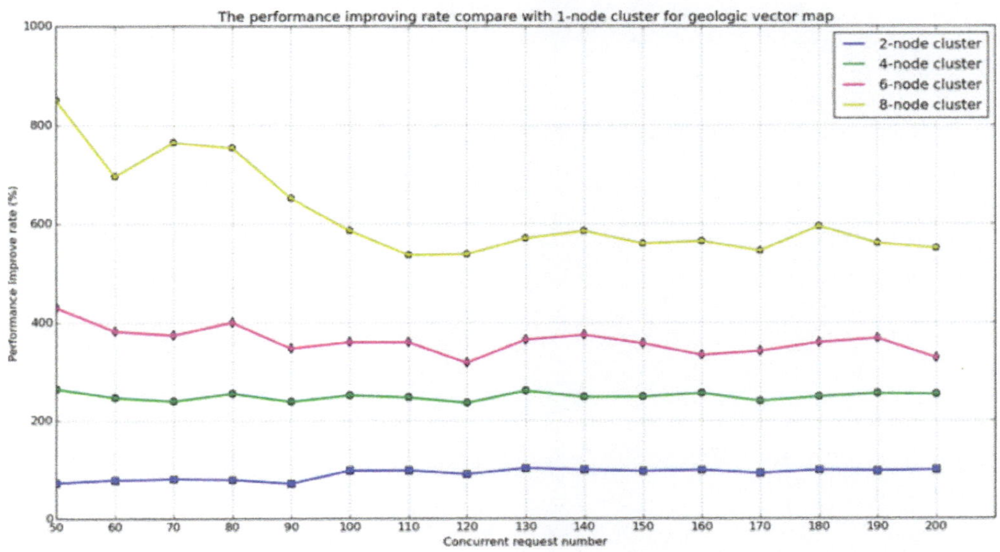

Figure 21. Performance improving rate of vector map service compared with 1-node cluster.

Theresponsetimeisusedtoevaluatetheclusterperformance, and the response time improving rate is used to evaluate the variation of the performance compared with a 1-node cluster. As shown in the following expression, $RTIR^n$ indicates the following: compared with a 1-node cluster, the response time improving rate of *n-node* cluster. RT_c^n represents the response time of an *n-node* cluster when the concurrent number is *c*.

$$RTIR^n = (\frac{RT_c^1}{RT_c^n} - 1) \times 100\% \quad (7)$$

From Fig 18 and Fig 20, it can be observed that the response time for the map service linearly increases with increasing concurrent number. The vector map service response time is substantially longer than the tile map response time. This is because the vector map service must perform spatial processing on the cluster server, the service must dynamically compute the map extent and clip map. In addition, the communication between nodes also increases with increasing number of cluster nodes, which could consume system resources and increase the response time. Fig 19 and Fig 21 show the performance improving rate compared with the 1-node cluster, these two figures demonstrate that the performance is clearly improved with an increasing number of cluster nodes, especially for the geologic tile map service.

Spatial Data Processing Performance

The polygon clip work flow was used to test the performance of spatial data processing in GSICCP. Polygon clip is a common operation in GIS processing; thus, utilizing the polygon clip to test the performance could closely represent the actual use situation. The entire environment was deployed as follows: 1) Hardware environment: includes a cluster manager server, task loader server and task executing server, where each server has 8 GB RAM and a 2.4 GHz CPU with 8 computing cores. 2) Software environment: the.Net and related geospatial middleware were deployed on the task-executing server machine, load Runner 11 (a task runner manager) was deployed on the task loader server, and the IGServer cluster manager was deployed on the cluster manager server.

During the performance test, the single work flow and batch work flow were tested to verify whether the polygon clip performance would vary with the number of cluster nodes. The geologic vector map for Luzhou, China, was adopted as the testing data. In this geologic vector map, the point layers include 185,159 features, the line layers include 644,802 features, and the polygon layers include 207,498 features. For the single work flow, each user sends a URL request, a free load node will process the request, and each request will execute the polygon clip operation only once. Three types of clusters were designed when executing the single workflow, the number of nodes in each cluster was 1, 2, and 3, and the concurrent number varied from 12 to 41. The test results are given in Table 2. For the batch work flow, each user sends a URL request, and different nodes in the cluster will execute the polygon clip operation in a distributed manner. In addition, the request will be executed more than once. Three types of cluster were designed when executing the batch workflow, the number of nodes in each cluster was 1, 2, and 3, and the concurrent number varied from 3 to 12. The test results are listed in Table 3.

Table 2. Performance test of different clusters for polygon clip operation in single workflow.

NN[a]		1			2			3	
Indicator	CN[b]	RT[c]	TP[d]	CN	RT	TP	CN	RT	TP
Point	12	58.407	163.269	29	57.569	329.615	41	58.368	495.577
Line	12	58.356	163	29	58.634	326.965	41	57.429	491.433
Polygon	12	60.333	157.508	29	58.305	321.139	41	58.724	481.958

[a]Node Number
[b]Concurrent Number
[c]Response Time (s)
[d]Throughput (bytes/s)

doi:10.1371/journal.pone.0145312.t002

Table 3. Performance test of different clusters for polygon clip operation in batch workflow.

NN[a]		1			2			3	
e	CN[b]	RT[c]	TP[d]	CN	RT	TP	CN	RT	TP
Point	4	59.83	145.031	6	58.942	220.975	12	58.084	454.284
Line	4	59.607	148.891	6	59.724	219.596	12	59.261	445.97
Polygon	4	60.129	146.188	6	60.171	210.036	12	60.271	430.715

[a]Node Number
[b]Concurrent Number
[c]Response Time (s)
[d]Throughput (bytes/s)

doi:10.1371/journal.pone.0145312.t003

Table 2 and Table 3 show the variation of the response time and throughput as a function of the cluster node and concurrent number in the polygon clip work flow. Overall, for a given time, a cluster with more nodes could process more user requests; in addition, the data throughput increased. During the performance test, the CPU rate was always lower than 75%, which means more cluster nodes could help improve the performance of the entire system.

DISCUSSION

Many geoprocessing services were built upon the architecture of GSICCP. The geological data service and geological processing service were introduced above. There are other services that have been deployed on the GSICCP such as a catalog service, geological production scheduling service, and GIS interoperation service. All these services and applications have greatly benefited from the geological work. Below, several intentions of this research are discussed.

It is evident that the newly emerged area of cloud computing can be implemented as easy-to-use tools[30]. Our research also adopts the concept of cloud computing to produce initial work; however, our work concentrates more on "how to build a geological cloud environment", not "how to utilize an existing cloud environment well". For historical reasons, substantial geological data and numerous services and applications have been developed and can be very complex to integrate. For a particular application or geological thematic problem, we can deploy such services and applications on existing cloud environments such as Azure[1,16,31]; however, for the entire geological domain, an open framework or platform that can integrate all geology-related data, services, and applications may be greatly beneficial. In such an environment, regardless of who integrates their service into the platform, some standards must be observed. This means that all integrated services use some common interfaces to share their information and obtain new information from other systems. Our research focuses on this objective, from hardware to the application. Considering data description, discovery, integration, management and sharing, according to the p2p node manager, we built a geological cloud environment. The entire cloud environment was deployed on more than 20 nodes. On the GSICCP, existing applications, such as geospatial data services, catalog services, geological production scheduling services, and GIS interoperation services, could achieve proper data sharing and cooperation. Furthermore, more geological systems could be integrated or developed within the GSICCP in the future to gradually form a geological service environment.

CONCLUSIONS AND OUTLOOK

This study built a Geological Survey Information Cloud-computing Platform that integrates and shares distributed geological spatial data and services and provides users with related geological cloud services on software, platform and infrastructure levels, which are known as SaaS, PaaS and IaaS, respectively. Our work primarily focused on the following aspects: 1) the design of the Geological Survey Information Cloud-computing Platform structure, 2) the introduction of geological ontology theory to universally organize and describe the geological spatial data and to utilize the MapGIS platform to manage the geological spatial data, and 3) the design of the P2P node manager used to organize the computing and storage nodes in the GSICCP.

Using the developed GSICCP, related studies can be performed in the future to improve the performance of the entire system. The GSICCP integrated massive geological spatial data. Thus, a framework for large geological data mining has been established. In the future, a data mining application should be developed on the GSICCP to help mine geological knowledge and to expand geology-related information, knowledge, services and applications.

ACKNOWLEDGMENTS

This project was supported by the National Science Foundation of China (Grant Nos. 41401443) and the Key Research Project, supported by the Natural Science Foundation of Hubei Province (Grant Nos. 2015CFA012). The authors thank the Development and Research Center of China Geological Survey for providing technical support. We thank the NERCGIS (the National Engineering Research Center for Geographic Information System of China) for providing hardware support.

AUTHOR CONTRIBUTIONS

Conceived and designed the experiments: LW CLL ZX. Performed the experiments: LX XL ZLC MQG. Analyzed the data: LW CLL MQG ZX. Contributed reagents/materials/analysis tools: XL ZLC MQG. Wrote the paper: LW LX ZLC MQG.

REFERENCES

1. Yang C, Goodchild M, Huang Q, Nebert D, Raskin R, Xu Y, et al. (2011) Spatial cloud computing: how can the geospatial sciences use and help shape cloud computing? International Journal of Digital Earth 4: 305–329. doi: 10. 1080/17538947. 2011. 587547
2. Li Z, Yang C, Jin B, Yu M, Liu K, Sun M, et al. (2015) Enabling Big Geoscience Data Analytics with a Cloud-Based, MapReduce-Enabled and Service-Oriented Workflow Framework. Plos One 10. doi: 10. 1371/journal. pone. 0116781
3. Li Z, Yang CP, Wu H, Li W, Miao L (2011) An optimized framework for seamlessly integrating OGC Web Services to support geospatial sciences. International Journal of Geographical Information Science 25: 595–613. doi: 10. 1080/13658816. 2010. 484811
4. Ji X, Huang Z, Fang Y, Chen B, Sui Z (2010) Weight of Evidence Method Based on Grid GIS and Its Applications on Evaluation of Mineral Resources. 2010 18th International Conference on Geoinformatics.
5. Yang C, Raskin R (2009) Introduction to distributed geographic information processing research. International Journal of Geographical Information Science 23: 553–560. doi: 10. 1080/13658810902733682
6. Gui Z, Yang C, Xia J, Liu K, Xu C, Li J, et al. (2013) A performance, semantic and service quality-enhanced distributed search engine for improving geospatial resource discovery. International Journal of Geographical Information Science 27: 1109–1132. doi: 10. 1080/13658816. 2012. 739692

7. Yang C, Li W, Xie J, Zhou B (2008) Distributed geospatial information processing: sharing distributed geospatial resources to support Digital Earth. International Journal of Digital Earth 1: 259–278. doi: 10. 1080/17538940802037954
8. Vaccari L, Shvaiko P, Marchese M (2009) A geo-service semantic integration in spatial data infrastructures. International Journal of Spatial Data Infrastructures Research 4: 24–51.
9. Evangelidis K, Ntouros K, Makridis S, Papatheodorou C (2014) Geospatial services in the Cloud. Computers & Geosciences 63: 116–122. doi: 10. 1016/j. cageo. 2013. 10. 007
10. Moon J, Park S, Lee J (2008) Resource management through resource virtualization in distributed network environments. In: Gervasi O, Lagana A, Mun Y, Murgante B, Taniar D et al. , editors. Computational Science and Its Applications—Iccsa 2008, Pt 2, Proceedings. pp. 360–370.
11. Song M, Xie Z, Luo X, Wu L, Li C (2010) Research of Catalogue Service System Based on China Geological Survey Information Grid Platform. 2010 18th International Conference on Geoinformatics.
12. Zhang H, Song Z, Zhu H, Zhang F (2015) Research on Association and Search Services of Massive Geospatial Information Based on Cloud Computing. In: Liu M, Zhang X, editors. Proceedings of the International Conference on Advances in Mechanical Engineering and Industrial Informatics. pp. 1238–1243.
13. Schaeffer B, Baranski B, Foerster T (2010) Towards Spatial Data Infrastructures in the Clouds. In: Painho M, Santos MY, Pundt H, editors. Geospatial Thinking. pp. 399–418.
14. Liu R, Huang R, Xie G (2011) A New Architecture of Geospatial Information Service for Cloud Computing. In: Zhiguo G, Luo XF, Chen J, Wang FL, Lei JS, editors. Emerging Research in Web Information Systems and Mining. pp. 426–432.
15. Gui Z, Yang C, Xia J, Huang Q, Liu K, Li Z, et al. (2014) A Service Brokering and Recommendation Mechanism for Better Selecting Cloud Services. Plos One 9. doi: 10. 1371/journal. pone. 0105297
16. Shao Y, Di L, Bai Y, Guo B, Gong J, Ieee (2012) Geoprocessing on the Amazon cloud computing platform—AWS. 2012 First International Conference on Agro-Geoinformatics (Agro-Geoinformatics): 286–291.
17. Papagianni C, Leivadeas A, Papavassiliou S, Maglaris V, Cervello-Pastor C, Monje A (2013) On the Optimal Allocation of Virtual Resources in Cloud Computing Networks. Ieee Transactions on Computers 62: 1060–1071. doi: 10. 1109/tc. 2013. 31
18. Wang J, Wan J, Liu Z, Wang P. Data mining of mass storage based on cloud computing; 2010. IEEE. pp. 426–431.
19. Lin F-C, Chung L-K, Ku W-Y, Chu L-R, Chou T-Y (2013) The Framework of Cloud Computing Platform for Massive Remote Sensing Images. 2013 Ieee 27th International Conference on Advanced Information Networking and Applications (Aina): 621–628.
20. Bildosola I, Rio-Belver R, Cilleruelo E, Garechana G (2015) Design and Implementation of a Cloud Computing Adoption Decision Tool: Generating a Cloud Road. Plos One 10. doi: 10. 1371/journal. pone. 0134563
21. Ezaki Y, Matsumoto H (2011) Integrated Management of Virtualized Infrastructure That Supports Cloud Computing: ServerView Resource Orchestrator. Fujitsu Scientific & Technical Journal 47: 247–254.
22. Zhang H, Li C, Shi Z, Zhang X (2012) Resource Pool-Oriented Resource Management for Cloud Computing. In: Zhu M, editor. Business, Economics, Financial Sciences, and Management. pp. 829–832.
23. Zhong L, Zhu B, Yang L, Song H (2011) Research on Layered Resource Discovery Model in Grid. In: Zhou Q, editor. 2011 2nd International Conference on Challenges in Environmental Science and Computer Engineering. pp. 77–84.
24. Kambayashi Y, Harada Y (2007) A resource discovery method based on multi-agents in P2P systems. In: Nguyen NT, Grzech A, Howlett RJ, Jain LC, editors. Agent and Multi-Agent Systems: Technologies and Applications, Proceedings. pp. 364–374.
25. Castella D, Solsona F, Gine F (2015) DisCoP: A P2P Framework for Managing and Searching Computing Markets. Journal of Grid Computing 13: 115–137. doi: 10. 1007/s10723-014-9318-3
26. He Q, Li Z, Zhang X. Study on cloud storage system based on distributed storage systems. Proceedings—2010 International Conference on Computational and Information Sciences, ICCIS 2010; 2010; Chengdu, Sichuan, China. IEEE Computer Society. pp. 1332–1335.
27. Zhou J, Shi Z (2010) Unstructured P2P-Enabled Service Discovery in the Cloud Environment. In: Shi ZZ, Vadera S, Aamodt A, Leake D, editors. Intelligent Information Processing V. pp. 173–182.
28. Xu H-M, Shi Y-J, Liu Y-L, Gao F-B, Wan T (2012) Integration of Cloud Computing and P2P: A Future Storage Infrastructure; Huang HZ, Zuo MJ, Liu Y, editors. 1489–1492 p.
29. Huang Q, Yang C, Liu K, Xia J, Xu C, Li J, et al. (2013) Evaluating open-source cloud computing solutions for geosciences. Computers & Geosciences 59: 41–52. doi: 10. 1016/j. cageo. 2013. 05. 001
30. Liu Y, Sun AY, Nelson K, Hipke WE (2013) Cloud computing for integrated stochastic groundwater uncertainty analysis. International Journal of Digital Earth 6: 313–337. doi: 10. 1080/17538947. 2012. 687778
31. Xia J, Yang C, Liu K, Gui Z, Li Z, Huang Q, et al. (2015) Adopting cloud computing to optimize spatial web portals for better performance to support Digital Earth and other global geospatial initiatives. International Journal of Digital Earth 8: 451–475. doi: 10. 1080/17538947. 2014. 929750
32. Wen Y, Chen M, Lu G, Lin H, He L, Yue S (2013) Prototyping an open environment for sharing geographical analysis models on cloud computing platform. International Journal of Digital Earth 6: 356–382. doi: 10. 1080/17538947. 2012. 716861

33. Kalabokidis K, Athanasis N, Vasilakos C, Palaiologou P (2014) Porting of a wildfire risk and fire spread application into a cloud computing environment. International Journal of Geographical Information Science 28: 541–552. doi: 10. 1080/13658816. 2013. 858257

34. Dube N, Ramakrishnan R, Dasgupta KS (2013) GEOID: GRID Services for Earth Observation Image Data Processing. International Journal of Digital Earth 6: 185–195. doi: 10. 1080/17538947. 2011. 608814

35. Lee D, Liang SHL (2011) Geopot: a Cloud-based geolocation data service for mobile applications. International Journal of Geographical Information Science 25: 1283–1301. doi: 10. 1080/13658816. 2011. 558017

36. Devarakonda R, Palanisamy G, Wilson BE, Green JM (2010) Mercury: reusable metadata management, data discovery and access system. Earth Science Informatics 3: 87–94. doi: 10. 1007/s12145-010-0050-7

37. Xu L, Wu L, Che D, Cai Z, Wu L, Ieee (2006) The Formal Representation of Semantic on Stratum Attribute Data Oriented 3D Geo-Modeling. 899–902 p. doi: 10. 1109/igarss. 2006. 231

38. Li W, Yang C, Nebert D, Raskin R, Houser P, Wu H, et al. (2011) Semantic-based web service discovery and chaining for building an Arctic spatial data infrastructure. Computers & Geosciences 37: 1752–1762. doi: 10. 1016/j. cageo. 2011. 06. 024

39. An Y, Zhao B (2007) Geo ontology design and comparison in geographic information integration; Lei JS, Yu J, Zhou SG, editors. 608–612 p.

40. Chen Y (2015) Mineral potential mapping with a restricted Boltzmann machine. Ore Geology Reviews 71: 749–760. doi: 10. 1016/j. oregeorev. 2014. 08. 012

41. Yuanyuan C, Keyan X, Shaobin Z, Yajian LIU (2007) Weight of Evidence Method Based on SIG and Its Application on Evaluation on Mineral Resources. Journal of Jilin University Earth Science Edition 37: 54–58.

42. Zhang J, Xiao J (2011) Architecture and application of integrated spatial information service platform for digital mine. Transactions of Nonferrous Metals Society of China 21: S706–S711. doi: 10. 1016/s1003-6326(12)61666-5

43. Zheng T, Yuan F, Zhang M, Li X, Jia C (2015) Metallogenic prognosis of iron mineral resources in Zhonggu area based on weights of evidence method and GIS. Journal of Hefei University of Technology Natural Science 38: 851–856.

44. Liu X, Wu S. Internet information extraction evaluation of mineral resources based on WebGIS. 2010 2nd Conference on Environmental Science and Information Application Technology, ESIAT 2010; 2010; Wuhan, China. IEEE Computer Society. pp. 150–153.

CHAPTER 10 A COMPARISON STUDY ON SIMILARITY AND DISSIMILARITY MEASURES IN CLUSTERING CONTINUOUS DATA

Ali Seyed Shirkhorshidi[1], Saeed Aghabozorgi[2], Teh Ying Wah[1]

[1] Department of Information Systems, Faculty of Computer Science and Information Technology, University of Malaya, 50603, Kuala Lumpur, Malaysia

[2] IBM Analytics, Platform, Emerging Technologies, IBM Canada Ltd., Markham, Ontario L6F 1C7, Canada

ABSTRACT

Similarity or distance measures are core components used by distance-based clustering algorithms to cluster similar data points into the same clusters, while dissimilar or distant data points are placed into different clusters. The performance of similarity measures is mostly addressed in two or three-dimensional spaces, beyond which, to the best of our knowledge, there is no empirical study that has revealed the behavior of similarity measures when dealing with high-dimensional datasets. To fill this gap, a technical framework is proposed in this study to analyze, compare and benchmark the influence of different similarity measures on the results of distance-based clustering algorithms. For reproducibility purposes, fifteen publicly available datasets were used for this study, and consequently, future distance measures can be evaluated and compared with the results of the measures discussed in this work. These datasets were classified as low and high-dimensional categories to study the performance of each measure against each category. This research should help the research community to identify suitable distance measures for datasets and also to facilitate a comparison and evaluation of the newly proposed similarity or distance measures with traditional ones.

INTRODUCTION

One of the biggest challenges of this decade is with databases having a variety of data types. Variety is among the key notion in the emerging concept of big data, which is known by the 4 Vs: Volume, Velocity, Variety and Variability [1,2]. Currently, there are a variety of data types available in databases, including: interval-scaled variables (salary, height), binary variables (gender), categorical variables (religion: Jewish, Muslim, Christian, etc.) and mixed type variables (multiple attributes with various types). Despite data type, the distance measure is a main component of distance-based clustering algorithms. Partitioning algorithms, such as k-means, k-medoids and more recently soft clustering approaches for instance fuzzy c-means [3] and rough clustering [4], are mainly dependent on distance measures to recognize clusters in a dataset.

In data mining, ample techniques use distance measures to some extent. Clustering is a well-known technique for knowledge discovery in various scientific areas, such as medical image analysis [5–7], clustering gene expression data [8–10], investigating and analyzing air pollution data [11–13], power consumption analysis [14–16], and many more fields of study. Improving clustering performance has always been a target for researchers. Since in distance-based clustering similarity or dissimilarity (distance) measures are the core algorithm components, their efficiency directly influences

Citation: Shirkhorshidi AS, Aghabozorgi S, Wah TY (2015) A Comparison Study on Similarity and Dissimilarity Measures in Clustering Continuous Data. PLoS ONE 10(12): e0144059. doi:10.1371/journal.pone.0144059.

the performance of clustering algorithms. These algorithms use similarity or distance measures to cluster similar data points into the same clusters, while dissimilar or distant data points are placed into different clusters. Examples of distance-based clustering algorithms include partitioning clustering algorithms, such as k-means as well as k-medoids and hierarchical clustering [17].

Although there are various studies available for comparing similarity/distance measures for clustering numerical data, but there are two difference between this study and other existing studies and related works: first, the aim in this study is to investigate the similarity/distance measures against low dimensional and high dimensional datasets and we wanted to analyse their behaviour in this context. Second thing that distinguish our study from others is that our datasets are coming from a variety of applications and domains while other works confined with a specific domain. In essence, the target of this research is to compare and benchmark similarity and distance measures for clustering continuous data to examine their performance while they are applied to low and high-dimensional datasets. For the sake of reproducibility, fifteen publicly available datasets [18,19] were used for this study, so future distance measures could consequently be evaluated and compared with the results of traditional measures discussed in this study. These datasets are classified into low and high-dimensional, and each measure is studied against each category. But before doing the study on similarity or dissimilarity measures, it needs to be clarified that they have significant influence on clustering quality and are worthwhile to be studied. In sections 3 (methodology) it is elaborated that the similarity or distance measures have significant influence on clustering results.

The key contributions of this paper are as follows:

- Twelve similarity measures frequently used for clustering continuous data from various fields are compiled in this study to be evaluated in a single framework. Most of these similarity measures have not been examined in domains other than the originally proposed one.
- A technical framework is proposed in this study to analyze, compare and benchmark the influence of different similarity measures on the result of distance-based clustering algorithms.
- Similarity measures are evaluated on a wide variety of publicly available datasets. Particularly, we evaluate and compare the performance of similarity measures for continuous data against datasets with low and high dimension.

The rest of paper is organized as follows: in section 2, a background on distance measures is discussed. In section 3, we have explained the methodology of the study. Experimental results with a discussion are represented in section 4, and section 5 summarizes the contributions of this study.

BACKGROUND ON DISTANCE MEASURES FOR CONTINUOUS DATA

Utilization of similarity measures is not limited to clustering, but in fact plenty of data mining algorithms use similarity measures to some extent. To reveal the influence of various distance measures on data mining, researchers have done experimental studies in various fields and have compared and evaluated the results generated by different distance measures. Although it is not practical to introduce a "Best" similarity measure or a best performing measure in general, a comparison study could shed a light on the performance and behavior of measures. For instance, Boriah et al. conducted a comparison study on similarity measures for categorical data and evaluated similarity measures in the context of outlier detection for categorical data [20]. It was concluded that the performance of an outlier detection algorithm is significantly affected by the similarity measure. In their research, it was not possible to introduce a best performing similarity measure, but they analyzed and reported the situations in which a measure has poor or superior performance. In another research work, Fernando et al. [21] reviewed, compared and benchmarked binary-based similarity measures for categorical data. With some cases studies, Deshpande et al. focused on data from a single knowledge area, for example biological data, and conducted a comparison in favor of profile similarity measures for genetic interaction networks. They concluded that the Dot Product is consistent among the best measures in different conditions and genetic interaction datasets [22].

Similarly, in the context of clustering, studies have been done on the effects of similarity measures., In one study Strehl and colleagues tried to recognize the impact of similarity measures on web clustering [23]. In another, six similarity measure were assessed, this time for trajectory clustering in outdoor surveillance scenes [24]. In chemical databases, Al Khalifa et. al. [25] examined performance of twelve coefficients for clustering, similarity searching and compound selection. From the results they concluded that no single coefficient is appropriate for all methodologies.

Despite these studies, no empirical analysis and comparison is available for clustering continuous data to investigate their behavior in low and high dimensional datasets. At the other hand our datasets are coming from a variety of applications and domains and while they are limited with a specific domain. In this study, we gather known similarity/distance measures available for clustering continuous data, which will be examined using various clustering algorithms and against 15 publicly available datasets. It is not possible to introduce a perfect similarity measure for all kinds of datasets, but in this paper we will discover the reaction of similarity measures to low and high-dimensional datasets. The similarity measures with the best results in each category are also introduced. Before presenting the similarity measures for clustering continuous data, a definition of a clustering problem should be given. Assuming that the number of clusters required to be created is an input value k, the clustering problem is defined as follows [26]:

Definition 1

Given a dataset $D = \{v_1, v_2, \ldots, v_n\}$ of data vectors and an integer value k, the clustering problem is to define a mapping $f: D \rightarrow \{1, \ldots, k\}$ where each v_i is assigned to one cluster C_j, $1 \leq j \leq k$. A cluster C_j contains precisely those data vectors mapped to it; that is, $C_j = \{v_i \mid f(t_i) = C_j, 1 \leq i \leq n, \text{ and } v_i \in D\}$.

In the rest of this study, v_1, v_2 represent two data vectors defined as $v_1 = \{x_1, x_2, \ldots, x_n\}$, $v_2 = \{y_1, y_2, \ldots, y_n\}$, where x_i, y_i are called attributes.

Subsequently, similarity measures for clustering continuous data are discussed. Some of these similarity measures are frequently employed for clustering purposes while others have scarcely appeared in literature.

Minkowski

The Minkowski family includes Euclidean distance and Manhattan distance, which are particular cases of the Minkowski distance [27–29]. The Minkowski distance is defined by $d_{min} = (\sum_{i=1}^{n} |x_i - y_i|^m)^{\frac{1}{m}},\ m \geq 1$ where m is a positive real number and x_i and y_i are two vectors in n-dimensional space. The Minkowski distance performs well when the dataset clusters are isolated or compacted; if the dataset does not fulfil this condition, then the large-scale attributes would dominate the others [30,31]. Another problem with Minkowski metrics is that the largest-scale feature dominates the rest. Thus, normalizing the continuous features is the solution to this problem [31].

A modified version of the Minkowski metric has been proposed to solve clustering obstacles. For example, Wilson and Martinez presented distance based on counts for nominal attributes and a modified Minkowski metric for continuous features [32].

Manhattan distance

Manhattan distance is a special case of the Minkowski distance at m = 1. Like its parent, Manhattan is sensitive to outliers. When this distance measure is used in clustering algorithms, the shape of clusters is hyper-rectangular [33]. A study by Perlibakas demonstrated that a modified version of this distance measure is among the best distance measures for PCA-based face recognition [34]. This measure is defined as $d_{man} = \sum_{i=1}^{n} |x_i - y_i|$.

Euclidean distance

The most well-known distance used for numerical data is probably the Euclidean distance. This is a special case of the Minkowski distance when m = 2. Euclidean distance performs well when deployed to datasets that include compact or isolated clusters [30,31]. Although Euclidean distance is very common in clustering, it has a drawback: if two data vectors have no attribute values in common, they may have a smaller distance than the other pair of data vectors containing the same attribute values [31,35,36]. Another problem with Euclidean distance as a family of the Minkowski metric is that the largest-scaled feature would dominate the others. Normalization of continuous features is a solution to this problem [31].

Average Distance

Regarding the above-mentioned drawback of Euclidean distance, average distance is a modified version of the Euclidean distance to improve the results [27,35]. For two data points x, y in n-dimentional space, the average distance is defined as $d_{ave} = (\frac{1}{n}\sum_{i=1}^{n}(x_i - y_i)^2)^{\frac{1}{2}}$.

Weighted Euclidean Distance

If the relative importance according to each attribute is available, then the Weighted Euclidean distance—another modification of Euclidean distance—can be used [37]. This distance is defined as $d_{we} = (\sum_{i=1}^{n} w_i(x_i - y_i)^2)^{\frac{1}{2}}$, where w_i is the weight given to the ith component.

This distance measure is the only measure which is not included in this study for comparison since calculating the weights is closely related to the dataset and the aim of researcher for cluster analysis on the dataset. As an instance of using this measure reader can refer to Ji et. al. research work. They used this measure for proposing a dynamic fuzzy cluster algorithm for time series [38].

Chord Distance

Chord distance is one more Euclidean distance modification to overcome the previously mentioned Euclidean distance shortcomings. It can solve problems caused by the scale of measurements as well. Chord distance is defined as the length of the chord joining two normalized points within a hypersphere of radius one. This distance can be calculated from non-normalized data as well [27]. Chord distance is defined as $d_{chord} = \left(2 - 2\frac{\sum_{i=1}^{n} x_i y_i}{\|x\|_2 \|y\|_2}\right)^{\frac{1}{2}}$, where $\|x\|_2$ is the L^2-norm $\|x\|_2 = \sqrt{\sum_{i=1}^{n} x_i^2}$.

Mahalanobis Distance

Mahalanobis distance is a data-driven measure in contrast to Euclidean and Manhattan distances that are independent of the related dataset to which two data points belong [20,33]. A regularized Mahalanobis distance can be used for extracting hyperellipsoidal clusters [30]. On the other hand, Mahalanobis distance can alleviated distortion caused by linear correlation among features by applying a whitening transformation to the data or by using the squared Mahalanobis distance [31]. Mahalanobis distance is defined by $d_{mah} = \sqrt{(x - y)S^{-1}(x - y)^T}$ $d_{mah} = \sqrt{(x - y)S^{-1}(x - y)^T}$ where S is the covariance matrix of the dataset [27,39].

Cosine deasure

The Cosine similarity measure is mostly used in document similarity [28,33] and is defined as $Cosine(x, y) = \frac{\sum_{i=1}^{n} x_i y_i}{\|x\|_2 \|y\|_2}$, where $\|y\|_2$ is the Euclidean norm of vector $y = (y_1, y_2, \ldots, y_n)$ defined as $\|y\|_2 = \sqrt{y_1^2 + y_2^2 + \ldots + y_n^2}$. The Cosine measure is invariant to rotation but is variant to linear transformations. It is also independent of vector length [33].

Pearson correlation

Pearson correlation is widely used in clustering gene expression data [33,36,40]. This similarity measure calculates the similarity between the shapes of two gene expression patterns. The Pearson correlation is defined by

$Pearson(x,y) = \frac{\sum_{i=1}^{n}(x_i-\mu_x)(y_i-\mu_y)}{\sqrt{\sum_{i=1}^{n}(x_i-y_i)^2}\sqrt{\sum_{i=1}^{n}(x_i-y_i)^2}}$, where μ_x and μ_y are the means for x and y respectively. The Pearson correlation has a disadvantage of being sensitive to outliers [33,40].

The similarity measures explained above are the most commonly used for clustering continuous data. Table 1 represents a summary of these with some highlights of each.

Table 1. Similarity Measures for continuous data (in time complexity, n **is the number of dimensions of** x **and** y).

Distance Measure	Equation	Time complexity	Advantages	Disadvantages	Applications
Euclidean Distance	$d_{euc} = \left[\sum_{i=1}^{n}(x_i-y_i)^2\right]^{\frac{1}{2}}$	O(n)	Very common, easy to compute and works well with datasets with compact or isolated clusters [27,31].	Sensitive to outliers [27,31].	*K*-means algorithm, Fuzzy *c*-means algorithm [38].
Average Distance	$d_{ave} = \left(\frac{1}{n}\sum_{i=1}^{n}(x_i-y_i)^2\right)^{\frac{1}{2}}$	O(n)	Better than Euclidean distance [35] at handling outliers.	Variables contribute independently to the measure of distance. Redundant values could dominate the similarity between data points [37].	*K*-means algorithm
Weighted Euclidean	$d_{we} = \left(\sum_{i=1}^{n}w_i(x_i-y_i)^2\right)^{\frac{1}{2}}$	O(n)	The weight matrix allows to increase the effect of more important data points than less important one [37].	Same as Average Distance.	Fuzzy *c*-means algorithm [38]
Chord	$d_{chord} = \left(2-2\frac{\sum_{i=1}^{n}x_iy_i}{\lVert x\rVert_2\lVert y\rVert_2}\right)^{\frac{1}{2}}$	O(3n)	Can work with un-normalized data [27].	It is not invariant to linear transformation [33].	Ecological resemblance detection [35].
Mahalanobis	$d_{mah} = \sqrt{(x-y)S^{-1}(x-y)^T}$	O(3n)	Mahalanobis is a data-driven measure that can ease the distance distortion caused by a linear combination of attributes [35].	It can be expensive in terms of computation [33]	Hyperellipsoidal clustering algorithm [30].
Cosine Measure	$Cosine(x,y) = \frac{\sum_{i=1}^{n}x_iy_i}{\lVert x\rVert_2\lVert y\rVert_2}$	O(3n)	Independent of vector length and invariant to rotation [33].	It is not invariant to linear transformation [33].	Mostly used in document similarity applications [28,33].
Manhattan	$d_{man} = \sum_{i=1}^{n}(x_i-y_i)$	O(n)	Is common and like other Minkowski-driven distances it works well with datasets with compact or isolated clusters [27].	Sensitive to the outliers. [27,31]	*K*-means algorithm
Mean Character Difference	$d_{MCD} = \frac{1}{n}\sum_{i=1}^{n}\lvert x_i-y_i\rvert$	O(n)	*Results in accurate outcomes using the K-medoids algorithm.	*Low accuracy for high-dimensional datasets using K-means.	Partitioning and hierarchical clustering algorithms.
Index of Association	$d_{IOA} = \frac{1}{n}\sum_{i=1}^{n}\left\lvert\frac{x_i}{\sum_{i=1}^{n}x_i}-\frac{y_i}{\sum_{i=1}^{n}y_i}\right\rvert$	O(3n)	-	*Low accuracy using K-means and K-medoids algorithms.	Partitioning and hierarchical clustering algorithms.
Canberra Metric	$d_{canb} = \sum_{i=1}^{n}\frac{\lvert x_i-y_i\rvert}{(x_i+y_i)}$	O(n)	*Results in accurate outcomes for high-dimensional datasets using the K-medoids algorithm.	-	Partitioning and hierarchical clustering algorithms.
Czekanowski Coefficient	$d_{czekan} = 1-\frac{2\sum_{i=1}^{n}min(x_i,y_i)}{\sum_{i=1}^{n}(x_i+y_i)}$	O(2n)	*Results in accurate outcomes for medium-dimensional datasets using the K-means algorithm.	-	Partitioning and hierarchical clustering algorithms.
Coefficient of Divergence	$d_{canb} = \left(\frac{1}{n}\sum_{i=1}^{n}\left(\frac{x_i-y_i}{x_i+y_i}\right)^2\right)^{\frac{1}{2}}$	O(n)	*Results in accurate outcomes using the K-means algorithm.	-	Partitioning and hierarchical clustering algorithms.
Pearson coefficient	$Pearson(x,y) = \frac{\sum_{i=1}^{n}(x_i-\mu_x)(y_i-\mu_y)}{\sqrt{\sum_{i=1}^{n}(x_i-y_i)^2}\sqrt{\sum_{i=1}^{n}(x_i-y_i)^2}}$	O(2n)	*Results in accurate outcomes using the hierarchical single-link algorithm for high dimensional datasets.	-	Partitioning and hierarchical clustering algorithms.

*Points marked by asterisk are compiled based on this article's experimental results.

doi:10.1371/journal.pone.0144059.t001

METHODOLOGY OF THE STUDY

Experimental design

This section is devoted to explain the method and the framework which is used in this study for evaluating the effect of similarity measures on clustering quality. The main objective of this research study is to analyse the effect of different distance measures on quality of clustering algorithm results. As it is illustrated in Fig 1 there are 15 datasets used with 4 distance based algorithms on a total of 12 distance measures. All the distance measures inTable 1 are examined except the Weighted Euclidean distance which is dependent on the dataset and the aim of clustering.

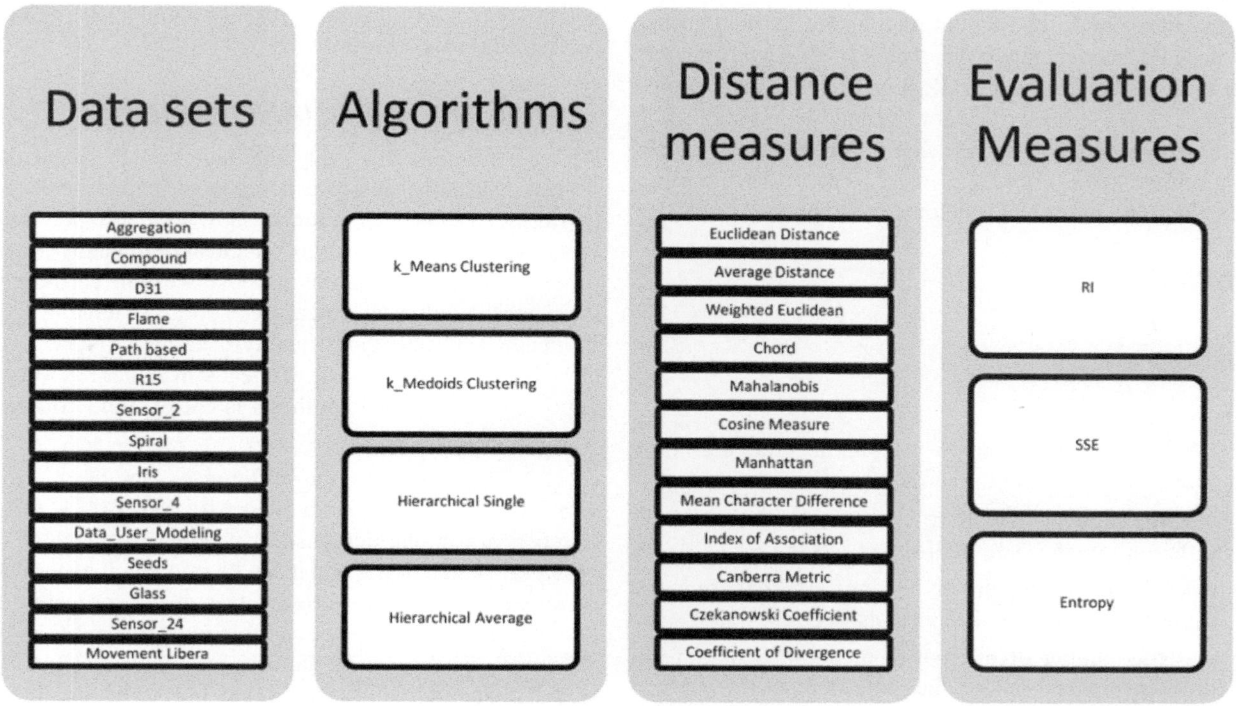

Figure 1. Overview of experimental study.

Fig 2 explains the methodology of the study briefly. For each dataset we examined all four distance based algorithms, and each algorithms' quality of clustering has been evaluated by each 12 distance measures as it is demonstrated in Fig 1. It makes a total of 720 experiments in this research work to analyse the effect of distance measures. Representing and comparing this huge number of experiments is a challenging task and could not be done using ordinary charts and tables. Consequently we have developed a special illustration method using heat mapped tables in order to demonstrate all the results in the way that could be read and understand quickly. This method is described in section 4.1.1.

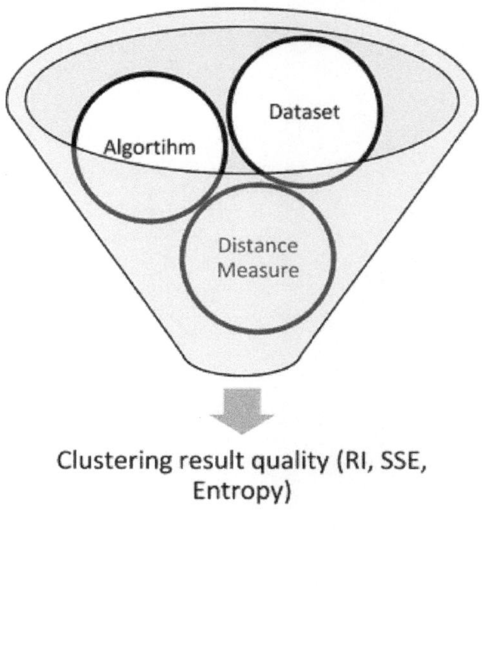

Figure 2. Arrangement of experiments.

Rand Index

In this study, we used Rand Index (RI) for evaluation of clustering outcomes resulted by various distance measures. This section is an overview on this measure and it investigates the reason that this measure has been chosen.

Rand index is frequently used in measuring clustering quality. It is a measure of agreement between two sets of objects: first is the set produced by clustering process and the other defined by external criteria. Although there are different clustering measures such as Sum of Squared Error, Entropy, Purity, Jaccard etc. but among them the Rand index is probably the most used index for cluster validation [17,41,42]. Assuming $S = \{o_1, o_2, \ldots, o_n\}$ is a set of$n$ elements and two partitions of S are given to compare $C = \{c_1, c_2, \ldots, c_r\}$, which is a partition of S into r subsets and $G = \{g_1, g_2, \ldots, g_s\}$, a partition of S into s subsets, the Rand index (R) is defined as follows:

Definition 2

$$RI = \frac{a+b}{a+b+c+d} \qquad 1$$

where:

- *a* is the number of pairs of vectors in S that are in the same set in *C* and in the same set in G.
- *b* is the number of pairs of elements in S that are in different sets in *C* and in different sets in G.
- *c* is the number of pairs of elements in S that are in the same set in *C* and in different sets in G.
- *d* is the number of pairs of elements in S that are in different sets in *C* and in the same set in G.

There is a modified version of rand index called Adjusted Rand Index (ARI) which is proposed by Hubert and Arabie [42] as an improvement for known problems with RI. These problems happen when the expected value of the RI of two random partition does not take a constant value (zero for example) or the Rand statistic approaches its upper limit of unity as the number of cluster increases. However, since our datasets don't have these problems and also owing to the fact that the results generated using ARI were following the same pattern of RI results, we have used Rand Index in this study due to its popularity in clustering community for clustering validation.

In this study we normalized the Rand Index values for the experiments. The normalized values are between 0 and 1 and we used following formula to approach it:

$$z_i = \frac{r_i - \min(r)}{\max(r) - \min(r)} \qquad 2$$

where $r = (r_1, \ldots, r_n)$ is the array of rand indexes produced by each similarity measure.

Analysis of variance (ANOVA) test

Before continuing this study, the main hypothesis needs to be proved: "distance measure has a considerable influence on clustering results". In order to show that distance measures cause significant difference on clustering quality, we have used ANOVA test. For this purpose we will consider a null hypothesis: "distance measures doesn't have significant influence on clustering quality". Using ANOVA test, if the p value be very small, it means that there is very small opportunity that null hypothesis is correct, and consequently we can reject it.

ANOVA analyzes the differences among a group of variable which is developed by Ronald Fisher [43]. ANOVA is a statistical test that demonstrate whether the mean of several groups are equal or not and it can be said that it generalizes the t-test for more than two groups. It is useful for testing means of more than two groups or variable for statistical significance. Statistical significance in statistics is achieved when a p-value is less than the significance level [44]. The p-value is the probability of obtaining results which acknowledge that the null hypothesis is true [45].

For ANOVA test we have considered a table with the structure shown in Table 2 which covers all RI results for all four algorithms and each distance/similarity measure and for all datasets. Table is divided into 4 section for four respective algorithms. In each sections rows represent results generated with distance measures for a dataset.

Table 2. Rand Index values used for ANOVA test (in the table HAverage stands for Hierarchical Average algorithm and HSingle stands for Hierarchical Single link).

Dataset	Distance/Similarity Measures										
	Euclidean	Average	Cosine	Chord	Mahalanobis	Canberra	CoeffDiv	Czekan	IndOfAssoc	Manhattan	MCharDiff	Pearson
k-Means												
sensor_2	0.722	0.733	0.659	0.659	0.725	0.744	0.741	0.765	0.662	0.729	0.729	0.403
Aggregation	0.929	0.929	0.798	0.799	0.927	0.921	0.904	0.949	0.799	0.927	0.927	0.636
Compound	0.919	0.914	0.746	0.746	0.926	0.890	0.908	0.886	0.744	0.906	0.904	0.497
Flame	0.756	0.756	0.569	0.569	0.750	0.716	0.498	0.710	0.557	0.750	0.750	0.536
Pathbased	0.750	0.750	0.639	0.639	0.758	0.735	0.733	0.746	0.637	0.748	0.748	0.635
R15	0.999	0.999	0.949	0.948	0.999	0.999	0.998	0.998	0.947	0.998	0.998	0.552
Spiral	0.554	0.554	0.562	0.562	0.555	0.550	0.552	0.553	0.562	0.556	0.556	0.496
D31	0.994	0.992	0.956	0.956	0.995	0.992	0.992	0.994	0.956	0.994	0.994	0.528
Iris	0.880	0.880	0.966	0.966	0.880	0.942	0.950	0.927	0.958	0.874	0.874	0.776
sensor_4	0.612	0.624	0.637	0.637	0.619	0.745	0.709	0.737	0.649	0.726	0.728	0.670
Data_User_Modeling	0.725	0.725	0.668	0.668	0.719	0.711	0.706	0.713	0.668	0.712	0.711	0.657
Seeds	0.876	0.874	0.884	0.884	0.876	0.859	0.782	0.891	0.890	0.872	0.872	0.359
Glass	0.741	0.742	0.737	0.740	0.732	0.604	0.602	0.734	0.732	0.734	0.731	0.342
sensor_24	0.610	0.615	0.614	0.617	0.596	0.618	0.621	0.613	0.610	0.604	0.611	0.626
Libras movement	0.914	0.917	0.913	0.917	0.915	0.911	0.914	0.910	0.913	0.914	0.912	0.918
k-Medoids												
sensor_2	0.777	0.736	0.661	0.661	0.729	0.804	0.806	0.797	0.675	0.785	0.796	0.403
Aggregation	0.949	0.949	0.790	0.790	0.950	0.928	0.901	0.958	0.787	0.941	0.953	0.636
Compound	0.925	0.911	0.734	0.733	0.920	0.890	0.890	0.900	0.740	0.916	0.913	0.497
Flame	0.762	0.762	0.538	0.538	0.756	0.705	0.498	0.716	0.565	0.744	0.744	0.536
Pathbased	0.746	0.746	0.606	0.606	0.756	0.743	0.745	0.745	0.667	0.741	0.741	0.635
R15	0.999	0.999	0.947	0.945	0.988	0.998	0.988	0.998	0.947	0.999	0.998	0.552
Spiral	0.555	0.554	0.555	0.555	0.555	0.571	0.555	0.557	0.551	0.556	0.564	0.496
D31	0.994	0.992	0.956	0.956	0.992	0.990	0.988	0.991	0.956	0.991	0.994	0.528
Iris	0.912	0.912	0.966	0.966	0.824	0.927	0.950	0.906	0.950	0.880	0.880	0.776
sensor_4	0.707	0.711	0.711	0.711	0.656	0.740	0.722	0.709	0.690	0.696	0.716	0.656
Data_User_Modeling	0.725	0.712	0.654	0.654	0.728	0.285	0.285	0.285	0.646	0.734	0.745	0.659
Seeds	0.874	0.874	0.842	0.842	0.798	0.872	0.771	0.876	0.865	0.867	0.867	0.359
Glass	0.735	0.736	0.738	0.732	0.711	0.633	0.582	0.737	0.735	0.737	0.739	0.342
sensor_24	0.624	0.623	0.623	0.622	0.588	0.652	0.634	0.630	0.629	0.620	0.617	0.613
Libras movement	0.907	0.909	0.908	0.905	0.720	0.897	0.905	0.901	0.906	0.904	0.904	0.907
HSingle												
sensor_2	0.432	0.432	0.355	0.355	0.432	0.432	0.432	0.431	0.365	0.432	0.432	0.405
Aggregation	0.926	0.926	0.574	0.574	0.926	0.619	0.927	0.927	0.550	0.926	0.926	0.635
Compound	0.890	0.890	0.415	0.415	0.896	0.895	0.898	0.891	0.415	0.712	0.712	0.497
Flame	0.541	0.541	0.522	0.522	0.541	0.531	0.531	0.541	0.522	0.541	0.541	0.538
Pathbased	0.338	0.338	0.362	0.362	0.340	0.339	0.338	0.338	0.362	0.338	0.338	0.635
R15	0.910	0.910	0.817	0.817	0.910	0.856	0.857	0.856	0.817	0.911	0.911	0.574
Spiral	1.000	1.000	0.383	0.383	1.000	0.781	0.781	0.781	0.383	1.000	1.000	0.497
D31	0.779	0.779	0.818	0.818	0.754	0.740	0.731	0.730	0.518	0.755	0.755	0.536
Iris	0.777	0.777	0.772	0.772	0.343	0.753	0.753	0.772	0.772	0.776	0.776	0.772
sensor_4	0.341	0.341	0.345	0.345	0.346	0.451	0.339	0.333	0.345	0.338	0.338	0.651
Data_User_Moceling	0.309	0.309	0.301	0.301	0.304	0.302	0.302	0.305	0.302	0.299	0.299	0.311
Seeds	0.357	0.357	0.340	0.340	0.337	0.340	0.337	0.340	0.340	0.340	0.340	0.358
Glass	0.304	0.304	0.308	0.308	0.309	0.293	0.294	0.308	0.308	0.308	0.308	0.342
sensor_24	0.347	0.347	0.346	0.346	0.353	0.346	0.347	0.346	0.346	0.345	0.345	0.349
Libras movement	0.187	0.187	0.202	0.202	0.131	0.183	0.183	0.187	0.192	0.187	0.187	0.296
HAverage												
sensor_2	0.466	0.466	0.634	0.634	0.506	0.466	0.729	0.716	0.634	0.466	0.466	0.404
Aggregation	1.000	1.000	0.778	0.778	0.997	0.930	0.948	0.927	0.778	0.991	0.991	0.643
Compound	0.921	0.921	0.676	0.676	0.921	0.850	0.852	0.829	0.697	0.933	0.933	0.511
Flame	0.721	0.721	0.503	0.503	0.847	0.512	0.529	0.501	0.503	0.689	0.689	0.538
Pathbased	0.738	0.738	0.699	0.699	0.754	0.438	0.377	0.708	0.629	0.724	0.724	0.635
R15	0.999	0.999	0.917	0.917	0.999	0.981	0.963	0.990	0.914	0.998	0.998	0.566
Spiral	0.537	0.537	0.528	0.528	0.557	0.424	0.499	0.498	0.428	0.540	0.540	0.497
D31	0.994	0.994	0.950	0.950	0.996	0.977	0.979	0.986	0.952	0.996	0.996	0.537
Iris	0.892	0.892	0.772	0.772	0.343	0.753	0.753	0.778	0.772	0.886	0.886	0.776
sensor_4	0.338	0.338	0.561	0.561	0.338	0.479	0.479	0.480	0.544	0.376	0.376	0.653
Data_User_Modeling	0.659	0.659	0.301	0.301	0.337	0.302	0.302	0.307	0.309	0.645	0.645	0.594
Seeds	0.887	0.887	0.691	0.691	0.337	0.879	0.581	0.802	0.688	0.802	0.802	0.362
Glass	0.329	0.329	0.570	0.570	0.309	0.328	0.323	0.415	0.415	0.415	0.415	0.369
sensor_24	0.353	0.353	0.538	0.538	0.347	0.498	0.516	0.518	0.521	0.428	0.428	0.446
Libras movement	0.886	0.886	0.892	0.892	0.131	0.582	0.613	0.827	0.844	0.861	0.861	0.886

doi:10.1371/journal.pone.0144059.t002

ANOVA test is performed for each algorithm separately to find if distance measures have significant impact on clustering results in each clustering algorithm.

The ANOVA test result on above table is demonstrated in the Tables 3–6.

Table 3. ANOVA results for k-means.

K_means	SS	df	MS	F	Prob>F
Columns	0.68317	11	0.06211	2.96	0.0013
Error	3.52624	168	0.02099		
Total	4.20942	179			

doi:10.1371/journal.pone.0144059.t003

Table 4. ANOVA results for k-medoids.

K_medoids	SS	df	MS	F	Prob>F
Columns	0.69565	11	0.06324	2.62	0.0042
Error	4.05766	168	0.02415		
Total	4.75331	179			

doi:10.1371/journal.pone.0144059.t004

Table 5. ANOVA results for HSingle.

HAvrage	SS	df	MS	F	Prob>F
Columns	0.47251	11	0.04296	2.62	0.0043
Error	2.52617	154	0.0164		
Total	8.91175	175			

doi:10.1371/journal.pone.0144059.t005

Table 6. ANOVA results for HSingle.

HSingle	SS	df	MS	F	Prob>F
Columns	0.3194	11	0.02903	2.38	0.0095
Error	1.8788	154	0.0122		
Total	10.2233	179			

doi:10.1371/journal.pone.0144059.t006

The small Prob values indicates that differences between means of the columns are significant. From that we can conclude that the similarity measures have significant impact in clustering quality. In the rest of this study we will inspect how these similarity measures influence on clustering quality.

EXPERIMENTAL RESULTS

It is noted that references to all data employed in this work are available in acknowledgment section. A diverse set of similarity measures for continuous data was studied on low and high-dimensional continuous datasets in order to clarify and compare the accuracy of each similarity measure in different datasets with various dimensionality situations and using 15 datasets [18,19,46–49]. Details of the datasets applied in this study are represented inTable 7.

Table 7. Dataset Details.

Dataset Name	Dimensions	Clusters	Vectors
Aggregation	2	7	788
Compound	2	6	399
D31	2	31	3100
Flame	2	2	240
Path based	2	3	300
R15	2	15	600
Sensor_2	2	4	5456
Spiral	2	3	312
Iris	4	3	150
Sensor_4	4	4	5456
Data_User_Modeling	5	4	258
Seeds	7	3	210
Glass	9	7	214
Sensor_24	24	4	5456
Movement Libera	90	15	360

doi:10.1371/journal.pone.0144059.t007

The experiments were conducted using partitioning (k-means and k-medoids) and hierarchical algorithms, which are distance-based. As it is discussed in section 3.2 the Rand index served to evaluate and compare the results. The results for each of these algorithms are discussed later in this section.

The k-means and k-medoids algorithms were used in this experiment as partitioning algorithms, and the Rand index served accuracy evaluation purposes. Due to the fact that the k-means and k-medoids algorithm results are dependent on the initial, randomly selected centers, and in some cases their accuracy might be affected by local minimum trap, the experiment was repeated 100 times for each similarity measure, after which the maximum Rand index was considered for comparison.

Illustration Technique

A summary of the normalized Rand index results is illustrated in color scale tables in Fig 3and Fig 4. Since the aim of this study is to investigate and evaluate the accuracy of similarity measures for different dimensional datasets, the tables are organized based on horizontally ascending dataset dimensions. After the first column, which contains the names of the similarity measures, the remaining table is divided in two batches of columns (low and high-dimensional) that demonstrate the normalized Rand indexes for low and high-dimensional datasets, respectively. The final column considered in this table is 'overall average' in order to explore the most accurate similarity measure in general. This illustrational structure and approach is used for all four algorithms in this paper.

	Low Dimensional								Higher Dimentional								Overall Average
Dimensions	2	2	2	2	2	2	2	2	4	4	5	7	9	24	90		
	sensor_2	Aggregation	Compound	Flame	Pathbased	R15	Spiral	D31	Iris	sensor_4	User_Mod	Seeds	Glass	sensor_24	Libras movement		
Euclidean	0.881	0.934	0.982	1.000	0.932	1.000	0.880	0.999	0.546	0.000	1.000	0.972	0.999	0.488	0.505		0.808
Average	0.912	0.934	0.972	1.000	0.932	1.000	0.881	0.995	0.546	0.091	1.000	0.968	1.000	0.655	0.941		0.855
Cosine	0.708	0.518	0.580	0.273	0.027	0.887	1.000	0.918	1.000	0.186	0.158	0.987	0.988	0.596	0.364		0.613
Chord	0.708	0.520	0.580	0.273	0.027	0.886	1.000	0.918	1.000	0.186	0.161	0.987	0.996	0.707	0.941		0.659
Mahalanobis	0.891	0.929	1.000	0.977	1.000	1.000	0.883	1.000	0.546	0.050	0.909	0.972	0.976	0.000	0.677		0.787
Canberra	0.942	0.910	0.915	0.844	0.815	0.999	0.817	0.994	0.874	1.000	0.793	0.939	0.654	0.754	0.166		0.828
CoeffDiv	0.934	0.855	0.958	0.000	0.797	0.998	0.839	0.994	0.915	0.730	0.711	0.795	0.649	0.853	0.587		0.774
Czekan	1.000	1.000	0.906	0.823	0.899	0.998	0.851	1.000	0.794	0.941	0.826	1.000	0.981	0.572	0.000		0.839
IndOfAssoc	0.715	0.519	0.576	0.227	0.014	0.883	0.986	0.918	0.957	0.274	0.159	0.997	0.977	0.482	0.417		0.607
Manhattan	0.901	0.929	0.953	0.977	0.914	0.998	0.901	0.998	0.515	0.860	0.801	0.963	0.980	0.279	0.495		0.831
MCharDiff	0.901	0.929	0.948	0.977	0.914	0.998	0.898	0.999	0.515	0.870	0.789	0.963	0.974	0.509	0.254		0.829
Pearson	0.000	0.000	0.000	0.147	0.000	0.000	0.000	0.000	0.000	0.438	0.000	0.000	0.000	1.000	1.000		0.172

Figure 3. K-means color scale table for normalized Rand index values (green represents the highest and it changes to red, which is the lowest Rand index value).

	Low Dimensional								Higher Dimensional							Overal Average
Dimensions	2	2	2	2	2	2	2	2	4	4	5	7	9	24	90	
	sensor_2	Aggregatio	Compound	Flame	Pathbased	R15	Spiral	D31	Iris	sensor_4	User_Mod	Seeds	Glass	sensor_24	Libras movement	
Euclidean	0.928	0.437	1.000	1.000	0.932	1.000	0.787	1.000	0.719	0.607	0.957	0.996	0.990	0.569	0.990	0.861
Average	0.825	0.972	0.967	1.000	0.932	1.000	0.785	0.996	0.719	0.649	0.928	0.996	0.992	0.543	1.000	0.887
Cosine	0.641	0.480	0.555	0.152	0.000	0.883	0.793	0.918	1.000	0.651	0.802	0.934	0.997	0.544	0.998	0.690
Chord	0.641	0.480	0.551	0.152	0.000	0.880	0.793	0.918	1.000	0.657	0.802	0.934	0.982	0.528	0.980	0.686
Mahalanobis	0.809	0.975	0.987	0.977	1.000	0.976	0.790	0.995	0.250	0.000	0.962	0.849	0.928	0.000	0.000	0.700
Canberra	0.996	0.909	0.918	0.783	0.916	0.998	1.000	0.992	0.794	1.000	0.000	0.991	0.734	1.000	0.941	0.865
CoeffDiv	1.000	0.825	0.918	0.000	0.929	0.975	0.786	0.988	0.915	0.784	0.000	0.796	0.604	0.716	0.982	0.748
Czekan	0.978	1.000	0.941	0.824	0.929	0.998	0.824	0.994	0.682	0.632	0.000	1.000	0.994	0.663	0.961	0.828
IndOfAssoc	0.674	0.468	0.568	0.255	0.409	0.884	0.743	0.919	0.915	0.408	0.784	0.978	0.991	0.635	0.987	0.708
Manhattan	0.947	0.949	0.979	0.932	0.903	0.999	0.806	0.995	0.546	0.477	0.977	0.981	0.994	0.501	0.976	0.864
MCharDiff	0.975	0.986	0.972	0.932	0.903	0.998	0.910	0.999	0.546	0.712	1.000	0.981	1.000	0.456	0.974	0.890
Pearson	0.000	0.000	0.000	0.143	0.196	0.000	0.000	0.000	0.000	0.006	0.813	0.000	0.000	0.400	0.990	0.170

Figure 4. K-medoids color scale table for normalized Rand index values (green is the highest and changes color to red, which is the lowest Rand index value).

Benchmarking Similarity Measures for Partitioning Algorithms

Fig 3 represents the results for the k-means algorithm. According to the figure, for low-dimensional datasets, the Mahalanobis measure has the highest results among all similarity measures. On the other hand, for high-dimensional datasets, the Coefficient of Divergence is the most accurate with the highest Rand index values. Fig 4 provides the results for the k-medoids algorithm. Mean Character Difference is the most precise measure for low-dimensional datasets, while the Cosine measure represents better results in terms of accuracy for high-dimensional datasets. Overall, Mean Character Difference has high accuracy for most datasets.

As a general result for the partitioning algorithms used in this study, average distance results in more accurate and reliable outcomes for both algorithms. It is the most accurate measure in the k-means algorithm and at the same time, with very little difference, it stands in second place after Mean Character Difference for the k-medoids algorithm.

From another perspective, similarity measures in the k-means algorithm can be investigated to clarify which would lead to the k-means converging faster. However the convergence of k-means and k-medoid algorithms is not guaranteed due to the possibility of falling in local minimum trap. For this reason we have run the algorithm 100 times to prevent bias toward this weakness. Fig 5 shows two sample box charts created by using normalized data, which represents the normalized iteration count needed for the convergence of each similarity measure. Results were collected after 100 times of repeating the k-means algorithm for each similarity measure and dataset.

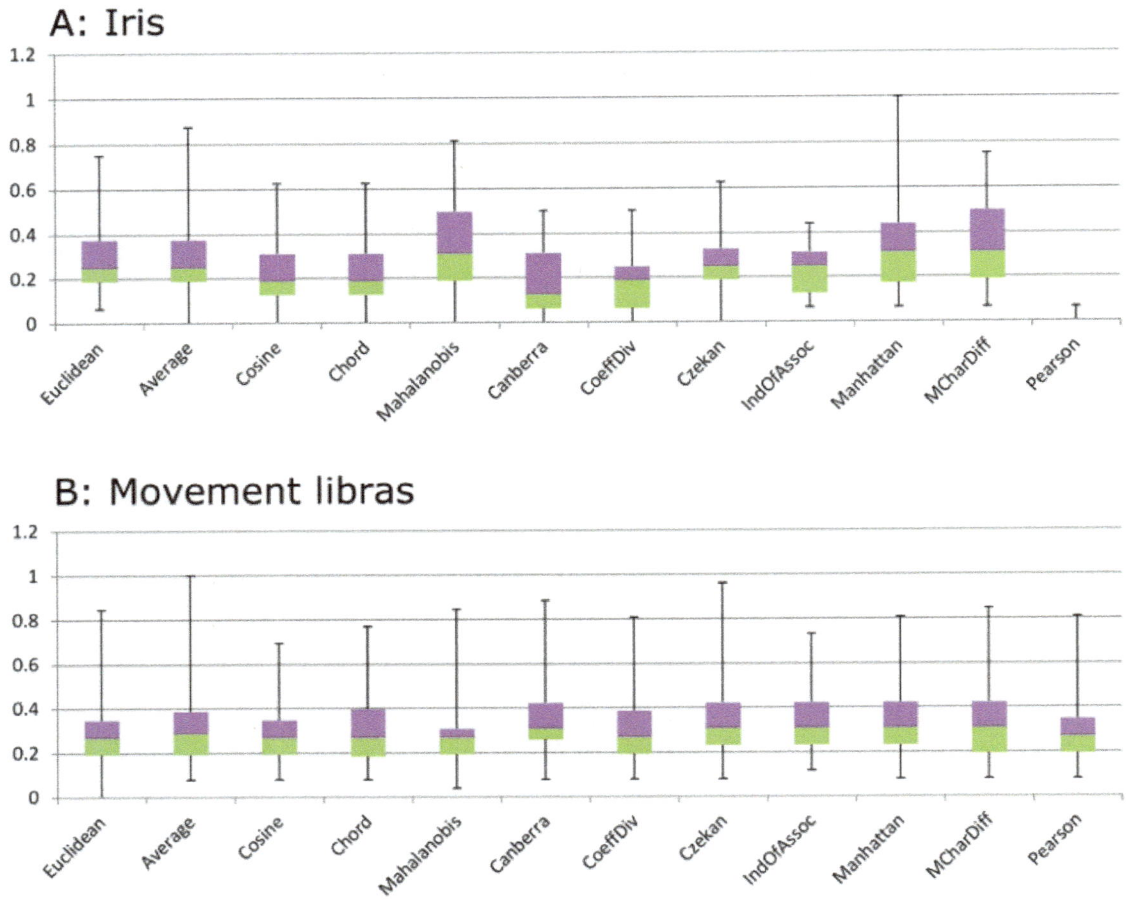

Figure 5. Sample box charts for k-means iteration counts created with a collection of normalized results after 100 times of repeating the algorithm for each similarity measure and dataset.

Fig 6 is a summarized color scale table representing the mean and variance of iteration counts for all 100 algorithm runs. Pearson has the fastest convergence in most datasets. After Pearson, Average is the fastest similarity measure in terms of convergence.

dimensions	2	2	2	2	2	2	2	2	4	4	5	7	9	24	90
	sensor_2	Aggregation	Compound	Flame	Pathbased	R15	Spiral	D31	Iris	sensor_4	Data_User_Modeling	Seeds	Glass	sensor_24	Libras movement
Euclidean	0.1682 (0.0686)	0.2040 (0.1007)	0.1728 (0.0969)	0.3277 (0.1516)	0.1728 (0.0969)	0.1094 (0.045)	0.3349 (0.1932)	0.1317 (0.0445)	0.3037 (0.1667)	0.1267 (0.0646)	0.1434 (0.1034)	0.1804 (0.0688)	0.2900 (0.1254)	0.2199 (0.1616)	0.2817 (0.1265)
Average	0.1658 (0.0689)	0.1922 (0.1011)	0.1643 (0.0806)	0.3504 (0.1594)	0.1643 (0.0806)	0.1073 (0.0391)	0.3558 (0.2448)	0.1349 (0.0503)	0.3018 (0.181)	0.1354 (0.0843)	0.1462 (0.0926)	0.1784 (0.0749)	0.2783 (0.1188)	0.2159 (0.1541)	0.3190 (0.1688)
Cosine	0.3265 (0.1725)	0.4033 (0.1966)	0.5253 (0.2831)	0.4179 (0.1491)	0.5253 (0.2831)	0.3191 (0.1617)	0.3166 (0.1904)	0.4018 (0.1468)	0.2254 (0.1191)	0.2176 (0.1216)	0.1104 (0.0695)	0.3076 (0.2268)	0.3150 (0.1455)	0.1762 (0.116)	0.2758 (0.1208)
Chord	0.2912 (0.1503)	0.3701 (0.2014)	0.5373 (0.2953)	0.4331 (0.1471)	0.5373 (0.2953)	0.2773 (0.1246)	0.2973 (0.1858)	0.3827 (0.1792)	0.2298 (0.1259)	0.2337 (0.1294)	0.1173 (0.0818)	0.3472 (0.2752)	0.3320 (0.1776)	0.1856 (0.1116)	0.3034 (0.1583)
Mahalanobis	0.1737 (0.0649)	0.2073 (0.0997)	0.1775 (0.0771)	0.3769 (0.1769)	0.1775 (0.0771)	0.1068 (0.0414)	0.2955 (0.168)	0.1333 (0.0482)	0.3415 (0.1849)	0.1242 (0.0745)	0.1636 (0.0958)	0.1867 (0.0727)	0.2741 (0.1265)	0.2034 (0.1173)	0.2859 (0.1305)
Canberra	0.2099 (0.0883)	0.2934 (0.1412)	0.2192 (0.0932)	0.4792 (0.1942)	0.2192 (0.0932)	0.1145 (0.0586)	0.2704 (0.1349)	0.1835 (0.068)	0.1824 (0.1349)	0.2236 (0.1733)	0.2243 (0.1569)	0.2124 (0.0819)	0.1486 (0.0704)	0.2873 (0.1987)	0.3477 (0.1487)
CoeffDiv	0.1965 (0.096)	0.2813 (0.1306)	0.2314 (0.0893)	0.4154 (0.1508)	0.2314 (0.0893)	0.1076 (0.0511)	0.2546 (0.1034)	0.1660 (0.0555)	0.1730 (0.1123)	0.1840 (0.0949)	0.1481 (0.0957)	0.2329 (0.0988)	0.1459 (0.1025)	0.3643 (0.2578)	0.3159 (0.1661)
Czekan	0.1976 (0.0787)	0.2755 (0.1197)	0.1780 (0.0808)	0.3592 (0.1417)	0.1780 (0.0808)	0.1269 (0.061)	0.2326 (0.0889)	0.1446 (0.0649)	0.2639 (0.1334)	0.1806 (0.1043)	0.1730 (0.1094)	0.1639 (0.0607)	0.2850 (0.1323)	0.1999 (0.1484)	0.3260 (0.1427)
IndOfAssoc	0.4238 (0.2591)	0.3800 (0.1871)	0.4116 (0.2462)	0.5385 (0.1706)	0.4116 (0.2462)	0.2824 (0.1639)	0.3177 (0.1794)	0.3686 (0.1423)	0.2254 (0.0988)	0.1636 (0.0745)	0.1480 (0.0953)	0.3033 (0.2167)	0.2640 (0.1029)	0.1893 (0.1007)	0.3442 (0.1354)
Manhattan	0.2578 (0.1074)	0.1807 (0.0654)	0.1748 (0.0721)	0.4040 (0.1764)	0.1748 (0.0721)	0.1310 (0.0617)	0.2477 (0.1458)	0.1261 (0.0489)	0.3371 (0.2081)	0.1857 (0.0798)	0.1365 (0.0807)	0.1830 (0.0755)	0.2682 (0.1116)	0.2109 (0.1283)	0.3302 (0.1397)
MCharDiff	0.2841 (0.1307)	0.1966 (0.0767)	0.1676 (0.0776)	0.4003 (0.2006)	0.1676 (0.0776)	0.1231 (0.055)	0.2323 (0.1332)	0.1251 (0.0519)	0.3333 (0.1874)	0.1828 (0.0797)	0.1496 (0.088)	0.1997 (0.076)	0.2693 (0.1355)	0.1943 (0.1288)	0.3302 (0.1496)
Pearson	0.0000 (0)	0.0000 (0)	0.0000 (0)	0.0000 (0)	0.0000 (0)	0.0000 (0)	0.0023 (0.0068)	0.0000 (0)	0.0006 (0.0062)	0.0255 (0.0256)	0.1272 (0.094)	0.0035 (0.0093)	0.0112 (0.0159)	0.1886 (0.1052)	0.2712 (0.1235)

Figure 6. Color scale table for iteration count mean and variance (green is the lowest and it changes color to red, which shows the greatest iteration count value).

Regarding the discussion on Rand index and iteration count, it is manifested that the Average measure is not only accurate in most datasets and with both k-means and k-medoids algorithms, but it is the second fastest similarity measure after Pearson in terms of convergence, making it a secure choice when clustering is necessary using k-means or k-medoids algorithms.

Benchmarking Similarity Measures for Hierarchical Algorithms

In a previous section, the influence of different similarity measures on k-means and k-medoids algorithms as partitioning algorithms was evaluated and compared. In this section, the results for Single-link and Group Average algorithms, which are two hierarchical clustering algorithms, will be discussed for each similarity measure in terms of the Rand index. Fig 7 and Fig 8 represent sample bar charts of the results. The bar charts include 6 sample datasets. Because bar charts for all datasets and similarity measures would be jumbled, the results are presented using color scale tables for easier understanding and discussion. As discussed in the last section, Fig 9 and Fig 10 are two color scale tables that demonstrate the normalized Rand index values for each similarity measure. The results inFig 9 for Single-link show that for low-dimensional datasets, the Mahalanobis distance is the most accurate similarity measure and Pearson is the best among other measures for high-dimensional datasets. The overall average column in this figure shows that generally, Pearson presents the highest accuracy and the Average and Euclidean distances are among the most accurate measures. For the Group Average algorithm, as seen in Fig 10, Euclidean and Average are the best among all similarity measures for low-dimensional datasets. For high-dimensional datasets, Cosine and Chord are the most accurate measures. Generally, in the Group Average algorithm, Manhattan and Mean Character Difference have the best overall Rand index results followed by Euclidean and Average. Considering the overall results, it is clear that the Average measure is constantly among the best measures, and for both Single-link and Group Average algorithms.

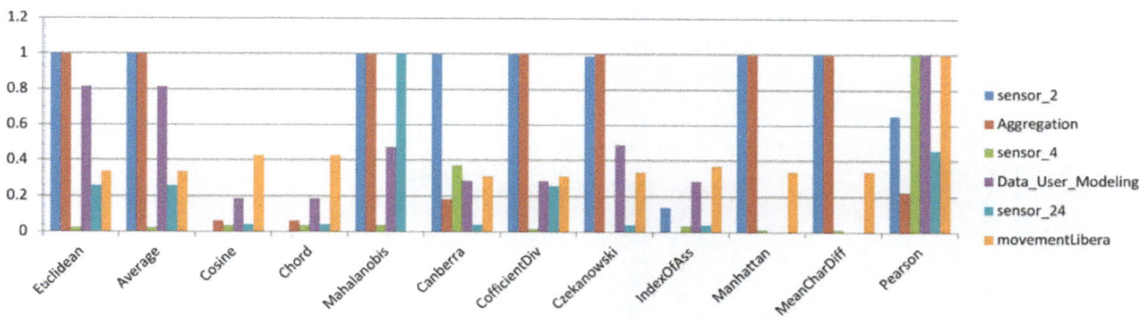

Figure 7. Bar chart of normalized Rand index values for selected datasets using the Single-link algorithm.

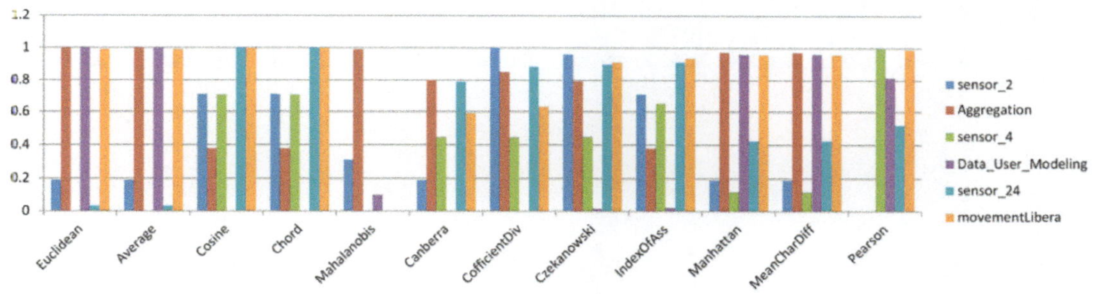

Figure 8. Bar chart of normalized Rand index values for selected datasets using the Group Average algorithm.

	Low Dimensional								Higher Dimensional							Overall Average
Dimension	2	2	2	2	2	2	2	2	4	4	5	7	9	24	90	
	sensor_2	Aggregatior	Compound	Flame	Pathbased	R15	Spiral	D31	Iris	sensor_4	User_Mod	Seeds	Glass	sensor_24	Libras movement	
Euclidean	1.000	0.996	0.984	0.000	0.996	0.194	1.000	0.869	1.000	0.025	0.814	0.939	0.212	0.257	0.337	0.642
Average	1.000	0.996	0.984	0.000	0.996	0.194	1.000	0.869	1.000	0.025	0.814	0.939	0.212	0.257	0.337	0.642
Cosine	0.000	0.063	0.000	0.080	0.722	0.007	0.000	1.000	0.989	0.036	0.186	0.160	0.298	0.041	0.428	0.267
Chord	0.000	0.063	0.000	0.080	0.722	0.007	0.000	1.000	0.989	0.036	0.186	0.160	0.298	0.041	0.428	0.267
Mahalanobis	1.000	0.998	0.995	0.008	0.996	1.000	1.000	0.786	0.000	0.040	0.474	0.000	0.326	1.000	0.000	0.575
Canberra	1.000	0.182	0.992	0.004	0.837	0.007	0.519	0.739	0.945	0.370	0.285	0.151	0.000	0.041	0.313	0.426
CoeffDiv	1.000	1.000	1.000	0.000	0.840	0.007	0.519	0.709	0.945	0.019	0.285	0.004	0.011	0.257	0.313	0.461
Czekan	0.988	1.000	0.984	0.000	0.837	0.007	1.000	0.705	0.989	0.000	0.489	0.151	0.298	0.041	0.338	0.522
IndOfAssoc	0.139	0.000	0.000	0.080	0.722	0.007	0.000	0.000	0.989	0.036	0.285	0.151	0.298	0.041	0.369	0.208
Manhattan	1.000	0.996	0.614	0.000	1.000	0.000	1.000	0.789	0.999	0.016	0.000	0.151	0.298	0.000	0.340	0.480
MCharDiff	1.000	0.996	0.614	0.000	1.000	0.000	1.000	0.789	0.999	0.016	0.000	0.151	0.298	0.000	0.340	0.480
Pearson	0.654	0.225	0.169	1.000	0.000	0.601	0.874	0.057	0.989	1.000	1.000	1.000	1.000	0.458	1.000	0.669

Figure 9. Color scale table of normalized Rand index values for the Single-link method (green is the highest and it changes color to red, which represents the lowest Rand index value).

	Low Dimensional								Higher Dimensional							Overall Average
Dimensions	2	2	2	2	2	2	2	2	4	4	5	7	9	24	90	
	sensor_2	Aggregatio	Compound	Flame	Pathbased	R15	Spiral	D31	Iris	sensor_4	User_Mod	Seeds	Glass	sensor_24	Libras movement	
Euclidean	0.190	1.000	0.972	0.958	1.000	1.000	0.636	0.996	1.000	0.000	1.000	1.000	0.079	0.032	0.992	0.724
Average	0.190	1.000	0.972	0.958	1.000	1.000	0.636	0.996	1.000	0.000	1.000	1.000	0.079	0.032	0.992	0.724
Cosine	0.709	0.379	0.391	0.856	0.811	0.539	0.004	0.901	0.781	0.706	0.000	0.645	1.000	1.000	1.000	0.648
Chord	0.709	0.379	0.391	0.856	0.811	0.539	0.004	0.901	0.781	0.706	0.000	0.645	1.000	1.000	1.000	0.648
Mahalanobis	0.313	0.992	0.973	1.000	1.000	0.000	1.000	1.000	0.000	0.000	0.100	0.000	0.000	0.000	0.000	0.425
Canberra	0.190	0.804	0.803	0.163	0.959	0.495	0.030	0.959	0.746	0.448	0.003	0.987	0.073	0.791	0.593	0.536
CoeffDiv	1.000	0.853	0.808	0.000	0.917	0.460	0.081	0.963	0.746	0.448	0.003	0.444	0.056	0.885	0.633	0.553
Czekan	0.961	0.797	0.754	0.879	0.981	0.644	0.000	0.978	0.791	0.450	0.018	0.846	0.407	0.899	0.914	0.688
IndOfAssoc	0.709	0.378	0.440	0.669	0.803	0.780	0.004	0.904	0.781	0.652	0.022	0.640	0.407	0.914	0.937	0.603
Manhattan	0.190	0.974	1.000	0.922	0.999	0.644	0.543	0.999	0.988	0.119	0.962	0.846	0.407	0.425	0.960	0.732
MCharDiff	0.190	0.974	1.000	0.922	0.999	0.644	0.543	0.999	0.988	0.119	0.962	0.846	0.407	0.425	0.960	0.732
Pearson	0.000	0.000	0.000	0.685	0.000	0.869	0.107	0.000	0.789	1.000	0.818	0.047	0.230	0.521	0.992	0.404

Figure 10. Color scale table of normalized Rand index values for Group Average (green is the highest and it changes color to red, which signifies the lowest Rand index value).

A review of the results and discussions on the k-means, k-medoids, Single-link and Group Average algorithms reveals that by considering the overall results, the Average measure is regularly among the most accurate measures for all four algorithms.

According to heat map tables it is noticeable that Pearson correlation is behaving differently in comparison to other distance measures. It specially shows very weak results with centroid based algorithms, k-means and k-medoids. Based on the results in this research, in general, Pearson correlation doesn't work properly for low dimensional datasets while it shows better results for high dimensional datasets.

Fig 11 illustrates the overall average RI in all 4 algorithms and all 15 datasets also uphold the same conclusion. Fig 12 at the other hand shows the average RI for 4 algorithms separately. It can be inferred that Average measure among other measures is more accurate.

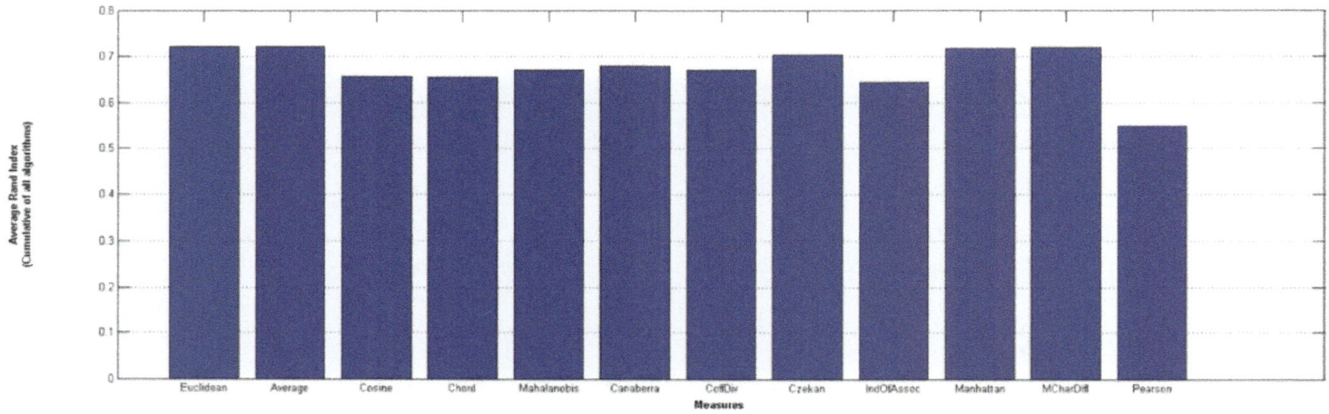

Figure 11. Overall RI Average.

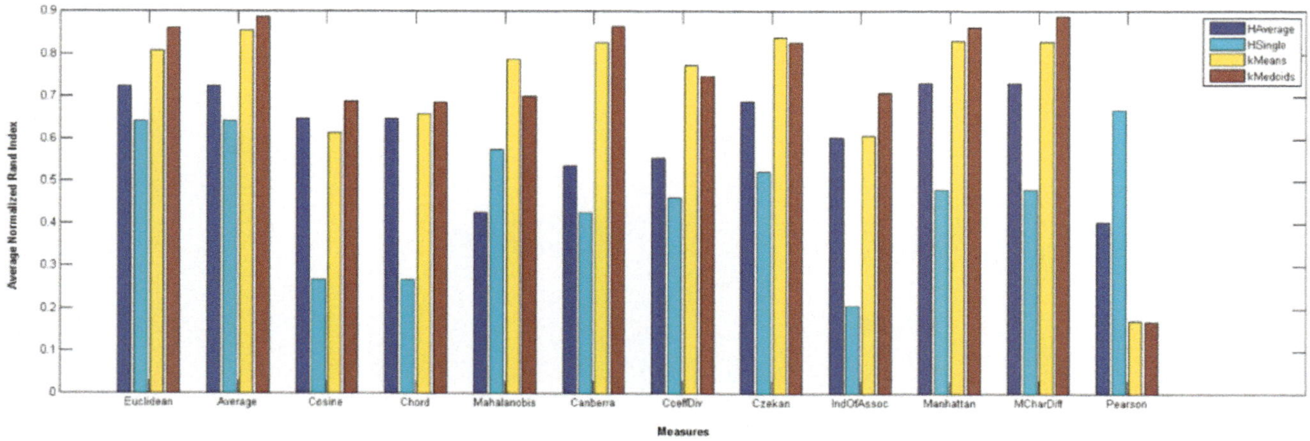

Figure 12. Average RI for four algorithms.

Furthermore, by using the k-means algorithm, this similarity measure is the fastest after Pearson in terms of convergence.

CONCLUDING REMARKS

Selecting the right distance measure is one of the challenges encountered by professionals and researchers when attempting to deploy a distance-based clustering algorithm to a dataset. The variety of similarity measures can cause confusion and difficulties in choosing a suitable measure. Similarity measures may perform differently for datasets with diverse dimensionalities. The aim of this study was to clarify which similarity measures are more appropriate for low-dimensional and which perform better for high-dimensional datasets in the experiments. In this work, similarity measures for clustering numerical data in distance-based algorithms were compared and benchmarked using 15 datasets categorized as low and high-dimensional datasets. The accuracy of similarity measures in terms of the Rand index was studied and the best similarity measures for each of the low and high-dimensional datasets were discussed for four well-known distance-based algorithms. Overall, the results indicate that Average Distance is among the top most accurate measures for all clustering algorithms employed in this article. Moreover, this measure is one of the fastest in terms of convergence when k-means is the target clustering algorithm. Based on results in this study, in general, Pearson correlation is not recommended for low dimensional datasets. It also is not compatible with centroid based algorithms. However, this measure is mostly recommended for high dimensional datasets and by using hierarchical approaches.

ACKNOWLEDGMENTS

Ali Seyed Shirkhorshidi would like to express his sincere gratitude to Fatemeh Zahedifar and Seyed Mohammad Reza Shirkhorshidi, who helped in revising and preparing the paper.

AUTHOR CONTRIBUTIONS

Conceived and designed the experiments: ASS SA TYW. Performed the experiments: ASS SA TYW. Analyzed the data: ASS SA TYW. Contributed reagents/materials/analysis tools: ASS SA TYW. Wrote the paper: ASS SA TYW.

REFERENCES

1. Shirkhorshidi AS, Aghabozorgi S, Wah TY, Herawan T. Big Data Clustering: A Review. Computational Science and Its Applications–ICCSA 2014. Springer; 2014. pp. 707–720. doi: 10. 1007/978-3-319-09156-3_49.
2. Mohebi A, Aghabozorgi S, Ying Wah T, Herawan T, Yahyapour R. Iterative big data clustering algorithms: a review. Softw Pract Exp. 2015; n/a–n/a. doi: 10. 1002/ spe. 2341.
3. Bezdek JC, Ehrlich R, Full W. FCM: The fuzzy c-means clustering algorithm [Internet]. Computers & Geosciences. 1984. pp. 191–203. doi: 10. 1016/0098-3004(84)90020-7.
4. Peters G. Some refinements of rough k-means clustering. Pattern Recognit. 2006;39: 1481–1491. doi: 10. 1016/j. patcog. 2006. 02. 002.
5. Cui W, Wang Y, Fan Y, Feng Y, Lei T. Localized FCM clustering with spatial information for medical image segmentation and bias field estimation. Int J Biomed Imaging. 2013;2013: 930301. doi: 10. 1155/2013/930301. pmid:23997761
6. Ye J, Lazar NA, Li Y. Sparse geostatistical analysis in clustering fMRI time series. J Neurosci Methods. 2011;199: 336–345. doi: 10. 1016/j. jneumeth. 2011. 05. 016. pmid:21641934
7. Meyer G. Chinrungrueng F. J. Spatiotemporal clustering of fMRI time series in the spectral domain. Med Image Anal. 2004;9: 51–68. doi: 10. 1016/j. media. 2004. 07. 002
8. An L, Doerge RW. Dynamic Clustering of Gene Expression [Internet]. ISRN Bioinformatics. 2012. pp. 1–12. doi: 10. 5402/2012/537217.
9. De Souto MCP, Costa IG, de Araujo DS a, Ludermir TB, Schliep A. Clustering cancer gene expression data: a comparative study. BMC Bioinformatics. 2008;9: 497. doi: 10. 1186/1471-2105-9-497. pmid:19038021
10. Ernst J, Nau GJ, Bar-Joseph Z. Clustering short time series gene expression data. Bioinformatics. 2005;21: i159 –i168. doi: 10. 1093/bioinformatics/bti1022. pmid:15961453
11. Moolgavkar SH, Mcclellan RO, Dewanji A, Turim J, Georg Luebeck E, Edwards M. Time-series analyses of air pollution and mortality in the United States: A subsampling approach. Environ Health Perspect. 2013;121: 73–78. doi: 10. 1289/ehp. 1104507. pmid:23108284
12. Ignaccolo R, Ghigo S, Bande S. Functional zoning for air quality. Environ Ecol Stat. 2013;20: 109–127. doi: 10. 1007/s10651-012-0210-7.
13. Carbajal-Hernández JJ, Sánchez-Fernández LP, Carrasco-Ochoa J a. , Martínez-Trinidad JF. Assessment and prediction of air quality using fuzzy logic and autoregressive models. Atmos Environ. Elsevier Ltd; 2012;60: 37–50. doi: 10. 1016/j. atmosenv. 2012. 06. 004.
14. Shen W, Babushkin V, Aung Z, Woon WL. An ensemble model for day-ahead electricity demand time series forecasting. Proc fourth Int Conf Futur energy Syst—e-Energy '13. New York, New York, USA: ACM Press; 2013; 51. doi: 10. 1145/2487166. 2487173.
15. Iglesias F, Kastner W. Analysis of Similarity Measures in Times Series Clustering for the Discovery of Building Energy Patterns. Energies. 2013;6: 579–597. doi: 10. 3390/en6020579.
16. Wijk J Van, Selow E Van. Cluster and calendar based visualization of time series data. Proc 1999 IEEE Symp Inf Vis. IEEE Comput. Soc; 1999; 4–9. doi: 10. 1109/ INFVIS. 1999. 801851.
17. Aghabozorgi S, Seyed Shirkhorshidi A, Ying Wah T. Time-series clustering–A decade review. Inf Syst. 2015;53: 16–38. doi: 10. 1016/j. is. 2015. 04. 007.
18. Bache K, Lichman M. UCI Machine Learning Repository [Internet]. 2013. Available:http://archive. ics. uci. edu/ml
19. Speech and Image Processing Unit, University of Eastern Finland [Internet]. Available: http://cs. joensuu. fi/sipu/datasets/
20. Boriah S, Chandola V, Kumar V. Similarity measures

for categorical data: A comparative evaluation. In Proceedings of the eighth SIAM International Conference on Data Mining. 2008. pp. 243–254. doi: 10. 1137/1. 9781611972788. 22.

21. Lourenco F, Lobo V, Bacao F. Binary-based similarity measures for categorical data and their application in Self-Organizing Maps. 2004; 1–18.
22. Deshpande R, VanderSluis B, Myers CL. Comparison of Profile Similarity Measures for Genetic Interaction Networks. PLoS One. 2013;8: e68664. doi: 10. 1371/ journal. pone. 0068664. pmid:23874711
23. Strehl A, Ghosh J, Mooney R. Impact of similarity measures on web-page clustering. Work Artif Intell Web .... 2000; 58–64. Available:http://www. aaai. org/Papers/ Workshops/2000/WS-00-01/WS00-01-011. pdf
24. Zhang Z, Huang K, Tan T. Comparison of similarity measures for trajectory clustering in outdoor surveillance scenes. Proceedings—International Conference on Pattern Recognition. IEEE; 2006. pp. 1135–1138. doi: 10. 1109/ICPR. 2006. 392.
25. Khalifa A Al, Haranczyk M, Holliday J. Comparison of Nonbinary Similarity Coefficients for Similarity Searching, Clustering and Compound Selection. J Chem Inf Model. 2009;49: 1193–1201. doi: 10. 1021/ ci8004644. pmid:19405526
26. Dunham MH. Data Mining Introductor and Advanced Topics. Upper Saddle River, New Jersey: Prentice Hall; 2003.
27. Gan G, Ma C, Wu J. Data Clustering theory, Algorithms, and Applications. ASASIAM Series on Statistics and Applied. Society for Industrial and Applied Mathematics; 2007.
28. Han J, Kamber M, Pei J. Data mining: concepts and techniques. Morgan Kaufmann; 2006.
29. Cha Sung-Hyuk. Comprehensive survey on distance/ similarity measures between probability density functions. Int J Math Model methods Appl Sci. 2007;1: 300–307. doi: 10. 1. 1. 154. 8446
30. Mao J, Jain AK. A self-organizing network for hyperellipsoidal clustering (HEC). IEEE Trans Neural Networks. 1996;7: 16–29. doi: 10. 1109/72. 478389. pmid:18255555
31. Jain AK, Murty MN, Flynn PJ. Data clustering: a review. ACM Computing Surveys. ACM; 1999. pp. 264–323. doi: 10. 1145/331499. 331504.
32. Wilson D, Martinez T. Improved heterogeneous distance functions. JAIR. 1997;6: 1–34. Available: http://arxiv. org/abs/cs/9701101
33. Xu R, Wunsch D. Survey of clustering algorithms [Internet]. IEEE Transactions on Neural Networks. 2005. pp. 645–678. doi: 10. 1109/TNN. 2005. 845141. pmid:15940994
34. Perlibakas V. Distance measures for PCA-based face recognition. Pattern Recognit Lett. 2004;25: 711–724. doi: 10. 1016/j. patrec. 2004. 01. 011.
35. Legendre P, Legendre L. Numerical ecology. Elsevier; 2012.
36. Wang H, Wang H, Wang W, Wang W, Yang H, Yang H, et al. Clustering by pattern similarity in large data sets. 2002 ACM SIGMOD international conference on Management of Data. New York, New York, USA: ACM Press; 2002. p. 394. doi: 10. 1145/564691. 564737.
37. Hand D, Mannila H, Smyth P. Principles of data mining(adaptive computation and machine learning). Drug safety. 2001.
38. Ji M, Xie F, Ping Y. A dynamic fuzzy cluster algorithm for time series. Abstr Appl Anal. 2013;2013: 1–7. doi: 10. 1155/2013/183410.
39. János Abonyi BF. Cluster Analysis for Data Mining and System Identification. Springer; 2007.
40. Jiang D, Tang C, Zhang A. Cluster analysis for gene expression data: A survey. IEEE Trans Knowl Data Eng. 2004;16: 1370–1386. doi: 10. 1109/TKDE. 2004. 68.
41. Santos JM, Embrechts M. On the Use of the Adjusted Rand Index as a Metric for Evaluating Supervised Classification. Lecture Notes in Computer Science (including subseries Lecture Notes in Artificial Intelligence and Lecture Notes in Bioinformatics). 2009. pp. 175–184. doi: 10. 1007/978-3-642-04277-5_18.
42. Hubert L, Arabie P. Comparing partitions. J Classif. Springer; 1985;2: 193–218. doi: 10. 1007/BF01908075.
43. Fisher R. Statistical methods for research workers [Internet]. Edinburgh: Oliver and Boyd; 1925. Available: https://scholar. google. com/scholar?hl=en&q=Statistical+Methods+for+Research+Workers&btnG=&as_sdt=1%2C5&as_sdtp=#0
44. Cumming G. Understanding the new statistics: Effect sizes, confidence intervals, and meta-analysis [Internet]. 2013. Available: https://books. google. com/books?hl=en&lr=&id=1W6laNc7Xt8C&oi=fnd&pg=PR1&dq=Understanding+The+New+Statistics:+Effect+Sizes,+Confidence+Intervals,+and+Meta-Analysis&ots=PuHRVGc5 5O&sig=cEg6l3tSxFHlTI5dvubr1j7yMpI
45. Schlotzhauer S. Elementary statistics using JMP [Internet]. 2007. Available:https://books. google. com/ books?hl=en&lr=&id=5JYM1WxGDz8C&oi=fnd&pg=PR3&dq=Elementary+Statistics+Using+JMP&ots=MZOht9zZOP&sig=IFCsAn4Nd9clwioPf3qS_QXPzKc
46. Gionis A, Mannila H, Tsaparas P. Clustering aggregation. ACM Trans Knowl Discov Data. 2005;1: Article 4. doi: 10. 1109/ICDE. 2005. 34.
47. Zahn CT. Graph-Theoretical Methods for Detecting and Describing Gestalt Clusters. IEEE Trans Comput. 1971;C-20: 68–86. doi: 10. 1109/T-C. 1971. 223083.
48. Veenman CJ, Reinders MJT, Backer E. A maximum variance cluster algorithm. IEEE Trans Pattern Anal Mach Intell. 2002;24: 1273–1280. doi: 10. 1109/TPAMI. 2002. 1033218.
49. Fu L, Medico E. FLAME, a novel fuzzy clustering method for the analysis of DNA microarray data. BMC Bioinformatics. 2007;8: 3. doi: 10. 1186/1471-2105-8-3. pmid:17204155

CHAPTER 11

RE-IDENTIFICATION RISK VERSUS DATA UTILITY FOR AGGREGATED MOBILITY RESEARCH USING MOBILE PHONE LOCATION DATA

Ling Yin[1], Qian Wang[1], Shih-Lung Shaw[2,3], Zhixiang Fang[3], Jinxing Hu[1], Ye Tao[4], Wei Wang[1]

[1] Shenzhen Institutes of Advanced Technology, Chinese Academy of Sciences, Shenzhen, Guangdong, China

[2] Department of Geography, The University of Tennessee, Knoxville, TN, United States of America

[3] State Key Laboratory of Information Engineering in Surveying, Mapping, and Remote Sensing, Wuhan University, Wuhan, Hubei, China

[4] Department of Urban Planning and Design, The University of Hong Kong, Hong Kong, China

ABSTRACT

Mobile phone location data is a newly emerging data source of great potential to support human mobility research. However, recent studies have indicated that many users can be easily re-identified based on their unique activity patterns. Privacy protection procedures will usually change the original data and cause a loss of data utility for analysis purposes. Therefore, the need for detailed data for activity analysis while avoiding potential privacy risks presents a challenge. The aim of this study is to reveal the re-identification risks from a Chinese city's mobile users and to examine the quantitative relationship between re-identification risk and data utility for an aggregated mobility analysis. The first step is to apply two reported attack models, the top N locations and the spatio-temporal points, to evaluate the re-identification risks in Shenzhen City, a metropolis in China. A spatial generalization approach to protecting privacy is then proposed and implemented, and spatially aggregated analysis is used to assess the loss of data utility after privacy protection. The results demonstrate that the re-identification risks in Shenzhen City are clearly different from those in regions reported in Western countries, which prove the spatial heterogeneity of re-identification risks in mobile phone location data. A uniform mathematical relationship has also been found between re-identification risk (x) and data (y) utility for both attack models: $y = -ax^b+c$, (a, b, c>0; 0<x<1), where the exponent b increases with the background knowledge of the attackers. The discovered mathematical relationship provides data publishers with useful guidance on choosing the right tradeoff between privacy and utility. Overall, this study contributes to a better understanding of re-identification risks and a privacy-utility tradeoff benchmark for improving privacy protection when sharing detailed trajectory data.

INTRODUCTION

As a routine procedure, mobile phone operators collect users' location data with certain sampling methods for billing, troubleshooting, or other technical measurement purposes. The ability to obtain massive numbers of individual trajectories automatically and remotely opens up unprecedented opportunities to study human mobility with a large sample size at low cost [1]. With mobile phone location data, a number of studies over the past few years have made progress in formulating universal human mobility patterns [2–4], predicting human mobility [5–6], estimating origin-destination (OD) flows [7–9], modeling human movement [10], revealing population dynamics and hot spots [11–12], identifying important activity places [13], and mining daily activity structures [14]. These studies have suggested that

Citation: Yin L, Wang Q, Shaw S-L, Fang Z, Hu J, Tao Y, et al. (2015) Re-Identification Risk versus Data Utility for Aggregated Mobility Research Using Mobile Phone Location Data. PLoS ONE 10(10): e0140589. doi:10.1371/journal.pone.0140589.

mobile phone location data have the potential to become a major data source to study human mobility for transportation, urban planning, epidemiology, and sociology research.

However, the rich spatio-temporal information embedded in such trajectory data may result in privacy breach. Two recent studies have pointed out that from anonymized mobile phone location datasets, and with only a little outside information, the uniqueness of individual trajectories can cause identity exposure (re-identification) for a considerable number of mobile users. The MobiCom 2011 study proposed an attack model based on the top *N* locations and demonstrated that at the spatial granularity of the mobile sector or mobile cell level, the top two or three locations from mobile users' trajectories yielded unique identifications of 10%–50% of individuals in the United States [15]. The Scientific Report 2013 study proposed an attack model based on spatial-temporal points and revealed that four randomly selected spatio-temporal points could uniquely identify 95% of the mobile users in a European country [16].

The severe re-identification risks revealed by these studies and the increasing number of studies using mobile phone location data impel the community to engage in a deeper discussion about the right way to safeguard privacy when working with these kinds of data [17]. On the one hand, researchers and policy-makers would like to have detailed trajectory data to learn important information that would benefit society; on the other hand, data publishers must apply privacy protection procedures on original data to make sure that sharing the data does not lead to privacy breach. Researchers have proposed some approaches to protecting trajectory privacy [18–21], such as adding dummy data [22] or suppressing or generalizing sensitive information [23–27]. However, existing research on other datasets has suggested that the more privacy we protect, the more data utility will be lost [28–32]. Generally, it is challenging to find an optimal tradeoff between these two conflicting goals. In terms of data utility for human mobility research, some studies have aimed to analyze the mobility patterns of a particular individual, such as identifying activity locations with a spatial resolution of hundreds of meters [13–14]. In this case, the changes to individual traces introduced by a privacy protection procedure such as location perturbation are likely to have a significant impact on the results of the analysis. On the other hand, many policy-making applications focus only on aggregated mobility patterns such as OD flows between regions with a spatial resolution of thousands of meters, a fact which likely enlarges the space for compromise between privacy protection and data utility.

To deepen our understanding of the privacy risks in mobile phone location data and to help develop useful privacy protection approaches when sharing such data, this study uses an anonymized mobile phone location dataset from a major city in China to address three issues. First, do the high re-identification risks in mobile phone location datasets from the United States [15] and a European country [16] also apply to a major city in China that has a different population size, culture, and lifestyle? To the best of our knowledge, a comparative study across countries has not yet been published. Second, how do generalization-based approaches, as suggested in [15] and [16], reduce re-identification risk and affect human mobility analysis, especially at the aggregated analysis level of policy-making? Third, this study seeks to explore the possibility of a quantitative relationship between re-identification risk and data utility for aggregated mobility analysis. If there is such a relationship, what is the math formula? Answers to these questions could help to estimate re-identification risks in different regions and to understand the tradeoff between privacy risk and data utility, thus making it possible to design better privacy protection approaches and to improve sustainable use of mobile phone location data.

MATERIALS AND METHODS

Dataset

Because previous studies [15] and [16] conducted their privacy risk measurements based on call detail records (CDR), which are a common type of mobile phone location dataset, the same data type was chosen for this study to enable rigorous comparison of results. The local transportation department provided the CDR dataset and permitted this research and publication of its results. Each CDR contains the location and time when a user initiates or receives a call, thus providing an individual trajectory data source. The CDR dataset used in this study was collected by a major telecom operator in Shenzhen City, a metropolis with the highest population density and fourth highest economic output among Chinese cities (http://english.sz.gov.cn/). Shenzhen City covers an area of 1952 km^2, where there are 3036 base stations owned by the telecom operator. This CDR dataset includes call records of 4.57 million mobile users in 2011 (nearly 30% of the total population) and covers a span of 34 days, including 25 weekdays and 9 weekend days. Each entry in the dataset is made up of six attribute fields (S1 Table): (*ID*) the user's ID (encrypted by the operator), (*t*) time when the call was connected, (*lat*, *long*) latitude and longitude of the user's connected base station, (*f*) a flag representing whether the call was initiated or received, and (*reg*) the regional phone code. This dataset itself uses three methods to protect privacy: encrypting users' mobile phone numbers; generalizing every user's precise location with a base station coverage area; and inhibiting exposure of user trajectories through sparse location sampling only triggered by call events.

Re-identification Risk Evaluation

This study defines individual privacy risk as the probability of being re-identified. To compare privacy risks in different geographical regions, the same methods proposed in [15] and [16] were used to evaluate the privacy risk in this dataset. These methods include two attack models using the top *N* locations [15] and spatio-temporal points [16] as quasi-identifiers.

The top *N* locations refer to the locations observed to be most frequently visited by a mobile user. This model assumes that attackers have background knowledge of a target's top *N* locations. In reality, the top *N* locations are usually important places for residents. For instance, the top two locations likely correspond to a user's home and work places, and the third top location is likely to be a kindergarten, school, or shopping mall that a user often visits. In today's information society, it is not difficult for attackers to obtain such outside knowledge. Therefore, the attack scenario using the top *N* locations is reasonable and generally applicable.

Specifically, a person's re-identification risk is quantified by the *k-anonymity value* ($k \in \mathbf{N}^*$), of which k represents the size of an anonymity set that includes users with the same top N locations [24]. The re-identification risk decreases with the size of the anonymity set k. In the extreme case where k equals 1 (i.e., there is only one user in the anonymity set), the re-identification risk of this user reaches 100%. The top N location model also has another two extended forms: the unordered top N locations, and the variable-length top locations. The unordered top N location model treats top locations identically regardless of their order. The variable-length top location model calculates the number of "preferred" locations for each user, and the number of top locations N varies for each user. For details of these two extended forms, interested readers can refer to [15]. Besides, the top N location model only works for frequent call users. For mobile users who made or received very few calls during the observation period, it is difficult to infer their top N locations accurately. Study [15] defines frequent call users as mobile users who made or received at least one call per day in average.

The second attack model represents a user U's trace by $Trace_U = \{lat_1\text{-}long_1\text{-}t_1, lat_2\text{-}long_2\text{-}t_2, lat_3\text{-}long_3\text{-}t_3, \ldots\ldots lat_n\text{-}long_n\text{-}t_n\}$, where the spatio-temporal point ($lat_i\text{-}long_i\text{-}t_i$) represents the location of U at time t_i and n is the number of observed spatio-temporal points in the trajectory. This model supposes that attackers know p spatio-temporal points of the target and simulates this uncertain background knowledge by randomly selecting p points. This attack assumption also has wide applicability, especially with the extensive use of mobile social media such as Twitter that can be used to acquire self-reported whereabouts. The k-anonymity method is also used to quantify privacy risks. In this case, k represents the size of the anonymity set composed of users with the same selected spatio-temporal points. Similarly, users in an anonymity set with size k equals to one can be 100% re-identified. This spatio-temporal point model works for all mobile users.

A uniquely identified population ratio x (x = population with k equal to 1/total population) has been suggested as a useful indicator to represent the re-identification risk in a population [16]. This study therefore uses this identified population ratio x to evaluate the impact of privacy protection on privacy risk reduction and to formulate the relationship between privacy risk and data utility.

Privacy Protection Procedure

This study proposes a privacy protection method which reduces the spatial precision of a user's location, which is a generalization-based approach. As Fig 1a shows, a base station coverage area can be represented by a Voronoi polygon. Many factors can influence the coverage area, including its surrounding topography and buildings and the height and angle of its antennas. If only the locations of base stations are available, the best approximation is to use Voronoi polygons [2,5,16]. Then a grid with a given spatial aggregation resolution is created for the study area (Fig 1b). Base stations with centroids located in the same grid block are aggregated (Fig 1c), and the aggregated base station is treated as a new spatial unit for data publication (Fig 1d). For instance, as shown in Fig 1, an original CDR record at base station 2 (lat_2, $long_2$, t) will be changed to ({(lat_1, $long_1$), (lat_2,$long_2$), (lat_3, $long_3$)}, t). With a larger location range, mobile users will more likely to co-locate with others, and their trace uniqueness can be expect to decrease.

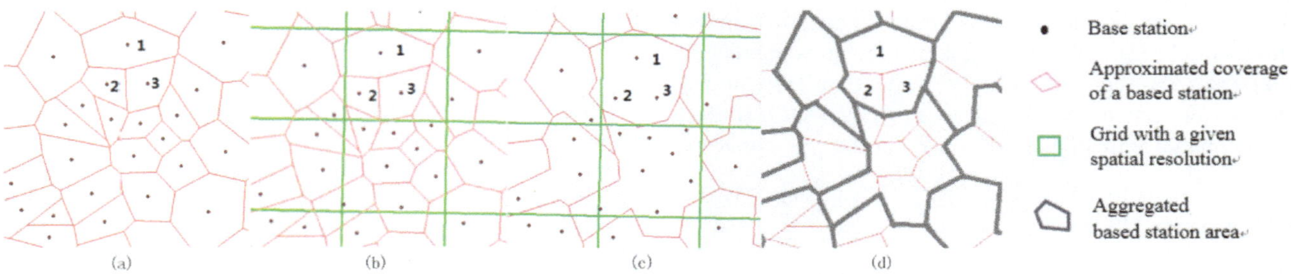

Figure 1. Privacy protection method for mobile phone location dataset by aggregating base stations. (a) Original base stations. (b) Grid creation. (c) Base station aggregation. (d) Aggregation results.

To measure the impact of spatial aggregation resolution on privacy protection systematically, the base stations were aggregated into a series of grids ranging from 200 m × 200 m to 2800 m × 2800 m with an increment of 200 m. S1 Fig shows the results of this aggregation.

Data Utility Evaluation

Because an OD flow matrix is a basic input for many transportation models and is of prime importance for studies based on human mobility, generation of an OD flow matrix was chosen here as a representative kind of aggregated analysis among various data utilities for mobile phone location data.

To measure data utility loss, the differences between two OD flow matrices derived from the dataset before and after privacy protection were assessed. Then data utility loss was calculated as the percentage of the total flow difference over the total flow during a time period T (Eq 1):

$$utility\ loss = \frac{\sum_{i=1}^{N}\sum_{j=1}^{N}|OD_{ij} - OD'_{ij}|}{\sum_{i=1}^{N}\sum_{j=1}^{N}OD_{ij}} \quad (1)$$

where OD_{ij} is the original flux from region i to region j during T, OD'_{ij} is the flux from region i to region j during T after privacy protection, and N is the number of regions.

As the regional unit in Eq 1, traffic analysis zones (TAZs) were chosen. TAZs are designed for mobility studies, usually by planning practitioners based on regional socioeconomic characteristics, and many transportation models require TAZ-based OD flow matrices OD^{TAZ} as inputs. TAZs may have different spatial resolutions according to application requirements. To compare the impacts on data utility of different spatial resolutions, this study used two sets of TAZs, one having 1112 TAZs with an average radius of 636 meters, and the other having 491 TAZs with an average radius of 994 meters. The radius of a TAZ is measured by the radius of a circle with the same area. The two sets of TAZs are provided by*City Urban Planning, Land & Resources Commission of Shenzhen Municipality*(http://www.szpl.gov.cn/). To represent the impact on whole dataset, the time period T is set as the entire time span of the CDR dataset (i.e., 34 days).

For the OD flow matrix before privacy protection, the first step was to apply the concept of transient-origin-destination [12] to identify movements between base stations. This method identifies a movement by searching for two consecutive non-identical locations from a trajectory and sets the two locations as origin and destination respectively according to their temporal order. This study named these OD flows as *All flows-Raw*, which represent the mobility patterns inherent in a CDR dataset. Because call events have been proved to be non-uniformly distributed over time [33] and a CDR dataset contains only a user's locations when a call event happens, the CDR is sparsely sampled, and this sampling method greatly influences the accuracy of estimating OD flows. For instance, a person may make a first call at place A in the morning, then make several trips without any calls, and finally make a second call at place B in the evening. The OD A→B derived from her/his CDR obviously provides wrong travel information for mobility studies. Moreover, in mobile networks, signal transitions between neighboring base stations will produce false short-distance movements [14]. To reduce these two types of errors in *All flows-Raw*, travel time of a single trip was used as a constraint to refine the identified movements. Based on a travel dairy of Shenzhen compiled only six months before the collection date of the mobile dataset used in this study, 98% of trips have a travel time between 5 minutes and 100 minutes (as shown inS2 Fig). This study excluded the movements with time intervals less than 5 minutes or greater than 100 minutes, and named the remaining OD flows as *All flows-Constraint*. Then the spatial unit of the OD flow matrix was converted from base stations to TAZs. The flow OD_{ij}^{TAZ} from TAZ i to TAZ j is generated by Eq 2:

$$OD_{ij}^{TAZ} = \sum_{k=1}^{M}\sum_{l=1}^{M}\frac{A_i^k}{A^k}\cdot\frac{A_j^l}{A^l}\cdot OD_{kl}^{BS} \quad (2)$$

where base station k with area A^k has an overlapping area A^k_i with TAZ i, base station l with area A^l has an overlapping area A^l_j with TAZ j, OD^{BS}_{kl} is the flux from base station k to base station l, and M is the number of base stations.

After privacy protection, suppose there are S aggregated base stations. The first step is to create flow OD^{AgrBS}_{pq} from aggregated base station p to q using Eq 3. Then Eq 4 is used to generate the TAZ-based OD'^{TAZ}_{ij} after privacy protection. Finally, Eq 1 is used to calculate the utility loss:

$$OD_{pq}^{AgrBS} = \sum_{u=1}^{U}\sum_{v=1}^{V} OD_{uv}^{BS} \quad (3)$$

where aggregated base station p includes U base stations, aggregated base station $q$includes V base stations, and OD^{BS}_{uv} is the flux from base station u to base station v:

$$OD\prime_{ij}^{TAZ} = \sum_{p=1}^{S}\sum_{q=1}^{S}\frac{A_i^p}{A^p}\cdot\frac{A_j^q}{A^q}\cdot OD_{pq}^{AgrBS} \quad (4)$$

where aggregated base station p with area A^p has an overlapping area A^p_i with TAZ i, and aggregated base station q with area A^q has an overlapping area A^q_j with TAZ j.

Moreover, the *Pareto principle* (also known as the *80–20 rule*) broadly exists in transportation systems. This principle states that roughly 20% of road segments (i.e., major roads) carry 80% of the total traffic flow. The Pareto rule suggests that a small proportion of OD pairs contributes most of the flows, and these OD pairs are more important than the remaining ones in a transportation system. Obviously, there exist some major flows that received impact from privacy protection procedures should be particularly examined in the results analysis. Because the definition of major flows can be various and may affect our analysis results, this study adopted three ways to define major flows. The first one was designed simply according to the Pareto principle. This study ranked OD pairs by their flux from high to low and selected the top 80% of flows as major flows, named *Major flows-Pareto*. We found that the top 80% of flows was contributed by less than 2% of OD pairs (seeS3 Fig for details), which is an extreme example of the Pareto principle. The second definition of major flows followed the network's backbone proposed by the study [34]. It filters a network's backbone from a weighted network by considering local heterogeneity and local correlations among relevant edges, so that it does not belittle small-scale interactions. This study names the backbone of networks as *Major flows-Backbone*. The third one defines major flows as the flows that start from or end with hotspots based on the study [35]. This study defined the hotspots as TAZs whose population are higher than a threshold. We estimated the population of a TAZ by summing up hourly caller volume in this TAZ through the study period. The population threshold is derived from the Lorenz curve of the population distribution [36]. This study names the flows selected by the third definition as *Major flows-Hotspot*. For details of the second and third definitions, interested readers can refer to [34–36]. This study calculated the above three types of major flows respectively based on All flows-Raw and All flows-Constraint, and labeled them with '-Raw' and–'Constraint' in the results analysis.

RESULTS AND DISCUSSION

Re-identification Risk

For the attack model using the top N locations, the size of the anonymity set (k-anonymity value) was calculated for each frequent call user, and the k-anonymity value was plotted for the proportion of users with $K \leq k$ (Fig 2). The three curves representing the top one, two, and three locations show that the k-anonymity value in general decreases with increasing number of top locations, which demonstrates the increased re-identification risk with additional background knowledge about top locations. As illustrated in Fig 2a and Table 1(see "For frequent call users"), almost no users are uniquely identified by their top one location, which means that if only the most frequently visited location is exposed, there is almost nothing to worry about. However, when the top two and top three locations are revealed, the uniquely identified population increases to **17%** and **49%** respectively. Fig 2bshows the *k*-anonymity values for the top one, two, and three locations unordered, and Fig 2c compares the two curves for the ordered and unordered top two locations. The re-identification risk from the unordered top two locations is nearly 5% less than that from the ordered top two locations. In other words, the additional background knowledge about the order of the top two locations increases the re-identification risk for users by approximately 5%. Fig 2c also shows the cases using the variable-length top locations ordered and unordered. The two curves are close to the curves of the top two locations. When the *k*-anonymity value is smaller than 10–20, the curves of the variable-length top locations are located below the curves of the top two locations. As the size of the anonymity set increases, the two curves of the variable-length top locations move higher than the curves of the top two locations, and gradually the two curves become identical. These results indicate that most users with relatively high re-identification risks (higher than 1/20–1/10) have only two preferred locations, and most users with relatively low re-identification risks have only one preferred location.

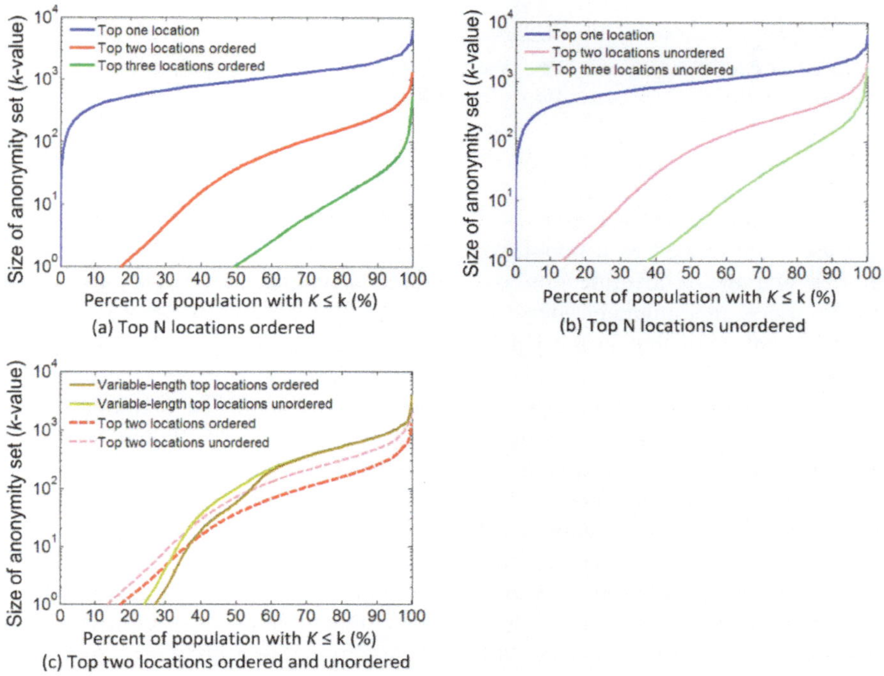

Figure 2. Size of anonymity set for the top N locations. (a) Top N locations ordered. (b) Top N locations unordered. (c) Top two locations ordered and unordered.

Table 1. Percentage of population with *k*-anonymity value = 1 in Shenzhen City and the United States.

User group	Region	Top 1 location (%)	Top 2 locations (%)	Top 3 locations (%)
Frequent call users	Shenzhen	~0	17	49
	United States *	~0	15	50
All mobile users	Shenzhen	~0	6	18
	United States*	~0	12	40

* The results in the United States for frequent users are reported in [15]. The results in the United States for all users are not reported in [15], but were calculated by the authors of this study based on the reported percentage of users with $k = 1$ among frequent users and the percentage of frequent call users among all users.

The *k*-anonymity values for the 1st, 5th, 10th, and the 50th percentiles of frequent call users were then compared in the results of this study and those for the entire United States as reported in [15] (Table 2). Shenzhen City had a re-identification risk fairly similar to that of the overall United States in terms of frequent call users. Without results from other regions in the world, the authors currently consider this consistency to be coincidental.

Table 2. *k*-anonymity value with top *N* **locations (*N* = 1, 2, 3) in Shenzhen City and the United States.**

User group	Region	Top 1 location (%ile)				Top 2 locations (%ile)				Top 3 locations (%ile)			
		1st	5th	10th	50th	1st	5th	10th	50th	1st	5th	10th	50th
Frequent call users	Shenzhen	82	246	376	943	1	1	1	38	1	1	1	1
	United States	92	220	331	967	1	1	1	9	1	1	1	1

* The results in the United States for frequent users are reported in [15].

doi:10.1371/journal.pone.0140589.t002

The percentage of frequent call users with *k*-anonymity value = 1 was also compared in the results of this research and in results from various cities in the United States [15] (Table 3). The percentage of frequent users with *k*-anonymity value = 1 in Shenzhen is between that of Sacramento and that of Chicago. Study [15] suggests that re-identification risk might be related to the differences between urban and rural lifestyles. A more urban lifestyle causes more diversified activities, thus generating smaller anonymity sets. According to this explanation, the degree of urban lifestyle in Shenzhen might be between that of Sacramento and that of Chicago.

Table 3. Percentage of frequent users with *k*-anonymity value = 1 in different cities (*N* = **2).**

Cities	Shenzhen (China)	Kansas City* (U.S.)	Sacramento* (U.S.)	Chicago* (U.S.)	Los Angeles* (U.S.)	San Francisco* (U.S.)
Percent of frequent users with *k*-anonymity value = 1 (%)	17	10	15	25	25	30
Population density (persons per mi²)	20,205	1,168	4,660	11,868	12,451	17,246

* The percentages of the population with *k* = 1 in various cities in the United States are reported in [15]. The population densities of cities in the United States were estimated based on the 2010 United States census results. They might vary according to the definition of city boundaries.

doi:10.1371/journal.pone.0140589.t003

These results and discussions are based on frequent call users. If non-frequent call users are treated as a population with no re-identification risk and the re-identification risk is calculated for all mobile users, the uniquely identified population in Shenzhen City is only half that in the United States for the top two locations and less than half for the top three locations (see "For all mobile users" in Table 1). Shenzhen City has only 37% frequent call users among its mobile users, whereas United States has 80% frequent call users. The significant higher ratio of inactivity mobile users in Shenzhen City could be related with several situations, such as mobile users in Shenzhen City make much fewer calls than in the United States, many Shenzhen mobile users use more than one telephone number or some telephone numbers have been left nearly unused. One or several of the above possible reasons lead to lower trajectory exposure and lower overall privacy risk for mobile users in Shenzhen City than in the United States.

In the attack model using spatio-temporal points, as shown in Fig 3, the population with 100% re-identification risk increases very fast until the number of spatio-temporal points reaches four. Nearly **75%** of the population can be uniquely identified by four spatio-temporal points. The re-identification risk then shows a convergent trend with a maximum risk of nearly **80%.**

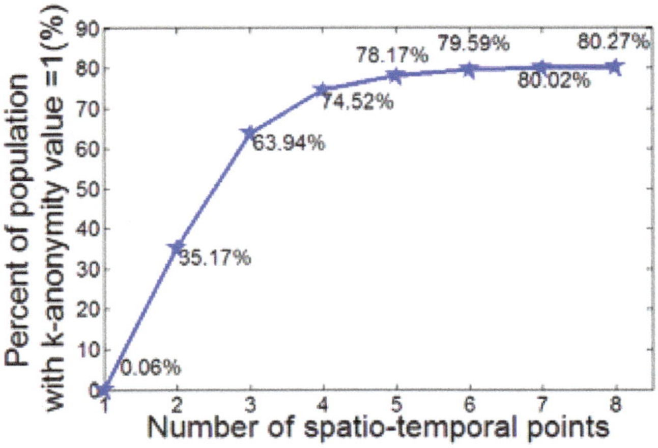

Figure 3. Population with 100% re-identification risk under different number of spatio-temporal points.

As reported in [16], four spatio-temporal points are enough to identify uniquely 95% of mobile users in a small European country. Study [16] also suggested that their results should generalize to higher population densities based on the following considerations. On the one hand, higher population density tends to increase the anonymity set; on the other hand, more mobile base stations will locate in areas with high population density, thus increasing the spatial precision of trajectories, which should offset the influence of high population density. However, the results of this research suggest significantly lower privacy risks in Shenzhen City, an area very likely having a much higher population density than the small European country. According to the results presented here, more mobile base stations as a result of higher population density might not fully offset the influence of high population density. However, the distributions of mobile base stations and population density used in study [16] are not available, and therefore the offsetting effect of base station density against population density cannot be evaluated. Moreover, as shown inTable 3, the re-identification risks in various cities in the United States increase with population density. Therefore, according to the results of this study and of studies [15–16], besides population density, factors such as degree of urban lifestyle must be considered to explain the spatial heterogeneity of re-identification risks.

Re-Identification Risk Reduction after Privacy Protection

The spatial generalization approach proposed by this study can effectively reduce the re-identification risks for the top two and three locations, and the re-identification risk declines more sharply for the top three locations (Fig 4a). When spatial aggregation scale increases to 2800 m, the uniquely identified population drops from 17% to 1% for the top two locations and from 49% to 12% for the top three locations.

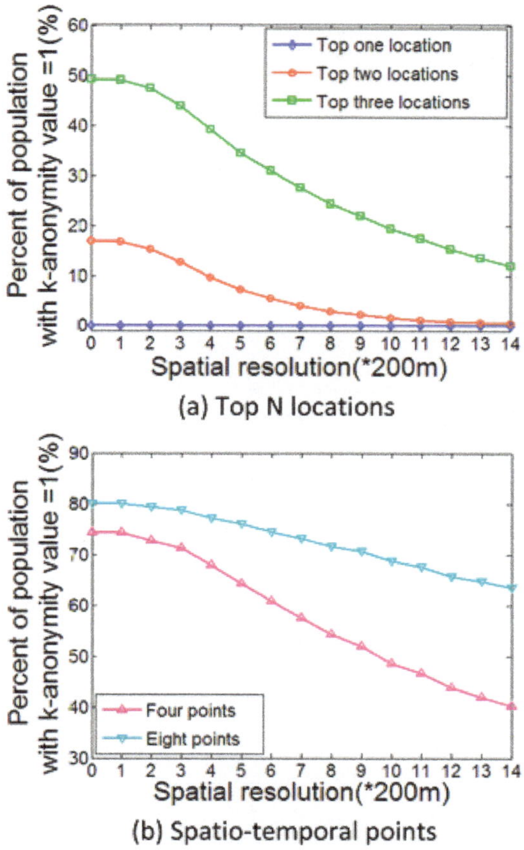

Figure 4. Privacy risk reduction of two privacy models. (a) Top N locations. (b) Spatio-temporal points.

As for the attack model using spatio-temporal points, to illustrate the effect of the spatial generalization approach on reducing re-identification risk, four and eight spatio-temporal points were chosen, because they are two critical points on the curve shown in Fig 3. When the spatial aggregation scale increased to 2800 m, the uniquely identified population dropped from 75% to 40% when using four spatio-temporal points and from 80% to 64% when using eight spatio-temporal points. The slower rate of decrease when using eight spatio-temporal points indicates the increased difficulty of reducing re-identification risk by spatial generalization when attackers know more target footprints.

Data Utility Loss after Privacy Protection

Using OD flow analysis as a data utility, Fig 5 shows that when spatial generalization scale increases from 200 m to 2800 m, data utility loss significantly increases while the differences between various data utility measurements gradually expand. When the spatial generalization scale increases to larger than 1000 m, the impact of privacy protection on major flows becomes slightly less than that of all flows. Because of the significant importance of major flows in transportation systems, the authors suggest using the major flow curves as a more important reference in practice. Besides, the data utility loss in an analysis based on TAZs with larger spatial units (491 TAZs with an average radius of 994 m) is clearly less than that in an analysis based on TAZs with smaller spatial units (1112 TAZs with an average radius of 636 m). This pattern can also be found in Figs 6–13 in the next section.

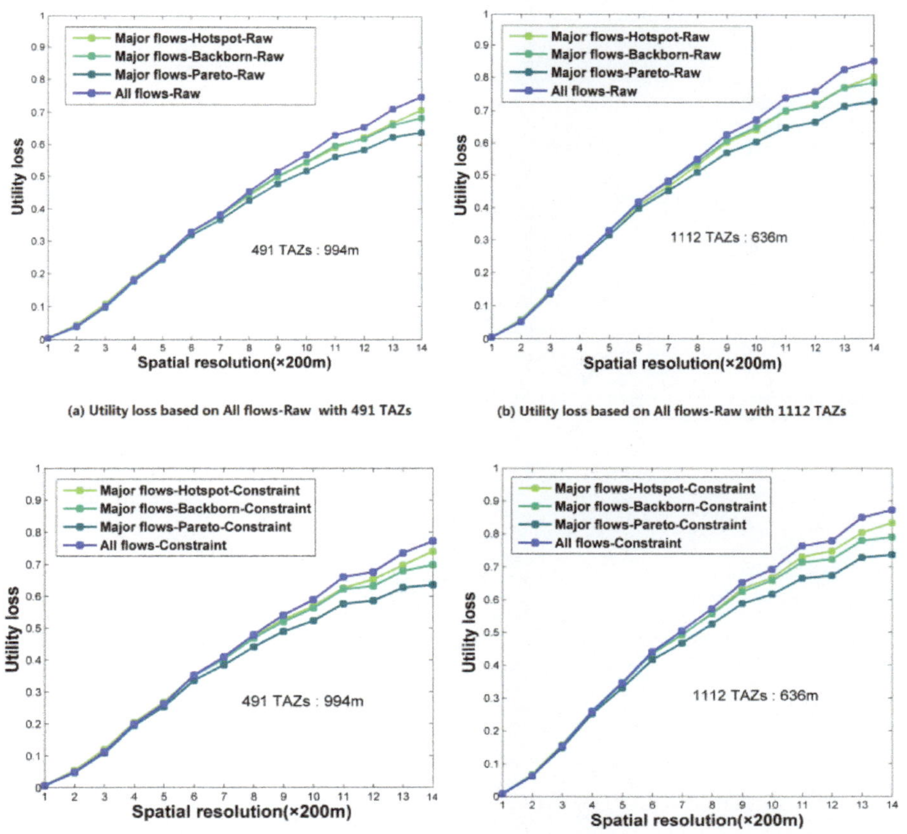

Figure 5. Data utility loss on analyzing OD flows with spatial generalization resolution. (a) Utility loss based on All flows-Raw with 491 TAZs. (b) Utility loss based on All flows-Raw with 1112 TAZs. (c) Utility loss based on All flows-Constraint with 491 TAZs. (d) Utility loss based on All flows-Constraint with 1112 TAZs.

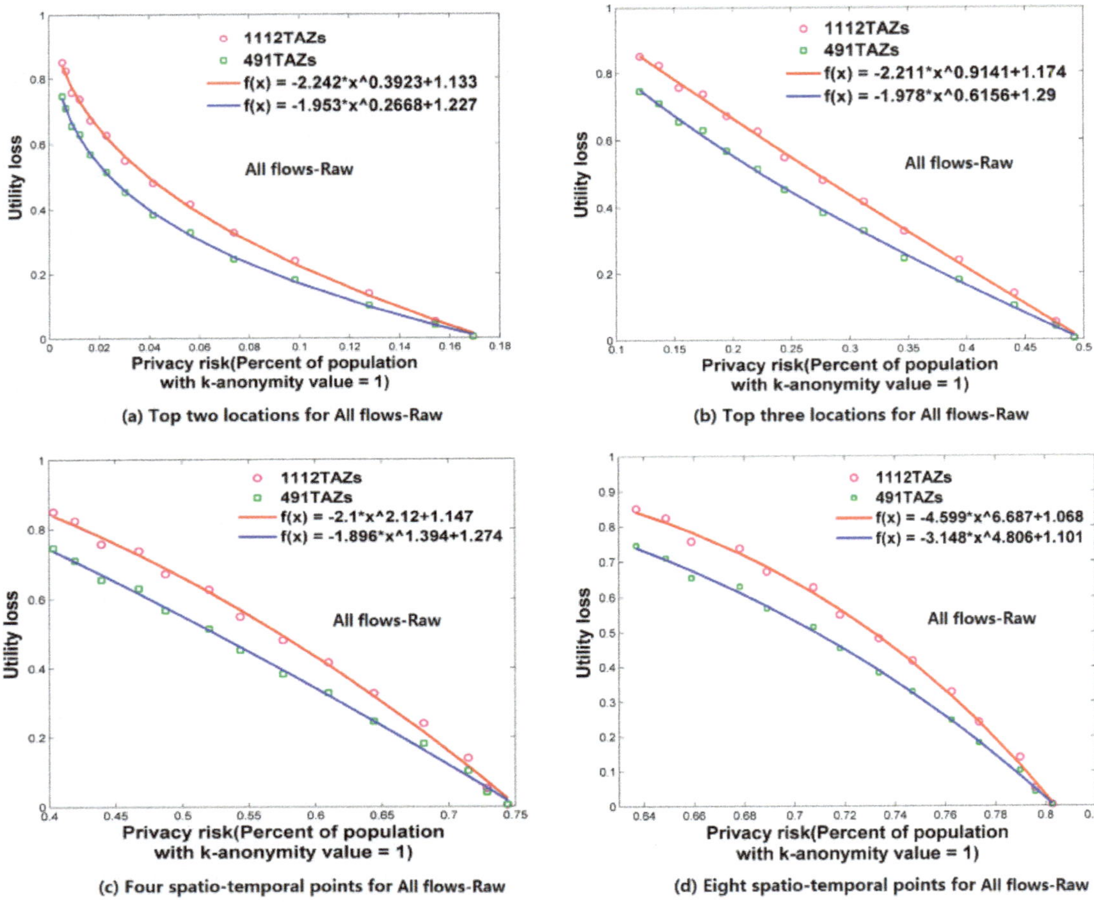

Figure 6. Relationships between privacy risk and data utility using All flows-Raw. (a) Top two locations. (b) Top three locations. (c) Four spatio-temporal points. (d) Eight spatio-temporal points.

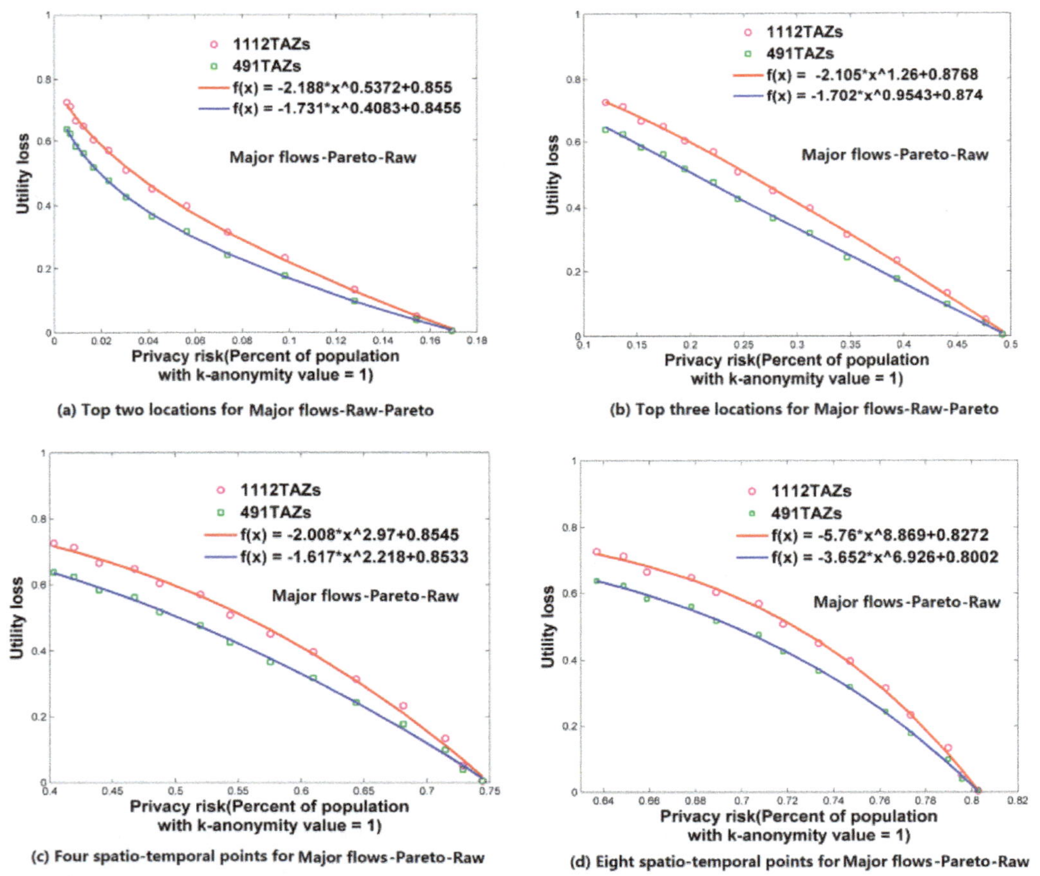

Figure 7. Relationships between privacy risk and data utility using Major flows-Pareto-Raw. (a) Top two locations. (b) Top three locations. (c) Four spatio-temporal points. (d) Eight spatio-temporal points.

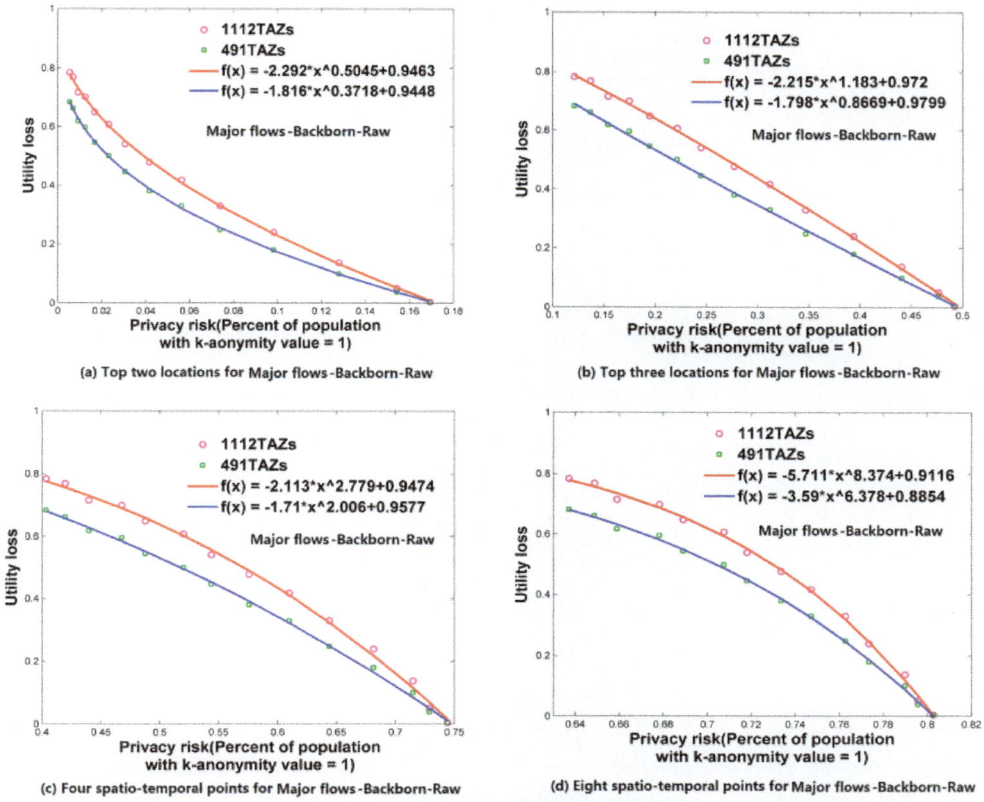

Figure 8. Relationships between privacy risk and data utility using Major flows-Backborn-Raw. (a) Top two locations. (b) Top three locations. (c) Four spatio-temporal points. (d) Eight spatio-temporal points.

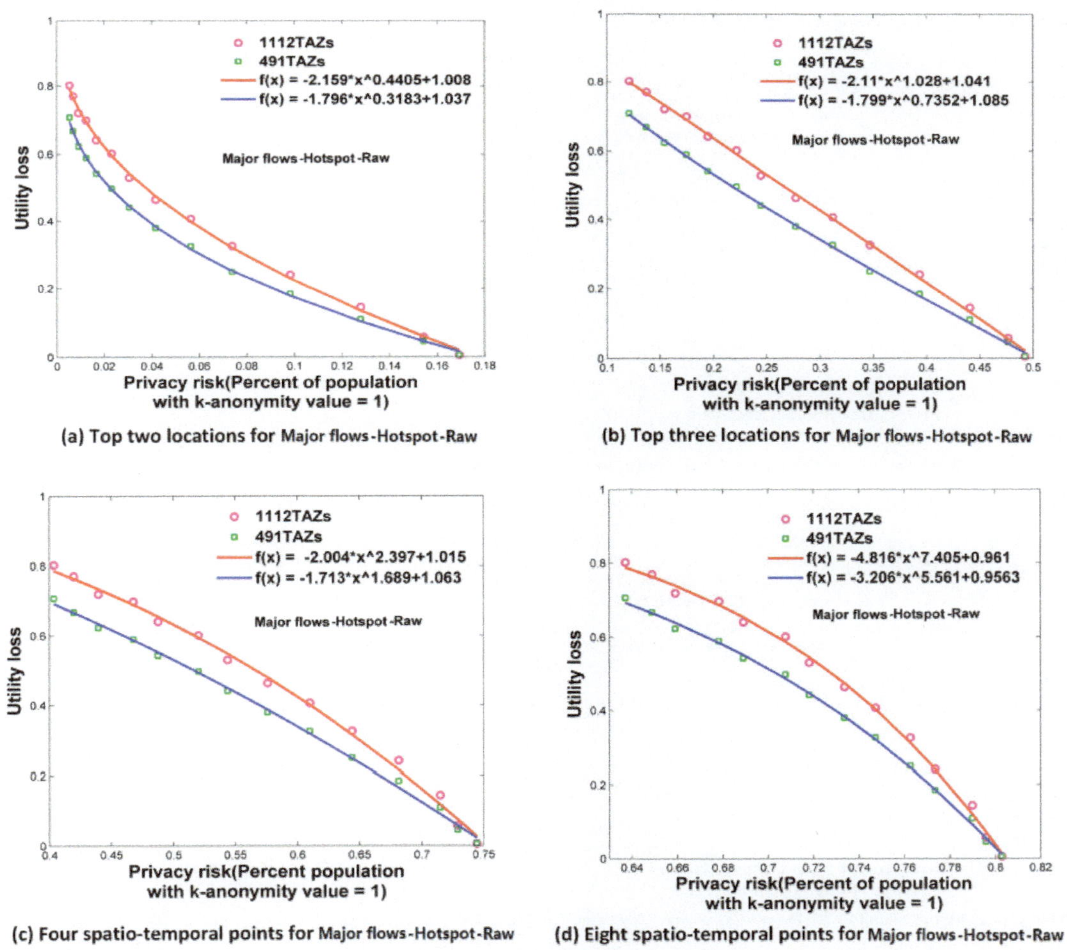

Figure 9. Relationships between privacy risk and data utility using Major flows-Hotspot-Raw. (a) Top two locations. (b) Top three locations. (c) Four spatio-temporal points. (d) Eight spatio-temporal points.

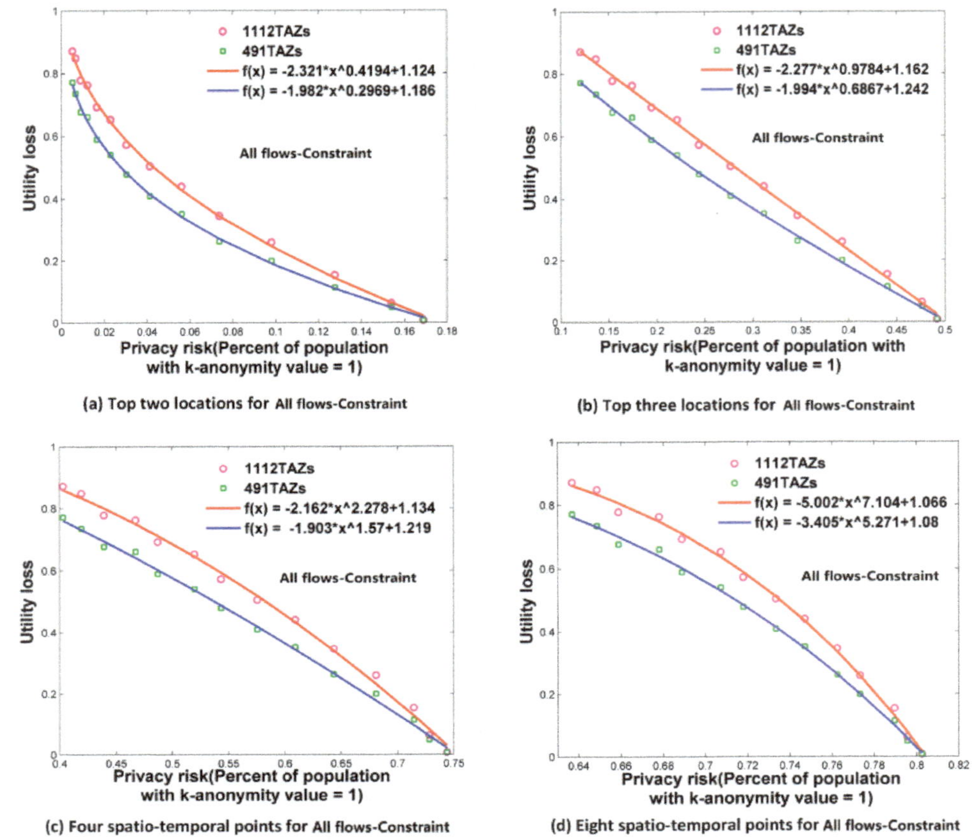

Figure 10. Relationships between privacy risk and data utility using All flows-Constraint. (a) Top two locations. (b) Top three locations. (c) Four spatio-temporal points. (d) Eight spatio-temporal points.

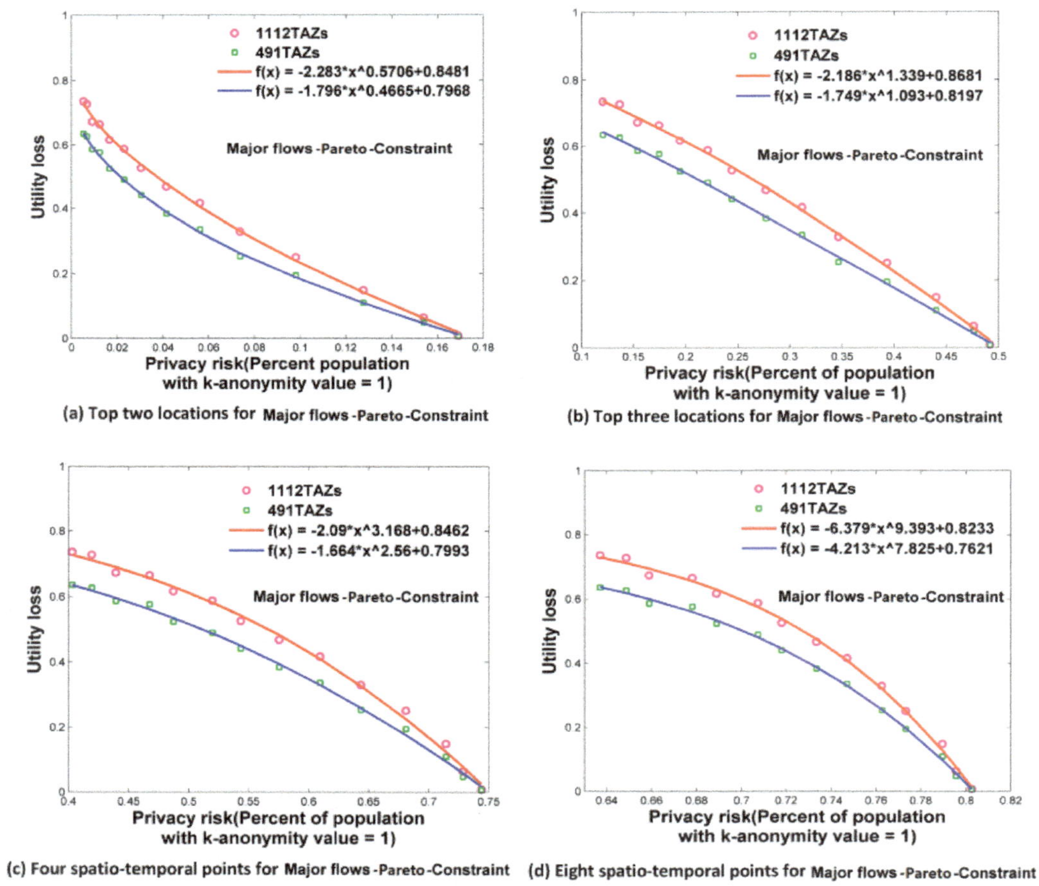

Figure 11. Relationships between privacy risk and data utility using Major flows-Pareto-Constraint. (a) Top two locations. (b) Top three locations. (c) Four spatio-temporal points. (d) Eight spatio-temporal points.

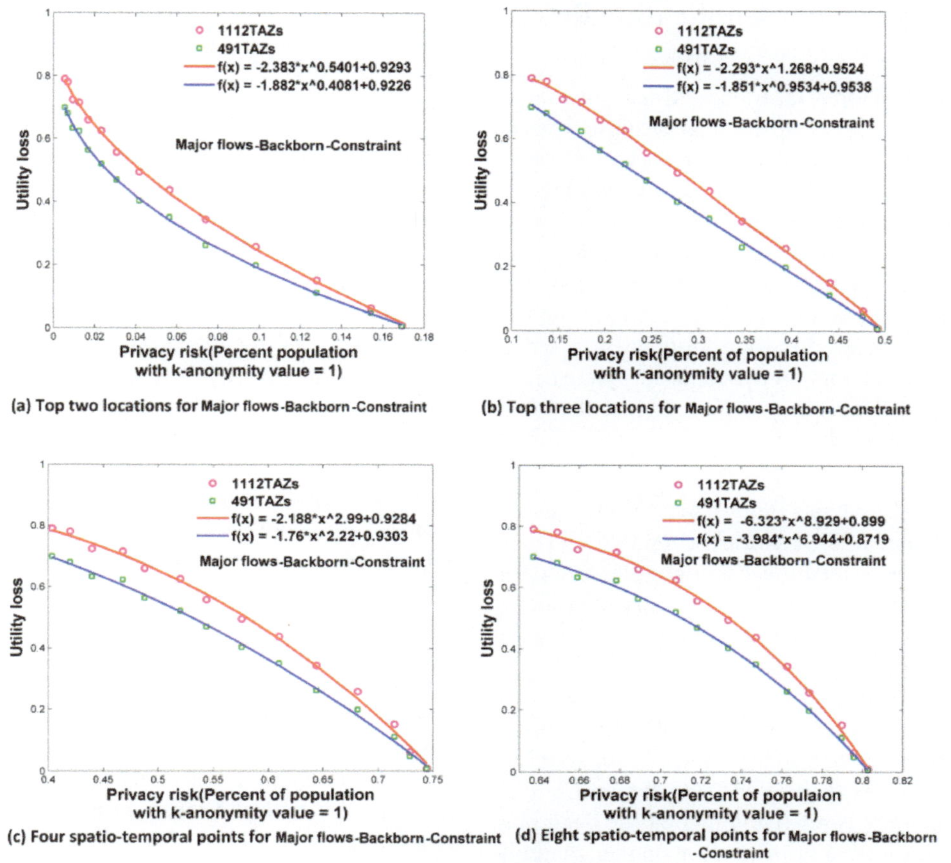

Figure 12. Relationships between privacy risk and data utility using Major flows-Backborn-Constraint. (a) Top two locations. (b) Top three locations. (c) Four spatio-temporal points. (d) Eight spatio-temporal points.

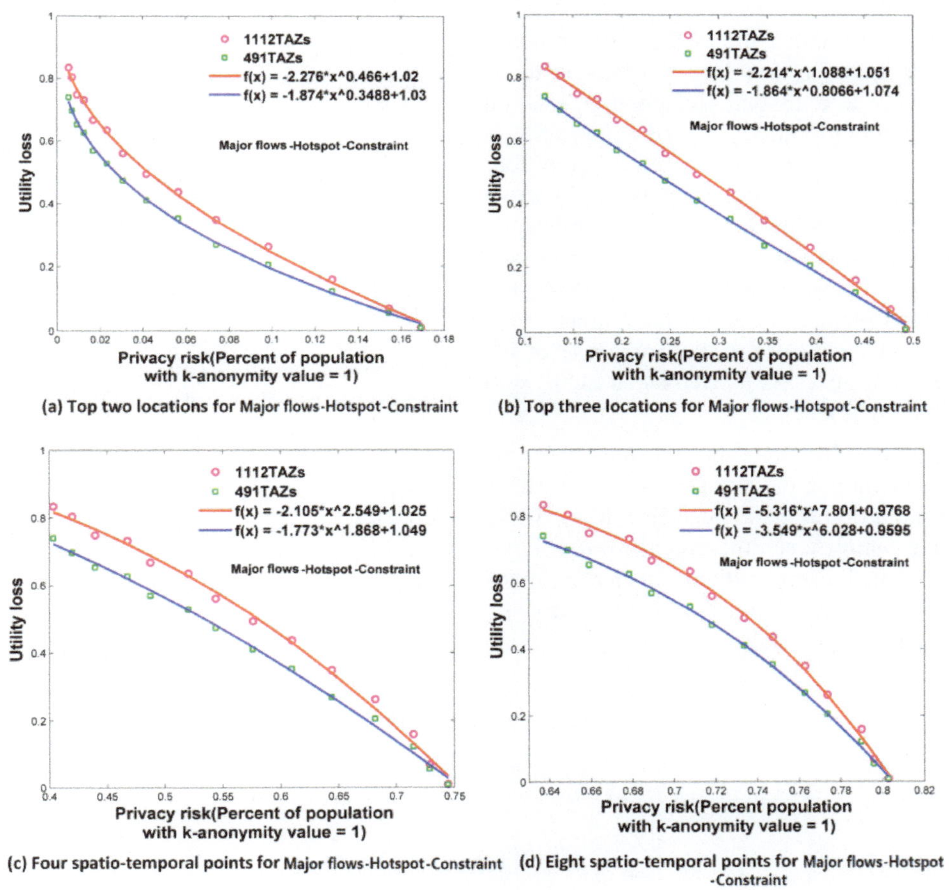

Figure 13. Relationships between privacy risk and data utility using Major flows-Hotspot-Constraint. (a) Top two locations. (b) Top three locations. (c) Four spatio-temporal points. (d) Eight spatio-temporal points.

Relationships between Re-Identification Risk and Data Utility

Using the attack models of top *N* locations and spatio-temporal points, Figs 6–9 and 10–13present the relationships between re-identification risk and data utility loss respectively based on the original OD flows (i.e. the '-Raw' series) and the OD flows with 5~100 min time constraints (i.e. the '-Constraint' series). It was found that all the relationships between re-identification risk **x** (the percentage of the population with 100% re-identification risk) and data utility loss **y** for the two attack models can be expressed by one formula: $y = -ax^b+c$ $(a,b,c>0;0<x<1)$. All estimators for *a*, *b*, and *c* are statistically significant ($p<0.001$), and the values of R^2 are more than 0.99 for all cases (see S2 Table), which indicate the goodness of fit of the proposed function.

The exponent *b* determines the shape of the curves. When *b* is between 0 and 1, such as for the top two locations (Fig 6a), to diminish the re-identification risk (please look at the *x*axis from right to left), the cost in data utility of reducing the re-identification risk is relatively low at the beginning, but gradually increases. When *b* is close to 1, such as for the top three locations (the red curve in Fig 6b for 1112 TAZs), the tradeoff between re-identification risk and data utility loss is close to linear. When *b* is larger than 1, such as for four and eight spatio-temporal points (Fig 6c and 6d), the cost in data utility for reducing privacy is relatively high at the beginning and gradually becomes lower. In general, a smaller *b*implies a larger marginal utility of the tradeoff for data utility, thus providing an easier way to protect privacy in the beginning phase that is more helpful in practice.

As shown in Figs 6–13, either for all flows or for major flows, the exponent *b* increases from the top two locations to the top three locations, to four spatio-temporal points, and then to eight spatio-temporal points. This trend indicates an increase in background knowledge of attackers in these four models and accordingly the increasing difficulty of protecting privacy. The uniform relationship between re-identification risk and data utility for the two attack models also offers a way to compare the two attack models. For example, the slightly larger*b* in the four spatio-temporal points model than in the top three locations model indicates a slight increase in the background knowledge of attackers as well as an increase in the difficulty of protecting privacy.

This study designed five different data utility measurements for OD flow analysis, including the raw OD flows, OD flows with time constraints, and three types of major flows. If the raw OD flows form a complete set, the others are four types of subsets with different filtering methods. In terms of the relationship between re-identification risk and data utility loss, our results show that subsets of OD flows created by a filtering method have the same relationship with the complete set of OD flows, and the filtering method does not affect the relationship.

Contributions and Future Work

The contributions of this research include the following two aspects. First, this study strengthens the argument that spatial heterogeneity exists in the re-identification risks in call detail records. Study [15] has demonstrated the spatial heterogeneity of different American cities under the attack model using the top *N* locations. Study [16] did not address this issue, but it inferred a spatial homogeneity under the attack model using spatial-temporal points. The results of this research clearly show that the re-identification risks of Shenzhen's mobile phone users lie between those of Sacramento and those of Chicago and are significantly lower than those in the reported European country when using spatial-temporal points. This study has therefore demonstrated that spatial heterogeneity not only occurs in the attack model using the top *N* locations, but is also valid in the attack model using spatial-temporal points. This finding raises awareness that the re-identification risks in call detail records vary across regions, and therefore that methods and institutions of protecting privacy when sharing detailed individual trajectory data should be considered in a local context. Second, a uniform relationship was found between re-identification risks (*x*) and the selected data utility (*y*) for both the top *N* location model and the spatio-temporal point model: $y = -ax^b+c$ $(a,b,c>0;0<x<1)$where the exponent *b* increases with the background knowledge of the attackers and a larger *b* implies more difficulty in reducing re-identification risk in the early phase. This relationship offers a tradeoff reference for other aggregated analyses based on mobile phone location data. It also provides data publishers with useful guidance on choosing the right tradeoff between privacy and utility.

This study raises several issues that need to be addressed in future work. (1) Based on the findings of this research and on previous studies [15–16], the spatial heterogeneity of the re-identification risks in call detail records likely comes from many reasons such as phone usage habits, population density, and lifestyle. To obtain an in-depth understanding of the factors influencing re-identification risks, it is necessary to investigate the quantitative relationship between privacy risk in mobile traces and possible influencing factors. (2) The proposed spatial generalization method is able to reduce re-identification risks in mobile traces. However, the data utility of generating an OD flow matrix, which is a typical aggregated mobility analysis, decreases rapidly when this procedure is applied to the dataset. Therefore, efforts are still needed to improve privacy protection methods for mobile phone location datasets. (3) Besides aggregated mobility analysis, the impact of privacy protection on analyses at an individual level requires further study. (4) If data is available in future, a study comparing with other regions would be worth pursuing.

SUPPORTING INFORMATION

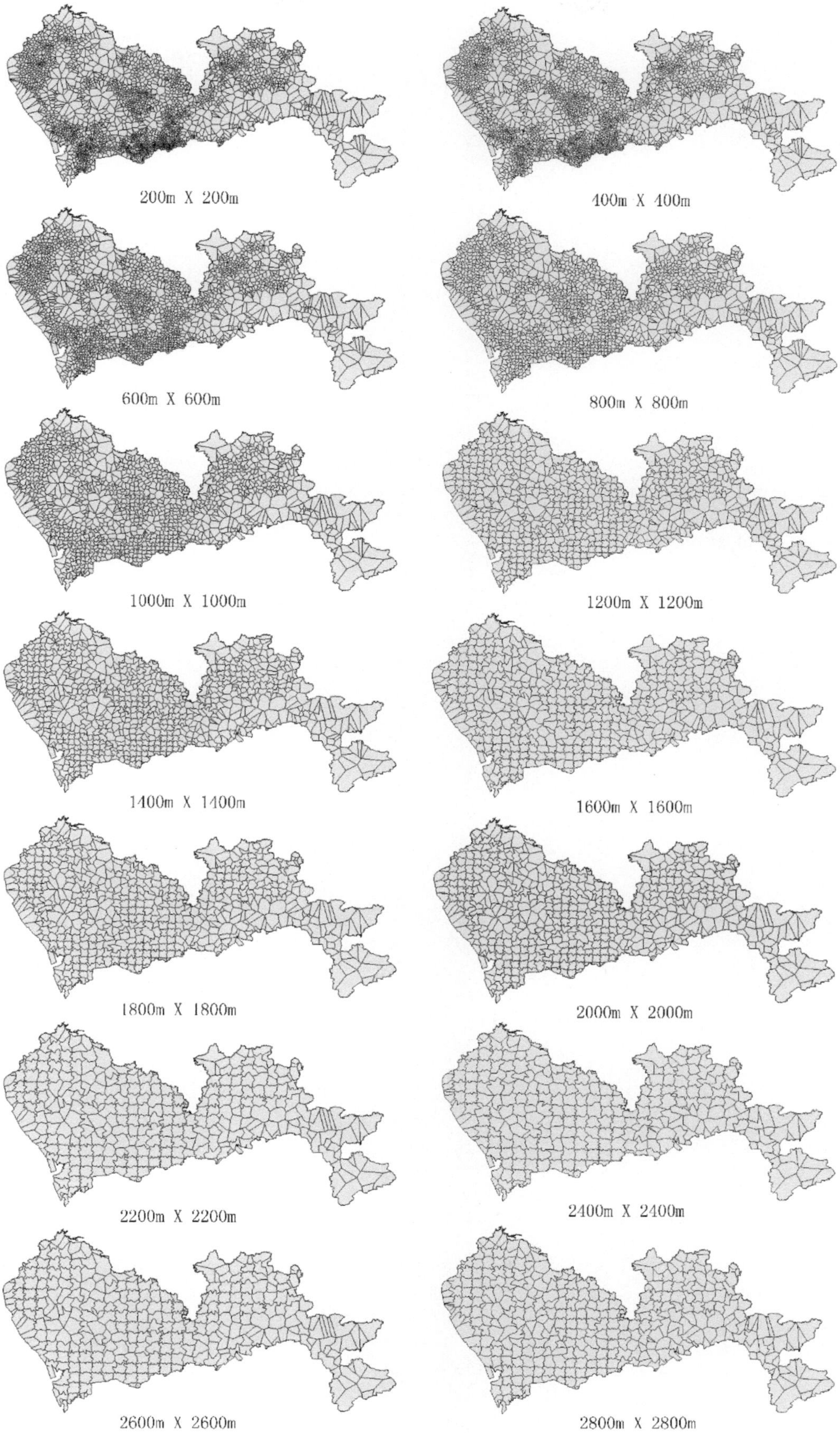

S1 Fig. Aggregated base stations by a series of grids ranging from 200 m × 200 m to 2800 m × 2800 m with an increment of 200 m.

doi:10.1371/journal.pone.0140589.s001

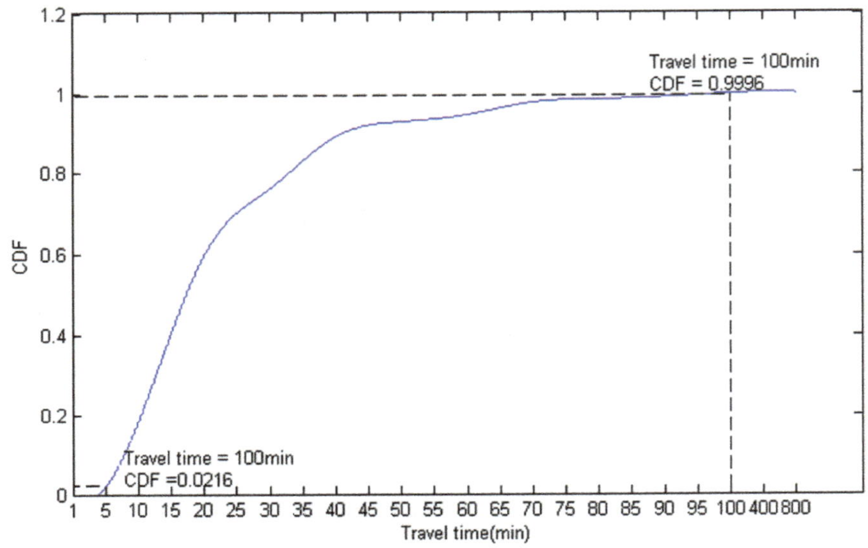

S2 Fig. The travel time distribution of a single trip in the travel dairy of Shenzhen City (sample size = 190,000).

doi:10.1371/journal.pone.0140589.s002

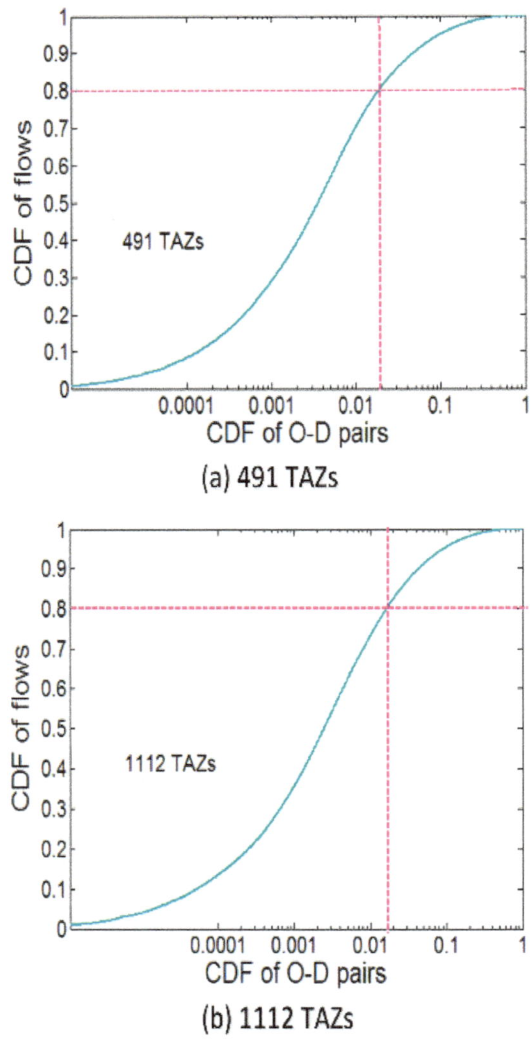

S3 Fig. The cumulative distribution of flows based on two sets of TAZs. (a) 491 TAZs. (b) 1112 TAZs.

doi:10.1371/journal.pone.0140589.s003

S1 Table. A snapshot of the CDR dataset.

ID	Time	Latitude	Longitude	Flag	Regional code
000****850	201*/*/1 6:03	22.542534	114.11719	1	755
000****850	201*/*/1 9:42	22.542534	114.11719	1	755
000****850	201*/*/1 10:27	22.542534	114.11719	0	755
000****850	201*/*/1 15:38	22.542534	114.11719	0	755
000****850	201*/*/1 16:06	22.542534	114.11719	1	755
000****850	201*/*/1 16:15	22.544722	114.119444	0	755
000****850	201*/*/1 16:56	22.546667	114.120306	1	755
000****850	201*/*/1 18:00	22.550833	114.122222	1	755
000****850	201*/*/1 19:46	22.548929	114.111791	1	755
000****850	201*/*/1 20:22	22.546667	114.120306	0	755
000****850	201*/*/1 20:24	22.546667	114.120306	0	755
000****850	201*/*/1 20:47	22.546667	114.120306	0	755
000****850	201*/*/1 21:15	22.546667	114.120306	0	755
000****850	201*/*/1 21:34	22.546667	114.120306	0	755
000****850	201*/*/1 22:00	22.546667	114.120306	1	755
000****850	201*/*/1 22:24	22.55195	114.12525	0	755
000****850	201*/*/1 22:52	22.55195	114.12525	1	755
000****850	201*/*/1 22:53	22.55195	114.12525	1	755
000****850	201*/*/1 23:12	22.550833	114.125833	0	755

doi:10.1371/journal.pone.0140589.s004

S2 Table. The goodness of fit of the proposed function *($y = -ax^b+c$)*

Case	Value of R-square
Based on All flows-Raw:	
Top two locations for All flows with 1112 TAZs	0.9988
Top two locations for All flows with 491 TAZs	0.9993
Top two locations for Major flows-Pareto with 1112 TAZs	0.9990
Top two locations for Major flows- Pareto with 491 TAZs	0.9996
Top two locations for Major flows-Backborn with 1112 TAZs	0.9993
Top two locations for Major flows-Backborn with 491 TAZs	0.9995
Top two locations for Major flows-Hotspot with 1112 TAZs	0.9986
Top two locations for Major flows-Hotspot with 491 TAZs	0.9992
Top three locations for All flows with 1112 TAZs	0.9987
Top three locations for All flows with 491 TAZs	0.9990
Top three locations for Major flows-Pareto with 1112 TAZs	0.9990
Top three locations for Major flows-Pareto with 491 TAZs	0.9991
Top three locations for Major flows-Backborn with 1112 TAZs	0.9991
Top three locations for Major flows-Backborn with 491 TAZs	0.9991
Top three locations for Major flows-Hotspot with 1112 TAZs	0.9986
Top three locations for Major flows-Hotspot with 491 TAZs	0.9992
Four spatio-temporal points for All flows with 1112 TAZs	0.9965
Four spatio-temporal points for All flows with 491 TAZs	0.9978
Four spatio-temporal points for Major flows-Pareto with 1112 TAZs	0.9962

Four spatio-temporal points for Major flows-Pareto with 491 TAZs	0.9983
Four spatio-temporal points for Major flows-Backborn with 1112 TAZs	0.9973
Four spatio-temporal points for Major flows- Backborn with 491 TAZs	0.9983
Four spatio-temporal points for Major flows-Hotspot with 1112 TAZs	0.9960
Four spatio-temporal points for Major flows-Hotspot with 491 TAZs	0.9975
Eight spatio-temporal points for All flows with 1112 TAZs	0.9974
Eight spatio-temporal points for All flows with 491 TAZs	0.9983
Eight spatio-temporal points for Major flows-Pareto with 1112 TAZs	0.9978
Eight spatio-temporal points for Major flows-Pareto with 491 TAZs	0.9987
Eight spatio-temporal points for Major flows-Backborn with 1112 TAZs	0.9980
Eight spatio-temporal points for Major flows- Backborn with 491 TAZs	0.9986
Eight spatio-temporal points for Major flows-Hotspot with 1112 TAZs	0.9973
Eight spatio-temporal points for Major flows-Hotspot with 491 TAZs	0.9984

doi:10.1371/journal.pone.0140589.s005

AUTHOR CONTRIBUTIONS

Conceived and designed the experiments: LY QW SS ZF JH YT WW. Performed the experiments: LY QW WW. Analyzed the data: LY QW YT WW. Contributed reagents/materials/analysis tools: LY JH. Wrote the paper: LY QW SS ZF JH YT WW.

REFERENCES

1. Jiang S, Fiore GA, Yang Y, Ferreira J Jr, Frazzoli E, González MC. A review of urban computing for mobile phone traces: current methods, challenges and opportunities. In Proceedings of the 2nd ACM SIGKDD International Workshop on Urban Computing, UrbComp. 2013.
2. Gonzalez MC, Hidalgo CA, Barabasi AL. Understanding individual human mobility patterns. Nature. 2008; 453(7196): 779–782. doi: 10. 1038/nature06958. pmid:18528393
3. Phithakkitnukoon S, Smoreda Z, Olivier P. Socio-geography of human mobility: A study using longitudinal mobile phone data. PloS one. 2012; 7(6), e39253. doi: 10. 1371/journal. pone. 0039253. pmid:22761748
4. Kang C, Ma X, Tong D, Liu Y. Intra-urban human mobility patterns: An urban morphology perspective. Physica A: Statistical Mechanics and its Applications, 2012; 391, 1702–1717. doi: 10. 1016/j. physa. 2011. 11. 005
5. Song C, Qu Z, Blumm N, Barabási AL. Limits of predictability in human mobility. Science, 2010; 327(5968), 1018–1021. doi: 10. 1126/science. 1177170. pmid:20167789
6. Qin SM, Verkasalo H, Mohtaschemi M, Hartonen T, Hartonen T, Alava M. . Patterns, entropy, and predictability of human mobility and life. PloS one, 2012; 7, e51353. doi: 10. 1371/journal. pone. 0051353. pmid:23300542
7. Wang M H, Schrock SD, Vander Broek N, Mulinazzi T. Estimating Dynamic Origin-Destination Data and Travel Demand Using Cell Phone Network Data. International Journal of Intelligent Transportation Systems Research, 2013; 11(2), 76–86. doi: 10. 1007/s13177-013-0058-8
8. Iqbal MS, Choudhury CF, Wang P, González MC. Development of origin–destination matrices using mobile phone call data. Transportation Research Part C: Emerging Technologies, 2014; 40: 63–74. doi: 10. 1016/j. trc. 2014. 01. 002
9. Friedrich M, Immisch K, Jehlicka P, Otterstätter T, Schlaich J. . Generating origin-destination matrices from mobile phone trajectories. Transportation Research Record: Journal of the Transportation Research Board, 2010, 2196(1): 93–101. doi: 10. 3141/2196-10
10. Buckee CO, Wesolowski A, Eagle N N, Hansen E, Snow RW. Mobile phones and malaria: modeling human and parasite travel. Travel medicine and infectious disease, 2013, 11(1): 15–22. doi: 10. 1016/j. tmaid. 2012. 12. 003. Epub 2013 Mar 9. pmid:23478045
11. Ahas R, Aasa A, Silm S, Tiru M. Daily rhythms of suburban commuters' movements in the Tallinn metropolitan area: Case study with mobile positioning data. Transportation Research Part C: Emerging Technologies, 2010; 18, 45–54. doi: 10. 1016/j. trc. 2009. 04. 011
12. Kang C, Liu Y, Ma X, Wu L. Towards estimating urban population distributions from mobile call data. Journal of Urban Technology, 2012; 19, 3–21. doi: 10. 1080/10630732. 2012. 715479
13. Isaacman S, Becker R, Caceres R, Kobourov S, Martonosi M, Rowland J, Varshavsky A. Identifying important places in people's lives from cellular network data. Pervasive Computing. Springer Berlin Heidelberg, 2011; 133–151.
14. Schneider C M, Belik V, Couronné T, Smoreda Z, González MC. Unravelling daily human mobility motifs. Journal of The Royal Society Interface, 2013; 10(84): 246–253. doi: 10. 1098/rsif. 2013. 0246

15. Zang H, Bolot J. Anonymization of location data does not work: A large-scale measurement study. In: Proceedings of the 17th annual international conference on Mobile computing and networking, ACM, 2011; 145–156.

16. de Montjoye Y A, Hidalgo C A, Verleysen M, Blondel VD. Unique in the Crowd: The privacy bounds of human mobility. Scientific reports, 2013, 3. doi: 10. 1038/srep01376

17. Butler D. Data sharing threatens privacy. Nature News, 2007; 449(7163): 644–645. doi: 10. 1038/449644a

18. Wernke M, Skvortsov P, Dürr F, Rothermel K. A classification of location privacy attacks and approaches. Personal and Ubiquitous Computing, 2014; 18(1): 163–175. doi: 10. 1007/s00779-012-0633-z

19. Giannotti F, Pedreschi D. Mobility, data mining and privacy: Geographic knowledge discovery. Springer Science & Business Media, 2008.

20. Fung B, Wang K, Chen R & Yu PS. Privacy-preserving data publishing: A survey of recent developments. ACM Computing Surveys (CSUR), 2010; 42(4), 14. doi: 10. 1145/1749603. 1749605

21. Terrovitis M, Mamoulis N. Privacy preservation in the publication of trajectories. In Mobile Data Management, 2008. MDM'08. 9th International Conference on. 2008:65–72.

22. Hoh B, Gruteser M. Protecting location privacy through path confusion. In Security and Privacy for Emerging Areas in Communications Networks, 2005. SecureComm 2005. First International Conference on (p. 194–205).

23. Chen R, Fung B, Mohammed N, Desai BC, Wang K. Privacy-preserving trajectory data publishing by local suppression. Information Sciences, 2013; 231, 83–97. doi: 10. 1016/j. ins. 2011. 07. 035

24. Sweeney L. Achieving k-anonymity privacy protection using generalization and suppression. International Journal of Uncertainty, Fuzziness and Knowledge-Based Systems, 2002; 10(05), 571–588. doi: 10. 1142/s021848850200165x

25. Nergiz ME, Atzori M, Saygin Y. Towards trajectory anonymization: a generalization-based approach. In Proceedings of the SIGSPATIAL ACM GIS 2008 International Workshop on Security and Privacy in GIS and LBS. ACM, 2008; 52–61.

26. Mohammed N, Fung B, Debbabi M. Walking in the crowd: anonymizing trajectory data for pattern analysis. In Proceedings of the 18th ACM conference on Information and knowledge management. 2009; p. 1441–1444.

27. Domingo-Ferrer J, Sramka M, Trujillo-Rasúa R. Privacy-preserving publication of trajectories using microaggregation. In Proceedings of the 3rd ACM SIGSPATIAL International Workshop on Security and Privacy in GIS and LBS. 2010; p. 26–33.

28. Rastogi V, Suciu D, Hong S. The boundary between privacy and utility in data publishing. In Proceedings of the 33rd international conference on Very large data bases. 2007; p. 531–542.

29. Brickell J, Shmatikov V. The cost of privacy: destruction of data-mining utility in anonymized data publishing. In Proceedings of the 14th ACM SIGKDD international conference on Knowledge discovery and data mining. 2008; p. 70–78.

30. Loukides G, Shao, J. Data utility and privacy protection trade-off in k-anonymisation. In Proceedings of the 2008 international workshop on Privacy and anonymity in information society 2008; p. 36–45.

31. Li T, Li N. On the tradeoff between privacy and utility in data publishing. In Proceedings of the 15th ACM SIGKDD international conference on Knowledge discovery and data mining. 2009; p. 517–526.

32. Guo S, Chen K. Mining Privacy Settings to Find Optimal Privacy-Utility Tradeoffs for Social Network Services. In Privacy, Security, Risk and Trust (PASSAT), 2012 International Conference on and 2012 International Confernece on Social Computing (SocialCom) 2012; p. 656–665.

33. Barabasi A L. The origin of bursts and heavy tails in human dynamics, Nature, 2005; 435(7039): 207–2011. pmid:15889093 doi: 10. 1038/nature03459

34. Serranoa M Á, Boguñáb M, Vespignanl A. Extracting the multiscale backborn of complex weighted networks. In Proceedings of the National Academy of Sciences of the United States of America. 2009; 106(16):6483–8. doi: 10. 1073/pnas. 0808904106.

35. Louail T, Lenormand M, Picornell M, Gantú O G, Herranz R, Frias-Martinez E, Ramasco J J, Barthelemy M. Uncovering the spatial structure of mobility networks. Nature Communications. 2015; 6, 6007. doi: 10. 1038/ncomms7007. pmid:25607690

36. Louail T, Lenormand M, Gantú O G, Picornell M, Herranz R, Frias-Martinez E, Ramasco J J, Barthelemy M. From mobile phone data to the spatial structure of cities. Scientific Reports. 2014; 4, 5276. doi: 10. 1038/srep05276. pmid:24923248

CHAPTER 12 FCTCLUS: A FAST CLUSTERING ALGORITHM FOR HETEROGENEOUS INFORMATION NETWORKS

Yang J[1], Chen L[2], Zhang J[1]

[1] Institute of Computer Science and Technology, Harbin Engineering University, Harbin, China

[2] Institute of Computer Science and Technology, Mudanjiang Teachers College, Mudanjiang, China

ABSTRACT

It is important to cluster heterogeneous information networks. A fast clustering algorithm based on an approximate commute time embedding for heterogeneous information networks with a star network schema is proposed in this paper by utilizing the sparsity of heterogeneous information networks. First, a heterogeneous information network is transformed into multiple compatible bipartite graphs from the compatible point of view. Second, the approximate commute time embedding of each bipartite graph is computed using random mapping and a linear time solver. All of the indicator subsets in each embedding simultaneously determine the target dataset. Finally, a general model is formulated by these indicator subsets, and a fast algorithm is derived by simultaneously clustering all of the indicator subsets using the sum of the weighted distances for all indicators for an identical target object. The proposed fast algorithm, FctClus, is shown to be efficient and generalizable and exhibits high clustering accuracy and fast computation speed based on a theoretic analysis and experimental verification.

INTRODUCTION

Information networks are ubiquitous and include social information networks and DBLP bibliographic networks. Numerous studies on homogeneous information networks, which consist of a single type of data object, have been performed; however, little research has been performed on the clustering of heterogeneous information networks, which consist of multiple types of data objects. Clustering on a heterogeneous network may lead to better understanding the hidden structures and deeper meanings of the networks[1].

The star network schema is popular and important in the field of heterogeneous information networks. The star network schema includes one data object target type and multiple data object attribute types, whereby each relation is the target data objects and all attribute data objects linking to it.

Algorithms based on compatible bipartite graphs can effectively consider multiple types of relational data. Various classical clustering algorithms, such as algorithms based on semi-definite programming[2,3], algorithms based on information theory[4] and spectral clustering algorithms for multi-type relational data[5], have been proposed for heterogeneous data from the compatible point of view. These algorithms are generalizable, but the computational complexity of these algorithms is too great for use in clustering heterogeneous information networks.

Sun et al. presents an algorithm, NetClus[6], and a PathSim-based clustering algorithm[7] for clustering heterogeneous information networks. NetClus is effective

Citation: Yang J, Chen L, Zhang J (2015) FctClus: A Fast Clustering Algorithm for Heterogeneous Information Networks. PLoS ONE 10(6): e0130086. doi:10.1371/journal.pone.0130086.

for DBLP bibliographic networks, but the algorithm is not a general model for clustering other heterogeneous information networks; NetClus is not sufficiently stable. The concept behind NetClus is also used for clustering service webs[8,9]. The PathSim-based clustering algorithm requires a user guide, and the clustering quality reflects the requirements of users rather than the requirements of the network. ComClus[10] is a derivation algorithm of NetClus for use with hybrid networks that simultaneously include heterogeneous and homogeneous relations. NetClus and ComClus are not general and depend on the given application.

Dynamic link inference in heterogeneous networks[11] requires more accurate initial clustering. A high clustering quality is necessary for network analysis, but low computation speed is intolerable because of the large network scales involved. The accuracy of the LDCC algorithm[12] is improved, while both the heterogeneous and homogeneous data relations are explored. The CESC algorithm[13] is very effective for clustering homogeneous data using an approximate commute time embedding. A heterogeneous information network with a star network schema can transform into multiple compatible bipartite graphs from the compatible point of view. When the relation between any two nodes of the bipartite graph is presented with the commute time, the relation of both heterogeneous and homogenous data objects can be explored; the clustering accuracy can also be improved. The heterogeneous information networks are large but very sparse; therefore, the approximate commute time embedding of each bipartite graph can be quickly computed using random mapping and a linear time solver[14]. All of the indicator subsets in each embedding indicate the target dataset, and subsequently, a general model for clustering heterogeneous information networks is formulated based on all indicator subsets. All weighted distances between the indicators and the cluster centers in the respective indicator subsets are computed. All indicator subsets can be simultaneously clustered according to the sum of the weighted distances for all indicators for an identical target object. Based on the above discussion, an effective clustering algorithm, FctClus, which is based on the approximate commute time embedding for heterogeneous information networks, is proposed in this paper. The computation speed and clustering accuracy of FctClus are high.

METHODS

Commute Time Embedding of the Bipartite Graph

Given two types of datasets, $X_0 = \{x_1^{(0)}, x_2^{(0)}, \cdots, x_{n_0}^{(0)}\}$ and $X_1 = \{x_1^{(1)}, x_2^{(1)}, \cdots, x_{n_1}^{(1)}\}$, the graph $G_b = \langle V, E\rangle$ is called a bipartite graph if $V(G_b) = X_0 \cup X_1$ and $E(G_b) = \{\langle x_i^{(0)}, x_j^{(1)}\rangle\}$, where $1 \le i \le n_0$, $1 \le j \le n_1$. $W_{n_0 \times n_1}$ is the relation matrix between X_0 and X_1, where the element w_{ij} is the edge weight between $x_i^{(0)}$ and $x_j^{(1)}$. Then, the adjacency matrix of the bipartite graph G_b can be denoted as

$$\tilde{W}_{n\times n} = \begin{bmatrix} 0 & W_{n_0\times n_1} \\ (W^T)_{n_1\times n_0} & 0 \end{bmatrix}$$

D_1 and D_2 are the diagonal matrices, where the diagonal element of D_1 is $d_i = \sum_{j=1}^{n_1} w_{ij}$ and the diagonal element of D_2 is $d_j = \sum_{i=1}^{n_0} w_{ij}$.

$$D = \begin{bmatrix} D_1 & 0 \\ 0 & D_2 \end{bmatrix}$$

thus the Laplacian matrix of the bipartite graph G_b is $L = D - \tilde{W}$. L can be eigen-decomposed into $L = \Phi\Lambda\Phi^T$, where $\Lambda = diag(\lambda_1, \lambda_2, \cdots, \lambda_n)$ is a diagonal matrix composed of the eigenvalues of L and $\lambda_1 \le \lambda_2 \le \cdots \le \lambda_n$, $\Phi = (\phi_1, \phi_2, \cdots, \phi_n)$ is an eigenmatrix and ϕ_i is an eigenvector corresponding to the eigenvalue λ_i. Let L^+ be a pseudo-inverse matrix of L and $L^+ = \sum_{i=2}^{n} \frac{1}{\lambda_i}\phi_i\phi_i^T$. The bipartite graph is also an undirected weighted graph. According to the literature[15], the commute time c_{ij} between nodes i and j of G_b can be computed by the pseudo-inverse matrix L^+.

$$c_{ij} = g_v(l_{ii}^+ + l_{jj}^+ - 2l_{ij}^+) = g_v(e_i - e_j)^T L^+(e_i - e_j) \qquad (1)$$

where l_{ij}^+ is the (i, j) element of L^+, $g_v = \sum w_{ij}$, e_i is a unit column vector in which the i-th element is 1; that is, $e_i = [\underset{1}{0}, \cdots, \underset{i-1}{0}, \underset{i}{1}, \underset{i+1}{0}, \cdots, \underset{n}{0}]^T$.

According to the literature[15,16], the commute time c_{ij} between nodes i and j of G_b is

$$\begin{aligned} c_{ij} &= g_v(e_i - e_j)^T L^+(e_i - e_j) \\ &= g_v(e_i - e_j)^T \Phi\Lambda^{-1}\Phi^T(e_i - e_j) \\ &= [\sqrt{g_v}\Lambda^{-1/2}\Phi^T(e_i - e_j)]^T[\sqrt{g_v}\Lambda^{-1/2}\Phi^T(e_i - e_j)] \end{aligned}$$

Thus, the commute time c_{ij} is the square pairwise Euclidean distance between the row vectors in the space $(\sqrt{g_v}\Lambda^{-1/2}\Phi^T)^T$ or the column vectors in the space $\sqrt{g_v}\Lambda^{-1/2}\Phi^T$ [13]. $(\sqrt{g_v}\Lambda^{-1/2}\Phi^T)^T$ or $\sqrt{g_v}\Lambda^{-1/2}\Phi^T$ is called the commute time embedding of the bipartite graph G_b. c_{ij} is the average path length between two nodes rather than the shortest path between two nodes. Using the commute time for clustering the noisy data increases robustness and captures the complex clusters. Therefore clustering in the commute time embedding can also effectively capture the complex clusters. $\sqrt{g_v}\Lambda^{-1/2}\Phi^T$ is used in this paper. If a normal Laplacian matrix $L_n = D^{-1/2}LD^{-1/2}$ is used, the commute time embedding is $\sqrt{g_v}\Lambda^{-1/2}\Phi^T D^{-1/2}$ [13].

Approximate Commute Time Embedding of the Bipartite Graph

If directly computing $\sqrt{g_v}\Lambda^{-1/2}\Phi^T$ or $\sqrt{g_v}\Lambda^{-1/2}\Phi^T D^{-1/2}$,

, the process requires $O(n^3)$ time for the eigen-decomposition of the Laplacian matrix L or L_n. $n = n_0+n_1$ is the number of nodes and s is the number of edges in the bipartite graph G_b. According to the literature[17], if the edges in G_b are oriented and

$$B(i,j) = \begin{cases} 1 & i \text{ is tail}, j \text{ is head} \\ -1 & i \text{ is head}, j \text{ is tail} \\ 0 & \text{others} \end{cases}$$

where i and j are nodes of G_b, then $B_{s\times n}$ is a directed edge-node incidence matrix. Using $\hat{W}_{s\times s}$ as a diagonal matrix whose entries are the edge weights, thus $L = B^T \hat{W} B$. Furthermore,

$$\psi = \sqrt{g_v}\hat{W}^{1/2}BL^+ \in R^{s\times n} \quad (2)$$

thus, ψ is the commute time embedding of the bipartite graph G_b, where the square root of the commute time is the Euclidean distance between i and j in ψ because

$$\begin{aligned} c_{ij} &= g_v(e_i - e_j)^T L^+(e_i - e_j) \\ &= g_v(e_i - e_j)^T L^+LL^+(e_i - e_j) \\ &= g_v(e_i - e_j)^T L^+B^T\hat{W}BL^+(e_i - e_j) \\ &= [\sqrt{g_v}\hat{W}^{1/2}BL^+(e_i - e_j)]^T[\sqrt{g_v}\hat{W}^{1/2}BL^+(e_i - e_j)] \end{aligned}$$

According to the literature[18], given vectors $v_1,\cdots, v_n \in R^s$ and $\varepsilon > 0$, $Q_{k_r\times s}$ is a random matrix of row vectors, where $Q(i,j) = \pm 1/\sqrt{k_r}$ is equivalent when $k_r = O(\log n / \varepsilon^2)$. With probability $1-1/n$, at least

$$(1-\varepsilon)\|v_i - v_j\|^2 \le \|Qv_i - Qv_j\|^2 \le (1+\varepsilon)\|v_i - v_j\|^2 \quad (3)$$

for all pairs.

Therefore, given the bipartite graph G_b with n nodes and s edges, $\varepsilon > 0$, and a matrix $Y_{k_r\times n} = \sqrt{g_v}Q\hat{W}^{1/2}BL^+$ with probability of at least $1-1/n$:

$$(1-\varepsilon)c_{ij} \le \|Y(e_i - e_j)\|^2 \le (1+\varepsilon)c_{ij} \quad (4)$$

for any nodes $i, j \in G_b$, where $k_r = O(\log n / \varepsilon^2)$.

The proof of Eq (4) comes directly from Eq (2) and Eq (3). $c_{ij} \approx \|Y(e_i - e_j)\|^2$ with an error ε based on Eq (4). If directly computing $Y_{k_r\times n} = \sqrt{g_v}Q\hat{W}^{1/2}BL^+, L^+$, L^+ must first be computed, but the computational complexity of directly computing L^+ is excessive. However, using the method in the literature[19,20] to compute $Y_{k_r\times n}$, the complexity is decreased. Let $\theta = \sqrt{g_v}Q(\hat{W}^{1/2}B)$; then, $Y = \theta L^+$, which is equal to $YL = \theta$. First, $\theta = \sqrt{g_v}Q(\hat{W}^{1/2}B)$ is computed, and then, $YL = \theta$. Each row of Y, y_i, is computed by solving the system $y_iL = \theta_i$, where θ_i is the i-th row of θ. The linear time solver of Spielman and Teng[19,20] requires only $\tilde{O}(s)$ time to solve the system. Because $\|y_i - \hat{y}_i\|_L \le \varepsilon\|y_i\|_L$ [17], where $\hat{y}_i$ is the solution, $y_iL = \theta_i$ using the linear time solver. Then, [17]

$$(1-\varepsilon)^2 c_{ij} \le \|\hat{Y}(e_i - e_j)\|^2 \le (1+\varepsilon)^2 c_{ij}$$

Therefore, $c_{ij} \approx \|\hat{Y}(e_i - e_j)\|^2$ with an error bound of ε^2. The component of the algorithm for the approximate commute time embedding of the bipartite graph is illustrated as follows.

Algorithm1 ApCte (Approximate Commute Time Embedding of the Bipartite Graph)

- input the relation matrix $W_{n_0\times n_1}$;
- compute the matrices B, $\hat{W}$ and L using $W_{n_0\times n_1}$;
- compute $\theta = \sqrt{g_v}Q(\hat{W}^{1/2}B)$;
- compute each $\hat{y}_i$ using the system $y_iL = \theta_i$ by calling to the Spielman-Teng solver k_r times[14], $1 \le i \le k_r$;
- output the approximate commute time embedding $\hat{Y}$.

All data objects of X_0 and X_1 are mapped into a common subspace $\hat{Y}$, where the first n_0 column vectors of $\hat{Y}$ indicate X_0 and the last n_1 column vectors of $\hat{Y}$ indicate X_1. The dataset is composed of the $n = n_0+n_1$ column vectors of $\hat{Y}$ is called an indicator dataset. The input matrix $W_{n_0\times n_1}$ is a sparse matrix with s nonzero elements. Therefore, the complexity of computing the matrices B, $\hat{W}$ and L in step 2 is $O(2s) + O(s) + O(n)$. The sparse matrix B has $2s$ nonzero elements, and the diagonal matrix $\hat{W}$ has s nonzero elements. Computing $\theta = \sqrt{g_v}Q(\hat{W}^{1/2}B)$ takes $O(2sk_r + s)$ time in step 3. Because the linear time solver of Spielman and Teng[19,20] requires only $\tilde{O}(s)$ time to solve for each y_i of system $y_iL = \theta_i$, constructing $\hat{Y}$ takes $\tilde{O}(sk_r)$ time in step 4. Therefore, the complexity of algorithm1, ApCte, is only $O(2s) + O(s) + O(n) + O(2sk_r + s) + \tilde{O}(sk_r) = \tilde{O}(4s + n + 3sk_r)$. In practice, $k_r = O(\log n / \varepsilon^2)$ is small and does not vary between different datasets. The indicator dataset includes low-dimensional homogeneous data; therefore, traditional algorithms can be used for the indicator dataset.

A General Model Formulation

Given a dataset $\chi = \{X_t\}_{t=0}^T$ with T+1 types, where X_t is a dataset belonging to the t-th type, a weighted graph $G = < V, E, W >$ on χ is called an information network; if $V(G) = \chi$, the $E(G)$ is a binary relation on V and $W: E \rightarrow R^+$. Such an information network is called a heterogeneous information network when $T \ge 1$ and a homogeneous information network when $T = 0$[6].

An information network $G = < V, E, W >$ on χ is called a heterogeneous information network with a star network schema if $\forall e = \langle x_i, x_j\rangle \in E$, $x_i \in X_0$ and $x_j \in X_t$ $(t \neq 0)$. X_0 is the target dataset, and X_t $(t \neq 0)$ is the attribute dataset.

To derive a general model for clustering the target dataset, a heterogeneous information network with a star network schema using the dataset $\chi = \{X_t\}_{t=0}^T$ with T+1 types is given, where X_0 is the target dataset and $\{X_t\}_{t=1}^{T}$ are the attribute datasets. $X_t = \{x_1^{(t)}, x_2^{(t)}, \cdots, x_{n_t}^{(t)}\}$, where n_t is the object number of X_t. $W^{(0t)} \in R^{n_0 \times n_t}$ denotes the relation matrix between the target dataset X_0 and the attribute dataset X_t, where the element $w_{ij}^{(0t)}$ denotes the relation between $x_i^{(0)}$ of X_0 and $x_j^{(t)}$ of X_t. If an edge between $x_i^{(0)}$ and $x_j^{(t)}$ exists, its edge weight is $w_{ij}^{(0t)}$. If no edge exists, $w_{ij}^{(0t)} = 0$. T relation matrices $\{W^{(0t)}\}_{t=1}^{T}$ exist in the heterogeneous information network with a star network schema.

The target dataset X_0 and the attribute dataset X_t constitute a bipartite graph, $G^{(0t)}$, which corresponds to the relation matrix $W^{(0t)}$. The indicator dataset $Y^{(0t)} = \{y_1^{(0t)}, y_2^{(0t)}, \cdots, y_{n_0+n_t}^{(0t)}\}$ which also is the approximate commute time embedding of $G^{(0t)}$ can be quickly computed by ApCte, where the first n_0 data of $Y^{(0t)}$ indicate X_0 and the last n_t data of $Y^{(0t)}$ indicate the attribute dataset X_t. $Y_t^{(0)}$ consists of the first n_0 data of $Y^{(0t)}$, and $Y^{(t)}$ consists of the last n_t data of $Y^{(0t)}$. $Y_t^{(0)}$ and $Y^{(t)}$ are called the indicator subsets. $y_i^{(t)} \in Y_t^{(0)}$ indicates the i-th object of X_0 and is called an indicator for $1 \leq i \leq n_0$. There exists a one-to-one correspondence between the indicators of $Y_t^{(0)}$ and the objects of X_0. Because T bipartite graphs correspond to T indicator datasets, the target dataset X_0 is simultaneously indicated by the T indicator subsets $\{Y_t^{(0)}\}_{t=1}^{T}$, and each object of X_0 is simultaneously indicated by T indicators.

$\beta^{(t)}$ is the weight of the relation matrix $W^{(0t)}$, where $\sum_{t=1}^{T} \beta^{(t)} = 1$, $\beta^{(t)} > 0$. The target dataset X_0 is partitioned into K clusters. The indicators of $\{Y_t^{(0)}\}_{t=1}^{T}$, which indicate the identical object of X_0, belong to T clusters. The T clusters are in T different indicator subsets and are denoted using the same label. Let

$$F = \sum_{t=1}^{T}(\beta^{(t)}\gamma \| Y_t^{(0)} - \omega^{(t)} \|^2) = \sum_{t=1}^{T}(\beta^{(t)}\sum_{i=1}^{n_0}(\gamma_{ij}\sum_{j=1}^{K}\| y_i^{(t)} - \omega_j^{(t)} \|^2)) \tag{5}$$

where $\omega_j^{(t)}$ is the j-th cluster center of the indicator subset $Y_t^{(0)}$. There exists a one-to-one correspondence between the indicator function $\gamma = \{\gamma_{ij}\}_{i=1}^{n_0}$ and the objects of X_0. If all indicators, $\{y_i^{(t)}\}_{t=1}^{T}$, that indicates the i-th object of X_0 belong to the j-th cluster, $\gamma_{ij} = 1$; otherwise, $\gamma_{ij} = 0$.

If the objective function F in Eq (5) is minimized, the clusters of X_0 are optimal from the compatible point of view because each indicator subset reflects the relation between the target dataset and the attribute dataset. Obviously, determining the global minimum of Eq (5) is NP hard.

Derivation of Fast Algorithm for Clustering Heterogeneous Information Networks

The following steps allow for the local minimum of F in Eq (5) to be quickly achieved by simultaneously clustering all of the indicator subsets.

Setting the Cluster Label

When given the cluster label of each indicator subset, the modeling process can be simplified. Suppose that the labels of the K clusters of each $Y_t^{(0)}$ are set. Let $q_1, q_2 \in X_0$, $y_1^{(1)}, y_2^{(1)} \in Y_1^{(0)}$, $\cdots y_1^{(T)}, y_2^{(T)} \in Y_T^{(0)}$. $\{y_1^{(t)}\}_{t=1}^{T}$ indicate q_1, and $\{y_2^{(t)}\}_{t=1}^{T}$ indicate q_2. The clusters which indicators for an identical target object belong to have the same label. If one indicator of $\{y_1^{(t)}\}_{t=1}^{T}$ belongs to the j-th cluster, all of the other indicators of $\{y_1^{(t)}\}_{t=1}^{T}$ also belong to the j-th cluster in their respective indicator subset. If $\{y_1^{(t)}\}_{t=1}^{T}$ belongs to the j-th cluster, then all $\{y_2^{(t)}\}_{t=1}^{T}$ either belong to the j-th cluster in their respective indicator subset or none belong to the j-th cluster.

Each cluster of $Y_t^{(0)}$ has an initial center. K random objects are selected from the target dataset X_0. The indicators indicating the K objects are taken as the initial cluster centers for each $Y_t^{(0)}$ and for the clusters whose center indicates an identical target object with the same label. Then, all of the other indicators for an identical target object only belong to the j-th cluster in each $Y_t^{(0)}$ or no indicators belong to the j-th cluster, where $1 \leq j \leq K$. Therefore, the K clusters of $\{Y_t^{(0)}\}_{t=1}^{T}$ are set labels.

The sum of the Weighted Distances

An object of X_0 is indicated by T indicators. All of the T distances between the indicator and the center in each $Y_t^{(0)}$ affect the object allocation. The target object allocation is determined by the sum of the weighted distances for the T indicators. Setting $q_i \in X_0$, $y_i^{(1)} \in Y_1^{(0)}$, $\cdots y_i^{(T)} \in Y_T^{(0)}$, $\{y_i^{(t)}\}_{t=1}^{T}$ indicates q_i. The weighted distance between $y_i^{(t)}$ and the j-th cluster center in $Y_t^{(0)}$ is $\beta^{(t)}\|y_i^{(t)} - \omega_j^{(t)}\|^2$. The sum of the weighted distances is $dis = \sum_{t=1}^{T}(\beta^{(t)}\|y_i^{(t)} - \omega_j^{(t)}\|^2)$, which determines the cluster that the object q_i belongs.

$$j = \arg\min \sum_{t=1}^{T}(\beta^{(t)}\|y_i^{(t)} - \omega_j^{(t)}\|^2) \tag{6}$$

where j is the cluster label.

The Local Minimum of *F*

F in Eq (5) can also be expressed as

$$F = \sum_{t=1}^{T}(\beta^{(t)}\sum_{i=1}^{n_0}(\gamma_{ij}\sum_{j=1}^{K}\|y_i^{(t)} - \omega_j^{(t)}\|^2)) = \sum_{i=1}^{n_0}(\gamma_{ij}\sum_{j=1}^{K}\sum_{t=1}^{T}(\beta^{(t)}\|y_i^{(t)} - \omega_j^{(t)}\|^2)) \tag{7}$$

Obviously, Eq (7) is another representation of Eq (5).

Given the initial centers $\{\omega_j^{(t)}\}_{j=1}^K$ and the cluster labels in the T indicator subsets $\{Y_t^{(0)}\}_{t=1}^T$, $\{Y_t^{(0)}\}_{t=1}^T$ is first partitioned by computing Eq (6) and setting $F = F_0$ in Eq (7). The cluster centers of $\{Y_t^{(0)}\}_{t=2}^T$ remain the same, and γ_{ij} is unchanged. The new center $\{\hat{\omega}_j^{(1)}\}_{j=1}^K$ of each cluster in $Y_1^{(0)}$ is computed. The new center is the mean of all data of each cluster. The new centers $\{\hat{\omega}_j^{(1)}\}_{j=1}^K$ of $Y_1^{(0)}$ replace the old centers, and subsequently, Eq (7) is used to set $F := F_1$. Then,

$$F_1 = \sum_{i=1}^{n_0}(\gamma_{ij}\sum_{j=1}^{K}(\beta^{(1)}\|y_i^{(1)} - \hat{\omega}_j^{(1)}\|^2 + \sum_{t=2}^{T}(\beta^{(t)}\|y_i^{(t)} - \omega_j^{(t)}\|^2))) \leq F_0 \quad (8)$$

Proving

$$F_1 = \sum_{i=1}^{n_0}(\gamma_{ij}\sum_{j=1}^{K}(\beta^{(1)}\|y_i^{(1)} - \hat{\omega}_j^{(1)}\|^2 + \sum_{t=2}^{T}(\beta^{(t)}\|y_i^{(t)} - \omega_j^{(t)}\|^2)))$$

Because only the new centers $\{\hat{\omega}_j^{(1)}\}_{j=1}^K$ of $Y_1^{(0)}$ replace the old centers, γ_{ij} remains unchanged. Therefore

$$F_1 = \sum_{i=1}^{n_0}(\gamma_{ij}\sum_{j=1}^{K}(\beta^{(1)}\|y_i^{(1)} - \hat{\omega}_j^{(1)}\|^2 + \sum_{t=2}^{T}(\beta^{(t)}\|y_i^{(t)} - \omega_j^{(t)}\|^2)))$$

Because the cluster centers of $\{Y_t^{(0)}\}_{t=2}^T$ also remain unchanged,

$\sum_{i=1}^{n_0}(\gamma_{ij}\sum_{j=1}^{K}\sum_{t=2}^{T}(\beta^{(t)}\|y_i^{(t)} - \omega_j^{(t)}\|^2))$ is constant, and $\sum_{i=1}^{n_0}(\gamma_{ij}\sum_{j=1}^{K}(\beta^{(1)}\|y_i^{(1)} - \hat{\omega}_j^{(1)}\|^2))$ $\leq \sum_{i=1}^{n_0}(\gamma_{ij}\sum_{j=1}^{K}(\beta^{(1)}\|y_i^{(1)} - \omega_j^{(1)}\|^2))$. Subsequently,

$$F_1 \leq \sum_{i=1}^{n_0}(\gamma_{ij}\sum_{j=1}^{K}(\beta^{(1)}\|y_i^{(1)} - \omega_j^{(1)}\|^2)) + \sum_{i=1}^{n_0}(\gamma_{ij}\sum_{j=1}^{K}\sum_{t=2}^{T}(\beta^{(t)}\|y_i^{(t)} - \omega_j^{(t)}\|^2)) = F_0$$

Thus, the cluster centers of $Y_1^{(0)}$, for $F_1 \leq F_0$, are replaced.

The new centers $\{\hat{\omega}_j^{(1)}\}_{j=1}^K$ of $Y_1^{(0)}$ replace the old centers, while the centers of $\{Y_t^{(0)}\}_{t=2}^T$ remain unchanged. Re-clustering $\{Y_t^{(0)}\}_{t=1}^T$ using Eq (6), where the corresponding value is $F = F_2$ in Eq (7), gives $F_2 \leq F_1$.

Partitioning $\{Y_t^{(0)}\}_{t=1}^T$ using Eq (6) computes the new cluster centers $\{\hat{\omega}_j^{(1)}\}_{j=1}^K$ of $Y_1^{(0)}$; the new centers replace the old centers $\{\hat{\omega}_j^{(1)}\}_{j=1}^K$. Then, the same procedure is repeated for each $\{Y_t^{(0)}\}_{t=2}^T$. The value of F decreases in this case. The above procedures are repeated until F in Eq (7) converges; then, the local minimum of F in Eq (7) is obtained. The algorithm based on the approximate commute time embedding for heterogeneous information networks is shown below.

Algorithm 2 FctClus (Fast Clustering Algorithm based on the Approximate Commute Time Embedding for Heterogeneous Information Networks)

1. Input relation matrices $\{W^{(0t)} \in R^{n_0 \times n_t}\}_{t=1}^T$, weights $\{\beta^{(t)} > 0\}_{t=1}^T$ and cluster number K;
2. **for** $t = 1$ to T **do**
3. Compute indicator dataset $Y^{(0t)}$ of the bipartite graph corresponding to $W^{(0t)}$ using algorithm 1;
4. Constitute the indicator subset $Y_t^{(0)}$ that indicates X_0;
5. end for
6. Initialize the K initial cluster centers $\{\omega_j^{(t)}\}_{j=1}^K$ of $\{Y_t^{(0)}\}_{t=1}^T$ and set the cluster label;
7. loop
8. **for** $t = 1$ to T **do**
9. Partition $\{Y_t^{(0)}\}_{t=1}^T$ into K clusters by computing Eq (6);

10. Re-compute the new cluster centers $\{\hat{\omega}_j^{(t)}\}_{j=1}^{K}$ of $Y_t^{(0)}$;

$\{\omega_j^{(t)} = \hat{\omega}_j^{(t)}\}_{j=1}^{K}$;

11. end for
12. end loop
13. Output the clusters of X_0.

The computational complexity of steps 2~5 is $\tilde{O}(\sum_{t=1}^{T}(4s_t + n_t + 3s_tk_r))$ in algorithm 2, where T is the number of relational matrices in the heterogeneous information network and k_r is the data dimension of $Y_t^{(0)}$. n_t and s_t are the node number and edge number of the t-th bipartite graph, respectively. Step 6 requires only $O(K)$ time; the time is constant. The object number of X_0 is equal to the indicator number of each indicator subset, thus the computational complexity of steps 7~13 is $O(uTKk_rn_0)$, where K is the number of clusters of each $Y_t^{(0)}$; n_0 is the data number of each $Y_t^{(0)}$; and u is the iteration number for F in Eq (7) convergence. Therefore, the computational complexity of algorithm 2, FctClus, is $\tilde{O}(\sum_{t=1}^{T}(4s_t + n_t + 3s_tk_r))$ + $O(uTKk_rn_0)$, where k_r and u are small and T and K are constant.

EXPERIMENTS

The Experimental Dataset

The experimental datasets are composed of real data selected from the DBLP data. The DBLP is a typical heterogeneous information network in computer science domain and contains 4 types of objects, including papers, authors, terms and venues. Two different-scaled heterogeous datasets called S_{small} and S_{large} respectively are used in experiments.

S_{small} is the small test dataset and is called the "four-area dataset", as in the literature[6].S_{small} extracted from the DBLP dataset downloaded in 2011 contains four areas related to data mining: databases, data mining, information retrieval and machine learning. Five representative conferences for each area are chosen, and all papers and terms that appear in the titles are included. S_{small} is showed in S1 File.

S_{large} is the large test dataset and extracted from the Chinese DBLP dataset, which are sharing resources released by Institute of automation, Chinese Academy of Sciences. S_{large} includes 34 computer science journals, 16, 567 papers, 47, 701 authors and 52,262 terms(keywords). S_{large} is showed in S2 File.

When analyzing the papers, this object is the target dataset, and the other objects are the attribute datasets. There is no direct link between papers because the DBLP provided very limited citation information. When analyzing the authors, this object is the target dataset, while papers and venues are the attribute datasets. However, there is a direct link between authors because of the co-author relation between various authors; therefore, authors are another attribute dataset related to the target dataset.

The experiments are performed in the MATLAB 7.0 programming environment. The matlab source codes for our algorithm are showed in S3 File and are available online athttps://github.com/lsy917/chenlimin, which include a main program and three function programs. FctClus.m is the main program which output the clusters of the object dataset, and ApCte.m, Prematrix.m and Net_Branches.m are function programs. The Koutis CMG solver[14] is used in all experiments as the nearly linear time solver to create the embedding. The solver uses symmetric, diagonally dominant matrices that are available online at http://www.cs.cmu.edu/~jkoutis/cmg.html.

The Relational Matrix

Papers are the target dataset, while authors, venues and terms are the attribute datasets. X_0denotes papers, and X_1, X_2 and X_3 denote authors, venues and terms, respectively. $W^{(0t)}$ is the relation matrix between X_0 and X_t, $1 \le t \le 3$. The element of $\{W^{(0t)}\}_{t=1}^{3}$ is

$$w_{ij}^{(0t)} = \begin{cases} 1 & \text{if } i \in X_0, j \in X_1 \cup X_2, \text{ node } i \text{ links to } j; \\ p & \text{if } i \in X_0, j \in X_3, \text{ node } i \text{ appears } p \text{ times in node } j; \\ 0 & \text{otherwise;} \end{cases}$$

When authors are the target dataset, papers and venues are the attribute datasets. Authors are also an attribute dataset because of the co-author relation existing between authors. X_0denotes authors when X_1 and X_2 denote papers and venues, respectively. $W^{(0t)}$ is the relation matrix between X_0 and X_t, $0 \le t \le 2$. The element of $\{W^{(0t)}\}_{t=0}^{2}$ is

$$w_{ij}^{(0t)} = \begin{cases} 1 & \text{if } i \in X_0, j \in X_1 \cup X_2, \text{node } i \text{ links to } j; \\ p & \text{if } i \in X_0, j \in X_0, \text{ node } i \text{ and } j \text{ co} - \text{author } p \text{ papers;} \\ 0 & \text{otherwise;} \end{cases}$$

All the algorithms use the same relation matrix for all experiments.

Parameter Analysis

Analysis of Parameter k_r.

The equation [13] $Accuracy = \frac{\sum_{i=1}^{n}\delta[map(c_i) = label(i)]}{n}$ is used to compute the clustering accuracy in the experiments, where n is the object number of dataset, *label(i)* is the cluster label, and c_i is the predicted label of an object i. $\delta(\cdot)$ is an indicator function:

$$\delta(\cdot) = \begin{cases} 1 & map(i) = label(i) \\ 0 & map(i) \neq label(i) \end{cases}.$$

k_r is small in practice, and minimal differences exist among the various datasets[13]. The literature[13] has proved that the accuracy curve is flat for clustering different homogeneous datasets when $k_r \geq 50$.

Using the small dataset S_{small}, the clustering accuracy as a function of k_r in a heterogeneous information network is studied.

An experiment with different k_r is conducted in the small dataset, S_{small}. In the FctClus algorithm, the weight of

$\{W^{(0r)}\}_{t=1}^{3}$ is taken as $\beta^{(1)} = 0.3$, $\beta^{(2)} = 0.4$ and $\beta^{(3)} = 0.3$ for clustering papers; the weight of $\{W^{(0r)}\}_{t=0}^{2}$ is taken as $\beta^{(1)} = 0.4$, $\beta^{(2)} = 0.2$ and $\beta^{(3)} = 0.4$ for clustering authors. The clustering accuracy is affected by k_r, as shown in Fig 1 and Fig 2.

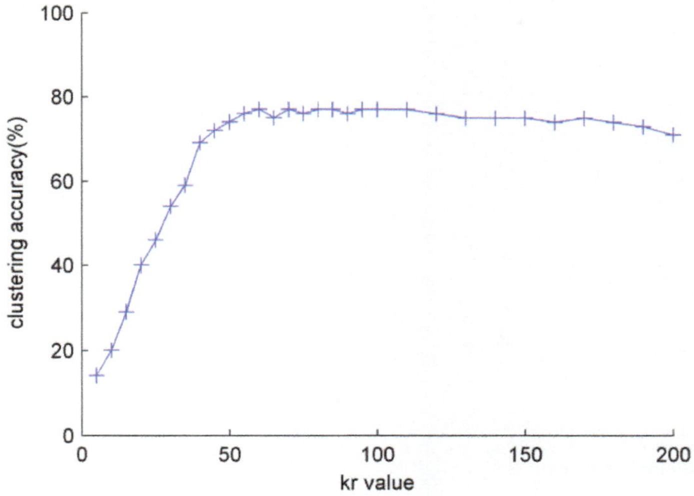

Figure 1. The influence of k_r for clustering papers on $s_{small.}$

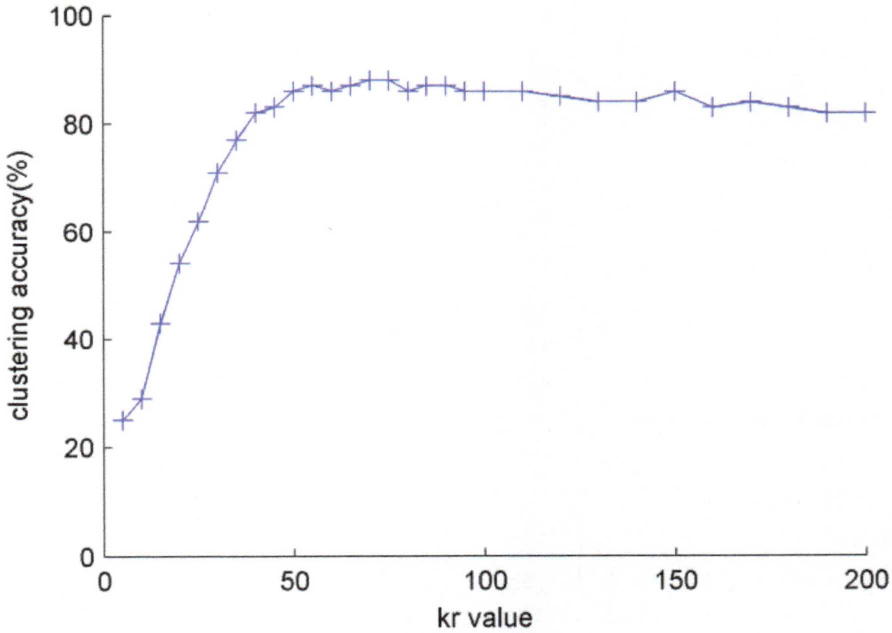

Figure 2. The influence of k_r for clustering authors on $s_{small.}$

The parameter k_r is quite small because the accuracy curve is flat when k_r obtains a certain value. $k_r = 60$ is suitable for the dataset in the experiment. k_r is small and does not considerably affect the computation speed of FctClus. It is advantageous that FctClus is not sensitive to k_r in terms of both accuracy and performance. All weights of the relation matrix and $k_r = 60$ are studied in other experiments.

Analysis of Iteration *u*

An experiment is conducted in the small dataset S_{small} to compare the influence of iteration$u$ on the clustering result, where $k_r = 60$. The influence of the iteration u on clustering papers and authors is shown in Fig 3 and Fig 4. The algorithm quickly convergences when $u = 30$.$u = 40$ is examined in the other experiments.

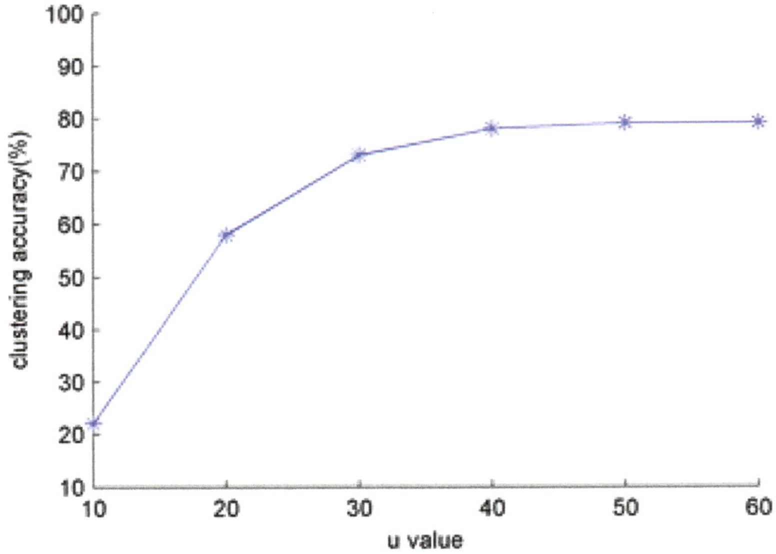

Figure 3. The influence of *u* **for clustering papers on** $s_{small.}$

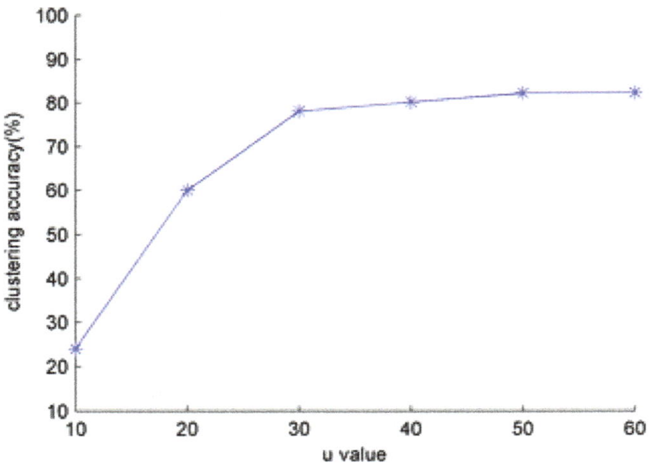

Figure 4. The influence of ***u*** **for clustering authors on** $s_{small.}$

Comparison of Clustering Accuracy and Computation Speed

The complexity of the algorithms is too high for large-scale networks based on semi-definite programming[2,3] and spectral clustering algorithms for multi-type relational data[5]. The low-complexity algorithms CIT[4], NetClus[6] and ComClus[10] are selected for comparison with the FctClus algorithm in terms of clustering accuracy and computation speed; the datasets S_{small} and S_{large} are also chosen for this experiment.

The initial cluster centers of FctClus or the initial cluster partitions of the other three algorithms are randomly selected 3 times. The best clustering accuracy of the 3 measurements is used as the clustering accuracy of the four algorithms, and the computation speed at this time is considered as the measured computation speed. The parameters in literature[6] are used as the parameters in NetClus, and the parameters in literature[10] are used as the parameters in ComClus in this experiment. The comparison results are shown in Table 1 and Table 2.

Table 1. Comparison of clustering accuracy (%).

target object &dataset	CIT	NetClus	ComClus	FctClus
Papers on s_{small}	73.91	71.54	72.83	78.87
Authors on s_{small}	74.41	69.13	74.91	81.33
Papers on s_{large}	70.84	71.28	72.93	76.36
Authors on s_{large}	71.02	68.29	73.01	77.94

doi:10.1371/journal.pone.0130086.t001

Table 2. Comparison of computation speed(s).

target object &dataset	CIT	NetClus	ComClus	FctClus
Papers on s_{small}	78.5	37.3	40.3	37.1
Authors on s_{small}	79.8	36.9	39.8	38.3
Papers on s_{large}	1469.3	802.6	827.3	808.4
Authors on s_{large}	1484.7	743.7	781.4	774.9

doi:10.1371/journal.pone.0130086.t002

The clustering accuracy of FctClus is the highest of all four algorithms. The clustering accuracy of CIT is lower than that of FctClus because the bipartite graphs of the heterogeneous information networks are sparse. The computational complexity of CIT is $O(n^2)$, and the convergence speed of CIT is low when the heterogeneous information network is sparse. The clustering accuracy of NetClus is low because only heterogeneous relations are used. Homogeneous and heterogeneous relations are both used in ComClus; therefore, the accuracy of ComClus is higher than that of NetClus. FctClus is an algorithm based on commute time embedding. The data relations are explored using commute time and the direct relations of the target dataset are considered. FctClus is not affected by the sparsity of networks; thus, FctClus is highly accurate.

The computation speed of FctClus is nearly as fast as NetClus. The experiment demonstrates that FctClus is effective. FctClus is more universal and can be adapted for clustering any heterogeneous information network with a star network schema. However, NetClus and ComClus can only be adapted for clustering bibliographic networks because NetClus and ComClus depend on a ranking function of a specific application field.

Comparison of Clustering Stability

To compare the stability of the FctClus, NetClus and CIT algorithms, the small dataset S_{small} is used for clustering papers in this experiment. ComClus is a derivation algorithm of NetClus; it has the same properties as NetClus. ComClus is not considered in this study.

The initial cluster centers of FctClus and the initial cluster partitions of NetClus and CIT are randomly recorded 10 times, and the three algorithms are executed 10 times respectively. The clustering accuracy of the three algorithms for 10 times is shown in Fig 5. Although the computation speeds of FctClus and NetClus are both high, Fig 5 shows that the stability of FctClus is higher than that of NetClus and that the initial centers do not greatly impact the clustering result of FctClus. However, NetClus is very unstable, and the initial clusters greatly impact the clustering accuracy and convergence speed of NetClus. CIT is more stable than NetClus, but the clustering accuracy is low.

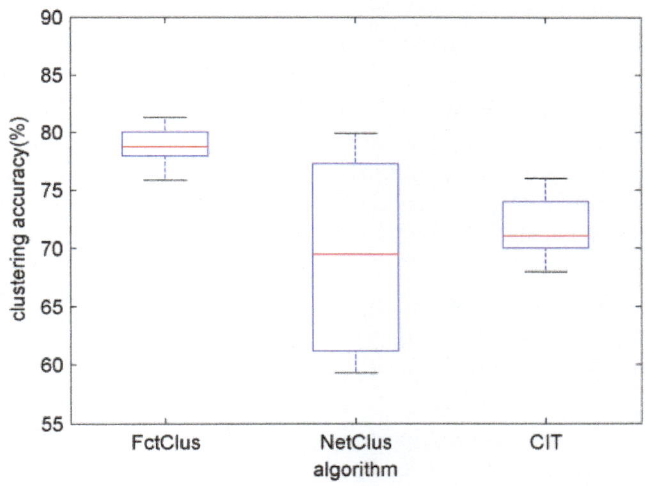

Figure 5. A stability comparison of the 3 algorithms for 10 times.

Running Time Analysis of the FctClus Algorithm

The running time distributions of FctClus on the two datasets are shown in Table 3. The experimental data show that FctClus is effective. The running time for serial computing the three embedding is less than 50% of the total running time. When utilizing parallel computing for the three embedding, the computation speed is higher. When clustering indicator subsets in parallel, the computation speed may also be increased.

Table 3. Distribution of running time for FctClus.

target object &dataset	Embedding time(s)	Clustering time(s)	Total time(s)
Papers on s_{small}	19.6	17.5	37.1
Authors on s_{small}	18.1	20.2	38.3
Papers on s_{large}	398.8	409.6	808.4
Authors on s_{large}	382.4	392.5	774.9

doi:10.1371/journal.pone.0130086.t003

CONCLUSIONS

The relation between the original data described by the commute time guarantees the accuracy and performance of the FctClus algorithm. Because heterogeneous information networks are sparse, FctClus can use random mapping and a linear time solver[14] to compute the approximate commute time embedding, which guarantees the high computation speed. FctClus is effective and may be broadly implemented for large heterogeneous information networks, as demonstrated in theory and experimentally. The weight of the relation matrix impacts the target function, but the weight cannot be determined self-adaptively; this requires further research. The relations of data in the real world are typically high-order heterogeneous, so effective clustering algorithms for heterogeneous information networks with any schema will be studied in the future.

AUTHOR CONTRIBUTIONS

Conceived and designed the experiments: JY LMC. Performed the experiments: LMC. Analyzed the data: JPZ. Contributed reagents/materials/analysis tools: JY LMC. Wrote the paper: LMC.

REFERENCES

1. Sun Y, Han J (2012) Mining heterogeneous information networks: principles and methodologies. Synthesis Lectures on Data Mining and Knowledge Discovery, 3 (2). pp. 1–159. doi: 10. 2200/s00433ed1v01y201207dmk005
2. Gao B, Liu TY, Qin T, Zheng X, Cheng QS, Ma WY (2005) Web image clustering by consistent utilization of visual features and surrounding texts. In Proceedings of the 13th annual ACM international conference on Multimedia. pp. 112-121.
3. Gao B, Liu TY, Zheng X, Cheng QS, Ma WY (2005) Consistent bipartite graph co-partitioning for star-structrured high-order heterogeneous data co-clustering. In Proceedings of the eleventh ACM SIGKDD international conference on Knowledge discovery in data mining. pp. 41-50.
4. Gao B, Liu TY, Ma WY (2006) Star-structured high-order heterogeous data co-clustering based on cosistent information theory. In Data Mining, 2006. ICDM'06. Sixth International Conference on. pp. 880-884.
5. Long B, Zhang ZM, Wu X, Yu PS (2006) Spectral clustering for multi-type relational data. In Proceedings of the 23rd international conference on Machine learning. pp. 585-592.
6. Sun Y, Yu Y, Han J (2009) Rankclus: ranking-based clustering of heterogeneous information networks with star network schema. In Proceedings of the 15th ACM SIGKDD international conference on Knowledge discovery and data mining. pp. 797-806.
7. Sun Y, Norick B, Han J, Yan X, Yu PS, Yu, X (2012) Integrating meta-path selection with user-guided object clustering in heterogeneous information networks, In Proceedings of the 18th ACM SIGKDD international conference on Knowledge discovery and data mining. pp. 1348-1356.
8. Li P, Wen J, Li X (2013) SNTClus: A novel service clustering algorithm based on network analysis and service tags. Przegląd Elektrotechniczny. pp. 89.
9. Li P, Chen L, Li X, Wen J (2013) RNRank: Network-based ranking on relational tuples, In Behavior and Social Computing. Springer International Publishing. pp. 139–150.
10. Wang R, Shi C, Yu PS, Wu B (2013) Integrating clustering and ranking on hybrid heterogeneous information network. In Advances in Knowledge Discovery and Data Mining. pp. 583-594.
11. Aggarwal CC, Xie Y, Philip SY (2012) Dynamic link inference in heterogeneous networks. In SDM. pp. 415-426.
12. Zhang L, Chen C, Bu J, Chen Z, Cai D, Han J (2012) Locally discriminative coclustering. Knowledge and Data Engineering, IEEE Transactions on, 24 (6). pp. 1025–1035. doi: 10. 1109/tkde. 2011. 71
13. Khoa NLD, Chawla S (2011) Large scale spectral clustering using approximate commute time embedding. arXiv preprint arXiv:1111. 4541.
14. Koutis I, Miller GL, Tolliver D (2011) Combinatorial preconditioners and multilevel solvers for problems in computer vision and image processing. Computer Vision and Image Understanding, 115 (12). pp. 1638–1646. doi: 10. 1016/j. cviu. 2011. 05. 013
15. Fouss F, Pirotte A,Renders JM, Saerens M (2007)Random walk computation of similarities between nodes of a graph with application to collaborative recommendation. Knowledge and Data Engineering, IEEE Transactions on,19 (3). pp. 355–369. doi: 10. 1109/tkde. 2007. 46
16. Qiu H, Hancock ER (2007)Clustering and embedding using commute times. Pattern Analysis and Machine Intelligence, IEEE Transactions on,29 (11). pp. 1873–1890. pmid:17848771 doi: 10. 1109/tpami. 2007. 1103
17. Spielman DA, Srivastava N (2008) Graph sparsification by effective resistances. In Proceedings of the 40th annual ACM symposium on Theory of computing, STOC '08. pp. 563-568.
18. Achlioptas D (2001) Database-friendly random projections, in Proceedings of the twentieth ACM SIGMOD SIGACT SIGART symposium on Principles of database systems, PODS '01. pp. 274-281.
19. Spielman DA, Teng SH (2004) Nearly-linear time algorithms for graph partitioning, graph sparsification, and solving linear systems. In Proceedings of the thirty-sixth annual ACM symposium on Theory of computing, STOC '04. pp. 81-90.
20. Spielman DA, Teng SH (2014) Nearly-linear time algorithms for preconditioning and solving symmetric, diagonally dominant linear systems. SIAM Journal on Matrix Analysis and Applications, 35 (3). pp. 835–885. doi: 10. 1137/090771430

CHAPTER 13

LARGE-SCALE TRANSPORTATION NETWORK CONGESTION EVOLUTION PREDICTION USING DEEP LEARNING THEORY

Xiaolei Ma,[1,2] Haiyang Yu,[1,2,] Yunpeng Wang,[1,2] and Yinhai Wang[3]

[1] School of Transportation Science and Engineering, Beijing Key Laboratory for Cooperative Vehicle Infrastructure, Systems, and Safety Control, Beihang University, Beijing, China,

[2] Jiangsu Province Collaborative Innovation Center of Modern Urban Traffic Technologies, SiPaiLou #2, Nanjing, China,

[3] Department of Civil and Environmental Engineering, University of Washington, Seattle, Washington, United States of America

ABSTRACT

Understanding how congestion at one location can cause ripples throughout large-scale transportation network is vital for transportation researchers and practitioners to pinpoint traffic bottlenecks for congestion mitigation. Traditional studies rely on either mathematical equations or simulation techniques to model traffic congestion dynamics. However, most of the approaches have limitations, largely due to unrealistic assumptions and cumbersome parameter calibration process. With the development of Intelligent Transportation Systems (ITS) and Internet of Things (IoT), transportation data become more and more ubiquitous. This triggers a series of data-driven research to investigate transportation phenomena. Among them, deep learning theory is considered one of the most promising techniques to tackle tremendous high-dimensional data. This study attempts to extend deep learning theory into large-scale transportation network analysis. A deep Restricted Boltzmann Machine and Recurrent Neural Network architecture is utilized to model and predict traffic congestion evolution based on Global Positioning System (GPS) data from taxi. A numerical study in Ningbo, China is conducted to validate the effectiveness and efficiency of the proposed method. Results show that the prediction accuracy can achieve as high as 88% within less than 6 minutes when the model is implemented in a Graphic Processing Unit (GPU)-based parallel computing environment. The predicted congestion evolution patterns can be visualized temporally and spatially through a map-based platform to identify the vulnerable links for proactive congestion mitigation.

INTRODUCTION

Traffic congestion costs billions of dollars in each year due to lost time, wasted fuel, excessive air pollution, and reduced productivity. The 2012 Urban Mobility Report indicates that the annual average delay per person was 38 hours in 2011 for the 498 surveyed urban areas, which is equivalent to a 238% increase compared to that in 1982. Traffic congestion incurred a total of 5.5 billion hours of travel delays and 2.9 billion gallons of extra fuel consumption in 2009, which corresponds to a congestion cost of 121 billion dollars [1].

Diagnosing congestion onset and predicting congestion evolution patterns are considered strategic countermeasures to locate traffic bottlenecks and adopt proactive measures for congestion mitigation. Many research efforts have been made to achieve these goals [2, 3]. However, most of previous studies tend to view congestion spots separately in a small-scale network. As mentioned by Yang[4], the number of network links for almost all the existing traffic congestion prediction

Citation: Ma X, Yu H, Wang Y, Wang Y (2015) Large-Scale Transportation Network Congestion Evolution Prediction Using Deep Learning Theory. PLoS ONE 10(3): e0119044. doi:10.1371/journal.pone.0119044.

methods do not exceed 100. In addition, these studies rely on either mathematical equations or simulation techniques to depict the network congestion evolution. This often results in suboptimality since transportation activities involve human factors which are difficult to represent or model accurately using mathematics-driven approaches. Previous network-wide congestion studies mainly resort to either complex network theory [5–11] or visualization techniques [12] to understand the evolution of network-wide traffic congestion. In complex network theory, transportation networks can be abstracted as scale-free networks [9], and traffic flow dynamics over the network are generated based on the power law distribution [11] However, these assumptions are not always adherent to the reality, and lack sufficient traffic sensor data to validate their findings. Visualization techniques can intuitively display the spatial and temporal distribution of network congestion through a map-based platform, but are incapable of explaining the mechanism of congestion generation and predicting future trend of congestion evolution.

Over the past decades, tremendous traffic sensors have been deployed on the existing freeway networks, generating a huge amount of data at relatively high time resolutions. The increasing availability of network data makes it possible to simultaneously examine traffic flows on a large-scale roadway network and observe the evolution of congestion on that network through data mining techniques. Transportation network consists of thousands of links with changing traffic condition over time. This is equivalent to a high-dimensional space where congestion prorogates temporally and spatially. This is challenging to model using traditional data mining approaches due to the curse of dimensionality: when the input dimensionality increases, the required training data grow exponentially [13]. The recent emergence of deep learning theory can address the curse of dimensionality issue through distributed representations, and thereby holds great promise in learning high-dimensional features with tremendous data. Compared to those shallow learning architectures, deep learning is able to model complex non-linear phenomenon using distributed and hierarchical feature representation [14, 15], and has received numerous success in the domain of computer vision, speech recognition, natural language processing and music composition [16]. Deep learning theory began to exhibits its superiority of predicting traffic flow over a single road segment [14]. However, to the best of our knowledge, no research has been conducted to apply deep learning theory into large-scale transportation network modeling and analysis. To assist transportation professionals in congestion diagnosis and operational strategy assessment, this study aims at developing a data-driven and network-wide congestion analysis paradigm based on traffic sensor measurements using deep learning theory.

The remainder of this paper is organized as follows: Section 2 presents a methodological framework to model network-wide traffic congestion, where GPS data are collected to depict the roadway traffic condition and a deep learning architecture Recurrent Neural Network and Restricted Boltzmann Machine (RNN-RBM) is introduced to predict the temporal-spatial congestion evolution pattern. To validate the effectiveness of the proposed algorithm, a numerical experiment with a city roadway network of over 500 links is undertaken in Section 3. The prediction results are demonstrated through a GIS platform to observe the future congestion evolution, followed by a sensitivity analysis with various congestion speed thresholds. In addition, a comparative study with conventional neural network and support vector machine methods is conducted to demonstrate the advantage of the proposed algorithm. Finally, discussion and conclusion are made in the last section.

METHODOLOGY

Traffic condition on each link is classified into a binary state, where 1 represents congested and 0 represents uncongested. The link traffic condition changes over time, and essentially becomes a binary sequence with varying length. Considering the size of a typical transportation network, the network-wide congestion pattern is equivalent to a high-dimensional matrix arranged in time (number of time steps) and space (number of links). The key of network-wide traffic congestion evolution prediction model is to understand how each matrix element evolves spatially and temporally. The initial step is to identify the traffic condition of each link using taxi GPS data. Missing and erroneous data will be reviewed and corrected to ensure satisfying quality. Finally, processed GPS data are aggregated into varying time intervals for representing network-wide traffic patterns. Inspired by polyphonic music generation and transcription approach [17](Boulanger-Lewandowski, 2012), a combination of Restricted Boltzmann Machine (RBM) and Recurrent Neural Network (RNN) is then utilized to learn the high-dimensional traffic congestion patterns. To fully take advantages of Graphics Processing Unit (GPU)-based parallel computing architecture, the proposed algorithm is implemented in the NVIDIA Compute Unified Device Architecture (CUDA) environment to accelerate the model learning procedure.

Transportation Network Representation

A GPS-equipped taxi can record its location and timestamp information, and the travel speed can be directly measured. For each link *n*, the average speed at time *t* is denoted asctn, If the average speed is lower than a threshold (20 km/hour), the link is considered congested, and thereby is set as 1. Due to the sampling error, GPS-equipped taxis may not fully travel along the entire network at any time. For those links without GPS data, vehicle speed is calculated by using the historical records for the same link. Based on the above discussion, traffic congestions for a network with *N* links within *T* time intervals can be expressed as:

$$\begin{bmatrix} c_1^1 & c_1^2 & \cdots & c_1^T \\ c_2^1 & c_2^1 & \cdots & c_2^T \\ \vdots & \vdots & \cdots & \vdots \\ c_N^1 & c_N^2 & \cdots & c_N^T \end{bmatrix} \tag{1}$$

Where ctn represents the traffic congestion condition on *n*th link at time *t*, which is a binary value. The next step is to predict the elements in each row (link). This can be treated as the single sequence learning problem. When multiple rows (links) are predicted simultaneously, this is known as the high-dimensional sequence learning problem. A deep learning architecture with temporal processing capabilities is desired.

RNN-RBM: A Deep Learning Architecture for High-Dimensional Temporal Sequence Prediction

Restricted Boltzmann Machine (RBM)

Restricted Boltzmann Machine (RBM) is an energy based model that includes one visible layer and one hidden layer [15]. As demonstrated in Fig. 1, units in both visible layer and hidden layer are mutually connected.

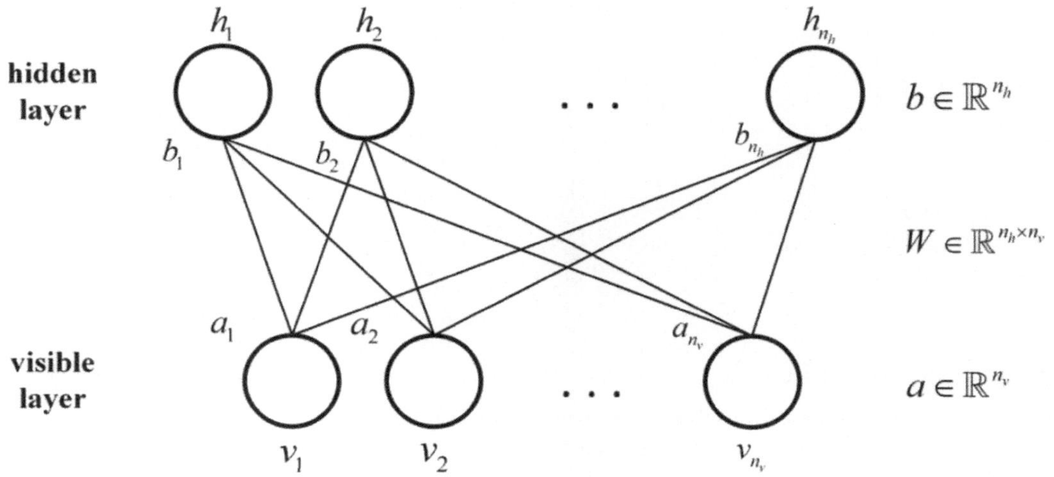

Figure 1: RBM Structure.

In Fig. 1, n_v and n_h respectively represent the number of units in hidden layer and visible layer. $v = (v_1,v_2,\ldots v_{nv})^T$represents the state vector for visible layer, where v_i is the state of the ith unit in visible layer. $h= (h_1,h_2,\ldots h_{nh})^T$represents the state vector value for hidden layer, where h_i is the state of the ith unit in hidden layer. $a = (a_1,a_2,\ldots a_{nv})^T$represents the bias vector for visible layer, where a_i is the bias of the ith unit in visible layer. $b = (b_1,b_2,\ldots b_{nh})^T$represents the bias vector for hidden layer, where b_i is the bias of the ith unit in hidden layer. $W= (w_{i,j}) \in \mathbb{R}^{n_h \times n_v}$ represents the weight matrix between visible layer and hidden layer, where $w_{i,j}$ is the connecting weight for the ith unit in visible layer and the jth unit in hidden layer. The units in both hidden and visible layers are binary-valued.

Based on the above notations, the energy function for a given **(v,h)** is defined as:

$$E_\theta(\mathbf{v},\mathbf{h}) = -\mathbf{a}^T\mathbf{v} - \mathbf{b}^T\mathbf{v} - \mathbf{h}^T W\mathbf{v} \tag{2}$$

The joint probability distribution function can be expressed as:

$$P_\theta(\mathbf{v},\mathbf{h}) = \frac{1}{Z_\theta}e^{-E_\theta(\mathbf{v},\mathbf{h})} \tag{3}$$

Where $\theta = (W,\mathbf{a},\mathbf{b})$, $Z_\theta = \sum_{\mathbf{v},\mathbf{h}} e^{-E_\theta(\mathbf{v},\mathbf{h})}$ is defined as the partition function to normalize the probability function.

The conditional probability that hidden unit h_k is activated given hidden vector v and the conditional probability that visible unit v_k is activated given visible vector h can be respectively calculated as:

$$P(h_k = 1|\mathbf{v}) = sigmoid(b_k + \sum_{i=1}^{n_v} w_{k,i}v_i) \tag{4}$$

$$P(v_k = 1|\mathbf{h}) = sigmoid(a_k + \sum_{i=1}^{n_h} w_{k,i}h_i) \tag{5}$$

sigmoid means the sigmoid activation function. Because there is no dependency within visible layer and hidden layer, both conditional probability functions can be written as:

$$P(\mathbf{h}|\mathbf{v}) = \prod_{k=1}^{n_h} P(h_k = 1|\mathbf{v}) \tag{6}$$

$$P(\mathbf{v}|\mathbf{h}) = \prod_{k=1}^{n_v} P(v_k = 1|\mathbf{h}) \tag{7}$$

To find the parameters θ, RBM is required to maximize the probability of training set V:

$$\arg\max_\theta \prod_{v \in V} P(v) \tag{8}$$

This is equal to maximize the log likelihood of P(v). A common optimization method is gradient descent algorithm. The mathematical form can be expressed in (Equation 9), where the derivative of ln $P(v)$ should be calculated as (Equation 10) in advance.

$$\theta = \theta + \eta\frac{\partial lnP(v)}{\partial\theta} \tag{9}$$

$$\frac{\partial lnP(v)}{\partial\theta} = -\langle\frac{\partial E(\mathbf{v},\mathbf{h})}{\partial\theta}\rangle_{P(\mathbf{h}|v)} + \langle\frac{\partial E(\mathbf{v},\mathbf{h})}{\partial\theta}\rangle_{P(\mathbf{v},\mathbf{h})} \tag{10}$$

Where η is known as the learning rate, and it is responsible to control the speed of convergence to find the optimal solution. $\langle\cdot\rangle_P$denotes the expectation value with respect to probability distribution P. Solving (equation 8) is computational intensive, Hilton [18] proposed the famous Contrastive Divergence (CD) approach to train RBM in an efficient fashion. The key of this algorithm is to perform n-step Gibbs sampling for approximating the expectation value of (Equation 10), the equation can be further simplified into the following three equations:

$$\frac{\partial \ln P(v)}{\partial \theta} = \begin{cases} \frac{\partial \ln P(\mathbf{v})}{\partial w_{i,j}} \approx P(h_i = 1|\mathbf{v}^{(0)})v_j^{(0)} - P(h_i = 1|\mathbf{v}^{(n)})v_j^{(n)} \\ \frac{\partial \ln P(\mathbf{v})}{\partial a_i} \approx v_i^{(0)} - v_i^{(n)} \\ \frac{\partial \ln P(\mathbf{v})}{\partial b_i} \approx P(h_i = 1|\mathbf{v}^{(0)}) - P(h_i = 1|\mathbf{v}^{(n)}) \end{cases} \quad (11)$$

The probability distribution function for RBM can be modified as a conditional probability distribution function depending on the previous state of RBM [19], and this leads to a variant of RBM model for efficiently modeling complex time series [20].

Recurrent Neural Network (RNN)

Recurrent Neural Network (RNN) is a special form of neural network family, and contains at least one feed-back connection as an internal state from neurons' outputs to their inputs. This loop structure grants the capability of temporal processing and sequence learning for the network. Due to RNN's short-term memory, it is widely used to model non-linear time series data [21]. Fig. 2 presents a State Space Neural Network (SSNN), which a widely used structure of RNN. Delay units are introduced to feed back the previous hidden unit activations with the inputs into the neural network. $x(t)$ and $h(t)$ respectively represent the vectors in input layer as well as delay units at time t. $h(t+l)$ and $y(t+l)$ respectively represent the vectors in hidden layer and output layer at time $t+l$. W_{IH} is the weight matrix from input layer to hidden layer. W_{HH} is the weight matrix from the delay units to hidden layer. W_{HO} is the weight matrix from hidden layer to output layer. A hidden layer connects both input layer and output layer. The hidden states are delayed by l time step, and fed back to the network as additional inputs. This procedure can be described in (Equation 12) and (13).

$$h(t+l) = \sigma(W_{IH}x(t) + W_{HH}h(t)) \quad (12)$$

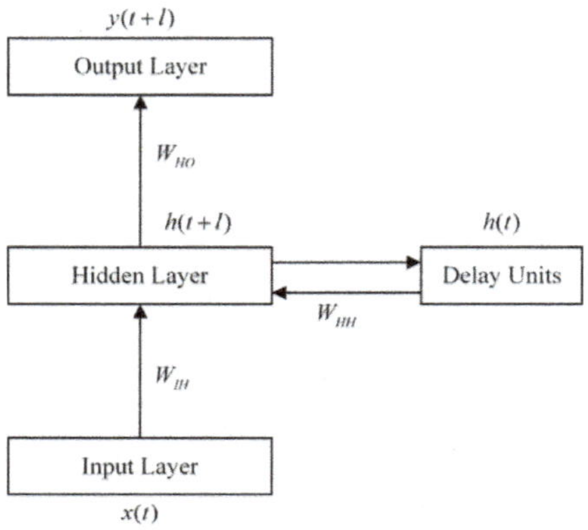

Figure 2: State Space Neural Network Structure.

$$y(t+l) = \sigma(W_{HO}h(t+l)) \quad (13)$$

Where $\sigma(\cdot)$ denote the activation function such as sigmoid function, tangent function and linear function.

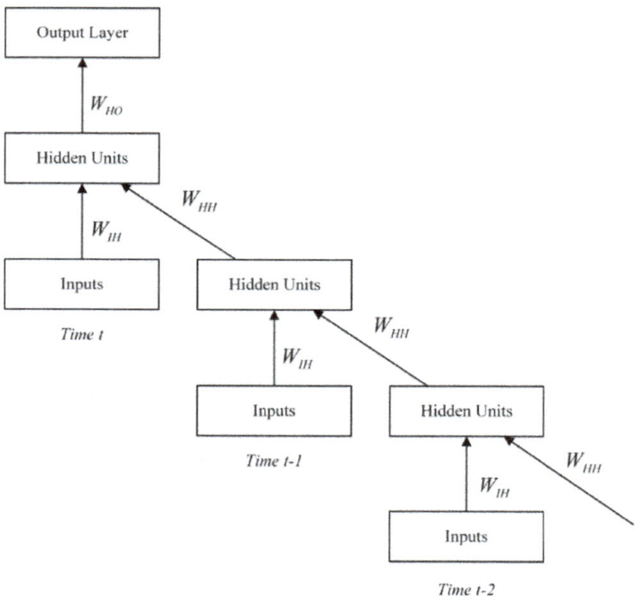

Figure 3: BackPropagation Through Time for RNN.

Training RNN is similar with training traditional multilayer Feed Forward Neural Network (FFNN). By unfolding the RNN structure over time, each feedback loop will be expanded as single layer feed-forward neural network at each time stamp in Fig. 3. In this case, RNN can be efficiently trained using the well-known back prorogation algorithm over time. This is also known as BackPropagation Through Time (BPTT). However, BPTT has difficulty training the sequence with long-term dependency since it can be converted into a deep architecture with multiple layers, and results in vanishing gradient as well as exploding gradient issues [22]. Although there are a certain number of algorithms proposed to solve these issues such as long short term memory network [23], it is still worth investigating in the context of deep learning theory.

RNN-RBM

Both RBM and RNN models have the capability of predicting a temporal sequence. A natural thought is to take advantage of the merits from both models. This triggers a deep architecture called RNN-RBM model to depict the temporal dependencies in high-dimensional sequences [17]. The architecture of RBB-RBM is given in Fig. 4:

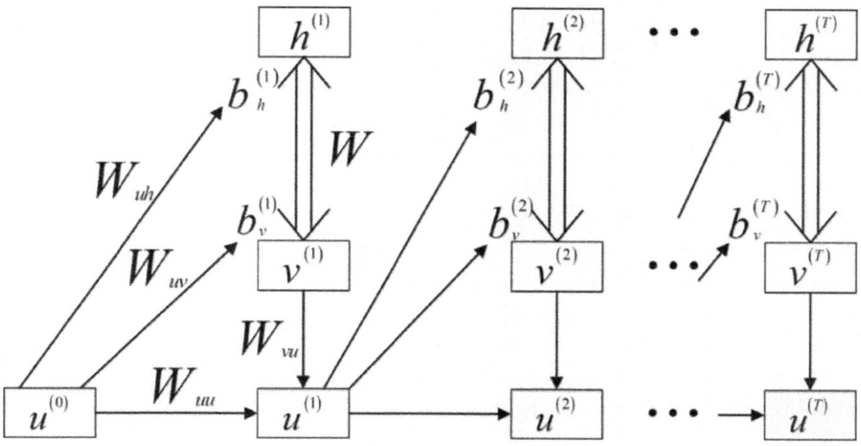

Figure 4: RBM-RNN Architecture.

The conditional RBM and RNN are stacked to construct a RNN-RBM model. Conditional RBM is an extension of conventional RBM, and it is designed to process temporal sequence by providing a feedback loop between visible layer and hidden layer. The bias values for both visible layer and hidden layer are updated based on the previous visible units [24]. The similar concept can be applied in the RNN-RBM model. b(t)vandb(t)hrespectively represent the bias vectors for visible layer and hidden layer in RBM model at time *t*, and are updated through the hidden units $u^{(t-1)}$ in RNN model at time *t*-1. Weight matrices W_{uv} andW_{uh} are provided to connect the RNN model and RBM model. The above procedure can be described in (Equation 14) and (Equation 15).

$$b_v^{(t)} = b_v + W_{uu}u^{(t-1)} \tag{14}$$

$$b_h^{(t)} = b_h + W_{uh}u^{(t-1)} \tag{15}$$

Where b_v and b_h are the initial biases in visible layer and hidden layer for RBM model. The RNN model is unfolded over time, and is utilized to generate the previous hidden states in RBM model based on the input layer $v^{(t)}$ and hidden layer $u^{(t)}$ in RNN model. The activation of hidden units in the hidden layer can be then calculated as:

$$u^{(t)} = sigmoid(b_u + W_{uu}u^{(t-1)} + W_{vu}v^{(t)}) \tag{16}$$

The algorithm execution is summarized below:

Step 1: Generate the value of hidden units in RNN model using (Equation 16).

Step 2: Update the biases in the RBM model using (Equation 14) and (15) based on the estimated $u^{(t-1)}$ in*Step 1*, and calculated the RBM parameters.

Step 3: Calculate the log-likelihood gradient $\frac{\partial lnP(v)}{\partial \theta}$ in RBM model using (Equation 11)

Step 4: The estimated gradient is propagated into RNN model, and the weight W_{uv} and W_{vu} are updated over time to train RNN model for prediction.

Temporal-Spatial Congestion Evolution Prediction

As previously mentioned, traffic condition on each roadway segment can be converted into a binary value denoting congestion status. Considering historical traffic patterns and number of links in a large-scale traffic network, the congestion evolution prediction problem becomes a high-dimensional temporal sequence learning problem. The RNN-RBM model can be applied to predict the temporal-spatial network congestion evolution pattern. To implement the RNN-RBM model in an efficient manner, the mini-batches gradient descent optimization method is applied: the training set is divided into a number of small samples, and each sample set can be parallelly processed using standard gradient descent optimization method. GPU is designed on a parallel throughput architecture that can execute multiple tasks concurrently [25]. This feature is especially suitable to accelerate the computation of RNN-RBM model. CUDA is a parallel computing platform developed by NVIDIA [26], and it offers a flexible programming library for users to manipulate the computational elements in GPUs.

NUMERICAL STUDY

Model Development

To validate the effectiveness and efficiency of the proposed network-wide congestion prediction approach, a transportation network in Ningbo City, China is used for the numerical experiment. The network consists of 515 road links where approximately 4000 GPS-equipped taxis traveled from April 13, 2014 to May 9, 2014. The GPS data are updated every 2 minutes. A series of data quality control methods are applied to remedy the missing or erroneous data, and this generates 5,521,294 GPS records with speed information. Each GPS record is associated with a unique link ID, and this link ID corresponds to a specific geospatial polyline in a GIS platform. These GPS data are further aggregated into 5 minutes, 10 minutes, 30 minutes and 60 minutes time intervals to evaluate the network traffic congestion prediction performance. The data from the first 22 days (i.e. from April 13, 2014 to May 4, 2014) are utilized for training the RNN-RBM model, and the remaining data are used for testing.

Minimizing cross-entropy error is set as the optimization objective during the RNN-RBM model training procedure. This is because that the cross-entropy indicates the distance between the probability distributions of computed outputs and target outputs, and thus it is preferable to using mean squared error for a neural network classifier with binary values [27]. The cross-entropy error is defined in (Equation 17).

$$\text{Cross} - \text{Entropy Error (CEE)} = -\frac{1}{T}\sum_{n=1}^{N}\sum_{t=1}^{T} c_n^t ln(\hat{c}_n^t) + (1 - c_n^t) ln(1 - \hat{c}_n^t) \tag{17}$$

In addition, both training accuracy and testing accuracy are presented to measure the algorithm effectiveness. The estimated congestion status for link n at time t is denoted asc^tn. According to (Equation 1), the ground-true congestion status for link n at time t is denoted asctn. Because both c^tn and ctn are binary values, the prediction accuracy can be defined in (Equation 18) given a transportation network with N links within Ttime intervals:

$$\text{Accuacy (Acc)} = (1 - \frac{\sum_{n=1}^{N}\sum_{t=1}^{T} |c_n^t - \hat{c}_n^t|}{NT}) \times 100\% \tag{18}$$

If a positive result refers to each link that is correctly identified as either congested or uncongested, then the sensitivity and specificity can be respectively defined as:

$$\text{Sensitivity} = \frac{\text{number of links correctly identifed as congested}}{\text{total number of congested links}} \tag{19}$$

$$\text{Specificity} = \frac{\text{number of links correctly identifed as uncongested}}{\text{total number of uncongested links}} \tag{20}$$

Algorithm runtime is used to evaluate the efficiency of the proposed approach.

Parameters in the RNN-RBM model are set optimally as follows:

Number of hidden units in the RNN model = 100

Number of hidden units in the RBM model = 150

Learning rate for gradient descent optimization method = 0.05

The weight matrix W for RNN-RBM model is initialized by following a Normal distribution with mean = 0 and variance = 0.01, and other matrices $W_{uu'}, W_{uv'}, W_{vu}$ and W_{uh} are initialized by following a Normal distribution with mean = 0 and variance = 0.0001. All the bias vectors in the model are set as zero initially.

Result Analysis

GPS speed data with four different aggregation levels were tested using the RNN-RBM model, and the trained model was then utilized to generate the future network-wide congestion evolution patterns from May 5, 2014 to May 9, 2014 for prediction. Each model was run for 200 iterations to ensure the algorithm's successful convergence. The algorithm was implemented using Python Theano [28] and was executed on a desktop computer with Intel i7 3.4GHz CPU, 8GB memory and NVIDIA GeForce GTX650 GPU (2GB RAM). The comparison results are demonstrated in Table 1:

Table 1: Comparison of traffic congestion prediction performance with different data aggregation levels.

Aggregation Level	Training Accuracy (%)	Cross-Entropy Error	Runtime (seconds)	Testing Accuracy (%)
60 minutes	95.1	-38.7	354	88.2%
30 minutes	88.4	-102.52	643	80.8%
10 minutes	80.2	-172.3	1729	73.4%
5 minutes	72.2	-239.8	4642	68.9%

doi:10.1371/journal.pone.0119044.t001

Results in Table 1 demonstrate that the overall algorithm prediction performance improves as the data aggregation level increases. This is probably due to the less data fluctuation (i.e. traffic condition does not change dramatically) as the time interval becomes longer. When the aggregation level achieves to one hour, the training accuracy is 95%, and more than 88% of congestion conditions can be correctly identified, while the algorithm can be successfully executed within 6 minutes. Both testing accuracy and training accuracy degrade when the data resolution becomes higher. However, the sensitivity and specificity do not straightly increase as the data aggregation level becomes larger. For instance, only 43% of congested linked can be correctly predicted when the aggregation level is set as 10 minutes. This implies that the data aggregation level influences the prediction outcomes, and should be carefully selected.

In addition, CUDA-based GPU parallel computing engine presents its superior capability of concurrently accelerating the computational intensive tasks. Compared with the CPU-based algorithm implementation, the proposed GPU-based framework can approximately improve the algorithm efficiency by 5 times.

The training accuracy changing curves for the above four scenarios are plotted in Fig. 5:

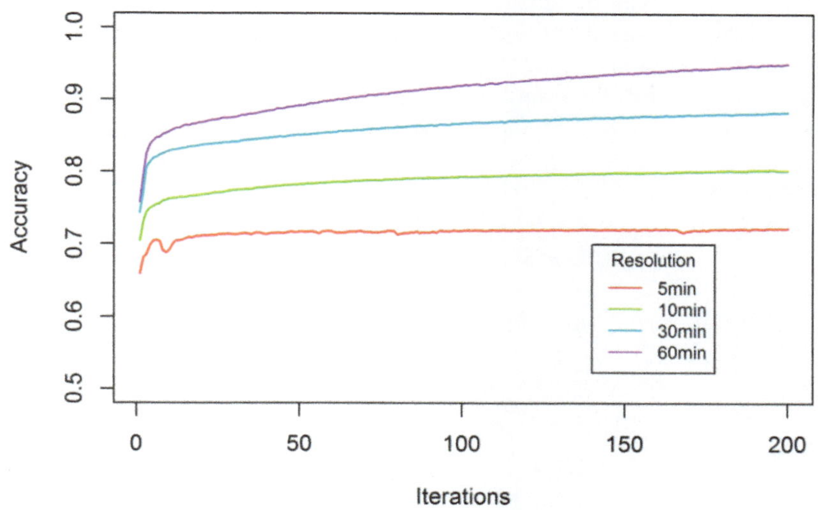

Figure 5: Training Accuracy Changing Curves with Different Data Aggregation Levels.

RNN-RBM models with varying data aggregation levels can converge after 150 iterations, and the training accuracy remains almost constant. This indicates that the RNN-RBM model is able to learn the network-wide traffic congestion patterns in a fast and reliable fashion.

Visualization

Based on the trained RNN-RBM models, the network congestion evolution patterns from May 5, 2014 to May 9, 2014 can be thereby predicted. As previously mentioned, each binary congestion status can be mapped on a GIS platform using the unique link ID. To visualize the spatial and temporal network congestion onset and growth, a series of dynamic GIS networks with colored links were created in Fig. 6A-Fig. 6D based on the predicted traffic congestion patterns on May 9, 2014.

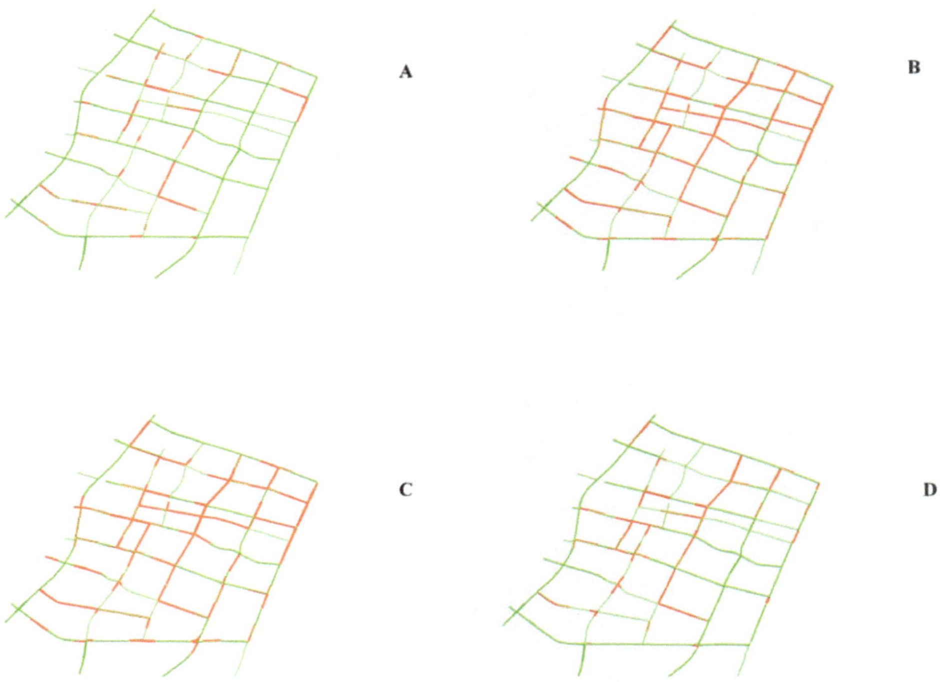

Figure 6: Predicted Network Congestion Evolution Patterns on May 09, 2014 with Varying Times of Day.

The congested link (less than 20 km/hour) is marked in red, and the uncongested link (equal to or greater than 20 km/hour) is marked in green. The traffic condition in the early morning was generally good with only a small number of congested links, and the network became more and more congested during morning peak hours. Similarly, when most people commuted during evening peak hours, network-wide traffic congestion reached highest. Finally, traffic jam dissipated at midnight since the majority of passengers engaged in less or no activities during that time. As presented in Fig. 6A-Fig. 6D, traffic congestion initially concentrated in the central of network, and gradually spread to the network boundary. There are several links that consistently experience traffic congestion, and should be taken special attention for congestion mitigation in advance.

The temporal distribution for number of congested links is summarized in Table 2 and visualized in Fig. 7. There are 35.9% of road links experiencing traffic congestion during morning peak hour (9:00AM-10:00AM), while 41.1% of network was congested during evening peak hour (5:00PM-6:00PM). This indicates that the evening peak traffic is worse than morning peak traffic, and causes more delay. People may tend to return home earlier than usual week days for weekend activities, and thus higher traffic volumes on Friday's evening peak hours can be observed.

Table 2: Statistics for number of congested links on May 9, 2014.

Time	Number of congested links	Percentage (%)
5:00–6:00	53	10.3
6:00–7:00	72	14.0
7:00–8:00	121	23.5
8:00–10:00	162	31.5
9:00–10:00	185	35.9
10:00–11:00	168	32.6
11:00–12:00	163	31.7
12:00–13:00	168	32.6
13:00–14:00	146	28.3
14:00–15:00	160	31.1
15:00–16:00	178	34.6
16:00–17:00	183	35.5
17:00–18:00	213	41.4
18:00–19:00	189	36.7
19:00–20:00	174	33.8
20:00–21:00	153	29.7
21:00–22:00	119	23.1
22:00–23:00	111	21.6
23:00–00:00	94	18.3

doi:10.1371/journal.pone.0119044.t002

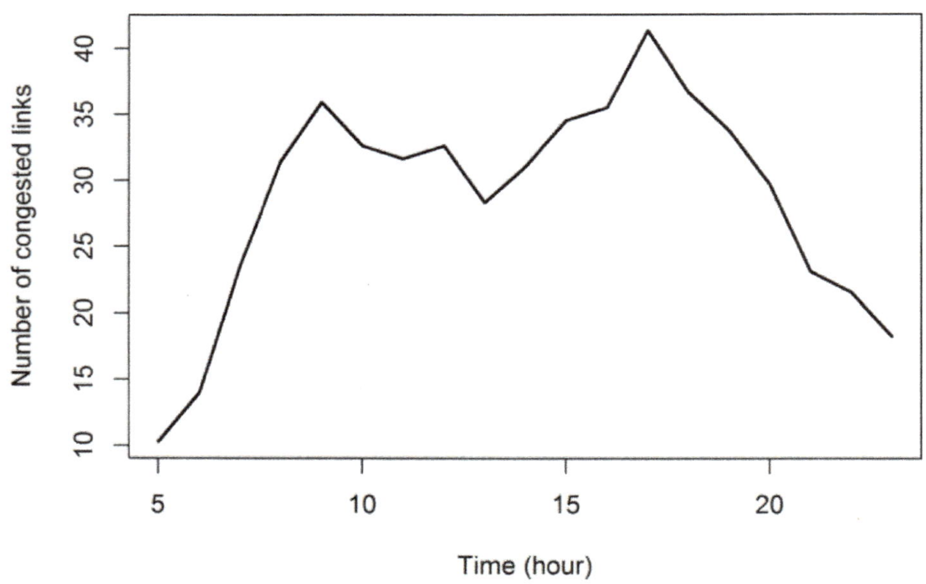

Figure 7: Temporal distribution for number of congested links on May 9, 2014.

Comparison

To further evaluate the advantages of RNN-RBM algorithm for large-scale transportation network congestion prediction, a study was conducted by comparing RNN-RBM, Back Propagation Neural Network (BPNN) and Support Vector Machine (SVM) methods. To remain a fair comparison environment, the same dataset and computing platform was adopted. The topology for BPNN was set as one input layer, one hidden layers with 10 processing units and one output layers\. For the SVM method, Radial Basis Function (RBF) was utilized with three adjustable parameters: cost C, width parameter g, and epsilon ε. These parameters were calibrated using 5-fold cross validation. The rolling horizon (i.e. the size of moving window defining previous network congestion statuses) was set as 2 time steps. To eliminate the randomness, both BPNN and SVM were executed for 10 times. Table 3 presents the performances for three algorithms with 60-minute data aggregation level.

Table 3: Comparison of traffic congestion prediction performance for different algorithms with 60-minute data aggregation level.

Algorithms	Runtime (seconds)	Prediction Accuracy (%)	Sensitivity (%)	Specificity (%)
RNN-RBM	354	88.2%	64.1%	91.1%
BPNN	13498	69.7%	38.2%	77.5%
SVM	14979	71.0%	36.6%	80.3%

doi:10.1371/journal.pone.0119044.t003

Due to the limit of computational resources, only 60-minute data aggregation level is utilized for testing. As demonstrated in table 3, the RNN-RBM outperforms the other two algorithm in terms of efficiency and effectiveness: The algorithm execution time for RNN-RBM is only 3% of that for BPNN, and 2.3% of that for SVM. The gain in computational efficiency for RNN-RBM does not sacrifice the algorithm accuracy. Compared with BPNN and SVM, the prediction accuracy for RNN-RBM increases by at least 17%. Moreover, both sensitivity and specificity for RNN-RBM are significantly higher than those for BPNN and SVM. This is owing to the deep and parallel architecture of RNN-RBM for learning multidimensional features in an efficient and effective manner.

Sensitivity Analysis

Congestion identification relies on the setting of speed threshold when traffic congestion occurs. To understand how various speed thresholds influence the congestion pattern prediction performance, a sensitivity analysis was conducted to examine the prediction capability of RNN-RBM model. Three different speed settings were adopted: 10 minutes, 20 minutes and 30 minutes. When the calculated average GPS link speed is lower than the specified speed threshold, the link is considered congested. The GPS speed data were aggregated into 60-minute interval, and followed the similar model training and testing procedure in the model development. The results are presented in table 4:

Table 4: Sensitivity analysis of congestion evolution prediction performance with various speed thresholds.

Speed Threshold	Number of Congested Links	Training Accuracy (%)	Runtime (seconds)	Testing Accuracy (%)
10 km/hour	1895	98.6%	290	93.8%
20 km/hour	13611	95.1%	354	88.2%
30 km/hour	20238	84.0%	419	79.9%

doi:10.1371/journal.pone.0119044.t004

There are a total of 59,225 traffic conditions from May 5, 2014 to May 9, 2014 for GPS data with 60-minute aggregation level. When the speed threshold is set as 10 km/hour, only 1895 congested links can be detected. Surprisingly, the model training and testing accuracies are not significantly higher than those with 20km/hour speed threshold, even though the number of congested links with 20km/hour speed threshold is approximately 7 times more than that with 10km/hour speed threshold. However, when the speed threshold increases to 30 km/hour, more than 30% of network links are congested. The training accuracy decreases to 84%, which is much lower than the scenario with 20 km/hour speed threshold. This is probably because that traffic congestion temporal patterns fluctuate more significantly as the speed threshold is higher, and thus incurs difficulties in predicting congestion evolution. In practice, the setting of congestion speed threshold should be carefully determined.

CONCLUSION

Properly understanding the temporal and spatial patterns of congestion evolution is crucial to effectively mitigate congestion. This study proposed a data-driven method to predict the network traffic congestion onset and evolution patterns. Based on the tremendous GPS taxi speed data, the network congestion onset, propagation and dissipation can be modeled using a deep RNN-RBM architecture. To the best of our knowledge, this is the first study to utilize the deep learning theory into large-scale transportation network analysis. Compared with the traditional equation-driven or simulation-driven network studies, the proposed method relies on less assumption to model traffic congestion dynamics. A numerical experiment in Ningbo, China is conducted to validate the effectiveness and efficiency of the proposed method. A transportation network with 515 links is constructed, where the speed information generated from 4000 taxis are mapped and converted into a binary value to represent traffic congestion for each link. The RNN-RBM model has the capability of learning high-dimensional temporal sequences in an accurate and efficient manner, and is implemented in a CUDA-based parallel environment to accelerate the computational procedure. The training accuracy can achieve as high as 95.1% using the GPS data with one hour aggregation level while the algorithm execution time is only less than 6 minutes, and the trained model can be utilized to correctly predict network-wide traffic congestion on more than 88% links. The inferred network congestion patterns are further visualized on a GIS-based map platform to investigate the temporal and spatial evolution of traffic congestion. By comparing with conventional data mining approaches (i.e. BPNN and SVM), the RNN-RBM algorithm demonstrates its superiority in terms of effectiveness and efficiency. In addition, a sensitivity analysis is conducted to understand how different speed thresholds impact the congestion prediction accuracy. The finding of this study is important for large-scale roadway network planning, operations, and investment decisions. Understanding which congested locations are autonomously generated and how congestion propagates over transportation network will allow researchers and practitioners to focus the limited resources on the primary congestion locations, and adopt the proactive countermeasures to mitigate congestion.

Although the proposed method is promising to model and predict large-scale transportation network congestion, there is still plenty of room to be improved in the future research. For instances, the pretraining techniques such as Hessian-free optimization method should be considered to initialize the parameters more rationally. In addition, the spatial interaction among the adjacent roadway segments should be taken into account to increase training and prediction accuracy.

Funding Statement

This research is supported by the Beijing Nova Programme, National Natural Science Foundation of China (Grant No. 51308021, No. 51408019, and No. 71402011) and National Basic Research Program of China (2012CB725404). The funders had no role in study design, data collection and analysis, decision to publish, or preparation of the manuscript.

DATA AVAILABILITY

All relevant data are within the paper and its Supporting Information files.

REFERENCES

1. Schrank D, Eisele B, Lomax T. TTI's 2012 urban mobility report. Proceedings of the 2012 annual urban mobility report Texas A&M Transportation Institute, Texas, USA. 2012.
2. Aligawesa AK. The detection and localization of traffic congestion for highway traffic systems using hybrid estimation techniques: Purdue University; 2009.
3. Long J, Gao Z, Ren H, Lian A. Urban traffic congestion propagation and bottleneck identification.Science in China Series F: Information Sciences. 2008;51(7):948–64.
4. Yang S. On feature selection for traffic congestion prediction. Transportation Research Part C: Emerging Technologies. 2013;26:160–9.
5. Wang J, Li Y, Liu J, He K, Wang P. Vulnerability analysis and passenger source prediction in urban rail transit networks. PloS one. 2013;8(11):e80178 doi: 10.1371/journal.pone.0080178
6. Wang J, Wang L. Congestion analysis of traffic networks with direction-dependant heterogeneity. Physica A: Statistical Mechanics and its Applications. 2013;392(2):392–9.
7. Liu C, Zhang Q-p, Zhang X. Emergence and disappearance of traffic congestion in weight-evolving networks. Simulation Modelling Practice and Theory. 2009;17(10):1566–74.
8. Colak S, Schneider CM, Wang P, González MC. On the role of spatial dynamics and topology on network flows. New Journal of Physics. 2013;15(11):113037.
9. Zhao L, Lai Y-C, Park K, Ye N. Onset of traffic congestion in complex networks. Physical Review E. 2005;71(2):026125.
10. Wang P, Hunter T, Bayen AM, Schechtner K, González MC. Understanding road usage patterns in urban areas. Scientific reports. 2012;2.
11. Chen S, Huang W, Cattani C, Altieri G. Traffic dynamics on complex networks: a survey. Mathematical Problems in Engineering. 2011;2012.
12. Cheng T, Tanaksaranond G, Brunsdon C, Haworth J. Exploratory visualisation of congestion evolutions on urban transport networks. Transportation Research Part C: Emerging Technologies. 2013;36:296–306.
13. Bellman R, Bellman RE, Bellman RE, Bellman RE. Adaptive control processes: a guided tour: Princeton University Press Princeton; 1961.
14. Huang WH, Song GJ, Hong HK, Xie KQ. Deep Architecture for Traffic Flow Prediction: Deep Belief Networks With Multitask Learning. Ieee Transactions on Intelligent Transportation Systems. 2014;15(5):2191–201.
15. Hinton GE, Salakhutdinov RR. Reducing the dimensionality of data with neural networks. Science. 2006;313(5786):504–7.
16. Bengio Y. Learning deep architectures for AI. Foundations and trends® in Machine Learning. 2009;2(1):1–127.
17. Boulanger-Lewandowski N, Bengio Y, Vincent P. Modeling temporal dependencies in high-dimensional sequences: Application to polyphonic music generation and transcription. arXiv preprint arXiv:12066392. 2012.
18. Hinton GE. Training products of experts by minimizing contrastive divergence. Neural computation. 2002;14(8):1771–800.
19. Längkvist M, Karlsson L, Loutfi A. A review of unsupervised feature learning and deep learning for time-series modeling. Pattern Recognition Letters. 2014;42:11–24.
20. Sutskever I, Hinton GE, Taylor GW. The recurrent temporal restricted boltzmann machine. Advances in Neural Information Processing Systems; 2009.
21. Hüsken M, Stagge P. Recurrent neural networks for time series classification. Neurocomputing. 2003;50:223–35.

22. Bengio Y, Simard P, Frasconi P. Learning long-term dependencies with gradient descent is difficult.Neural Networks, IEEE Transactions on. 1994;5(2):157–66.
23. Hochreiter S, Schmidhuber J. Long short-term memory. Neural computation. 1997;9(8):1735–80.
24. Sutskever I, Hinton GE, editors. Learning multilevel distributed representations for high-dimensional sequences. International Conference on Artificial Intelligence and Statistics; 2007.
25. Schatz MC, Trapnell C, Delcher AL, Varshney A. High-throughput sequence alignment using Graphics Processing Units. BMC bioinformatics. 2007;8(1):474.
26. Documentation CT. v6. 0. Santa Clara (CA, USA): NVIDIA Corporation. 2014.
27. Golik P, Doetsch P, Ney H, editors. Cross-entropy vs. squared error training: a theoretical and experimental comparison. INTERSPEECH; 2013.
28. Bergstra J, Breuleux O, Bastien F, Lamblin P, Pascanu R, Desjardins G, et al. . Theano: a CPU and GPU math expression compiler. Proceedings of the Python for scientific computing conference (SciPy); 2010.

CHAPTER 14

COMBINATIONAL REASONING OF QUANTITATIVE FUZZY TOPOLOGICAL RELATIONS FOR SIMPLE FUZZY REGIONS

Bo Liu[1,2], Dajun Li[1] , Yuanping Xia[1] , Jian Ruan[1] , Lili Xu[1] , Huanyi Wu[1]

[1] Faculty of Geomatics, East China Institute of Technology, 330013, Nanchang, PR, China

[2] State Key Laboratory of Information Engineering in Surveying, Mapping and Remote Sensing, Wuhan University, 430079, Wuhan, PR, China

ABSTRACT

In recent years, formalization and reasoning of topological relations have become a hot topic as a means to generate knowledge about the relations between spatial objects at the conceptual and geometrical levels. These mechanisms have been widely used in spatial data query, spatial data mining, evaluation of equivalence and similarity in a spatial scene, as well as for consistency assessment of the topological relations of multi-resolution spatial databases. The concept of computational fuzzy topological space is applied to simple fuzzy regions to efficiently and more accurately solve fuzzy topological relations. Thus, extending the existing research and improving upon the previous work, this paper presents a new method to describe fuzzy topological relations between simple spatial regions in Geographic Information Sciences (GIS) and Artificial Intelligence (AI). Firstly, we propose a new definition for simple fuzzy line segments and simple fuzzy regions based on the computational fuzzy topology. And then, based on the new definitions, we also propose a new combinational reasoning method to compute the topological relations between simple fuzzy regions, moreover, this study has discovered that there are (1) 23 different topological relations between a simple crisp region and a simple fuzzy region; (2) 152 different topological relations between two simple fuzzy regions. In the end, we have discussed some examples to demonstrate the validity of the new method, through comparisons with existing fuzzy models, we showed that the proposed method can compute more than the existing models, as it is more expressive than the existing fuzzy models.

INTRODUCTION

Geographical information sciences (GIS) commonly deal with geographical phenomena modeled by crisp points, lines, and regions, which are clearly defined or have crisp boundaries. However, geospatial data are always uncertain or fuzzy due to inaccurate data acquisition, incomplete representation, dynamic change, and the inherent fuzziness of geographical phenomena itself. In GIS, many studies have been devoted to modeling topological relations, specifically the modeling of quantitative fuzzy topological relations between simple spatial objects. Topology is a fundamental challenge when modeling spatial relations in geospatial data that includes a mix of crisp, fuzzy and complex objects. Two mechanisms, the formalization and reasoning of topological relations, have become popular in recent years to gain knowledge about the relations between these objects at the conceptual and geometrical levels. These mechanisms have been widely used in spatial data query [1–2], spatial data mining [3], evaluation of equivalence and

Citation: Liu B, Li D, Xia Y, Ruan J, Xu L, Wu H (2015) Combinational Reasoning of Quantitative Fuzzy Topological Relations for Simple Fuzzy Regions. PLoS ONE 10(3): e0117379. doi:10.1371/journal.pone.0117379.

similarity in a spatial scene [4], and for consistency assessment of the topological relations of multi-resolution spatial databases [5–7]. Dilo et al. [8] defined several types and operators for modeling spatial data systems to handle fuzzy information. Shi et al. [9] and Liu et al. [10] developed a new object extraction and classification method based on fuzzy topology.

However, the uncertain topological relations themselves must be modeled due to the existence of indeterminate and uncertain boundaries between spatial objects in GIS. Fuzzy topology theory can potentially be applied to the modeling of fuzzy topological relations among spatial objects.

To date, many models have been designed to formalize topological relations between simple fuzzy objects, they can be implemented on spatial databases at less cost than other uncertainty models and are useful when managing, storing, querying, and analyzing uncertain data. For example, Egenhofer and Franzosa [5, 11] and Winter [12] modeled the topological relations between two spatial regions in two dimensional space (2-D) based on the 4-intersection model and ordinary point set theory. Li et al. [13], Long and Li [14] produced a Voronoi-based 9-intersection model based on Voronoi diagrams. Cohn et al. [15, 16] discovered forty-six topological relations between two regions with indeterminate boundaries based on the region connection calculus (RCC) theory [17]. Clemmentini and Di Felice [18–20] used extended 9-intersection model to classify forty-four topological relations between simple regions with broad boundaries. The extended 9-intersection model substantially agrees with the RCC model, though the former removes two relations considered as invalid in the geographical environment. The extended 9-intersection model can be extended to represent topological relations between objects with different dimensions, like regions and lines, while the RCC model can only be applied to relations between regions. Tang and Kainz [21], Tang et al. [22], Tang [23] applied fuzzy theory and a 9-intersection matrix, discovered forty-four topological relations between two simple fuzzy regions. Shi and Liu [24] discussed fuzzy topological relations between fuzzy spatial objects based on the theory of fuzzy topology. Du et al. [25, 26] proposed computational methods for fuzzy topological relations description, as well as a new fuzzy 9-intersection model. These models provided a framework to conceptually describe the topological relations between two regions and can be considered as an extension of the crisp case. In order to define and describe spatial relations qualitatively and to compute the fuzzy topological relations quantitatively, Liu and Shi [27, 28], Shi and Liu [29] defined a computational fuzzy topology to compute the interior, boundary, and exterior parts of spatial objects, and based on these definitions, Liu and Shi [28] proposed a computational 9-intersection model, and discovered sixteen topological relations between simple fuzzy region and line segment; forty-six topological relations between simple fuzzy line segments; three topological relations between simple fuzzy region and fuzzy point; and three topological relations between simple fuzzy line segment and fuzzy point, but it did not give the topological relations between two simple fuzzy regions, and it did not compute the topological relations between one simple fuzzy spatial region and one simple crisp spatial region.

To obtain the quantitative fuzzy topological relations between simple fuzzy regions in GIS, based on the previous researches, this paper develops a new method of describing quantitative fuzzy topological relations for simple fuzzy regions. The new method not only computes the topological relations between one simple fuzzy spatial region and one simple crisp spatial region, but also computes the topological relations between two simple fuzzy regions.

The remainder of this paper is organized as follows. In section 2, some basic concepts of fuzzy topology, computational fuzzy topology and the definitions of simple fuzzy spatial objects in GIS are reviewed; In Section 3, the new definitions of simple fuzzy spatial objects are introduced, and we proposed a new combinational reasoning method of quantitative fuzzy topological relations for simple fuzzy regions; In Section 4, by comparing the proposed method with existing fuzzy models, we demonstrated that it can make finer distinctions and is more expressive; Finally, some conclusions are drawn in Section 5.

A BRIEF SUMMARY OF COMPUTATIONAL FUZZY TOPOLOGY

In this section, coherent fuzzy topologies, induced by interior and closure operators [27–30], are reviewed. Mathematically, point set topology is the fundamental theory for modeling topological relations between crisp spatial objects in a GIS. By extension, fuzzy topology is a generalization of ordinary topology that introduces the concept of membership value and can be adopted for modeling topological relations between spatial objects with uncertainties. Zadeh [31] introduced the concept of fuzzy sets, and fuzzy set theory. Fuzzy topology was further developed based on the fuzzy sets [30, 32–34]. Liu and Shi [27, 28] and Shi and Liu [29] define a computational fuzzy topology to compute the interior, boundary and exterior of spatial objects. The computation is based on two operators, the interior operator and the closure operator. Each interior operator corresponds to one fuzzy topology and that each closure operator also corresponds to one fuzzy topology [30]. The research detailed in this paper extends this work by defining fuzzy spatial objects. However, it is important to review basic concepts in fuzzy set theory as well as simple fuzzy objects in a GIS.

Basic Concepts

We focus on the two-dimensional Euclidean plane R^2, with the usual distance and topology. Fuzzy topology is an extension of ordinary topology that fuses two structures, order structure and topological structure. Furthermore, the fuzzy interior, boundary, and exterior play an important role in the uncertain relations between GIS objects. Therefore, Shi and Liu [29] gave those items a very clean concept and the definition on fuzzy topological space.

In this section, we present the basic definitions for fuzzy sets and fuzzy mapping briefly, details on these definitions are given in related references [27–30, 32]. Fuzzy sets, open fuzzy sets, and closed fuzzy sets are the basic elements of fuzzy topology. The following are several definitions of fuzzy sets.

Definition 1 (Fuzzy subset). Let X be a non-empty ordinary set and I be the closed interval [0, 1].

An I-fuzzy subset on X is a mapping (called the membership function of A) $\mu_A : X \to I$, i.e., the family of all the [0,1]-fuzzy or I-fuzzy subsets on X is just I^X consisting of all the mappings from X to I. Here, I^X is called an I-fuzzy space. X is called the carrier domain of each I-fuzzy subset on it, and I is called the value domain of each I-fuzzy subset on X. $A \in I^X$ is called a crisp subset on X, if the image of the mapping is the subset of $\{0,1\} \subset I$.

Definition 2 (Rules of set relations). Let A and B be fuzzy sets in X with membership functions $\mu_A(x)$ and $\mu_B(x)$, respectively. Then,

1. $A = B$, *iff* $\mu_A(x) = \mu_B(x)$ *for all x in X*;
2. $A \leq B$, *iff* $\mu_A(x) \leq \mu_B(x)$ *for all x in X*;
3. $C = A \vee B$, *iff* $\mu_C(x) = \max[\mu_A(x), \mu_B(x)]$ *for all x in X*;
4. $D = A \wedge B$, *iff* $\mu_D(x) = \min[\mu_A(x), \mu_B(x)]$ *for all x in X*;
5. $E = A \setminus B$, *iff* $\mu_E(x) = 1 - \mu_A(x)$ *for all x in X*.

The fuzzy interior, boundary, and exterior play an important role in the uncertain relations between GIS spatial objects [29]. In the following, we will introduce the concept of fuzzy topology, which will be a basis for the description of uncertain relations between simple spatial objects in GIS. Furthermore, and the following are the commonly used definitions of fuzzy topological space, fuzzy interior, fuzzy closure, fuzzy complement, and fuzzy boundary [30].

Definition 3 (Fuzzy topological space). Let X be a non-empty ordinary set and $I = [0, 1]$, $\delta \subset I^X$. δ is called an I-fuzzy topology on X, and (I^X, δ) is called an I-fuzzy topological space (I-fts), if δ satisfies the following conditions:

- $0,1 \in \delta$;
- *If* $A, B \in \delta$, *then* $A \wedge B \in \delta$;
- *Let* $\{A_i : i \in J\} \subset \delta$, *where J is an index set, then* $\vee_{i \in J} A_i \in \delta$.

Where, $0 \in \delta$ means the empty set and $1 \in \delta$ means the whole set X. The elements in δ are called open elements and the elements in the complement of δ are called closed elements, and the set of the complement of open set is denoted by δ'.

Definition 4 (Interior and closure). For any fuzzy set $A \in I^X$, the interior of A is defined as the join of all the open subsets contained in A, denoted by A°, and the closure of A as the meeting of all the closed subsets containing A, denoted by $\overline{A}$.

Definition 5 (Fuzzy complement). For any fuzzy set A, we defined the complements of A by $A^C(x) = 1 - A(x)$, denoted by A^C.

Definition 6 (Fuzzy boundary). The boundary of a fuzzy set A is defined as $\partial A = \overline{A} \wedge \overline{A^C}$.

Definition 7 (Closure operator). An operator $\alpha : I^X \to I^X$ is a fuzzy closure operator if the following conditions are satisfied:

1. $\alpha(0) = 0$;
2. $\alpha(A) \leq A$, *for all* $A \in I^X$;
3. $\alpha(A \vee B) = \alpha(A) \vee \alpha(B)$;
4. $\alpha(\alpha(A)) = \alpha(A)$, *for all* $A \in I^X$.

Definition 8 (Interior operator). An operator $\alpha : I^X \to I^X$ is a fuzzy interior operator if the following conditions are satisfied:

1. $\alpha(1) = 1$;
2. $A \leq \alpha(A)$, *for all* $A \in I^X$;
3. $\alpha(A \wedge B) = \alpha(A) \wedge \alpha(B)$;
4. $\alpha(\alpha(A)) = \alpha(A)$, *for all* $A \in I^X$.

Definition 9 (Interior and closure operators). For any fixed $\alpha \in [0,1]$, both operators, interior and closure, are defined as $A_\alpha(x) = \begin{cases} A(x) & if \quad A(x) > \alpha \\ 0 & if \quad A(x) \leq \alpha \end{cases}$ and $A^{1-\alpha}(x) = \begin{cases} 1 & if \quad A(x) \geq 1-\alpha \\ A(x) & if \quad A(x) < 1-\alpha \end{cases}$, respectively. And induced an I-fuzzy topology $(X, \tau_\alpha, \tau^{1-\alpha})$ in X, where $\tau_\alpha = \{A_\alpha : A \in I^X\}$ is the open sets and $\tau^{1-\alpha} = \{A^{1-\alpha} : A \in I^X\}$ is the closed sets. The elements in τ_α and $\tau^{1-\alpha}$ satisfy the relations $(A_\alpha)^C = (A^C)^{1-\alpha}$, for all fuzzy set A, i.e., the complement of the element in the τ_α closed set. Details on how these two operators can induce a coherent I-fuzzy topology are given in Liu and Shi [27].

To study topological relations, it is essential to firstly understand the properties of a fuzzy mapping, especially the homeomorphic mapping since topological relations are invariant in homeomorphic mappings. The following section presents a number of definitions related to fuzzy mapping.

Let I^X, I^Y be I-fuzzy spaces, $f: X \to Y$ an ordinary mapping. Based on $f: X \to Y$, define I-fuzzy mapping $f^{\to} : I^X \to I^Y$ and its I-fuzzy reverse mapping $f^{\to} : I^X \to I^Y$ by

$$f^{\to} : I^X \to I^Y, f^{\to}(A)(y) = \begin{cases} V\{A(x)\}, if & x \in f^{-1}(y) \\ 0 & otherwise \end{cases}, \forall A \in I^X, \forall y \in Y$$

$f^{\leftarrow} : I^Y \to I^X, f^{\leftarrow}(B)(x) = B(f(x)), \forall B \in I^Y, \forall x \in X$ While $I = [0,1]$.

Let (I^X, δ), (I^Y, δ) be I-fts's, $f^{\to} : (I^X, \delta) \to (I^Y, \mu)$ is called I-fuzzy homeomorphism, if it is bijective continuous and open [30]. One important theorem to check an I-fuzzy homeomorphism is that, as proved by Shi and Liu [29]. Let $A \in I^X$, $B \in I^Y$, let (I^X, δ), (I^Y, δ) be I-fts's induces by interior operator and closure operators. Then $f^{\to} : (I^X, \delta) \to (I^Y, \mu)$ is an I-fuzzy homeomorphism if and only if $f: X \to Y$ is bijective mapping. Meanwhile, for the topology induced by these two operators, for checking homeomorphic map, actually, we only have to check whether it is one-one corresponding between domain and range only.

Modeling Simple Fuzzy Spatial Objects in GIS

Geometrically, GIS features can be classified as points, lines, and regions, and within the framework of crisp objects modeling in GIS, we first need to model simple objects before we model the topological relations between the objects. Similarly, within the framework of fuzzy objects modeling in GIS, we first need to model simple fuzzy objects before we can model the fuzzy topological relations between the objects [19]. Many researchers also have been working on modeling fuzzy topological relations and simple fuzzy objects [21, 27–29]. For example, Tang and Kainz [21] defined a simple fuzzy region based on fuzzy topology; Liu and Shi [27–29] have provided definitions of simple fuzzy points, simple fuzzy line segments and simple fuzzy regions.

In this research, the mentioned fuzzy definitions of the basic elements(simple fuzzy points, lines, and regions) in GIS are summarized briefly as follows, details on these definitions are given in related references [27–29].

Definition 10 (fuzzy point, Fig. 1(a)). An *I*-fuzzy point on *X* is an *I*-fuzzy subset $X_\alpha \in I^X$, defined as:

$$x_\alpha(y) = \begin{cases} \alpha & if \quad y = x \\ 0 & otherwise \end{cases}.$$

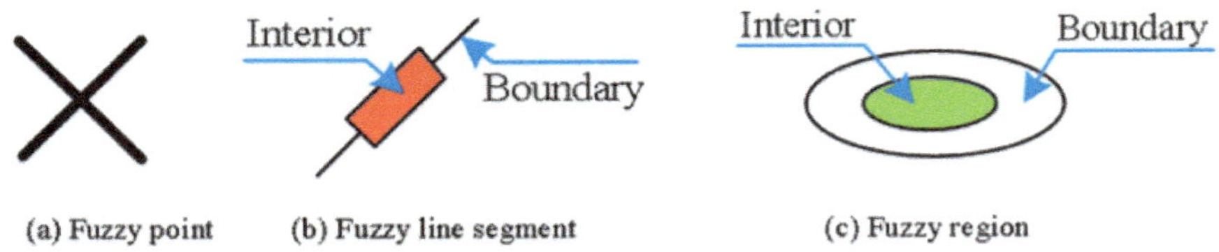

Figure 1. (a) Fuzzy point for given α; (b) Fuzzy line segment for given β; (c) Fuzzy region for given γ [28].

Definition 11 (Simple fuzzy line). A fuzzy subset in *X* is called a simple fuzzy line (*L*), if *L* is a supported connected line in the background topology (i.e., a crisp line in the background topology).

Definition 12 (Simple fuzzy line segment, Fig. 1(b)). The simple fuzzy line segment (*L*) is a fuzzy subset in *X* with: 1) for any $\beta \in (0,1)$, the fuzzy line L_β is a supported connected line segment (i.e., a crisp line segment in the background topology) in the background topology and 2) ∂L $(= (L_\beta)^C \wedge L^{1-\beta})$ has at most two supported connected components.

Definition 13 (Simple fuzzy region, Fig. 1(c)). A simple fuzzy region is a fuzzy region in a polygon feature *X* which: 1) for any $\gamma \in (0,1)$, the fuzzy set A_γ and $\partial A(A_\gamma)^C \wedge L^{1-\gamma}$ are two supported connected regular bounded open sets in the background topological space; 2) in the background topological space, any outward normal from $Supp(A_\gamma)$ must meet $Supp(\partial A)$ and have only one component.

On the basic definitions of simple fuzzy points, line segments and regions, Shi and Liu [29] provide an example of computing the interior, boundary, and exterior of spatial objects for different α values, and the interior, boundary, and exterior of spatial objects were confirmed for each given α value. Based on the fuzzy objects' definitions, Liu and Shi [28] proposed a new 3 × 3 integration model to compute sixteen topological relations between a simple fuzzy region to a simple fuzzy line segment, three topological relations between a simple fuzzy region to a simple fuzzy point, forty-six topological relations between a simple fuzzy line segment and a simple fuzzy line segment, and three topological relations between a simple fuzzy line segment and a simple fuzzy point. However, the relations between two simple fuzzy regions were not computed, and the element $f_X A \wedge BdV$ of the 3 × 3 integration model is the ratio of the area (or volume) of meet of two fuzzy spatial objects in a join of two simple spatial object (here a join of two fuzzy objects means 'union' of two fuzzy objects; meet of two fuzzy objects means 'intersection' of two fuzzy objects [28]), and was difficult to describe the topological relations between simple crisp spatial regions and simple fuzzy spatial regions.

Based on existing related studies, in next section, we will discuss the newly combinational reasoning method to compute the topological relations between simple fuzzy regions.

COMBINATIONAL REASONING OF QUANTITATIVE FUZZY TOPOLOGICAL RELATIONS FOR SIMPLE FUZZY REGIONS

The Basic Topological Relations between Two Simple Crisp Regions

Many models have been designed to formalize topological relations between simple crisp objects, such as the 4-Intersection Model (4IM) [11, 35], the 9-Intersection Model (9IM) [36], Region Connection Calculus (RCC) theory [17], and the Voronoi-based 9-Intersection Model (V9I) [13, 14]. All of the existing models can determine the eight basic topological relations possible for 2-dimensional simple crisp regions in the physical world: *disjoint, meet,overlap, cover, contain, equal, inside, and covered-by*, respectively as seen in Fig. 2. In point set topology, the 4IM, 9IM, and V9I models divide a simple crisp region into three parts: interior (A°), boundary (∂A), and exterior A^- / A^V. In this paper, we used 9IM (as Eq. (1)) to compute the eight basic topological relations of

simple crisp regions.

$$R_9(A,B) = \begin{bmatrix} A^\circ \cap B^\circ & A^\circ \cap \partial B & A^\circ \cap B^- \\ \partial A \cap B^\circ & \partial A \cap \partial B & \partial A \cap B^- \\ A^- \cap B^\circ & A^- \cap \partial B & A^- \cap B^- \end{bmatrix} \quad \textbf{(1)}$$

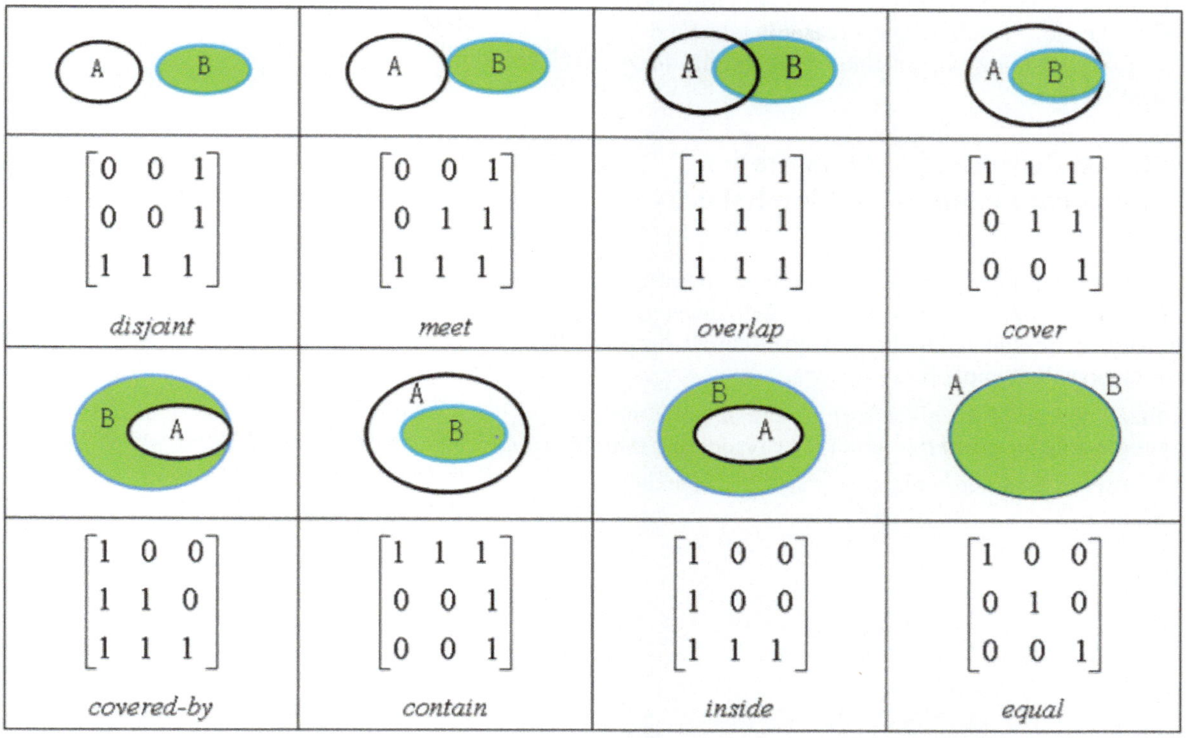

Figure 2. The eight basic topological relations between two simple crisp regions [36]

Since the intersection of two sets can be either 0 or 1, the topological relation between two simple crisp regions as follows.

The New Definitions of Simple Fuzzy Spatial Objects

A given α, a simple fuzzy spatial line segment and region in GIS has a certain interior and boundary as shown in Fig. 1. We developed a new definition for a simple fuzzy spatial line segment and region by applying the definition in the previous section, and on fuzzy topological space [32], the fuzzy point definition remains the same as Definition 10.

Definition 14 (inner and outer boundary of simple fuzzy line segment, Fig. 3(a)), for givenα, the interior and boundary of simple line segment *L(as shown in Fig. 1(b))* are confirmed, in the same way as a simple crisp line segment. Hence, we define ∂L_α^- as the outer-boundary of *L*, and ∂L_α^o as the inner-boundary of *L*, L_α^o as the interior of *L*, and ∂L_α as the boundary of *L (as shown in Fig. 3(a))*: $\partial L_\alpha = \partial L_\alpha^- - \partial L_\alpha^o$. So, a simple fuzzy line segment *L*for given α can be expressed as: $L_\alpha = \partial L_\alpha^- \cup \partial L_\alpha \cup \partial L_\alpha^o \cup L_\alpha^o$.

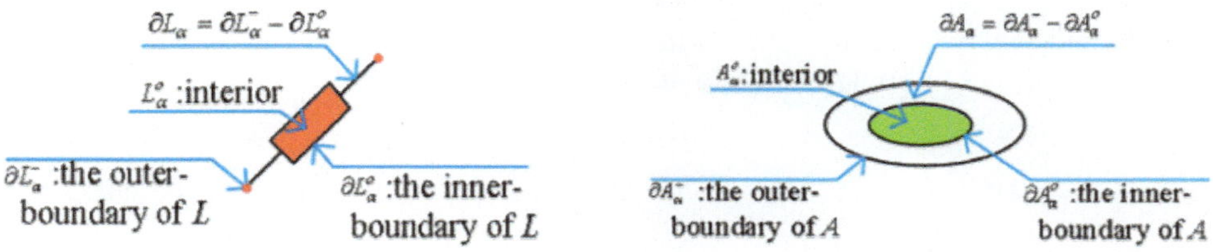

(a) Fuzzy line segment L (b) Fuzzy region A

Figure 3. (a) The inner-outer boundary of simple fuzzy line segment *L* **for given** $\boldsymbol{\alpha}$; (b) the inner-outer boundary of simple fuzzy region *A* **for given** $\boldsymbol{\alpha}$.

Definition 15 (inner and outer boundary of simple fuzzy region, Fig. 3(b)), for a given α, the interior and boundary of fuzzy region *A (as shown in Fig. 1(c))* is confirmed. Just as for a crisp region, we defined ∂A_α^- as the outer-boundary of *A*, and ∂A_α^o as the inner-boundary of*A*, A_α^o as the interior of *A* and ∂A_α as the boundary of *A (as shown in Fig. 3(b))*: $\partial A_\alpha = \partial A_\alpha^- - \partial A_\alpha^o$. So the fuzzy region *A* for given α can be expressed as: $A_\alpha = \partial A_\alpha^- \cup \partial A_\alpha \cup \partial A_\alpha^o \cup A_\alpha^o$. Meanwhile, ∂A_α^- and ∂A_α^o can be considered as two simple crisp regions.

Based on the above definitions, 1) to a simple fuzzy line segment *L* for given α, if $\partial L_\alpha^- = \partial L_\alpha^o$, that is $\partial L_\alpha = 0$, and $L = L_\alpha = \partial L_\alpha^- \cup L_\alpha^o$, it means *L* is a simple crisp line segment; 2) to a fuzzy region *A* for given α, if ∂A_α^-, that is $\partial A_\alpha = 0$, $A = A_\alpha = \partial A_\alpha^- \cup A_\alpha^o$, it means *A* is a simple crisp region.

On the basis of these definitions, we will primarily focus on discussing the new combinational reasoning method of quantitative fuzzy topological relations for simple fuzzy regions in next section.

Combinational Reasoning of Quantitative Fuzzy Topological Relations for Simple Fuzzy Regions

In this section, we will only discuss the topological relations between the simple fuzzy regions, and we will develop a new combinational reasoning method of quantitative fuzzy topological relations for simple fuzzy regions.

For a fuzzy region *A1* for given α (Fig. 4 (a)), while the other fuzzy region *A2* for given β (Fig. 4 (b)), Considering the relationship between the outer-boundary ($\partial A1_\alpha^- / \partial A2_\beta^-$), boundary ($\partial A1_\alpha / \partial A2_\beta$), inner-boundary ($\partial A1_\alpha^o / \partial A2_\beta^o$), and interior ($A1_\alpha^o / A2_\beta^o$) of the simple fuzzy region *A* and *B* (as shown in Fig. 4), their topological relations have three different situations:

i If $\partial A1_\alpha^- = \partial A1_\alpha^o$, that is $\partial A1_\alpha = 0$, and $A1 = A1_\alpha = \partial A1_\alpha^- \cup A1_\alpha^o$. If $\partial A2_\beta^- = \partial A2_\beta^o$, that is $\partial A2_\beta = 0$, and $\partial A2_\beta$. *A1* and *A2* are simple crisp regions, the eight topological relations *R*(*A*1, *A*2) between *A1* and *A2* (as shown in Fig. 2). So, *R*(*A*1, *A*2) can be computed by 4IM [11], 9IM [36], or other existing models.

iii If $\partial A1_\alpha^- = \partial A1_\alpha^o$, that is $\partial A1_\alpha = 0$, and $A1 = A1_\alpha = \partial A1_\alpha^- \cup A1_\alpha^o$. If $\partial A2_\beta^- \neq \partial A2_\beta^o$, that is $\partial A2_\beta \neq 0$, $A2 = A2_\beta = \partial A2_\beta^- \cup \partial A2_\beta \cup \partial A2_\beta^o \cup A2_\beta^o$. *A1* is a crisp region, *A2* is a fuzzy region, and comprised of four components $\partial A2_\beta^-, \partial A2_\beta$, $\partial A2_\beta^o$ and $A2_\beta^o$. The topological relations between *A1* and *A2* can be described as $R(A1, A2_\beta^-)$ and $R(A1, A2_\beta^o)$ which can be computed by 4IM [11], 9IM [36], or other existing models.

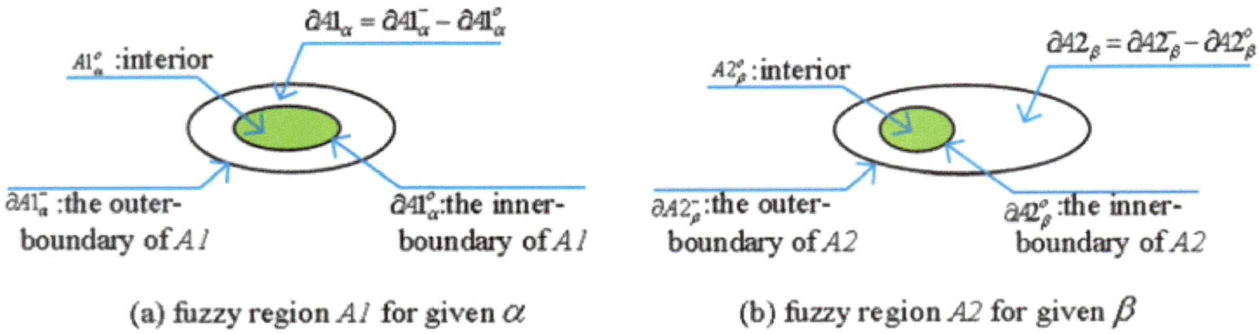

Figure 4. (a) Fuzzy region *A1* **for given α**; (b) Fuzzy region *A2* **for given β**.

Since all of the existing models can determine eight basic topological relations, such as{*disjoint, meet, overlap, cover, contain, equal, inside, and covered-by*}, each topological relation between two simple crisp regions $R(A1, A2_\beta^-)$ and $R(A1, A2_\beta^o)$ can be any one of the eight basic topological relations, hence in theory, $R(A1, A2_\beta^-)$ and $R(A1, A2_\beta^o)$ can determine $8^2 = 64$ topological relations, but only 23 basic relations for 2-dimensional simple regions in the physical world have been defined, and the relevant topological relations between *A1* and *A2* are included within the Supporting Information (S1 Table).

If $R(A1, A2_\beta^-) = disjoint$ $R(A1, A2_\beta^o) = disjoint$

If $R(A1, A2_\beta^-) = meet$ $R(A1, A2_\beta^o) = disjoint$

If $R(A1, A2_\beta^-) = overlap$

$R(A1, A2_\beta^o) = \{disjoint,\ meet,\ overlap,\ covered-by,\ inside\}$

If $R(A1, A2_\beta^-) = cover$

$R(A1, A2_\beta^o) = \{disjoint\ ,meet\ ,overlap\ ,covered-by\ ,inside\}$

If $R(A1, A2_\beta^-) = contain$

$R(A1, A2_\beta^o) = \{disjoint,\ meet,\ overlap,\ cover,\ contain,\ equal,\ inside,\ covered-by\}$

If $R(A1, A2_\beta^-) = covered-by$, $R(A1, A2_\beta^o) = \{inside\}$.

If $R(A1, A2_\beta^-) = inside$ $R(A1, A2_\beta^o) = inside$

If $R(A1, A2_\beta^-) = equal$ $R(A1, A2_\beta^o) = inside$

iii) If $\partial A1_\alpha^- \neq \partial A1_\alpha^o$, that is $\partial A1_\alpha \neq 0$, and $A1 = A1_\alpha = \partial A1_\alpha^- \cup \partial A1_\alpha \cup \partial A1_\alpha^o \cup A1_\alpha^o$. If $\partial A2_\beta^- \neq \partial A2_\beta^o$, that is $\partial A2_\beta \neq 0$, and $A2 = A2_\beta = \partial A2_\beta^- \cup \partial A2_\beta \cup \partial A2_\beta^o \cup A2_\beta^o$. *A1* and *A2*are fuzzy regions, *A1* comprised of four components $\partial A1_\alpha^-$, $\partial A1_\alpha$, $\partial A1_\alpha^o$ and $A1_\alpha^o$, meanwhile, $\partial A1_\alpha = \partial A1_\alpha^- - \partial A1_\alpha^o$, *A2* also comprised of four components $\partial A2_\beta^-$, $\partial A2_\beta$, $\partial A2_\beta^o$, and $A2_\beta^o$, meanwhile, $\partial A2_\beta = \partial A2_\beta^- - \partial A2_\beta^o$. The topological relations between *A1*and *A2*, can be described as by $R(A1_\alpha^-, A2_\beta^-)$, $R(A1_\alpha^-, A2_\beta^o)$, $R(A1_\alpha^o, A2_\beta^-)$, and $R(A1_\alpha^o, A2_\beta^o)$, which can be computed by 4IM [11], 9IM [36], or other existing models.

Corresponding to conditions (ii), each topological relation between two simple crisp region $R(A1_\alpha^-, A2_\beta^-)$, $R(A1_\alpha^-, A2_\beta^o)$, $R(A1_\alpha^o, A2_\beta^-)$ and $R(A1_\alpha^o, A2_\beta^o)$ can be any one of the eight basic topological relations. Hence in theory, $R(A1_\alpha^-, A2_\beta^-)$, $R(A1_\alpha^-, A2_\beta^o)$, $R(A1_\alpha^o, A2_\beta^-)$, and $R(A1_\alpha^o, A2_\beta^o)$ can determine $8^4 = 4096$ topological relations, but only 152 basic relations for 2-dimensional simple regions in the physical world have been defined, and the relevant topological relations between *A1* and *A2* are included within the Supporting Information (S2 Table).

1. $If\ R(A1^-_\alpha, A2^-_\beta) = disjoint\ R(A1^-_\alpha, A2^o_\beta) = R(A1^o_\alpha, A2^-_\beta) = R(A1^o_\alpha, A2^o_\beta) = disjoint$

2. $If\ R(A1^-_\alpha, A2^-_\beta) = meet\ R(A1^-_\alpha, A2^o_\beta) = R(A1^o_\alpha, A2^-_\beta) = R(A1^o_\alpha, A2^o_\beta) = disjoint$;

3. $If\ R(A1^-_\alpha, A2^-_\beta) = overlap\ R(A1^-_\alpha, A2^o_\beta) = disjoint$
$R(A1^o_\alpha, A2^-_\beta) = \{disjoint, meet, overlap, covered-by, inside\}\ R(A1^o_\alpha, A2^o_\beta) = disjoint$

4. $If\ R(A1^-_\alpha, A2^-_\beta) = overlap\ R(A1^-_\alpha, A2^o_\beta) = meet$
$R(A1^o_\alpha, A2^-_\beta) = \{disjoint, meet, overlap, covered-by, inside\}$ and $R(A1^o_\alpha, A2^o_\beta) = disjoint$

5. $If\ R(A1^-_\alpha, A2^-_\beta) = overlap$, $R(A1^-_\alpha, A2^o_\beta) = overlap$, $R(A1^o_\alpha, A2^-_\beta) = disjoint$, $R(A1^o_\alpha, A2^o_\beta) = disjoint$;

6. $If\ R(A1^-_\alpha, A2^-_\beta) = overlap$, $R(A1^-_\alpha, A2^o_\beta) = overlap$, $R(A1^o_\alpha, A2^-_\beta) = meet$, $R(A1^o_\alpha, A2^o_\beta) = disjoint$;

7. $If\ R(A1^-_\alpha, A2^-_\beta) = overlap$, $R(A1^-_\alpha, A2^o_\beta) = overlap$, $R(A1^o_\alpha, A2^-_\beta) = overlap$,
$R(A1^o_\alpha, A2^o_\beta) = \{disjoint, meet, overlap\}$

8. $If\ R(A1^-_\alpha, A2^-_\beta) = overlap$, $R(A1^-_\alpha, A2^o_\beta) = overlap$, $R(A1^o_\alpha, A2^-_\beta) = covered-by$,
$R(A1^o_\alpha, A2^o_\beta) = \{disjoint, meet, overlap\}$;

9. $If\ R(A1^-_\alpha, A2^-_\beta) = overlap$, $R(A1^-_\alpha, A2^o_\beta) = overlap$, $R(A1^o_\alpha, A2^-_\beta) = inside$,
$R(A1^o_\alpha, A2^o_\beta) = \{disjoint, meet, overlap, covered-by, inside\}$

10. $If\ R(A1^-_\alpha, A2^-_\beta) = overlap$, $R(A1^-_\alpha, A2^o_\beta) = cover$, $R(A1^o_\alpha, A2^-_\beta) = disjoint$, $R(A1^o_\alpha, A2^o_\beta) = disjoint$;

11. $If\ R(A1^-_\alpha, A2^-_\beta) = overlap$, $R(A1^-_\alpha, A2^o_\beta) = cover$, $R(A1^o_\alpha, A2^-_\beta) = overlap$,
$R(A1^o_\alpha, A2^o_\beta) = \{disjoint, meet, overlap\}$;

12. $If\ R(A1^-_\alpha, A2^-_\beta) = overlap$, $R(A1^-_\alpha, A2^o_\beta) = cover$, $R(A1^o_\alpha, A2^-_\beta) = covered-by$,
$R(A1^o_\alpha, A2^o_\beta) = \{disjoint, meet, overlap\}$

13. $If\ R(A1^-_\alpha, A2^-_\beta) = overlap$, $R(A1^-_\alpha, A2^o_\beta) = cover$, $R(A1^o_\alpha, A2^-_\beta) = inside$,
$R(A1^o_\alpha, A2^o_\beta) = \{disjoint, meet, overlap, covered-by, inside\}$;

14. $If\ R(A1^-_\alpha, A2^-_\beta) = overlap$, $R(A1^-_\alpha, A2^o_\beta) = contain$, $R(A1^o_\alpha, A2^-_\beta) = disjoint$, $R(A1^o_\alpha, A2^o_\beta) = disjoint$;

15. $If\ R(A1^-_\alpha, A2^-_\beta) = overlap$, $R(A1^-_\alpha, A2^o_\beta) = contain$, $R(A1^o_\alpha, A2^-_\beta) = meet$, $R(A1^o_\alpha, A2^o_\beta) = disjoint$;

16. $If\ R(A1^-_\alpha, A2^-_\beta) = overlap$, $R(A1^-_\alpha, A2^o_\beta) = contain$, $R(A1^o_\alpha, A2^-_\beta) = meet$, $R(A1^o_\alpha, A2^o_\beta) = disjoint$;

17. $If\ R(A1^-_\alpha, A2^-_\beta) = overlap$, $R(A1^-_\alpha, A2^o_\beta) = contain$, $R(A1^o_\alpha, A2^-_\beta) = overlap$,
$R(A1^o_\alpha, A2^o_\beta) = \{disjoint, meet, overlap, cover, contains\}$

18. $If\ R(A1^-_\alpha, A2^-_\beta) = overlap$, $R(A1^-_\alpha, A2^o_\beta) = contain$, $R(A1^o_\alpha, A2^-_\beta) = covered-by$,
$R(A1^o_\alpha, A2^o_\beta) = \{disjoint, meet, overlap, cover, contains\}$

19. $If\ R(A1^-_\alpha, A2^-_\beta) = overlap$, $R(A1^-_\alpha, A2^o_\beta) = contain$, $R(A1^o_\alpha, A2^-_\beta) = inside$,
$R(A1^o_\alpha, A2^o_\beta) = \{disjoint, meet, overlap, cover, contain, covered-by, inside, equal\}$;

20. $If\ R(A1^{-}_{\alpha}, A2^{-}_{\beta}) = cover,\ R(A1^{-}_{\alpha}, A2^{o}_{\beta}) = contain,\ R(A1^{o}_{\alpha}, A2^{-}_{\beta}) = disjoint,\ R(A1^{o}_{\alpha}, A2^{o}_{\beta}) = disjoint;$

21. $If\ R(A1^{-}_{\alpha}, A2^{-}_{\beta}) = cover,\ R(A1^{-}_{\alpha}, A2^{o}_{\beta}) = contain,\ R(A1^{o}_{\alpha}, A2^{-}_{\beta}) = meet,\ R(A1^{o}_{\alpha}, A2^{o}_{\beta}) = disjoint;$

22. $If\ R(A1^{-}_{\alpha}, A2^{-}_{\beta}) = cover,\ R(A1^{-}_{\alpha}, A2^{o}_{\beta}) = contain,\ R(A1^{o}_{\alpha}, A2^{-}_{\beta}) = overlap,$
$R(A1^{o}_{\alpha}, A2^{o}_{\beta}) = \{disjoint,\ meet,\ overlap,\ cover,\ contain\}$

23. $If\ R(A1^{-}_{\alpha}, A2^{-}_{\beta}) = cover,\ R(A1^{-}_{\alpha}, A2^{o}_{\beta}) = contain,\ R(A1^{o}_{\alpha}, A2^{-}_{\beta}) = covered-by,$
$R(A1^{o}_{\alpha}, A2^{o}_{\beta}) = \{disjoint,\ meet,\ overlap,\ cover,\ contain\}$

24. $If\ R(A1^{-}_{\alpha}, A2^{-}_{\beta}) = cover,\ R(A1^{-}_{\alpha}, A2^{o}_{\beta}) = contain,\ R(A1^{o}_{\alpha}, A2^{-}_{\beta}) = inside,$
$R(A1^{o}_{\alpha}, A2^{o}_{\beta}) = \{disjoint,\ meet,\ overlap,\ cover,\ contain,\ covered-by,\ inside,\ equal\}$

25. $If\ R(A1^{-}_{\alpha}, A2^{-}_{\beta}) = covered-by,\ R(A1^{-}_{\alpha}, A2^{o}_{\beta}) = disjoint,\ R(A1^{o}_{\alpha}, A2^{-}_{\beta}) = inside,\ R(A1^{o}_{\alpha}, A2^{o}_{\beta}) = disjoint;$

26. $If\ R(A1^{-}_{\alpha}, A2^{-}_{\beta}) = covered-by,\ R(A1^{-}_{\alpha}, A2^{o}_{\beta}) = meet,\ R(A1^{o}_{\alpha}, A2^{-}_{\beta}) = inside,\ R(A1^{o}_{\alpha}, A2^{o}_{\beta}) = disjoint$

27. $If\ R(A1^{-}_{\alpha}, A2^{-}_{\beta}) = covered-by,\ R(A1^{-}_{\alpha}, A2^{o}_{\beta}) = overlap,\ R(A1^{o}_{\alpha}, A2^{-}_{\beta}) = inside,$
$R(A1^{o}_{\alpha}, A2^{o}_{\beta}) = \{disjoint,\ meet,\ overlap,\ covered-by,\ inside\}$

28. $If\ R(A1^{-}_{\alpha}, A2^{-}_{\beta}) = covered-by,\ R(A1^{-}_{\alpha}, A2^{o}_{\beta}) = cover,\ R(A1^{o}_{\alpha}, A2^{-}_{\beta}) = inside,$
$R(A1^{o}_{\alpha}, A2^{o}_{\beta}) = \{disjoint,\ meet,\ overlap,\ covered-by,\ inside\}$

29. $If\ R(A1^{-}_{\alpha}, A2^{-}_{\beta}) = covered-by,\ R(A1^{-}_{\alpha}, A2^{o}_{\beta}) = contain,\ R(A1^{o}_{\alpha}, A2^{-}_{\beta}) = inside,$
$R(A1^{o}_{\alpha}, A2^{o}_{\beta}) = \{disjoint,\ meet,\ overlap,\ cover,\ contain,\ covered-by,\ inside,\ equal\}$

30. $If\ R(A1^{-}_{\alpha}, A2^{-}_{\beta}) = contain,\ R(A1^{-}_{\alpha}, A2^{o}_{\beta}) = contain,\ R(A1^{o}_{\alpha}, A2^{-}_{\beta}) = disjoint,\ R(A1^{o}_{\alpha}, A2^{o}_{\beta}) = disjoint;$

31. $If\ R(A1^{-}_{\alpha}, A2^{-}_{\beta}) = contain,\ R(A1^{-}_{\alpha}, A2^{o}_{\beta}) = contain,\ R(A1^{o}_{\alpha}, A2^{-}_{\beta}) = meet,\ R(A1^{o}_{\alpha}, A2^{o}_{\beta}) = disjoint;$

32. $If\ R(A1^{-}_{\alpha}, A2^{-}_{\beta}) = contain,\ R(A1^{-}_{\alpha}, A2^{o}_{\beta}) = contain,\ R(A1^{o}_{\alpha}, A2^{-}_{\beta}) = overlap,$
$R(A1^{o}_{\alpha}, A2^{o}_{\beta}) = \{disjoint,\ meet,\ overlap,\ cover,\ contain\}$

33. $If\ R(A1^{-}_{\alpha}, A2^{-}_{\beta}) = contain,\ R(A1^{-}_{\alpha}, A2^{o}_{\beta}) = contain,\ R(A1^{o}_{\alpha}, A2^{-}_{\beta}) = cover,\ R(A1^{o}_{\alpha}, A2^{o}_{\beta}) = contain$

34. $If\ R(A1^{-}_{\alpha}, A2^{-}_{\beta}) = contain,\ R(A1^{-}_{\alpha}, A2^{o}_{\beta}) = contain,\ R(A1^{o}_{\alpha}, A2^{-}_{\beta}) = covered-by,$
$R(A1^{o}_{\alpha}, A2^{o}_{\beta}) = \{disjoint,\ meet,\ overlap,\ cover,\ contain\}$

35. $If\ R(A1^{-}_{\alpha}, A2^{-}_{\beta}) = contain,\ R(A1^{-}_{\alpha}, A2^{o}_{\beta}) = contain,\ R(A1^{o}_{\alpha}, A2^{-}_{\beta}) = contain,\ R(A1^{o}_{\alpha}, A2^{o}_{\beta}) = contain$

36. $If\ R(A1^{-}_{\alpha}, A2^{-}_{\beta}) = contain,\ R(A1^{-}_{\alpha}, A2^{o}_{\beta}) = contain,\ R(A1^{o}_{\alpha}, A2^{-}_{\beta}) = inside,$
$R(A1^{o}_{\alpha}, A2^{o}_{\beta}) = \{disjoint,\ meet,\ overlap,\ cover,\ contain,\ covered-by,\ inside,\ equal\}$

37. $If\ R(A1^{-}_{\alpha}, A2^{-}_{\beta}) = contain,\ R(A1^{-}_{\alpha}, A2^{o}_{\beta}) = contain,\ R(A1^{o}_{\alpha}, A2^{-}_{\beta}) = equal,\ R(A1^{o}_{\alpha}, A2^{o}_{\beta}) = contain$

38. $If\ R(A1^{-}_{\alpha}, A2^{-}_{\beta}) = inside,\ R(A1^{-}_{\alpha}, A2^{o}_{\beta}) = inside,\ R(A1^{o}_{\alpha}, A2^{-}_{\beta}) = disjoint,\ R(A1^{o}_{\alpha}, A2^{o}_{\beta}) = disjoint;$

39. $If\ R(A1^{-}_{\alpha}, A2^{-}_{\beta}) = inside,\ R(A1^{-}_{\alpha}, A2^{o}_{\beta}) = inside,\ R(A1^{o}_{\alpha}, A2^{-}_{\beta}) = meet,\ R(A1^{o}_{\alpha}, A2^{o}_{\beta}) = disjoint;$

40. $If\ R(A1_{\alpha}^{-},A2_{\beta}^{-})=inside, R(A1_{\alpha}^{-},A2_{\beta}^{o})=inside, R(A1_{\alpha}^{o},A2_{\beta}^{-})=overlap,$
$R(A1_{\alpha}^{o},A2_{\beta}^{o})=\{disjoint,\ meet,\ overlap,\ covered-by,\ inside\}$

41. $If\ R(A1_{\alpha}^{-},A2_{\beta}^{-})=inside, R(A1_{\alpha}^{-},A2_{\beta}^{o})=inside, R(A1_{\alpha}^{o},A2_{\beta}^{-})=cover,$
$R(A1_{\alpha}^{o},A2_{\beta}^{o})=\{disjoint,\ meet,\ overlap,\ covered-by,\ inside\}$

42. $If\ R(A1_{\alpha}^{-},A2_{\beta}^{-})=inside, R(A1_{\alpha}^{-},A2_{\beta}^{o})=inside, R(A1_{\alpha}^{o},A2_{\beta}^{-})=contain,$
$R(A1_{\alpha}^{o},A2_{\beta}^{o})=\{disjoint,\ meet,\ overlap,\ cover,\ contain,\ covered-by,\ inside,\ equal\}$

43. $If\ R(A1_{\alpha}^{-},A2_{\beta}^{-})=inside, R(A1_{\alpha}^{-},A2_{\beta}^{o})=inside, R(A1_{\alpha}^{o},A2_{\beta}^{-})=covered-by, R(A1_{\alpha}^{o},A2_{\beta}^{o})=inside;$

44. $If\ R(A1_{\alpha}^{-},A2_{\beta}^{-})=inside, R(A1_{\alpha}^{-},A2_{\beta}^{o})=inside, R(A1_{\alpha}^{o},A2_{\beta}^{-})=covered-by, R(A1_{\alpha}^{o},A2_{\beta}^{o})=inside;$

45. $If\ R(A1_{\alpha}^{-},A2_{\beta}^{-})=inside, R(A1_{\alpha}^{-},A2_{\beta}^{o})=inside, R(A1_{\alpha}^{o},A2_{\beta}^{-})=equal, R(A1_{\alpha}^{o},A2_{\beta}^{o})=inside;$

46. $If\ R(A1_{\alpha}^{-},A2_{\beta}^{-})=equal, R(A1_{\alpha}^{-},A2_{\beta}^{o})=R(A1_{\alpha}^{o},A2_{\beta}^{-})=contain,$
$R(A1_{\alpha}^{o},A2_{\beta}^{o})=\{disjoint,\ meet,\ overlap,\ cover,\ contain,\ covered-by,\ inside,\ equal\}$

COMPARISON WITH EXISTING MODELS

In dealing with fuzzy spatial objects, Cohn and Gotts [15] proposed the 'egg-yolk' model with two concentric sub-regions, indicating the degree of 'membership' in a vague/fuzzy region. In this model, the 'yolk' represents the precise part and 'egg' represents the vague/fuzzy part of a region. The 'egg-yolk' model is an extension of RCC theory [17] into the vague/fuzzy region, a total of forty-six relations can be identified [15]. Based on the 9-intersection model (9IM, Eq. (1)), Clemmentini and Di Felice defined a region with a broad boundary, by using two simple regions [18, 20], this broad boundary is denoted by ΔA. Based on empty and non-empty invariance, Clementini and Di Felice's Algebraic Model asequation (2):

$$R_9(A,B)=\begin{bmatrix} A^{\circ}\cap B^{\circ} & A^{\circ}\cap \Delta B & A^{\circ}\cap B^{-} \\ \Delta A\cap B^{\circ} & \Delta A\cap \Delta B & \Delta A\cap B^{-} \\ A^{-}\cap B^{\circ} & A^{-}\cap \Delta B & A^{-}\cap B^{-} \end{bmatrix} \quad \textbf{(2)}$$

Equation (2) gave a total of forty-four relations between two spatial regions with a broad boundary. The extended 9-intersection model (Eq. (2)) substantially agrees with the 'egg-yolk' model, though the former removes two relations considered as invalid in the geographical environment.

For example, in the table 2 (18) and (21), as shown in Fig. 5(a, b), the equation (2) yielded the same matrix, $R_9(A,B)=\begin{bmatrix} 0 & 1 & 1 \\ 1 & 1 & 1 \\ 0 & 1 & 1 \end{bmatrix}$. That is to say, the topological relations are same, but they are obviously different from each other as shown in Fig. 5 (a, b). And then, we'll discuss the topological relations (as shown in Fig. 5) of using the new combinational reasoning method in this paper.

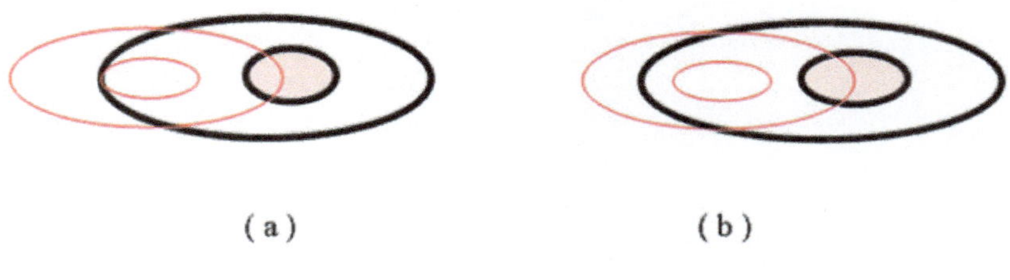

Figure 5. Two different topological relations between *A1* **and** *A2*.

Fuzzy topology is dependent on the value of αorβ used in leveling cuts. Different values ofαandβ generate different fuzzy topologies and may have different topological structures. Therefore, we can generate the suitable fuzzy topology by adjusting the value ofαorβ, and the generated fuzzy topology can thus match the cases of the application concerned. Moreover, different values of αandβcan provide a multi-directional spatial analysis in GIS [29]. Details about calculating the value of αorβ in fuzzy topology and fuzzy sets, we can see the relevant literatures [27, 29]. In this paper, based on the research of Liu and Shi, we propose a new definition for simple fuzzy line segments and simple fuzzy regions, and also propose a new combinational reasoning method to compute the fuzzy topological relations between two simple spatial regions. Therefore, it's important to note that the values ofαandβin the Fig. 5 only used to demonstrate the validity of the new method, in the actual application and analysis, an optimal value ofαorβcan be obtained by investigating these fuzzy topologies, and generated a suitable fuzzy topological relations [29]. We can generate a suitable fuzzy topology by adjusting the value of αorβ, and then more information can be generated for spatial queries by applying fuzzy topology.

In Fig. 5 (a) and (b), the simple fuzzy region *A1* for givenα, *A2* for givenβ, the topological relation between *A1* and *A2* can be obtained by calculating $R(A1_{\alpha}^{-}, A2_{\beta}^{-})$, $R(A1_{\alpha}^{-}, A2_{\beta}^{o})$, $R(A1_{\alpha}^{o}, A2_{\beta}^{-})$, and $R(A1_{\alpha}^{o}, A2_{\beta}^{o})$.

For Fig. 5 (a), we used 9IM (Eq. (1)) to compute $R(A1_{\alpha}^{-}, A2_{\beta}^{-})$, $R(A1_{\alpha}^{-}, A2_{\beta}^{o})$, $R(A1_{\alpha}^{o}, A2_{\beta}^{-})$, and $R(A1_{\alpha}^{o}, A2_{\beta}^{o})$, so the topological relation can be described as follows:

a): $R(A1_{\alpha}^{-}, A2_{\beta}^{-})=overlap$, $R(A1_{\alpha}^{-}, A2_{\beta}^{o})=overlap$, $R(A1_{\alpha}^{o}, A2_{\beta}^{-})=covered-by$, $R(A1_{\alpha}^{o}, A2_{\beta}^{o})=disjoint$

$$R(A1_{\alpha}^{-}, A2_{\beta}^{-}) = \begin{bmatrix} 1 & 1 & 1 \\ 1 & 1 & 1 \\ 1 & 1 & 1 \end{bmatrix},$$

$$R(A1_{\alpha}^{-}, A2_{\beta}^{o}) = \begin{bmatrix} 1 & 1 & 1 \\ 1 & 1 & 1 \\ 1 & 1 & 1 \end{bmatrix},$$

$$R(A1_{\alpha}^{o}, A2_{\beta}^{-}) = \begin{bmatrix} 1 & 0 & 0 \\ 1 & 1 & 0 \\ 1 & 1 & 1 \end{bmatrix},$$

$$R(A1_{\alpha}^{o}, A2_{\beta}^{o}) = \begin{bmatrix} 0 & 0 & 1 \\ 0 & 0 & 1 \\ 1 & 1 & 1 \end{bmatrix};$$

For Fig. 5 (b), we used 9IM (Eq. (1)) to compute $R(A1_{\alpha}^{-}, A2_{\beta}^{-})$, $R(A1_{\alpha}^{-}, A2_{\beta}^{o})$, $R(A1_{\alpha}^{o}, A2_{\beta}^{-})$, and $R(A1_{\alpha}^{o}, A2_{\beta}^{o})$, so the topological relation can be described as follows:

b): $R(A1_{\alpha}^{-}, A2_{\beta}^{-})=overlap$, $R(A1_{\alpha}^{-}, A2_{\beta}^{o})=overlap$, $R(A1_{\alpha}^{o}, A2_{\beta}^{-})=inside$, $R(A1_{\alpha}^{o}, A2_{\beta}^{o})=disjoint$

$$R(A1_{\alpha}^{-}, A2_{\beta}^{-}) = \begin{bmatrix} 1 & 1 & 1 \\ 1 & 1 & 1 \\ 1 & 1 & 1 \end{bmatrix},$$

$$R(A1_{\alpha}^{-}, A2_{\beta}^{o}) = \begin{bmatrix} 1 & 1 & 1 \\ 1 & 1 & 1 \\ 1 & 1 & 1 \end{bmatrix},$$

$$R(A1_{\alpha}^{o}, A2_{\beta}^{-}) = \begin{bmatrix} 1 & 0 & 0 \\ 1 & 0 & 0 \\ 1 & 1 & 1 \end{bmatrix},$$

$$R(A1_{\alpha}^{o}, A2_{\beta}^{o}) = \begin{bmatrix} 0 & 0 & 1 \\ 0 & 0 & 1 \\ 1 & 1 & 1 \end{bmatrix}.$$

Through the above comparison analysis, the new proposed combinational reasoning method (when taking different values ofαandβ) not only can obtain the topological relations of simple fuzzy regions as listed in existing studies [15, 16, 18, 20], but also the topological relations not currently listed.

CONCLUSION

Fuzzy topological relations between simple spatial objects can be used for fuzzy spatial queries, fuzzy spatial analyses, and other questions. This paper presented a combinational reasoning method of quantitative fuzzy topological relations for simple spatial regions in GIS. Based on the research of Liu and Shi, we proposed a new definition for simple fuzzy line segments and simple fuzzy regions based on the computational fuzzy topology, we also proposed a new combinational reasoning method to compute the fuzzy topological relations between simple spatial regions, an analysis of the new method exposes: (1) 23 different topological relations between a simple crisp region and a simple fuzzy region; (2) 152 different topological relations between two simple fuzzy regions. Based on the new definitions, the proposed method in this study not only computes the topological relations between a simple crisp region and a simple fuzzy region, but also computes the topological relations between two simple fuzzy regions. In the end, we have discussed some examples to demonstrate the validity of the new method. Through comparisons of results, we showed that the proposed method can make finer distinctions, as it is more expressive than the existing fuzzy models.

SUPPORTING INFORMATION

S1 Table. The 23 relations between a simple crisp region and a simple fuzzy region inR^2.

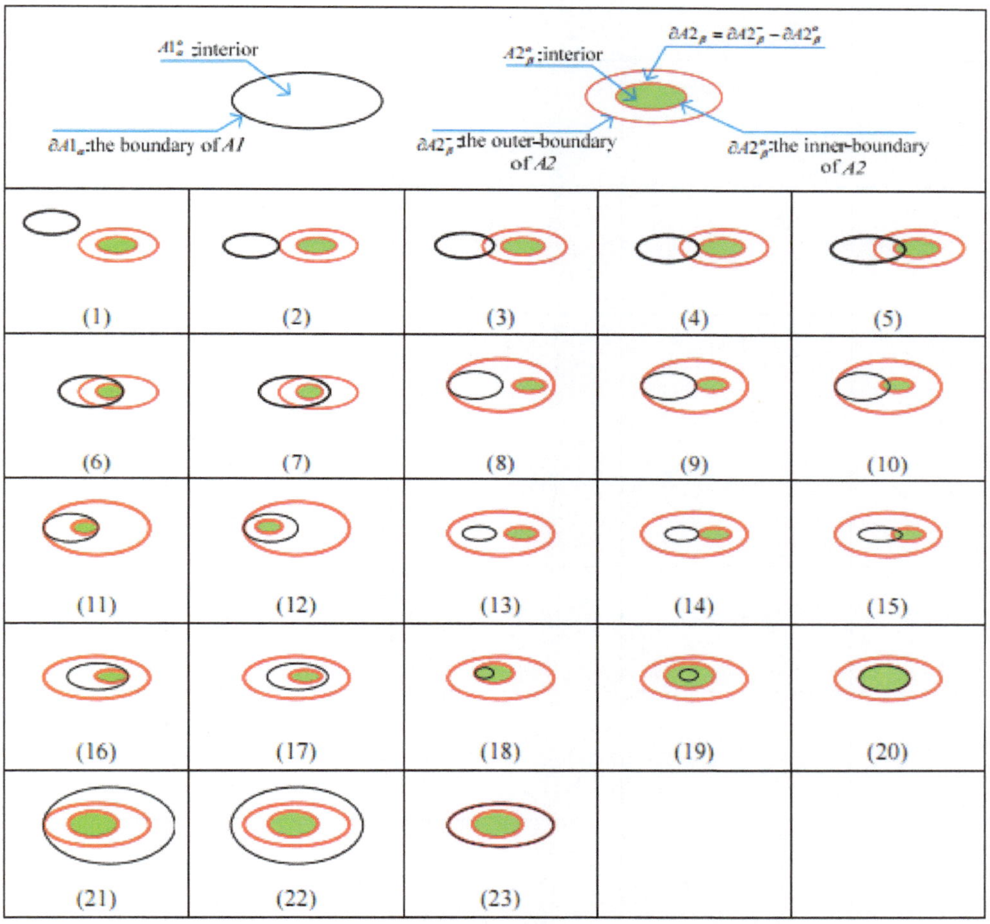

doi:10.1371/journal.pone.0117379.s001

S2 Table. The 152 relations between two simple fuzzy regions in R^2.

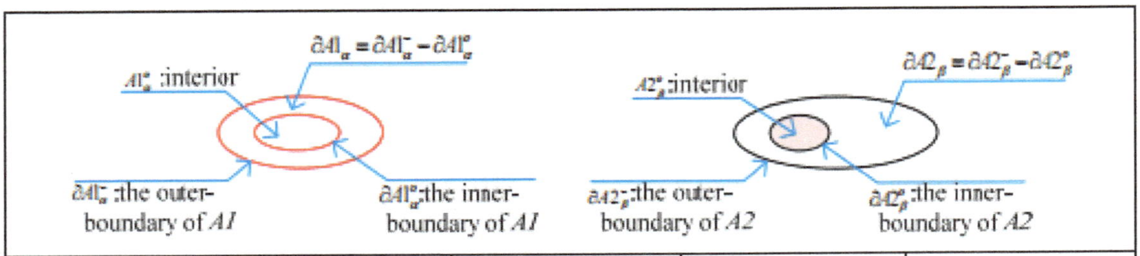

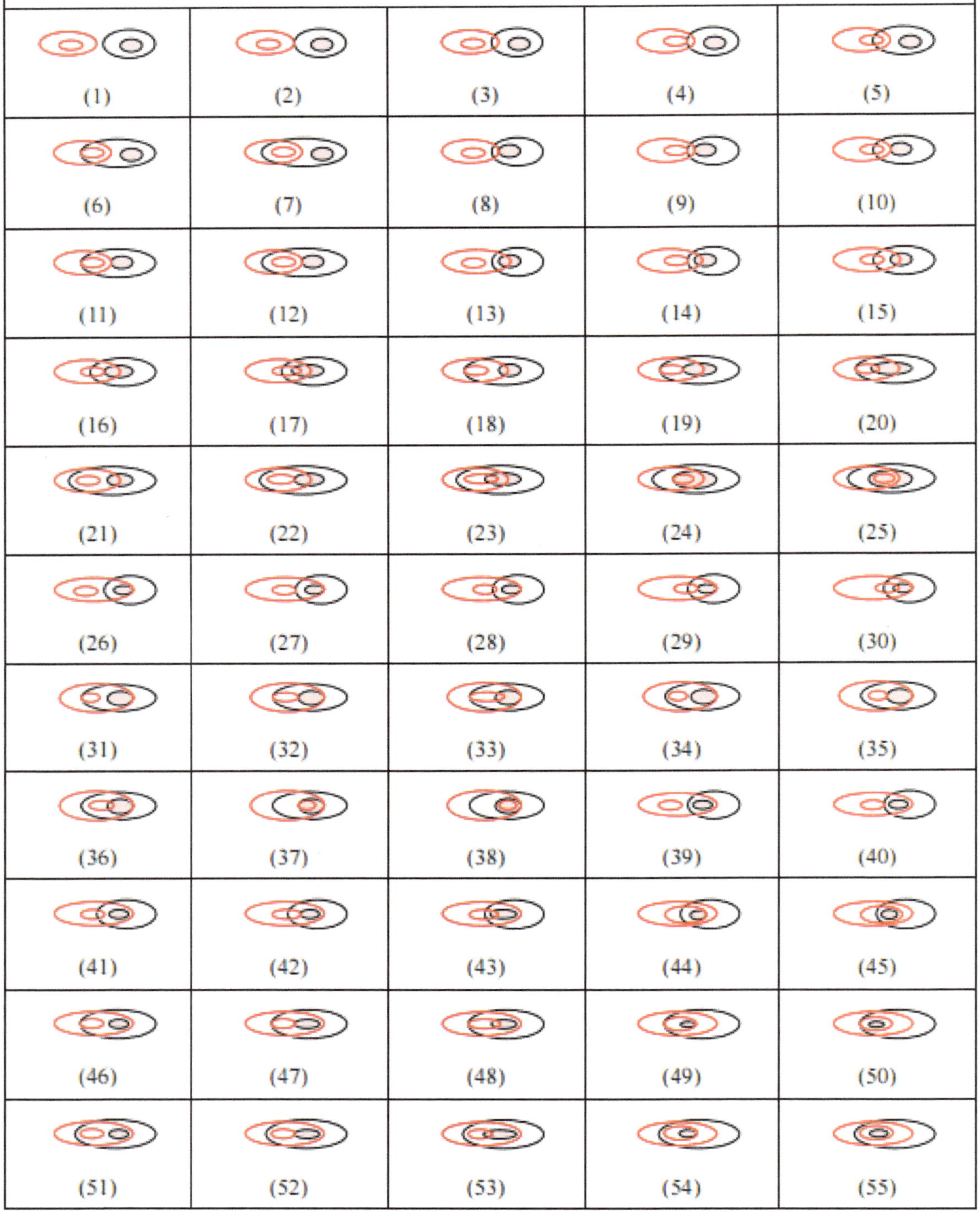

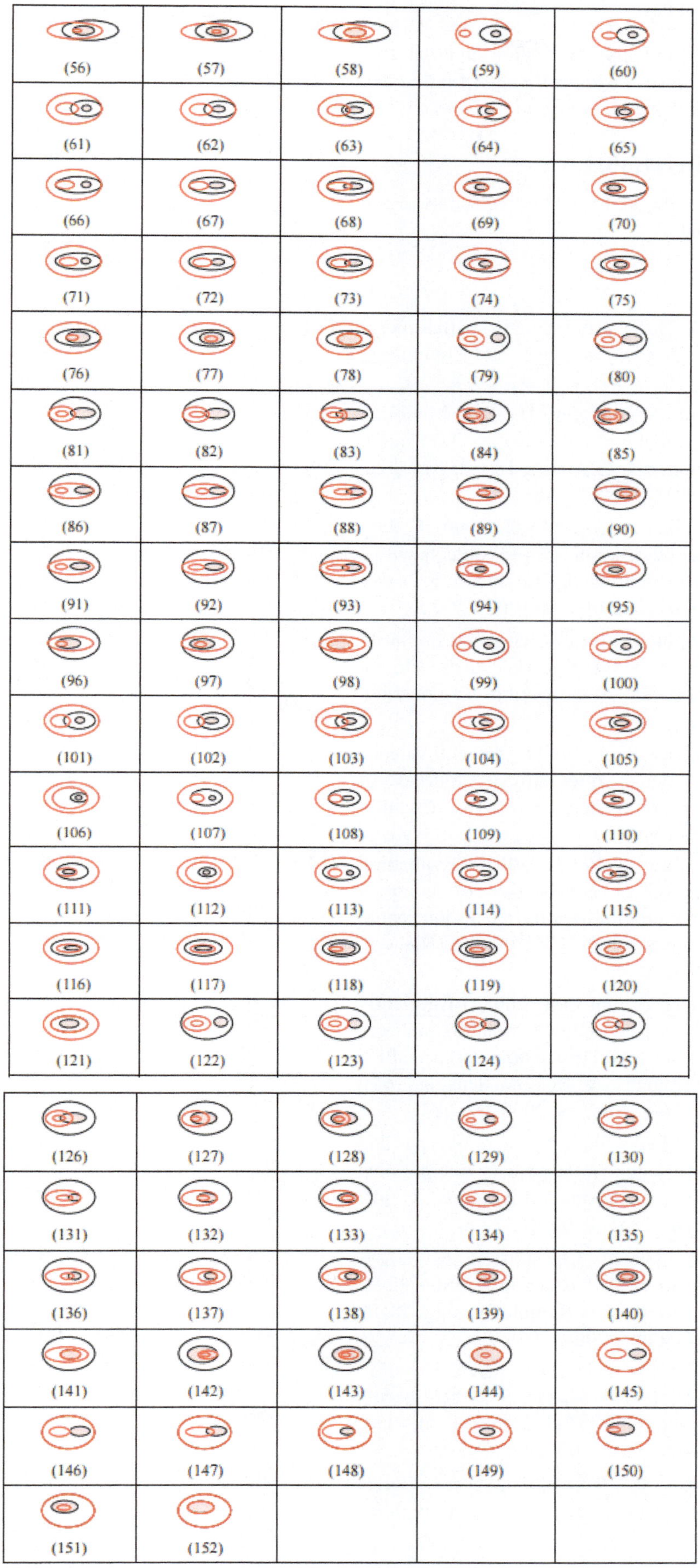

doi:10.1371/journal.pone.0117379.s002

ACKNOWLEDGMENTS

The authors would like to thank the Editor and the two anonymous reviewers whose insightful suggestions have significantly improved this letter.

AUTHOR CONTRIBUTIONS

Wrote the paper: BL DJL YPX JR LLX HYW. Conceived and analyzed the paper: BL DJL.

REFERENCES

1. Egenhofer MJ (1997) Query processing in spatial-query-by-sketch. Journal of Visual Languages and Computing, 8 (4): 403–424. doi: 10. 1006/jvlc. 1997. 0054
2. Clementini E, Sharma J, Egenhofer MJ (1994) Modeling topological spatial relations: Strategies for query processing. Computers and Graphics, 18 (6): 815–822. doi: 10. 1016/0097-8493(94)90007-8
3. Clementini E, Di Felice P, Koperski K (2000) Mining multiple level spatial association rules for objects with a broad boundary. Data & Knowledge Engineering, 34 (3): 251–270. doi: 10. 1016/s0169-023x(00)00017-3
4. Paiva JAC (1998) Topological equivalence and similarity in multi-representation geographic databases. Ph. D. Dissertation. Department of Surveying Engineering, University of Maine.
5. Egenhofer M, Franzosa R (1994) On the equivalence of topological relations. International Journal of Geographical Information Systems, 8 (6): 133–152. doi: 10. 1080/02693799508902030
6. Du SH, Qin QM, Wang Q, Ma H (2008a) Evaluating structural and topological consistency of complex regions with broad boundaries in multi-resolution spatial databases. Information Sciences, 178(2008): 52–68. doi: 10. 1016/j. ins. 2007. 07. 023
7. Du SH, Guo L, Wang Q, Qin QM (2008b) Efficiently computing and deriving topological relation matrices between complex regions with broad boundaries. ISPRS Journal of Photogrammetry & Remote Sensing, (63): 593–609. doi: 10. 1016/j. isprsjprs. 2008. 02. 004
8. Dilo A, de By RA, Stein A (2007) A system of types and operators for handling vague spatial objects. International Journal of Geographical Information Systems, 21 (4): 397–426. doi: 10. 1080/13658810601037096
9. Shi WZ, Liu KF, Huang CQ (2010) A Fuzzy-Topology-Based Area Object Extraction Method. IEEE Transactions on Geoscience and Remote Sensing, 48(1): 147–154. doi: 10. 1109/tgrs. 2009. 2024302
10. Liu KF, Shi WZ, Zhang H (2011) A fuzzy topology-based maximum likelihood classification, ISPRS Journal of Photogrammetry and Remote Sensing, (66): 103–114. doi: 10. 1016/j. isprsjprs. 2010. 09. 007
11. Egenhofer M, Franzosa R (1991a) Point-set topological spatial relations. International Journal of Geographical Information Systems, 5 (2): 161–174. doi: 10. 1080/02693799108927841
12. Winter S (2000) Uncertain topological relations between imprecise regions. International Journal of Geographical Information Science, 14 (5): 411–430. doi: 10. 1080/13658810050057579
13. Li CM, Chen J, Li ZL (1999) Raster-based method or the generation of Voronoi diagrams for spatial entities. International Journal of Geographical Information Systems, 13 (3): 209. doi: 10. 1080/136588199241328
14. Long ZG, Li SQ (2013) A complete classification of spatial relations using the Voronoi-based nine-intersection model. International Journal of Geographical Information Science, 27(10): 2006–2025. doi: 10. 1080/13658816. 2013. 781607
15. Cohn AG, Gotts NM (1996) The 'egg-yolk' representation of regions with indeterminate boundaries. In Geographic Objects with Indeterminate Boundaries, Burrough P. A. , Frank A. U. (Eds.). Taylor & Francis, London and Bristol: 171–187.
16. Cohn AG, Bennett B, Gooday J, Gotts NM (1997) Qualitative spatial representation and reasoning with the region connection calculus. GeoInformatica, 1 (1): 1–44. doi: 10. 1007/978-0-585-28322-7_4
17. Randell DA, Cui Z, Cohn AG (1992) A spatial logic based on regions and connection. In Proceedings 3rd International Conference on Knowledge Representation and Reasoning, 25–29 October 1992, San Mate, M. Kaufmann, California, 165–176.
18. Clemmentini E, Di Felice DP (1996a) An algebraic model for spatial objects with indeterminate boundaries. In Geographic Objects with Indeterminate Boundaries, Burrough P. A. , Frank A. U. (Eds.). Taylor & Francis, London and Bristol: 155–169.
19. Clementini E, Di Felice P (1996b) A model for representing topological relationships between complex geometric features in spatial databases. Information Sciences, 90 (1): 121–136. doi: 10. 1016/0020-0255(95)00289-8
20. Clementini E, Di Felice P (1997). Approximate topological relations. International Journal of Approximate Reasoning, 16 (2): 173–204. doi: 10. 1016/s0888-613x(96)00127-2
21. Tang XM, Kainz W (2002) Analysis of topological relations between fuzzy regions in general fuzzy topological space. In The SDH conference 02, 9–12 July 2002, Ottawa Congress Centers, Ottawa, Canada, 114–123.
22. Tang XM, Kainz W, Yu F (2005) Reasoning about changes of land cover with fuzzy settings. International Journal of Remote Sensing, 26 (14): 3025–3046. doi: 10. 1080/01431160500057863
23. Tang XM (2004) Spatial object modeling in fuzzy topological spaces: with applications to land cover change. Ph. D. Dissertation. University of Twente, ITC publications, The Netherlands.
24. Shi WZ, Liu KF (2004) Modelling fuzzy topological relations between uncertain objects in GIS. Photogrammetric Engineering and Remote Sensing, 70(8): 921–930. doi: 10. 14358/pers. 70. 8. 921
25. Du SH, Qin QM, Wang Q (2005a) Fuzzy description of topological relations I: a unified fuzzy 9-intersection

model. In: Advances in Natural Computation, Wang L. , Chen K. , Ong Y. S. (Eds.), Lecture Notes in Computer Science, vol. 3612: 1260–1273.

26. Du SH, Qin QM, Wang Q (2005b) Fuzzy description of topological relations II: computation methods and examples. In: Advances in Natural Computation, Wang L. , Chen K. , Ong Y. S. (Eds.), Lecture Notes in Computer Science, vol. 3612: 1274–1279.
27. Liu KF, Shi WZ (2006) Computation of fuzzy topological relations of spatial objects based on induced fuzzy topology. International Journal of Geographical Information Systems, 20 (8): 857–883. doi: 10. 1080/13658810600711345
28. Liu KF, Shi WZ (2009) Quantitative fuzzy topological relations of spatial objects by induced fuzzy topology. International Journal of Applied Earth Observation and Geoinformation, (11): 38–45. doi: 10. 1016/j. jag. 2008. 06. 001
29. Shi WZ, Liu KF (2007) A fuzzy topology for computing the interior, boundary, and exterior of spatial objects quantitatively in GIS. Computer and Geoscience, 33 (7): 898–915. doi: 10. 1016/j. cageo. 2006. 10. 013
30. Liu YM, Luo MK (1997) Fuzzy Topology (Singapore: World Scientific).
31. Zadeh LA (1965) Fuzzy Sets. Information and Control, (8): 338–353. doi: 10. 1016/s0019-9958(65)90241-x
32. Chang CL (1968) Fuzzy topological spaces. Journal of Mathematical Analysis and Applications, 24: 182–190. doi: 10. 1016/0022-247x(68)90057-7
33. Wong CK (1974) Fuzzy points and local properties of fuzzy topology. Journal of Mathematical Analysis and Applications, (46): 316–328. doi: 10. 1016/0022-247x(74)90242-x
34. Wu G, Zheng C (1991) Fuzzy boundary and characteristic properties of order homomorphisms. Fuzzy Sets and Systems, (39): 329–337. doi: 10. 1016/0165-0114(91)90102-v
35. Egenhofer M, Mark D (1995) Modeling Conceptual Neighborhoods of Topological Line-Region Relations. International Journal of Geographical Information Systems, 9 (5): 555–565. doi: 10. 1080/02693799508902056
36. Egenhofer M, Herring J (1991b) Categorizing Binary Topological Relationships between Regions, Lines, Points in Geographic Databases. Oronoi: Technical Report, Department of Surveying Engineering, University of Maine, Oronoi, ME

CHAPTER 15

A TRANSPARENT AND TRANSFERABLE FRAMEWORK FOR TRACKING QUALITY INFORMATION IN LARGE DATASETS

Derek E. Smith[1], Stefan Metzger[1,2], Jeffrey R. Taylor[1,2]

[1] National Ecological Observatory Network, Boulder, Colorado, United States of America

[2] Institute of Arctic and Alpine Research, University of Colorado, Boulder, Colorado, United States of America

ABSTRACT

The ability to evaluate the validity of data is essential to any investigation, and manual "eyes on" assessments of data quality have dominated in the past. Yet, as the size of collected data continues to increase, so does the effort required to assess their quality. This challenge is of particular concern for networks that automate their data collection, and has resulted in the automation of many quality assurance and quality control analyses. Unfortunately, the interpretation of the resulting data quality flags can become quite challenging with large data sets. We have developed a framework to summarize data quality information and facilitate interpretation by the user. Our framework consists of first compiling data quality information and then presenting it through 2 separate mechanisms; a quality report and a quality summary. The quality report presents the results of specific quality analyses as they relate to individual observations, while the quality summary takes a spatial or temporal aggregate of each quality analysis and provides a summary of the results. Included in the quality summary is a final quality flag, which further condenses data quality information to assess whether a data product is valid or not. This framework has the added flexibility to allow "eyes on" information on data quality to be incorporated for many data types. Furthermore, this framework can aid problem tracking and resolution, should sensor or system malfunctions arise.

INTRODUCTION

Advancements in sensor measurement techniques and data collection continue to increase both the accuracy and quantity of measurements we are able to capture. Yet, without some indication of a data set's validity it is seemingly useless. Similarly, while the demand on the quality of data can vary from one research question to another, it is paramount that the data quality is known. One organization that is confronted by this challenge is the National Ecological Observatory Network (NEON). Set to begin full operations in 2017, the NEON is designed to collect and provide a wide array of environmental data freely to the public for a period of 30 years, from sites located throughout the United States [1], [2]. When the observatory is complete, the NEON will consist of over 14,000 automated sensors and stream more than 55,000 variables. The sheer number of measurements that the NEON will capture has in turn necessitated the automation of much of the data processing. While historically data quality has been assessed manually using an "eyes on" approach, this is no longer

Citation: Smith DE, Metzger S, Taylor JR (2014) A Transparent and Transferable Framework for Tracking Quality Information in Large Datasets. PLoS ONE 9(11): e112249. doi:10.1371/journal.pone.0112249.

feasible for datasets of this magnitude. This has subsequently led the NEON to develop various automated quality assessment and quality control (QA/QC) analyses [3]. In turn this has necessitated the development of a framework that automates the propagation and interpretation of data quality information, which is discussed here.

Ideally, in order to evaluate whether data is acceptable, the intended data use should first be identified [4]. Herein lies a major challenge for the NEON because it is impossible to account for all potential ways the resulting data products may be used. Thus, in order to accommodate varying use cases and levels of expertise, we developed a framework that condenses data quality information, while retaining several levels of detail. The reliable generation of data products can be summarized into 3 main components: (i) Quality requirements for the raw data, components/assemblies and data products. (ii) Quality verification of raw data and the final data products, and (iii) Corrective actions taken for data products that do not meet their requirements [5]. Here components (ii) and (iii) are addressed. The data quality framework summarizes quality information by condensing individual sensor tests and QA/QC analyses into quality metrics and generates an overall quality summary, which will be discussed in the Sect. "*Materials and Methods*". In turn one's ability to assess the overall quality of a data product is vastly simplified through the data quality framework.

NEON has implemented this framework for atmospheric sensor data in order to provide transparent data quality information to its users. Here we present how this framework can be used to assess the data quality of a NEON tower sensor. To put the ability of the framework to condense data quality information into perspective, at a typical NEON site over 150 atmospheric and terrestrial sensor measurements are made. Generally, 1- and 30-minute averages are produced from sensor measurements, which are often acquired at a rate of 1 Hz and include 8 different QA/QC analyses. Accordingly, the QA/QC results for atmospheric and terrestrial sensors are upwards of 1×10^8 a day, 2×10^9 a month, and 3×10^{10} a year. Through the presented framework, the QA/QC information can be condensed by roughly 4 orders of magnitude for 1-minute averages and 6 orders of magnitude for 30-minute averages. It becomes increasingly apparent that one would be unable to digest and interpret all of the individual quality information from sensors sampling at a rate of 20 Hz. Thus, we sought to formulate an automated framework that allows the results from sensor tests and QA/QC analyses to be summarized in a way that is transparent and easily interpretable. This will enable users to determine whether corrective actions are necessary if a data product has not met the requirements needed for a specific use case.

Data quality assessment techniques employed by the eddy-covariance community were used as a foundation for this framework, since they routinely assess large data sets and scrutinize their data quality [6], [7], and [8]. These approaches were designed to determine the quality of a reported data product that originated from multiple input data products. Briefly, these schemes define a set of criteria that individually map the quality of inputs to a data product. This information is then incorporated into a rank-based scheme that determines the overall quality of the reported data product. A caveat of these rank-based approaches is that they do not easily transfer and integrate among different types of measurements, as they are typically designed to be used for 1 specific application.

Therefore, we chose to (initially) refrain from grouping/ranking data into different categories based on the magnitude of their deviation for a specific analysis. Instead, we first derive a simplistic approach that allows the framework to be applied across a greater number of data types. This, in turn, allows for data quality information to be propagated in a less ambiguous manor across varying use cases. The methodology was initially conceived for use with ecological data, nonetheless it can be readily applied to various data types. Even in the scope of NEON, ecological data may not be big data when viewed through the lens of data mining, but it is comparatively complex. As such, it quickly becomes problematic to use existing rank-based approaches to create and implement a standardized and transparent methodology to summarize quality across varying data types. In addition, existing rank-based approaches limit the degree to which quality information can be propagated since the approaches generally require that they are tailored to specific questions, methods, use cases, and so forth.

Here, we advance existing rank-based approaches to create a data quality assessment scheme that is modular in form so it can easily be transferred among a variety of sensor measurements and physical samples. It is also shown how, at a later stage, means for gradation can be re-inserted. For example, the framework can assess and propagate information for sensor measurements and physical samples from an array of sources, e.g., atmospheric, terrestrial, and/or aquatic. In addition, the data quality framework enables all the quality information to be condensed into a final flag. This final quality flag signifies whether a data product is valid or invalid based on predetermined and user-defined thresholds for the various sensor tests and QA/QC analyses that are in place. Here we present the principal components of this framework as well as an example of how it can be used to assess data quality. The majority of the paper will focus on the Sect. "*Materials and Methods*", which provides an overview of the data quality framework methodology, its various components, and how it is constructed. The Sect. "*Application of Data Quality Framework*" provides an example of how the framework can be applied to ecological data using sensor-based measurements from a NEON tower site. We conclude with discussing the applicability and expandability of the framework to various data types and use cases.

MATERIALS AND METHODS

Each of the following sub-sections provide an overview of an individual component that collectively compose the entire data quality framework. As presented, each component of the framework is sequential in nature, incorporating the components from previous sections in order to construct the framework. Initially, quality flags and their various states are defined. This is followed by an overview of how quality flags relate to quality metrics. Quality metric information is then further condensed into a final quality flag for a data product. Lastly, a system for summarizing and presenting the data quality information is presented.

Quality Flags

Quality flags are defined as quality information provided through sensor tests and/or QA/QC analyses. In Eq. (1) we depict a quality flag for an arbitrary analysis, x, as having 1 of 3 possible states. However, a quality flag with greater or fewer number of states could be incorporated into the framework in the same fashion, an example of this is shown in Sect. "*Application of Data Quality Framework*".

$$QF_x = \begin{cases} 1 & \textit{if a test } \textbf{failed} \\ 0 & \textit{if a test } \textbf{passed} \\ -1 & \textit{if a test was not run } \textbf{(NA)} \textit{ due to a lack of ancillary data} \end{cases} \quad \textbf{(1)}$$

It is important to note that results from sensor tests and QA/QC analyses can be continuous. In order to discretize such results for use in the present framework, a user-defined threshold or logic for a range of states needs to be applied, such as described in Sect. "*Computation of Final Quality Flag*" and Table 1, respectively.

Table 1. Treatment of temperature sensor data based on results from pair-wise comparisons, i.e., Eq. (9)–(11).

Inputs A B C	Averaging Operator	Averaging Flag (QF_{AVE})
T T T	$\frac{1}{3}(T_1+T_2+T_3)$	0
T T F	$median(T_1,T_2,T_3)$	1
T F T	$median(T_1,T_2,T_3)$	2
T F F	$\frac{1}{2}(T_1+T_2)$	3
F T T	$median(T_1,T_2,T_3)$	4
F T F	$\frac{1}{2}(T_2+T_3)$	5
F F T	$\frac{1}{2}(T_1+T_3)$	6
F F F	$median(T_1,T_2,T_3)$	7

doi:10.1371/journal.pone.0112249.t001

Quality Metrics

Quality metrics simply summarize the quality flag information for a given period of time or spatial extent by their frequency of occurrence. Respectively, there is 1 quality metric for each possible state a quality flag could take, which is represented as a percentage of the total number of measurements. Accordingly, our example of a quality flag in Eq. (1) has 3 corresponding quality metrics ($QM_{x,1}, QM_{x,0}, QM_{x,-1}$), which relate to the individual quality flag's state.

$$QM_{x,1} = \frac{\sum_{i=1}^{n}(QF_{x_i} \equiv 1)}{n} \cdot 100\% \quad \textbf{(2)}$$

$$QM_{x,0} = \frac{\sum_{i=1}^{n}(QF_{x_i} \equiv 0)}{n} \cdot 100\% \quad \textbf{(3)}$$

$$QM_{x,-1} = \frac{\left|\sum_{i=1}^{n}(QF_{x_i} \equiv -1)\right|}{n} \cdot 100\% \quad \textbf{(4)}$$

Where, n is the number of measurements for a given period of time, and QF_x is the quality flag result for a specific quality analysis that corresponds to an individual measurement obtained during the period of time. The total sum for all of the quality metrics related to a specific quality flag is always 100%, independent of the number of states that the quality flags and associated quality metrics may have. The relationship between quality metrics and quality flags for an arbitrary data product with a set of f quality flags and n measurements is displayed in Table 2.

Table 2. Illustration of how quality flags and quality metrics are determined for a data product with n **measurements and** f **quality** flags.

Observation	QF_1			⋯	QF_f		
1	$1 \vee 0 \vee -1$			⋱	$1 \vee 0 \vee -1$		
⋮	⋮			⋱	⋮		
n	⋮			⋱	⋮		
	$QM_{1,1}$	$QM_{1,0}$	$QM_{1,-1}$		$QM_{f,1}$	$QM_{f,0}$	$QM_{f,-1}$
	$\frac{\sum_{i=1}^{n}(QF_1 \equiv 1)}{n} \cdot 100\%$	$\frac{\sum_{i=1}^{n}(QF_1 \equiv 0)}{n} \cdot 100\%$	$\frac{\left\|\sum_{i=1}^{n}(QF_1 \equiv -1)\right\|}{n} \cdot 100\%$	⋯	$\frac{\sum_{i=1}^{n}(QF_f \equiv 1)}{n} \cdot 100\%$	$\frac{\sum_{i=1}^{n}(QF_f \equiv 0)}{n} \cdot 100\%$	$\frac{\left\|\sum_{i=1}^{n}(QF_f \equiv -1)\right\|}{n} \cdot 100\%$

doi:10.1371/journal.pone.0112249.t002

Alpha and Beta Quality Flags and Metrics

The calculation of α and β quality flags and quality metrics are very similar to one another and are specific to a measurement. The difference between the 2 of them is that, αdetermines whether or not 1 or more of the quality flags failed for a measurement, while βdetermines whether or not 1 or more of the results of the quality flags could not be determined due to a lack of ancillary data. The calculation of QF_α and QF_β for an individual measurement are shown in Eq. (5) and (6).

$$QF_\alpha = \begin{cases} 1 & if \ \sum_{j=1}^{f}(QF_j \equiv 1) > 0 \\ 0 & otherwise \end{cases} \quad (5)$$

$$QF_\beta = \begin{cases} 1 & \sum_{j=1}^{f}(QF_j \equiv -1) > 0 \\ 0 & otherwise \end{cases} \quad (6)$$

Following the calculation of QF_α and QF_β, i.e., Eq. (5) and (6), α and β quality metrics, QM_α and QM_β, are determined. It is important to mention that for a given observation, QF_α and QF_β can both be set to 1 in the event an associated quality flag is set to 1 and another associated quality flag could not be computed due to a lack of ancillary data. Thus, while the quality metrics derived from individual quality flags always sum to 100%, quality metrics for QF_α and QF_β always sum to $\leq 200\%$. A visual representation of how α and βquality flags and quality metrics are determined and fit into the overall framework is shown in Table 3.

Table 3. Overview of the data quality framework and how the various sections/modules fit in.

Observation	QF_1			⋯	QF_f			QF_α	QF_β
1	$1 \vee 0 \vee -1$			⋱	$1 \vee 0 \vee -1$			*Eq. (5)*	*Eq. (6)*
⋮	⋮			⋱	⋮			⋮	⋮
n	⋮			⋱	⋮			⋮	⋮
	Eq. (2)	*Eq. (3)*	*Eq. (4)*	⋯	*Eq. (2)*	*Eq. (3)*	*Eq. (4)*	*Eq. (2)*	*Eq. (2)*

doi:10.1371/journal.pone.0112249.t003

Computation of Final Quality Flag

To increase the comprehensiveness of the data quality framework, information is then further condensed into a final quality flag. The final quality flag, QF_{FINAL}, offers users a way to quickly assess the quality of a data product and to determine whether or not data has passed or failed an overall assessment. The QF_{FINAL} threshold is defined by relating QM_α and QM_β in a meaningful way to the variable of interest. Therefore, the validity of a data product is based on an acceptable amount of failed quality tests, and subsequently removed observations, as well as an acceptable amount of inconclusive tests. If a data product reaches or exceeds this threshold it is flagged as invalid (i.e., $QF_{FINAL} = 1$) and valid (i.e., $QF_{FINAL} = 0$) otherwise. The threshold is user-defined, which enables its application across a multitude of varying data types.

Here we present the QF_{FINAL} threshold arbitrarily as a 2:1 ratio of QM_α to QM_β with maximum fractions of 10% QM_α and 20% for QM_β, Eq. (7). Hence, in this example a data product is considered invalid if 10% or more of the data used to create it has failed a set of quality tests and were removed, more than 20% of quality test results remain inconclusive, or a combination of the 2. Figure 1 represents the ratio of QM_α to QM_β in a graphical form for this threshold.

$$QF_{FINAL} = \begin{cases} 1 & if \ QM_\beta + (2QM_\alpha) \geq 20\% \\ 0 & otherwise \end{cases} \quad (7)$$

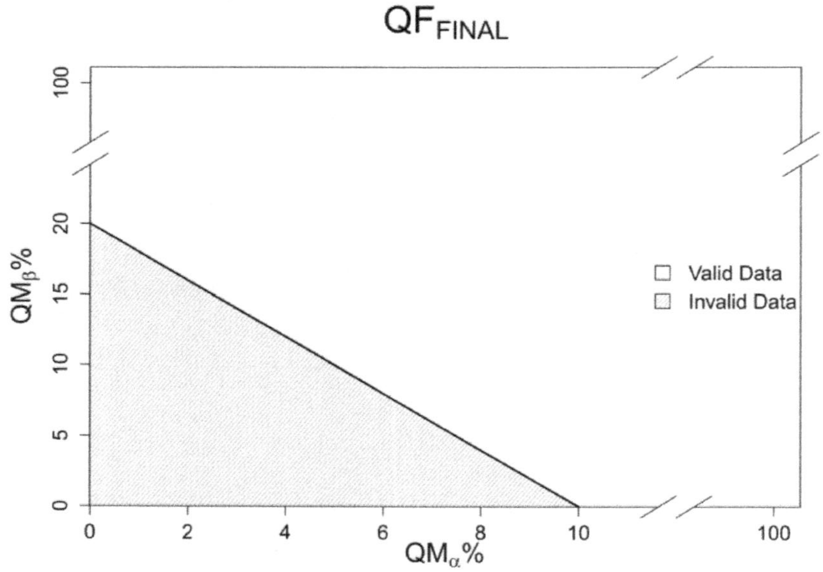

Figure 1. Representation of QF_{FINAL} **using Eq. (7) to determine whether or not a data product is valid.**

Quality Summary and Quality Report

Ultimately, all of the quality information for a data product (i.e., quality flags and quality metrics) and the final quality flag, are compiled and summarized in 2 separate schemes; a quality report and a quality summary. The quality report presents the result of all sensor tests and QA/QC analyses as they relate to individual observations, i.e., the individual quality flag results. For example, a quality report for a 30-minute temperature average, sampled at a rate of 1 Hz, allows users to differentiate the 1800 outcomes for each sensor test and QA/QC analysis. Alternatively, the quality summary provides the quality metric results for each quality flag as well as the final quality flag, which allows for a quick assessment of the validity of a data product. An overview of what information is contained in the quality report and quality summary is shown in Table 4. This approach presents and retains several levels of detail, which facilitates data transparency and usability. In addition, this allows backtracking through the results, thus aiding problem tracking and resolution, as shown in the Sect. "*Application of Data Quality Framework*".

Table 4. Overview of the information contained in the quality summary and quality report.

Observation	*QF_1*			*QF_2*			*QF_3*			*QF_α*	*QF_β*	
1	0			0			0			0	0	
2	0			0			0			0	0	
3	0			0			0			0	0	
6	0			0			0			0	0	
7	0			0			0			0	0	
8	0			0			1			1	0	
9	1			0			1			1	0	
10	1			0			0			1	0	
11	0			0			0			0	0	
12	0			0			0			0	0	
13	0			0			0			0	0	
14	0			0			0			0	0	
15	0			−1			−1			0	1	
	$QM_{1,1}$ 13%	$QM_{1,0}$ 87%	$QM_{1,-1}$ 0%	$QM_{2,1}$ 0%	$QM_{2,0}$ 93%	$QM_{2,-1}$ 7%	$QM_{3,1}$ 13%	$QM_{3,0}$ 80%	$QM_{3,-1}$ 7%	QM_α 20%	QM_β 7%	QF_{FINAL} 1

This example displays the quality report and quality summary information for 15 sensor measurements and 3 arbitrary quality analyses. The quality report contains the individual quality flag outcomes for each sensor measurement, i.e., rows 1–15. The quality summary includes the corresponding quality metrics and the final quality flag information, i.e., the bottom row.

doi:10.1371/journal.pone.0112249.t004

Furthermore, depending on the use case the amount of quality information reported can be substantially reduced by including only specific information. For example, a sensor sampled at 1 Hz reports 1800 measurements for a 30-minute average. If 1 sensor test and 7 different QA/QC analyses are run on the individual observations, a 30-minute average has 14400 related quality flag outcomes. Applying the data quality framework, the 14400 outcomes are summarized into 24 quality metrics (Figure 2, panel 1). Similarly, if one is only interested in sensor measurements that failed sensor tests and QA/QC analyses, the number of quality metrics can be reduced to 8, i.e., the $QM_{1.1-1.8}$ (Figure 2, panel 2). The outcomes of the quality flags can be further reduced to a single quality metric if one is only interested in the percent of sensor measurements that have 1 or more failed quality flags, (Figure 2, panel 3). Additionally, the data quality information can be entirely condensed into a single quality flag by applying the final quality flag concept (Figure 2, panel 4).

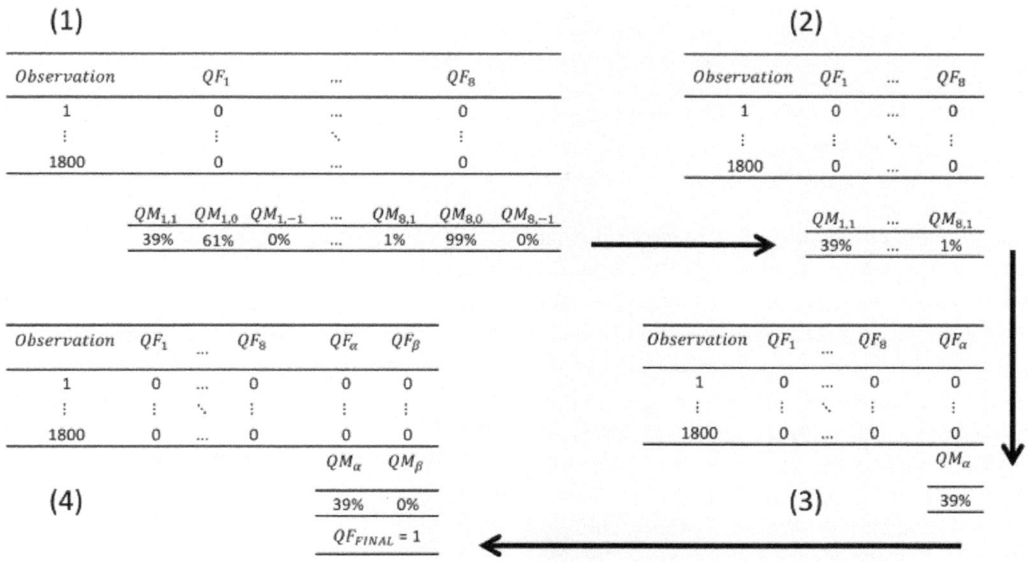

Figure 2. Different ways data quality information can be condensed for a 30-minute average of a sensor sampled at 1 Hz with 8 quality flags. (1) The 14400 flag outcomes are condensed into 24 quality metrics. (2) The 14400 flag outcomes are condensed down to 8 quality metrics representing failed analyses only. (3) The 14400 flag outcomes are reduced to 1 quality metric representing the percentage of sensor measurements that failed 1 or more analysis. (4) The 14400 flag outcomes are condensed to a final quality flag.

Data Description

Preliminary, error-injected data from a NEON tower site in Sterling, Colorado, from January 2013, is used to illustrate how this framework can be applied to ecological data. The Sterling tower site (40.461903° N, -103.029266° E, altitude: 1364 m asl) is located in an agricultural field in the eastern plains of Colorado. Here, the triple redundant aspirated air temperature (TRAAT) measurement, which is located on the top of the Sterling tower, is assessed. The temperature measurement is captured at a rate of 1 Hz, however the techniques presented here can be applied to any sampling rate.

The tower top temperature measurement is made via 3 platinum resistance thermometers (PRTs) that are housed in a fan aspirated radiation shield. Under the NEON's current framework each 1 Hz TRAAT observation has 1 sensor test and 8 associated QA/QC analyses, which inform the overall data quality of 1- and 30-minute average data products. However, for simplicity here we only examine the outcome of 3 of these quality analyses for a 10-minute TRAAT average. First, the range test flags TRAAT measurements that are outside of a realistic temperature range for a given location and season. Second, the null test assesses the number of dropped observations over a given period of time. Third, the averaging flag indicates how the final 1 Hz TRAAT measurement is calculated from the 3 PRT measurements. The averaging flag consists of 8 possible outcomes, which represent the different ways the PRTs can be averaged to determine a 1 Hz TRAAT measurement. In order to understand how the 8 averaging flag outcomes originate, the algorithm used to calculate a TRAAT measurement is briefly discussed.

Following the conversion of the 3 PRT measurements to degrees Celsius, pairwise differences are computed among the PRT measurements (i.e., T_{1-3}) with corresponding time stamps, as follows:

$$\Delta T_{12} = |T_1 - T_2|$$
$$\Delta T_{23} = |T_2 - T_3|$$
$$\Delta T_{31} = |T_3 - T_1| \quad \textbf{(8)}$$

Next, the differences among the sensor measurements are compared to their associated uncertainties (i.e., $u12$, $u23$ and $u31$), and true and false statements are used to determine whether the PRTs within the TRAAT sensor are operating normally. Under normal operation, if sufficient aspiration is present and the PRTs are functioning properly, the variation among the 3 sensor measurements should not be greater than their associated measurement uncertainties, Eq. (9)–(11).

The uncertainty of the PRT measurements can be attributed to a number of quantifiable and unquantifiable sources. For example, we can quantify uncertainties that arise from the sensor calibration and the data acquisition system. Alternatively, temperature bias from radiative forcing can be minimized through active aspiration. Yet, we cannot entirely quantify its residual effect on the sensor measurement. NEON is currently in the process of determining uncertainty estimates for both PRT calibrations as well as the data acquisition system. Thus, for this example, a manufacturer accuracy specification of $\pm 0.3^\circ C$ at $0^\circ C$ in addition to an estimated aspiration bias of $\pm 0.03^\circ C$ are combined to an uncertainty threshold of $\pm 0.66^\circ C$ for the pairwise differences. However, once the sensor calibration and data acquisition system uncertainty have been fully characterized, the uncertainty estimates will become specific to each individual sensor and temperature specific.

$$A = \begin{vmatrix} True & if\ (\Delta T_{12} \leq u_{12}) \\ False & otherwise \end{vmatrix} \quad \textbf{(9)}$$

$$B = \begin{vmatrix} True & if\ (\Delta T_{23} \leq u_{23}) \\ False & otherwise \end{vmatrix} \quad \textbf{(10)}$$

$$C = \begin{vmatrix} True & if\ (\Delta T_{31} \leq u_{31}) \\ False & otherwise \end{vmatrix} \quad \textbf{(11)}$$

Once the differences among sensor measurements have been compared to their respective uncertainties, the results from Eq. (9)–(11) are evaluated against the logic shown in Table 1. This determines which averaging operator is used to compute the resulting, 1 Hz averaged TRAAT measurement. For problem tracking purposes an averaging flag is set to correspond to the averaging operator that was used, which under normal operation should remain set to zero.

The assessed 10-minute period of error-injected TRAAT data consists of 600 1 Hz temperature averages and 1800 individual PRT sensor measurements (Figure 3). Since quality analyses are applied to the averaged 1 Hz TRAAT measurements, a total of 1800 quality flag outcomes associated with the averaging flag (600), range (600), and null (600) quality analyses were generated for the 10-minute temperature average of $-2.73^\circ C$.

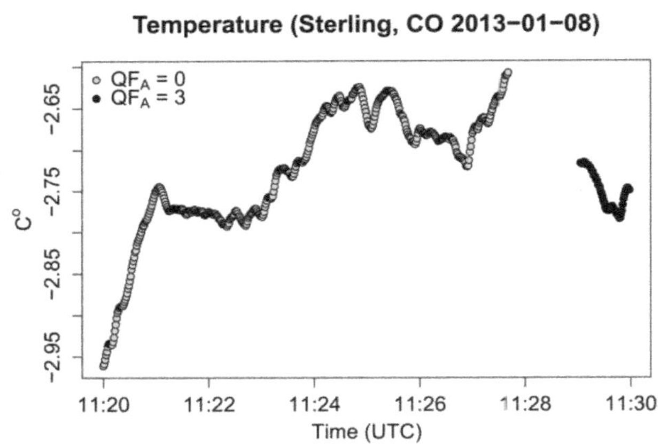

Figure 3. TRAAT from the NEON Sterling CO site, each circle indicates an averaged 1 Hz sensor measurement. The open gray circles indicate that the average of the 3 PRTs was used in the TRAAT calculation. Alternatively, the full black circles indicate that the TRAAT 1 Hz sensor measurement was calculated as the average of PRT 1 and PRT 2, i.e., averaging flag set to 3 in Table 1.

Application of Data Quality Framework

Applying the quality framework to the TRAAT sensor tests and QA/QC analyses, the 1800 quality flag outcomes were condensed to the 14 quality metrics shown in Table 5. $QM_\alpha = 14\%$ and $QM_\beta = 9\%$ were determined based on the criterion shown in Eq. (12)and (13). Using Eq. (7) we found $QF_{FINAL} = 1$, i.e., the 10-minute TRAAT average was deemed not valid.

$$QF_\alpha = \begin{cases} 1 & if\ QF_{RANGE} = 1 \vee QF_{NULL} = 1 \vee QF_{AVE}(7) = 1 \\ 0 & otherwise \end{cases} \quad \textbf{(12)}$$

Table 5. The associated quality metrics for the 10-minute TRAAT average.

Quality Metric	Outcome (%)
$QM_{RANGE}(0)$	100
$QM_{RANGE}(1)$	0
$QM_{RANGE}(-1)$	0
$QM_{NULL}(0)$	86
$QM_{NULL}(1)$	14
$QM_{NULL}(-1)$	0
QM_{AVE} (0)	77
$QM_{AVE}(1)$	0
$QM_{AVE}(2)$	0
QM_{AVE} (3)	9
QM_{AVE} (4)	0
QM_{AVE} (5)	0
QM_{AVE} (6)	0
$QM_{AVE}(7)$	0

QM_{RANGE} represent the quality metric results from the range test, QM_{NULL} represent the quality metric results from the null test, and QM_{AVE} represent the quality metric results from the averaging flag as shown in Table 1.
doi:10.1371/journal.pone.0112249.t005

$$QF_{\beta}=\begin{cases}1 & \text{if } QF_{RANGE}=-1 \vee QF_{NULL}=-1 \vee QF_{AVE}(1,...,6)=1\\ 0 & \text{otherwise}\end{cases} \quad \textbf{(13)}$$

The quality metrics indicated that the observed PRT temperatures remained within a realistic range throughout 10-minute time period. However, the quality metric for the null analysis indicated that 14% of the observations were missing. In order to determine when the null flags occurred the quality report was examined to identify the individual flag results. The quality report indicated that all of the null flags were consecutive, which was verified when plotting the averaged 1 Hz TRAAT measurements (Figure 3).

Assessing the quality metrics produced by the averaging flag indicated that the majority of 1 Hz TRAAT measurements were made by averaging all 3 PRTs. However, 9% of the observations had an averaging flag of 3, indicating that only PRT 1 and PRT 2 within the TRAAT sensor were used (Table 5). The averaging flag was used to backtrack which of the 1 Hz TRAAT averages were calculated from less than 3 PRT observations (highlighted in black in Figure 3).

Through the assessment of the quality analyses it became apparent that after a series of consecutive nulls, the averaged TRAAT measurements changed from being determined by the average of the 3 PRTs to the average of only 2 of the PRTs. This may indicate that either a PRT or another part of the sensor malfunctioned. In practice, data following this 10-minute average should be inspected to determine whether it is necessary to issue a trouble ticket and have the TRAAT sensor physically inspected.

The error-injected result from the TRAAT sensor is just 1 example of the quality framework's ability to allow a user to more efficiently assess data quality. If the final quality flag indicates that there may be issues with the data, one can subsequently inspect the quality summary and quality report to extract specific information. This enables one to efficiently identify areas of interest for detailed inspection, instead of having to inspect the entire data set. In addition, as seen with the TRAAT results, the quality framework can expedite trouble shooting and backtracking procedures, as well as assist with algorithm development. For example, if one wanted to test new QA/QC analyses the quality summary could aid in quickly identifying whether or not these analyses were generating too many false positives and/or negatives, while the quality report could be used to target the specific problem areas.

DISCUSSION AND CONCLUSIONS

Coupled with the increasing number of measurements collected by researchers, comes the need for a framework to interpret their quality. Manual assessments of data quality may still be possible for physically collected samples. Yet, automated data collection often necessitates the automation of data quality assessments as well, which can become difficult to interpret for large data sets. Thus, in order to add the final automation step for assessing data quality, we have presented an integrated, transferable, and scalable data quality framework methodology. These methods could be readily refined and expanded upon to develop more complex summarization methodologies for specific issues and/or data types.

The data quality framework is flexible and allows its components to be altered or recombined in various ways to support specific areas of interest. For instance, the framework supports assessing the track record of a sensor because all of the sensor test and quality analysis information remains embedded. Thus, a sensor's track record is represented through the quality report and quality summary. The time period that is summarized through the data quality framework could be altered if one wanted to examine a sensor's track record at different granularities.

Similarly, a degrading sensor could be identified by assessing its quality metrics for a particular test of interest. There are a number of quality analyses that have and/or could be developed to aid in tracking the degradation of a sensor, and the quality framework could be employed to summarize the results so that they could be readily interpreted. Additionally, quality metrics could be incorporated into automated routines to generate trouble tickets for specific issues, and could be used as inputs for further in-depth quality analyses.

The most notable property of the presented data quality framework is its modular nature, which permits its use with a freely selectable array of data types, tests, and processing steps. The quality framework can be constructed or deconstructed in different forms, in order to allow it to be used on different spatial and temporal scales. For example, terrestrial physical sampling such as species counts, may initially only utilize the QF_x portion of the framework to determine whether or not an observation had 1 or more failed quality analyses. Likewise, physical samples collected for aquatic analyses, such as phytoplankton biomass, may employ similar components of the quality framework. On the other hand, aquatic sensor measurements are likely to use components of the quality framework that are similar to those used by the TRAAT sensor. The framework can also be arranged in a cascading manor to handle multiple data streams and processing steps that result in a single estimate, e.g., of the surface-atmosphere exchange.

ACKNOWLEDGMENTS

We wish to thank Ted Hart for his valuable suggestions and discussions throughout the preparation of the manuscript as well as the anonymous reviewers for their insightful comments. Data was provided by the NEON.

AUTHOR CONTRIBUTIONS

Conceived and designed the experiments: DES SM JRT. Performed the experiments: DES SM. Analyzed the data: DES. Contributed reagents/materials/analysis tools: DES SM. Wrote the paper: DES SM JRT.

REFERENCES

1. Schimel D, Keller M, Berukoff S, Kao R, Loescher HW, et al.. (2011) NEON science strategy: Enabling continental-scale ecological forecasting. National Ecological Observatory Network, Boulder, Colorado, Available:www.neoninc.org/science/sciencestrategy, Accessed 20 October 2014.
2. Keller M, Schimel DS, Hargrove WW, Hoffman FM (2008) A continental strategy for the National Ecological Observatory Network. Frontiers in Ecology and the Environment 6: 282–284 doi:[]10.1890/1540-9295(2008)6[282:ACSFTN]2.0.CO.
3. Taylor JR, Loescher HL (2013) Automated quality control methods for sensor data: A novel observatory approach. Biogeosciences 10: 4957–4971 doi:10.5194/bg-10-4957-2013.
4. EPA (2006) Data quality assessment: A reviewers guide (QA/G-9R). Technical report, Environmental Protection Agency, Available:http://www.epa.gov/quality/qa_docs.html, Accessed 2014 October 20.
5. Wang RY, Storey VC, Firth CP (1995) A framework for analysis of data quality research. IEEE Transactions on Knowledge and Data Engineering 7: 623–643 doi:10.1109/69.404034.
6. Mauder M, Cuntz M, Drüe C, Graf A, Rebmann C, et al. (2013) A strategy for quality and uncertainty assessment of long-term eddy-covariance measurements. Agricultural and Forest Meteorology 169: 122–135 doi:10.1016/j.agrformet.2012.09.006.
7. Mauder M, Foken T (2011) Documentation and instruction manual of the eddy-covariance software package TK3. Arbeitsergebnisse, Universität Bayreuth, Abt. Mikrometeorologie, 46, 60 p., Available: http://www.bayceer.uni-bayreuth.de/mm/de/software/software/software_dl. php?id_obj=96786, Accessed 2014 October 20.
8. Göckede M, Rebmann C, Foken T (2004) A combination of quality assessment tools for eddy covariance measurements with footprint modelling for the characterization of complex sites. Agricultural and Forest Meteorology 127: 175–188 doi:10.1016/j.agrformet.2004.07.012.

CHAPTER 16

ITEPE: A SOURCE TRACING ALGORITHM FOR THE MICROBLOG

Xueyan Zhou[1,2], Jing Yang[1], Zehong Lin[2], Jianpei Zhang[1]

[1] College of Computer Science and Technology, Harbin Engineering University, Harbin, China

[2] College of Engineering, Harbin University, Harbin, China

ABSTRACT

Finding the true source of a social network is a crucial component of social network information tracing. Using the new media microblog as an example, this paper provides a source tracing algorithm ITEPE (Initiators and Early Participants Extraction) to solve this problem. First, the cascade (session tree) is built according to the retweeting of a microblog, after which the cascade set (session forest) is clustered by topical relevance. Second, real initiators are identified through the user relationship network and information cascade network. The influence index and conformity index of every node is then iteratively calculated according to text sentiment analysis and information cascades and the early important participants are extracted. Finally, the real initiators and early participants are evaluated through an experiment.

INTRODUCTION

As an online social media tool, the microblog has experienced rapid development in recent times. Microblogs allow users to broadcast messages and share feelings and information at any time, and these messages are automatically pushed to friends' homepages, forming the automatic propagation mechanism. The microblog has become a concentrated expression and reflection of public opinion on the Internet, which largely affects public opinion in general [1]. Although the spread range of messages in daily life is small, the development of social networks has amplified it greatly. For example, public opinion originating on social networks spreads quickly and easily due to diverse information, powerful interactivity and other advantages that traditional media cannot match; however, fuzzy and false information can also appear on social media. Harmful information can be propagated across regions and borders through open-ended communication, particularly reactionary rhetoric attacking social stability. Thus, source tracing research is necessary to quell rumors. The current study focuses on topic detection and tracking. Source tracing research is limited. Information propagated through microblogging spreads quickly, reaching larger audiences and exerting a wider influence than information disseminated through other channels, rendering it difficult to trace. Source tracing and the identification of events and key figures in microblog propagation has become a significant problem in need of a solution. Therefore, quantifying the participation degree of users, confirming the topic source and extracting key persons are the key foci of this paper.

Source tracing includes mining the true initiator and early important participants because some users simply repost or directly copy other's blog messages, with the result that the early participants are sometimes more important than the

Citation: Zhou X, Yang J, Lin Z, Zhang J (2014) ITEPE: A Source Tracing Algorithm for the Microblog. PLoS ONE 9(10): e111380. doi:10.1371/journal.pone.0111380.

initiators. To determine these important nodes, this paper presents the ITEPE source tracing algorithm. The forwarded cascades (session tree) are built and the cascade sets (session forest) are then clustered according to topic relevance. Second, the real initiators are determined through a combination of user networks and information cascade networks. The influence index and conformity index of every node are then iteratively calculated according to text sentiment analysis and information cascades and the early important participants are extracted. The real initiators and early participants will be obtained and evaluated through an experiment. Compared to previous studies, the ITEPE algorithm has the ability to trace back to the information source through microblog retweeting cascades. Related research has not been identified.

There have been recent several studies on the social network information diffusion model, and multiple algorithms extract social networks from a group of the most influential nodes. The basic idea is that these nodes will disseminate information more widely, including information dissemination predicted by analyzing the blog information cascade [2], [3]. According to Dabeer [4], who analyzed the factors affecting microblog information dissemination, including information characteristics and the activity, response and out-degree of fan nodes, the information dissemination speed of microblogs is faster than that of traditional blogs and their propagation models differ. Dabeer further proposed a decision making framework based on Markov to measure the effectiveness of information dissemination. Lehmann [5] tracked the hashtag diffusion process in the Twitter network and discovered that epidemic spread models play an important role. Yang [6] predicted the speed, size and scope of microblog information dissemination, and Tsur [7] combined content and network topology by using linear regression to predict the diffusion of information within a given timeframe.

This paper differs from the existing studies in two ways. First, most of the existing algorithms extract and sort the high-influence nodes but do not consider topic relevancy. Yang [8] presented a linear influence model using microblog network relationships to predict the diffusion path and provide the global diffusion capacity of each node. The number of studies focusing on the information source remains relatively small. Recent studies show that the dissemination of information does not depend on the most influential person but on the mutual influence among those likely to be affected [9]. An important conclusion of the study is that early important participants are more influential than the message initiator in the information dissemination cascade. Our research will focus on the traceability research of the microblog information spread cascade, including the true information initiator and early important participants. Second, the topic-based emotion subgraph is proposed to analyze the influence and conformity index in cascade sets to mine the key person.

Retweets from microblogs are the main data mining objects because retweets are the basis of information dissemination, influence analysis, sentiment analysis, topic discovery and evolution, and so on. Therefore, the study of microblog retweeting helps us understand the information diffusion mechanism. Macskassy [10] showed that the majority of users do not necessarily retweet familiar topics. Yang [11] studied the Twitter retweeting mechanism with results indicating that approximately 1/4 of published microblog tweets are retweets of friends' posts. Welch [12] studied the semantic information of the follow and retweeting relationship and found that the latter has stronger topical relevance. Pal and Counts [13] assessed and sorted users' authority using the number of original tweets, participants in the session and retweeting as a primary index; their model used a large calculation quantity Gaussian mixture model to calculate the user influence, which is not suitable for traceability research. Meanwhile, the user influence assessment based on information must address many different languages, dialects, pictures and videos, and so on. Therefore, we must use a simple method to gather accurate information such that only the cascade and the topology are used to study traceability without semantic mining, and only positive and negative emotions are used to assess influence while ignoring the impact of information in different formats.

The influence of microblogs can be understood as a user being affected by other users in such a way as to change his or her behavior. There are two separate approaches to key person extraction in social networks: the approach based on context roles and that based on social network structures. The most common key person extraction methods rely on various centrality measures for each node separately. These algorithms, however, lack a holistic view, and the node position in a social community is determined by its neighborhoods, such as degree prestige and degree centrality. There are also global algorithms, such as proximity prestige, rank prestige, node position, eccentricity and closeness centrality. Many studies have examined various domains (influence spread, public opinion analysis and terrorist group analysis) in this area [14]–[17]. Most existing influence analysis algorithms are improved using traditional algorithms. Cha et al. used indegree, retweets and mentions to measure individual influence on Twitter. Additionally, influence can be measured by diffusion ability, as in Bakshy [19], who used Twitter data URL structures to build the cascade propagation tree and measured node influence on its diffusion range. Steeg [20] suggested a measure of causal relationships between nodes based on the information-theoretic notion of transfer entropy, or information transfer. Most of these methods, however, only consider node influence and ignore the conformity assessment. The purpose of social network traceability is to find the information source. Thus, the information initiators and early important nodes are the main mining objects. However, the existing algorithms cannot meet this demand, so we use the topic-based cascade and users' topologies to confirm the information source by calculating the influence index and conformity index. The result sets include true information initiators and early participants.

METHODS

We introduce some of the related terms and concepts of the microblog information cascade in Table 1.

Table 1. Symbol profile.

Symbols	Semantics
C^i	Cascade i
T^i	Timestamp when the first message appears in C^i
φ^i	Set of all message that appeared in C^i
ς	Topic-based cascade set
G_T	Social network cascade set based on topic T
$\Phi(v)$	Node Influence Index
$\Omega(v)$	Node Conformity Index
IT_T	Effective initiator of topic T
EP_T	Early participants of topic T
KP_T	Key persons for the sourcing of topic T

doi:10.1371/journal.pone.0111380.t001

The cascade in microblogs

Users can publish their feelings and ideas via microblogs, which are composed of text, pictures and corresponding comments. A very important element of a post is the comments section, which allows for discussions. The microblog has become an important tool for information dissemination and for this reason, learning more about the microblog information diffusion mechanism is important for the establishment of a new concept of rapid development communication.

We build the user relationship network and retweeting network for the microblog. The retweeting network is the topic-based cascade. Fig. 1 presents the two networks.

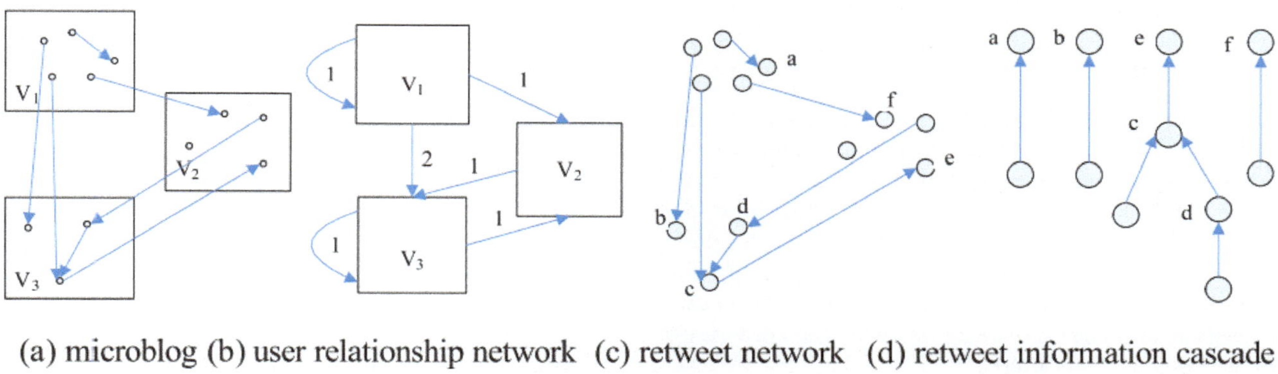

Figure 1. Relationship in microblog.

Fig. 1 (a) describes the microblog relationship, G=(V, E). V is the user and E is the retweet or comment. Fig. 1 (b) is the user relationship network, where the weighted edges represent the number of interactions. The network reflects the users' friends' relationships, but everyone has different interests and individuals will not retweet all of their friends' posts. Thus, the user relationship network cannot reflect true influence and can be used to assist analysis topic-based key people. The retweeting network (Fig. 1(c)) breaks through the friend relationship limitation and solely considers the information cascade (Fig. 1(d)) of retweeting and commenting behavior in a time sequence. An information cascade is also known as a session tree, and the outdegree of its initiator is 0. The other out-degrees link to the initiator or participators to form the information cascade through retweeting, sharing, comments, and so forth. Thus, the outdegrees have the opposite influence of the directed edge. The isolated nodes do not possess retweeted information from others (for instance, the isolated node in Fig. 1(c)). This study considers only the information that can be retweeted at least once.

Influence Index and Conformity Index

The influence index measures an individual's capacity to influence others, while the conformity index is the degree to which an individual is affected by others. High-influence individuals' social networks are those whose views and opinions are always accepted, indicating that emotional factors need to be considered in microblog key person extraction. Similar to the behavior of other networks, microblog retweeting mainly includes positive and negative emotions. In Fig. 1 (b), an edge from node a to node b means agree or disagree with b, where the agreement edges are marked as positive (+) or negative (−). Studies have shown that network information dissemination depends on mutual influence among people who are easily affected by others. Thus, the conformity index should be considered along with the influence analysis. Using the emotional inclination analysis method [18], we can find the emotional labeled directed graph G (V, E), where each edge is marked as positive or negative. The emotional labeling of the information is shown in Fig. 2 (a).

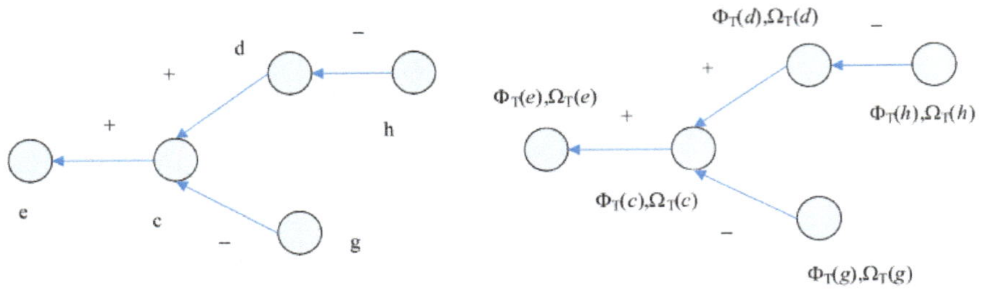

(a) information cascade after emotional labeling (b) indices results of cascade

Figure 2. Information cascade after emotional labeling and index calculation.

$E^{+}=\{ce, dc\}$ indicates positive emotion and $E^{-}=\{hd,gc\}$ indicates negative emotion. The G(V,E) is composed of the positive subgraph $G^{+}(V,E^{+})$ and the negative subgraph $G^{-}(V,E^{-})$. The influence index $\Phi(v)$ and conformity index $\Omega(v)$ of node v in G are as follows: $\Phi(v)=\sum_{uv\in E+}\Omega(u)-\sum_{uv\in E-}\Omega(u)$ $\Omega(v)=\sum_{vu\in E+}\Phi(u)-\sum_{vu\in E-}\Phi(u)$

The two indices should be calculated using a recursive loop. All $v\in V$ in a certain subject T can be initialized by $\Phi_T(v)=\Omega_T(v)=1$. The convergence results are shown in Fig. 2 (b).

ITEPE Algorithm

The size of the information propagation is determined in the first steps, so the extraction of information initiators and early important participants is important in public opinion analysis. Initiators are those users with the original information, but some users have the habit of directly copying others' blog posts. Thus, these nodes must be deleted using the user relationship network. The term 'early important participants' refers to early participants with higher levels of influence. The core idea of ITEPE is shown in Algorithm 1.

Algorithm 1: The ITEPE algorithm

Input: Social Network $G\ (V, E)$

Output: Keyperson$_T$ for each topic T

1) Begin
2) $C\leftarrow$**ExtractCascade** (G);
3) IF C is context-aware then
4) $\varsigma\leftarrow$**ExtractSubgraph**(C);
5) else
6) $\varsigma=\{C\}$
7) for each $G_T\in\varsigma$ do
8) $IT_T\leftarrow$**ExtractInitiator**(G_T)
9) if G_T is not a signed network then
10) $(G^{+}_T(V_T,E^{+}_T))$, $(G^{-}_T(V_T,E^{-}_T))$ $\leftarrow$**EdgeLabel**(G_T);
11) (Φ_T, Ω_T) $\leftarrow$**IndexCompute**$(G^{+}_T(V_T,E^{+}_T))$, $(G^{-}_T(V_T,E^{-}_T))$;
12) $EP_T\leftarrow$ **EarlyParticipants**(Φ_T, Ω_T)
13) $KP_T\leftarrow(IT_T,EP_T)$
14) End

First, the retweeting cascades are extracted from microblog data from defined periods and divided into several cascade sets based on context awareness. Second, true initiators IT_T are confirmed for a certain topic T using the user relationship network. The emotional label, influence index and conformity index are then calculated to obtain the early important participants EP_T. The union set of IT_T and EP_T is the key person K_T for microblog information traceability. The algorithm includes six main parts: ExtractCascade, ExtractSubgraph, ExtractInitiator, EdgeLabel, IndexCompute and EarlyParticipants six main parts.

(1) ExtractCascade is shown in Algorithm 2, where edge E in the social network can be understood as a minimum cascade. The two existing cascades are merged if they intersect. Linear and explosive spreads are two extreme cases, with the actual cascade generally falling somewhere in between.

Algorithm 2: The ExtractCascade algorithm.

Input: Social network G (V, E), E= $\{e_1, e_2, \ldots e_m\}$ is the retweet relationship

Output: A set of isolated cascades $C=\{c^1, c^2,\ldots, c^s\}$

1) Begin
2) initialize each cascade as a single link $C\leftarrow E$;
3) **while** $\exists c^p$, c^q and $c^p\cap c^q\neq\emptyset$ **do**
4) **forall** c^i, $c^j\in C$ **and** $c^i\neq c^j$ **do**
5) **if** $\varphi^i\cap\varphi^j$ **then**
6) add j to i: $c^i\leftarrow c^i, c^j$;
7) remove j: $C\leftarrow C\backslash\{c^j\}$;
8) End

(2) There are many latent semantic mining algorithms that have useful applications for social networking data (e.g., LDA). The microblog contains more obvious topic information, and most microblog posts on the same topic are nearly identical. Thus, the keyword matching method can be used for the topic-based

subgraph extraction, the core idea being to cluster the cascade based on the same keywords. For example, topic T has keywords $\{k_1,k_2,k_3\}$, and the cascade set G_T is composed of the cascades that contain those three keywords.

(3) Based on G_T, the ExtractInitiator extraction algorithm finds all of the source nodes and the corresponding timestamps to determine an effective initiator. Some users directly copy other users' blog posts, so these nodes must be deleted using the user relationship network. The goal is to analyze the relationships among all of the source nodes and delete the nodes that republish the same topical information to their friends.

(4) $E=\{uv\}$ means u retweets v, and $\forall E\in c^i\subset G_T$. E is identified as positive emotions E^+ with no comments; the emotion word table was used to calculate the emotional inclination of comments [21]. If the comments contain several emotional words, we take the average. Make $E\rightarrow E^+$ when the value is greater than 0.5, and $E\rightarrow E^-$ otherwise.

(5) If $\forall v\in c^i\subset G_T,\Phi(v)=\Omega(v)=1$, then the influence index $\Phi(v)$ and conformity index $\Omega(v)$ are iteratively calculated and normalized.

(6) T^T=Earliest$\{T^i|c_i\subset G_T\}$ is the timestamp of G_T, $\forall v\in c^i\subset G_T$, and $\tau=\Phi(v)/\Omega(v)$. Thus, the early important participants v should satisfy earlier T^v and higher τ.

EXPERIMENTS

Dataset

The dataset comes from China's well-known Sina microblog. The Sina microblog opened to the public in October 2009 and today possesses nearly 600 million registered users, nearly 100 million of whom are daily users. Microblog information is characterized by timeliness, and most topics will fade quickly from view. The experimental dataset uses partial data from January 2013 (a total of 85,116,132 posts) for analysis. Because the proposed algorithm analyzes microblog information traceability, the isolated nodes should be deleted. Subjects of blog posts include people's work, the economy, entertainment, education, sports and other fields (e.g., Spring Festival travel was the subject of 4,728,674 posts and haze, the subject of 2,389,428 posts).

Cascade Extraction

Although the isolated nodes have been deleted, nearly 76% of the cascade extraction results are less than or equal to 3. Table 2 compares the cascade extraction results of microblogs and blogs [3]. The 204 cascades with different topologies were extracted from the data. The most common cascade is a simple cascade with only one retweet. The 12 highest frequency topology structures are shown is Fig. 3. First, the cascades are arranged in descending order according to the frequency of occurrence (G1 has the highest frequency). Second, the cascade shape is divided into chain and star two categories. The chain with a node in a layer focuses on depth dissemination, and the star with several nodes in a layer focuses on the breadth of spread. In our experiments, the star appears more frequently than the chain in the same cascade scale (e.g., G2 has a higher frequency than G4, and G8 has a higher frequency than G12). Additionally, multiple initiations cannot occur in microblog retweeting, so the cascade topology has only one root node.

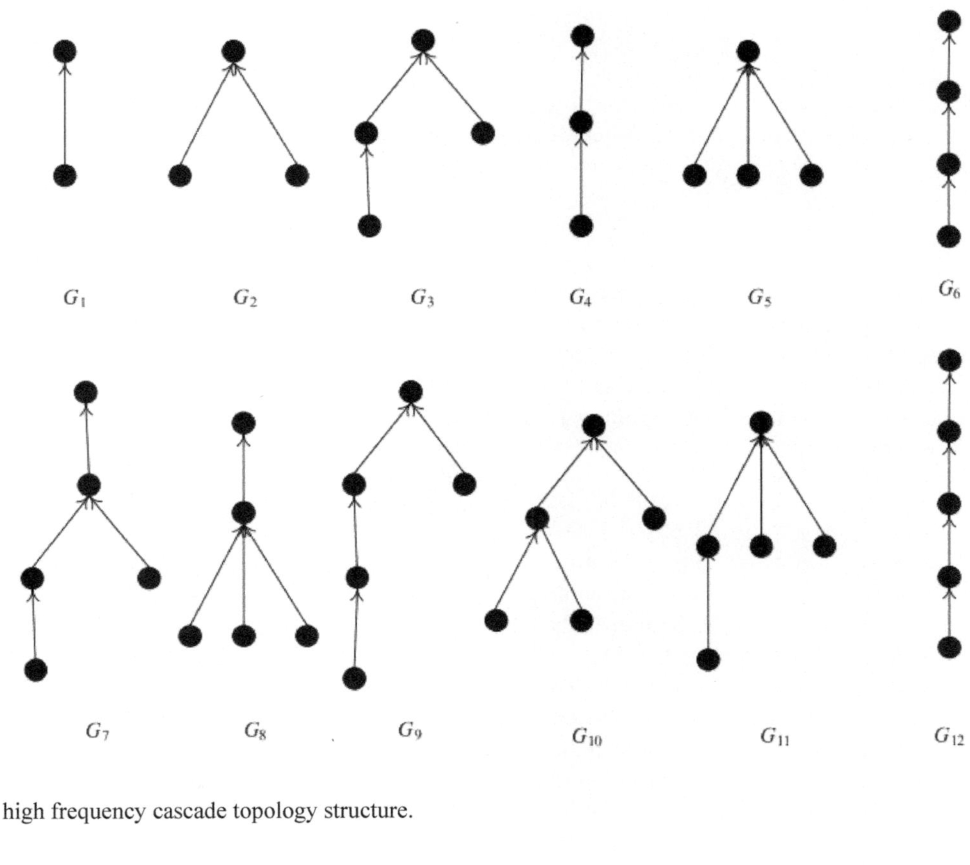

Figure 3. Basic high frequency cascade topology structure.

Table 2. Comparison of cascade extraction data.

Microblog index		Blog index	
Nodes (User ID)	1,824,955	Number of blogs	156,195
Edges (Number of retweets)	96,439	Edges (Number of hyperlinks)	340,124
Number of microblog texts	82,123,008	Number of posts	873,469
Number of cascades	48743	Number of cascades	7,269
Cascades size ≤2	24529	Cascades size ≤2	5674
Cascades size =3	12472	Cascades size =3	883
Cascades size ≥3	11742	Cascades size ≥3	712

doi:10.1371/journal.pone.0111380.t002

The microblog cascades that appear in table 2 are also largely simple cascades, but the probability that a cascade forms is higher than a blog, which indicates that the information in a microblog is more fluid. The significant difference in the high frequency simple cascade topology has two main aspects: (1) blogs have more chains and microblogs have more star structures because on a microblog, every piece of information is pushed on to friends, which increases the probability of it being retweeted simultaneously; and 2) blog cascades can contain multiple initiators and blog posts can contain multiple hyperlinks, but retweeting behavior in a microblog setting can only be performed by an initiator.

Topic-based Subgraph Extractions

The keyword matching method can complete the topic-based subgraph extraction, the core idea of which is clustering the cascades around the same keywords, i.e., topic T has keywords $\{k_1,k_2,k_3\}$ and cascade set G_T is composed of the cascades that contain those three keywords. For instance, the keywords for January 2013 describe new traffic rules {running yellow lights, new traffic rules, 6-point deduction} and the cascades contain any keywords composed of a new set for information traceability mining. Some particularly widespread events of relatively long durations (e.g., Spring Festival travel and the Spring Festival Gala) will have larger cascade sets. For instance, there are 4,728,674 posts regarding Spring Festival travel, 2,389,428 posts regarding haze and 1,425,510 posts containing the phrase "I am a singer." This type of information attracts public discussion and comments and the traceability is insignificant. Thus, this paper mainly focuses on emergencies and false information traceability, which are of relatively short duration but have a greater influence on public opinion. Table 3 shows the microblog events set for subsequent traceability research.

Table 3. Events and main index.

No.	Microblog events	Version numbers	Retweeting numbers
1	Homeowners series of events cited attention	2812	19991
2	Heilongjiang women's petitions	1427	12797
3	Yuan Longping recommended that the government should treat waste as a criminal act	1347	22218
4	Wenzhou posted two session road closures annunciate cited attention	943	24803
5	Jiangxi Secondary School students punished in playground	742	14510
6	Stewardess purchasing sentenced to 11 years and second trial made controversy	630	11609
7	Hubei Huangshi mobilized preparation the country unannounced inspection 98 days in advance	574	5772
8	Censorship of James Bond film	544	18391
9	Li Yundi was elected as Chongqing CPPCC members	319	12546

doi:10.1371/journal.pone.0111380.t003

The version numbers in the experiments are the number of cascades; a post and its associated retweets form a cascade. Because the same posts are often copied or minimally edited for reposting, the version numbers are generally much larger than the news numbers. True information initiator mining is the first step in traceability studies.

Initiators

Although they will have the same keywords, posts about an event will focus on various interpretations of it due to different perspectives and the passage of time. S_i is the source node in cascade C_i in topic T, and the true information initiators reduce elements in set S. This mainly includes two aspects: (1) cascades of high similarity are classified as one version and only retain the earliest timestamp source node; and (2) the nodes that subsequently publish the same topic information to friends are deleted using the user relationship network. Specific ideas include analyzing the relationship between all of the source nodes and deleting the nodes that subsequently publish the same topic information to friends through horizontal text similarity. Classical text similarity measurement methods include KL relative entropy, TF-IDF, cosine distance, editing distance, and so on. The Sina microblog is similar to Twitter, allowing users to post short messages of up to 140 characters and to obtain followers. The majority of the text of similar short messages does not change, so the simple word repetition rate is used to measure text similarity, as shown in the following equation: $sim(S_i,S_j)=\frac{num(text(S_i)\cap text(S_j))}{\max\{len(S_i),len(S_j)\}}$ where $len(S_i)$ is the number of characters of S_i, $num(text(S_i)\cap text(S_j))$ is the repeated total number of characters of S_i and S_j, and a higher $sim()$ value indicates greater similarity, with a value of 1 when a post is copied directly. If $sim(S_i,S_j)$ is greater than the threshold 0.71 in the experiment, cascades C_i and C_j can be about a similar message. Table 4 shows the news version number of 9 popular microblog issues, which is far lower than the number of cascades. To mine the true information initiator, the source nodes with the earliest timestamps of every new version are examined. For instance, there are 734 versions of the No. 1 issue, which means that there are 734 possible initiators. Thus, the user relationship should be analyzed further. If a user's message is similar to that of his or her friend's earlier messages, the user can be identified as a false initiator. If $sim(S_i,S_j)$ is greater than the threshold 0.47 in the experiment and the timestamp is later than that of a friend's, then the source node will be identified as a copier. The initiators of the different issues are all within 80 in Table 4 compared to the tens of thousands of microblog information disseminators. Thus, this magnitude benefits traceability and the control of public opinion.

Table 4. Cascade set of issues.

No.	1	2	3	4	5	6	7	8	9
Cascade numbers	2812	1427	1347	943	742	630	574	544	319
Version numbers	734	254	240	334	659	226	239	289	221
Initiators	63	53	67	71	24	36	43	29	58

doi:10.1371/journal.pone.0111380.t004

A special phenomenon common to microblogs cannot be ignored: if a highly influential node retweets a message that is then widely retweeted, then the participants are more important than the initiators. Therefore, only mining the initiators in the information traceability is insufficient.

Early Important Participants

The time factor is very important in information traceability studies, whereas the average new edges of every node changes little over time and the cascade edge generation decreases exponentially [9]. Experiments show that the user relationship network is in line with the former, whereas users participating in a cascade follow the latter. Fig. 4 shows that the number of retweets together with the corresponding time of the largest cascade in the number 1 issue.

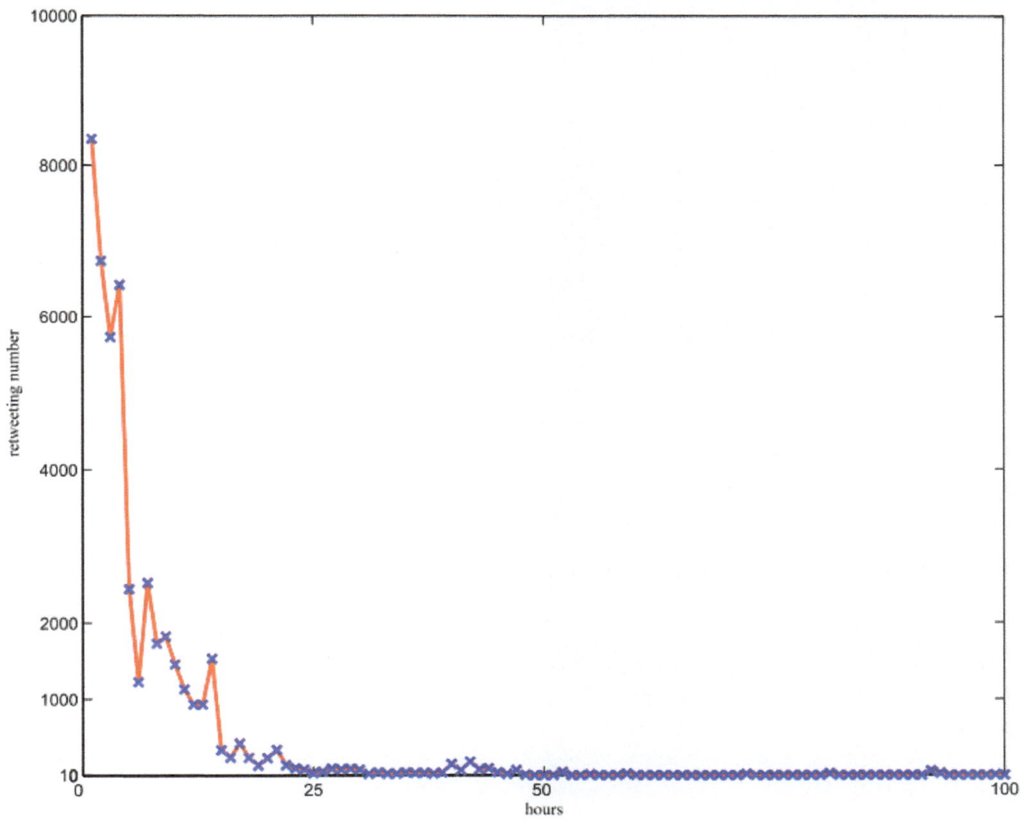

Figure 4. Retweets in a cascade over time.

Eighty-four percent of retweets are posted within 10 hours, which also highlights the rapidity of information transmission on microblogs. To identify the source accurately, the influence index and conformity index of every node will be iteratively calculated according to the text sentiment analysis and information cascade, following which the early important participants will be extracted. The early important participants have the following characteristics: (1) earlier participant time; and (2) high influence index and low conformity index.

The emotional terms and phrases were counted in the comment data [18], including both supportive words and opposing words, and the 30 items with the greatest frequency were selected. The negative terms were valued between 0.5 and 1, with larger values indicating greater opposition; likewise, the positive terms were valued between 0 and 0.5, with smaller values indicating greater support. E was identified as positive emotions E^{+} with no comments, and the emotion word table was used to calculate the emotional inclination of comments. If the comments contained several emotional words, we took the average. $E \rightarrow E^{+}$if the value is greater than 0.5; Otherwise $E \rightarrow E^{-}$.

For any $v \in c^{i} \subset G_{T}$, let $\Phi(v) = \Omega(v) = 1$. The influence index $\Phi(v)$ and conformity index $\Omega(v)$ are then iteratively calculated and normalized. The $\tau = \Phi(v)/\Omega(v)$ is defined to measure the user comprehensive influence, and the users' τ distribution across different topics is shown in Fig. 5.

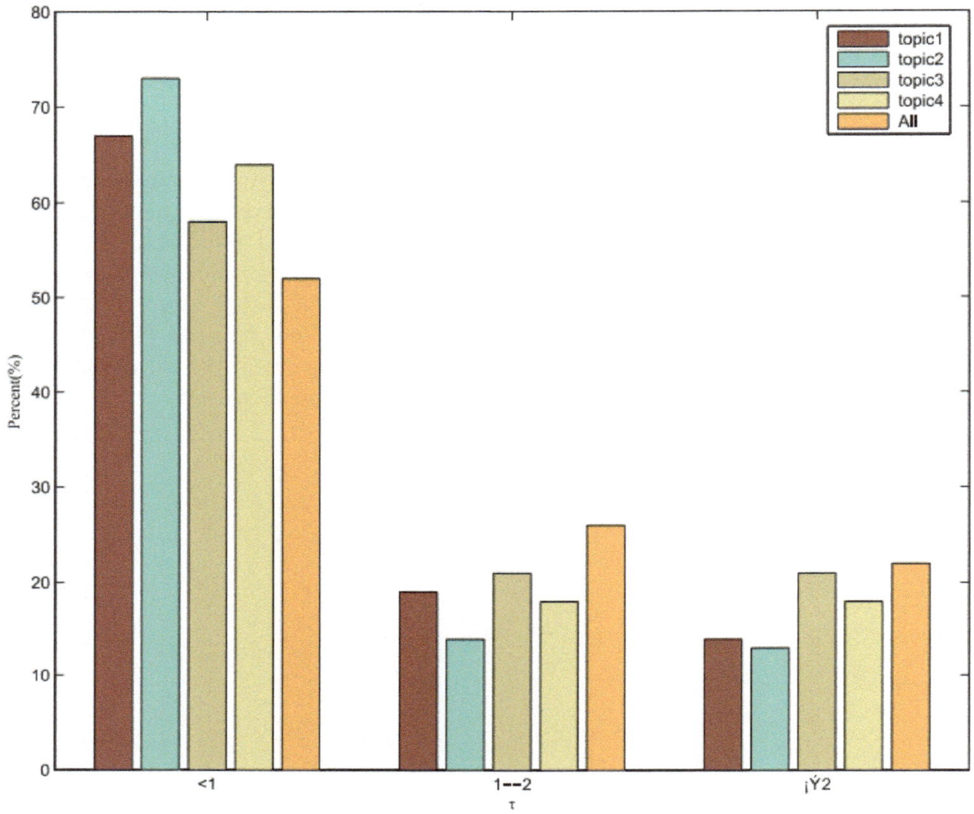

Figure 5. Comprehensive influence distribution in various topics.

The comprehensive influence indices τ for all 9 issues were analyzed. Fig. 4 presents four issues and their averages. $\tau \geq 2$ means that the influence index $\Phi(v)$ is significantly greater than the conformity index. The partial users, who make up less than 20%, can influence other users and cannot easily be affected. This indicates that there a few people who can affect the information dissemination model of the majority on microblogs.

The time factor is important in information traceability studies. Early important participant $v$should satisfy an earlier timestamp T^{v} and higher comprehensive influence indexτ. The T^{T}= Earliest $\{T^{i}|c_{i} \subset G_{T}\}$ is defined as the timestamp of G_{T}. The T^{*}= Latest $\{T^{i}|c_{i} \subset G_{T}\}$ is defined as the latest timestamp of G_{T}. For any$\forall v \in c^{i} \subset G_{T}$, T^{v} is the timestamp of v participating in cascade c^{i}. Thus, $t = T^{v} - T^{T}$. To find the early important participants with a small Δt and largerτ, the time and comprehensive influence of the users involved in different issues are analyzed in Fig. 6.

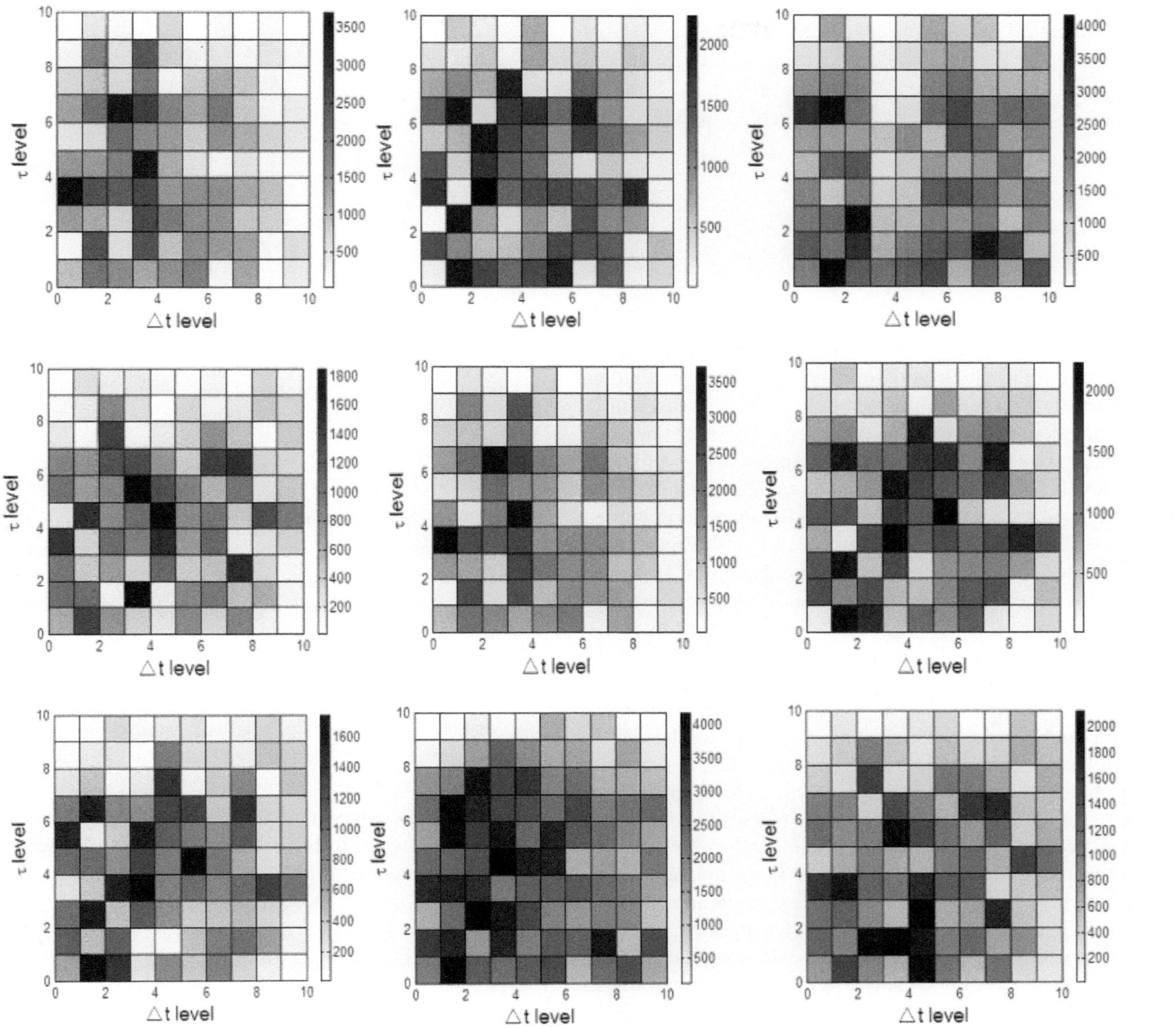

Figure 6. User influence and participation time statistics.

Because different issues have different scales over time, the quantitative classification method is adopted for comparison. Δt level divides the total during time $T^*–T^T$ into 10 sections, and the comprehensive influence level divides the difference in influence in the issue into 10 sections where for any $v \in c^i \subset G_T$, $\tau_{max}=max(\tau_v)$,$\tau_{min}=min(\tau_v)$. Thus, the coordinates of v are $(10(T^v–T^T)/(T^*–T^T)$, $10(\tau_v–\tau_{min})/(\tau_{max}–\tau_{min}))$. Additionally, a deeper color indicates that more users have different magnitudes through different issues.

It can be seen that most of the events have more active first halves and less active second halves. Some events have a second peak in the number of participants, which may be due to the propagation of a new message that reignites the issue. The users with high comprehensive influence levels are a minority, particularly in the 9th and 10th levels. The nodes in the upper left corner of the first square are the early important participants with the highest τ level and lowest Δt level, and the maximum value in all 9 topics is 101.

The Assessment and Validation of Traceability Results

Early important participants may include some initiators, so the results are the union of both. The results of all of the events in Table 3 are shown in Table 5. Thus, the information traceability results are basically locked within 131 IDs that reached the mining results. To evaluate the accuracy of the results, the following aspects must be considered: (a) whether the result set contains the earliest initiator; (b) whether a friend relationship exists between the nodes; (c) manual analysis of whether tweeted text is related to the event; and (d) whether the tweet and follower numbers are collected to analyze if they are the active nodes. √ means that the traceability results satisfy the index, and × means that the traceability results do not satisfy the index.

Table 5. Results of ITEPE.

No.	1	2	3	4	5	6	7	8	9
Initiator	63	53	67	71	24	36	43	29	58
Early important participants	86	74	101	81	61	50	39	57	37
Source nodes	120	113	104	131	74	71	69	78	85
(a)	√	√	√	√	√	√	√	√	√
(b)	×	×	×	×	√	×	×	×	√
(c)	√	√	√	√	√	√	√	√	√
(d)	√	√	√	×	√	√	×	√	√

doi:10.1371/journal.pone.0111380.t005

All of the events that reached Index (a) show that the traceability nodes contain the initiator, which also illustrates that the true information initiator is not to be missed. Finding the earliest initiator is required by the conventional sense source tracing method. From the above analysis, it can be seen that only finding one node in the traceability process is insufficient. For Index (b), if there are friends in the same cascade, then the nodes that subsequently publish the same information to their friends will be deleted, so the source nodes in the majority of the events are isolated nodes without friendship ties. However, friendships appear in the 5th and 9th issues because more than half of the subsequent messages were altered for posting. Thus, these nodes are retained to carry new information. All of the events satisfy Index (c) that tweeted text is related to an event, which is determined by the algorithm characteristic because the topic and cascade locked in by the keywords lessen the possibility of topic drift. Index (d) measures the activity of the nodes and the active nodes with more followers and larger tweet numbers. Only the 4th and 7thissues have minority inactive nodes. The inactive nodes are easily eliminated in the cascade extraction process because those messages have a smaller chance of being seen by others. Sometimes inactive nodes are independent-minded or well informed, such as a military enthusiast posting a new message to a microblog even though he does not usually use this kind of platform. In summary, the traceability results contain the earliest initiator, and most nodes are active. The algorithm controls topic drift and ensures accuracy.

CONCLUSIONS

Microblog source tracing must quickly lock in the information source, which is critical to public opinion analysis and early warning. To confirm these important nodes, ITEPE is proposed. First, the cascade (session tree) is built according to retweets in microblogs, and the cascade set (session forest) is clustered by topic relevance. Second, real initiators are identified through the user relationship network and information cascade network. The influence index and conformity index of every node is then iteratively calculated according to the text sentiment analysis and information cascade, and the early important participants are extracted. Finally, the real initiators and early participants are identified and evaluated through an experiment. Analysis of data from the Sina microblog from January 2013 yielded 9 popular events. The source tracing process combines news features, microblog information propagation characteristics, textual emotional features and user characteristics to analyze and evaluate, and the result set has high accuracy.

Author Contributions

Conceived and designed the experiments: XZ JY. Performed the experiments: ZL. Analyzed the data: JZ. Contributed reagents/materials/analysis tools: XZ. Wrote the paper: ZL.

REFERENCES

1. Zhaoyun D, Yan J, Bin Z (2014) Survey of Data Mining for Microblog. Journal of Computer Research and Development 51(4): 691–706.
2. Leskovec J, McGlohon M, Faloutsos C, Glance N, Hurst M (2007) Patterns of Cascading Behavior in Large Blog Graphs: 551–556.
3. Li H, Bhowmick SS, Sun A, Cui JT (2014) Affinity-driven blog cascade analysis and prediction. Data Mining and Knowledge Discovery 28(2): 442–474. doi: 10.1007/s10618-013-0307-0
4. Dabeer O, Mehendale P, Karnik A, Saroop A (2011) Timing Tweets to Increase Effectiveness of Information Campaigns: 105–112.
5. Lehmann J, Gonçalves B, Ramasco JJ (2012) Dynamical classes of collective attention in twitter//Proceedings of the 21st international conference on World Wide Web. ACM: 251–260.
6. Yang J, Counts S (2010) Predicting the Speed, Scale, and Range of Information Diffusion in Twitter. ICWSM 10: 355–358.
7. Tsur O, Rappoport A (2012) What's in a hashtag?: content based prediction of the spread of ideas in microblogging communities//Proceedings of the fifth ACM international conference on Web search and data mining. ACM: 643–652.
8. Yang J, Leskovec J (2010) Modeling information diffusion in implicit networks//Data Mining (ICDM): 599–608.
9. Watts DJ, Dodds PS (2007) Influentials, networks, and public opinion formation. Journal of consumer research 34(4): 441–458. doi: 10.1086/518527
10. Macskassy SA, Michelson M (2011) Why do people retweet? anti-homophily wins the day!//ICWSM: 209–216.
11. Yang Z, Guo JY, Cai KK, Tang J, Li JZ, et al.. (2010) Understanding retweeting behaviors in social networks//Proceedings of the 19th ACM international conference on Information and knowledge management. ACM: 1633–1636.
12. Welch MJ, Schonfeld U, He D, Cho JH (2011) Topical

semantics of twitter links//Proceedings of the fourth ACM international conference on Web search and data mining. ACM: 327–336.

13. Pal A, Counts S (2011) Identifying topical authorities in microblogs//Proceedings of the fourth ACM international conference on Web search and data mining. ACM: 45–54.

14. Wasserman S (1994) Social network analysis: Methods and applications. Cambridge university press.

15. Carrington PJ (2005) Models and methods in social network analysis. Cambridge university press.

16. Sabidussi G (1996) The centrality index of a graph. Psychometrika 31(4): 581–603. doi: 10.1007/bf02289527

17. Degenne A, Forsé M (1999) Introducing social networks.

18. Cha M, Haddadi H, Benevenuto F, Gummadi KP (2010) Measuring User Influence in Twitter: The Million Follower Fallacy. ICWSM 10: 10–17.

19. Bakshy E, Hofman JM, Mason WA, Watts DJ (2011) Everyone's an influencer: quantifying influence on twitter, ACM: 65–74.

20. Ver Steeg G, Galstyan A (2012) Information transfer in social media. ACM: 509–518.

21. Zhou X, Yang J, Zhang J, Lin Z (2014) A BBS Opinion Leader Mining Algorithm Based on Topic Model. Journal of Computational Information Systems 10 (6): 2571–2578.

CHAPTER 17

A HIDDEN MARKOV MODEL FOR URBAN-SCALE TRAFFIC ESTIMATION USING FLOATING CAR DATA

Xiaomeng Wang[1,2], Ling Peng[1], Tianhe Chi[1] , Mengzhu Li[3] , Xiaojing Yao[1,2], Jing Shao[1,2]

[1] Institute of Remote Sensing and Digital Earth, Chinese Academy of Sciences, Beijing, China

[2] University of Chinese Academy of Sciences, Chinese Academy of Sciences, Beijing, China

[3] College of Economics and Management, Southwest University, Chongqing, China

ABSTRACT

Urban-scale traffic monitoring plays a vital role in reducing traffic congestion. Owing to its low cost and wide coverage, floating car data (FCD) serves as a novel approach to collecting traffic data. However, sparse probe data represents the vast majority of the data available on arterial roads in most urban environments. In order to overcome the problem of data sparseness, this paper proposes a hidden Markov model (HMM)-based traffic estimation model, in which the traffic condition on a road segment is considered as a hidden state that can be estimated according to the conditions of road segments having similar traffic characteristics. An algorithm based on clustering and pattern mining rather than on adjacency relationships is proposed to find clusters with road segments having similar traffic characteristics. A multi-clustering strategy is adopted to achieve a trade-off between clustering accuracy and coverage. Finally, the proposed model is designed and implemented on the basis of a real-time algorithm. Results of experiments based on real FCD confirm the applicability, accuracy, and efficiency of the model. In addition, the results indicate that the model is practicable for traffic estimation on urban arterials and works well even when more than 70% of the probe data are missing.

INTRODUCTION

Traffic congestion has become a severe problem in metropolises, resulting in widespread wastage of time and energy [1]. Traffic monitoring and estimation is an important method for obtaining information on traffic conditions; thus, it plays a vital role in reducing traffic congestion [2]. Static sensors (inductive loop detectors [3], video cameras [4], etc.), deployed at fixed locations on roads, are used to detect traffic state (e.g., flow velocity and traffic density). However, it is difficult for these traditional approaches to cover all roads because they involve extensive infrastructure deployment and high maintenance costs [5].

With the rapid development of mobile technologies, recent years have witnessed the emergence of a new method known as floating car data (FCD) for collecting valuable real-time information on traffic conditions. In this method, vehicles (e.g. taxis and buses) equipped with global positioning systems (GPS), accelerometers, and other sensors can provide data such as position, velocity, and acceleration of the vehicle. FCD is not as expensive as traditional data acquisition methods because it requires no dedicated infrastructure. Moreover, it has the potential to provide good spatiotemporal coverage of the transportation network and useful data given a certain penetration rate in the population [6, 7].

Citation: Wang X, Peng L, Chi T, Li M, Yao X, Shao J (2015) A Hidden Markov Model for Urban-Scale Traffic Estimation Using Floating Car Data. PLoS ONE 10(12): e0145348. doi:10.1371/journal.pone.0145348

In some previous studies, FCD has been used to estimate traffic conditions on highways, providing good results with a low penetration rate (1%–3%) [7–9]. Compared to traffic estimation on freeways, traffic estimation on arterials is more complex because of the traffic lights and intersections, and it requires a greater number of samples for analysis. Several researches have discussed the minimum penetration rate required. For example, Breitenberger et al. [10] proposed a penetration rate of 10% on arterial and urban roads. In addition, Vandenberghe et al. [11] discussed the maximum sample interval and the maximum transmission interval of aggregated samples, where the former defines the time between two consecutive FCD samples captured by the same floating car and the latter defines the time between two consecutive server uploads of all new samples by a floating car.

However, it is difficult for FCD to meet the sampling requirements in practice, and the distribution of observed probe data may be sparse and uneven. Traffic state estimation using sparse probe data has not been explored extensively. Herring et al. [12] proposed a probabilistic modeling framework for estimating arterial travel time distribution using sparse probe data. They modeled the evolution of traffic states as a coupled hidden Markov model (HMM), in which the traffic states of nearby road segments are correlated and evolve over time in a Markov manner. The present study differs from their study in that it considers links with similar traffic conditions instead of adjacent links of the road network, which may improve the modeling accuracy. Yanmin et al. [13] revealed the hidden structures within the traffic conditions of a road network using principal component analysis (PCA) and proposed a compressive sensing-based algorithm for obtaining the missing traffic conditions. However, they simply developed an offline data analytics algorithm that cannot be applied to real-time traffic estimation.

The present study proposes an HMM-based model that focuses on overcoming the problem of data sparseness for traffic estimation using FCD. It is assumed that the traffic state of a road segment is invisible and that each road segment belongs to a cluster of road segments having similar traffic characteristics. The traffic conditions of the other road segments in the cluster are considered as observations, based on which an HMM can be constructed. An algorithm based on clustering and pattern mining is proposed to find all road segment clusters in which segments have similar traffic characteristics, and a multi-clustering strategy is adopted to achieve a trade-off between clustering accuracy and coverage. Through data analysis, two exponential distribution functions are used for computing emission probability and transition probability. Finally, a real-time estimation algorithm is developed for online traffic application. The results of extensive experiments conducted using real floating car data show that our model works well even when more than 70% of the probe data are missing.

The remainder of this paper is organized as follows. Section 2 describes the problem of traffic estimation using sparse probe data. Section 3 discusses the construction of an HMM-based traffic estimation model, outlines the main steps of the proposed approach, and presents an algorithm for real-time traffic estimation. Section 4 describes the implementation of the proposed model and as well as a case study for assessing the accuracy of the model. Finally, Section 5 summarizes our findings and concludes the paper.

Problem Description

There are numerous floating cars running on the roads. They upload their state information, such as location, speed, and direction, from time to time. The state of a floating car at time t is expressed as s<id, l, v, t>, where id, l, and v denote the ID, location, and speed, respectively, of the vehicle. A road network G is divided into a set of road segments, $R = \{r_n \mid n = 1, 2, \ldots, N\}$, by intersections. A map-matching algorithm is used to find the road segment on which the vehicle is traveling at time t. In order to facilitate statistical analysis, a set of predefined time slots, $T = \{t_m \mid m = 1, 2, \ldots, M\}$, instead of continuous time, is employed for traffic condition estimation. Then, the state of vehicle s is converted into s<id, r, v, t>.

In the field of traffic engineering, several metrics have been proposed for quantifying the traffic condition of a link, such as speed [14], density [15], flow [16], and queues at intersections [17]. Furthermore, Many traffic flow models [18–29] have been proposed to study complex traffic conditions. The present study employs the velocity of the traffic flow on a road segment, as in some previous studies [1, 13, 14, 30, 31]. The floating cars are part of the traffic flow; hence, it is reasonable to consider their speed as the speed of the traffic flow. The speed of the traffic flow on segment n at time slot m, $x^{n,m}$, is approximated as the average speed of all vehicles moving within the traffic flow on this road segment at time slot m. Then, the traffic condition of the road network can be expressed by matrix X as follows:

$$X = \begin{bmatrix} x^{1,1} & \cdots & x^{1,M} \\ \vdots & x^{r,t} & \vdots \\ x^{N,1} & \cdots & x^{N,M} \end{bmatrix} \quad (1)$$

Here, the row $X_r = \{x^{r,m} \mid m = 1, 2, \ldots, M\}$ represents the traffic condition sequence of road segment r over time. Because of the randomness and unevenness of the floating car data, it is difficult to obtain a complete traffic condition matrix, as there are many spatiotemporal vacancies with no probe measurements. As shown in Fig 1, for the traffic condition sequence of a road segment, there may be some sub-sequences without sample data. Hence, in this study, the main objective of traffic estimation is to estimate the values of these missing states, which can approximate the true states.

r_4	1	0	1	0	1	0	0	1
r_3	0	1	1	1	1	0	0	0
r_2	1	1	0	0	1	0	0	1
r_1	0	0	0	1	1	0	0	1
	t_1	t_2	t_3	t_4	t_5	t_6	t_7	t_8

Figure 1. Traffic condition sequences. The value 1 indicates the presence of sample data and 0 indicates the absence of sample data at a time slot.

METHODS

Estimation Model Based on HMM

In this paper, an HMM-based estimation model is proposed to estimate missing traffic state sequences. An HHM, which is based on the concept of Markov process and Markov chain, is characterized by five elements: observation, hidden state, state transition probability, emission probability, and initial state.

The first step in HMM construction is to establish the observations and hidden states of the model. In this study, the traffic condition of the target road segment r at time slot t is the hidden state $x^{r,t}$. It is assumed that the road segment r belongs to a cluster C in which all road segments have similar traffic characteristics. Then, the observations $y^{r,t}$ are defined as the traffic conditions of the other road segments in the cluster. In some previous studies [16, 32], adjacent road segments have been assumed to be correlated with each other. However, in practice, such an assumption may be not very accurate. A method based on clustering and frequent pattern mining is proposed in Section 3.2 in order to find clusters having road segments with similar traffic characteristics. In this study, speed, which is a continuous variable, is employed as the traffic condition; thus, the hidden state has an infinite number of values. Therefore, it is necessary to select finite candidate states for the HMM process. The state value range at t can be limited according to the observation $y^{r,t}$ and previous state $x^{r,t-1}$; then, the range should be discretized to a candidate state set $CS^{r,t} = \{x_i^{r,t} | i = 1, 2, \ldots, k\}$.

The emission probability, $Pr(y^{r,t}|x^{r,t})$, is the likelihood of observing the traffic condition $y^{r,t}$ conditional on the traffic condition $x^{r,t}$ being the true condition of the road segment r at time slot t. The transition probability, $Pr(x^{r,t}, x^{r,t+1})$, is the probability that the traffic condition of the road segment r will transform from a state $x^{r,t}$ at time t to another state $x^{r,t+1}$ at time t+1. The methods for measuring and calculating the emission probability and transition probability are discussed in Section 3.3.

The HMM sequentially generates candidate traffic condition sequences and evaluates them on the basis of their likelihood, which is measured by the joint probability (Fig 2). Past hypotheses of the solution are extended to account for new observations over time. Then, the surviving sequence with the highest joint probability is selected from among the remaining candidates of the previous stage as the final solution. The joint probability is expressed as

$$J^{r,t+1} = Pr(y^{r,t+1}|x^{r,t+1}) \max_{x^{r,t} \in CS^{r,t}} \{Pr(x^{r,t}, x^{r,t+1}) J^{r,t}\} \quad (2)$$

where $J^{r,1} = Pr(y^{r,1}|x^{r,1})$ and $CS^{r,t}$ denotes the set of candidate states of the road segment r at time slot t. After the HMM process, the last traffic condition sequence with the maximum joint probability can be found:

$$x^{r,T} = argmax_{x^{r,T} \in CS^{r,T}} \{J_T\}.$$

Then, the system works backwards to find the traffic condition sequence $x_{T-1}, \ldots, x_1$ of the road segment.

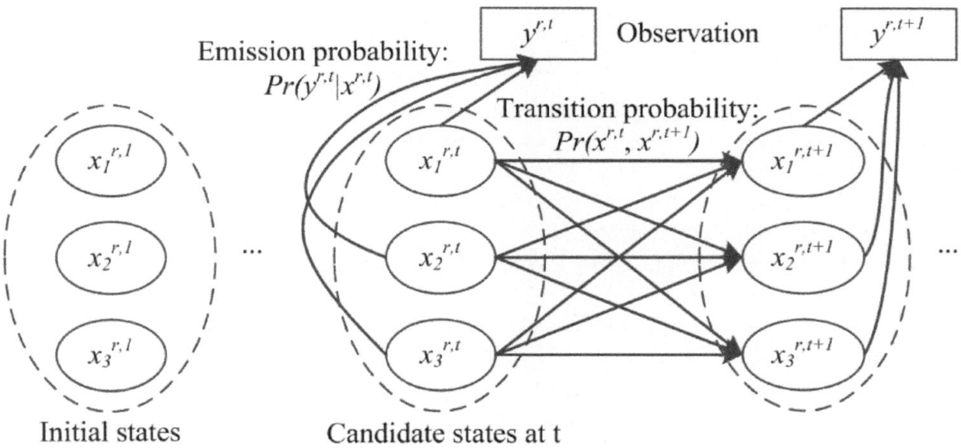

Figure 2. HMM process of traffic condition estimation.

Traffic Similarity Analysis

Clustering Analysis

In this study, the traffic condition sequence, $X_r = \{x^{r,t} | t = 1, 2, \ldots, M\}$, is considered as the traffic characteristic of the road segment r over a period of time. A spectral clustering algorithm is adopted to divide the road segment set into clusters based on historical data, and the road segments in the same cluster have similar traffic characteristics.

In the spectral clustering algorithm, the set of points in an arbitrary feature space can be represented as a complete weighted undirected graph G(V, E). The vertices of the graph G are the points in the feature space and the weight w_{ij} of an edge (v_i, v_j) in E is a measure of the similarity between vertex v_i and v_j. In this context, we can formulate the clustering problem as a graph-partitioning problem that requires partitions V_1, $V_2, \ldots, V_k$ of the vertex set V according to some measure; then, the vertices in any set V_i have a high degree of similarity, and the vertices in two different sets V_i, V_j have a low degree of similarity.

For road segment clustering, the road segments are considered as vertices of the graph G. The weight w_{ij} between the road segments i and j is the difference between the traffic characteristics of the two road segments; it can be expressed by a Euclidean distance as follows:

$$w_{ij} = \sqrt{\sum_{t=1}^{M} \left(x^{i,t} - x^{j,t}\right)^2} \quad \textbf{(3)}$$

where M is the number of time slots in the traffic condition sequence and $x^{i,t}$ is the traffic condition of road segment i at time slot t. A normalized spectral clustering algorithm (Box 1) is constructed according to previous research [33]:

Box 1. Spectral Clustering Algorithm.

Algorithm 1 SpectralClustering: spectral clustering

Input: G(V, E): Traffic condition graph; k: Number of clusters;

Output: C = $\{V_1, V_2, \ldots V_k\}$: clusters;

1: Get weighted adjacency matrix W of G(V, E);

2: Calculate degree matrix D of W;

3: $L \leftarrow I - D^{-\frac{1}{2}}.W.D^{-\frac{1}{2}}$; //Compute normalized Laplacian

3: Compute the first k eigenvectors $_1$,... u_k of L;

4: Let U be the matrix containing the vectors u_1, … , u_k as columns;

5: Use the k-means algorithm to cluster U, then get the clusters C;

6: return C;

In practice, it is difficult to determine a suitable number of clusters for road segment clustering. Therefore, a modified clustering algorithm is proposed, and the average weight w_{av} of a cluster, instead of the cluster number k, is set as a constraint for controlling the clustering process. In order to simplify the computation, w_{av} is defined as the average weight between the centroid of a cluster and other objects. The centroid is given by

$$vc_k = \frac{1}{|V_k|} \sum_{v_i \in V_k} v_i \quad \textbf{(4)}$$

where V_k denotes the vertices of the k-th cluster, $|V_k|$ is the number of vertices in V_k, v_i is the i-th vertex of V_k, and vc_k is the centroid of V_k,. Then, the average weight of V_k can be expressed as

$$w_{av} = \frac{1}{|V_k|} \sum_{v_i \in V_k} \left\| v_i - vc_k \right\| \quad \textbf{(5)}$$

In the algorithm (Box 2) based on the constraint ω, the vertices of G are divided into small clusters step by step, and the cluster whose w_{av} is greater than the threshold value ω should be divided into smaller clusters until the constraint is met. Because clusters with only one object are meaningless, it is reasonable to set a minimum number of objects in a cluster (N_{min}). A small value k is set as the number of clusters in every clustering step. In this study, both k and N_{min} are set as 2.

Box 2. Clustering Algorithm Based on Constraint.

Algorithm 2 ConstraintClustering: Clustering based on constraint

Input: G(V, E): Traffic condition graph; ω: Threshold value; k: Number of clusters at every step; N_{min}: Minimum number of objects in a cluster;

Output: C = $\{V_1, V_2, \ldots V_K\}$: clusters;

1: **if** $|V| > N_{min}$ and $|V| > k$

2: C ← SpectralClustering(G, k);

3: $C_{temp} \leftarrow \emptyset$;

4: **for** i ← 1 to k do

5: **if** the average weight w_{av} of V_i is greater than ω

6: Get sub-graph G_i from G corresponding to V_i;

7: $C_{temp} \leftarrow C_{temp} \cup$ SpectralClustering(G_i, k);

8: **else**

9: $C_{temp} \leftarrow C_{temp} \cup \{V_i\}$;

10: **end if**

11: **end for**

12: $C \leftarrow C_{temp}$;

13: **else**

14: C ← {V};

15: **end if**

16: return C;

Pattern Mining

To avoid coincidental clusters, it is reasonable to perform clustering multiple times for different days and find frequent clusters with a better representation of traffic similarity between road segments. In general, the traffic condition exhibits different patterns on weekdays and weekends. As shown in Fig 3, the traffic conditions of arterial roads in Beijing have similar characteristics on weekdays but significantly different characteristics on weekends. Therefore, the traffic conditions should be discussed separately.

The road segment set, R = $\{r_n \mid n = 1, 2, \ldots, N\}$, is divided into cluster set $C_d = \{R_k \mid k = 1, 2, \ldots, K\}$ according to the traffic condition of the d-th day using the clustering algorithm proposed in Section 3.2.1. The cluster set list, L = $\{C_d \mid d = 1, 2, \ldots, D\}$, contains all clusters of the last Ddays (weekdays or weekends) from the target day. The objective of the frequent pattern mining approach adopted in this study is to find the frequent cluster set, P = $\{R_j \subset R \mid j = 1, 2, \ldots, J\}$, where the cluster R_j appears frequently in L. An indicator function is used to indicate whether R_j appears in the cluster set C_d:

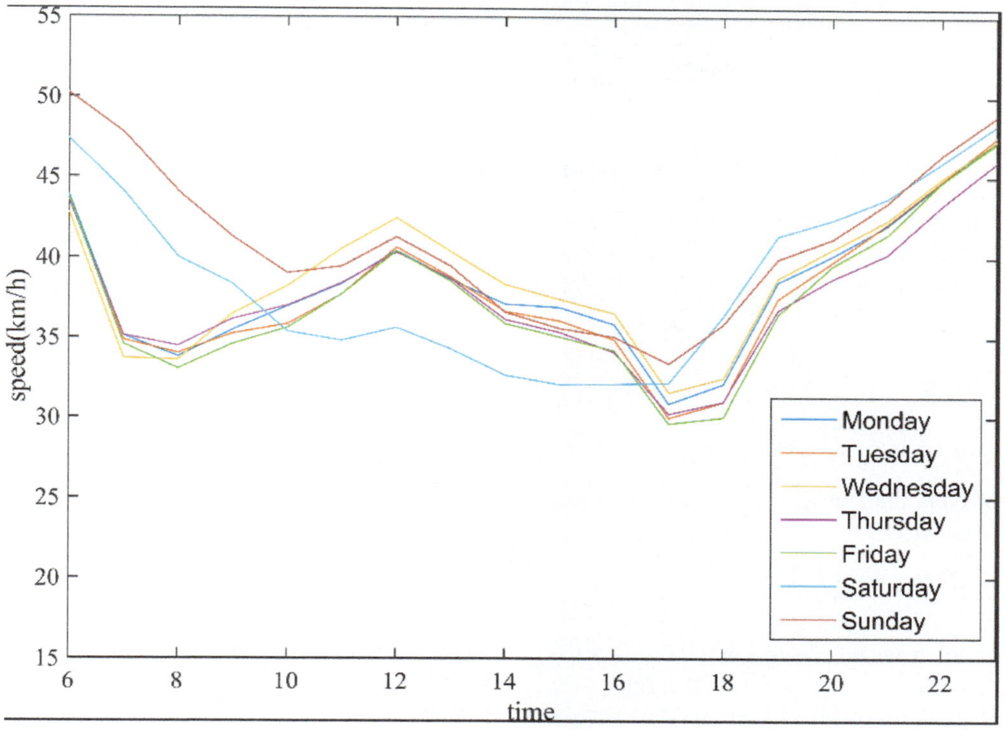

Figure 3. Average speed of arterial roads in Beijing.

$$f(R_j, C_d) = \begin{cases} 1 \; if \; \exists R_k \in C_d, \; let \; R_j \subset R_k \\ 0 \; if \; \nexists R_k \in C_d, \; let \; R_j \subset R_k \end{cases} \quad \textbf{(6)}$$

In this study, the number of times the cluster R_j appears in the cluster set L is defined as the support, and it can be calculated as follows:

$$support(R_j, L) = \sum_{C_d \in L} f(R_j, C_d) \quad \textbf{(7)}$$

The frequent cluster must meet the minimum support, Sup_{min}; then, the frequent cluster set can be defined as follows:

$$P(L) = \{R_j \subset R | j = 1, 2, \ldots J, and \; support(R_j, L) \geq Sup_{min}\} \quad \textbf{(8)}$$

It is difficult for traditional pattern mining algorithms (e.g., the Apriori algorithm) to compute and find the frequent clusters, as the number of road segments and clusters is extremely large. To overcome this problem, a frequent pattern mining approach based on intersection is proposed. The intersection between two cluster sets is expressed as

$$intersection(C_1, C_2) = \{R_k | R_k = R_i \cap R_j, R_i \subset C_1, R_j \subset C_2, and \; |R_k| > 1\} \quad \textbf{(9)}$$

where C_1 and C_2 are the cluster sets of two days, R_i and R_j are arbitrary clusters of sets $C_1$and C_2, respectively, and R_k is the intersection of R_i and R_j. Note that R_k is meaningful for estimation only if it includes more than one road segment. Therefore, in the intersection process, the cluster R_k will be discarded when $|R_k|<2$. As shown in Fig 4, the frequent cluster set can be obtained by gradual intersection.

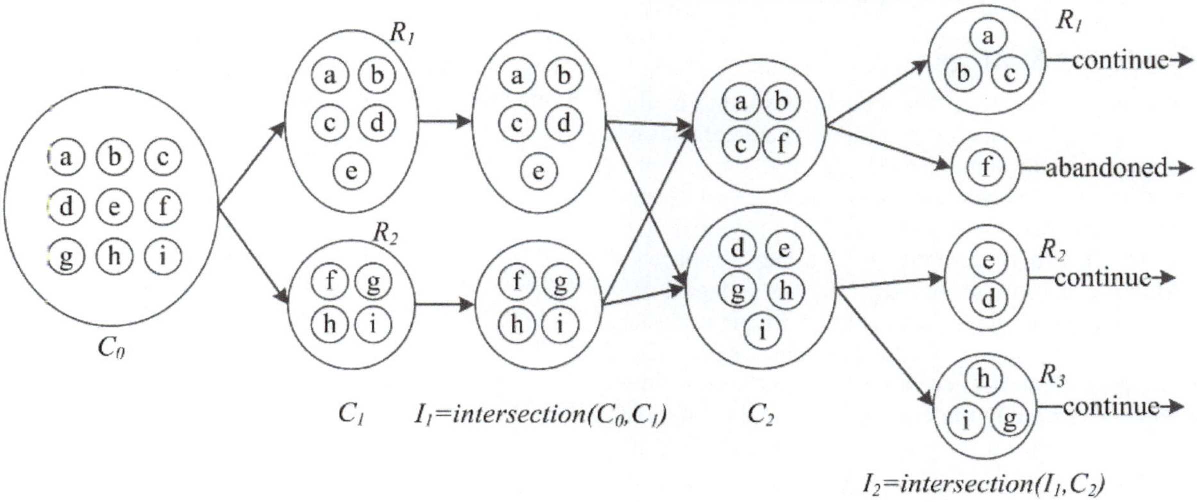

Figure 4. Frequent clusters are obtained by gradual intersection.

For a cluster set list L_i, which has i cluster sets, the frequent clusters that appear i times in L_i can be found by a recursive algorithm based on intersection; this algorithm can be expressed as

$$Pattern(L_i) = intersection(C_j, Pattern(L_i - C_j)) \quad \textbf{(10)}$$

where C_j is an arbitrary cluster set in the list L_i; if L_i contains only one cluster set C_j, then Pattern(L_i) will return C_j. In order to find all frequent clusters that appear i times in L, it is necessary to obtain the combination set, given by

$$L^i_{com} = \{L^k_i | k = 1, 2, \ldots, \binom{|L|}{i}\} \quad \textbf{(11)}$$

where L^i_{com} includes all combinations that contain i cluster sets of L; the number of combinations is $\binom{|L|}{i}$. Then, the frequent cluster set can be obtained as

$$FC_i = \bigcup_{l \in L^i_{com}} Pattern(l) \quad \textbf{(12)}$$

where FC_i contains all frequent clusters whose support is i. Then, all frequent clusters that appear more than Sup_{min} times can be obtained using the following algorithm (Box 3):

Box 3. Traffic Frequent Pattern Mining Algorithm.

Algorithm 3 TrafficPatternMining: Traffic frequent pattern mining

Input: L = {C_1, C_2, …, C_D}; Sup_{min}: minimum support

Output: FC = {FC_i|i = Sup_{min}, Sup_{min} +1, …, D};

1: FC ← Ø;

2: **for** i ←Sup_{min} to D

3: FC_i ← Ø;

4: L_{com} ← i-combinations from L;

5: FC_i ← Get all frequent clusters from (12);

6: FC ← FC ∪ {FC_i};

7: **end for**

8: return FC;

Multi-Clustering Strategy

As discussed in Section 3.2.1, the smaller the value of the constraint ω, the more similar are the traffic characteristics of the road segments in the same cluster; this may improve the estimation accuracy. However, the frequent cluster set covers fewer road segments because of the more stringent constraint. To resolve this conflict, a multiple-clustering strategy is adopted. Multiple constraints ω_1, ω_2,…ω_m are selected for clustering and pattern mining; then, a list of frequent cluster sets, FCL = {FC_ω |ω = ω_1, ω_2, …, ω_m}, is generated, where FC_ω is the frequent cluster set corresponding to the constraint ω. In the process of finding the cluster that contains the road segment r, the frequent cluster set with smaller ω should be considered first.

Probability Calculation

Emission probability.

For a road segment r that belongs to the frequent cluster C, its traffic condition $x^{r,t}$ at time slot tapproximates the traffic conditions $y^{r,t}$ of other road segments in C. Thus, the difference diffbetween $x^{r,t}$ and $y^{r,t}$ can be adopted to calculate the emission probability $Pr(y^{r,t}|x^{r,t})$. According to observations, the emission probability follows an exponential distribution; hence, it can be calculated as

$$Pr(y^{r,t}|x^{r,t}) = \lambda e^{-\lambda \cdot diff} = \lambda e^{-\lambda \frac{1}{|C'|} \sum_{i \in C'} |x^{r,t} - x^{i,t}|} \quad \textbf{(13)}$$

where, λ is the parameter of the exponential distribution (λ>0) anddiff is the average traffic condition difference between the road segment r and road segments in C' = {r'∈C| r'≠r}.

In order to find the appropriate frequent cluster C, the frequent cluster set FC_ω with a smaller constraint value ω should be considered preferentially, and in the frequent cluster set FC = {FC_i|i = Sup_{min}, Sup_{min} +1, …, D}, the clusters that appear more frequently should be considered first.

Transition Probability

Through data analysis, in a relatively short time interval, the traffic condition at time slot t+1 is close to that at time slot t. Thus, the traffic state change Δx = $|x^{r,t} - x^{r,t+1}|$ is employed to measure the state transition. According to observations, the state transition probability follows an exponential distribution, and it can be expressed as

$$Pr(x^{r,t}, x^{r,t+1}) = \beta e^{-\beta \cdot \Delta x} \quad \textbf{(14)}$$

where, β is the parameter of the exponential distribution (β>0).

Candidate Selection

As discussed in Sections 3.2 and 3.3, the state $x^{r,t+1}$ may approximate the previous state $x^{r,t}$and the observations $y^{r,t+1}$ = {$x^{i,t+1}$|i∈C and i≠r}, where C is the frequent cluster that contains the road segment r. Then, the value range of $x^{r,t+1}$ is set as [x_{min}-μ, x_{max}+μ], where x_{min} =min({$x^{r,t}$}∪$y^{r,t+1}$), x_{max} = max({$x^{r,t}$}∪$y^{r,t+1}$), and μ is used to avoid missing valid values. For computational convenience, the range should be discretized to finite candidates denoted by the set

$$CS = \left\{ x_i \middle| x_i = x_{min} - \mu + i \cdot \frac{x_{max} - x_{min} + 2\mu}{N_{cand} - 1}, i = 0, 1, 2 \ldots, N_{cand} - 1 \right\} \quad \textbf{(15)}$$

where N_{cand} is the number of candidates. In order to facilitate algorithm design, the candidate set is CS = {$x^{r,t+1}$} when the state at time slot t+1 is obtained from the samples. Then, it is not necessary to find the missing state sub-sequences discussed in Section 2; the entire state sequence can be estimated in a single process.

Real-Time Algorithm

For the road segment r at time slot t, a list PreSList = $\{Se_i \mid i = 1,2,\ldots m\}$ is used to store previous surviving state sequences. A sequence is denoted by Se = (SS, JP), where SS = $\{x^{r,1},x^{r,2},\ldots,x^{r,t-1}\}$ stores previous consecutive candidate states and JP is the joint probability. Using Algorithm 4 (Box 4), the current candidate sequence list SList is obtained according toPreSList and the candidate states CS_t of road segment r at time slot t. Then, the state sequence with the maximum joint probability in SList is the optimal solution of road segment r at time slot t; the sequence is given by $\arg\max_{Se\in SList}\{Se.JP\}$. For the first state, the initial joint probability of the state sequence is the emission probability of the candidate states. Obviously, the algorithm can output the estimated states in real time; thus, it is applicable to online application.

Box 4. Real-Time Traffic Estimation Algorithm Based on HMM.

Algorithm 4 TrafficEstimation: Real-time traffic estimation based on HMM

Input: PreSList: List of surviving sequences of road segment r at time slot t-1; t: time.

Output: SList: List of surviving sequences of road segment r at time slot t.

SList ← PreSList; //SList is a current surviving sequence list

CS_t ← Get candidate states; //Discussed in Section 3.4;

SListTemp ← ∅;

if t = = 1

for x in CS_t

Construct a new state sequence Se; Set x as the starting state;

Se.JP ← $Pr(y^{r,t}|x)$; //Discussed in Section 3.2;

Add Se into SList;

end for

else

for x in CS_t

Se ← $\arg\max_{Se\in SList}\{Se.JP\cdot Pr(x^{r,t-1},x)\}$;

Set x as the t-th state of Se;

Se.JP ← $Pr(y^{r,t}|x)\cdot Se.JP\cdot Pr(x^{r,t-1},x)$;

Add Se to the temporary list SListTemp;

end for

SList ← SListTemp;

end if

output $\arg\max_{Se\in SList}\{Se.JP\}$; //Real-time output current solution;

return SList;

RESULTS AND DISCUSSION

For the experiments, 8559 arterial road segments were selected; the roads cover the main regions of central Beijing. The traffic conditions between 6:00 and 24:00 were considered, and the time was divided into 108 time slots at 10-min intervals (e.g., the first time slot was 6:00–6:10 and the 12th time slot was 7:50–8:00).

The taxi trajectory data in Beijing during November 2012 served as the FCD data, obtained from 12,600 taxis. The data samples of six weekdays were selected for a case study; five of these days were used for frequent cluster mining and parameter estimation, and the remaining day was used to test the estimation model. Before the experiments were performed, the trajectory data were matched to the road network using map-matching methods [34–36], and anomalous samples were eliminated.

The model was implemented using a Java platform on a computer having a quad-core CPU (2.2 GHz) and 8-GB memory.

Frequent Cluster Mining

Six constraint values $\{\omega \mid \omega = 10, 15, 20, 25, 30, 35\}$ were considered in the clustering analysis stage. The average weight w_{av} discussed in Section 3.2.1 was employed to measure the degree of similarity, which decreased as w_{av} increased. As shown in Table 1, the mean w_{av} of the cluster set and the average number of objects in each cluster, $ON_{average}$, increase with ω. Clusters having a single object cannot be used for estimation; the proportion of such clusters,r_{single}, decreases as ω increases. For traffic estimation, a perfect cluster set has small averagew_{av}, large $ON_{average}$, and small r_{single}. A cluster set having small average w_{av} is more likely to have small $ON_{average}$ and large r_{single}, which confirms the existence of the contradiction discussed in Section 3.2.3. Therefore, it is necessary to adopt a multi-clustering strategy.

Table 1. Accuracy and coverage of cluster sets corresponding to different **ω**

ω	mean w_{av}	$ON_{average}$	r_{single}(%)
10	12.29	2.34	21.51
15	12.97	2.69	15.06
20	14.61	3.67	9.21
25	16.58	5.09	4.71
30	18.71	7.29	2.34
35	20.77	11.04	1.03

doi:10.1371/journal.pone.0145348.t001

As shown in Fig 5, the traffic characteristics of the road segments in the same cluster have a very high degree of similarity when the average weight w_{av} is small, such as clusters a, b, and c. As the average weight w_{av} increases, the degree of similarity of the cluster decreases and the number of the objects in the cluster increases.

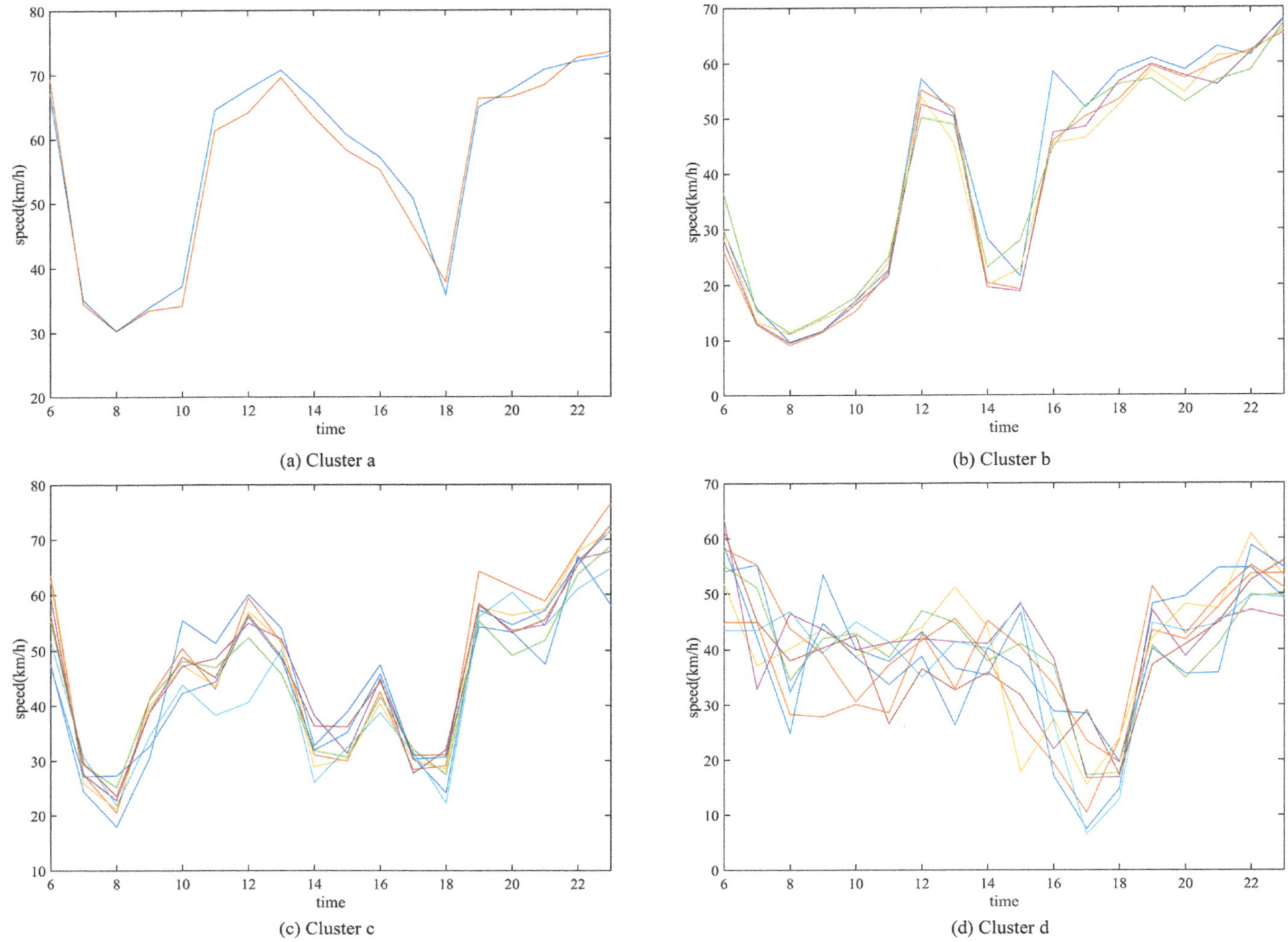

Figure 5. Traffic condition sequences of the road segments in four clusters. (a) The average weight of cluster a is 4.71, (b) the average weight of cluster b is 9.75, (c) the average weight of cluster c is 14.58, and (d) the average weight of cluster d is 24.93.

Samples of five days were selected for frequent cluster mining, and the minimum supportSup_{min} was set as 3. Table 2 lists the coverage rates of the frequent clusters, which is given by the ratio $R_{cover} = N_{cover}/N_{total}$, where N_{cover} is the number of road segments in the frequent cluster set and N_{total} is the total number of road segments. The coverage rate increases with ω, and the support of the most frequent clusters is less than or equal to 4. When ω increases to 35, the coverage rate of the frequent cluster set reaches 96.76%, which indicates that the set of these ω is sufficient and appropriate for this study.

Table 2. Coverage rate of the frequent cluster set for each ω (%)

ω/support	**≥5**	**≥4**	**≥3**
10	0.71	4.79	16.75
15	1.33	6.49	20.13
20	1.77	8.8	28.68
25	2.67	14.13	45.76
30	4.84	26.04	75.58
35	7.2	39.1	96.76

doi:10.1371/journal.pone.0145348.t002

The road segments that are adjacent to each other may have similar traffic characteristics; this property can be used instead of clustering for finding similar road segments. However, in contrast to our assumption, this is not very likely in practice. As shown in Fig 6, although the proportion of road segments whose adjacent segments are in the same cluster increases with ω, this proportion is still low. Therefore, it is more reasonable to find similar road segments by clustering rather than by adjacency relationships.

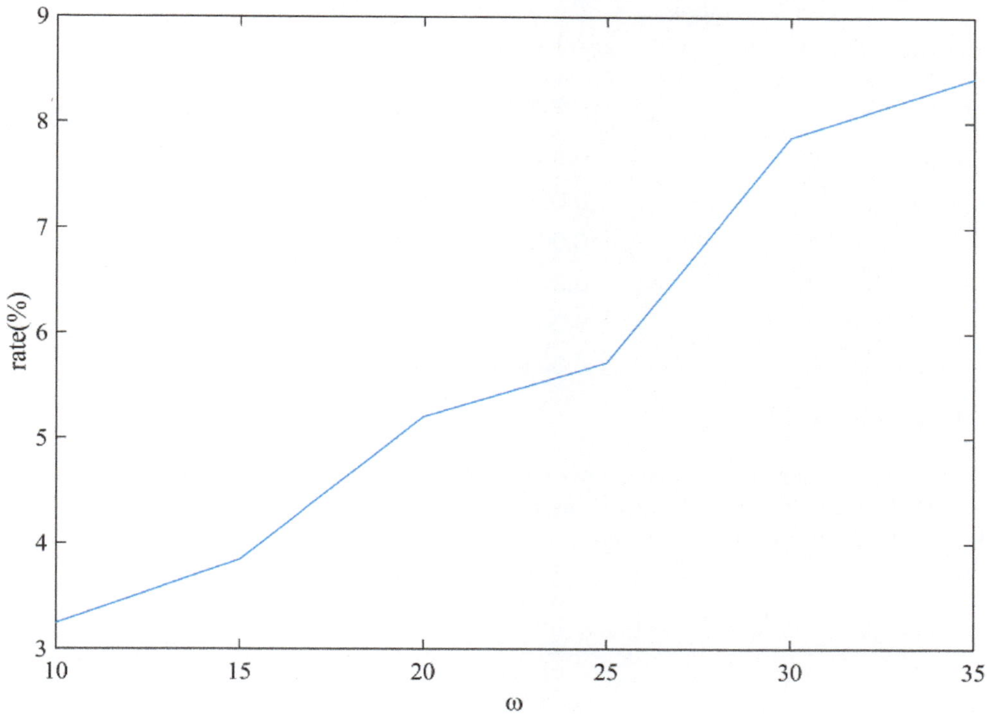

Figure 6. Proportion of road segments whose adjacent road segments are also in the same cluster.

Parameter estimation

Statistical analysis of the distribution of diff was carried out in order to estimate the parameter λin (13). In different frequent cluster sets corresponding to specific values of ω, the distribution ofdiff is different. In order to observe the distribution of diff, we calculated the ratio of each diff value to the total number of samples. As shown in Fig 7, the steepness of the distribution curve increases with ω, which indicates that the road segments in the frequent cluster generated on the basis of a smaller ω are more likely to have a higher degree of similarity, because the probability that diff takes a smaller value is higher.

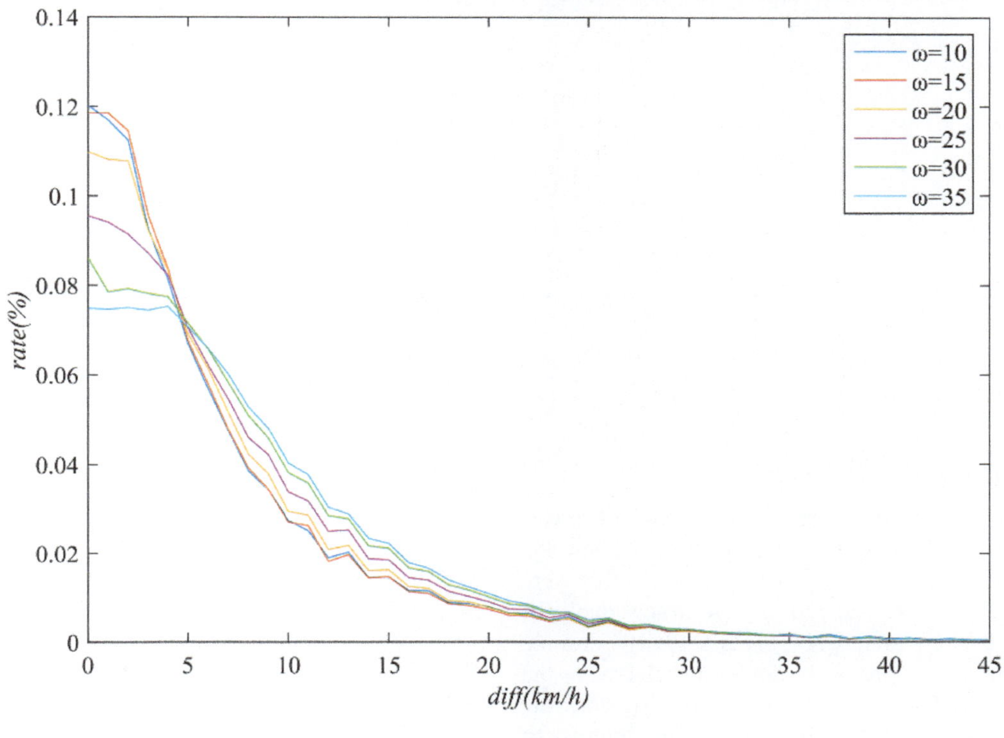

Figure 7. Distribution of diff in frequent cluster sets corresponding to different values of ω.

The parameter λ was calculated as 1/E(diff), where E(diff) is the expectation of diff, and the equation was initialized with an initial parameter λ^*; then, the parameter was learned by iterative computation until it converged to a specific value. Table 3 lists λ values for six frequent cluster sets, FCL = $\{FC_\omega | \omega = 10, 15, 20, 25, 30, 35\}$, as well as the sum of squared errors (SSE), root-mean-square error (RMSE), and R-square, which indicate that the equation works well for the samples.

Table 3. Estimated parameters of the emission probability equation corresponding to different frequent cluster sets

ω	λ	SSE	R-square	RMSE
10	0.1337	0.000689	0.988	0.0030
15	0.1351	0.000847	0.986	0.0033
20	0.1251	0.000775	0.986	0.0032
25	0.1123	0.000694	0.986	0.0030
30	0.1012	0.000902	0. 980	0.0034
35	0.09267	0.001353	0. 966	0.0042

doi:10.1371/journal.pone.0145348.t003

As shown in Fig 8, the traffic state change Δx follows an exponential distribution. The parameter β is calculated as 1/E(Δx), where E(Δx) is the expectation of Δx; after iterative computation, the estimated values of β, SSE, RMSE, and R-square are 0.09451, 0.000528, 0.002436, and 0.9871, respectively.

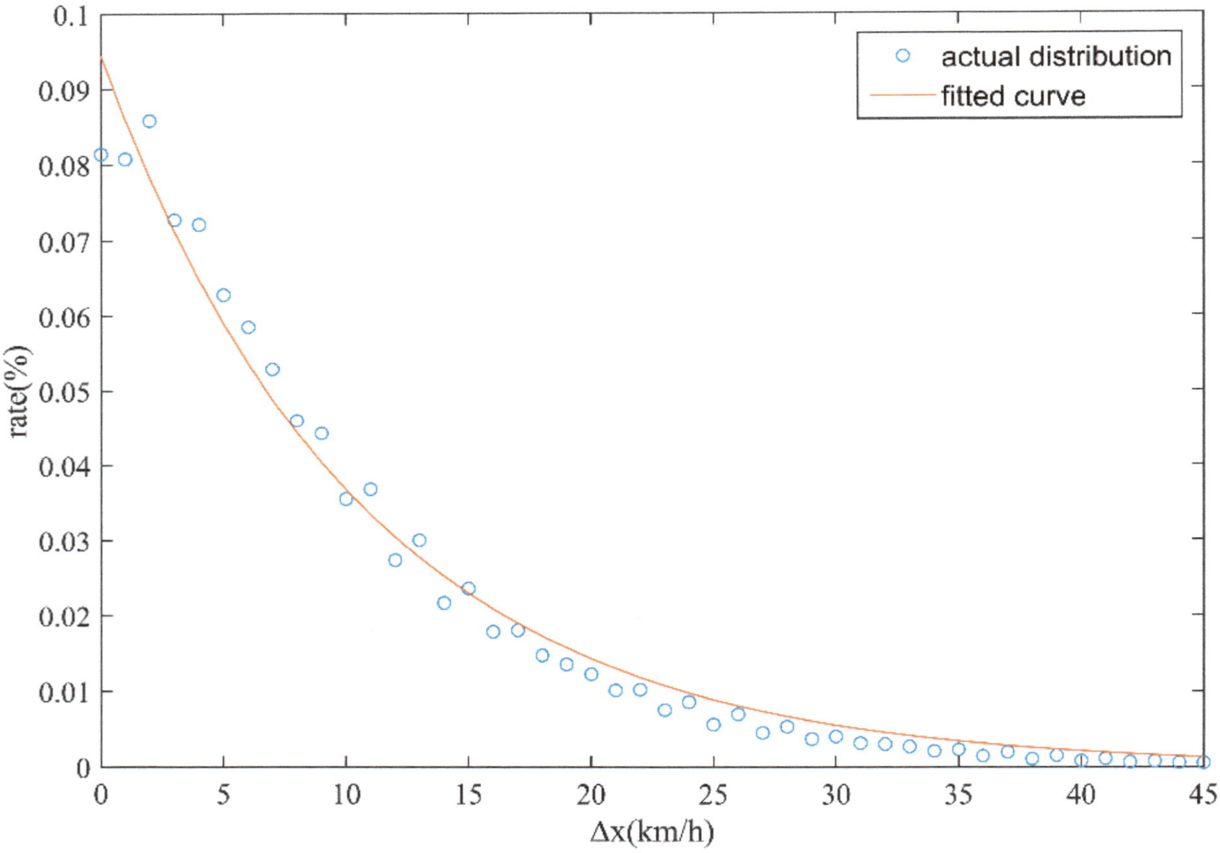

Figure 8. Distribution of the traffic state change Δx.

Model accuracy and efficiency

A state sequence set of 8559 arterial road segments was prepared for testing. Because it is difficult to obtain the complete state set of these road segments, the states that were actually obtained were considered for accuracy analysis; the total number of these states, N_{base}, was 6.19×10^5. Among these states, a number of states were randomly selected as the missing states that need to be estimated. The missing state rate is denoted by $R_{miss} = N_{miss}/N_{base}$, where N_{miss} is the number of missing states. The mean absolute error (MAE) was employed to measure the estimation accuracy, and it is given by

$$MAE = \frac{1}{N_{estim}} \sum_{i=1}^{N_{estim}} |\hat{x}_i - x_i| \tag{16}$$

where N_{estim} is the number of states estimated, $\hat{x}_i$ is the estimated value of the i-th state, and x_i is the true value of the i-th state.

The accuracies of two models, Model 1 and Model 2, were compared. Model 1 is the proposed model, which finds road segments with similar traffic states via clustering and frequent pattern mining, whereas Model 2 assumes that adjacent road segments have similar traffic conditions. As shown in Fig 9, MAE increases with R_{miss}, and the MAE of Model 2 is significantly higher than that of Model 1, which implies that the proposed model is more accurate.

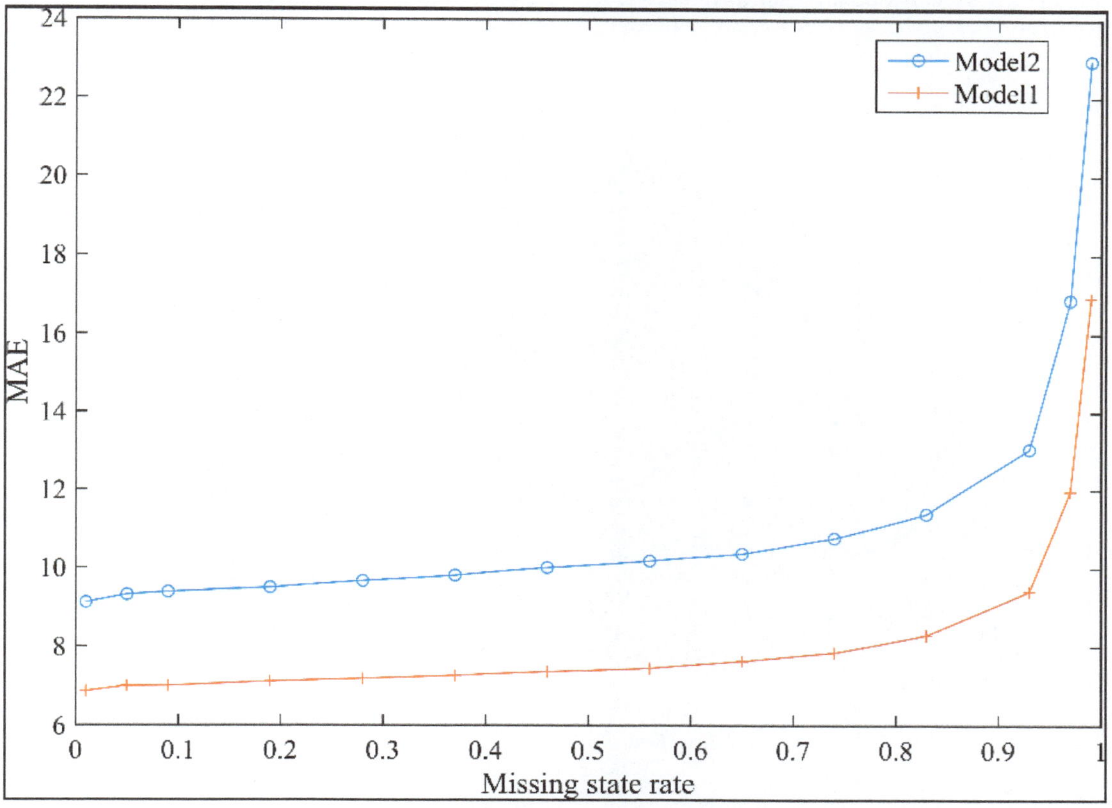

Figure 9. Comparison of accuracies of the two models.

If there is no reference state, such as the previous state or the states of similar road segments, for the state $x^{r,t}$, the state cannot be estimated. The rate of the states that cannot be estimated is R_{miss}-R_{estim}; then, the number of states that can be estimated is R_{valid} = 1-(R_{miss}-R_{estim}), where R_{estim} = N_{estim}/N_{base}. As shown in Table 4, MAE increases gradually before R_{miss} reaches 83.33%, and R_{valid} remains high until R_{miss} reaches 92.59%, which indicates that the model is applicable to very sparse sample data.

Table 4. Estimation accuracy and coverage corresponding to different values of the missing state rate R_{miss}

R_{miss}(%)	MAE(km/h)	R_{estim}(%)	R_{valid}(%)
0.93	6.86	0.92	99.99
4.63	6.99	4.61	99.98
9.26	7.01	9.2	99.94
18.52	7.11	18.24	99.72
27.78	7.18	26.77	98.99
37.04	7.26	35.88	98.84
46.3	7.36	44.93	98.63
55.56	7.44	53.92	98.36
64.81	7.64	62.8	97.99
74.07	7.84	71.51	97.44
83.33	8.29	79.41	96.08
92.59	9.41	85.12	92.53
97.22	11.96	82.05	84.83
99.07	16.91	64.58	65.51

doi:10.1371/journal.pone.0145348.t004

The cumulative distribution function (CDF) of the estimation error E is given by

$$F_E(e) = P(E \leq e) = \frac{N(E \leq e)}{N_{estim}} \quad (17)$$

where estimation error E is the absolute value of the difference between the estimated and observed values, N_{estim} is the number of estimated states, and $N(E \leq e)$ is the number of estimated states whose error is less than or equal to e. Fig 10 shows the CDFs of estimation errors corresponding to different values of the missing state rate R_{miss}. Before R_{miss} reaches 83.33%, the CDF curve is steeper, which indicates that most errors are small. For example, when R_{miss} = 83.33%, more than 52.79% of the errors are less than or equal to 5 and more than 76.88% of the errors are less than or equal to 10.

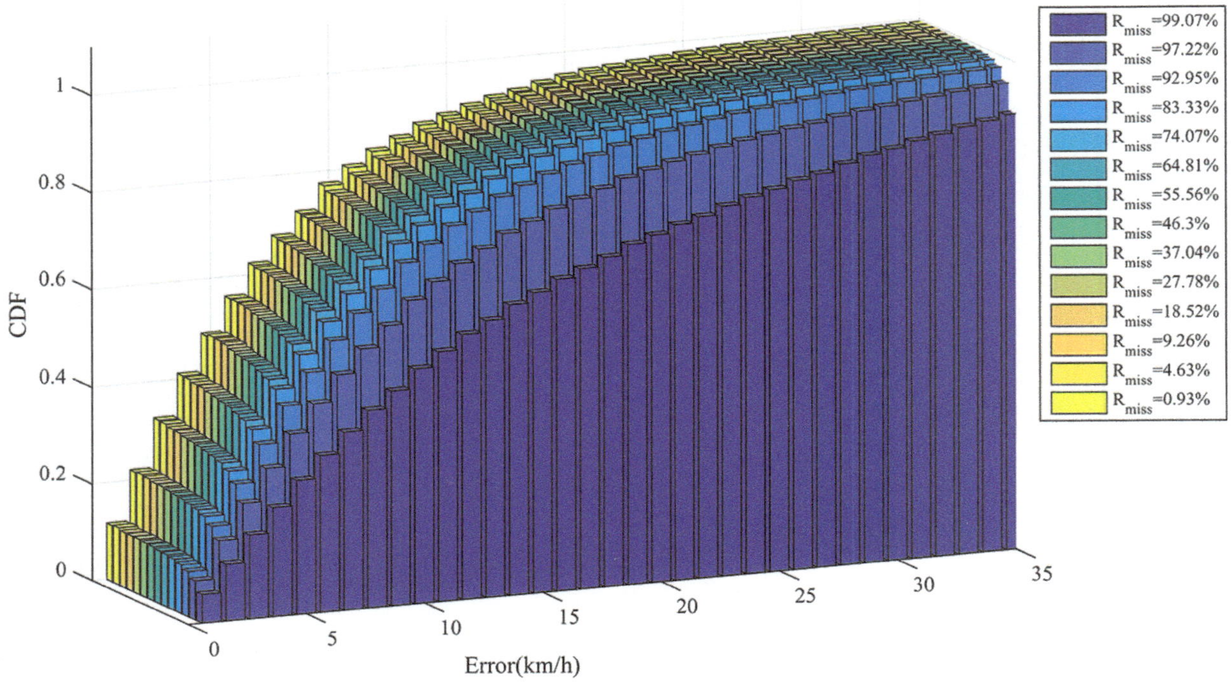

Figure 10. Estimation error CDF corresponding to different values of the missing state rate R_{miss}.

The states that are obtained are considered as the true states; then, the estimated error distribution function in the global scope is given by

$$F'(e) = 1 - R_{miss} + F_E(e) \cdot R_{estim} \quad \textbf{(18)}$$

Table 5 summarizes the global distribution of the estimated error, which reflects the accuracy of the model corresponding to different values of the missing state rate R_{miss}. According to the error distribution, it is easy to determine whether the accuracy of the model meets the requirements of the application. For example, in an application that requires 90% of the errors are to be less than 5 km/h, if the missing state rate is less than 18.52%, then the model may be suitable for the application.

Table 5. Global cumulative distribution of the estimated error corresponding to different values of the missing state rate R_{miss}

R_{miss}(%)	F'(5)(%)	F'(10) (%)	F'(20) (%)	F'(30) (%)
0.93	99.59	99.81	99.96	99.98
4.63	97.96	99.06	99.79	99.94
9.26	95.90	98.09	99.55	99.86
18.52	91.66	95.98	98.92	99.54
27.78	87.06	93.43	97.75	98.70
37.04	82.66	91.26	97.16	98.47
46.30	78.22	89.00	96.45	98.12
55.56	73.71	86.61	95.66	97.68
64.81	68.84	83.9	94.64	97.10
74.07	63.68	80.91	93.32	96.28
83.33	57.43	76.58	90.79	94.41
92.59	48.53	68.92	84.88	89.67
97.22	37.74	56.32	72.91	79.33
99.07	21.94	34.32	48.19	56.34

doi:10.1371/journal.pone.0145348.t005

In our data source, the missing state rate of the arterial roads was around 33%, while the missing state rate of the other roads was around 65%. Samples of 8559 arterial roads were considered. The error was less than or equal to 5 (resp. 10) for more than 84.84% (resp. 92.61%) of the states; this indicates a high estimation accuracy. Fig 11(A) shows the traffic state map of the arterial roads in Beijing at the 50th time slot (14:10–14:20) before estimation, and Fig 11(B) shows the states of the roads after estimation. Most of the missing states were estimated, and the estimated values were very close to the true values.

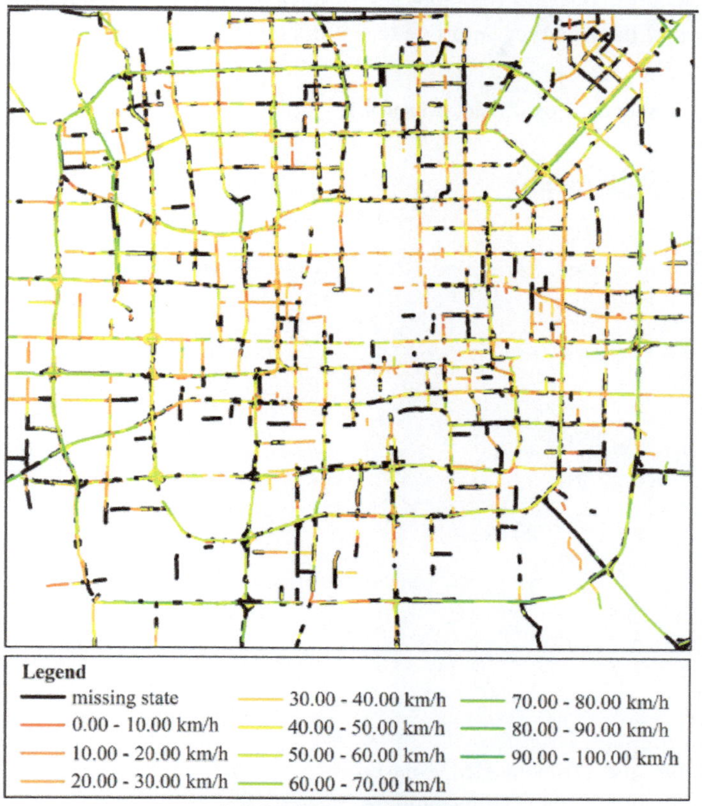

(a) Before estimation

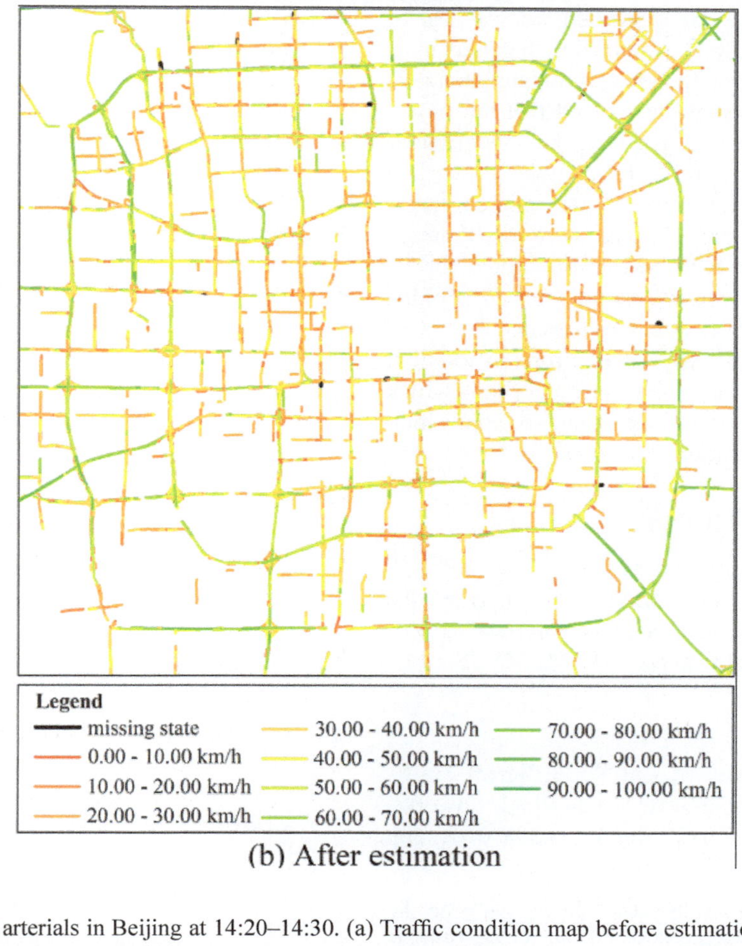

(b) After estimation

Figure 11. Traffic condition of arterials in Beijing at 14:20–14:30. (a) Traffic condition map before estimation, and (b) traffic condition map after estimation; the black regions represent missing states.

The main factor that affects the efficiency of the model is the number of candidates for the hidden states, N_{cand}, which has been discussed in Section 3.4. Several values of N_{cand} were selected for the experiments, where the missing state rate was around 74%. The results show that the accuracy improved as N_{cand} increased; however, the time cost increased significantly (Table 6). When N_{cand} reached around 12, the accuracy stabilized and the model could estimate approximately 4169.22 states per second. From the viewpoint of practical application, the model can meet the efficiency requirements of metropolitan real-time traffic estimation.

Table 6. Efficiency of the model corresponding to different values of N_{cand}

N_{cand}	MAE (km/h)	cost (s)	speed (states/s)
4	8.35	21	19456.38
6	7.9	25	16343.36
8	7.82	52	7857.38
10	7.78	66	6190.66
12	7.76	98	4169.22
14	7.76	130	3142.95
16	7.76	154	2653.14
18	7.76	213	1918.23
20	7.76	243	1681.41

doi:10.1371/journal.pone.0145348.t006

CONCLUSION

This paper presented an effective and efficient HMM-based model for urban-scale traffic estimation using floating car data. Clustering analysis and pattern mining were adopted to analyze a large data set of real probe data collected from a fleet of 12,600 taxis in Beijing, China, and it was found that there exist frequent clusters in which the road segments have similar traffic characteristics. Comparative analysis showed that the model based on clustering is more effective than the model based on adjacency relationships for traffic estimation. In order to achieve a trade-off between clustering accuracy and coverage, a multi-clustering strategy was adopted in the estimation process. Experimental results showed that the model can be applied to different scenarios; even when more than 70% of the original data are missing, the model can guarantee that more than 80% of the states have relatively small errors. In addition, the model was implemented using a real-time algorithm, which offers higher precision and has a broader scope for application than some offline traffic estimation algorithms.

AUTHOR CONTRIBUTIONS

Conceived and designed the experiments: XW LP TC. Performed the experiments: XW ML XY JS. Analyzed the data: XW ML XY JS. Contributed reagents/materials/analysis tools: XW ML XY JS. Wrote the paper: XW ML XY JS.

REFERENCES

1. Kong QJ, Zhao QK, Wei C, Liu YC. Efficient Traffic State Estimation for Large-Scale Urban Road Networks. Ieee T Intell Transp. 2013 Mar;14(1):398–407. doi: 10.1109/tits.2012.2218237
2. Leontiadis I, Marfia G, Mack D, Pau G, Mascolo C, Gerla M. On the Effectiveness of an Opportunistic Traffic Management System for Vehicular Networks. Intelligent Transportation Systems, IEEE Transactions on. 2011;12(4):1537–48. doi: 10.1109/tits.2011.2161469
3. Yeon J, Elefteriadou L, Lawphongpanich S. Travel time estimation on a freeway using Discrete Time Markov Chains. Transportation Research Part B: Methodological. 2008;42(4):325–38. doi: 10.1016/j.trb.2007.08.005
4. Bramberger M, Brunner J, Rinner B, Schwabach H. Real-time video analysis on an embedded smart camera for traffic surveillance. Real-Time and Embedded Technology and Applications Symposium, 2004 Proceedings RTAS 2004 10th IEEE; 2004 May 25–28; 2004. p. 174–181.
5. Herrera JC, Bayen AM. Traffic Flow Reconstruction Using Mobile Sensors and Loop Detector Data. TRB 87th Annual Meeting Compendium; 2007.
6. Hiribarren G, Herrera JC. Real time traffic states estimation on arterials based on trajectory data. Transport Res B-Meth. 2014 Nov;69:19–30. doi: 10.1016/j.trb.2014.07.003
7. Herrera JC, Work DB, Herring R, Ban X, Jacobson Q, Bayen AM. Evaluation of traffic data obtained via GPS-enabled mobile phones: The Mobile Century field experiment. Transportation Research Part C: Emerging Technologies. 2010;18(4):568–83. doi: 10.1016/j.trc.2009.10.006
8. de Fabritiis C, Ragona R, Valenti G. Traffic Estimation And Prediction Based On Real Time Floating Car Data. Intelligent Transportation Systems, 2008 ITSC 2008 11th International IEEE Conference on; 2008 Oct 12–15; 2008. p. 197–203.
9. Bar-Gera H. Evaluation of a cellular phone-based system for measurements of traffic speeds and travel times: A case study from Israel. Transportation Research Part

C: Emerging Technologies. 2007;15(6):380–91. doi: 10.1016/j.trc.2007.06.003

10. Breitenberger S, Grueber B, Neuherz M, Kates R. Traffic information potential and necessary penetration rates. Traffic Engineering & Control. 2004;45(11):396–401.

11. Vandenberghe W, Vanhauwaert E, Verbrugge S, Moerman I, Demeester P. Feasibility of expanding traffic monitoring systems with floating car data technology. Iet Intell Transp Sy. 2012 Dec;6(4):347–54. doi: 10.1049/iet-its.2011.0221

12. Herring R, Hofleitner A, Abbeel P, Bayen A. Estimating arterial traffic conditions using sparse probe data. Intelligent Transportation Systems (ITSC), 2010 13th International IEEE Conference on; 2010 Sept 19–22; 2010. p. 929–36.

13. Zhu YM, Li Z, Zhu HZ, Li ML, Zhang Q. A Compressive Sensing Approach to Urban Traffic Estimation with Probe Vehicles. Ieee T Mobile Comput. 2013 Nov;12(11):2289–302. doi: 10.1109/tmc.2012.205

14. Bejan AI, Gibbens RJ. Evaluation of velocity fields via sparse bus probe data in urban areas. Intelligent Transportation Systems (ITSC), 2011 14th International IEEE Conference on; 2011 Oct 5–7; 2011. p. 746–53.

15. Seo T, Kusakabe T, Asakura Y. Estimation of flow and density using probe vehicles with spacing measurement equipment. Transport Res C-Emer. 2015 Apr;53:134–50. doi: 10.1016/j.trc.2015.01.033

16. Fowe AJ, Chan YP. A microstate spatial-inference model for network-traffic estimation. Transport Res C-Emer. 2013 Nov;36:245–60. doi: 10.1016/j.trc.2013.08.011

17. Ramezani M, Geroliminis N. Queue Profile Estimation in Congested Urban Networks with Probe Data. Comput-Aided Civ Inf. 2015 Jun;30(6):414–32. doi: 10.1111/mice.12095

18. Tang TQ, Shi WF, Shang HY, Wang YP. An extended car-following model with consideration of the reliability of inter-vehicle communication. Measurement. 2014; 58:286–293. doi: 10.1016/j.measurement.2014.08.051

19. Gupta A.K.; Sharma S.; Redhu P. Analyses of lattice traffic flow model on a gradient highway. Commun Theor Phys. 2014; 62:393–404. doi: 10.1088/0253-6102/62/3/17

20. Gupta A.K.; Redhu P. Jamming transition of a two-dimensional traffic dynamics with consideration of optimal current difference. Phys Lett A. 2013; 377:2027–2033. doi: 10.1016/j.physleta.2013.06.009

21. Gupta A.K. A section approach to a traffic flow model on networks. Int J Mod Phys C. 2013,24. doi: 10.1142/s0129183113500186

22. Tang TQ, Li CY, Huang HJ. A new car-following model with the consideration of the driver's forecast effect. Physics Letters A. 2010; 374(38):3951–3956. doi: 10.1016/j.physleta.2010.07.062

23. Yu SW, Shi ZK. Dynamics of connected cruise control systems considering velocity changes with memory feedback. Measurement. 2015; 64:34–48. doi: 10.1016/j.measurement.2014.12.036

24. Ge J, Orosz G. Dynamics of connected vehicle systems with delayed acceleration feedback. Transportation Research Part C. 2014; 46:46–64. doi: 10.1016/j.trc.2014.04.014

25. Tang TQ, Huang HJ, Shang HY. A dynamic model for the heterogeneous traffic flow consisting of car, bicycle and pedestrian. International Journal of Modern Physics C. 2010; 21:159–176. doi: 10.1142/s0129183110015038

26. Yu SW, Shi ZK. An extended car-following model considering vehicular gap fluctuation. Measurement. 2015; 70:137–147. doi: 10.1016/j.measurement.2015.03.031

27. Yu SW, Shi ZK. An extended car-following model at signalized intersections. Physica A, 2014; 407:152–159. doi: 10.1016/j.physa.2014.03.081

28. Yu SW, Shi ZK. An improved car-following model considering headway changes with memory. Physica A, 2015; 421:1–14. doi: 10.1016/j.physa.2014.11.008

29. Yu S, Liu Q, Li X. Full velocity difference and acceleration model for a car-following theory. Communications in Nonlinear Science & Numerical Simulation. 2013; 18(5):1229–1234. doi: 10.1016/j.cnsns.2012.09.014

30. Wang JW, Wang YS, Yun MP, Yang XG. Development of Urban Road Network Traffic State Dynamic Estimation Method. Math Probl Eng. 2015. doi: 10.1155/2015/714149

31. Work DB, Blandin S, Tossavainen O-P, Piccoli B, Bayen AM. A Traffic Model for Velocity Data Assimilation. Applied Mathematics Research eXpress. 2010 January 1; 2010(1):1–35. doi: 10.1093/amrx/abq002

32. Hofleitner A, Herring R, Abbeel P, Bayen A. Learning the Dynamics of Arterial Traffic From Probe Data Using a Dynamic Bayesian Network. Intelligent Transportation Systems, IEEE Transactions on. 2012;13(4):1679–93. doi: 10.1109/tits.2012.2200474

33. von Luxburg U. A tutorial on spectral clustering. Stat Comput. 2007;17(4):395–416. doi: 10.1007/s11222-007-9033-z

34. Chen BY, Yuan H, Li QQ, Lam WHK, Shaw SL, Yan K. Map-matching algorithm for large-scale low-frequency floating car data. Int J Geogr Inf Sci. 2014 Jan 2;28(1):22–38. doi: 10.1080/13658816.2013.816427

35. He ZC, She XW, Zhuang LJ, Nie PL. On-line map-matching framework for floating car data with low sampling rate in urban road networks. Iet Intell Transp Sy. 2013 Dec;7(4):404–14. doi: 10.1049/iet-its.2011.0226

36. Raymond R, Morimura T, Osogami T, Hirosue N. Map matching with Hidden Markov Model on sampled road network. International Conference on Pattern Recognition (ICPR); 11–15 Nov. 2012; Tsukuba: IEEE; 2012. p. 2242–5.

CHAPTER 18

OBJECT-ORIENTED CLASSIFICATION OF SUGARCANE USING TIME-SERIES MIDDLE-RESOLUTION REMOTE SENSING DATA BASED ON ADABOOST

Zhen Zhou[1,2], Jingfeng Huang[1,3], Jing Wang[1,2], Kangyu Zhang[1,2], Zhaomin Kuang[4] , Shiquan Zhong[4] , Xiaodong Song[1,2]

[1] Institute of Remote Sensing and Information Application, Zhejiang University, Hangzhou, China

[2] Key Laboratory of Agricultural Remote Sensing and Information System, Zhejiang Province, Hangzhou, China

[3] Key Laboratory of Environmental Remediation and Ecological Health, Ministry of Education, Zhejiang University, Hangzhou, China

[4] Guangxi Zhuang Autonomous Region Institute of Meteorological and Disaster-Mitigation Research, Nanning, China

ABSTRACT

Most areas planted with sugarcane are located in southern China. However, remote sensing of sugarcane has been limited because useable remote sensing data are limited due to the cloudy climate of this region during the growing season and severe spectral mixing with other crops. In this study, we developed a methodology for automatically mapping sugarcane over large areas using time-series middle-resolution remote sensing data. For this purpose, two major techniques were used, the object-oriented method (OOM) and data mining (DM). In addition, time-series Chinese HJ-1 CCD images were obtained during the sugarcane growing period. Image objects were generated using a multi-resolution segmentation algorithm, and DM was implemented using the AdaBoost algorithm, which generated the prediction model. The prediction model was applied to the HJ-1 CCD time-series image objects, and then a map of the sugarcane planting area was produced. The classification accuracy was evaluated using independent field survey sampling points. The confusion matrix analysis showed that the overall classification accuracy reached 93.6% and that the Kappa coefficient was 0.85. Thus, the results showed that this method is feasible, efficient, and applicable for extrapolating the classification of other crops in large areas where the application of high-resolution remote sensing data is impractical due to financial considerations or because qualified images are limited.

INTRODUCTION

Sugar is a major food additive and is one of the most important raw bioenergy materials. Sugar made from sugarcane accounts for approximately 80% of the total sugar production in China [1]. The areas of sugarcane planting and production in China are ranked third in the world after those of India and Brazil. Regarding safety and policy making, it is important to quickly estimate sugarcane planting status over large areas. Conventionally, the local government usually estimates the sugarcane planting area by using a field survey; however, the survey coverage is usually very limited and time consuming.

As a powerful alternative, remote sensing provides an effective method for monitoring crop growth and estimating crop yield due to its unique capabilities in terms of its spectral, temporal and spatial resolutions [2]. In the literature, many different types of optical remote sensing data, such as the Moderate Resolution Imaging Spectroradiometer (MODIS), Advanced Spaceborne Thermal Emission and Reflection Radiometer (ASTER), Landsat-5 Thematic Mapper (TM), High Resolution Imaging Camera (CCD) on board of China-Brazil Earth Resources Satellite-2 and -2B (CBERS-2 and

Citation: Zhou Z, Huang J, Wang J, Zhang K, Kuang Z, Zhong S, et al. (2015) Object-Oriented Classification of Sugarcane Using Time-Series Middle-Resolution Remote Sensing Data Based on AdaBoost. PLoS ONE 10(11): e0142069. doi:10.1371/journal.pone.0142069

-2B), Landsat-7 Enhanced Thematic Mapper Plus (ETM+), SPOT-5 High Resolution Geometrical (HRG), and ENVISAT Advanced SAR (ASAR), have been applied for discriminating between sugarcane varieties, mapping sugarcane planting areas and estimating sugarcane yields [1–6].

Nevertheless, approximately 90% of China's sugarcane crop is grown in southern and southwest regions [1] where the landscape is highly heterogeneous and is covered by cloudy weather during the sugarcane growing season. Consequently, only a few qualified remote sensing images are available. Additionally, cross cultivation in the above-mentioned sugarcane growing regions is common; thus, the extraction of sugarcane information from remote sensing data is compromised by spectral mixing with other types of crops [7].

The unique phenology of sugarcane, which is longer than rice and peanut and shorter than evergreen plants, such as banana and eucalyptus, may provide valuable information for remote sensing classification in the study area. By properly using time-series remote sensing images, the phenology of sugarcane, which can be used to differentiate the sugarcane planting area from the other land cover types, may decrease the interference of similar spectra from the other vegetation in the spectrum and increase the classification accuracy [8].

Conventional remote sensing classification algorithms, e.g., the unsupervised/supervised classifiers, the Iterative Self-Organizing Data Analysis Technique (ISOData), the Maximum Likelihood (ML) classifier, the Neural Network (NN) and the Support Vector Machine (SVM), are applied directly to pixels and do not consider contextual information [9–11]. However, pixel-based classification procedures, particularly those only using single imagery, may cause problems in automatic pattern recognition due to phenological crop variability, different cropping systems and non-uniform measurement conditions [12]. Alternatively, object-oriented techniques based on multi-temporal remote sensing images have been widely applied for land cover classification[13].

Compared with traditional pixel-based remote sensing classification methods, object-oriented methods (OOMs) consider the analysis of an "object in space" instead of a "pixel in space" [14]. The objects in OOMs have geographical features such as shape and length; texture features such as the gray level co-occurrence matrix (GLCM); and topological entities such as adjacency [15]. All of the attributes of a specific object form a knowledge base for the sample objects and can be applied in the classification process using data mining (DM) techniques [16].

DM is a separate stage within a process known as knowledge discovery in database (KDD) [17]. In the KDD process, decision tree (DT) classification techniques have been used to classify remote sensing data and have several advantages over the maximum likelihood method and artificial neural network algorithms. DT has the ability to handle data measured on different scales, but lacks any assumptions concerning the frequency distributions of data in each of the classes and the ability to handle non-linear relationships between features and classes [9]. For high-dimensional data, DT has no obvious advantages compared with the ANN and MLC classifiers [18]. However, the boosting method in machine learning is more robust than traditional DT. The basic idea of boosting is to create a highly accurate prediction rule by combining many relatively weak and inaccurate rules [19]. The AdaBoost (Adaptive Boosting) algorithm was the first practical boosting algorithm and remains one of the most widely used and studied data mining algorithms [20].

The small sun-synchronous satellites for environmental and disaster monitoring and forecasting (HJ-1 A/B) of China were launched in 2008, with a spatial resolution of 30 m, four spectral bands ranging from 0.43–0.90°μm and a revisit cycle of four days (the revisit cycle of the constellation is 2 days) [11]. Considering the influences of climate and the affordability of high spatial resolution remote sensing data, this study aimed to demonstrate the feasibility of using OOMs and the AdaBoost algorithm based on HJ-1 A/B data to classify sugarcane growing areas in regions with limited data and complex land cover. Thus, this study aimed to classify sugarcane production at a large regional scale in southern China. The phenological information regarding the major crops in the study area was used to facilitate the selection of remote sensing data and the interpretation of the results. The accuracy of this classification was evaluated using an independent validation data set.

MATERIALS AND METHODS

Ethics statement

No specific permissions were required for the field investigation in Suixi County, China. We confirm that the field investigation in Suixi County did not involve endangered or protected species.

Study area

The study area, Suixi County, is located north of the Leizhou Peninsula in Guangdong Province (Fig 1). The terrain in this area is relatively flat, and the mean elevation is approximately 40 m above sea level. Suixi County has a subtropical maritime monsoon climate with a mean annual temperature of approximately 22.8°C and an annual precipitation between 1700–1800 mm. Suixi County is a major sugarcane planting area in Guangdong Province, with approximately 467 km^2 of planted area year round. In addition to sugarcane, the major vegetation in this region includes rice, peanut, banana, grass, pineapple, pitaya, mango and eucalyptus. However, the dominant types of crops in terms of area are rice and peanut.

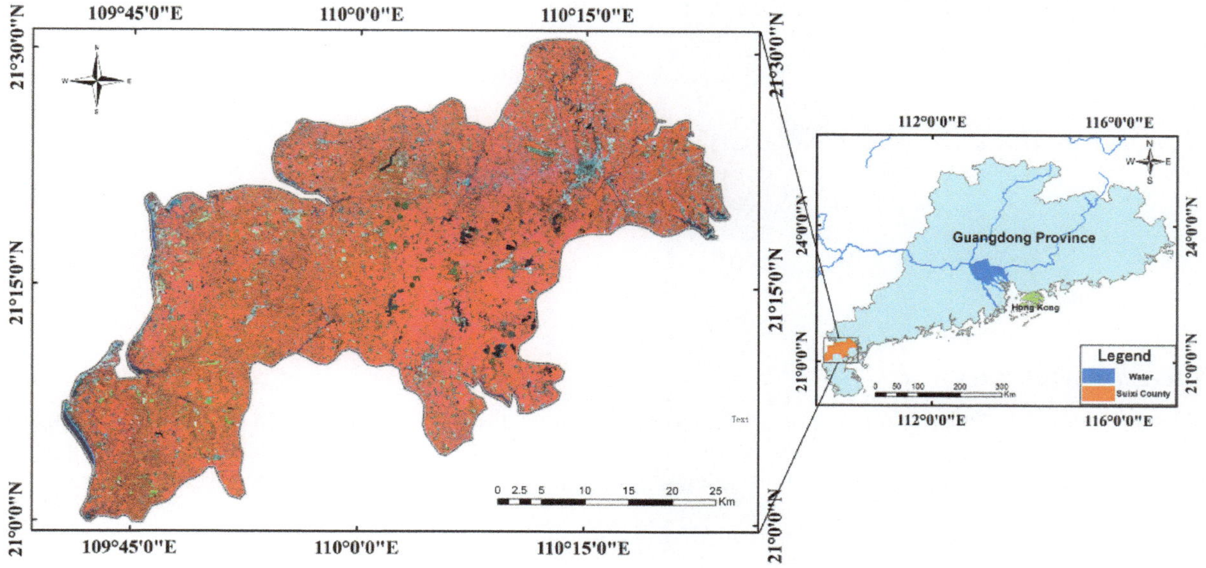

Figure 1. Study area in Suixi County, China. HJ-1 CCD image acquired on 26 October 2013 with a composition of R (4), G (3) and B (2). The HJ-1 CCD images were downloaded from the China Center for Resources Satellite Data and Application. I request permission for the open-access journal PLOS ONE to publish **Fig 1** under the Creative Commons Attribution License (CCAL) CC BY 3.0.

Crop phenologies

Crop phenology is well correlated with changes in the spectral features of vegetation and is an important reference parameter for selecting remote sensing images [21, 22]. For sugarcane, the seedling period is from March to early June (including ratoon crops), the stem elongation period is from early June to the end of September, the sugar accumulation period is in October, the maturation period is from November to December, and harvest begins in late December and lasts until March of the next year. As mentioned above, of the other crops, only rice and peanut were considered because they cover large growing areas. The corresponding phenologies are listed in Table 1.

Table 1. Summary of the major phenological periods of the three major crops grown in the study area

Crop	Year (2013)							Year (2014)				
	Jun.	Jul.	Aug.	Sep.	Oct.	Nov.	Dec.	Jan.	Feb.	Mar.	Apr.	May
Sugarcane	ST	ST	ST	ST	SA	MA	MA/HA	HA	HA	HA/SE	HA/SE	SL
Rice	HA	SO	VE	RE	MA	HA	FA	FA	FA	SO	VE	RE/MA
Peanut	MA/HA	SE	SL	FP	MA	HA	FA	FA	FA	SE	SL	FP

Note: HA: harvest stage; SE: seeding stage; SL: seedling stage; ST: stem elongation stage; SA: sugar accumulation stage; MA: maturation stage; SO: sowing-transplanting stage; VE: vegetative stage; RE: reproductive stage; FA: fallow; FP: flowering-podding stage.

doi:10.1371/journal.pone.0142069.t001

Remote Sensing Images

The sensor characteristics of the HJ-1 CCD images are presented in Table 2. To better differentiate sugarcane from the other land cover classes, 6 HJ-1 CCD images (Table 3) were obtained based on the sugarcane phenological periods shown in Table 1. The HJ-1 CCD images were geometrically corrected (the total root mean square error<0.5 pixel) by using Landsat-8 OLI data (acquired on 14/11/2014, path/row: 124/45) of the entire study area for the reference image. Atmospheric correction was performed using the FLAASH module in the ENVI package.

Table 2. Specifications of the HJ-1 A/B satellites

Satellite	Payload	Band	Spectral range (μm)	Spatial resolution (m)	Swath width (km)	Revisit cycle (day)
HJ-1 A/B	Multispectral CCD camera	1	0.43–0.52	30	360 (700 for two)	4 (2 for constellation)
		2	0.52–0.60	30		
		3	0.63–0.69	30		
		4	0.76–0.90	30		

doi:10.1371/journal.pone.0142069.t002

Table 3. HJ-1 A/B CCD images used in the classification

No.	Satellite	Sensor	Date (dd/mm/yyyy)	Phenology of sugarcane
1	HJ-1 A	CCD2	13/06/2013	Stem elongation
2	HJ-1 A	CCD1	03/10/2013	Sugar accumulation
3	HJ-1 A	CCD1	26/10/2013	Sugar accumulation
4	HJ-1 B	CCD2	28/12/2013	Maturation
5	HJ-1 A	CCD1	23/01/2014	Harvest
6	HJ-1 B	CCD2	13/05/2014	Seedling

doi:10.1371/journal.pone.0142069.t003

Classification Methods

The proposed approach includes two major steps: image segmentation and data mining. The first part includes object-oriented multi-resolution image segmentation and attribute table generation, and the second part includes building the training set, using the AdaBoost algorithm and boosted classifiers, and interpreting and evaluating the classification results (Fig 2).

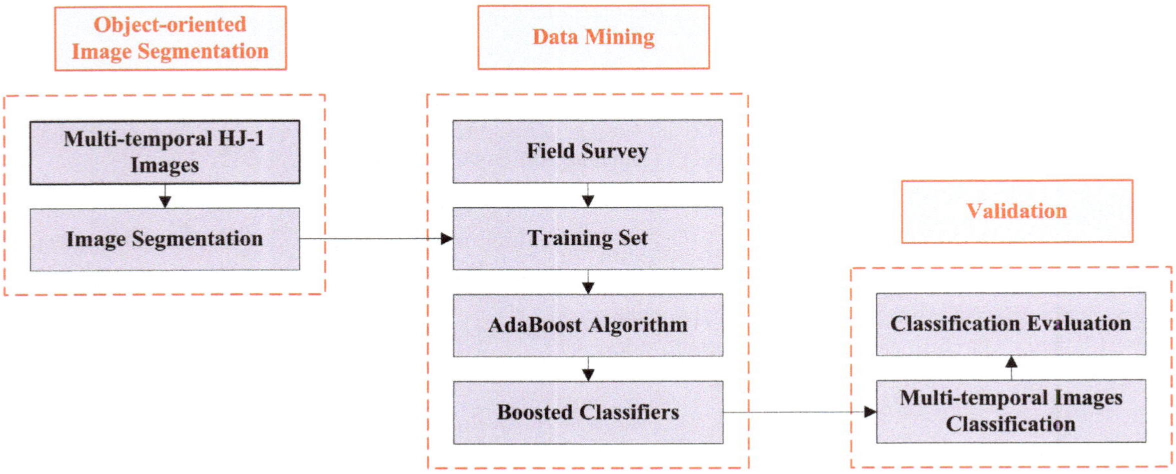

Figure 2. Schematic diagram illustrates the primary processes in the extraction of sugarcane growing areas. I request permission for the open-access journal PLOS ONE to publish Fig 2 under the Creative Commons Attribution License (CCAL) CC BY 3.0.

Image Segmentation

Object-oriented image segmentation was performed using the eCognition software [23]. The generation of objects was subjected to the heterogeneity criteria by adjusting the spectral band weight, scale parameter, form factor, and compactness factor. To guarantee the homogeneity of objects, all bands of the HJ-1 CCD time-series images were selected for segmentation. The object attributes used in the following classification are shown in Table 4. The selected attributes were spectral, spatial, textural and customized attributes, such as the normalized difference vegetation index (NDVI) [24], which has been demonstrated as closely correlated with the leaf area, biomass, percent ground cover and crop productivity [25, 26]; the enhanced vegetation index (EVI) [27]; and the 2-band enhanced vegetation index (EVI2) [28].

Table 4. Object attributes used to characterize sugarcane and the other classes in the selected HJ-1 CCD time-series images

Type	Attribute	Description	Reference value range
Customized	NDVI	Vegetation index	[-1, 1]
	EVI	Vegetation index	[-1, 1]
	EVI2	Vegetation index	[-1, 1]
Spectral	Mean	Mean spectral intensity of an image object	$[C_k^{min}, C_k^{max}]^a$
	Standard deviation	Standard deviation of the spectral intensity of an image object	$[0, \frac{1}{2}C_k^{range}]$
Spatial	Area	Total area of an image object	[0, scene size]
	Border length	Sum of outer and inner borders, if existing, of an image object	[0, ∞]
	Pixel number	Number of pixels forming an image object	[0, scene size]
	Asymmetry	Relative length of an image object compared to a regular polygon	[0, 1]
	Border index	Ratio between the border length of the image object and the smallest enclosing rectangle	[1, ∞], 1 = ideal
	Compactness	Product of the length and width divided by the number of pixels of the image object	[0, ∞], 1 = ideal
	Elliptic fit	Describing how well an image object fits into an ellipse of similar size and proportion	[0, 1], 1 = complete fit, and 0 = no fit
	Main direction	Direction of the eigenvector belonging to the larger of the two eigenvalues derived from the covariance matrix of the spatial distribution of the image object	[0, 180]
	Rectangular fit	Describing how well an image object fits into a rectangle of similar size and proportion	[0, 1], where 1 represents a perfect rectangle
	Roundness	Describing how similar an image object fits into an ellipse	[0, ∞], 0 = ideal
	Shape index	Describing the smoothness of the surface of an image object border	[0, 1]
Texture	GLCM[b]contrast	Measure of the amount of local variation in the image	[0, 65025]
	GLCM homogeneity	Opposite of the contrast	[0, 1]
	GLCM dissimilarity	Similar to contrast but increases linearly	[0, 255]
	GLCM entropy	A measure of textural uniformity of an image	[0, 10404]
	GLCM mean	Average intensity of all pixels in a 2-D image object that belonged to the GLCM	[0, 255]
	GLCM std. dev	Standard deviation of all pixels in a 2-D image object that belonged to the GLCM	[0, 255]
	GLCM correlation	Linear dependency of gray levels of neighboring pixels	[0, 1]

[a]C_k^{min}: the darkest possible intensity; C_k^{max}: the brightest possible intensity.

[b]GLCM: gray level co-occurrence matrix.

doi:10.1371/journal.pone.0142069.t004

Training Data Sets

A field campaign was conducted in 2014 in the study area, and 382 field samples were collected using a portable GPS (Trimble SA). Among the samples, 146 were sugarcane, while the rest of the samples belonged to the other land cover types, e.g., water body, impervious surface/buildings, and other types of vegetation.

Data mining.

Data mining involv.es the selection and application of intelligent techniques to extract patterns of interest for the effective production of knowledge [17]. In this study, the overall goals of data mining were to extract information from a data set (i.e., the 382 samples) and transform it into an understandable structure for further use. For this purpose, the boosting technique was applied.

Boosting is a machine learning ensemble meta-algorithm that can be used to reduce bias and variance in supervised learning. The basic principle of boosting is to learn multiple classifiers (weak classifiers) by changing the weights of the training samples and then combine these classifiers to improve classification performance. In this study, we used the AdaBoost algorithm.

AdaBoost is a generic iterative supervised learning algorithm that combines the other learning algorithms (weak learners) into a weighted linear boosted classifier to obtain a much higher accuracy [29]. Itis the first practical boosting algorithm and works by changing the weights of training data at each iteration (i.e., increasing the weights of the misclassified samples in the previous weak classifier and reducing the weights of the correctly classified samples). Thus, the misclassified samples will receive more attention due to their increased weights. Using this method, we should obtain a series of weak classifiers. Second, the algorithm adopts a weighted majority vote strategy in which the weights of the weak classifiers with small classification error rates are increased to improve their importance in the vote and vice versa [20, 30]. The package 'adabag' in the R environment was used for this purpose [31].

To evaluate the classification model generated by the AdaBoost algorithm, a standard statistics tool known as cross validation was used to provide an objective measure of quality for the generated model [32]. Specifically, a k-fold cross-validation method was adopted. The k-fold cross-validation involves partitioning a data set into k randomly complementary subsets. Of the k subsets, the decision tree built from the remaining k-1 subsets (called the training sets) will be validated by the retained single one. The cross validation process is then repeated k times (the folds), with each of the k subsets used exactly once as the validation data. Additional details on the cross-validation concept may be found in [33, 34]. We used a 10-fold cross validation to test the prediction model and summarized information regarding the classification error, such as the mean absolute error and relative absolute error.

Classification of multi-temporal images and evaluation.

Using the verified predict model generated by the AdaBoost algorithm, the segmented HJ-1 CCD multi-temporal series data were classified into two classes of interest, sugarcane and others, by using the rules defined by the attributes and their respective thresholds, which were identified by AdaBoost.

Another 500 randomly selected sampling points (not involved in the training) were used to evaluate the classification accuracy. The confusion matrix assessment method was applied, and the global accuracy and Kappa coefficients were evaluated.

RESULTS

Image Segmentation

In the process of segmenting the multi-temporal HJ-1 CCD time-series images, image objects were generated based on several adjustable criteria of homogeneity or heterogeneity in color and shape. The four parameters listed in Table 5 (i.e., scale, shape, color and compactness) need to be calibrated. We focused on adjusting the scale parameter because this parameter affects the average image object size (a larger value leads to larger objects and vice versa). To achieve better classification results, four different scale parameter values were used, and the results were compared using visual interpretation to determine the most suitable scale parameter value (Fig 3).

Table 5. Multi-resolution segmentation criteria used for the multi-temporal HJ-1 CCD images.

Parameter	(a)	(b)	(c)	(d)
Scale	50	40	30	35
Shape	0.2	0.2	0.2	0.2
Color	0.8	0.8	0.8	0.8
Compactness	0.5	0.5	0.5	0.5

doi:10.1371/journal.pone.0142069.t005

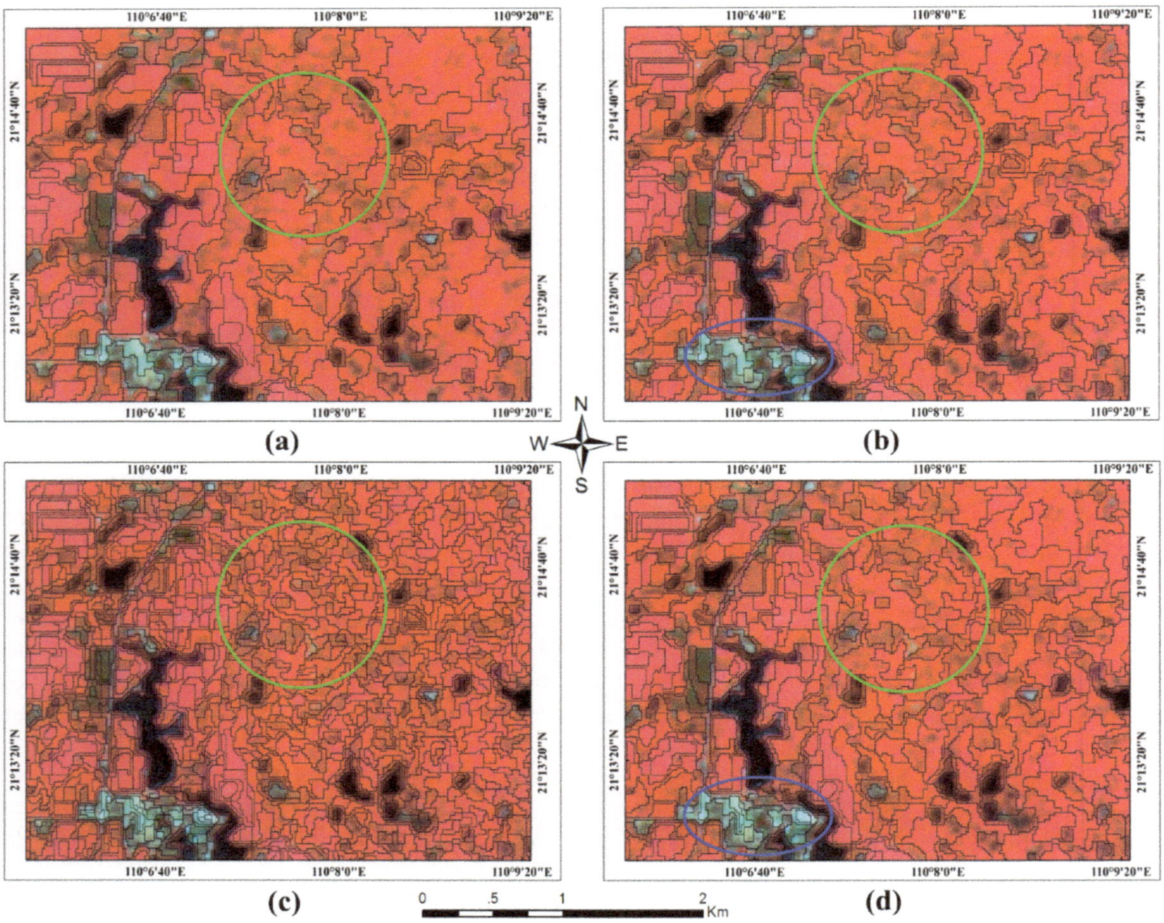

Figure 3. Multi-resolution segmentation using four different segmentation criteria. The base map of the multi-temporal HJ-1 CCD multi-spectral images with the following composition: R (4), G (3) and B (2). I request permission for the open-access journal PLOS ONE to publish **Fig 3** under the Creative Commons Attribution License (CCAL) CC BY 3.0.

We tuned the scale parameter using four different settings, i.e., 50, 40, 35 and 30. In Fig 3a, the segmentation was inadequate and the mixing of different types of cropland was severe (e.g., in the green circle). In Fig 3b, the pattern was more reasonable and the value of the scale parameter decreased to 40, which split the large mixed croplands into smaller mixed croplands. When the scale parameter decreased to 30, as shown in Fig 3c, over-segmentation occurred, indicating that further reducing the scale parameter would not improve the effect of segmentation. However, when the scale parameter was set to 35, as shown in Fig 3d, the segmentation effect showed no obvious changes (in green circles) compared with Fig 3b; however, the residential areas (in blue circles) were over-segmented. Thus, we selected the parameters in column (b) in Table 5 and segmented the HJ-1 CCD time-series images into 22,763 objects to form the test set (including the training set).

Data Mining

To determine suitable boosting iteration number ranges, we gradually increased the boosting iteration number from 1 to 100 and calculated the classification error rate as shown in Fig 4. The error rate decreased quickly as the boosting iteration number increased from 1 to 25. Beyond 25, increasing the boosting iteration number did not improve the error rate significantly, and the error rate was approximately 0.036.

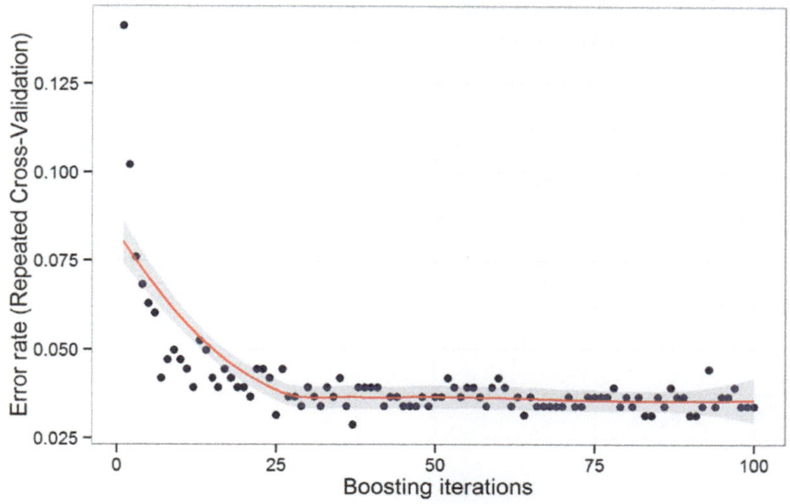

Figure 4. Relationship between the boosting iteration number and the corresponding error rate. I request permission for the open-access journal PLOS ONE to publish **Fig 4** under the Creative Commons Attribution License (CCAL) CC BY 3.0.

We further tested the changes in the relative importance of each attribute in the boosting tree as the boosting iteration number increased from 100 to 1000. Fig 5 shows the relative importance of each attribute after 100 iterations. We increased the iteration number to 1000, retrieved the relative importance of each attribute again, and then compared our findings with the results shown in Fig 5. The ranks of the first four attributes remained unchanged, while the ranks of the other attributes (importance≥1) only exhibited minor changes. Thus, we ran the AdaBoost algorithm using 100 iterations, and the overall accuracy was 96.35% with a Kappa coefficient of 0.92.

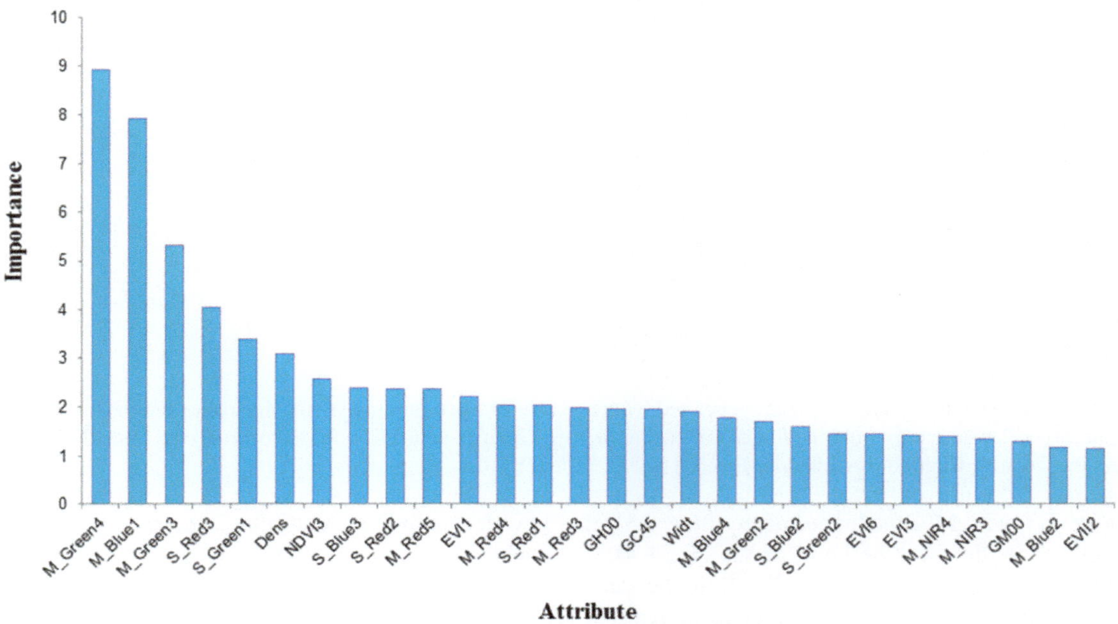

Figure 5. The relative importance of each attribute in the classification task (only those attributes with importance ≥ 1 are shown here). The nomenclature of the attributes are explained as follows. The prefix "M_" means the mean value of the specific spectral band that follows, e.g.,

Green, Blue, Red and NIR; the prefix "S_" represents the standard difference of the following band; and the suffix numbers, e.g., 1 to 6, correspond to the image numbers given in Table 3. The Dens, Widt and Asym are the abbreviations of Density, Width and Asymmetry, respectively. The GH00 is short for the GLCM homogeneity of an object at the angle of 0°; GC45 is short for the GLCM contrast of an object at the angle of 45°; and GM00 is short for the GLCM mean of an object at the angle of 0°. I request permission for the open-access journal PLOS ONE to publish **Fig 5** under the Creative Commons Attribution License (CCAL) CC BY 3.0.

Decision Rules

By applying the AdaBoost algorithm iteratively, 100 DTs were generated. We chose the DT with the largest weight to illustrate the reasonability of the generated decision rules from the HJ-1 multi-temporal CCD time-series images (Fig 6).

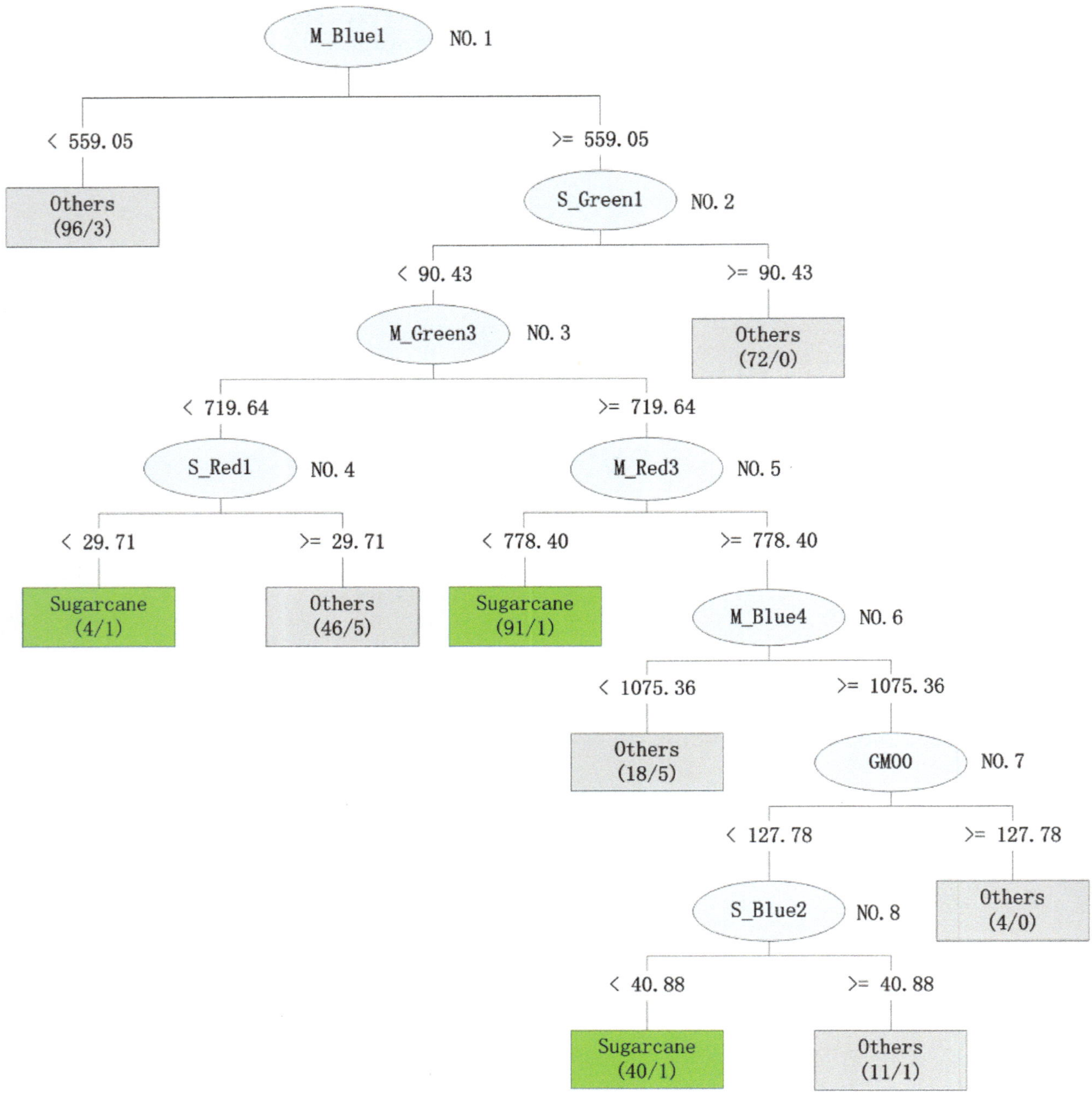

Figure 6. The decision tree with the largest weight generated by the AdaBoost algorithm to classify sugarcane and the other land cover types (note that the spectral reflectance was multiplied by a scale factor of 10^4). I request permission for the open-access journal PLOS ONE to publish **Fig 6** under the Creative Commons Attribution License (CCAL) CC BY 3.0.

The root of DT was M_Blue1, the mean value (M) of the spectral reflectance in the blue band of the No. 1 HJ-1 data (see Table 3, and all the attributes will follow the same nomenclature) and most of the eucalyptus and banana samples fell on the left side of the DT. During this period, the sugarcane was in the early stem elongation stage with small plants and low chlorophyll content in the canopy; thus, the reflectance in the blue band was obviously higher than that of eucalyptus and banana.

The No. 2 node was S_Green1, which is the standard deviation (S) of the spectral reflectance in the green band of the No. 1 HJ-1 data, and most of the residential objects fell on the right side of the branch. For crop objects, the spectral reflectance in the green band and its standard deviation were much more uniform than those of the residential land (particularly the village, where scattered tree canopies usually mixed with houses).

The No. 3 node classified most of the sugarcane into the right branch. Except for several sugarcane objects, most of the samples (i.e., eucalyptus, banana and the mixture of evergreen forest and bare land) were classified into the right branch of the No. 4 node. Thus, at this stage (sugar accumulation for sugarcane, and maturation for rice and peanut), the average green band spectral reflectance was suitable for separating the major crops from the other plants.

At the same stage as the No. 3 node, the No. 5 node used the average red band spectral reflectance and classified a large portion of the sugarcane into the left branch. As mentioned above, the sugarcane was at its most vigorous growing stage (i.e., the sugar accumulation stage), and the relatively high chlorophyll content of the sugarcane canopy compared with the rice and peanut canopies decreased the spectral reflectance of the red band (the red band is a major chlorophyll absorption spectral region).

In December, i.e., the No. 6 node (HJ-1 image No. 4), the rice and peanut crops had been harvested and the corresponding croplands were in the fallow state. During this period, sugarcane harvesting had recently began, and 5 sugarcane samples were misclassified. However, most of the sugarcane samples, which had relatively higher blue band spectral reflectance, fell on the right branch.

Finally, the remaining sugarcane samples were identified by lower mean GLCM values and lower blue reflectance standard deviations in the No. 2 HJ-1 image, and bare lands and roads were classified as other objects with higher GLCM mean values. Additionally, the objects with higher blue reflectance standard deviations in the No. 2 HJ-1 image were classified as residential areas.

Classification Results

The prediction model built by the AdaBoost algorithm was applied to the entire study area; the classification results for the sugarcane growing area are shown in Fig 7. The total growing area of sugarcane was approximately 481.58 km^2 in the 2013–2014 harvest year. According to the statistical data of the local agriculture department in 2014, the total acreage of sugarcane was 492.97 km^2, and the relative classification accuracy was approximately 97.68%.

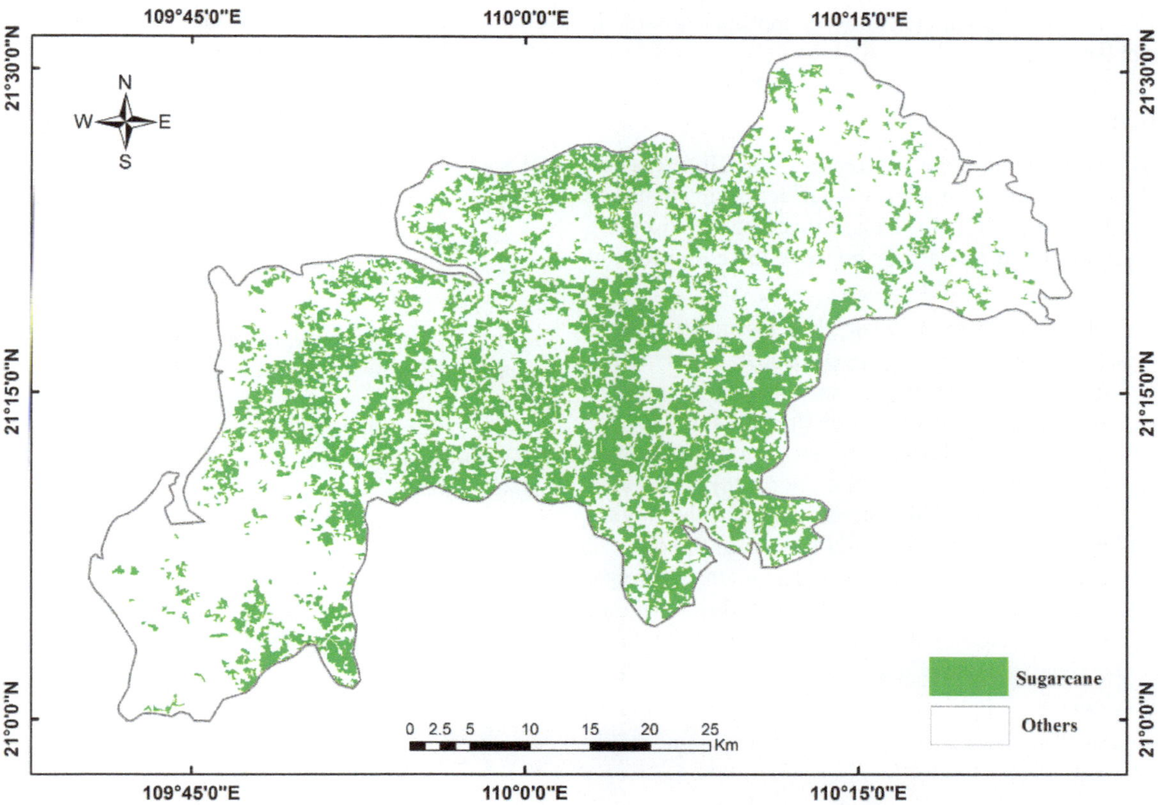

Figure 7. Thematic map of sugarcane areas in Suixi County. I request permission for the open-access journal PLOS ONE to publish Fig 7 under the Creative Commons Attribution License (CCAL) CC BY 3.0.

The confusion matrix shown in Table 6 was generated using another 500 sampling points, which are mentioned in section 2.4.4. Among the 500 reference sampling points, 159 points belonged to the sugarcane class and 24 points were misclassified into the "others" class. Overall, 341 points belonged to the "others" class, and only 8 points were misclassified into the sugarcane class. Finally, the overall classification accuracy and Kappa coefficient were 93.60% and 0.85, respectively.

Table 6. Confusion matrix of the classification verified using independent sampling points

		Reference map		
	Class	Sugarcane	Others	Total
Classification result	Sugarcane	135	8	143
	Others	24	333	357
	Total	159	341	500

doi:10.1371/journal.pone.0142069.t006

DISCUSSIONS

Image Segmentation

Image segmentation is a fundamental step in object-oriented classification; however, the effectiveness of segmentation, which is determined by the segmentation parameter settings, heavily relies on the experience of the expert and the specific objects of interest [35]. In this study, we adopted a trial and error strategy, calibrated the scale parameter values from 50 to 30, and compared the different segmentation results. The results showed that setting the scale parameter to 50 is too loose and that setting the scale parameter to 30 is too tight. Furthermore, no obvious differences were observed when the scale parameter was set to 40 or 35 for croplands; however, when 35 was adopted, the fragmentation of residential land became severe and classification could not be performed. Thus, setting the scale parameter to 40 is appropriate for this specific problem.

Data Mining

The classification error rate decreased significantly and converged quickly when we used the AdaBoost algorithm (Fig 4). Compared with traditional DT classification, the ensemble classifier AdaBoost can effectively improve the classification accuracy.

The object attributes involved in the classification were generally classified as customized, spectral, spatial and texture (Table 4). Fig 5 only shows the 28 attributes with relative importance greater than 1 in the prediction model. Most of these attributes (18/28) belonged to the spectral category, followed by the customized (5/28), texture (3/28) and spatial (2/28) attribute categories. We speculated that the highly fragmented landscape in the study area (common in southern China) resulted in the extremely diversified geometric patterns, even for the same crops. The effects of the texture attributes on the classification were not significant and were potentially caused by the relative coarse spatial resolution of the HJ-1 CCD image data.

Among the 18 spectral attributes, 6, 5 and 5 attributes were related to the red, green and blue bands, respectively. Only two attributes (i.e., M_NIR4 and M_NIR3) were related to the NIR band, and the relative importance of these attributes was minor. This finding may be directly related to the low importance of vegetation indices (customized attributes) in the prediction model. Furthermore, this finding indicated that the combined single bands could achieve sound classification results without fully using the vegetation index information.

Regarding temporal attributes, the 4 (M_Blue1, S_Green1, EVI1 and S_Red1), 6 (S_Red2, M_Green2, S_Blue2, S_Green2, M_Blue2 and EVI12), 7 (M_Green3, S_Red3, NDVI3, S_Blue3, M_Red3, EVI3 and M_NIR3), 4 (M_Green4, M_Red4, M_Blue4 and M_NIR4), 1 (M_Red5) and 1 (EVI6) attributes were related to HJ-1 images 1–6, respectively, as shown inTable 3. These findings clearly show that the images from the early and middle phenology stages of sugarcane were more critical than the latter ones.

Function of Crop Phenology in the Classification

The phenologies of the major crops in the study area could provide key information for selecting remote sensing images [36]. The six images used in this study (Table 3) covered the entire sugarcane growing season and included the major phenologies of rice and peanut (Table 1). For example, the 1st temporal period was June, when the blue band spectral reflectance could be used to clearly discriminate the crops (sugarcane, rice and peanut) from eucalyptus and banana. In Fig 6, the No. 5 node, which corresponds to the image from October, used the maximum red light absorption capability of sugarcane at that stage to differentiate between rice and peanut. When using knowledge of the phenologies of the major crops in the specific study area, the image selection should be very specific and the prediction model should be easy to interpret.

From Figs 5 and 6, we observed that the first four images dominated the building processes of the decision rules (i.e., the left two images might be redundant). Thus, under this technical framework, we built knowledge regarding which critical temporal window should be used to guide image selection. Next, the redundant images of these ranges could be safely omitted. For this specific study, if only several qualified images covering the early and middle sugarcane phenologies can be obtained, then the classification accuracy should be guaranteed. Additionally, the remote sensing images obtained during the latter phenologies after sugar accumulation may not be necessary.

CONCLUSION

The classification of sugarcane in southern China in large areas faces two challenges: (1) a limited amount of qualified (and affordability in practical applications) remote sensing data due to pervasive cloudy weather and (2) the complex mixture of land cover and their similar spectral reflectances. In this context, our goal was to fully use the spectral and textural differences in various croplands in limited middle-resolution remote sensing images to facilitate the classification of sugarcane. Additionally, we aimed to determine whether a suitable temporal window exists to guide the selection of key remote sensing images in sugarcane classification.

In this study, six HJ-1 CCD images with a spatial resolution of 30 m and covering the entire sugarcane growing season (2013–2014) were used. The composite image, including the vegetation indices, was segmented into 22,763 objects using an object-oriented method. Next, the AdaBoost algorithm was used to build the DT model using 100 iterations. A 10-fold cross-validation method was applied to 382 field samples and showed that the overall classification and Kappa coefficient were 96.35% and 0.92, respectively. The DT model was applied to the entire study area to classify sugarcane and was tested using another 500 independent sampling points in the field. The overall accuracy achieved was 93.6%, and the Kappa coefficient was 0.85.

The classification model (i.e., a boosting tree) was built using the AdaBoost algorithm, and the categories and temporal features of the object attributes (Table 4) with relative importance greater than 1 were specifically checked (Fig 5). According to the proportion, most of the attributes belonged to the spectral category, followed by the customized, texture and spatial categories. Most of the spectral attributes were related to visible bands, and the effects of NIR bands and vegetation indices were minor. Only three texture and two spatial attributes with relative importance greater than 1 were identified, which might be caused by the relative coarse spatial resolution of the HJ-1 CCD data and the highly fragmented and irregular landscape in the study area.

Interestingly, we found that most of the attributes belonged to the early and middle temporal HJ-1 images and that the images during the early and middle phenology stages of sugarcane were clearly more critical compared with the latter images. Thus, under this technical framework, constructing an optimized image selection principle to guide remote sensing classification in similar regions is possible.

ACKNOWLEDGMENTS

We thank the China Center for Resources Satellite Data and Application for providing the free HJ-1 CCD data and the USGS for providing the free Landsat-8 OLI data. We also thank Pamela F. from American Journal Experts (https://www.aje.com) for linguistic assistance during the preparation of our manuscript. In addition, we thank the anonymous reviewers for their helpful comments.

AUTHOR CONTRIBUTIONS

Conceived and designed the experiments: ZZ XDS. Performed the experiments: ZZ KYZ. Analyzed the data: ZZ JW. Contributed reagents/materials/analysis tools: ZZ ZMK SQZ. Wrote the paper: ZZ XDS JFH.

REFERENCES

1. Lin H, Chen J, Pei Z, Zhang S, Hu X. Monitoring sugarcane growth using ENVISAT ASAR data. IEEE Tran Geosci Remote Sens. 2009;47(8):2572–80. doi: 10.1109/tgrs.2009.2015769
2. Xavier AC, Rudorff BF, Shimabukuro YE, Berka LMS, Moreira MA. Multi-temporal analysis of MODIS data to classify sugarcane crop. Int J Remote Sens. 2006;27(4):755–68. doi: 10.1080/01431160500296735
3. Rudorff BFT, Aguiar DA, Silva WF, Sugawara LM, Adami M, Moreira MA. Studies on the rapid expansion of sugarcane for ethanol production in São Paulo State (Brazil) using Landsat data. Remote Sens. 2010;2(4):1057–76. doi: 10.3390/rs2041057
4. El Hajj M, Bégué A, Guillaume S, Martiné J-F. Integrating SPOT-5 time series, crop growth modeling and expert knowledge for monitoring agricultural practices—The case of sugarcane harvest on Reunion Island. Remote Sens Environ. 2009;113(10):2052–61. doi: 10.1016/j.rse.2009.04.009
5. Fortes C, Dematte̊ J. Discrimination of sugarcane varieties using Landsat 7 ETM+ spectral data. Int J Remote Sens. 2006;27(7):1395–412. doi: 10.1080/01431160500383863
6. Almeida T, De Souza Filho C, Rossetto R. ASTER and Landsat ETM+ images applied to sugarcane yield forecast. Int J Remote Sens. 2006;27(19):4057–69. doi: 10.1080/01431160600857451
7. Townshend JR, Justice C, Kalb V. Characterization and classification of South American land cover types using satellite data. Int J Remote Sens. 1987;8(8):1189–207. doi: 10.1080/01431168708954764
8. Wolter PT, Mladenoff DJ, Host GE, Crow TR. Improved forest classification in the Northern Lake States using multi-temporal Landsat imagery. Photogramm Eng Rem S. 1995;61(9):1129–44.
9. Friedl MA, Brodley CE. Decision tree classification of land cover from remotely sensed data. Remote Sens Environ. 1997;61(3):399–409. doi: 10.1016/s0034-4257(97)00049-7
10. Li C, Wang J, Wang L, Hu L, Gong P. Comparison of Classification Algorithms and Training Sample Sizes in Urban Land Classification with Landsat Thematic Mapper Imagery. Remote Sens. 2014;6(2):964–83. doi: 10.3390/rs6020964.
11. Wang J, Huang J, Zhang K, Li X, She B, Wei C, et al. Rice Fields Mapping in Fragmented Area Using Multi-Temporal HJ-1A/B CCD Images. Remote Sens. 2015;7(4):3467–88. doi: 10.3390/rs70403467.
12. Vieira MA, Formaggio AR, Rennó CD, Atzberger C, Aguiar DA, Mello MP. Object based image analysis and data mining applied to a remotely sensed Landsat time-series to map sugarcane over large areas. Remote Sens Environ. 2012;123:553–62. doi: 10.1016/j.rse.2012.04.011
13. Bock M, Xofis P, Mitchley J, Rossner G, Wissen M. Object-oriented methods for habitat mapping at multiple scales–Case studies from Northern Germany and Wye Downs, UK. J Nat Conserv. 2005;13(2):75–89. doi: 10.1016/j.jnc.2004.12.002
14. Navulur K. Multispectral image analysis using the object-oriented paradigm: CRC Press/Taylor&Francis, Boca Raton; 2006.
15. Baatz M, Benz U, Dehghani S, Heynen M, Höltje A, Hofmann P, et al. eCognition professional user guide 4. Definiens Imaging, Munich. 2004.
16. dos Santos Silva MP, Camara G, Escada MIS, de Souza RCM. Remote-sensing image mining: detecting

agents of land-use change in tropical forest areas. Int J Remote Sens. 2008;29(16):4803–22. doi: 10.1080/01431160801950634

17. Fayyad U, Piatetsky-Shapiro G, Smyth P. From data mining to knowledge discovery in databases. AI Mag. 1996;17(3):37.
18. Pal M, Mather PM. An assessment of the effectiveness of decision tree methods for land cover classification. Remote Sens Environ. 2003;86(4):554–65. doi: 10.1016/s0034-4257(03)00132-9
19. Schapire RE. Explaining adaboost. Empirical inference: Springer Berlin Heidelberg; 2013. p. 37–52.
20. Freund Y, Schapire RE. A decision-theoretic generalization of on-line learning and an application to boosting. J Comput Syst Sci. 1997;55(1):119–39. doi: 10.1006/jcss.1997.1504
21. Sakamoto T, Yokozawa M, Toritani H, Shibayama M, Ishitsuka N, Ohno H. A crop phenology detection method using time-series MODIS data. Remote Sens Environ. 2005;96(3–4):366–74. doi: 10.1016/j.rse.2005.03.008.
22. Boschetti M, Stroppiana D, Brivio PA, Bocchi S. Multi-year monitoring of rice crop phenology through time series analysis of MODIS images. Int J Remote Sens. 2009;30(18):4643–62. doi: 10.1080/01431160802632249.
23. Definiens A. Definiens eCognition Developer 8 Reference Book. Definiens AG, München. 2009.
24. Rouse J, Haas R, Schell J, Deering D, Harlan J. Monitoring the vernal advancements and retrogradation of natural vegetation. NASA/GSFC, Final Report, Greenbelt, MD, USA. 1974:1–137.
25. Hansen PM, Schjoerring JK. Reflectance measurement of canopy biomass and nitrogen status in wheat crops using normalized difference vegetation indices and partial least squares regression. Remote Sens Environ. 2003;86(4):542–53. doi: 10.1016/s0034-4257(03)00131-7.
26. Lu L, Li X, Huang CL, Ma MG, Che T, Bogaert J, et al. Investigating the relationship between ground-measured LAI and vegetation indices in an alpine meadow, north-west China. Int J Remote Sens. 2005;26(20):4471–84. doi: 10.1080/01431160500114938.
27. Huete A, Didan K, Miura T, Rodriguez EP, Gao X, Ferreira LG. Overview of the radiometric and biophysical performance of the MODIS vegetation indices. Remote Sens Environ. 2002;83(1):195–213. doi: 10.1016/s0034-4257(02)00096-2
28. Jiang Z, Huete A, Didan K, Miura T. Development of a two-band enhanced vegetation index without a blue band. Remote Sens Environ. 2008;112(10):3833–45. doi: 10.1016/j.rse.2008.06.006.
29. SK Lodha D F, DP Helmbold. Aerial Lidar Data Classification using AdaBoost. 2007.
30. Miao X, Heaton JS, Zheng S, Charlet DA, Liu H. Applying tree-based ensemble algorithms to the classification of ecological zones using multi-temporal multi-source remote-sensing data. Int J Remote Sens. 2012;33(6):1823–49. doi: 10.1080/01431161.2011.602651
31. Alfaro E, Gámez M, Garcia N. Adabag: An R package for classification with boosting and bagging. J Stat Softw. 2013;54(2):1–35. doi: 10.18637/jss.v054.i02
32. Stone M. Cross-validatory choice and assessment of statistical predictions. J Roy Stat Soc B Met. 1974:111–47.
33. Steele BM. Maximum posterior probability estimators of map accuracy. Remote Sens Environ. 2005;99(3):254–70. doi: 10.1016/j.rse.2005.09.001
34. Witten IH, Frank E. Data Mining: Practical machine learning tools and techniques: Morgan Kaufmann; 2005.
35. Kim M, Madden M, Warner T. Estimation of optimal image object size for the segmentation of forest stands with multispectral IKONOS imagery. Object-based image analysis: Springer; 2008. p. 291–307.
36. Peña-Barragán JM, Ngugi MK, Plant RE, Six J. Object-based crop identification using multiple vegetation indices, textural features and crop phenology. Remote Sens Environ. 2011;115(6):1301–16. doi: 10.1016/j.rse.2011.01.009.

CHAPTER 19

SKIPCOR: SKIP-MENTION COREFERENCE RESOLUTION USING LINEAR-CHAIN CONDITIONAL RANDOM FIELDS

Slavko Žitnik[1], Lovro Šubelj[2], Marko Bajec[2]

[1] Laboratory for Data Technologies, University of Ljubljana and Optilab d.o.o., Ljubljana, Slovenia

[2] Laboratory for Data Technologies, University of Ljubljana, Ljubljana, Slovenia

ABSTRACT

Coreference resolution tries to identify all expressions (called mentions) in observed text that refer to the same entity. Beside entity extraction and relation extraction, it represents one of the three complementary tasks in Information Extraction. In this paper we describe a novel coreference resolution system SkipCor that reformulates the problem as a sequence labeling task. None of the existing supervised, unsupervised, pairwise or sequence-based models are similar to our approach, which only uses linear-chain conditional random fields and supports high scalability with fast model training and inference, and a straightforward parallelization. We evaluate the proposed system against the ACE 2004, CoNLL 2012 and SemEval 2010 benchmark datasets. SkipCor clearly outperforms two baseline systems that detect coreferentiality using the same features as SkipCor. The obtained results are at least comparable to the current state-of-the-art in coreference resolution.

INTRODUCTION

The field of Information Extraction (IE) deals with automatic extraction of structured information such as person names, locations, organizations etc. from unstructured or semi-structured text. The roots of IE dates back to 1970s when the first approaches emerged [1]. Since then a lot of effort has been put in finding solutions that would facilitate efficient and accurate IE. This has resulted in many different IE systems that are available today or at least described in the literature [2], [3]. Nevertheless, we are still not able to extract information with high precision and recall especially when performing IE on large unstructured datasets such as on the web for example. This and the fact that the amount of unstructured data is rapidly growing make the IE field more and more important.

The IE task can be divided into three subtasks: entity extraction, relation extraction and coreference resolution. As its name implies, the entity extraction focuses on the extraction of entities, i.e. parts of the text or expressions in text that can be categorized as one of the predefined categories, such as the names of places, persons, organizations, dates, etc. The relation extraction then seeks to identify relations among the identified entities (e.g. some expression that was identified as a name of a person is found to be related to some other expression identified as an organization). Finally, the coreference resolution tries to identify parts of the text or expressions that refer to the same entity in the analyzed text. The expressions that we observe in the coreference resolution are called "mentions" and can be one of the following types: named mentions (e.g. "*John Doe* was here"), nominal mentions (e.g. "*the boy* was here")

Citation: Žitnik S, Šubelj L, Bajec M (2014) SkipCor: Skip-Mention Coreference Resolution Using Linear-Chain Conditional Random Fields. PLoS ONE 9(6): e100101. doi:10.1371/journal.pone.0100101.

or pronominal mentions (e.g. "*he* was here") [4]. To detect mentions that refer to the same entity, a two-steps procedure is usually performed: (1) the identification of all mentions in the observed text and (2) the clustering of the identified mentions so that all mentions referring to the same entity fall into the same cluster.

Coreference resolution [5] represents an important step in IE as it provides bases for merging contextual information extracted through other tasks [6]. For example relations and attributes that are identified in entity [7] and relation extraction and are associated with a particular mention hold not only for that particular mention but also for other coreferent mentions, even the distance between them is several words or sentences [8]. The identification of coreferent mentions in text has already proved useful in various domains, ranging from mining news articles [9] to biological data [10].

In this paper we describe a novel coreference resolution system 'SkipCor', which is based on the well known conditional random fields algorithm [11]. The novelty of SkipCor lies in a special transformation of input data into the so called *n* skip-mention sequences, in which only every ($n+1$)-th mention is included. This allows the use of very simple first-order (i.e., linear-chain) models that enable much faster and exact training and inference than do the general models. Thus, in contrast to most other approaches, the proposed system is completely parallelizable with a linear time complexity (in the number of mentions in the text). We compare SkipCor to a baseline system, on seven standard benchmark datasets. It clearly outperforms the baseline system that uses only a single sequence of mentions and a standard pairwise system that, as in traditional approaches mentioned above, looks at all the mention pairs in order to identify the coreferent ones. Furthermore, the results obtained are at least comparable to the current state-of-the-art in coreference resolution. We also investigate the drop in accuracy to be expected in real-world scenarios, where systems are trained on one dataset, and adopted on another, something which may be of independent interest.

BACKGROUND

The majority of techniques for coreference resolution transform the problem into a pairwise classification task [12], [13] (i.e., the algorithm checks every pair of mentions for coreference). This enables the use of standard machine learning classifiers that rely on hand-labeled data sets. On the other hand, unsupervised techniques infer the coreferentiality based on sequences of mentions [14], [15], which are much harder to train and are not easily generalized to new problems or domains. In this section we will provide an overview of the different coreference resolution systems, with special focus on approaches based on graphical models [11] (as SkipCor).

One of the earliest supervised approaches used a decision tree algorithm and twelve informative feature functions [16]. That approach was the first to improve on the performance of previously state-of-the-art rule-based techniques. Even though the adopted features were based solely on pairs of mentions with local information, it was difficult to improve their results by only using more sophisticated algorithms. Therefore, a number of innovative and linguistic-rich feature functions [13], [17] along with different algorithms like maximum entropy [18], SVM classifiers [19] and Markov Logic Networks [20] have been proposed in the recent literature. Recently, Bengston and Roth [17] have systematically divided different feature functions into categories and clearly demonstrated their importance. In particular, they have shown that the development of well-designed features can greatly improve the performance of a coreference resolution system. Due to the similarities among the proposed supervised systems, the Reconcile platform [21] was developed in order to provide a common framework for new algorithms, features, and their evaluation.

Unsupervised approaches demand no training data. Nevertheless, unsupervised state-of-the-art systems still achieve comparable results to the supervised systems. Haghighi and Klein [15] proposed a modular unsupervised system using rich features. The system is based on a three-step procedure, consisting of the extraction of syntactic paths from the mentions, the evaluation of semantic compatibility between the mentions, and the selection of reference mentions, which serve as the basis for using pairwise decisions over transitive closures. Lee et al. [14] upgraded Raghunathan's system [22], which is based on a multi-pass sieve approach. They employed thirteen sieves (i.e., sequential processing steps) sorted by precision. During the execution of each sieve, the entire dataset is processed by applying a few manually written patterns. These hand-crafted patterns relate only to syntactic parse trees and extracted named entities, and are based on different heuristics and dataset specifications. Some unsupervised techniques have also been proposed. They infer coreferentiality based on sequences of mentions [23]–[25].

In the field of factor graphs, McCallum et al. [26] proposed three general conditional random fields (CRF) models to solve the coreference resolution problem. The first is a general model (i.e., the CRF structure is unrestricted) and the training or inference is therefore complex. In such cases exact inference is not possible and therefore approximation algorithms must be used to compute right marginal values for the underlying CRF structure [27]. The second model represents pairs of mentions by specific attributes, while the third represents the pairs as nodes in the model. Wellner et al. [28] successfully applied coreference resolution to citation matching, interestingly by using a special case of McCallum's first model combined with named entity extraction. Most similar to the linear models, a skip-chain CRF has been proposed in [29], which also supports the use of long-distance dependencies by incorporating additional cliques into the model. Still, longer times are needed for training and inference compared to linear-chain CRF. Cullota et al. [12] proposed the use of first-order probabilistic models over sets of mentions; thus, the algorithm operates directly on the entities. To avoid a combinatorial explosion of all possible entity subsets, they incrementally merged different mentions into sets. Later, they also included the step of canonicalization [28], which refers to the process of generating the underlying entities along with their attributes. Recently, Sundar et al. [30] proposed a CRF-based coreference resolution system. They further decomposed the problem into two subtasks: pronominal resolution using general CRFs that has only parse tree features, and non-pronominal resolution using linear-chain CRFs that has different string similarity features. Although the system is based on linear models, the input to the models still consists merely of sequences of length two.

In Table 1 we show the classification of some of the coreference resolution approaches that have been put forth in the literature. We categorize the systems along two dimensions: the type of input to the algorithm, and the type of model learning. As can be observed, the proposed SkipCor system is novel from the perspective of the selected dimensions. Among the unsupervised approaches, coreference resolution systems have been developed for both pairwise and sequence-based input types. In contrast, supervised approaches have mainly employed only pairwise comparisons. The system in [30] is similar to our baseline algorithm, SkipCorPair; however, it predicts whether two mentions are coreferent using a CRF algorithm. Also, [26] presents some CRF-based methods, but it evaluates only a version where each node represents a pair of mentions.

Table 1. Classification of coreference resolution approaches

	UNSUPERVISED	SUPERVISED
SEQUENCE-BASED	[23–25]	**SkipCor**
PAIRWISE	[14,15,22], etc.	[12,13,16–20,26,30]

According to the two-dimensional classification of coreference resolution systems, the proposed SkipCor system solves the problem in a novel fashion.
doi:10.1371/journal.pone.0100101.t001

In summary, SkipCor represents a novel CRF-based approach that identifies coreferences over mention chains and employs simple clustering to uncover all mentions in the text that refer to the same entity. In contrast to other systems, we adopt a supervised algorithm for training and inference on sequence-based data. Thus, instead of using a pairwise or set-based approach, we consider sequences of mentions in some document and use simple linear-chain CRF models. To enable the use of such simple models, we introduce an adequate transformation of the data into skip-mention sequences. Consequently, the feature functions also refer to non-local information and can detect distant mention coreferences. Note also that the training and inference of linear-chain CRFs can be solved with a fast and exact algorithm, which significantly reduces the time complexity of the system.

Conditional Random Fields

Conditional random fields (CRF) [11] is a discriminative model that estimates the joint distribution $p(\overline{y}|\overline{x},w)$ over the target sequence $\overline{y}$ conditioned on the observed sequence $\overline{x}$ and weight vector w (see below). We represent a sentence by a sequence of words x_i with additional corresponding sequences that represent attribute values such as part-of-speech tags $x_i^{k_1}$, lemmas $x_i^{k_2}$, relations $x_i^{k_3}$, and other observable values $x_i^{k_j}$. These values are used by feature functions f_l that are weighted during CRF training in order to model the target sequence $\overline{y}$. The sequence $\overline{y}$ corresponds to the source sequence and consists of the labels that we would like to automatically infer. For named entity recognition, we commonly use tags such as PER for person type, ORG for organization, and LOC for location. Similarly for relationship extraction, we use tags WORKS-AT, LIVES-IN, etc. For the coreference resolution task, we build sequences containing only mentions, as opposed to sequences containing all the words in a document. Then we use the label C if the current mention is coreferent with the previous one, and O otherwise.

In the field of IE, CRFs have been successfully employed for various sequence labeling tasks and have achieved state-of-the-art results. It can also deal with a large number of multiple, overlapping, and non-independent features.

Training a CRF is thus maximizing the conditional log-likelihood of the training data, by which we find a weight vector w that predicts the most probable sequence $\hat{y}$ for a given $\overline{x}$. Hence,

$$\hat{y} = \arg\max_{\overline{y}} p(\overline{y}|\overline{x},w) \quad (1)$$

where the conditional distribution is

$$p(\overline{y}|\overline{x},w) = \frac{\exp\left[\sum_{l=1}^{m} w_l \sum_{i=1}^{length(\overline{x})} f_l(\overline{y},\overline{x},i)\right]}{C(\overline{x},w)} \quad (2)$$

Here, m is the number of feature functions and $C(\overline{x},w)$ is a normalization constant computed over all possible sequences $\overline{y}$.

The structure of a CRF defines how the dependencies with target labels are modeled. A general graphical model (i.e., a graph denoting the conditional dependence structure) can depend on many labels and is therefore intractable for training or inference without complex approximation algorithms. Thus, we use only a simple linear-chain CRF (LCRF) model, which depends on the current and previous labels (i.e., a first order model). The structure of such a model is represented in Figure 1. Furthermore, with the use of a number of feature functions and special dataset transformations, our method achieves comparable results to the best known systems.

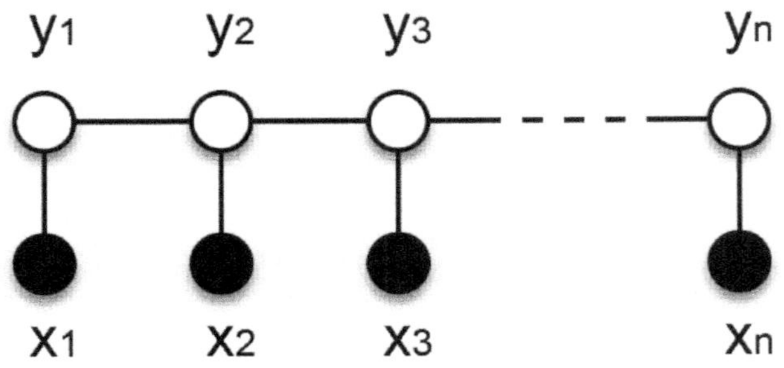

Figure 1. Linear-chain conditional random fields model. Black nodes represent observable values, which are in our case entity mentions. White nodes represent hidden labels that we need to predict and define whether the current observable value is coreferent with the previous one.

METHODS

In this section we introduce the proposed SkipCor algorithm. First, we overview and introduce new feature functions used by conditional random fields models in the present paper. Next, we explain the data representation using skip-mention sequences and illustrate the coreference resolution execution of the proposed system on an example document. We also support the proposed representation by examining the distribution of consecutive coreferent mention distances on a representative coreference dataset. Last, we explain the implementation [31] of the proposed SkipCor system and discuss the time complexity of the algorithm.

Feature Functions

The selection of informative features is the main source of an increase of precision and recall when training machine learning classifiers. Feature functions are usually implemented as templates and the final features are then generated by scanning the entire training data. In natural language processing, a few thousand or more features are commonly used, which can be efficiently handled by a CRF. A feature function that returns 1 if the current mention is of person type or the previous mention is equal to "Mr." and 0 otherwise, is defined by:

$f_l(\overline{y},\overline{x},i) = \text{if } (y_i == \text{PER} \vee x_{i-1} == \text{"Mr."})$

then return 1 else return 0

Although many feature functions have been proposed in the literature [7], [16], [17], [32]–[34], we introduce new feature functions for the purpose of this research. These can be sorted into the following categories:

Preprocessing

These feature functions use standard preprocessing labels, which are a result of the preprocessing step, such as lemmas, part-of-speech (POS) tags, chunks, and parse trees. The derived feature functions are "target label distribution", "do POS tags match on distances up to two mentions away", "distribution of POS tags", "mention type match", "is a mention pronoun of demonstrative/definitive noun phrase", "is mention a pronoun", "length between mentions within a parse tree", "parse tree path from the root node", "parse tree path between the two mentions", "depth of a mention within a parse tree", and "parse tree parent value match".

Location

Sometimes it is important to know where the mention resides. Location feature functions deal with the mention's location compared to the whole document, sentence, or other mentions. Our approach already implicitly uses mention distance at each skip-mention model, but we still employ some specific feature functions. These are "sentence/mention/token distance between the two mentions", "is first/last mention" and "are mentions within the same sentence".

Mention Shape

Mention constituents are represented as word phrases and by using mention shape features we are interested in whether two of them share some property. These feature functions are string-based and are implemented as follows: "does a mention start with an upper case", "do both mentions start with upper case", "does a prefix/postfix/whole of left/right mention on distances up to five mentions match", "does a mention text/extent match", "is one mention appositive of another", "is one mention prefix/suffix/substring of another", "Hearst mention co-occurrence rules", "is a mention within quotes", "does a mention contain head/extent words of another" and "length difference between the two mentions".

Semantic

This class of feature functions captures semantic relationships between mentions by employing additional semantic sources, such as WordNet [35], specialized lexicons, semantic gazeteer lists, and ontologies. The semantic feature functions are "do named entity types match", "do mentions agree on gender/number" [36], "is one mention appositive of another", "is a mention an alias of another" (heuristically), "edit distance similarity between two mentions", "WordNet relation (hypernym/hyponym/synonym) between the mentions", "do mentions share the same WordNet synset", "current mention word sense", "do both mentions represent an animate object" [37] and "do both mentions speak" (taking context words into account).

A brief description and exact list of feature functions that we use is presented in Table 2. Still, their exact implementations can be retrieved from our public source repository [31] (within the class FeatureFunctionPackages).

Table 2. Feature functions description

Name	Description	Model
Target label distribution	Distribution of target labels.	A, S, C
Starts upper	Does the mention start with an upper case letter.	A, S, C
Starts upper twice	Do two consequent mentions start with an upper case letter.	A, S, C
Prefix value	Value of the prefix (length of 2 and 3) for the mention on offset distance (distances from −5 to 5) from the current mention.	A, S, C
Suffix value	Value of the suffix (length of 2 and 3) for the mention on offset distance (distances from −5 to 5) from the current mention.	A, S, C
Consequent value	A combination of values of the consequent mentions on offset distance (distances from −4 to 4) from the current mention.	A, S, C
String match	Do consequent mention values match.	A, S, C
Gender match	Does the gender of two consequent mentions match.	A, S, C
Gender value	The gender value of the mention.	A, S, C
Is appositive	Is the mention appositive of the another.	A, S, C
Alias	Is the mention alias or abbreviation of the another.	A, S, C
Is prefix	Is the mention prefix of the another.	A, S, C
Is suffix	Is the mention suffix of the another.	A, S, C
Similarity value	How similar are the two mention values according to the Jaro Winkler [53] metric.	A, S, C
Is pronoun	Is the mention a pronoun.	A, S, C
Same sentence	Are consequent mentions in the same sentence.	A, S, C
Hearst co-occurence [54]	Does the text between the two mentions follow some predefined rules, e.g. m_i such as m_j.	A, S, C
Sentence distance	What is the distance between the sentences of the two mentions.	A, S, C
Is quoted	Is the mention within the parentheses.	A, S, C
Substring match	Is the mention a substring of the another.	A
Starts with	Does the mention starts with the another.	A, S, C
Ends with	Does the mention ends with the another.	A, S, C
Number match	Do the mentions match in number (i.e., singular, plural).	A, S, C
Mention type	Type of mention (i.e., pronoun, name, nominal).	A
Relative pronoun	Heuristic decision if the mention is a relative pronoun of the another.	A
WordNet [35]	How is the mention semantically connected to the another (e.g., is a hypernym, synonym).	A
WordNet synset	Are the two consequent mentions in the same synset.	S, C
Entity type	What is the named entity type or subtype of the mention.	A
Length difference	What is the difference in length of the two consecutive mentions.	A, S, C
Is demonstrative	Is the mention a demonstrative noun phrase.	A, S, C
Offset match	Do consecutive POS values on distances from −2 to 2 match.	A
Parse tree path	Path values between the two mentions in a parse tree.	A, S, C
Parse tree mention depth	Depth of the mention within the parse tree.	A, S, C
Parse tree parent value	Parse tree value of the mention on lengths of one, two or three.	A, S, C
Relation	Does a relationship exist between the two consecutive mentions.	S
Speaker	Who is the current speaker in a transcript text.	C

The feature functions are used by all skip-mention CRF models and are modeled as unigram or bigram features. The exact details (e.g., which mention values are used by a specific feature functions) and implementations can be retrieved from our public source repository [31] (within the class FeatureFunctionPackages). The abbreviations A, S and C define which feature functions were used when training the models for the ACE2004, SemEval2010 and CoNLL2012 datasets, respectively.
doi:10.1371/journal.pone.0100101.t002

Skip-mention Sequences

Since merely linear-chain CRF models are used, we can identify only coreferences over two directly consecutive mentions. Thus, to detect coreferences over mentions on larger distances, i.e., having one, two, three, or more mentions in between, we propose a skip-mention dataset transformation.

To support our transformation idea, we show the distribution of distances between two consecutive coreferent mentions (see Figure 2) in the SemEval2010 evaluation dataset. Although the figure shows the distribution for only one dataset, it is representative enough to illustrate the general problem, which is the same for all other datasets. According to the distribution, only 10% of the directly consecutive mention pairs are coreferent, while the highest number (i.e., 12.5%) of coreferent mention pairs are at distance one - i.e., having one other mention in between. Taking into account all mention pairs up to a distance of 20, cumulatively, 81% of the mention pairs can be identified. With distances up to 50, about 92% of the mention pairs can be identified. However, by using longer or all possible distances, the accuracy of a general coreference system is not expected to increase since more false positives are extracted. To overcome such problems, a promising cut-off point is selected (see Figure 3).

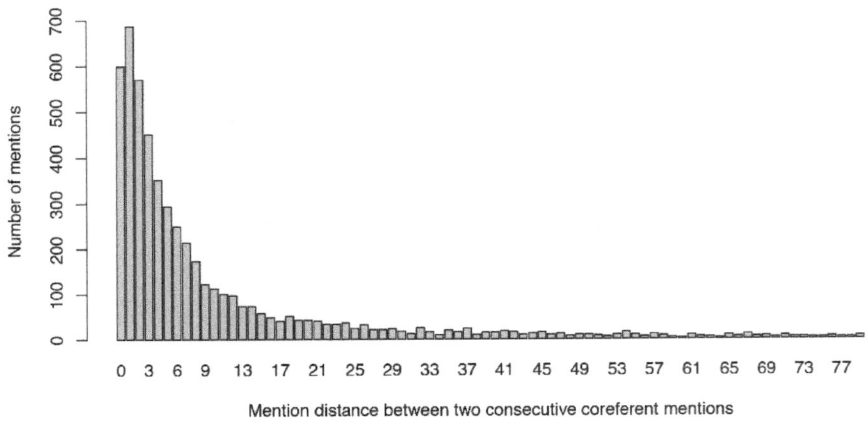

Figure 2. Distribution of distances between two consecutive coreferent mentions. The data was taken from the SemEval2010 [46] coreference dataset. Distance Xbetween two consecutive mentions means that there exist X other mentions between them.

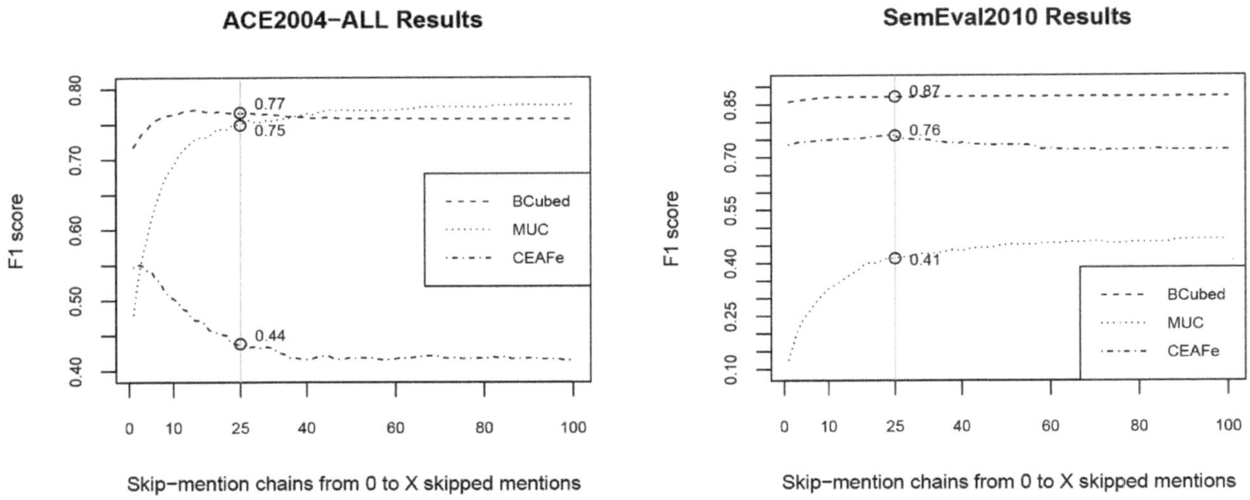

Figure 3. Coreference resolution results using different skip-mention sequences. Evaluation of the proposed system on the whole ACE2004 [45] and SemEval2010 [46]datasets using the metrics BCubed [41], MUC [9] and CEAFe [42].

Thus, to detect coreferences we form a zero skip-mention sequence from each document, which contains all the mentions from a document. Then we form specific S skip-mention sequences. Each S skip-mention sequence contains every (s+1)-th mention from a document and one linear-chain CRF model is trained for each value of S. In the next section we present an example of detecting coreferences using skip-mention sequences.

A Worked Example

In this section we illustrate the detection of coreferences using our approach from the following document: "John is married to Jena. He is a mechanic at OBI and she works there. It is a DIY market.". Let $\bar{x} = [x_1, x_2, x_3, \ldots, x_n]$ denote a sequence of all mentions within the document. Mentions x_i are ordered by their occurrence in the document. For example, from the document we select all entity mentions into one training mention sequence x:

$$x = [\text{John, Jena, He, OBI, she, there, It, DIY market}] \quad (3)$$

As mentions mostly consist of noun phrases we could also identify a mechanic as a mention. Due to the simplification of the process the phrase was not identified as a mention during the mention detection. Our goal is now to detect the target clusters for each entity x_{John},x_{Jena} and x_{OBI}:

$$x_{\text{John}} = \{\text{John, He}\}, \quad (4)$$

$$x_{\text{Jena}} = \{\text{Jena, she}\}, \quad (5)$$

$$x_{\text{OBI}} = \{\text{OBI, there, It, DIY market}\} \quad (6)$$

In some cases, a mention could overlap with another mention. We treat such pairs as separate mentions and order them lexicographically by the index of the first word and mention length.

First, we decide to use zero, one and two for S skip-mention sequences and this is also a parameter to the system. In Figure 4, we show a training mention sequence x, which is applicable to first-order probabilistic models. We call it a 'zero skip-mention sequence' because it includes all mentions from a document and there are no (i.e., zero) other mentions between any two consecutive mentions in it. To identify coreferent mentions in the sequences, we need to label them using the labels {O, C}. The label C states that the current mention is coreferent with the previous one, whereas O states that the current mention is not coreferent with the previous one. Our linear-chain CRF models are learned over these labels and are therefore able to infer new labels for unseen mention sequences. Observe that for the toy example above, first-order models detect just three coreferent mentions {there, It, DIY Market} from a zero skip-mention sequence.

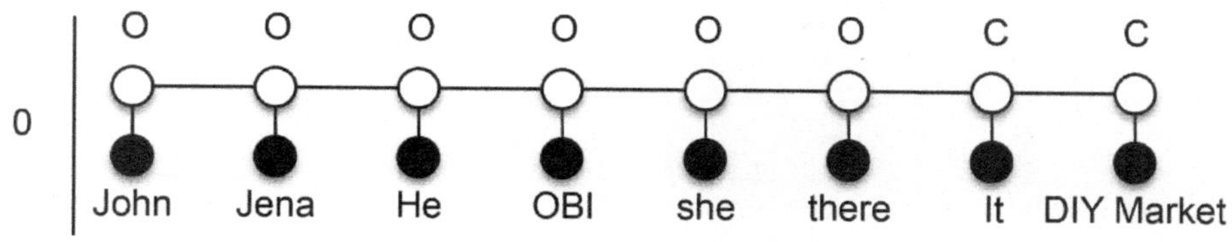

Figure 4. Zero skip-mention training sequence. Initial mention sequence that contains all mentions from the input text "*John* is married to *Jena. He* is a mechanic at *OBI* and *she* works *there. It* is a *DIY market.*" If the current mention is coreferent with the previous one, it is labeled with *C*, otherwise with *O*.

To solve the problem of identification of coreferent mentions at longer distances that contain other mention in between (e.g., OBI and there), we introduce further transformations. All additional skip-mention sequences are generated from the initial zero skip-mention sequence X and are labeled accordingly using {O, C} labels. We also train a separate linear-chain CRF model for each additional skip-mention sequence type, which enables us to tag new unseen data for specific skip-mention distance.

Next, we then generate one skip-mention sequences (see Figure 5), which contain every second mention from the x above. The trained model for one skip-mention sequences can therefore extend our results by two new pairs {John, He} and {OBI, there}. Analogously, for the two skip-mention sequences (see Figure 6) we could get our final missing pairs {OBI, It} and {Jena, She}.

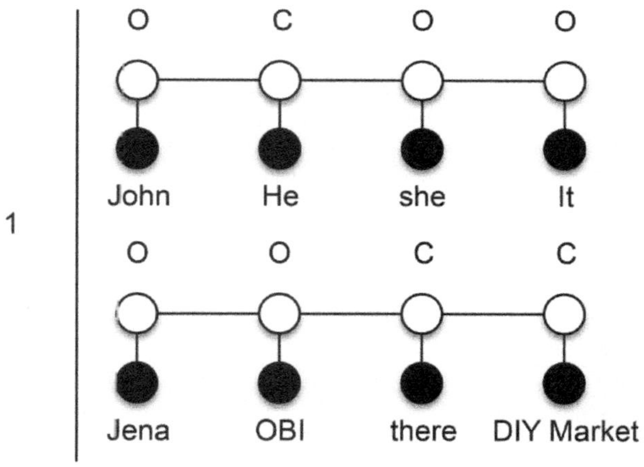

Figure 5. One skip-mention training sequences. Mention sequences that include every second mention (i.e., one skip-mention) from the input text "*John* is married to *Jena. He* is a mechanic at *OBI* and *she* works *there. It* is a *DIY market.*" If the current mention is coreferent with the previous one, it is labeled with *C*, otherwise with *O*.

Lastly, we perform mention clustering from the previously extracted results from all the skip-mention sequences and return target entity clusters.

x_{John}, xJ_{ena} and x_{OBI}

As shown in the example above, the transformation into higher skip-mention sequences returns more sequences per document. Intuitively, at distance zero, we get one training sequence per document (it contains all document mentions). At distance one, we get two sequences (each contains every second mention). At distance two, we get three sequences, etc. Therefore, the transformation into d skip-mention sequences returns $d+1$ sequences of length n/d, where n is the number of all mentions in the document.

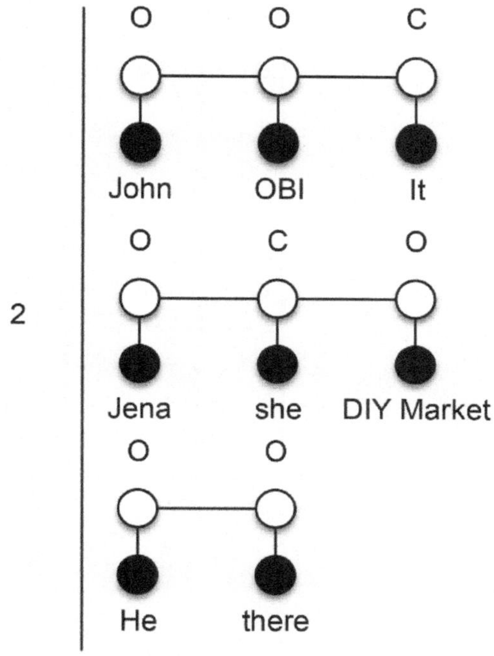

Figure 6. Two skip-mention training sequences. Mention sequences that include every third mention (i.e., two skip-mention) from the input text "*John* is married to *Jena. He* is a mechanic at *OBI* and *she* works *there. It* is a*DIY market.*" If the current mention is coreferent with the previous one, it is labeled with*C*, otherwise with *O*.

The SkipCor System

The SkipCor system takes a set of documents as input and returns a set of coreferent mention clusters, where each cluster represents an entity to which the mentions refer. The algorithm first reads mentions from the text and then transforms them into skip-mention sequences. Then, we load LCRF models specific to the generated skip-mention sequences and each of these independent models returns separately tagged skip-mention sequences, which are used at the clustering step. The final result is therefore a set of entities (represented as clusters of mentions) for each input document. We show a high level SkipCor data flow in Figure 7 and the detailed algorithms for training and inference are presented in Table 3 and Table 4, respectively.

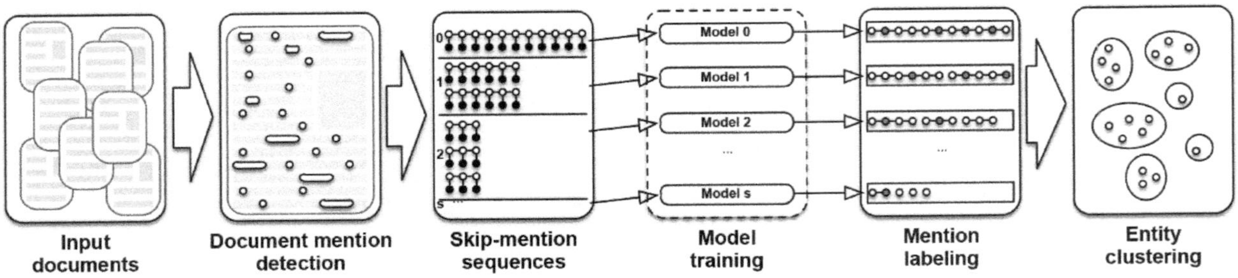

Figure 7. High level skip-mention coreference resolution data flow. The input to the system is given as a set of documents. For each document we select mentions and transform them into mention sequences. According to the system parameters, sequences contain every $s+1$th mention (i.e., s skip-mention). A model is trained for each sequence type and then used for labeling. After sequences are labeled, the mentions are then clustered. Each cluster of mentions represents a specific entity, which is also the final result of the system.

Table 3. Algorithm 1

Algorithm 1: Skip-mention classifier training

Input: training documents D, feature functions $f_i \in F$ and skip-mention distances $s_i \in S$

Output: skip-mention model $(skipMentionCRF, S, F)$

$sentences \leftarrow$ importTrainingData(D)

$sentences \leftarrow$ preprocessInputText($sentences$)

$mentionSequences \leftarrow$ readMentions($sentences$)

$skipMentionCRF \leftarrow []$ //empty list

parallel for each $s_i \in S$:

  $skipMentionSequences \leftarrow$ transform($mentionSequences, s_i$)

  initializeFeatureFunctions($skipMentionSequences, F$)

  $skipMentionCRF_i \leftarrow$ LCRFTrain($skipMentionSequences$)

return $(skipMentionCRF, S, F)$

doi:10.1371/journal.pone.0100101.t003

Table 4. Algorithm 2

Algorithm 2: Skip-mention classifier labeling

Input: document D and a skip-mention model $(skipMentionCRF, S, F)$

Output: coreferent mention clusters

$sentences \leftarrow$ preprocessInputText(D)

$mentionSequence \leftarrow$ detectMentions($sentences$)

$coreferentMentions \leftarrow \varnothing$

parallel for each $s_i \in S$:

  $skipMentionSequences \leftarrow$ transform($mentionSequence, s_i$)

  initializeFeatureFunctions($skipMentionSequences, F$)

  $coreferentMentions$ add LCRFLabel ($skipMentionCRF_i, skipMentionSequences$)

$mentionClusters \leftarrow$ cluster($coreferentMentions$)

return $mentionClusters$

doi:10.1371/journal.pone.0100101.t004

The training phase is similar to the inference phase. The only difference is that the training must occur before any inference (the dashed rectangle in Figure 7). Each of the trained LCRF models is then able to infer the labels for a specific skip-mention distance.

During the training phase, Table 3, we build a skip-mention coreference resolution model. The algorithm takes as input the training documents, a list of feature functions, and a list of skip-mention distances. First, in the pre-processing step, we import the training data in the form of sentences and enrich them with additional tags (e.g., part-of-speech tags, lemmas, parse trees). Then we generate mention sequences (i.e., with zero skip-mentions) for each document. These sequences contain references to the original sentences, therefore the feature functions can use context data from the original input text and not only from the mention sequences. The main part of training the algorithm is the for loop, in which we transform the original mention sequences into the appropriate s_i skip-mention sequences, generate features, and train a specific model for every s_i using the LCRFTrain function. Each for loop execution is independent of the others, thus, the algorithm can be parallelized. Lastly, the final result of training is a SkipCor model, which is a tuple consisting of a list of trained skip-mention linear-chain CRF models, a list of the corresponding skip-mention distances, and a list of the feature functions.

To detect coreferences in unseen documents, we follow the algorithm shown in Table 4. As input, we take a raw text document and a SkipCor model that was trained using the algorithm inTable 3. During the execution, similarly to the training phase, we preprocess the input document and generate the initial mention sequence. If the mentions were not already detected in the input document, we perform a rule-based mention detection [14] to generate the initial mention sequence. Due to fact that we are processing only one document, we get only one zero skip-mention sequence at this step (line 2). In the parallel for loop, we transform the initial mention sequence into s_i skip-mention sequences, generate the features, and execute the labeling of the specific s_i skip-mention LCRF model. All mention pairs that are identified as coreferring are stored in a set, which is the result of the parallel for loop. Lastly, during the clustering step we merge the coreferent mentions into mention clusters, where each cluster represents an underlying entity. These entity clusters are returned as the final result of the SkipCor coreference resolution.

The clustering step is performed using hierarchical agglomerative clustering. All the identified coreferent pairs that were extracted from the labeled zero-skip mention sequence are represented as initial mention clusters. If a mention is coreferent to no other mentions, it will form a singleton cluster. The initial clusters are then iteratively merged according to other labeled s_i skip-mention sequences. The final result of clustering is also the final result of the SkipCor labeling, and consists of a set of clusters that represent separate entities.

The time complexity of both proposed methods is mainly determined by the training and inference of the LCRF models (i.e., LCRFTrain and LCRFLabel), since other routines can be run in linear time. Still, some third-party methods used at pre-processing could consume more time. Due to the parallel execution of the for loop, we need to find the longest lasting execution. Let us say that the CRF training or inference has a time complexity of $O(EL^Q)$ [38], where $E$is the number of edges in the graph, L is the number of labels, and Q is the size of the maximal clique. In our type of CRF model, we use two possible labels: O, C, and the size of every clique is two. The number of edges E depends on the sequence input to the algorithm. Let us say that there are n mentions in a document, which results in a zero skip-mention sequence with 2n-1 = O(n) edges. Moreover, every other generated d skip-mention sequence contains $d(\frac{2n}{d}-1)=2n-d=O(n)$ edges. Thus, we conclude that by employing parallelization, CRF models would use O (2^2n) = O(n) of time. Additionally, next to other linear time procedures, it is also important to include the time for feature function initialization, which takes on the order of O (nm), where m is the number of input feature functions.

RESULTS AND DISCUSSION

In this section, we first explain the coreference resolution evaluation metrics, the system settings that are used during the analysis, and give an overview of the SkipCor baseline systems. Then we introduce the evaluation datasets with some general statistics, labeling specifics, and additional attributes used for training. Next, we show the evaluation results on all the datasets, compare the SkipCor system to two baseline systems, and discuss the results. Lastly, we see how the system accuracy drops when training it on one dataset and testing it on another, to show the expected accuracy in real life scenarios.

Experimental Framework

There is no general agreement on which metric to use for the coreference resolution task. We here adopt the measures most commonly used in the literature, which will be described below. Prior to the measures we use in this paper, a graph based scoring algorithm had been used, that produced very unintuitive results [39], [40]. There have been a number of metrics proposed, so we evaluate the system using the following most commonly used measures:

MUC

The key idea in developing the MUC measure [9] was to give an intuitive explanation of the results for coreference resolution systems. It is a link-based metric (it focuses on pairs of mentions) and is the most widely used. MUC counts false positives by computing the minimum number of links that need to be added in order to connect all the mentions referring to an entity. Recall, on the other hand, measures how many of the links must be removed so that no two mentions referring to different entities are connected in the graph. Thus, the MUC metric gives better scores to systems having more mentions per entity, while it also ignores entities with only one mention (singleton entities).

BCubed

The BCubed metric [41] tries to address the shortcomings of MUC by focusing on mentions, and measures the overlap of the predicted and true clusters by computing the values of recall and precision for each mention. If k is the key entity and r the response entity containing the mention m, the recall for mention m is calculated as $\frac{|k \cap r|}{|k|}$, and the precision for the same mention, as $\frac{|k \cap r|}{|r|}$. This score has the advantage of measuring the impact of singleton entities, and gives more weight to the splitting or merging of larger entities.

CEAF

The goal of the CEAF metric [42] is to achieve better interpretability. The result therefore reflects the percentage of correctly recognized entities. We use entity-based metric (in contrast to a mention-based version) that tries to match the response entity with at most one key entity. For CEAF, the value of recall is $\frac{\text{total similarity}}{|k|}$, while precision is $\frac{\text{total similarity}}{|k|}$.

For the evaluation in this paper, only exact mention matches are considered as correct, see[43] with some modifications proposed by Cai and Strube [5].

The majority of the state-of-the-art systems were evaluated on specialized shared tasks at MUC (Message Understanding Conference) [44], ACE (Automatic Content Extraction) [45], SemEval2010 (Semantic Evaluation) [46], and, most recently, at CoNLL-2011 and CoNLL-2012 (Conference on Computational Language Learning) [43], [47]. Some general information regarding the English datasets that we used in our evaluation is shown in Table 5. We focused primarily on newswire and broadcast news texts, which have been the most thoroughly studied in the past. To be more specific, we used the following datasets: (1) The ACE 2004 dataset, which in addition to broadcast news and newswire texts, also contains transcripts of conversations and various news reports transcribed and translated from Chinese and Arabic. It is the de facto standard dataset for all major information extraction tasks. (2) The SemEval 2010 dataset was designed specifically to evaluate coreference resolution systems in six languages. The English section of the dataset contains newswire and broadcast news from The Wall Street Journal and the TDT-4 collection. (3) The CoNLL 2012 corpus is one of the largest coreference resolution datasets. It tries to provide a much larger selection of coreferring entities, connecting together events and entities. The corpus consists of newswire texts, magazine articles, broadcast news, broadcast conversations, web data, conversational speech, and an English translation of the New Testament.

Table 5. Dataset descriptions

Dataset	# documents	# sentences	# tokens	# mentions	# entities
ACE2004-ALL	450	7,518	191,387	29,724	12,439
ACE2004-NW	127	2,865	74,987	11,188	4,701
ACE2004-BN	220	3,782	71,602	11,323	4,918
SemEval2010-Train	229	3,648	78,831	21,550	16,082
SemEval2010-Test	85	1,141	24,121	6,692	4,839
CoNLL2012-ALL-Train	1,914	75,185	1,299,310	154,760	33,113
CoNLL2012-ALL-Test	221	9,479	169,579	19,677	4,217
CoNLL2012-NW-Train	734	15,288	387,082	34,470	9,404
CoNLL2012-NW-Test	88	1,898	49,235	4,361	1,168
CoNLL2012-BN-Train	748	9,723	180,300	22,262	6,433
CoNLL2012-BN-Test	93	1,252	23,209	2,936	790

The acronyms ALL (i.e., whole), NW (i.e., newswire), BN (i.e., broadcast news) stand for different subdatasets of the whole dataset, which is further divided into training and test portions.

doi:10.1371/journal.pone.0100101.t005

The proposed system is trained to detect coreferences over all tagged mention types: named, nominal, and pronominal. Due to differences in annotator agreements and rules for tagging the mentions, we cannot compare the results between the corpora. For example, the ACE and CoNLL datasets both include tags for all three mention types, but CoNLL includes more general entities. The CoNLL dataset also includes exact mention phrase boundaries, without considering parse tree constituents (a subtree that identifies an exact token sequence). Therefore it is expected for the results to be lower on CoNLL. Furthermore, SemEval includes only nominal mention types and heuristically identified singleton mentions. Nevertheless, we still conducted additional experiments involving training on one dataset type or domain and testing on another. We will present these results since the main motivation for the whole IE field is to develop techniques that work on an unpredictable user text input, where a user does not know what kind of data the algorithms were trained on.

To get additional annotations for the datasets, we used Apache OpenNLP toolkit [48] sentence splitter, POS tagger, and a dependency parser. For the LCRF training and inference, we used CRFSuite [49] with a cut-off threshold of three features and a default setting, which uses the L-BFGS optimization method. The whole implementation along with the evaluation of the proposed skip-mention coreference resolution is available in a public source code repository[31].

Empirical Comparisons

As already mentioned, the accuracy of the system depends on the skip-mention sequence types: the accuracy may not increase when using larger and larger skip-mention distances. InFigure 3, we show the results of training the models using different skip-mention sequence distances. From the results, we observe that when taking into account skip-mention distances larger than 40, the F1 scores do not increase or change significantly because although the recall scores increase, the precision scores decrease. Therefore, the final F1 score remains almost stalled due to a compensation of both scores, or even starts to slightly decrease. The scores that we further present in the evaluation were recorded using all skip-mention distances from zero to 25 (cut-off lines in Figure 3). We did not perform any mention detection, and therefore we always compare the results to the settings with already detected mentions.

We compared the proposed SkipCor system to the baseline systems SkipCorZero and SkipCorPair, both using the same feature functions and settings as SkipCor. The only difference between them is the use of different skip-mention sequence types. SkipCorZero detects coreferences only over zero skip-mention sequences, while SkipCorPair checks every mention pair within a document and predicts whether the two mentions are coreferent or not. Due to the large number of mention pairs considered by SkipCorPair, we limited the distance of the mention pairs to ten mentions. SkipCorPair therefore consists of ten LCRF models, each of which is trained to label coreferentiality on skip-mention sequences of length of two mentions.

In Table 6 we present the results for the ACE2004 dataset. When using the newswire and broadcast news portion, we split the data into training and testing sets in the ratio 70:30. For the whole ACE dataset, we used 336 documents for training and the others for testing [12]. SkipCorZero and SkipCorPair achieved relatively good or best precision values but very low recall. Generally, SkipCorPair outperformed SkipCorZero, while the proposed SkipCor system outperformed both of them. In comparison to other proposed systems, SkipCor achieved a slightly better BCubed score but a lower MUC score. As the results are so close, and opposite for the two measures, it is hard to decide which system is better. On broadcast news, we achieved better MUC and BCubed scores, which are similar to the ones from the newswire section. On the other hand, the precision values are lower, but we achieved a lower difference between the precision and recall compared to the competitive systems. Therefore, we uncovered a lot more mention clusters that have more errors, but the overall results are better. Lastly, we tested the system over the whole dataset (ACE2004-ALL), where we achieved results comparable to those of other systems.

Table 6. Results of the proposed SkipCor system, baseline systems, and other approaches on the ACE2004 datasets

	MUC			BCubed		
	P	R	F	P	R	F
System	**ACE2004-NW**					
SkipCor	78.6	68.8	73.4	75.7	**78.6**	**77.1**
SkipCorZero	78.5	22.6	35.1	**96.3**	51.9	67.4
SkipCorPair	78.2	49.0	60.3	85.3	61.7	71.6
Finkel et al. [55]	78.7	58.5	67.1	86.8	65.2	74.5
Soon et al. [16][1]	**85.3**	37.8	52.4	94.1	56.9	70.9
Haghighi et al. [15]	77.0	**75.9**	**76.5**	79.4	74.5	76.9
Stoyanov et al. [21]	-	-	62.1	-	-	75.5
	ACE2004-BN					
SkipCor	76.3	**71.3**	**73.7**	76.2	**81.5**	**78.8**
SkipCorZero	79.3	28.3	41.7	**95.9**	57.3	71.8
SkipCorPair	80.9	59.4	68.5	86.3	70.7	77.7
Finkel et al. [55]	87.8	46.8	61.1	93.5	59.9	73.1
Soon et al. [16][1]	90.0	43.2	58.3	95.6	58.4	72.5
	ACE2004-ALL					
SkipCor	79.5	70.9	75.0	76.3	**81.1**	78.6
SkipCorZero	**81.3**	28.9	42.6	**95.6**	55.4	70.2
SkipCorPair	80.5	57.1	66.8	84.8	68.9	76.0
Cullota et al. [12]	-	-	-	86.7	73.2	79.3
Bengston et al. [17]	-	-	-	88.3	74.5	**80.8**
Haghighi et al. [15][2]	74.8	**77.7**	**76.2**	79.6	78.5	79.0

Coreference resolution systems evaluated on the ACE2004 dataset (i.e., ALL) [45] and its newswire (i.e., NW) and broadcast news (i.e., BN) subdatasets using the metrics MUC [9] and BCubed [41].

[1]Results were reported by Finkel and Manning [42].

[2]The MUC F1-score value does not agree with reported precision and recall and has been recalculated.

doi:10.1371/journal.pone.0100101.t006

The results for the CoNLL2012 dataset are shown in Table 7. The corpus is already separated into training, testing, and development datasets (we did not use the last when training). We used gold mention boundaries and additional manual tags, which are included in the data, therefore the results are comparable to the Gold Mention Boundaries setting. Fernandes et al.[34] proposed the shared task winning system and they are also the only ones who published their results on the broadcast news and newswire subdatasets (i.e., CONLL2012-BN, CONLL2012-NW). Similarly to the ACE2004 results, SkipCor performed better than SkipCorPair and SkipCorZero, except on the CoNLL2012-BN subdataset, where SkipCorPair outperformed SkipCor as it achieved the best precision and good recall. Otherwise, on most of the measures, SkipCor slightly outperformed the other systems and achieved better results with the MUC metric, generating cleaner mention clusters. For the full shared task, nine research teams submitted their results, but we show the results of only the top six. We significantly outperformed the others according to the MUC metric, where we increased the precision while having a comparable level of recall. According to the BCubed metric, the results are very similar, but in terms of CEAF we performed a little worse. The systems at the shared task were ranked using the CoNLL2012 measure, which is an average score of the MUC, the BCubed, and the CEAF F-scores. The winning Fernandes et al. [34] system achieved a CoNLL2012 score of 63.1 on English data, whereas our system achieved a score of 61.3, ranking as the second. The next then got the score of 60.7, with the others ranging down to the score of 43.0.

Table 7. Results of the proposed SkipCor system, baseline systems, and other approaches on the CoNLL2012 datasets

	MUC			BCubed			CEAF		
	P	R	F	P	R	F	P	R	F
System	**CoNLL2012-NW**								
SkipCor	76.1	**61.5**	**68.0**	69.6	**70.9**	**70.2**	39.9	**59.8**	**47.8**
SkipCorZero	76.7	16.8	27.5	**95.5**	36.7	53.0	35.1	35.3	35.2
SkipCorPair	**81.3**	45.9	58.7	86.4	56.7	68.5	**42.0**	54.7	47.5
Fernandes et al. [34]	-	-	61.6	-	-	70.0	-	-	46.6
	CoNLL2012-BN								
SkipCor	76.2	**62.0**	**68.4**	69.8	**71.3**	**70.5**	34.2	**59.2**	43.3
SkipCorZero	76.8	19.4	31.0	**95.9**	45.8	62.0	37.4	37.6	37.5
SkipCorPair	**81.9**	44.7	57.8	88.6	54.6	67.6	**39.1**	56.3	46.1
Fernandes et al. [34]	-	-	65.6	-	-	70.0	-	-	**49.1**
	CoNLL2012-ALL								
SkipCor	84.9	63.6	**72.7**	74.6	65.6	69.8	32.9	**57.2**	41.7
SkipCorZero	81.8	21.7	34.3	**95.7**	39.7	56.1	32.1	32.7	32.4
SkipCorPair	**85.9**	50.7	63.8	86.5	53.4	66.0	30.8	53.8	39.2
Fernandes et al. [34]	77.5	64.9	70.7	79.0	64.3	**70.9**	**41.7**	56.5	**48.0**
Björkelund et al. [56]	71.6	63.4	67.3	76.6	64.0	69.7	41.4	50.0	45.3
Chen et al. [57]	66.8	63.3	65.0	73.6	65.4	69.2	44.9	48.8	46.8
Stamborg et al. [58]	58.8	**66.2**	62.3	65.0	**71.2**	68.0	45.8	38.5	41.8
Zhekova et al. [51]	54.7	55.0	54.8	55.6	61.9	58.6	34.7	34.4	34.5
Li et al. [59]	33.7	44.2	38.2	53.9	66.4	59.5	36.5	27.5	31.4

Coreference resolution systems evaluated on the CoNLL2012 dataset (i.e., ALL) [43], and its newswire (i.e., NW) and broadcast news (i.e., BN) subdatasets using the metrics MUC [9], BCubed [41] and CEAF [42].
doi:10.1371/journal.pone.0100101.t007

In Table 8 we show the results for the SemEval2010 dataset, which is already separated into training and testing portions. We compared the systems using the Gold-standard Closed setting, for which systems can use only the provided attributes with true mention boundaries. On this dataset, SkipCor outperformed SkipCorZero on all three measures and outperformed SkipCorPair in terms of the CEAF and BCubed metrics. Interestingly, SkipCorPair achieved a significantly higher MUC precision score, and it therefore outperformed SkipCor in this measure. Compared to other systems, SkipCor achieved better BCubed and CEAF scores, but a lower MUC score. Interestingly, in the selected setting, the RelaxCor system performed the best, but our system outperformed it on all three measures. Focusing only on the MUC measure, we got the second place, as the SUCRE system achieved a better recall score.

Table 8. Results of the proposed SkipCor system, baseline systems, and other approaches on the SemEval2010 dataset

	MUC			BCubed			CEAF		
	P	R	F	P	R	F	P	R	F
System	**SemEval2010**								
SkipCor	68.8	30.1	41.8	94.8	**80.8**	**87.3**	74.0	78.5	**76.2**
SkipCorZero	67.0	3.6	6.8	**99.6**	75.1	85.7	73.0	73.1	73.1
SkipCorPair	**76.7**	35.6	48.7	97.1	79.0	87.1	72.7	**79.4**	75.9
RelaxCor [60]	72.4	21.9	33.7	97.0	74.8	84.5	**75.6**	75.6	75.6
SUCRE [61]	54.9	**68.1**	**60.8**	78.5	86.7	82.4	74.3	74.3	74.3
TANL-1 [33]	24.4	23.7	24.0	72.1	74.6	73.4	61.4	75.0	67.6
UBIU [50]	25.5	17.2	20.5	83.5	67.8	74.8	68.2	63.4	65.7

Coreference resolution systems evaluated on the SemEval2010 dataset [46] using the metrics MUC [9], BCubed [41] and CEAF [42].
doi:10.1371/journal.pone.0100101.t008

System UBIU [50], which entered the SemEval2010 shared task, also competed at the CoNLL2012 task, with a few modifications [51]. Our system significantly outperformed UBIU on both tasks and in terms of all three metrics. In contrast to our proposal, UBIU uses pairwise classification with a form of memory-based machine learning.

According to the results we showed, SkipCor outperformed both SkipCorZero and SkipCorPair. SkipCorZero mostly achieved good precision but very low recall. This is due to the identification of coreferences only between consecutive mentions within a document. SkipCor therefore uses skip-mention sequences to boost the recall values and consequently also the final result. SkipCorPair ranks somewhere between SkipCorZero and SkipCor. It checks for coreferences between mention pairs and is therefore very similar to other pairwise approaches. Due to a lot of pairwise comparisons, many mention sequences of length two must be generated, and therefore SkipCorPair executes more slowly than SkipCor.

Generally, SkipCor showed improvements on most of the datasets or achieved comparable results. We did not asses statistical significance of the differences in accuracy between the various systems because their implementations are not accessible and also referenced papers report single F score values only. Although some of the the existing rule-based systems are easy to implement and achieved good or best results, they may not be easily adapted to a different domain. This is also the reason why we proposed a simple machine-learned method for the task. SkipCor mostly obtained very good recall scores and a little bit lower precision. Other top performance systems use hybrid approaches, combining rule-based strategies with machine learning. All of them also employ feature engineering with a heavy use of lexicalized features. At the ACE2004 task, Haghighi et al. [15] used a completely deterministic approach, driven entirely by syntactic and semantic constraints. Bengston and Roth [17] focused especially on rich feature functions engineering with a simple pairwise classifier based on averaged perceptron. At the SemEval2010 shared task, the best two systems used a combination of manual rules and a set of machine learning classifiers (i.e., decision trees, naive Bayes, SVM, or maximum entropy models). Lastly, the CoNLL2012 task winner, Fernandes et al. [34], looked for the best mention clustering within a document using a specialized version of structure perceptron and represented mention clusters as coreference trees. The only system that used first-order probabilistic models was the one by Cullota et al. [12] on the ACE dataset. Their usage is completely different from that of our approach, because they still perform standard pairwise comparisons and then use first-order logic over mention clusters. Other CRF-based approaches, which were mentioned within the section on related work, were tested only against a limited version of a coreference resolution dataset or focused on an entity resolution task, which is a little similar to coreference resolution.

Performance in Real-world Scenarios

In addition to standard evaluation techniques, we trained SkipCor on one dataset and tested it on another (Table 9). Although the datasets do not have the same annotation guidelines or domain, this is interesting, as showing the results that can be expected by an end user on real data.

Table 9. Comparison of the results when training on one type of dataset or domain and testing on another

	Model				
Dataset	**A-BN**	**A-NW**	**C-BN**	**C-NW**	**SemEval2010**
A-BN	*74, 78, 54*	**72**, 77, 39	65, 70, 28	64, 69, 29	42, **71**, 49
A-NW	**72**, 73, 42	*73, 75, 58*	60, 64, 27	59, 69, 29	42, 67, **50**
C-BN	33, 56, 37	40, 58, 39	*68, 70, 43*	**65**, 70, 27	**57**, 64, 31
C-NW	39, 57, 39	41, 59, 41	**67**, 66, 28	*68, 70, 48*	56, 64, 32
SemEval2010	19, **82, 70**	23, **85, 74**	39, 76, 40	39, **77, 33**	*42, 87, 76*

Coreference resolution results comparison on ACE2004 (i.e., A), CoNLL2012 (i.e., C) and SemEval2010 newswire (i.e., NW) and broadcast news (i.e., BN) datasets. Each column represents a model trained on a specific dataset, while each row represents a dataset. Values represent F-scores of MUC [9], BCubed [41] and CEAF [42], respectively.

doi:10.1371/journal.pone.0100101.t009

First, we notice only a minor performance drop when testing within the datasets from the same shared task. For example, the results between broadcast news and newswire data remained almost the same as for the CoNLL and ACE2004 data separately. Furthermore, CoNLL models performed only a little worse on the ACE2004 dataset than originally. On the other hand, ACE2004 models performed less well on the CoNLL dataset, with a drop of roughly 20%. Both the CoNLL and ACE2004 models achieved low MUC scores on SemEval, but the best BCubed and CEAF scores. The difference is due to the fact that SemEval contains only nominal mentions and heuristically tagged singletons, which are more easily discovered, and they boost the scores. A model trained on SemEval performed the worst on both CoNLL and ACE2004. Interestingly, it achieved better MUC scores on CoNLL data than on the native SemEval testing dataset.

To conclude, the results typically show drops in accuracy on other domains or other datasets of the same or a different domain, from their performance on the same dataset. A similar analysis on different coreference datasets has also been conducted before [52], and their findings also show that evaluation on the same dataset the models were trained on gives the best results.

CONCLUSIONS

The present paper proposed 'SkipCor', a novel skip-mention coreference resolution system that is based solely on the linear-chain conditional random fields algorithm. To support the identification of all coreferent mentions in the text, the basic algorithm was extended with an adequate transformation of the data into different skip-mention sequences. In contrast to traditional approaches, the proposed system avoids checking all possible pairwise comparisons or using a single model. Thus, the system is completely parallelizable with a linear time complexity. Due to the amount of textual data available to date, the latter is of considerable importance in practical applications. We also stressed that the proposed skip-mention sequences could be adopted within other approaches in a straightforward fashion, which represents a prominent direction for future research.

The proposed system was evaluated on standard coreference resolution datasets that are the focus of evaluations for the majority of the techniques in the field. We compared the system to some baseline algorithms and also to the best performing coreference systems reported in the literature. The results obtained are comparable to the current state-of-the-art in coreference resolution, while we also more thoroughly analysed the contribution of the proposed skip-mention sequences. In addition, the analysis revealed that although accuracy in real-world scenarios can be even larger than expected, it decreases significantly when the system is trained on less reliable datasets.

Future work will focus on the development of more intelligent SkipCor mention clustering techniques (e.g., weighted scoring of coreference models) to minimize the number of merged conflicting mentions. Moreover, the system will be extended with a domain ontology that will provide an additional source of feature functions.

AUTHOR CONTRIBUTIONS

Conceived and designed the experiments: SŽ LŠ MB. Performed the experiments: SŽ. Analyzed the data: SŽ. Contributed reagents/materials/analysis tools: SŽ. Wrote the paper: SŽ LŠ MB.

REFERENCES

1. Andersen PM, Hayes PJ, Huettner AK, Schmandt LM, Nirenburg IB, et al.. (1992) Automatic extraction of facts from press releases to generate news stories. In: Proceedings of the third conference on Applied natural language processing. Pennsylvania: Association for Computational Linguistics, pp. 170–177.
2. Sarawagi S (2008) Information extraction. Foundations and Trends in Databases 1: 261–377. doi: 10.1561/1900000003
3. Wimalasuriya DC, Dou D (2010) Ontology-based information extraction: An introduction and a survey of current approaches. Journal of Information Science 36: 306–323. doi: 10.1177/0165551509360123
4. Luo X (2007) Coreference or not: A twin model for coreference resolution. In: Proceedings of the Conference of the North American Chapter of the Association for Computational Linguistics. New York: Association for Computational Linguistics, pp. 73–80.
5. Cai J, Strube M (2010) End-to-end coreference resolution via hypergraph partitioning. In: Proceedings of the 23rd International Conference on Computational Linguistics. Pennsylvania: Association for Computational Linguistics, pp. 143–151.
6. Bernardi R, Kirschner M, Ratkovic Z (2010) Context fusion: The role of discourse structure and centering theory. In: Proceedings of The International Conference on Language Resources and Evaluation. Valletta: European Language Resources Evaluation, pp. 1–8.
7. Ng V (2008) Unsupervised models for coreference resolution. In: Proceedings of the Conference on Empirical Methods in Natural Language Processing. Pennsylvania: Association for Computational Linguistics, pp. 640–649.
8. Clark JH, González-Brenes JP (2008) Coreference resolution: Current trends and future directions. Language and Statistics II Literature Review: 1–14.
9. Vilain M, Burger J, Aberdeen J, Connolly D, Hirschman L (1995) A model-theoretic coreference scoring scheme. In: Proceedings of the 6th conference on Message understanding. Pennsylvania: Association for Computational Linguistics, pp. 45–52.
10. Nguyen N, Kim JD, Miwa M, Matsuzaki T, Tsujii J (2012) Improving protein coreference resolution by simple semantic classification. BMC Bioinformatics 13: 1–21. doi: 10.1186/1471-2105-13-304
11. Lafferty J, McCallum A, Pereira F (2001) Conditional random fields: Probabilistic models for segmenting and labeling sequence data. In: Proceedings of the Eighteenth International Conference on Machine Learning. San Francisco: Morgan Kaufmann, pp. 282–289.
12. Culotta A, Wick M, Hall R, McCallum A (2007) First-order probabilistic models for coreference resolution. In: Human Language Technology Conference of the North American Chapter of the Association of Computational Linguistics. pp. 81–88.
13. Ng V, Cardie C (2002) Improving machine learning approaches to coreference resolution. In: Proceedings of the 40th Annual Meeting on Association for Computational Linguistics. Philadelphia: Association for Computational Linguistics, pp. 104–111.
14. Lee H, Peirsman Y, Chang A, Chambers N, Surdeanu M, et al.. (2011) Stanford's multi-pass sieve coreference resolution system at the CoNLL-2011 shared task. In: Proceedings of the Fifteenth Conference on Computational Natural Language Learning: Shared Task. Pennsylvania: Association for Computational Linguistics, pp. 28–34.
15. Haghighi A, Klein D (2009) Simple coreference resolution with rich syntactic and semantic features. In: Proceedings of the 2009 Conference on Empirical Methods in Natural Language Processing. Pennsylvania: Association for Computational Linguistics, volume 3 , pp. 1152–1161.
16. Soon WM, Ng HT, Lim DCY (2001) A machine learning approach to coreference resolution of noun phrases. Computational linguistics 27: 521–544. doi: 10.1162/089120101753342653
17. Bengtson E, Roth D (2008) Understanding the value of features for coreference resolution. In: Proceedings of the Conference on Empirical Methods in Natural Language Processing. Pennsylvania: Association for Computational Linguistics, pp. 294–303.
18. Luo X, Ittycheriah A, Jing H, Kambhatla N, Roukos S (2004) A mention-synchronous coreference resolution algorithm based on the bell tree. In: Proceedings of the 42nd Annual Meeting on Association for Computational Linguistics. Pennsylvania: Association for Computational Linguistics, pp. 136–143.
19. Rahman A, Ng V (2009) Supervised models for coreference resolution. In: Proceedings of the 2009 Conference on Empirical Methods in Natural Language Processing. volume 2 , pp. 968–977.
20. Huang S, Zhang Y, Zhou J, Chen J (2009) Coreference

resolution using markov logic networks. Advances in Computational Linguistics 41: 157–168.

21. Stoyanov V, Cardie C, Gilbert N, Riloff E, Buttler D, et al.. (2010) Coreference resolution with reconcile. In: Proceedings of the Association for Computational Linguistics 2010 Conference - Short Papers. Pennsylvania: Association for Computational Linguistics, pp. 156–161.

22. Raghunathan K, Lee H, Rangarajan S, Chambers N, Surdeanu M, et al.. (2010) A multi-pass sieve for coreference resolution. In: Proceedings of the 2010 Conference on Empirical Methods in Natural Language Processing. Pennsylvania: Association for Computational Linguistics, pp. 492–501.

23. Bejan C, Titsworth M, Hickl A, Harabagiu S (2009) Nonparametric bayesian models for unsupervised event coreference resolution. In: Advances in Neural Information Processing Systems. pp. 73–81.

24. Bejan CA, Harabagiu S (2010) Unsupervised event coreference resolution with rich linguistic features. In: Proceedings of the 48th Annual Meeting of the Association for Computational Linguistics. Stroudsburg: Association for Computational Linguistics, pp. 1412–1422.

25. Charniak E (2001) Unsupervised learning of name structure from coreference data. In: Proceedings of the second meeting of the North American Chapter of the Association for Computational Linguistics on Language technologies. Stroudsburg: Association for Computational Linguistics, pp. 1–7.

26. McCallum A, Wellner B (2004) Conditional models of identity uncertainty with application to noun coreference. In: Neural Information Processing Systems. pp. 1–8.

27. Fosler-Lussier E, He Y, Jyothi P, Prabhavalkar R (2013) Conditional random fields in speech, audio, and language processing. Proceedings of the IEEE 101: 1054–1075. doi: 10.1109/jproc.2013.2248112

28. Wellner B, McCallum A, Peng F, Hay M (2004) An integrated, conditional model of information extraction and coreference with application to citation matching. In: Proceedings of the 20th conference on Uncertainty in artificial intelligence. Arlington: AUAI Press, pp. 593–601.

29. Finkel JR, Grenager T, Manning C (2005) Incorporating non-local information into information extraction systems by Gibbs sampling. In: Proceedings of the 43rd Annual Meeting on Association for Computational Linguistics. Pennsylvania: Association for Computational Linguistics, pp. 363–370.

30. Ram RVS, Devi SL (2012) Coreference resolution using tree CRFs. In: Proceedings of Conference on Intelligent Text Processing and Computational Linguistics. Heidelberg: Springer, pp. 285–296.

31. Žitnik S (2013) Intelligent Ontology-based Information Extraction - IOBIE, source code repository. Available: https://bitbucket.org/szitnik/iobie. (Last accessed 15th May 2014).

32. Broscheit S, Poesio M, Ponzetto SP, Rodriguez KJ, Romano L, et al.. (2010) BART: a multilingual anaphora resolution system. In: Proceedings of the 5th International Workshop on Semantic Evaluation. Pennsylvania: Association for Computational Linguistics, pp. 104–107.

33. Attardi G, Rossi SD, Simi M (2010) TANL-1: coreference resolution by parse analysis and similarity clustering. In: Proceedings of the 5th International Workshop on Semantic Evaluation. Pennsylvania: Association for Computational Linguistics, pp. 108–111.

34. Fernandes ER, dos Santos CN, Milidiú RL (2012) Latent structure perceptron with feature induction for unrestricted coreference resolution. In: Proceedings of CoNLL 2012 Joint Conference on EMNLP and CoNLL. Pennsylvania: Association for Computational Linguistics, pp. 41–48.

35. Miller GA (1995) WordNet: a lexical database for english. Communications of the ACM 38: 39–41. doi: 10.1145/219717.219748

36. Bergsma S, Lin D (2006) Bootstrapping path-based pronoun resolution. In: Proceedings of the 21st International Conference on Computational Linguistics and the 44th annual meeting of the Association for Computational Linguistics. Pennsylvania: Association for Computational Linguistics, pp. 33–40.

37. Orasan C, Evans R (2007) NP animacy identification for anaphora resolution. Journal of Artificial Intelligence Research 29: 79–103.

38. Cohn T (2006) Efficient inference in large conditional random fields. In: Proceedings of the 17th European conference on Machine Learning. Heidelberg: Springer, pp. 606–613.

39. Chincor N (1991) MUC-3 evaluation metrics. In: Proceedings of the 3rd conference on Message understanding. Pennsylvania: Association for Computational Linguistics, pp. 17–24.

40. Chinchor N, Sundheim B (1993) MUC-5 evaluation metrics. In: Proceedings of the 5th conference on Message understanding. Pennsylvania: Association for Computational Linguistics, p. 6978.

41. Bagga A, Baldwin B (1998) Algorithms for scoring coreference chains. In: The first international conference on language resources and evaluation workshop on linguistics coreference. volume 1, pp. 1–7.

42. Luo X (2005) On coreference resolution performance metrics. In: Proceedings of the conference on Human Language Technology and Empirical Methods in Natural Language Processing. Pennsylvania: Association for Computational Linguistics, pp. 25–32.

43. Pradhan S, Moschitti A, Xue N, Uryupina O, Zhang Y (2012) CoNLL-2012 shared task: Modeling multilingual unrestricted coreference in OntoNotes. In: Proceedings of the Joint Conference on EMNLP and CoNLL: Shared Task. Association for Computational Linguistics, pp. 1–40.

44. Hirschman L, Chincor NA (1997) MUC-7 coreference task definition. In: Proceedings of the Seventh Message Understanding Conference. San Francisco: Morgan Kaufmann, pp. 1–17.

45. Doddington G, Mitchell A, Przybocki M, Ramshaw

L, Strassel S, et al.. (2004) The automatic content extraction (ACE) programtasks, data, and evaluation. In: Proceedings of LREC. volume 4, pp. 837–840.

46. Recasens M, Màrquez L, Sapena E, Mart AM, Taulé M, et al.. (2010) SemEval-2010 task 1: Coreference resolution in multiple languages. In: Proceedings of the 5th International Workshop on Semantic Evaluation. pp. 1–8.

47. Pradhan S, Ramshaw L, Marcus M, Palmer M, Weischedel R, et al.. (2011) CoNLL-2011 shared task: Modeling unrestricted coreference in ontonotes. In: Proceedings of the Fifteenth Conference on Computational Natural Language Learning: Shared Task. pp. 1–27.

48. Apache OpenNLP: a machine learning based toolkit for the processing of natural language text. Available: http://opennlp.apache.org/. (Last accessed 15th May 2014).

49. Okazaki N (2007) CRFsuite: a fast implementation of conditional random fields (CRFs). Available: http://www.chokkan.org/software/crfsuite. (Last accessed 15th May 2014).

50. Zhekova D, Kübler S (2010) UBIU: a language-independent system for coreference resolution. In: Proceedings of the 5th International Workshop on Semantic Evaluation. pp. 96–99.

51. Zhekova D, Kübler S, Bonner J, Ragheb M, Hsu YY (2012) UBIU for multilingual coreference resolution in OntoNotes. In: Joint Conference on EMNLP and CoNLL-Shared Task. pp. 88–94.

52. Gilbert N, Riloff E (2013) Domain-specific coreference resolution with lexicalized features. Pennsylvania: Association for Computational Linguistics, pp. 1–6.

53. Winkler WE (1990) String comparator metrics and enhanced decision rules in the fellegi-sunter model of record linkage. In: Proceedings of the Section on Survey Research Methods. American Statistical Association, pp. 354–359.

54. Bansal M, Klein D (2012) Coreference semantics from web features. In: Proceedings of the 50th Annual Meeting of the Association for Computational Linguistics: Long Papers-Volume 1. p. 389398.

55. Finkel JR, Manning CD (2008) Enforcing transitivity in coreference resolution. In: Proceedings of the 46th Annual Meeting of the Association for Computational Linguistics on Human Language Technologies: Short Papers. pp. 45–48.

56. Björkelund A, Farkas R (2012) Data-driven multilingual coreference resolution using resolver stacking. In: Proceedings of the Joint Conference on EMNLP and CoNLL: Shared Task. pp. 49–55.

57. Chen C, Ng V (2012) Combining the best of two worlds: A hybrid approach to multilingual coreference resolution. In: Proceedings of the Joint Conference on EMNLP and CoNLL: Shared Task. pp. 56–63.

58. Stamborg M, Medved D, Exner P, Nugues P (2012) Using syntactic dependencies to solve coreferences. In: Joint Conference on EMNLP and CoNLL-Shared Task. pp. 64–70.

59. Li X, Wang X, Liao X (2012) Simple maximum entropy models for multilingual coreference resolution. In: Proceedings of the Joint Conference on EMNLP and CoNLL: Shared Task. pp. 83–88.

60. Sapena E, Padró L, Turmo J (2010) RelaxCor: a global relaxation labeling approach to coreference resolution. In: Proceedings of the 5th International Workshop on Semantic Evaluation. pp. 88–91.

61. Kobdani H, Schtze H (2010) SUCRE: a modular system for coreference resolution. In: Proceedings of the 5th International Workshop on Semantic Evaluation. pp. 92–95.

CHAPTER 20

A NODE LINKAGE APPROACH FOR SEQUENTIAL PATTERN MINING

Osvaldo Navarro, Rene´ Cumplido, Luis Villaseñor-Pineda,, Claudia Feregrino-Uribe, Jesús Ariel Carrasco-Ochoa

Departamento de Ciencias Computacionales, Instituto Nacional de Astrofı´sica, O´ ptica y Electro´nica, Sta. Ma. Tonantzintla, Puebla, Me´xico

ABSTRACT

Sequential Pattern Mining is a widely addressed problem in data mining, with applications such as analyzing Web usage, examining purchase behavior, and text mining, among others. Nevertheless, with the dramatic increase in data volume, the current approaches prove inefficient when dealing with large input datasets, a large number of different symbols and low minimum supports. In this paper, we propose a new sequential pattern mining algorithm, which follows a pattern-growth scheme to discover sequential patterns. Unlike most pattern growth algorithms, our approach does not build a data structure to represent the input dataset, but instead accesses the required sequences through pseudo-projection databases, achieving better runtime and reducing memory requirements. Our algorithm traverses the search space in a depth-first fashion and only preserves in memory a pattern node linkage and the pseudo-projections required for the branch being explored at the time. Experimental results show that our new approach, the Node Linkage Depth-First Traversal algorithm (NLDFT), has better performance and scalability in comparison with state of the art algorithms.

INTRODUCTION

Since Agrawal [1] proposed the problem of sequential pattern mining, it has become an important data mining problem, mainly because of its wide variety of applications. Sequential pattern mining methods have been used in applications such as mining web usage behavior[2], [3], [4], Drug-drug interaction detection [5], text mining tasks such as document clustering[6], question answering [7], authorship atribution [8], touring path suggestion [9], CRM strategies for online shopping [10], mining anomalous events in surveillance videos from commercial environments [11], among others. This range of applications is possible likely because datasets from many domains contain some sort of sequential order between its elements; for instance, the sequential order of proteins in DNA sequences, time stamps on web access logs and business databases, the sequence of words in a document, among others. Furthermore, due to the dramatic pace at which data is collected nowadays, most of the current data mining methods are becoming inefficient. This is because most of the popular data mining methods were created when the common dataset size was several orders of magnitude smaller[12].

Thus, current datasets pose a significant challenge for current data mining approaches, which is part of the motivation for this work.

The two main approaches to tackle the sequential mining problem are: apriori-based and pattern growth-based [13]. The first strategy consists in generating a set of candidate patterns

Citation: Navarro O, Cumplido R, Villaseñor-Pineda L, Feregrino-Uribe C, Carrasco-Ochoa JA (2014) A Node Linkage Approach for Sequential Pattern Mining. PLoS ONE 9(6): e95418. doi:10.1371/journal.pone.0095418

and then testing them against the frequency threshold to find the sequential patterns. Pruning techniques are usually combined with this strategy, to generate a candidate pattern set as small as possible. However, approaches based on this strategy have to deal with a combinatorial explosion of candidate patterns when dealing with large datasets and low frequency thresholds. The pattern-growth strategy finds sequential patterns by appending symbols to an already know frequent sequence, forming new sequences, which then are evaluated to see if they are frequent as well. The pattern-growth based approaches usually do this by traversing a previously build data structure that represents the entire dataset. This data structures become huge when processing large databases, which usually has a negative impact on performance and memory usage.

In this paper, the Node Linkage Depth-First Traversal (NLDFT) algorithm for sequential pattern mining is proposed. Unlike most pattern growth approaches, the proposed algorithm does not build a data structure to represent the input dataset, but instead accesses the required sequences through pseudo-projection databases. The proposed algorithm traverses the search space in a depth-first fashion and only preserves in memory a pattern node linkage and the pseudo-projections required for the branch being explored at the time.

The rest of this paper is organized as follows. The *Related Work* section presents a summary of the related work about sequential pattern mining. The Preliminaries section presents the basic concepts and ideas necessary to understand the sequential pattern mining problem and its formal definition. In the *Proposed Algorithm* section, the NLDFT algorithm is described. The *Performance Evaluation* section describes the experiments made to evaluate the proposed algorithm and the results obtained from them. Next, the Complexity Analysis section presents a theoretical analysis and comparison of the performance of the NLDFT algorithm. Finally, the Conclusions *and Future Work* section presents general conclusions and suggestions for future work.

Related Work

There is a variety of problems that deal with mining frequent sequences, each one with different input and/or conditions. Among them, for instance, there is the problem of finding frequent sequences of symbols [1], frequent sequences of itemsets [14], maximal frequent word sequences [15], frequent closed sequences [16], frequent sequences with time constraints [17], among others. In this work we addressed the problem of mining frequent sequences of symbols, which will be referred to as *sequential pattern mining* in the rest of this article.

The sequential pattern mining problem was first defined in [1]. Since then, many other approaches have been proposed. These methods can be categorized, by the way they discover sequential patterns, in three categories: apriori-based approaches, pattern growth-based approaches and hybrid approaches.

The apriori-based approaches usually discover the sequential patterns in a breadth-first fashion, *i.e.*, they obtain the frequent sequences of size k together at the k iteration of the algorithm as it traverses the search space. Also, these methods depend on a feature named *generate-and-test* [18] to carry out the mining. This feature entails growing already found patterns by one item at a time and then testing the generated candidates against the minimum support.

The first algorithm that worked under the apriori-based scheme was Apriori All, which was proposed by Agrawal [1]. The AprioriAll algorithm was proposed to tackle the problem of finding sequential patterns in a database of customer transactions. This algorithm travels the search space in a first-breadth fashion, finding all the patterns of length k in the k iteration before moving on to the next one. To find the patterns in an iteration level, this method generates a set of candidate patterns, which are further tested against the minimum support. Also, the algorithm incorporates a pruning technique based on the antimonotonic property that states that if a sequence cannot pass the minimum support test, all of its super-sequences will also fail the test [18]. This method has the main disadvantage of generating an explosive number of candidates, particularly at early stages of the mining process, which consumes a lot of memory.

Another representative algorithm of the apriori-based scheme is SPADE [19]. This method not only discovers single item sequences, but sequences of subsets of items, as well. SPADE represents the search space as a lattice of frequent sequences, which can be traversed in either depth-first or breadth-first fashion. The algorithm traverses the lattice, testing candidates against the minimum support to find the set of frequent sequences. To achieve this, an id-list is generated for each frequent sequence in the lattice, which is a list of all the input-sequence identifiers and item set identifier pairs that contain that sequence. To obtain the support count of a candidate sequence k-pattern, the algorithm performs temporal joins over the id-lists of any two of its (k−1) subsequences. Moreover, as maintaining all the intermediate id-list in memory would not be possible for databases of considerable size, Zaki proposed to break the lattice into disjoint subsets called *equivalence classes*. Thus, each equivalence class can be loaded into main memory and processed separately. However, even with the improvement of not having to constantly read the original database, but only three times, this method still faces the problem of generating a huge number of candidates, specially when dealing with large databases and/or low minimum supports.

To tackle the issue of efficiently generating candidate patterns, Tan et al. [20] proposed *SEQUEST*, an algorithm that relies on a structure called Direct Memory Access Strips (DMA-Strips). A DMA-Strip represents a single sequence in a database, and is composed by an ordered list which stores a sequence of items' *label*, *scope* and *event-id*. The *event-id* groups items based on their timestamps and the *scope* is used to determine the relationship between two consecutive items in a strip. To generate a candidate pattern, the algorithm iterates through a DMA-Strim and extends one item at a time. Next, to test a candidate pattern against the minimum support, two approaches were proposed: a vertical join counting approach similar to the one used in [19] and a horizontal counting approach using a hash table. Experimental results indicated that the vertical approach performed better than the horizontal approach. However, the vertical approach performance could degrade if the frequency of extracted candidate patterns is high, as it usually occurs when the minimum support is low, due to the nature of the join approach complexity.

A recent apriori-based approach is *PRISM* [14]. In this approach, an encoding based on prime factorization theory is used to represent the input database, in order to efficiently calculate the frequency of candidate patterns. PRISM represents the search space as a tree structure, where each node represents a sequence, and generates candidate patterns by combining a node with each one of its siblings. Finally, PRISM uses join operations over the encoded database to find the frequency of the current candidate. Although PRISM outperforms previous apriori-based approached such as SPADE, it also has the issue of the combinatorial explosion of the candidate generation process, which would significantly increase the runtime of the algorithm when dealing with large databases and low minimum supports.

The pattern growth strategy is characterized by traversing the search space in a depth-first fashion. It offers the advantage of not having to generate candidate patterns, which avoids the combinatorial explosion of patterns when dealing with large databases. Because of this, the pattern growth strategy has become the most used scheme of action, preferred over the apriori-based strategy. Among these approaches, Ezeife and Lu [2] presents the algorithm *Pre-order Linked Wap-Tree (PLWAP)*, a method for mining sequential patterns from a web access sequence database, which uses a data structure named *PLWAP-tree* [21] to efficiently access the sequences to be mined. The algorithm then recursively mines the tree, using prefix conditional sequence search, to find all the sequential patterns. One of the benefits of this method is that it only reads the original database twice, which helps to reduce I/O access costs or extra storage requirements. Also, the algorithm doesn't have to build a data structure at each level of recursion, which yields an improvement in running time, compared with previous works, which used the same data structure [3]. Peterson and Tang [22] propose an algorithm which also uses a data structure based on the aggregate tree. However, this method does not link the elements of the same type in the aggregate tree, but instead builds a forest of *first-occurrence subtrees* as the basic data structure to represent database projections. Although this method improves in memory usage compared with the PLWAP algorithm, it still has to build the entire aggregate tree before the mining process. This would require a lot of memory when dealing with large databases, which is usually the case within the text mining area. Ezeife et al.[23] presents PLWAPLong, also based on the PLWAP algorithm. PLWAPLong uses a simpler numbering scheme than PLWAP, to identify ancestor and descendant relationships in the aggregate tree. In this way, PLWAPLong is capable of dealing with larger databases than PLWAP, with a lower impact in performance. Moreover, PLWAPLong uses a more efficient approach to find the first occurrences of a word in the aggregate tree, which is a recurrent operation in the mining process, used to determine the frequency of a word in a projected database. While PLWAPLong can process larger databases than PLWAP, the algorithm was tested against databases with rather small vocabularies and average document size, in comparison with the ones used in text mining tasks. Furthermore, PLWAPLong too has to build the entire aggregate tree before the mining process, which results costly when dealing with databases with large vocabularies and a large average document size.

The hybrid approaches comprehend methods that combine one or more features from both apriori-based and pattern growth-based approaches. Among them, Chen [13] proposes a novel data structure named *UpDown Directed Acyclic Graph* (UDDAG), which supports bidirectional pattern growth from both ends of the discovered patterns, in order to perform a fast conditional search. First, the algorithm finds the frequent words in the sequence database, and uses them to filter the database from infrequent elements. Next, a frequent word is chosen to be the root of an UDDAG, and two database projections are created; one projection is formed by the prefixes of the sequence database with respect to the root pattern and the other one is formed by the suffixes. Frequent words are then found in these projections, and are appended to the root pattern to form new frequent patterns; thus it is said that in each level of recursion the root pattern is grown from both ends. Finally, the algorithm combines the patterns found in both projections to form candidate patterns, which are tested against the minimum support, in order to find new frequent patterns. Each one of the projections created is treated as a new database and the previous process is repeated, recursively. The UDDAG algorithm is an hybrid approach, as it uses conditional search in combination with candidate generation, to find all the sequential patterns. One of the advantages of its novel data structure, is that in each level or recursion the root pattern is grown from both sides concurrently, in comparison with other pattern growth-based methods, that only grow the length of the root pattern in 1 at each recursion. However, the need to use a candidate generation phase at each level of recursion impacts negatively in the algorithm's performance, and this impact becomes unacceptable when processing large databases using low minimum supports, due to the explosive number of candidates generated.

Many approaches have been proposed to provide an efficient solution to sequential pattern mining problem. However, the current methods still have problems when dealing with large databases and low minimum supports, which is the case in areas like Text Mining, where the datasets are usually formed by a large number of documents of considerable size. Two of the most common issues that occur when processing a large dataset are the combinatorial explosion of candidates in apriori-based approaches, and the generation of huge data structures in pattern growth-based approaches. The proposed algorithm avoids the candidate generation phase, and does not build a data structure to represent the input database, but only access the required sequences through pseudo-projected databases, and only maintains in memory these pseudo-projections along with a pattern-node linkage required in the branch of the search space being explored at a time, thus avoiding the common issues previously mentioned.

Preliminaries

Before giving the formal definition of the sequential pattern mining problem, it is necessary to introduce the following definitions:

Definition 1. *Let* Σ *be the set of symbols and '$\cdot$' be the operation of concatenating any two symbols from* Σ. *A* **non-empty sequence** *s is a finite succession of symbols from* Σ, $s = s_1 \cdot \ldots \cdot s_m$, *such that* $s_i \in \Sigma$ *for all* $1 \leq i \leq m < \infty$ *and*

s_i and s_j are not necessarily different for $i \neq j$. The length of a sequence $s = s_1 \cdot ... \cdot s_m$ is m, and it will denoted as len(s). *A* **sequence database** *D is a finite set of non-empty sequences. A* **pattern** *is a non-empty sequence.*

Definition 2. *A non-empty sequence is a* **subsequence** *of another sequence if it is embedded in that sequence, i.e., a sequence $s' = s'_1 \cdot ... \cdot s'_n$ is a subsequence of a sequence $s = s_1 \cdot ... \cdot s_m$, denoted as $s' \subseteq s$, if and only if $n \leq m$ and there exist $i_1,...,i_n$ such that $1 \leq i_1 < ... < i_n \leq m$ and $s'_j = s_{i_j}$ for all $1 \leq j \leq n$.*

Definition 3. *A sequence s in D is said to support a pattern p if p is a subsequence of s. The* **support of a pattern** *p in D, denoted as Sup_D (p), is the number of sequences in D that support p. Given a threshold in* (0,1], *a pattern p is frequent with respect to and D if $Sup_D(p) \geq \xi|D|$, where $|D|$ is the number of sequences in D. $\xi|D|$ is called the absolute threshold and denoted as .*

Definition 4. *Given two sequences s and p, such that $p \subseteq s$, the* **p-prefix** *of s is the prefix of s from the first symbol (the leftmost symbol) to the first occurrence of p inclusive. This definition is a generalization of the one found in [24], for sequences of length greater than 1.*

For instance, considering $s = d \cdot e \cdot \mathbf{a} \cdot g \cdot \mathbf{b} \cdot f \cdot a \cdot g \cdot a \cdot b \cdot c$ and $p = a \cdot b$, the p-prefix of *s* is $d \cdot e \cdot a \cdot g \cdot b$. The subsequence $d \cdot e \cdot a \cdot g \cdot b \cdot f \cdot a \cdot g \cdot a \cdot b$ is not the p-prefix because the first occurrence of $a \cdot b$ in the sequence is the one that is in bold.

Definition 5. *Given two sequences s and p, such that $p \subseteq s$, s can be represented as $s = \hat{p} \cdot e$, where $\hat{p}$ is the p-prefix of s and e is the rest of the sequence. The subsequence e corresponds to the* **projection** *of s with respect to p, denoted as proj(s,p).*

Roughly speaking, the projection of a sequence s with respect to a sequence p can be constructed by taking out the symbols in s, from the first one to the last symbol in the first occurrence of p in s. The remaining symbols will constitute the projection. For instance, considering $s = d \cdot e \cdot a \cdot g \cdot \mathbf{b} \cdot f \cdot a \cdot g \cdot a \cdot b \cdot c$ and $p = a \cdot b$, the projection of s with respect to p is $f \cdot a \cdot g \cdot a \cdot b \cdot c$.

Definition 6. *Given a sequence database D and a sequence s, the* **projection database** *of D with respect to s, denoted as $Proj_s(D)$ is defined as the set of non-empty projections of every sequence in D with respect to sequence s. Formally:*

$$Proj_s(D) = \{proj(x,s) | x \in D, len(proj(x,s)) \neq 0\} \quad \textbf{(1)}$$

Definition 7. *Given a pair of sequences $s = s_1 \cdot s_2 \cdot ... \cdot s_n$ and w, such that $w \subseteq s$, and $proj(s,w) = s_i \cdot s_{i+1} \cdot ... \cdot s_n$, the* **pseudo-projection** *of s with respect to w, denoted as pproj(s,w) is defined as follows:*

$$pproj(s,w) = \begin{cases} (ID(s),i), & if \quad len(proj(s,w)) \geq 0 \\ (ID(s),-1), & if \quad len(proj(s,w)) = 0 \end{cases} \quad \textbf{(2)}$$

where ID(S) *gives a unique identifier for the sequence s. If the second entry of a pseudo-projection is* -1, *the pseudo-projection will be called* **empty pseudo-projection**.

Roughly speaking, a pseudo-projection of a sequence *s* with respect to a sequence *w* stores a pair of values: the identifier of *s* and the start position of the projection of *s* with respect to *w*.

Definition 8. *Similarly to definition 6, given a sequence database D and a sequence s, the* **pseudo-projection database** *of D with respect to s, denoted as $Proj_s(D)$ is defined as the set of non-empty pseudo-projections of every sequence in D with respect to sequence s. Formally:*

$$PProj_s(D) = \{pproj(x,s) | x \in D, len(proj(x,s)) \neq 0\} \quad \textbf{(3)}$$

Theorem 1. Given a sequence database *D*, a pattern *p*, and a symbol $e \in \Sigma$, the support of p.e, i.e., $p_1 \cdot p_2 \cdot ... \cdot p_n \cdot e$, in *D* is equal to the support of *e* in the projection database of *D* with respect to *p*. Formally:

$$sup_D(p \cdot e) = sup_{Proj_p(D)}(e) \quad \textbf{(4)}$$

The formal proof for this theorem is similar to the one provided in [25] for a similar theorem. The proof is as follows:

Proof. ($\geq$) Let *s* be a sequence in *D* that supports p.e. Then, *s* can be represented as $s = \hat{p} \cdot \hat{e}$, such that $\hat{p}$ is the *p*-prefix of *s*, where $p \subseteq \hat{p}$ and $e \subseteq \hat{e}$. Thus, ê is the projection of *s* with respect to *p*, then $\hat{e} \in Proj_p(D)$. Also, as $e \subseteq \hat{e}$ and $\hat{e} \in Proj_p(D)$, then for every sequence in *D* that supports p.e, there will be a sequence in $Proj_p(D)$ that supports *e*. This means that the support of *e* in $Proj_p(D)$ is at least equal to the support of p.e in D. Therefore, $sup_{Proj_p(D)}(e) \geq sup_D(p \cdot e)$.

($\leq$) Let $\tilde{e}$ be a sequence in $Proj_p(D)$ that supports *e*, that is, $e \subseteq \tilde{e}$. As $\tilde{e}$ is the projection of a sequence *s'* in *D* with respect to *p*, then $s' = \tilde{p} \cdot \tilde{e}$, where $\tilde{p}$ is the p-prefix of *s'*. Since $p \subseteq \tilde{p}$ and $e \subseteq \tilde{e}$, then $p \cdot e \subseteq \tilde{p} \cdot \tilde{e} = s'$. In this way, for every sequence in $Proj_p(D)$ that supports *e*, there will be a sequence in *D* that supports p.e. This means that the support of p.e in *D* is at least equal to the support of *e* in $Proj_p(D)$. Therefore, $sup_{Proj_p(D)}(e) \leq sup_D(p \cdot e)$.

Having defined the previous concepts, the **sequential pattern mining problem** can be defined as the task of finding all the frequent sequences in a given sequence database *D* with respect to a given threshold ξ. For instance, Figure 1 shows a database formed by 3 sequences, and its correspondent sequential patterns, for an absolute threshold (also called frequency threshold) of 2.

	Size 1	Size 2	Size 3
1. $a \cdot b \cdot c \cdot d$	1. a	1. $a \cdot c$	1. $a \cdot c \cdot d$
2. $a \cdot e \cdot c \cdot d$	2. e	2. $a \cdot d$	
3. $a \cdot e \cdot f \cdot g$	3. d	3. $a \cdot e$	
	4. c	4. $c \cdot d$	

a) b)

Figure 1. Example of a sequence database and its frequent sequences. Sequence database containing 3 sequences (a) and its correspondent frequent sequences (b), for a frequency threshold of 2.

METHODS

The main idea behind the proposed algorithm is to build frequent sequences by growing an already known frequent sequence *p* with a frequent symbol *w* found in the database projection with respect to *p*, creating the sequence p.w, which Theorem 1 guarantees that it is a frequent sequence. This process repeats recursively, until there are no more frequent symbols to append to the current frequent sequence. The process then rolls back to the previous frequent sequence found and continues growing it with another frequent symbol. The search space, therefore, is represented as a series of trees, one for each frequent sequence of length 1. Each node of a tree represents a frequent sequence, and they are located in the tree in a way that a sequence node will be the same as its parent node, but with a symbol appended at the end of the sequence. Figure 2 shows an example of the search space of a small sequence database with four different symbols.

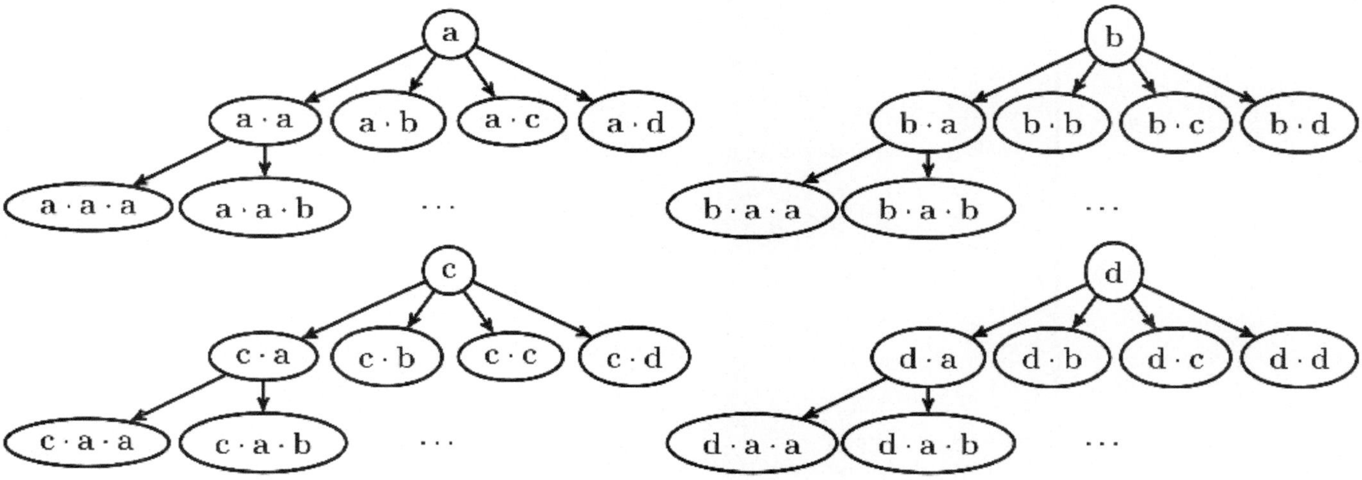

Figure 2. Example of search space. An example of the search space for a sequence database with $\Sigma = \{a, b, c, d\}$.

With each frequent sequence discovered, a new node is built and liked to its parent node. Each node contains a frequent sequence, and pointers to its parent node and its descendants, to maintain the structure of the current tree. Without loss of generality, the symbols in the implementation have been represented as positive integers. A sequence can be represented, then, as an array of integers.

Properly linking every frequent sequence found by the algorithm would result in a subtree of one of the search space trees. However, storing the whole tree in main memory during the mining process is not needed, only the branch where the sequence that is being grown belongs. This is because it is only required to access the ancestors of the current sequence, when the algorithm rollsback to a previous sequence and tries to grow it with another frequent symbol. This results in a significant memory saving, specially when dealing with a sequence database with a large set of different symbols (Σ).

Although the NLDFT algorithm does not generate candidate patterns, but grows frequent sequences from already found frequent sequences instead, the frequency of the found sequences still has to be ensured. To guarantee that, the proposed algorithm only uses symbols that meet the minimum support to build frequent sequences. Each time the algorithm search in a pseudo-projection database for symbols to build new frequent sequences, it only retrieves the symbols that meet the frequency threshold. In this way, when the algorithm uses those retrieved symbols to grow the current frequent sequence, it is assured that the new sequence is frequent as well.

The NLDFT algorithm is divided in three main steps. The first step comprises preliminary operations, which prepare the input data for the main mining process. The Algorithm 1 in Table 1 shows these operations. First of all, the algorithm reads the original database and finds the frequent symbols; these symbols correspond to the set of the frequent sequences of length 1. Next, the database is read again, and the symbols that are not on the set of frequent symbols are removed. Next, for each frequent symbols found, the pseudo-projection database with respect to that symbol is built. This is shown in Table 2. Next, a call to the mining process is made, having as input the symbol and the pseudo-projection database. The mining process then will recursively find the frequent sequences that start with the corresponding symbol. The union of the frequent sequence sets found with each iteration will constitute the set of the frequent sequences of input database.

Table 1. Algorithm 1

```
input:  D, a sequence database
        η, a minimum support.
output: F, a set containing all the frequent sequences in D.
Initialization
//STEP 1: Find frequent symbols and filter input database.
FW ← GetFrequentSymbols (D, η)
MinFrequency ← D.size * η
MainDB ← FilterDatabase (D, FW)
MainProj ← GetPseudoProjection (MainDB, −1)
F ← FW
foreach symbol a in FW do
|  Proj ← GetPseudoProjection (MainProj, a)
|  F ← F ∪ Mine (Proj, a, η)
end
Return F
```

NLDFT's main function.

doi:10.1371/journal.pone.0095418.t001

Table 2. Algorithm 2

```
input:  D, a pseudo-projection database
        a, a symbol
output: ProjDB, the pseudo-projection database of D with respect to a
GetPseudoProjection (D, a)
{
    ProjDB ← Ø
    foreach sequence d in D do
        for i ← d.Start to D.Size - 1 do
            if MainDB[d.ID][i] = = a then
                Proj ← new ProjSequence Proj.ID = d.ID if a= = −1 then
                    Proj.Start ← 0
                else
                    Proj.Start ← i + 1
                end
                ProjDB.add(Proj) break
            end
        end
        delete Proj
    end
    return ProjDB
}
```

NLDFT's GetPseudoProjection function. This function creates a pseudo-projection database from an input pseudo-projection database and a symbol.

doi:10.1371/journal.pone.0095418.t002

The second step of the algorithm occurs inside the main mining process, which receives as input data a pseudo-projection database, a sequence that will be grown to discover more frequent sequences and the minimum support. This step is shown in Table 3. The first operation made in the main mining process is finding the frequent symbols inside the input pseudo-projection database. This is done inside the function *GetFrequentSymbols*, which is shown in detail in Table 4. There, each sequence of the pseudo-projection database is read, and the occurrences of the symbols read in each sequence is counted. Once the function has read all the sequences, those symbols that met the minimum frequency are returned as output.

Table 3. Algorithm 3

```
input: D, a pseudo-projection database
        p, the growing sequence
        η, the minimum support
output: F, a set containing all the frequent sequences in D.
Mine (D, p, η)
{
  //STEP 2: Find frequent symbols in the given projection database.
  FW ← GetFrequentSymbols (D, η)
  //STEP 3: Form new frequent sequences by combining the sequence p with every symbol obtained in the previous step.
  foreach symbol a in FW do
  |   F ← F ∪{p · a}
  |   Proj ← GetPseudoProjection (D, a)
  |   Mine (Proj, {p · a}, η)
  end
  Return F
}
```

NLDFT's Mine function. This function recursively grows the input sequence *p*.

doi:10.1371/journal.pone.0095418.t003

Table 4. Algorithm 4

```
input:  D, a pseudo-projection database
        η, the minimum support
output: FWArray, the set of frequent symbols in D with respect to η
GetFrequentSymbols (D, η)
{
  foreach sequence d in D do
  |   Duplicates.clear()
  |   for i ← sequence.begin to sequence.end do
  |   |   if Duplicates.exists (MainDB [d.I D][i]) = = true then
  |   |   |   Duplicates.add(MainDB [d.ID][i])
  |   |   |   if FWArray exists (MainDB [d ID][i]) = =true then
  |   |   |   |   FWArray.count ++
  |   |   |   else
  |   |   |   |   FWArray.add(MainDB [d.ID][i])
  |   |   |   |   FWArray (w).count ← 1
  |   |   |   end
  |   |   end
  |   end
  end
  for wElem ← FWArray.begin to FWArray.end do
  |   if wElem.count < MinFrequency then
  |   |   wElem.delete
  |   end
  end
  return FWArray
}
```

NLDFT's GetFrequentSymbols function. This function finds the frequent symbols in the input pseudo-projection database.

doi:10.1371/journal.pone.0095418.t004

The third and final step of the proposed algorithm also occurs inside the function *Mine*, and comprises building new frequent sequences out of the input frequent sequence and the frequent symbols found in step 2. After returning from the function *GetFrequentSymbols*, and for each of the symbols returned from it, a new frequent sequence is formed, by appending that symbol to the end of the input frequent sequence. Finally, a projection of the input database is generated and used as the input of a new recursive call to the *Mine* function, along with the new frequent sequence built, and the minimum support. The process continues recursively, until no frequent symbols are found in the current input database.

Example

Next, an illustrative example about the proposed algorithm's functionality is shown. Figure 3shows a sequence database composed by six sequences, which is going to be processed by the proposed algorithm with a frequency threshold of 2. The first step in the algorithm is to read the database and find the frequent symbols, which are also the set of frequent sequences of length 1. Next, the non frequent symbols are removed. The resultant database appears in the lower part of the figure.

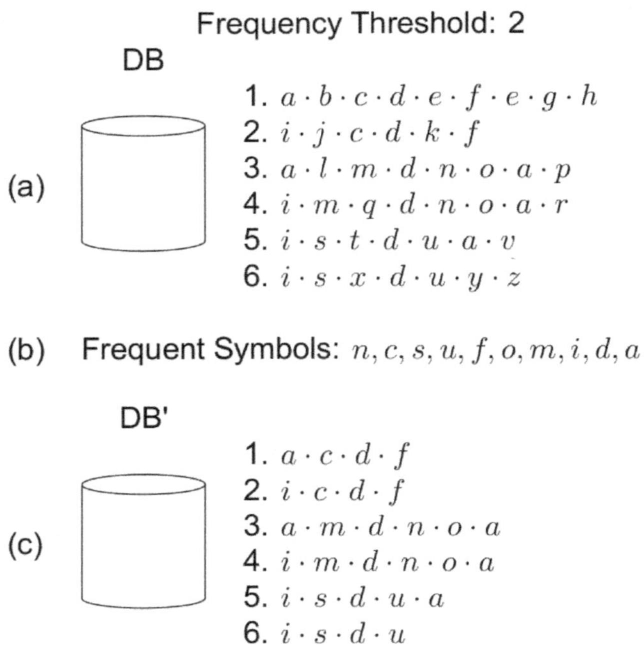

Figure 3. Example of the NLDFT algorithm's functionality (1 of 7). The figure shows a sequence database (a), the set of frequent symbols obtained from it (b) and the filtered database (c).

Next, one of the frequent sequences found is selected to be grown. This is shown in Figure 4. In this case, the chosen symbol is *n* and the pseudo-projection database with respect to that sequence is built. Next, the pseudo-projection database is searched for frequent symbols. From that search, two frequent symbols are found: *o* and *a*, which are used to build the frequent sequences n.o and n.a. Next, one of the frequent symbols is chosen, in this case the symbol *o*, and a pseudo-projection database is built with respect to that symbol and the current database. Finally, this new pseudo-projection database is used, along with the symbol *o* and the sequence ***n·o*** as the input for the next call of the mining process and the recursion continues; this part of the process corresponds to the Step 3 of NLDFT. From the input database of the new recursive call, the only frequent symbol found is *a*, which is used to build the frequent sequence n.o.a.

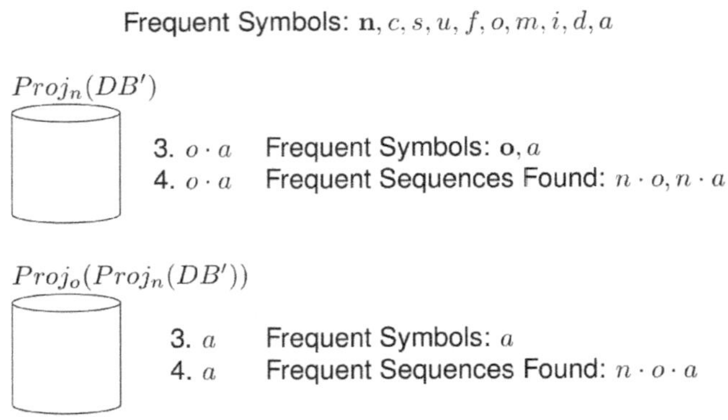

Figure 4. Example of the NLDFT algorithm's functionality (2 of 7). The figure shows two recursive calls to the main mining process, where 3 frequent sequences are found.

In the next recursive call, there are no more frequent sequences to be found, as the input database does not contain any symbol. This is shown in the upper part of Figure 5. The algorithm then has to go back to a previous frequent sequence which still has unprocessed frequent symbols in its associated frequent symbol set, in this case the sequence *n*, and now choses the symbol *a* to use in a subsequent recursive call. Also, in this recursive call there are no frequent sequences to be found, because the input database does not contain any symbols. This is shown in the lower part of Figure 5. Because there are no more frequent symbols to grow the sequence *n*, all the frequent sequences that start with that symbol have now been found. These frequent sequences and their ancestor/descendant relations are shown as a tree structure in Figure 6. Next, the frequent sequence *c* is chosen and the same process as the one with the frequent sequence *n* is followed, which is shown in Figure 7. The pseudo-projection database is then built with respect to the frequent sequence *c* and frequent symbols are searched for in that database. The frequent symbols found are *d* and *f*, which are then used, along with the frequent sequence *c* to build the frequent sequences c.d and c.f. Next, the symbol *d* is chosen from the new frequent symbol set and another pseudo-projection database is generated. In this database, *f* is the only frequent symbol found, so the sequence c.d.f is the only frequent sequence built. Now, the just discovered symbol *f* is chosen and another pseudo-projection database is generated, which does not have any symbols, so the recursion stops there, and the process continues with the symbol *f* associated with the frequent sequence *c*, until all the frequent sequences that start with the symbol *c* are found. This is shown in Figure 8. These frequent sequences and their ancestor/descendant relations are shown in Figure 9. The next step is to choose another frequent sequence of length 1 and repeat the process. The algorithm will continue until all of the frequent sequences of length 1 are processed. Then, the complete set *P* of frequent sequences is:

$$P = \{n, n \cdot o, n \cdot a, n \cdot o \cdot a, c, c \cdot d, c \cdot d \cdot f, s, s \cdot d, s \cdot d \cdot u, u, f, o, o \cdot a, i, i \cdot s, i \cdot s \cdot d, i \cdot s \cdot d \cdot u, d, d \cdot f, d \cdot n, d \cdot n \cdot o, d \cdot n \cdot o \cdot a, d \cdot o, d \cdot o \cdot a, a, a \cdot d\}$$

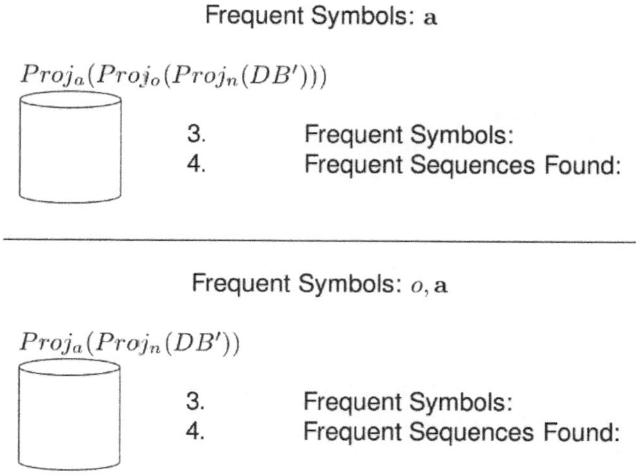

Figure 5. Example of the NLDFT algorithm's functionality (3 of 7). The upper part shows the next recursive call with respect to the Figure 4, where the input database does not contain any symbol. The algorithm goes back to the previous frequent sequence and makes another recursive call with a different frequent symbol (lower part of the figure), which does not contribute with any frequent sequence.

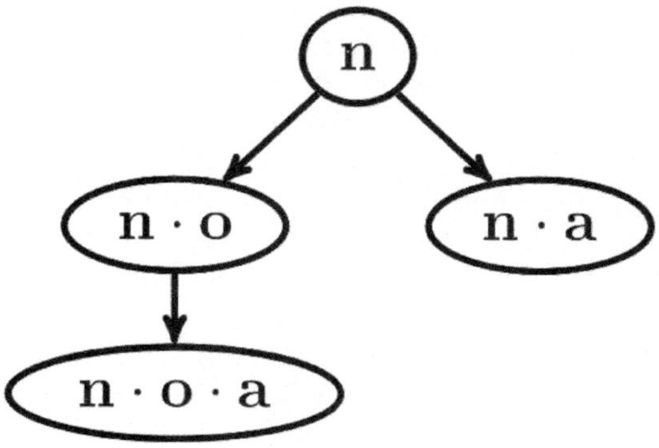

Figure 6. Example of the NLDFT algorithm's functionality (4 of 7). Frequent sequences found by growing the frequent sequence *n*.

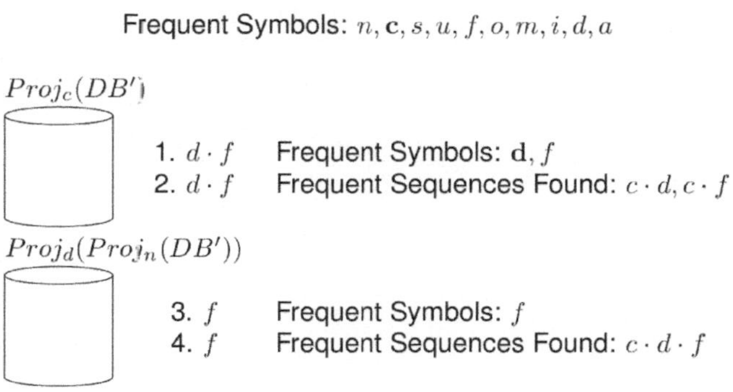

Figure 7. Example of the NLDFT algorithm's functionality (5 of 7). Recursive calls of the Mine function to grow the frequent sequence *c*.

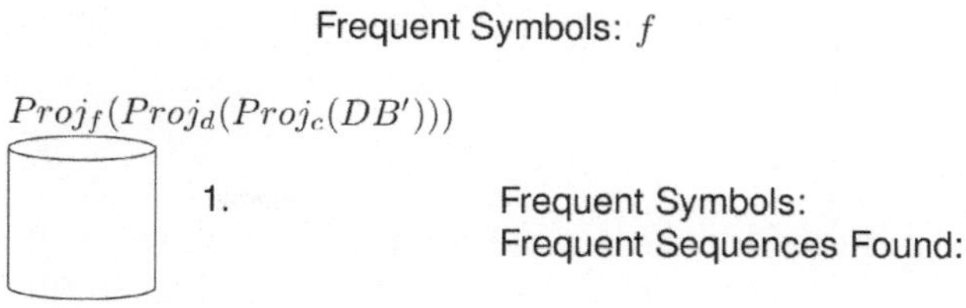

Figure 8. Example of the NLDFT algorithm's functionality (6 of 7). Last recursive call to grow the frequent sequence *c*. The projection database does not contain any symbol, so the recursion stops in this direction.

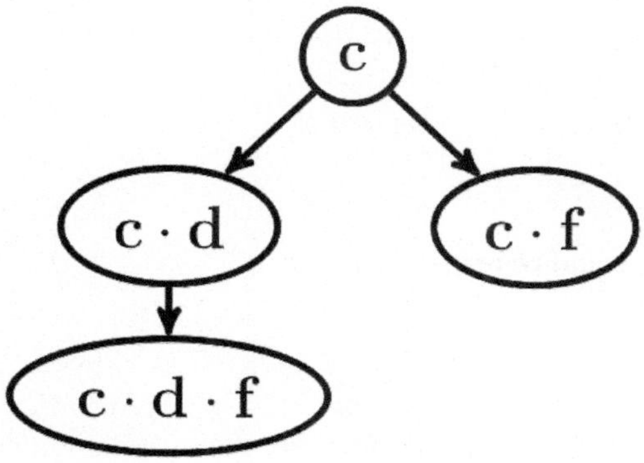

Figure 9. Example of the NLDFT algorithm's functionality (7 of 7). Frequent sequences found by growing the frequent sequence *c*.

The proof of the correctness of the proposed algorithm is given in the next section.

Correctness Proof

In this section, a proof is provided to demonstrate that the sequences found by the NLDFT algorithm in any given database and according to a minimum support from the complete set of frequent sequences. The correctness proof shows this in two parts: first proving that every sequence that meets the frequency threshold is found by the proposed algorithm; and second, that the proposed algorithm only discovers sequences that meet the given frequency threshold.

Let

- D be the input database.
- η be the frequency threshold.
- P_{alg} be the set of frequent sequences discovered by the algorithm.
- P be the set of sequences that meet the frequency threshold.

The correctness of the proposed algorithm can be demonstrated by providing the following two statements:

- Statement 1: If s is a sequence that meets the frequency threshold, then s is discovered by the NLDFT algorithm, i.e., if $s \in P$ then $s \in P_{alg}$.
- Statement 2: if s is a sequence discovered by the NLDFT algorithm, then s meets the frequency threshold, i.e., if $s \in P_{alg}$ then $s \in P$.

Proof of Statement 1.

It will be proven that if $s \in P$ then $s \in P_{alg}$, by mathematical induction over the length of *s*, len(s), for all the natural numbers, N.

Proof.

Basis: Show that the statement holds for len(s) = 1. The algorithm scans the input database and finds all the symbols whose frequency is equal or greater than the frequency threshold as a first step. These symbols correspond to the frequent sequences of length 1. Therefore, if *s* meets the frequency threshold, it is found by NLDFT, which shows that the statement 1 holds for the basis step.

Inductive step: Show that if the statement holds for a sequence *s'* of length *k*, then it also holds for a sequence *s* of length *k*+1 where $k \in \mathbb{N}$.

Starting from the sequence *s*:

$$s = s_1 \cdot s_2 \cdot s_3 \cdot \ldots \cdot s_k \cdot s_{k+1} \quad (5)$$

This could be rewritten as:

$$s = s' \cdot s_{k+1} \quad (6)$$

Since $s \in P$, then $s' \in P$ and s_{k+1} is frequent. Also, *s'* is found by the NLDFT algorithm, by the induction hypothesis. Moreover, in the Step 2 of NLDFT (shown in Algorithm 3, Table 3), the algorithm generates a list of symbols that meet the frequency threshold for the pseudo-projection database $pproj_{s_k}(D)$. Also, by Theorem 1, it is known that s_{k+1} also meets the frequency threshold for the pseudo-projection database $pproj_{s_k}(D)$. Therefore, s_{k+1} is included in the list of symbols generated in step 2, and then it will be appended at the end of *s'* in step 3, forming the frequent sequence *s*. Thus, it has been shown that $s \in P_{alg}$.

Proof of Statement 2.

It will be proven that if $s \in P_{alg}$ then $s \in P$, by mathematical induction over the length of *s*, len(s), for all the natural numbers, N.

Proof.

Basis: Show that the statement holds for len(s) = 1.

As $s \in P_{alg}$ and len(s) = 1, the NLDFT algorithm finds *s* in Step 1 (shown in Table 1), as it is in this step where all the frequent sequences of size 1 are discovered. Also, $s \in P$, as the NLDFT algorithm only retrieves the symbols that meet the frequency threshold. Thus, it has been shown that the statement 2 holds for the basis step.

Inductive step: Show that if the statement holds for a sequence *s'* of length *k*, then it also holds for a sequence *s* of length *k*+1 where $k \in \mathbb{N}$

Starting from the sequence *s*:

$$s = s_1 \cdot s_2 \cdot s_3 \cdot \ldots \cdot s_k \cdot s_{k+1} \quad (7)$$

This could be rewritten as:

$$s = s' \cdot s_{k+1} \quad (8)$$

Since $s \in P_{alg}$, then $s' \in P_{alg}$ and $s_{k+1} \in P_{alg}$. The NLDFT algorithm finds s_{k+1} in the Step 2 (shown in Algorithm 3, Table 3), as part of a set of frequent symbols in $PProj'_s(D)$, discovered with the function *GetFrequentSymbols*. Therefore, $s_{k+1} \in P$. Next, in step 3, the symbol s_{k+1} is appended at the end of the sequence *s'*, forming the sequence *s*. By the inductive hypothesis, $s' \in P$. Also, by the Theorem 1, it is known that if s_{k+1} meets the frequency threshold in the pseudo-projection database $PProj_{s'}(s_{k+1})$, then the sequence $s = s' \cdot s_{k+1}$ also meets the frequency threshold in *D*. Thus, *s* meets the minimum support. Therefore, it has been shown that $s \in P$.

Complexity Analysis

The running time of the sequential pattern mining problem depends not only in the dimensions of the input database and the minimum support, but in the form of the sequences as well, and it is unfeasible to consider an average case scenario, because that would depend on the domain of the input database. Therefore, a worst case scenario will be considered to analyze the NLDFT algorithm's performance.

Since lowering the minimum support yields a larger set of frequent sequences and increases the running time of the mining process, (see Figure 10 and Figure 11), the chosen frequency threshold in a worst case scenario will be the minimum, i.e., a threshold of 2 sequences. Considering this, a worst case scenario for an input database of size *mn* will have m/2 pairs of sequences, each of size *n*, and each pair of sequences will be composed by different symbols, unique to that pair. This would yield for each pair of sequences a set of frequent sequences with size equal to the size of the power set of its symbols (minus the empty set), which is the maximum number of frequent sequences that can be discovered in each pair of sequences. The union of the sets of frequent sequences of each pair of sequences will form the final set of frequent sequences. Thus, for a database of size *mn* and a frequency threshold of 2, the size of the set of frequent sequences is given by $P = \frac{m}{2}(2^n - 1)$. An example of an input database for a worst case scenario is shown in Figure 12.

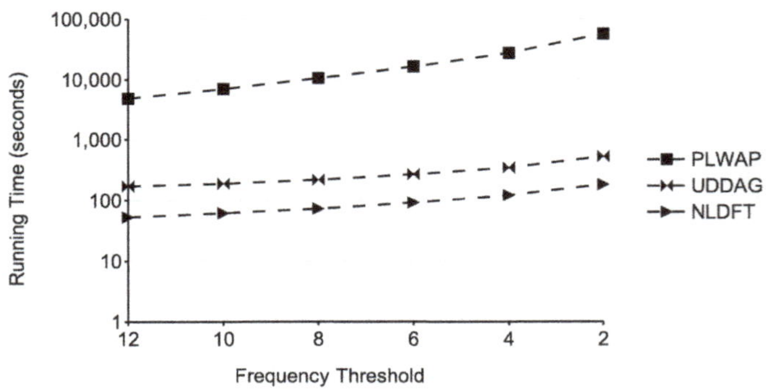

Figure 10. Comparison of runtime for different frequency thresholds. Processing C20.S5.N2k.D60k.

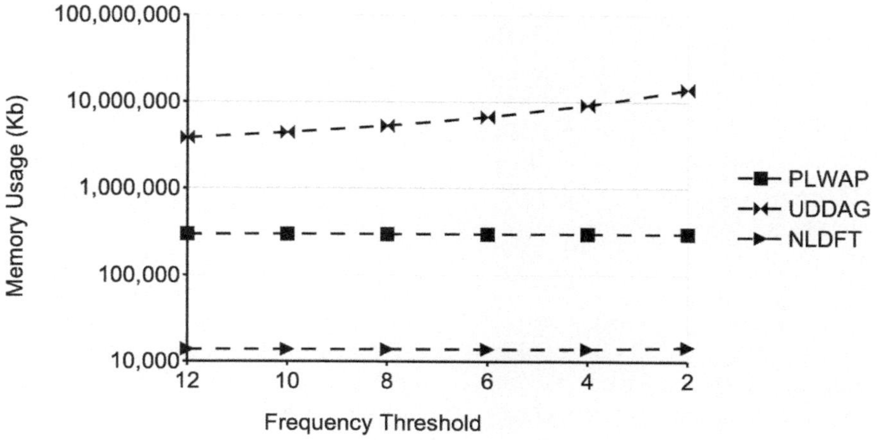

Figure 11. Comparison of runtime for different frequency thresholds in the study case. The figure shows the runtimes obtained when processing the study case database at frequency thresholds varying from 20 to 10 sequences.

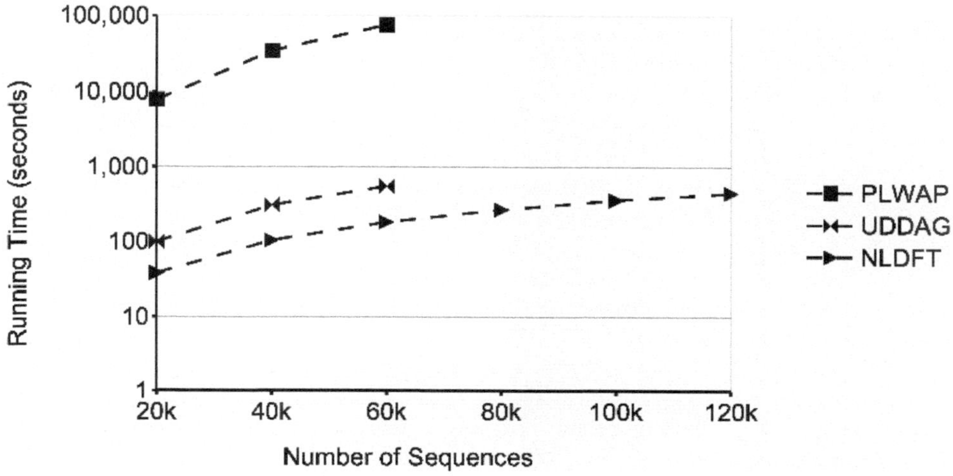

Figure 12. Example of an input sequence database in a worst case scenario. The figure shows a sequence database of size 4×4 (a)), formed by two pairs of sequences with different symbols, unique to each pair. The number of patterns of each pair is equal to the size of the power set (minus the empty set) of the set formed by the symbols in each pair (b)). The set of frequent sequences *P* in the database is the union of the sets of frequent sequences in each pair, $P_{1,2}$ and $P_{3,4}$.

The two main operations of the NLDFT algorithm are finding the frequent symbols in a given pseudo-projection database and building pseudo-projection databases. Since finding the frequent symbols entails checking every symbol in a given pseudo-projection database, at mostmn symbols have to be checked. Since checking a symbol takes constant time, the time needed to complete the entire operation is O(mn). Similarly, to build a pseudo-projection database entails checking at most every symbol in the previous pseudo-projection database, and to process a symbol takes a constant number of operations, thus the time needed to build a pseudo projection is also O(mn). Furthermore, these two main operations have to be performed everytime a recursive call is made. Since a recursive call is made for every frequent sequence discovered, in a worst case scenario $\frac{m}{2}(2^n-1)$ recursive calls are made. Therefore, in a worst case scenario, the running time of the NLDFT algorithm is O (m^2n (2^n-1)).

It is difficult to theoretically compare the performance of the NLDFT algorithm with the ones of the UDDAG and PLWAP algorithms. The authors of the UDDAG algorithm do not give a final running time bound of the algorithm, but only an upper bound on the number of projections made and a description of the operations made for the other parts of the algorithm. Although it appears that the UDDAG builds less database projections than the NLDFT algorithms, since it grows a pattern in both directions at each recursion level instead of one, it has to go through a candidate generation operation at each recursion level as well, which severely increases the running time. On the other hand, the authors of the PLWAP algorithm state that the time to build the PLWAP-tree is O (nl), where n is the number of frequent symbols and l is the length of the longest frequent sequence in the given database, and the time to perform the mine process is O (f,p), where f is the number of frequent symbols and p is the number of frequent sequences. However, is not clear if those bounds are of an average or worst case scenario. In a worst case scenario, the running time of the PLWAP's mining process is O (m^2n (2^n-1)), which is the same as the NLDFT algorithm's time complexity. This made necessary to perform running time experiments, in order to better understand the performance of the three algorithms and how they compare with each other.

From the memory requirements' point of view, the NLDFT algorithm maintains in main memory the filtered input database (without nonfrequent symbols), the node linkage of the pattern being growth, along with the set of frequent symbols and the pseudo-projection database associated with each node. Moreover, each pseudo-projection database and each frequent symbols set are smaller than the ones of the previous node, and once the frequent sequence being processed cannot be grown, its associated frequent symbols set and pseudo-projection database are deleted, releasing the occupied memory. On the other hand, the UDDAG also uses pseudo-projections to grow frequent sequences, but as it grows sequences bidirectionally, it has to store an extra pointer for each sequence in the pseudo-projection database, to indicate no only the start position of the sequence in the input database, but the ending position as well. Also, at each recursion level, the UDDAG algorithm generates candidate sequences, which are then stored and tested against the minimum support. The number of candidates stored severely increases when dealing with large databases and/or low minimum supports, which has a very negative impact on the memory consumption of the entire algorithm (see for instanceFigures 13 and 14). The PLWAP algorithm, on the other hand, does not rely on pseudo-projection databases and does not maintain the input database in main memory during the mining process. However, the PLWAP algorithm builds and maintains during the whole mining process an elaborated data structure. When dealing with large databases and/or low minimum supports, this data structure occupies a significant amount of memory. This is because the tree structure built has a branch for every sequence in the input database. Also, a queue is created for each frequent symbol, which contains all the occurrences of each frequent symbol in the tree structure.

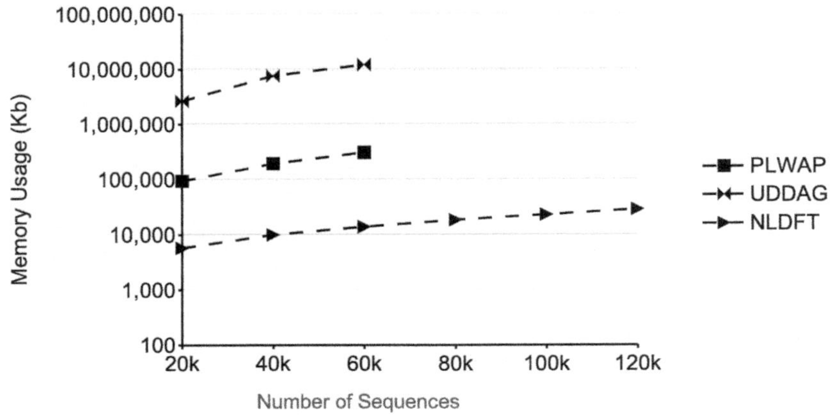

Figure 13. Comparison of memory usage for different number of sequences. The figure shows the memory usage obtained when processing databases with a number of sequences varying from 20k to 120k.

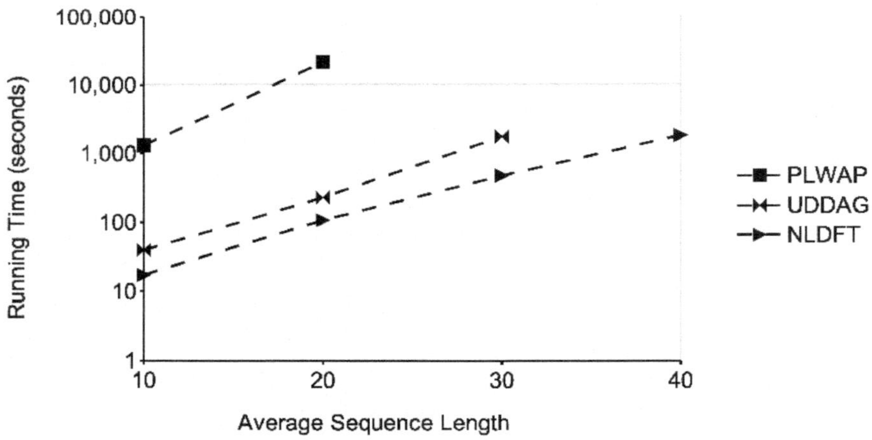

Figure 14. Comparison of memory usage for different average sequence lengths. The figure shows the memory usage of the tested algorithms when processing databases with an average sequence length varying from 10 to 40 symbols.

RESULTS AND DISCUSSION

Experimental Setup

A series of experiments were conducted to compare the proposed algorithm against representative approaches. The proposed algorithm was compared against the UDDAG [13] and PLWAP [2] algorithms. According to the authors of [13], the UDDAG algorithm is considerable faster than representative algorithms such as PrefixSpan, LapinSpan [26] and SPADE. Moreover, according to [18], PLWAP is the best model of pattern-growth tree projection sequential pattern mining techniques.

The PLWAP algorithm's code was obtained from the author's web page and the UDDAG algorithm was programmed. Both algorithms were coded in C++ and were compiled with g++. The proposed algorithm was also programmed in C++, and the experiments were performed in a computer with a core i7 processor of 3.40 GHz, 16 GiB of RAM and using GNU/

Linux with the Ubuntu 11.10 distribution, as operating system. To perform the experiments, synthetic sequence databases were used, which were created with MBSDG (*Market-Basket Synthetic Data Generator*), an open source application available at [27]. The application is based on the IBM Quest application, which was used to generate test databases for several sequential patter mining approaches (e.g. [2], [13], [1], among others). The following parameters were used to generate the databases:

- $|D|$: Number of sequences in the database.
- $|N|$: Number of different symbols in the database.
- $|S|$: Average length of maximal potentially frequent sequence.
- $|C|$: Average sequence length.

For instance, a database labeled as $C20{\cdot}S10{\cdot}N5k{\cdot}D50k$ means that $|C|=20, |S|=10, |N|=5k, |D|=50k$, i.e. a database with an average sequence length of 20 symbols, an average of 10 symbols length for the maximal potentially frequent sequence, 5,000 different symbols and 50,000 sequences. The increase of any of this parameters when generating a database will cause an increase in the execution time when finding sequential patterns in such database. The parameters were chosen to be the same as those used in [2] for testing the PLWAP algorithm, in order to have similar experimental conditions. However, the minimum supports used in this paper are lower than those used in [2], as its computational resources were more limited than the ones used in this article. The database format consists of a single file, with a line of positive integer numbers per sequence. The numbers correspond to the symbols of the sequences and are separated by spaces. No additional information about the database should be provided to the algorithm.

Figure 10 shows a comparison of running time for different frequency thresholds, using a database with parameters $C10{\cdot}S5{\cdot}N2k{\cdot}D60k$. The graph shows that the processing time of the three algorithms increases as the minimum support decreases. This is because with lower supports, the number of patterns that meet the frequency threshold increases, which entails more processing. However, the proposed algorithm performs significantly better than the other two algorithms, even having a running time of two orders of magnitude lower than the PLWAP algorithm. Also, Figure 15 shows the memory usage of the three approaches for the same tests. In this experiment, the NLDFT algorithm also requires less memory than the other two algorithms, even being two orders of magnitude below the UDDAG's memory. Also, although the UDDAG algorithm had a better running time than the PLWAP algorithm, it is much more memory consuming and this consumption significantly increased when the frequency threshold was lowered.

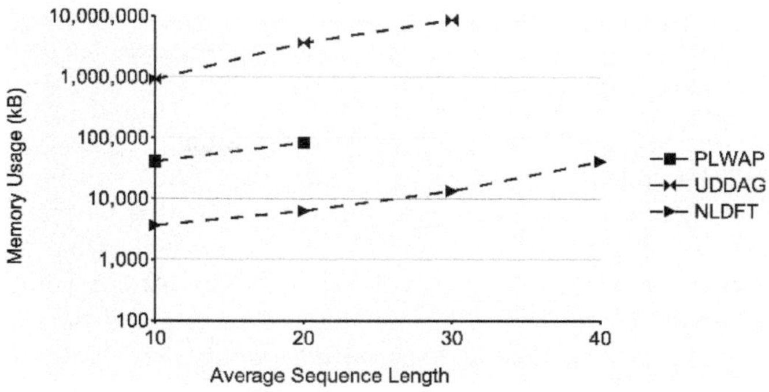

Figure 15. Comparison of memory usage for different frequency thresholds. Processing $C20{\cdot}S5{\cdot}N2k{\cdot}D60k$.

Figure 16 shows a comparison of running time for processing databases with different number of sequences. These databases were generated using $C20{\cdot}S5{\cdot}N2k$ for the first three parameters and $D20k$, $D40k$, $D60k$, $D80k$, $D100k$ and $D120k$ the last parameter, respectively. The frequency threshold was fixed at 2. The graph shows that as the number of sequences increases, the running time of the algorithms increases as well, as more patterns are likely to be discovered and more sequences have to be mined. When dealing with the database of 80 k sequences, the UDDAG algorithm ran out of memory. This is likely due the candidate generation phase that the UDDAG algorithm has to go through at each level of recursion, because it generates and stores a large amount of candidate sequences, and this amount gets larger when dealing with large databases and/or lower minimum supports. Moreover, the PLWAP algorithm did not finish in an acceptable time (less than 24 hours). The NLDFT algorithm, on the other hand, had a better running time than the other two algorithms and was capable of dealing with the largest database used in the experiment. Figure 13 shows the memory usage of the three approaches in this experiment. The memory consumption of the three approaches increased when dealing with larger datasets. In this experiment, the PLWAP algorithm also had a better memory consumption than the UDDAG algorithm, although the UDDAG had a better running time. The NLDFT algorithm also had a better memory consumption than those two algorithm, and always maintained the consumption below 100 MB.

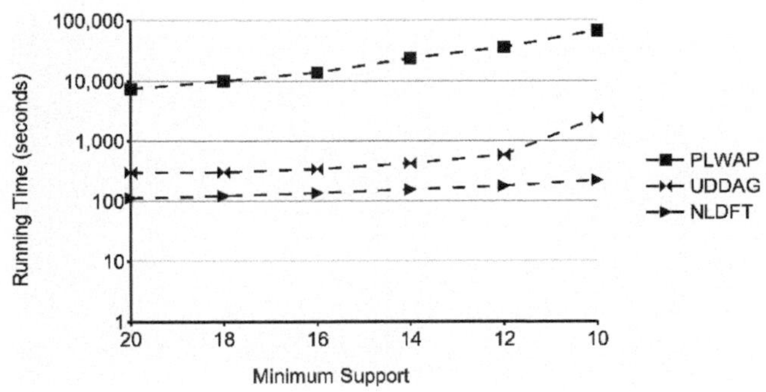

Figure 16. Comparison of runtime for different number of sequences. The figure shows the runtimes obtained when processing databases with a number of sequences varying from 20k to 120k.

Figure 17 shows the running times of the algorithms when processing databases with different average sequence lengths. Four databases were used, with parameters $C10{\cdot}S5{\cdot}N2k{\cdot}D10k$, $C20{\cdot}S8{\cdot}N2k{\cdot}D10k$, $C30{\cdot}S10{\cdot}N2k{\cdot}D10k$ and $C40{\cdot}S13{\cdot}N2k{\cdot}D10k$ and a frequency threshold of 2. The graph shows that the running times of the three algorithms increase with the average sequence length. This is likely because larger sequences can contain more patterns than smaller ones, and the patterns could be larger as well, which entails more processing and storage of these patterns. In this experiment, the NLDFT algorithm performed better than the other two algorithms and was capable of dealing with the largest average sequence length tested. When dealing with the database with an average sequence length of 30, the PLWAP did not finished in an acceptable time (less than 24 hours). Also, the UDDAG algorithm ran out of memory when dealing with the dataset with an average sequence length of 40 symbols. As mentioned before, this is likely because the amount of candidate sequences the UDDAG generates and stores at each level of recursion greatly increases when dealing with larger databases. Figure 14 shows the memory usage of the three approaches for this experiment. The graph shows that the memory consumption increases when dealing with larger average sequence lengths, as more and larger patterns have to be stored. The NLDFT algorithm had a better consumption than the other two algorithms in this experiment as well, and maintained its consumption below 100 k kB in all the tests. Finally, Table 5 shows the number of patterns found by the three algorithms in each database used in the experiments.

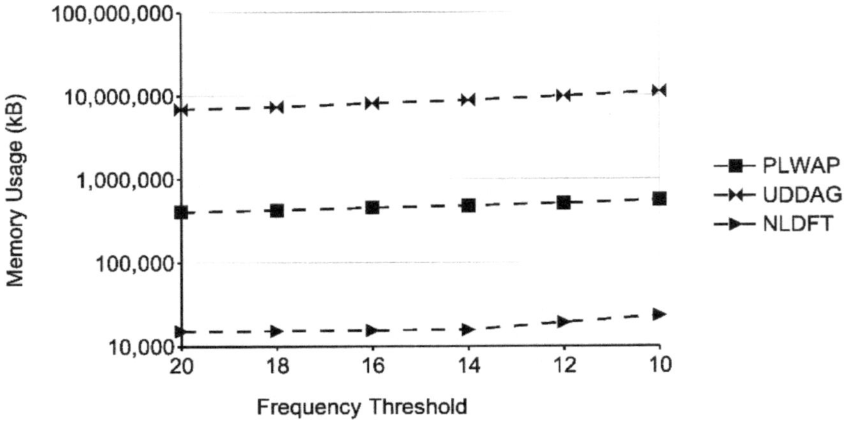

Figure 17. Comparison of runtime for different average sequence lengths. The figure shows the runtimes obtained when processing databases with an average sequence length varying from 10 to 40 symbols.

Table 5. Number of patterns per database

Database	Frequency Threshold	Patterns
$C10{\cdot}S5{\cdot}N2k{\cdot}D60k$	12	37,510
	10	55,941
	8	86,748
	6	142,563
	4	255,800
	2	700,242
$C10{\cdot}S5{\cdot}N2k{\cdot}D20k$	2	237,493
D40k	2	474,544
D60k	2	700,242
D80k	2	912,238
D100k	2	1,164,148
D120k	2	1,428,286
$C10{\cdot}S5{\cdot}N2k{\cdot}D10k$	2	115,714
$C20{\cdot}S8$	2	854,718
$C30{\cdot}S10$	2	4,735,950
$C40{\cdot}S13$	2	21,848,524

Number of patterns obtained with each tested database and frequency threshold.

A study case: text documents as a sequence database

The earliest sequential pattern mining algorithms were applied to databases comprised by web logs, where each sequence was formed by a series of web pages visited by a user in a period of time, or customer transactions, where each sequence was formed by the items bought by one customer in a period of time. However, sequential pattern mining algorithms can be applied to any database comprised by sequences. In the case of text documents, as text keeps a natural sequential order given by its characters and words, its possible to apply a sequential pattern mining algorithm to a set of documents, where a sequential element can be a single character, a word or even a contiguous sequence of items (*n-gram*), and the sequential order is given by the occurrence of such element in the document. Finding frequent sequences of text is an interesting task because the found patterns could contain information about the author's style, fixed expressions, similitude between documents, among others. Moreover, text corpora poses a challenge for current sequential pattern mining algorithms, because these datasets are usually comprised of a large number of documents, which can be of a large size. The above was the motivation to perform a series of experiments using a text database, which results are presented in this section.

In this study case the behavior of the proposed algorithm was tested when dealing with text documents and also aimed to find the terminology that represents the concepts of the documents' domain.

The dataset is composed of 57,653 text sequences with an average length of 20 symbols or words and a symbol set size of 28,547 symbols, that belong to a set of scientific articles of the oil extraction domain. To prepare the corpus, the stop words were removed and a numerical representation was generated, where a unique integer was assigned to each different word.

Figure 11 shows a comparison between the PLWAP, UDDAG and the proposed algorithm at different minimum supports. The figure shows the running times obtained from tests done with minimum supports from 20 to 10; when tested with a lower support, UDDAG and NLDFT algorithms ran out of memory and PLWAP was stopped after a week of processing. However, the proposed algorithm performed significantly better than the other two methods, specially at lower minimum supports. Moreover, the running time of the NLDFT algorithm increased with less pronunciation than the other two algorithms, when decreasing the frequency threshold. Figure 18 shows the memory usage of the three algorithms in the previous experiment. The graph shows that the UDDAG algorithm consumed much more memory than the other two algorithms, even at the highest minimum support tested, in which it consumes almost 6 gigabytes of memory. Also, the proposed algorithm consumed significantly less memory than the PLWAP algorithm, going from 25 megabytes to 87 megabytes approximately, at the lowest support in the graph, compared with the PLWAP algorithm, which starts at 390 megabytes and goes up to 547 megabytes approximately. This is likely because the PLWAP algorithm builds a tree data structure and queues for each frequent symbol, representing the input database, which could consume a great amount of memory when the input database is large, and maintains it during the whole mining process.

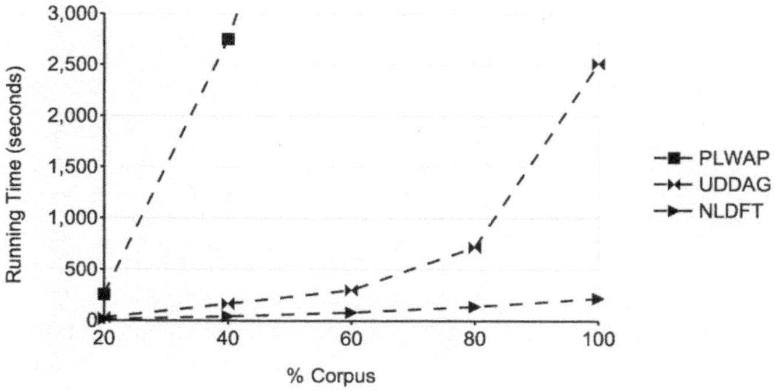

Figure 18. Comparison of memory usage for different frequency thresholds in the study case. The figure shows the memory usage of the tested algorithms when processing the study case database at frequency thresholds varying from 20 to 10 sequences.

Figures 19 and 20 show the running time during experiments done to test the scalability of the proposed algorithm. In the experiment of Figure 19, algorithms PLWAP, UDDAG and NLDFT's running time were tested using different percentages of the corpus, and a fixed frequency threshold of 10 sequences. It is important to notice that even at 40% of the corpus, the PLWAP algorithm tooks almost five times the running time of PLWAP and UDDAG algorithms, and tends to exponentially increase its running time as the number of sequences increases. UDDAG and NLDFT algorithms showed a similar performance until dealing with the 80% of the corpus, which is were the UDDAG algorithm takes almost two times the running time of NLDFT, and this difference increases when dealing with the 100% of the corpus. This is likely because when dealing with larger databases, the candidate-generation phase of the UDDAG algorithm generates a huge amount of candidate patterns, which testing consumes a significant amount of time.

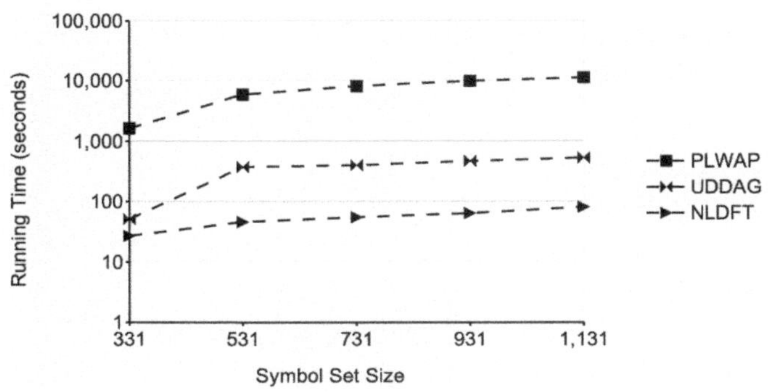

Figure 19. Comparison of runtime at different percentages of the corpus in the study case. The figure shows the runtimes of the tested algorithms, at different percentages of the study case database.

1. $a \cdot b \cdot c \cdot d$ | $P_{1,2} = \{a, a \cdot b, a \cdot b \cdot c, a \cdot b \cdot c \cdot d, a \cdot b \cdot d, a \cdot c, a \cdot c \cdot d, a \cdot d, b,$
2. $a \cdot b \cdot c \cdot d$ | $b \cdot c, b \cdot c \cdot d, b \cdot d, c, c \cdot d, d\}, |P_{1,2}| = 2^n - 1 = 15$

3. $e \cdot f \cdot g \cdot h$ | $P_{3,4} = \{e, e \cdot f, e \cdot f \cdot g, e \cdot f \cdot h, e \cdot f \cdot g \cdot h, e \cdot g, e \cdot g \cdot h, e \cdot h,$
4. $e \cdot f \cdot g \cdot h$ | $f, f \cdot g, f \cdot g \cdot h, f \cdot h, g, g \cdot h, h\}, |P_{3,4}| = 2^n - 1 = 15$

a) b)

$$P = P_{1,2} \cup P_{3,4}, \ |P| = \binom{m}{2}(2^n - 1) = 30$$

c)

Figure 20. Comparison of runtime at different symbol set sizes in the study case. The figure shows the runtimes of the tested algorithms, at different sizes of the symbol set of the study case database.

Figure 20 shows the running time obtained when varying the size of the symbol set (Σ). This was done by removing the least frequent symbols, those that occurred in less than a hundred sequences, and only maintaining those symbols that occur in at least one hundred sequences. The resultant symbol set had a size of 1131 symbols. From this symbol set, several test were done, by removing symbols from the set by its frequency, in an ascending order. The frequency threshold was fixed to 10 sequences. The graph shows that, when dealing with a larger symbol set, the running time of the three algorithms increased. This is likely because, as more frequent symbols were added, more frequent patterns arised, which entailed more storage and processing. Moreover, there is a significant difference between the running times obtained in the test done with a symbol set of 331 symbols and the test done with a symbol set of 531. This is because the number of frequent sequences that were created when adding the next 200 frequent symbols is significantly large, almost twice the number of frequent sequences found in the test with a symbol set of 331 symbols (see Table 6). Nevertheless, the NLDFT algorithm performed significantly better than the other two approaches in all the tests, achieving a running time lower than the PLWAP algorithm's in two orders of magnitude and lower than the UDDAG algorithm's in one order of magnitude when the symbol set had 531 or more symbols. Finally, Table 6 shows the number of patterns found in each database used in this study case.

Table 6. Patterns per text database in the study case

Database	Frequency Threshold	Patterns
*C*20·*N*28,547·*D*57,653	20	67,436
	18	88,852
	16	112,820
	14	161,871
	12	254,137
	10	528,737
*C*20·*N*28,547·*D*11,531 (20%)	10	32,823
D23,062 (40%)	10	102,582
D34,593 (60%)	10	135,029
D46,124 (80%)	10	255,674
D57,653 (100%)	10	528,737
*C*20·*N*331·*D*52,432	10	74399
*N*531·*D*53,810	10	209754
*N*731·*D*54,660	10	231354
*N*931·*D*55,071	10	262561
*N*1131·*D*55,316	10	268484

Number of patterns obtained with each variation of the study case database and each frequency threshold used.

doi:10.1371/journal.pone.0095418.t006

DISCUSSION

The experiments carried out showed that the proposed algorithm performs significantly better than the UDDAG and PLWAP algorithms, specially at lower supports. The experiments also showed how the processing time of the three algorithms increased as the minimum support was lowered, because this produces an increase in the number of patterns that meet the frequency threshold. Also, the proposed algorithm shows a better scalability than the UDDAG and PLWAP algorithms, as it maintains a good performance when increasing the number of sequences, the average sequence length or the size of the symbol set, while the UDDAG and PLWAP algorithms have a great decrease in performance when increasing the size of the dataset. Regarding memory efficiency, the NLDFT algorithm also performed better than the UDDAG and PLWAP algorithms. This is because the NLDFT algorithm, unlike the UDDAG and PLWAP algorithms, does not build a costly data structure holding the entire input database to perform the mining process, and neither stores candidate patterns to later test their frequency. The NLDFT algorithm only stores the necessary information for the pattern that is currently growing.

CONCLUSIONS

Based on the experimental and theatrical comparison with recent sequential pattern mining approaches, the NLDFT algorithm showed to be one of the most efficient for sequential pattern mining. The NLDFT algorithm has better performance in running time and memory consumption than popular approaches. Additionally, it has better scalability.

As future work, we will explore different approaches for improving the efficiency of the frequent symbol extraction process of the NLDFT algorithm, because this process is executed frequently. Approaches to solve the k-majority problem could be useful, since this problem is similar to the frequently symbol extraction process. Among these approaches we will explore: using hash operations and linked lists to store the frequency counters [28] and using a parallel scheme, discovering local frequent symbols and then reducing that set to find the final set of frequent symbols [29]. Moreover, NLDFT has no restriction over the distance between the symbols of a frequent sequence (known as *gap restriction*), however, it would be desirable to give the user the option of setting a gap restriction as an input parameter of the algorithm, in order to obtain frequent sequences useful in areas such as Text Mining, where frequent sequences whose symbols are separated by long distances are not meaningful. A possible way to achieve this, is by assigning a restriction value to each growing frequent sequence, which would indicate the maximum distance where frequent symbols could appear after the sequence to be considered within the gap restriction.

AUTHOR CONTRIBUTIONS

Conceived and designed the experiments: ON RC LVP CFU JACO. Performed the experiments: ON. Analyzed the data: ON RC LVP CFU JACO. Contributed reagents/materials/analysis tools: ON RC LVP CFU JACO. Wrote the paper: ON RC LVP CFU JACO.

REFERENCES

1. Agrawal R (1995) Mining sequential patterns. Data Engineering, 1995 Proceedings doi: 10.1109/icde.1995.380415
2. Ezeife C, Lu Y (2005) Mining web log sequential patterns with position coded pre-order linked wap-tree. Data Mining and Knowledge Discovery 10: 5–38. doi: 10.1007/s10618-005-0248-3
3. Pei J, Han J, Mortazavi-Asl B (2000) Mining access patterns efficiently from web logs. Discovery and Data Mining doi: 10.1007/3-540-45571-x_47
4. Tang P, Turkia MP (2007) Mining frequent web access patterns with partial enumeration. Proceedings of the 45th annual southeast regional conference on - ACM-SE 45: 226. doi: 10.1145/1233341.1233382
5. Garcia-Blasco S, Mola-Velasco SM, Danger R, Rosso P (2012) Automatic Drug-Drug Interaction Detection: A Machine Learning Approach With Maximal. In: Challenge Task on Drug-Drug Interaction Extraction.
6. Hernández-Reyes E, García-Hernández R, Carrasco-Ochoa A, Martínez-Trinidad F (2006) Document Clustering Based on Maximal Frequent Sequences. In: Proceedings of the 5th international conference on Advances in Natural Language Processing. pp. 257–267.
7. Denicia-Carral C, Montes-y Gómez M, Villaseñor Pineda L, Hernández García R (2006) A Text Mining Approach for Definition Question Answering. In: in Proceedings for the Fifth International Conference on Natural Language Processing (FinTal 2006). pp. 76–86.
8. Coyotl-Morales RM, Villaseñor Pineda L, Montes-y Gómez M, Rosso P (2006) Authorship Attribution Using Word Sequences. In: Proceedings of the 11th Iberoamerican conference on Progress in Pattern Recognition, Image Analysis and Applications. pp. 844–853.
9. Tsai CY, Liou JJ, Chen CJ, Hsiao CC (2012) Generating touring path suggestions using time interval sequential pattern mining. Expert Systems with Applications 39: 3593–3602. doi: 10.1016/j.eswa.2011.09.049
10. Shim B, Choi K, Suh Y (2012) Crm strategies for a small-sized online shopping mall based on association rules and sequential patterns. Expert Systems with Applications 39: 7736–7742. doi: 10.1016/j.eswa.2012.01.080
11. Anwara F, Petrouniasb I, Morrisc T, Kodogiannisd V (2012) Mining anomalous events against frequent sequences in surveillance videos from commercial environments. Expert Systems with Applications 39: 4511–4531. doi: 10.1016/j.eswa.2011.09.134
12. García-Pedrajas N, de Haro-García A (2011) Scaling up data mining algorithms: review and taxonomy. Progress in Artificial Intelligence 1: 71–87. doi: 10.1007/s13748-011-0004-4
13. Chen J (2009) An UpDown Directed Acyclic Graph Approach for Sequential Pattern Mining. — IEEE Transactions on Knowledge and Data Engineering 22: 913–928. doi: 10.1109/tkde.2009.135
14. Gouda K, Hassaan M, Zaki MJ (2010) Prism: An effective approach for frequent sequence mining via prime-block encoding. Journal of Computer and System

Sciences 76: 88–102. doi: 10.1016/j.jcss.2009.05.008

15. Ahonen-Myka H (2002) Discovery of frequent word sequences in text. Pattern Detection and Discovery 26: 180–189. doi: 10.1007/3-540-45728-3_14
16. Li C (2008) Efficiently mining closed subsequences with gap constraints. International Conference on Data Mining 313–322. doi: 10.1137/1.9781611972788.28
17. Masseglia F, Poncelet P, Teisseire M (2009) Efficient mining of sequential patterns with time constraints: Reducing the combinations. Expert Systems with Applications 36: 2677–2690. doi: 10.1016/j.eswa.2008.01.021
18. Mabroukeh NR, Ezeife CI (2010) A taxonomy of sequential pattern mining algorithms. ACM Computing Surveys 43: 1–41. doi: 10.1145/1824795.1824798
19. Zaki M (2001) SPADE: An efficient algorithm for mining frequent sequences. Machine Learning 42: 31–60.
20. Tan H, Dillon T, Hadzic F, Chang E (2006) SEQUEST: mining frequent subsequences using DMA Strips. In: Proceedings of the Seventh International Conference on Data Mining and Information Engineering. Southampton, UK: Citeseer, volume 1 of *WIT Transactions on Information and Communication Technologies*, *Vol* 37: , pp. 35–328. doi:10.2495/DATA060321
21. Spiliopoulou M (1999) WUM: a tool for web utilization analysis. The World Wide Web and Databases 1590: 184–203. doi: 10.1007/10704656_12
22. Peterson Ea, Tang P (2008) Mining frequent sequential patterns with first-occurrence forests. Proceedings of the 46th Annual Southeast Regional Conference on XX - ACM-SE 46: 34. doi: 10.1145/1593105.1593115
23. Ezeife C, Saeed K, Zhang D (2009) Mining very long sequences in large databases with PLWAP Long. In: Proceedings of the 2009 International Database Engineering & Applications Symposium. New York, New York, USA: ACM, pp. 234–241. doi:10.1145/1620432.1620457
24. Antunes C, Oliveira AL (2003) Generalization of pattern-growth methods for sequential pattern mining with gap constraints. In: Machine Learning and Data Mining in Pattern Recognition. pp. 239–251.
25. Tang P, Turkia M, Gallivan K (2007) Mining web access patterns with first-occurrence linked WAP-trees. In: SEDE. Citeseer, pp. 247–252.
26. Kitsuregawa M, Zhenglu Y (2005) LAPIN-SPAM: An Improved Algorithm for Mining Sequential Pattern. 21st International Conference on Data Engineering Workshops (ICDEW'05) 1222–1222. doi: 10.1109/icde.2005.235
27. Pitman A (2011) Website hosting the market-basket synthetic data generator application. URL http://synthdatagen.codeplex.com/.
28. Karp RM, Shenker S, Papadimitriou CH (2003) A simple algorithm for finding frequent elements in streams and bags. ACM Transactions on Database Systems 28: 51–55. doi: 10.1145/762471.762473
29. Cafaro M, Tempesta P (2011) Finding frequent items in parallel. Concurrency and Computation: Practice and Experience 23: 1774–1788. doi: 10.1002/cpe.1761

CHAPTER 21

FAST K-NNG CONSTRUCTION WITH GPU-BASED QUICK MULTI-SELECT

Ivan Komarov, Ali Dashti, Roshan M. D'Souza

Department of Mechanical Engineering, Complex Systems Simulation Lab, University of Wisconsin-Milwaukee, Milwaukee, Wisconsin, United States of America

ABSTRACT

In this paper, we describe a new brute force algorithm for building the k-Nearest Neighbor Graph (*k*-NNG). The *k*-NNG algorithm has many applications in areas such as machine learning, bio-informatics, and clustering analysis. While there are very efficient algorithms for data of low dimensions, for high dimensional data the brute force search is the best algorithm. There are two main parts to the algorithm: the first part is finding the distances between the input vectors, which may be formulated as a matrix multiplication problem; the second is the selection of the *k*-NNs for each of the query vectors. For the second part, we describe a novel graphics processing unit (GPU)-based multi-select algorithm based on quick sort. Our optimization makes clever use of warp voting functions available on the latest GPUs along with user-controlled cache. Benchmarks show significant improvement over state-of-the-art implementations of the *k*-NN search on GPUs.

INTRODUCTION

The *k*-nearest neighbor (*k*-NN) (illustrated in Figure 1) and the related *k*-nearest neighbor graph (*k*-NNG) are important algorithms for data classification with a wide variety of applications in areas such as bioinformatics [1], [2], data mining [3], machine learning [4]–[6], cluster analysis [7], and pattern recognition [8]. Given an initial set of data points called a corpus/training set and a set of query points, *k*-NN finds the nearest k neighbors in the corpus set for each member of the query set. For low dimensional data-sets, there are a variety of indexing data structures such as kd-trees [9], BBD-trees [10], random-projection trees (rp-trees) [11], and hashing based on locally sensitive hash [12] that can be built from the set of corpus/training data points. Next, the *k*-NN search can be accomplished very efficiently for each data point in the query set using these data structures. In the case of a k-NNG, every data point in the corpus is also a member of the query set.

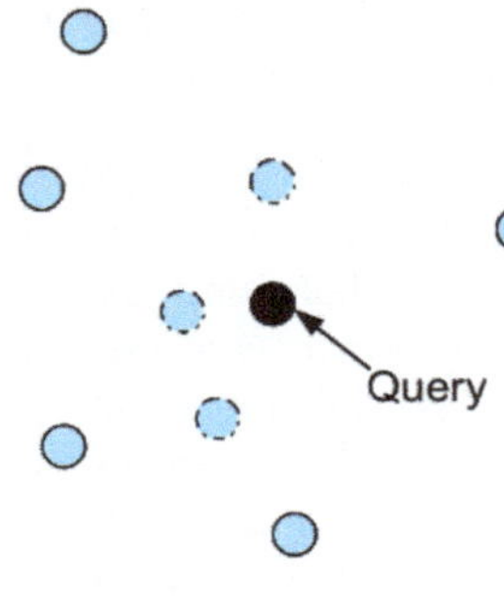

Figure 1. k-NN search. The blue dots are corpus data vectors. The blue dots with dashed lines are the 3 nearest neighbors to the query.

Citation: Komarov I, Dashti A, D'Souza RM (2014) Fast k-NNG Construction with GPU-Based Quick Multi-Select. PLoS ONE 9(5): e92409. doi:10.1371/journal.pone.0092409

Direct construction of an exact k-NNG has also been investigated by many researchers [13]–[18]. All of these methods have time complexity that increases exponentially with the data dimension. Approximate methods that can handle high-dimensional data with a trade-off between speed and accuracy have also been investigated. These techniques are based on a hybrid of spatial subdivision and small scale brute force refinement [19]–[21]. The spatial subdivision becomes grossly inaccurate for data sets that have dimensions exceeding 10^3.

For high dimensional data, the most efficient method for finding the k-NNG is in fact the brute force method [22]. The brute force algorithm consists of two fundamental steps. The first step finds the distances between the query point based on an user-defined metric. This process result in a distance matrix of size M×N where M is the number of query points and N is the number of corpus data points. The k-NNs in the corpus data points for each query points are then found by sorting each row of the matrix and finding the k indices of the k smallest distances. Recent efforts have accelerated the brute force k-NN and k-NNG methods by parallelizing on graphics processing units. These methods differ in the manner in which the k nearest indices are found. In [23], [24], each row of the distance matrix is processed by one thread. They use a modified insertion sort algorithm to select the k nearest neighbors. The data structure is stored in global memory, which in turn leads to un-coalesced memory access patterns. Moreover, each thread has divergent paths to find the k nearest neighbors, which leads to a loss in computational efficiency. In [25], every row in the distance matrix is processed by one thread block. A single heap in global memory maintains the current k nearest elements. Each thread strides through the row of the matrix and inserts an element into a buffer if it is smaller that the largest element in the heap. When the buffer fills up, all threads synchronize and push their elements into the heap serially. In [26], a thread block is used to process a single row. Each thread in the thread block strides through the array storing the k smallest elements in a local heap maintained in global memory. Next, all the thread heaps are merged into 32 heaps in shared memory threads in a single thread warp. Finally, a single thread merges the 32 heaps in shared memory to find the k nearest neighbors. Both methods dramatically slow down if k grows large because of branch divergence and un-coalesced global memory access. In [27], radix sort is used for finding k nearest neigbhors. Each row is processed in a separate kernel call and for the number n of data-corpus size that fits into GPU memory, this process underutilizes resources.

Graphics Processing Units: Architecture and Execution Model

Graphics Processing Units (GPUs) were originally developed to handle computations related to computer graphics tasks such as transformation and shading. Computational scientists used this functionality to accelerate scientific computing by posing such computations in terms of shading operations [28]. Subsequently, GPU vendors developed specialized C language extensions to facilitate direct access to the computing hardware for scientific computing. Our implementation uses CUDA [29], a C language extension developed by NVIDIA.

Architecturally, an NVIDIA GPU consists of several multiprocessors (MPs). Each MP has several serial processors. In addition to registers, each MP has access to on-chip user-controlled cache called shared memory. Logically, threads are organized into thread blocks (TBs). All threads in a TB are executed on a single MP. Threads in a TB can be synchronized and can communicate through shared memory. Depending on the amount of shared memory and registers required, there could be several TBs assigned to be executed on a MP. All threads can communicate through global main memory. Registers have the highest access speed, followed by the shared memory, and then by global memory. Of course, data in the registers cannot be shared among threads. Shared memory locations are accessed through specific memory banks.

At the hardware level, threads in a TB are divided into groups of 32 threads called thread warps. Thread warps are analogous to the threads in a typical symmetric multiprocessor architecture. All threads in a thread warp execute in lockstep. Any branching between threads in a thread warp will cause serialization (different types of serialization depending on the complexity of the branching). Therefore it is advisable to avoid branching between threads of the same warp. During global memory access, if the threads in a warp access locations outside of contiguous 128 byte segments, the memory access will be serialized. Also, if two or more threads try to access shared memory affiliated to the same memory bank, this memory access will be serialized. An exception is when all threads in a warp access the same shared memory location. In such cases, a broadcast mechanism is automatically engaged. Therefore, implementations of algorithms for GPU acceleration require careful consideration of architectural limitations as well as advantages.

In our implementation we use an NVIDIA Tesla C2050 GPU. It has 14 multiprocessors, each with 32 cores, for a total of 448 cores. The single precision peak performance is 1.0 TFlops. Each MP has 64 KB of shared memory and a 128 KB register file. The main memory is 3 GB GDDR5.

METHODS AND MATERIALS

In this paper, we present a hybrid parallelization approach for brute force computation of multiple k-NN queries. The first part of the brute force k-NN, namely, finding the distance metric matrix, is formulated as a matrix multiplication problem. Therefore efficient implementations of dense matrix operations can be used. The second part is finding the k-NN for each query data point. For this part of brute force k-NN, we have developed a two-level, parallel implementation of the quick select algorithm. At the top or coarse level, multiple queries are processed independently and in parallel. At the fine level of parallelism, every query is parallelized over all threads in a thread block or thread warp.

Related Work

Recently, there have been quite a few works focused on parallel k-NN queries on GPUs. In[30], a truncated bitonic sort based selection algorithm has been described. The results show a dramatic drop off in performance with an increase in both the number of data points n and number of nearest neighbors k. For example, the speedup over straight sort and selection using the CUDA thurst::sort for $n = 2^{16}$, $k = 2^8$, is barely 4X. In [31], a radix select implementation on the GPU is presented for selecting the kth element. This implementation is very efficient for large values of n and runs up to 190X faster than a single core CPU implementation of the serial n-select algorithm. In [32], a randomized selection algorithm is presented. This method, however, shows no improvement over CUDA thrust::sort for data sizes of up to $51e^5$. On the other hand, the implementation in [31] shows a 6.3X speedup. Both methods are however, only suited for single query operations on ultra-large data sets. A similar implementation has been presented by Alabi et al. [33]. The k-NN problem is slightly different from the method for selecting the kth element because extra work is necessary to track all the k smallest elements.

In [34], a data-parallel quick-sort algorithm for GPUs has been presented. They describe a two stage process. In the first stage, all thread blocks cooperatively work on partitioning the original list to a point where the size of each partition is small enough to be processed by a single thread block. The first stage needs inter-thread block synchronization since the results of two or more thread blocks needs to be merged to build the partitions. This can be done through atomic operations or through default synchronization by ending kernel execution. The latter needs a new kernel launch for each new phase of partitioning. The second stage is very similar to the first, but each partition in this case is handled by a single thread block.

The partitioning process is a two step process and uses an auxiliary output array (i.e., it is not an in-place write operation). In the first step, a pivot element is randomly selected. Next, each thread strides through the input array counting the number of elements that are greater than, equal to, and less than the pivot. These two counts are stored in two arrays in shared memory. A pre-fix sum on these arrays in shared memory gives the location in global memory where each thread needs to write into the auxiliary the elements in the partitioning process. At the end of each partitioning task, the input and auxiliary arrays are swapped. When the partition size falls below a pre-defined threshold, a direct sort algorithm such as a bitonic sort is used.

GPU-Based Quick Multi-Select

Our overall approach is illustrated in algorithm 1. Of the steps in the algorithm, distance computation and partitioning with pivot selection are done on the GPU by launching kernels. The decision process within the if-then-else statements are accomplished on the CPU. Each iteration of the while loop incurs a GPU kernel launch for partitioning with pivot selection. Our approach, while similar to the approach in [34], address some of the major drawbacks as related to the k-NN application: (1) the quick-sort algorithm in [34] is only suitable for sorting a single input array at a time; (2) inter thread block synchronization and synchronization between threads in the same thread block affects performance; (3) the pre-fix sum operation that is used during the partition process is quite an expensive operation; (4) the two step process of partitioning involves reading the same data from global memory twice (once for counting, once for writing); and (5) the write process into the auxiliary array is un-coalesced. Our approach, by contrast, operates on multiple arrays simultaneously. Each array is handled by a single thread warp. Threads in a warp are executed simultaneously on a single multi-processor are synchronized by default. Partitioning of an array is done incrementally in 32 element wide segments. We use shared memory to ensure coalesced memory writes of the results of partitioning into the auxiliary array in global memory. Our approach uses the warp voting function _ballot(p) to partition the input without reading the input array twice and without executing the parallel-prefix sum. The ballot function _ballot(p) fills a 32 bit unsigned integer, one bit per thread in the warp, based on the evaluation of the predicate p (see Algorithm 1 inTable 1).

Table 1. Algorithm 1: Overall data flow

Data: k (number of nearest neighbors), Q(set of query vectors), C (set of data corpus vectors)
Result: Matrices of size $k \times q$ (q is the number of vectors in Q) of the indices I and values V of k nearest vectors in C for each vector in Q
Compute the distance matrix D using matrix multiplication
Process for each row $D(i, :)$ using either a warp or thread block
Set $l=0$, $r=n$
While $l \neq r$ **do**
Select a pivot element $[l, n]$
Partition $D(i, :)$ based on pivot
if $k > L$ (*L is the length of the left side*) **then**
Set $k=k-L$
Set $l=L$ (keep the left side as is and partition the right side)
else
Set $r=L$ (discard the right side and partition the left side)
end
end

doi:10.1371/journal.pone.0092409.t001

Each thread in the warp first reads in an element into its register from global memory. Elements are then written to a 32 element wide shared memory array with elements greater than or equal to the pivot being written from the right end and elements less than the pivot being written from the left end. To do this, each thread needs to know where in shared memory to off load its element. We execute the warp voting function based on a predicate that checks if the element in the register is greater than or equal to the pivot or smaller than the pivot. Threads which have an element greater than or equal to the pivot set the corresponding bit to '1' and to '0' if the element is less than the pivot (Figure 2). If the element in the register is less than the pivot, then the thread needs to find how many of the threads before it have elements less than the pivot and vice-versa. We use a combination of bit shift operations and the _popc(x) function on the integer result of the warp voting operation to accomplish this. The _popc(x) function counts the number of bits set to '1' in the input integer 'x'. For example, if the warp vote integer in binary is B= 0101…., then it is clear that threads 0,2 have elements less than the pivot and threads 1,3 have elements greater than or equal to the pivot. Each thread i within the warp computes the result b = B>>(31-i). When the _popc(b) function is applied to the result of this step, it will indicate the position in shared memory at which thread i will off-load its element that happens to be less than the pivot (Figure 3). Similarly, $[31 - \_popc(\tilde{b})]$ will indicate the position from the right side at which which thread i will off load its element that happens to be greater than or equal to the pivot. In the example, thread 3 will bit shift B to the right by 29 bits and the result will be b = 0101. This implies that _popc(b)=2. Therefore thread 3 will off-load its element at the second location from the left in shared memory (Figure 4). Note that the total number of elements in shared memory that are less than the pivot is given by _popc(B). Two global counters, $g<$ and $g \leq$, are also maintained to keep track of the total number of elements less than the pivot and total number of elements greater than or equal to the pivot, respectively. These two counters indicate location in the auxiliary array at which the warp writes the incremental results of pivoting from shared memory. Next, the threads write the contents of the shared memory into global auxiliary array with threads whose id is less than _popc(B) (number of elements that are greater than the pivot) writing from the left side and other threads writing from the right side. This write process requires two coalesced writes, one for elements smaller than the pivot and one for elements greater than or equal to the pivot, into the auxiliary array (Figure 4).

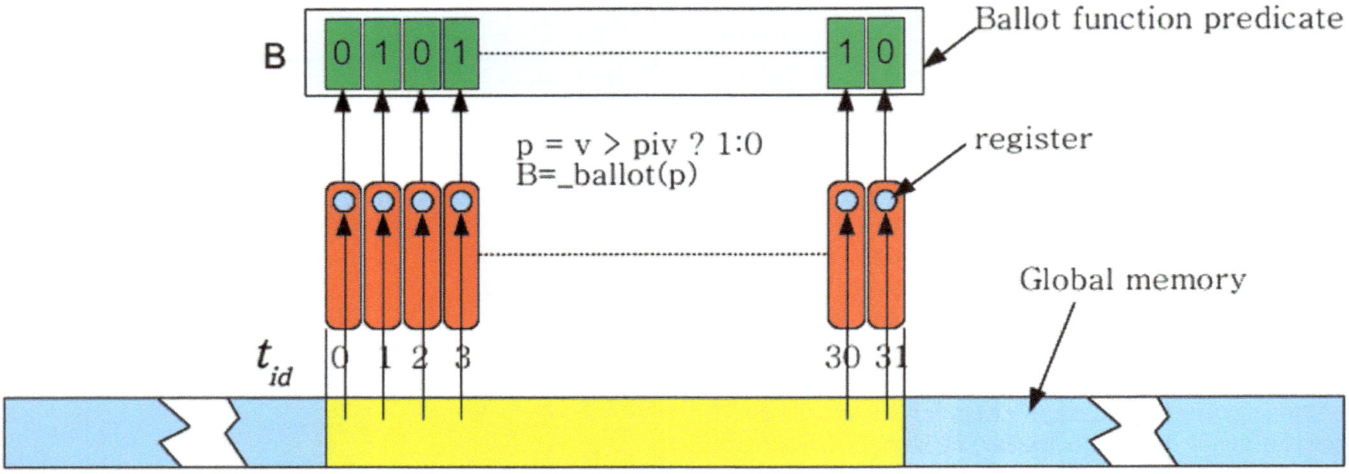

Figure 2. Read in process. Read in of the array is done incrementally in sets of 32 elements. As illustrated, the memory access is coalesced. The value is stored in a register. Simultaneously, the invocation of the warp voting function fills the bit array B based on the evaluation of the predicate, which indicates if the value in the register is greater than or equal to the pivot or less than the pivot.

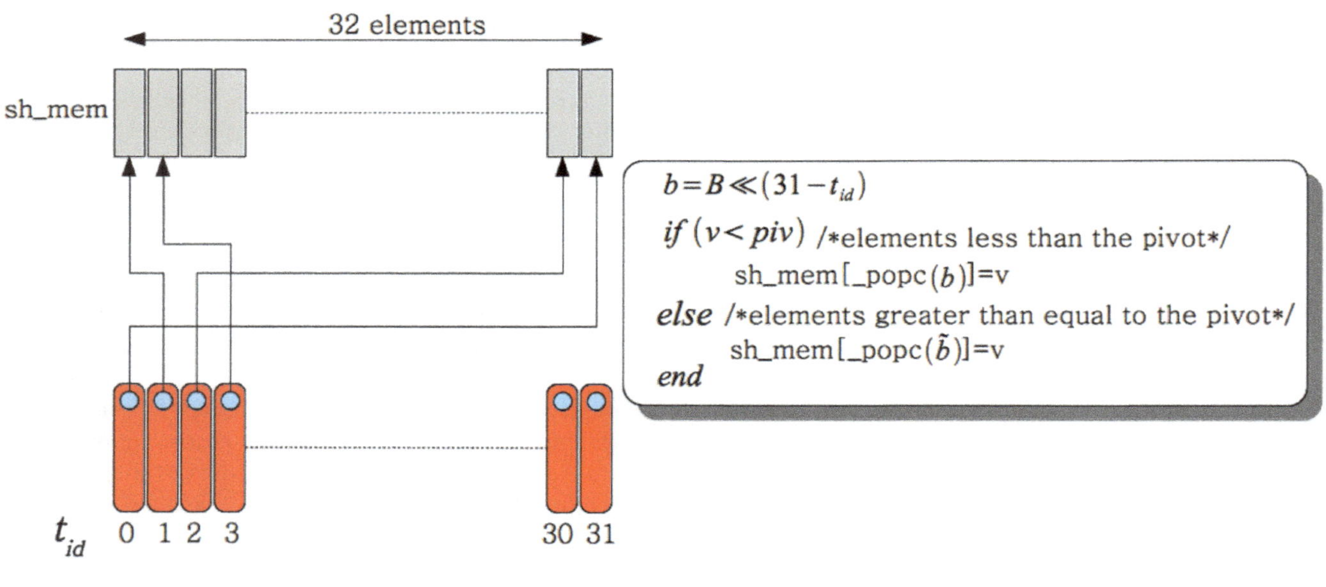

Figure 3. Pivot process. The pivot process is accomplished in shared memory. Each thread determines where in the shared memory the value has to be written. Values less than the pivot are accumulated on the left hand side and values greater than or equal to the pivot are accumulated on the right hand side. Since all threads write to different locations, there are no bank conflicts.

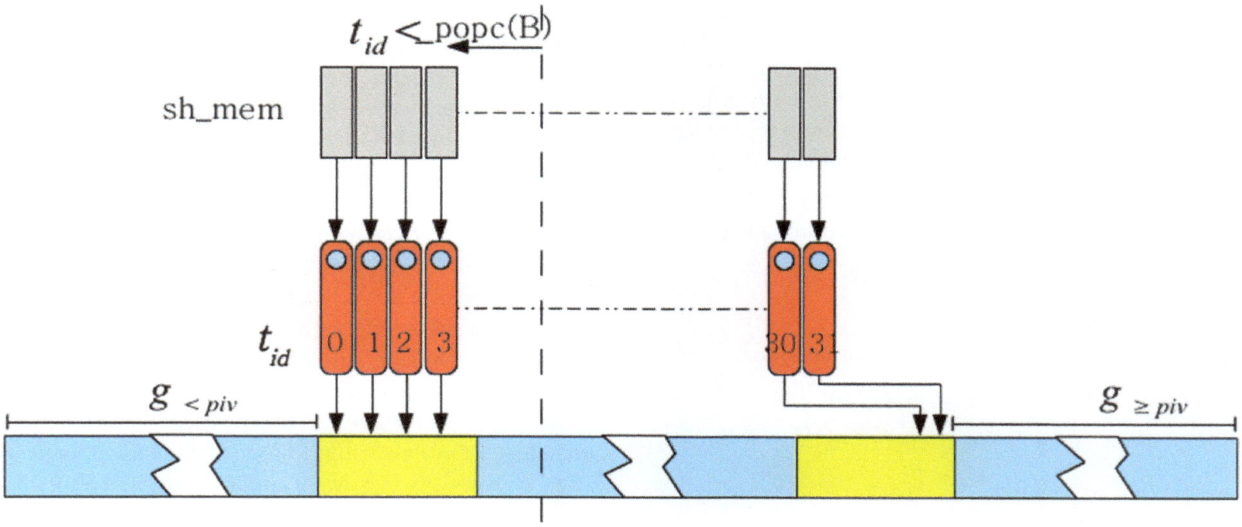

Figure 4. Write out process. The thread id indicates (based on the computation _popc(B)) whether a given thread is writing out an element less than the pivot or greater than or equal to the pivot. The values g < piv and $g \geq piv$, which are maintained in shared memory and updated incrementally, indicate the location in the global array of the location of the last element that is less than the pivot and greater than or equal to the pivot. This operation involves at most two coalesced memory writes.

With one warp per query, we must have a minimum of 1024 queries to fully utilize GPU resources. If we use one thread block per query, we can reduce the minimum number of queries for full GPU utilization to 128. When processing each row of the distance matrix using a thread block, each thread block will have several thread warps (depending on the thread count) that will cooperatively pivot elements. While writing the elements into shared memory, each thread has to determine its relative write position in shared memory with respect to all thread block threads. As a first step, each thread finds its write position with respect to threads in its own warp as described in the previous paragraph. Subsequently, all threads in the thread block are synchronized. An inter warp pre-fix sum step determines the write position of each thread with respect to the entire thread block. The maximum number of thread warps per block is 16 (the max. thread count in a thread block is 512, and the number of threads in a warp is 32). Because of the small number of elements, we use a single thread per thread block to conduct the inter warp prefix sum. This is much more economical than a multi-threaded pre-fix sum.

Once a partition is complete, the output array (auxiliary array) has a left side of length L elements, each of which is less than the pivot. The right side is of length R elements each of which is greater than or equal to the pivot. Suppose we need K nearest neighbors, and K < L, then we need to process only the left hand side. Suppose K > L, then we keep the left hand side as is, and partition the right hand side to find K-L elements. Since the input and auxiliary arrays are swapped at the end of the partition process, in the second case (K > L), we would have to copy the left hand side from the auxiliary array to the input array. We can avoid copying the data by instead storing a stack of references which indicate the start and end indices and the arrays (auxiliary or input) that the partitions that form the K nearest neighbors are to be found. This significantly reduces the memory transactions needed for the operations.

Distance Calculation

Our implementation supports three distance metrics, namely, Euclidian, Cosine, and Pearson. The Euclidian distance between two vectors $\vec{x}, \vec{y}$ is given by:

$$d_E(\vec{x}, \vec{y}) = \sqrt{\|\vec{x}\|^2 + \|\vec{y}\|^2 - 2\vec{x}\cdot\vec{y}}$$

The Cosine distance metric is given by:

$$d_C(\vec{x}, \vec{y}) = \frac{\vec{x}\cdot\vec{y}}{\|\vec{x}\|\,\|\vec{y}\|}$$

The Pearson distance is given by:

$$d_C(\vec{x},\vec{y}) = \frac{\hat{x}\cdot\hat{y}}{\|\hat{x}\|\,\|\hat{y}\|}$$

where, $\hat{x} = \vec{x} - \bar{x}$ and $\bar{x}$ is the mean of the entries in $\vec{x}$. Note that the Pearson distance coefficient is essentially the Cosine distance of the centered data sets.

The process of finding either of these distances requires operations for finding vector means, vector magnitudes, and dot products. For two data sets X, Y, where the columns of X and Y represent the data vectors $\vec{x}_i$ and $\vec{y}_j$ respectively, the n × m dot products

$$\vec{x}_i\cdot\vec{y}_j \begin{cases} i = 1,2\ldots n \\ j = 1,2..m \end{cases}$$

are easily formulated as a matrix product X^T, Y. There are very efficient libraries for dense matrix multiplication which can be used for this purpose [35]. The process of finding vector means and vector magnitudes are essentially vector reductions. The thrust library has optimized reduction_by_key which we have used to simultaneously find the vector means and magnitudes of all vectors in X, Y.

Finding the Eulcidian and Cosine distances require the same inputs (dot products and norms of $\vec{x}, \vec{y}$). In the first parallel kernel operation, we compute the vector norms of the vectors in X, Y using a combination of a transform iterator and reduction_by_key function. The transform iterator generates the square of individual elements and feeds the result into the reduction_by_key function, which in turn computes the square of the vector norms. The next step is to find the distance. In case the of the Euclidian distance, to find the k nearest vectors to $\vec{x}_i \in X$ from $\vec{y}_j \in Y$ the squared distance formula is given by:

$$d_{ij}^2 = \|\vec{x}_i\|^2 + \|\vec{y}_j\|^2 - 2\vec{x}_i \cdot \vec{y}_j$$

The comparison to find the k nearest neighbors of $\vec{x}_i$ is between the numbers d_{ij}^2. Furthermore, all of the d_{ij}^2 have a common addition factor $\|\vec{x}_i\|^2$. Therefore, it is sufficient to compare the distance metric $d'_{ij} = \|\vec{y}_j\|^2 - 2\vec{x}_i \cdot \vec{y}_j$. This saves an addition operation. To find the k nearest vectors to $\vec{y}_i \in Y$ from $\vec{X}_j \in X$, we follow the same process but find the matrix of dot products Y^TX by simply taking a transpose of the matrix X^TY that we computed earlier. The same analysis is valid for Cosine distances as well.

To find the Pearson distance, we need to pre-process the raw data to center it. We use the reduction_by_key to find the vector means. We then center each vector using one thread block per vector. Once the data is centered, the process of finding the distance metric is the same as that of the Cosine distance.

RESULTS

Our algorithms were written in NVIDIA's CUDA [29] and executed on a Tesla C2050 compute card. We used gcc4.2 with appropriate optimization flags. This card has 448 serial processors and a peak single precision performance of 1.03 TFlops. The RAM memory is 3 GB with a global memory bandwidth of 144 GB/s. We used CUDA 4.2 drivers for our implementation. We performed a comprehensive set of tests against implementations by Garcia et al. [23] and Sismanis et al. [30], both of which provide for *k*-NN. We also benchmarked our algorithm against the nth_element from the standard template library and the GPU-based radix/bucket select implementation of kth-element algorithm by Alabi et al. [33]. The work by Alabi et al., as indicated earlier, is slightly different since they just return the kth largest or smallest element and not the *k*-NNs. This means that they do not keep track of the *k*-NN elements and therefore perform less work than our algorithm and the implementations by Garcia and Sismanis. For accurate comparison, we downloaded all GPU codes (Sismanis, Garcia, Alabi) and recompiled it using the same compiler and CUDA drivers as the ones we used to compile our code. The test data was a matrix (Q × n, Q is the number of queries, and n is the size of the corpus data set) of uniformly random floating point numbers with indices. In some tests, indices were left out.

For large data sets, the code developed by Garcia et al. [23], batches execution of multiple queries. For large n, the size of the batches (i.e., the number of queries) can cause underutilization of GPU resources. We chose parameters in our data sets n, Q so that the algorithm by Garcia operated at its full potential. Figure 5 shows the results of the benchmarks where we kept Q constant and varied the parameters k,n. We set the number of simultaneous queries Q = 8192 = 2^{13}. We varied the number of closest neighbors as $6 \leq \log_2(k) \leq 9$. Also, we varied the size of the corpus data as $13 \leq \log_2(n) \leq 18$. We only benchmarked the search part of the algorithm, since the method for distance calculation is virtually identical between the two methods. Figure 6 shows the performance advantage of our algorithm. There is dramatic gain in speedup when k grows. As k grows, Garcia's algorithm shifts its k-NN stack from shared memory to global memory and is saddled with all the associated pitfalls, such as un-coalesced memory access. In Figure 6, we illustrate the effect of changing the number of queries. In this example, we kept the size of the corpus at n = 65536 and changed the number of queries as $8192 \leq Q \leq 65536$. Simultaneously, we changed the number of selections as $64 \leq k \leq 512$. For small queries, Garcia's method underutilizes the GPU. As we increase the number of queries, the GPU utilization increases, and therefore, we see a decrease in speedup from the peak. For the largest sizes of k=215 and Q = 65536 that fit in our GPU memory, our method is 80× faster.

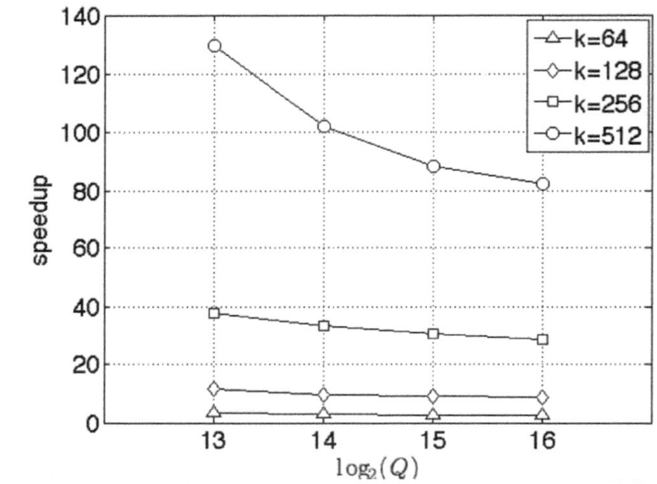

Figure 5. Benchmark against GPU k-NN by Garcia for selection alone with varying size of corpus data (n) [23]. We set the number of queries Q = 2^{13} to ensure full GPU utilization. The parameter n was varied from $2^{13} < n < 2^{16}$. The number of nearest neighbors k was varied as $64 \leq k \leq 512$. Except for k = 512, the speedup remains flat with respect to n. The dramatic gain in performance with k is because the Garcia algorithm shifts its k-NN stack from shared memory to global memory as k increases. This increases inefficiencies due to uncoalesced memory access. We achieved a speedup $\approx 130\times$ for k= 512 and n =2^{16}.

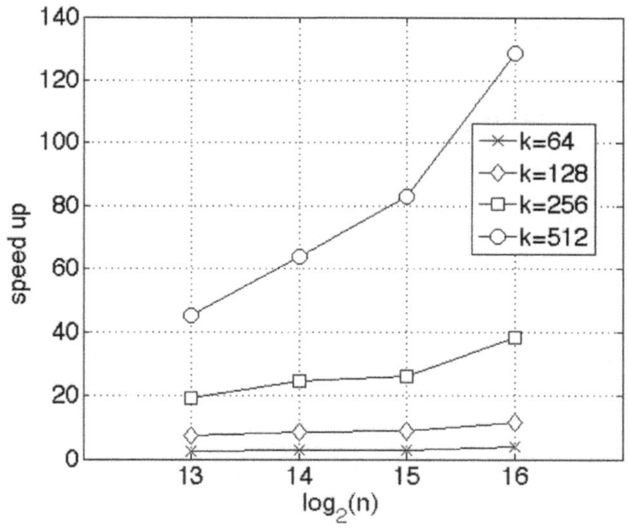

Figure 6. Benchmark of selection alone against GPU k-NN by Garcia for different query sizes (Q). We set n = 65536. We varied the number of queries as $2^{13} \leq Q \leq 2^{16}$. Simultaneously, we varied the number of nearest neighbors as $64 \leq k \leq 512$. Note that speedup falls as the number of queries Q increases. This is because the Garcia algorithm increases GPU utilization as the number of queries is increased. For the largest data sets that fit into GPU memory, corresponding to the level of full GPU utilization by Garcia ($Q = 2^{16}$) and for the largest number of nearest neighbors (k = 512), our algorithm is 80× faster.

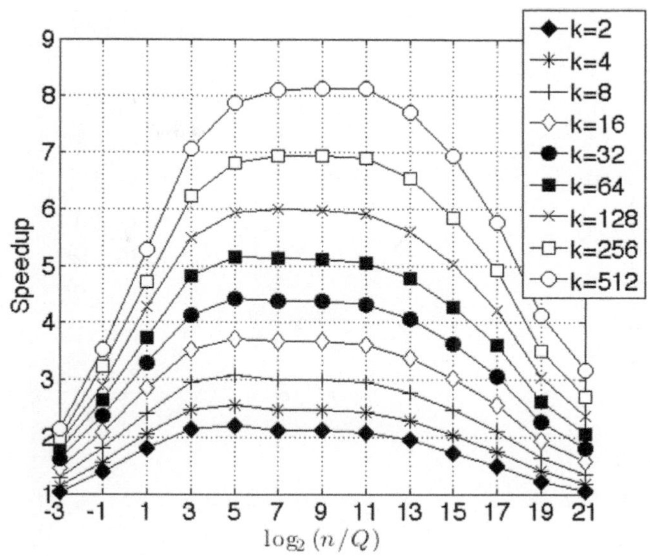

Figure 7. Benchmark against work by Sismanis et al. [30]. These tests were performed for elements that contained both values and indices. In this benchmark we varied $\log_2$ (n/Q) as $-3 \leq \log_2(n/Q) \leq 20$. We kept the product n × Q = 2^{27}. We simultaneously varied k as $2 \leq k \leq 512$. Performance peaks at $\log_2$ (n/Q) = 12 stays flat untill $\log_2$ (n/Q) = 11 and starts falling at $\log_2$ (n/Q) = 13. The decrease in performance corresponds to the number of queries Q falling below 128 where our method underutilizes GPU resources.

For the benchmarks against work by Sismanis (Figure 7), we compared the selection method alone. We kept the product n×Q = 2^{27} constant, where n is the number of data corpus elements (columns in the distance matrix) and Q is the number of query elements (rows in the distance matrix). We plotted our speedup against the ratio $\log_2$ (n/Q). We ran a thousand trials for each evaluation and averaged the results. As seen in Figure 7, the performance gains for various k rapidly rise with $\log_2$ (n/Q), reach a saturation level, and then fall for large values of $\log_2$ (n/Q). The degradation of performance occurs at $\log_2$ (n/Q) = 13. This point corresponds to Q = 128, i.e., where the number of thread blocks falls below 128. At this stage, our algorithm is not able to fully utilize GPU resources. We show in a subsequent test that our algorithm saturates the GPU only when the thread block count exceeds 128. The performance advantage grows with k. We were able to benchmark only up to k = 512 as the Sismaniss implementation cannot handle $k > 512$. With increased GPU RAM, we can handle larger distance matrices and therefore, have more queries Q for large values of n. For example, if we had a GPU with 18 GB of available RAM instead of the current 2 GB (usable), we would be easily able to handle distance matrices of sizes 128×2^{23}. This would push the point of performance degradation to a point given by $\log_2$ (n/Q) = 16. Consequently, we expect our algorithm to perform even better on fused GPU-CPU architectures that have unified memory access to main CPU RAM. Such processors will become mainstream in the next 2–3 years.

Our third set of benchmarks were against the radix/bucket select-based kth statistic algorithm implemented by [33]. This implementation takes one query at a time. Therefore, our comparison tests involved initially loading the entire distance matrix into GPU RAM and then invoking the radix select algorithm one query at a time. This approach adds kernel launch overhead to the time for calculation. However, the typical kernel launch overhead for the GPU in our tests is 5.7 micro seconds which is nearly two orders of magnitude smaller than the time required for task execution. Figure 8 shows the results of our benchmarks. For this battery of tests, we kept the product n×Q = 2^{28} constant. Once again, we ran a thousand trials for each evaluation and averaged the results. For low values of $\log_2$ (n/Q), our approach is significantly better. This is because in this regime, the implementation by [33] underutilizes GPU resources. As the ratio $\log_2$ (n/Q) increases, our performance advantage decreases. At $\log_2$ (n/Q) = 14, our algorithm starts underutilizing GPU resources because the number of thread blocks in operation falls below 128. The method of [33] achieves GPU saturation only at $\log_2$ (n/Q) = 18 (i.e., n = 2^{23}, Q = 2^5). Even at this point, our algorithm is slightly faster ($\approx 2\times$), even though it is underutilizing GPU resources and is performing a significantly larger amount of work keeping track of k-NNs instead of finding just the kth statistic.

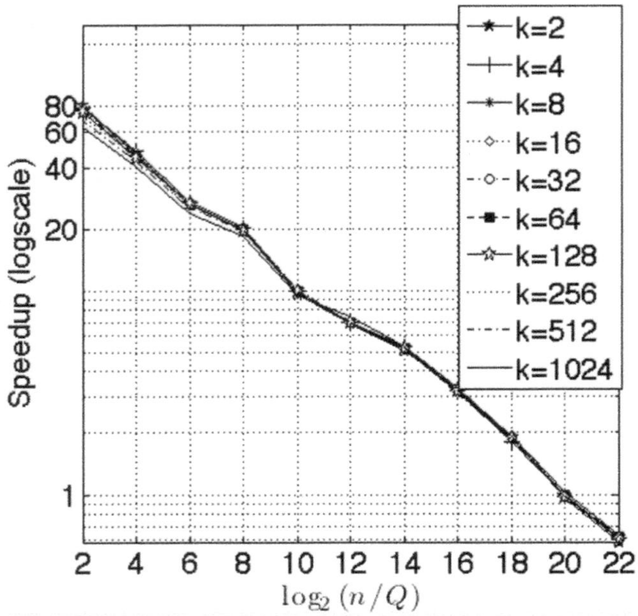

Figure 8. Benchmark against work by Alabi et al. [33]. Here the benchmark is comparing the speedup of selecting kth element vs selection of k-NN using our algorithm. These tests were performed for elements with values alone. We kept the product n × Q = 2^{28} and varied k as $2 \leq k \leq 1024$. Simultaneously, we varied $\log_2$ (n/Q) as $2 \leq \log_2 (n/Q) \leq 22$. There is a dramatic fall in performance gain because the method by Alabi increases GPU utilization as n/Q increases. It reaches saturation at n / Q = 2^{18} [33]. Our algorithm starts underutilizing GPU resources at n/Q=14. Even when Alabi et al. is saturated and our algorithm is significantly underutilizing GPU resources, we are 1.8× faster. Once again, with a larger GPU RAM, our algorithm would perform significantly better.

Figure 9 illustrates our tests to investigate GPU saturation. In these tests, we kept n=2^{20} constant and varied Q, the number of queries from Q = 2^3 to Q = 2^8. For various values of k, it can be seen that the time per query drops with the Q and flattens out at Q = 2^8. Since we are utilizing one thread block per query, we should have at least 128 queries to fully utilize GPU resources.

We benchmarked our selection algorithm against the Standard Template Library nth_select. Just as in [33], the nth_select algorithm works on a single query. We compared our implementation with a single threaded nth_select working one query at time. The data was loaded into memory ahead of time and queries were processed in a for loop. We used a Intel Core i5-3750K running at 3.8 GHz. This CPU has 4 cores with 32 KB L1 cache, 256 KB L2 cache, and 6 MB L3 cache shared between the 4 cores. Figure 10 shows the results of the benchmark. In this test, we varied the parameter k as $2 \leq k \leq 1024$ and the parameter n, as $16 \leq \log_2 (n) \leq 20$. The speedup increases with n and, as can be seen in the figure does not reach saturation even at n=2^{20}. There is a slight degradation with the increase in k, which is obvious since the larger k entails keeping track of a larger list of elements. In our tests, we achieved around 41× speedup for the largest k with the largest data sets that could be accommodated in our GPU RAM.

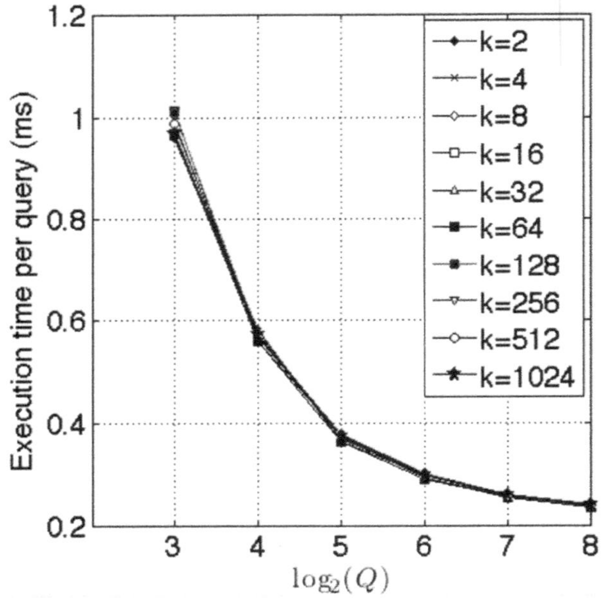

Figure 9. Effect of varying the number of queries Q. In this benchmark, we kept n=2^{20} and varied the number of queries as $8 \leq Q \leq 256$. As can be seen from the graph for various values of k, the time per query decreases with the increase in Q and roughly flattens out at Q=128.

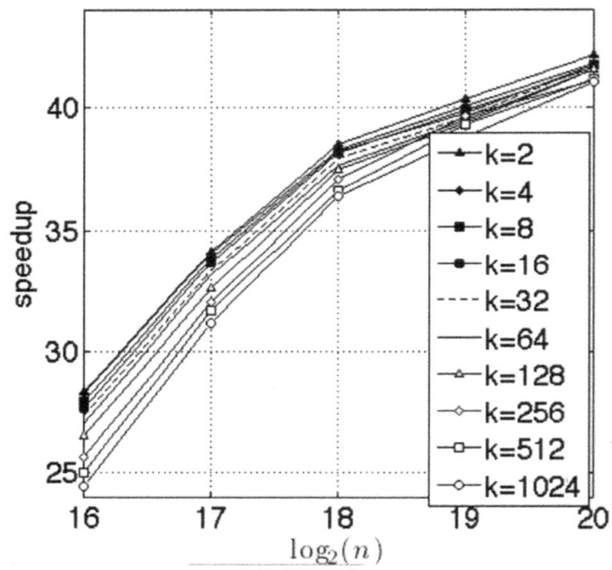

Figure 10. Benchmark against nth element. This benchmark is against a single core of the CPU. As can be seen, the performance degrades slightly with larger values of k. The number of queries were set to Q =256. We ran up to n=2^{20} and achieved around 41× speedup. As can be seen from the figure, the speedup graph has not been saturated for the largest values of n that can be accommodated on our GPU.

Finally, in Table 2, we show variation in time for different data sets. Time for execution is dependent on the data set. Therefore, we ran about 1000 trials for each setting and measured the mean and standard deviation. Table 2 lists the results. It appears that the standard deviation in timing decreases as k increases. Overall the standard is less than 0.5%.

Table 2. Execution time variation

n	$k=64$		$k=128$		$k=256$		$k=512$	
	mean	%std	mean	%std	mean	%std	mean	%std
2^{13}	138.03	0.37	144.4	0.27	151.36	0.24	159.35	0.31
2^{14}	163.55	0.33	170.04	0.311	177.27	0.25	185.91	0.27
2^{15}	208.83	0.29	215.3	0.37	222.97	0.28	232.10	0.245
2^{16}	288.44	0.29	294.85	0.28	302.34	0.27	311.8	0.26

In this study, we kept the number of queries $Q=2^{13}$ and varied n and k to study the mean and standard deviation of execution time over 1000 trials for each data set (n,k).

doi:10.1371/journal.pone.0092409.t001

DISCUSSION

We have successfully developed and implemented a multi-query k-NN algorithm on a GPU. Our algorithm is an implementation of the Quick Select method and uses the architectural advantages of modern GPUs. For corpus data that fit in GPU memory, based on our benchmarks, our algorithm outperforms all current state-of-the art methods. There are, however, many limitations to our method. To achieve full GPU saturation, we cannot have the number of queries Q < 128, i.e., we need to have at least 128 thread blocks running simultaneously. Given the roughly 2 GB available memory, this restricts the number of elements in the corpus data to n < 2097152. With the newer fused GPU-CPU processors, with unified RAM (up to 64 GB), we will be able to handle much larger data sets. We are also looking at batch execution with data partitioning for large corpus data that do not fit into GPU memory. We may be able to overlap computation with data transfer to and from the CPU RAM to reduce overall execution time. Batch execution will obviously require merging of results between executions and additional memory to store intermediate results. We believe there will be significant opportunities for optimization based on the number of queries, corpus data size, and the dimension of vectors in the corpus data. This research will be explored in subsequent publications.

AUTHOR CONTRIBUTIONS

Conceived and designed the experiments: IK RMD. Performed the experiments: IK RMD AD. Analyzed the data: RMD. Contributed reagents/materials/analysis tools: IK RMD. Wrote the paper: RMD. Designed the algorithm: RMD. Implemented the algorithm: IK.

REFERENCES

1. Roberts A, McMillan L, Wang W, Parker J, Rusyn I, et al. (2007) Inferring missing genotypes in large snp panels using fast nearest-neighbor searches over sliding windows. Bioinformatics 23: i401–i407. doi: 10.1093/bioinformatics/btm220
2. Weston J, Elisseeff A, Zhou D, Leslie CS, Noble WS (2004) Protein ranking: from local to global structure in the protein similarity network. Proc Natl Acad Sci U S A 101: 6559–6563. doi: 10.1073/pnas.0308067101
3. Zaki MJ, Ho CT, editors (2000) Large-Scale Parallel Data Mining, Workshop on Large-Scale Parallel KDD Systems, SIGKDD, August 15, 1999, San Diego, CA, USA, revised papers, volume 1759 of Lecture Notes in Computer Science. Springer.
4. Maier M, Hein M, von Luxburg U (2009) Optimal construction of k-nearest-neighbor graphs for identifying noisy clusters. Theor Comput Sci 410: 1749–1764. doi: 10.1016/j.tcs.2009.01.009
5. Liu W, He J, Chang SF (2010) Large graph construction for scalable semi-supervised learning. In: ICML. pp. 679–686.
6. Tenenbaum JB, Silva V, Langford JC (2000) A Global Geometric Framework for Nonlinear Dimensionality Reduction. Science 290: 2319–2323. doi: 10.1126/science.290.5500.2319
7. Fränti P, Virmajoki O, Hautamäki V (2006) Fast agglomerative clustering using a k-nearest neighbor graph. IEEE Trans Pattern Anal Mach Intell 28: 1875–1881. doi: 10.1109/tpami.2006.227
8. Duda RO, Hart PE, Stork DG (2001) Pattern Classification (2nd Edition). Wiley-Interscience.
9. Jones PW, Osipov A, Rokhlin V (2011) Randomized approximate nearest neighbors algorithm. Proceedings of the National Academy of Sciences 108: 15679–15686. doi: 10.1073/pnas.1107769108
10. Arya S, Mount DM, Netanyahu NS, Silverman R, Wu A (1994) An optimal algorithm for approximate nearest neighbor searching. In: Proceedings of the fifth annual ACM-SIAM symposium on Discrete algorithms. Philadelphia, PA, USA: Society for Industrial and Applied Mathematics, SODA '94, pp. 573–582. Available:http://dl.acm.org/citation.cfm?id=314464.314652.
11. Dasgupta S, Freund Y (2008) Random projection trees and low dimensional manifolds. In: Proceedings of the 40th annual ACM symposium on Theory of computing. New York, NY, USA: ACM, STOC '08, pp. 537–546.
12. Datar M, Immorlica N, Indyk P, Mirrokni VS (2004) Locality-sensitive hashing scheme based on p-stable distributions. In: Proceedings of the twentieth annual symposium on Computational geometry. New York, NY, USA: ACM, SCG '04, pp. 253–262.
13. Bentley JL (1980) Multidimensional divide-and-conquer. Commun ACM 23: 214–229. doi: 10.1145/358841.358850
14. Clarkson KL (1983) Fast algorithms for the all nearest neighbors problem. In: FOCS. pp. 226–232.
15. Vaidya PM (1989) An O(n log n) algorithm for the all-nearest-neighbors problem. Discrete & Computational

Geometry 4: 101–115. doi: 10.1007/bf02187718

16. Paredes R, Chávez E, Figueroa K, Navarro G (2006) Practical construction of k-nearest neighbor graphs in metric spaces. In: WEA. pp. 85–97.
17. Chan TM (1998) Approximate nearest neighbor queries revisited. Discrete & Computational Geometry 20: 359–373. doi: 10.1007/pl00009390
18. Connor M, Kumar P (2010) Fast construction of k-nearest neighbor graphs for point clouds. IEEE Trans Vis Comput Graph 16: 599–608. doi: 10.1109/tvcg.2010.9
19. Chen J, ren Fang H, Saad Y (2009) Fast approximate *k*-nn graph construction for high dimensional data via recursive lanczos bisection. Journal of Machine Learning Research 10: 1989–2012.
20. Wang J, Wang J, Zeng G, Tu Z, Gan R, et al. (2012) Scalable k-nn graph construction for visual descriptors. In: CVPR. pp. 1106–1113.
21. Dong W, Moses C, Li K (2011) Efficient k-nearest neighbor graph construction for generic similarity measures. In: Proceedings of the 20th international conference on World Wide Web. New York, NY, USA: ACM, WWW '11, pp. 577–586. doi:10.1145/1963405.1963487. Available:http://doi.acm.org/10.1145/1963405.1963487.
22. Indyk P (2004) Nearest neighbors in high-dimensional spaces. In: Goodman JE, O'Rourke J, editors, Handbook of Discrete and Computational Geometry, Boca Raton, FL: CRC Press LLC. 2nd edition.
23. Garcia V, Debreuve E, Nielsen F, Barlaud M (2010) K-nearest neighbor search: Fast gpu-based implementations and application to high-dimensional feature matching. In: ICIP. pp. 3757–3760.
24. Arefin AS, Riveros C, Berretta R, Moscato P (2012) Gpu-fs-*k*nn: A software tool for fast and scalable *k*nn computation using gpus. PLoS ONE 7: e44000. doi: 10.1371/journal.pone.0044000
25. Barrientos RJ, Gómez JI, Tenllado C, Prieto-Matias M, Marin M (2011) knn query processing in metric spaces using gpus. In: Euro-Par (1)'11. pp. 380–392.
26. Kato K, Hosino T (2009) Solving k-nearest vector problem on multiple graphics processors. CoRR abs/0906.0231.
27. Kuang Q, Zhao L (2009) A practical gpu based knn algorithm. In: Proceedings of the Second Symposium International Computer Science and Computational Technology (ISCSCT 09). pp. 151–155.
28. Owens JD, Luebke D, Govindaraju N, Harris M, Krger J, et al. (2007) A survey of general-purpose computation on graphics hardware. Computer Graphics Forum 26: 80–113. doi: 10.1111/j.1467-8659.2007.01012.x
29. Sanders J, Kandrot E (2010) CUDA by Example: An Introduction to General-Purpose GPU Programming. Addison-Wesley Professional, 1st edition.
30. Sismanis N, Pitsianis N, Sun X (2012) Parallel search of k-nearest neighbors with synchronous operations. In: High Performance Extreme Computing (HPEC), 2012 IEEE Conference on. pp. 1–6. doi:10.1109/HPEC.2012.6408667.
31. Baxter S (2011). Mgpu select. Available:http://www.moderngpu.com/select/mgpuselect.html.
32. Monroe L, Wendelberger J, Michalak S (2011) Randomized selection on the gpu. In: Proceedings of the ACM SIGGRAPH Symposium on High Performance Graphics. New York, NY, USA: ACM, HPG '11, pp. 89–98. doi:10.1145/2018323.2018338. Available:http://doi.acm.org/10.1145/2018323.2018338.
33. Alabi T, Blanchard JD, Gordon B, Steinbach R (2012) Fast *k*-selection algorithms for graphics processing units. J Exp Algorithmics 17 doi: 10.1145/2133803.2345676
34. Cederman D, Tsigas P (2010) Gpu-quicksort: A practical quicksort algorithm for graphics processors. J Exp Algorithmics 14 doi: 10.1145/1498698.1564500
35. Volkov V, Demmel JW (2008) Benchmarking gpus to tune dense linear algebra. In: Proceedings of the 2008 ACM/IEEE conference on Supercomputing. Piscataway, NJ, USA: IEEE Press, SC '08, pp. 31:1–31:11. Available: http://dl.acm.org/citation.cfm?id=1413370.1413402.

INDEX

N

O

P

Q

R

S

T

U

V

W